CATALOGUE OF THE PEPYS LIBRARY AT MAGDALENE COLLEGE, CAMBRIDGE

General Editor

ROBERT LATHAM

Fellow and Pepys Librarian

CATALOGUE
of the
PEPYS LIBRARY
at Magdalene College
Cambridge

VOLUME I : PRINTED BOOKS

Compiled by N. A. SMITH

assisted by H. M. Adams and D. Pepys Whiteley

With an appendix on Incunabula by J. C. T. OATES

D.S. BREWER LTD · ROWMAN & LITTLEFIELD

© *The Master and Fellows of Magdalene College Cambridge 1978*

Published by D. S. Brewer Ltd, 240 Hills Road, Cambridge
and PO Box 24, Ipswich IP1 1JJ
and Rowman & Littlefield, 81 Adams Drive, Totowa
New Jersey 07512, USA

First published 1978

British Library Cataloguing in Publication Data

Magdalene College, Cambridge
    Catalogue of the Pepys Library at Magdalene College, Cambridge
    Vol.1: Printed books.
    1. Pepys, Samuel — Library
    I. Title II. Latham, Robert, b.1912
    016.94206'6'0924   Z997.P/
    ISBN 0-85991-025-3

Printed in England by Dramrite Printers Ltd
Long Lane, Southwark, London SE1

CONTENTS

Preface by Robert Latham   ix
Introduction by N. A. Smith   xi
Abbreviations and contractions   xiii

Catalogue of Printed Books   1

Appendix: Catalogue of Incunabula by J. C. T. Oates   195
List of 'Collections'   199
Missing Books   201

TO F.E. CLEARY

BENEFACTOR

PREFACE

The Pepys Library consists of the collection made by Samuel Pepys during his lifetime (1633-1703), together with a few items added according to his directions in the year or so following his death mainly in order to round off incomplete sets. He made a will in 1701 which made no mention of his library, but in codicils added on 12 and 13 May 1703, a fortnight before his death, he made arrangements for its disposal.[1] It was to pass for life to his heir John Jackson (son of his sister Paulina), and after Jackson's death to Magdalene College, Cambridge, where both Pepys and Jackson had been educated. He asked that it should be housed in the 'new building' there in a chamber to be chosen by Jackson. The 3000 volumes arrived at the college in the summer of 1724, together with the twelve glazed presses and the library desk in which they had been contained. They have remained in the college's possession ever since virtually as Pepys left them. By the terms of his gift the college is forbidden to add to or to reduce their number.[2]

A descriptive catalogue (never completed) was planned before the First World War; the first volume appeared in 1914 and the fourth in 1940.[3] In addition certain parts of the collection have been listed in separate publications: the Spanish books by Sir Stephen Gaselee,[4] the Spanish chapbooks by Professor E.M.Wilson,[5] the engraved portraits by John Charrington,[6] and the 'Penny Merriments' by Dr R.Thompson.[7] At some points the present catalogue goes over the same ground as these previous works, and, where appropriate, gives reference to them.

It has now been decided to start afresh with a new design rather than attempt to complete the catalogue of 1914-40. The new catalogue will be contained in seven volumes, to be published at intervals over the next few years:

    I   Printed Books
    II   Broadside Ballads
    III   Prints and Drawings
    IV   Music, Maps, and Calligraphy
    V   Manuscripts
    VI   Bindings
    VII Pepys's Catalogue.

Each of volumes I-VI will carry an introduction explaining the arrangement and treatment of the items within it. The introduction to the last volume will include an account of the collection as a whole. The distribution of items between the volumes of the catalogue will be clear in most cases from the volume-titles. There are, however, certain categories about which further explanation is necessary. Books with mixed contents (there are many, for instance, which contain both printed and manuscript items) are given entries in whatever volumes of the catalogue are relevant. The entries

---

1. The will and its codicils, with a 'scheme' for the completion of the library, are printed in H.B.Wheatley, *Pepysiana* (1899), pp.251-70.

2. Eight volumes have been missing since at least 1912. Six are volumes of printed books, containing seven works: they are listed below, pp.199. The two missing manuscript volumes are listed in vol.V.

3. *Bibliotheca Pepysiana, A Descriptive Catalogue of the Library of Samuel Pepys:* Part I, *'Sea' Manuscripts,* by J.R. Tanner (1914); Part II, *Early Printed Books to 1558,* by E.Gordon Duff, with a General Introduction by F.Sidgwick (1914); Part III, *Medieval Manuscripts,* by M.R.James (1923); and Part IV, *Shorthand Books,* by W.J.Carlton (1940).

4. *The Spanish Books in the Library of Samuel Pepys* (1921).

5. *Trans. Cambridge Bibliog. Soc.,* II (1955-7), pp.127-54, 229-68, 305-22.

6. *A Catalogue of the Engraved Portraits in the Library of Samuel Pepys* (1936).

7. *The Library* (5th ser.), XXXI (1976), pp.223-34. Unfortunately this appeared too late to be used in the present volume.

concerning maps, atlases and calligraphical works, whether printed or in manuscript, are gathered together in vol.IV. In the case of music, it has been decided, in order to facilitate reference, to include books on the subject of music (as distinct from scores) in vol.I as well as in vol.IV, but not to include music manuscripts in vol.V. In all cases where an item is entered more than once cross-references are given.

Work on this project was started some years ago under the editorship of my predecessor as Pepys Librarian, Dr R.W.Ladborough. From the beginning a number of scholars acted as an advisory committee — Dr A.N.L.Munby, Miss Jane Norton, Professor Francis Wormald, Dr Graham Pollard, Professor Bruce Dickins (all five, alas, deceased), together with Mr J.C.T.Oates. The college is most grateful to them. The college also acknowledges with gratitude the generous grants made by the Calouste Gulbenkian Foundation, F.E.Cleary Esq., and the late Professor Wormald which have made the preparation of the work possible.

In carrying out my own duties as General Editor I have received invaluable help from Mr Oates and the late Dr Munby. I owe more than I can briefly say to their wise and kindly guidance.

Robert Latham

INTRODUCTION

ENTRIES

This catalogue[1] of the printed books in the Pepys Library is basically an author-title catalogue. Each book is entered under the name of its author, or under the first word (not an article) of the title if the author is unknown. Each book has only one entry; no entries will be found under the names of editors, translators or authors other than the first-named; nor have any subject entries been provided. Works by more than four authors have been entered under the title. References have been given from the titles of anonymous books whose authorship is known. The fact that a book was published anonymously is shown by enclosing the heading for the author within square brackets; those in which an author's name is represented only by initials have been entered under the last initial, with a reference from the title: but if the full name is known the book is entered there with references both from title and from the initial. In the case of reports of trials the defendants are treated as authors.

Treaties are entered under the first-named country, and liturgical books under the heading 'Liturgies', sub-divided by churches.

The title of each book has been recorded as it appears on the title-page; omissions from within the title quoted (apart from statements of authorship) are indicated by marks of omission, but no note is made of omissions at the end. Contractions and other special characters are reproduced as closely as possible; in transcribing I/J and U/V and in providing accents the normal usage of the book itself has been followed.

In the imprint, up to three printers or publishers have been named; all after the third have been omitted and replaced by 'etc.'.

NOTES

Following the main part of the entry, brief notes have been provided of any imperfections in the Pepys copy, of illustrations, and of autographs and certain manuscript additions.[2] Pepys himself hardly ever wrote in his books, apart from entering shelf-numbers on the fly-leaves, but in some cases previous owners (and readers) had added autographs and notes. His library clerks[3] also occasionally added notes of collations made with other copies. The autographs and the most important of the notes are recorded here. The manuscript lists of contents and indexes added by one or other of Pepys's clerks are not usually recorded. A large number of manuscript additions were made by Daniel Waterland, Master of Magdalene, 1713-40, who was the first Master to be responsible for the Library. He wrote brief comments in books concerning biblical history, and identified some of the anonymous authors of the pamphlets published in 1697-1703 concerning the Convocation controversy. These notes are unsigned but unmistakably in his hand. In addition, where the book is one of the pamphlets or other small items which Pepys had bound up by subject, the title and volume number of the collection is given. A list of these collections is given at the end of this volume.

REFERENCES TO OTHER CATALOGUES, ETC.

References in this catalogue to other printed catalogues and bibliographies fall into three categories:

a) Where appropriate, the entry-numbers in *STC, Wing* and *Adams* have been quoted.

---

1. This introduction concerns methods used in the main part of this volume. The methods used in the description of the incunabula are self-explanatory.

2. The notes on autographs and MS additions have been added by the General Editor.

3. These notes remain unattributed because it is virtually impossible to distinguish between the hands of the two clerks, Thomas Henderson and Paul Lorrain, who wrote most of them.

Wherever possible account has been taken of the second editions of vol.II of *STC* and vol.I of *Wing*.

b) References have been given to previous catalogues of parts of the Library, which in most cases supplement the present catalogue in that they contain fuller bibliographical descriptions.

c) References to Pepys's own writings have been given for the diary, the Tangier papers, and his published correspondence. Such references should be used with caution: Pepys's habit of updating his collection by buying new editions of works in his library means that the book now in the Library may not be that to which the reference properly applies.

The original entries upon which this catalogue is based were compiled by H.M.Adams and D.Pepys Whiteley; I should like to record my gratitude to them, to Dr D.W.Cruickshank of University College, Dublin for information about the Spanish plays, and finally to Mrs E.M.Coleman and Mrs D.Swallow for their help in preparing and reading the proofs of this volume.

N.A.S.

AUTHORITIES CITED

Adams	Catalogue of the books printed on the continent of Europe, 1501-1600, in Cambridge libraries. Compiled by H.M.Adams. Cambridge, 1967.
Carlton	Bibliotheca Pepysiana. A descriptive catalogue ... Part IV. Shorthand books, by W.J.Carlton. London, 1940.
Charrington	Catalogue of the engraved portraits in the Pepys Library, by J.Charrington. Cambridge, 1936.
De Ricci	A census of Caxtons, by S.de Ricci. (Bibliographical Soc.) Oxford, 1909.
Diary	The Diary of Samuel Pepys. Ed. by R.Latham and W.Matthews. London, 1970-
Duff	Bibliotheca Pepysiana. A descriptive catalogue ... Part II. Early printed books to 1558, by E.G.Duff. London, 1914.
Duff, Fifteenth Century	Fifteenth century English books ... By E.G.Duff. (Bibliographical Soc.) Oxford, 1917.
Gaselee	The Spanish books in the library of Samuel Pepys, by S.Gaselee. (Bibliographical Soc.) Oxford, 1921.
GW	Gesamtkatalog der Wiegendrucke. Leipzig, 1925-
Heath	The letters of Samuel Pepys and his family circle. Ed. by H.T.Heath. Oxford, 1955.
Howarth	Letters and the second diary of Samuel Pepys. Ed. by R.G.Howarth. London, 1932.
Naval Minutes	Samuel Pepys's Naval Minutes. Ed. by J.R.Tanner. (Navy Records Soc.) London, 1926.
STC	Short-title catalogue of books printed in England ... 1475-1640. Compiled by A.W.Pollard & G.R.Redgrave. London, 1926.
	———————— 2nd ed. Vol.II (I-Z). Ib., 1976.
Tangier Papers	The Tangier papers of Samuel Pepys. Transcribed ... by E.Chappell. (Navy Records Soc.) London, 1935.
Tanner	Bibliotheca Pepysiana. A descriptive catalogue ... Part I. 'Sea' manuscripts, by J.R.Tanner. London, 1914.
Wilson	Samuel Pepys's Spanish chap-books. *In* Transactions of the Cambridge Bibliographical Soc., vol.II, pts 2, 3 & 4, 1955-7.
Wing	Short-title catalogue of books printed in England ... 1641-1700. Compiled by D.Wing. New York, 1945-51.
	———————— 2nd ed. Vol.I (A-England). Ib., 1972.

Abbreviations and Contractions

brs.	broadside
col.	coloured
ed.	edition, edited
engr., engrs	engraved, engraving(s)
fo. [in imprint]	folio
ff. [in stating number of foliated leaves]	leaves
fp., fps	frontispiece(s)
impr.	impression
ll.	leaves
pl., pls	plate(s)
port., ports	portrait(s)
pr.	printed
s. sh.	single sheet

A

A.(J.). M.D.   *See* ARBUTHNOT (John).

A.(H.D.M.). A sober and temperate discourse,
1661.
See DAWBENY (Henry).   **1189(5)**

ABBADIE (Jacques). Traité de la divinité de Nôtre
Seigneur Jesus-Christ.   12mo.
Rotterdam, chez Reinier Leers, 1689   **496**

——————————Traité de la vérité de la religion
chrétienne.   2 pts in 2 vols.   8vo.
Rotterdam, chez Reinier Leers, 1684   **1499-1500**

ABENHOMIN, *pseud.*   *See* PÉREZ DE HITA
(Ginés).

ABENTARIQUE (Abulcacim Tarif), *pseud.*
See LUNA (Miguel).

ABLANCOURT (Jean Jacobé de Frémont d').
See FRÉMONT D'ABLANCOURT (Jean
Jacobé de).

ABREGÉ de la vie de Monsieur de Turenne.
12mo.
Ville-Franche, chez Charles de la Verité, 1680
    99(3)

ABREGÉ de la vie des peintres, 1699.
See PILES (Roger de).   **804**

ABRIDGEMENT (The) or summarie of the Scots
chronicles, 1671.
See MONIPENNIE (John).   **337**

ABSTRACT (An) of the orphans accounts, as
they were drawn out of the books in the Chamber
of London ... According to ... An Act for the relief of orphans and other creditors.   fo.
[London, 1694]   Bound in after p.660.
Wing A138A.   **2476**

ACADÉMIE FRANÇAISE. Le dictionnaire de
l'Académie françoise.   2 vols in 1.   fo.
*Paris, chez la veuve de Jean Baptiste Coignard, et
chez Jean Baptiste Coignard,* 1694   Engr. fp.
    2811

ACADÉMIE ROYALE DES SCIENCES. Recueil
d'observations, 1693.
See RECUEIL d'observations ...   **2617**

ACCADEMIA DEL CIMENTO. Essayes of natural
experiments made in the Academie del Cimento ...
Englished by R.Waller.   4to.
London, for Benjamin Alsop, 1684   Engr. fp.,
19 engr. pls.   Wing A161.   **1797**

ACCOUNT (An) of Denmark, 1694.
See MOLESWORTH (Robert, Viscount).   **1209**

ACCOUNT (An) of Mr.Blunts late book, entituled, King William and Queen Mary conquerors,
ordered by the House of Commons to be burnt.
2nd ed.   4to.
London, 1693   [Consutilia VII]   **1433(2)**

ACCOUNT (An) of several new inventions, 1691.
See HALE (Thomas).   **396**

ACCOUNT (An) of the arraignments and tryals of
Col.R.Kirkby, Capt.J.Constable, C.Wade, S.Vinc-
ent, and C.Fogg ... at a court-martial ... for coward-
ice.   fo.
*London, for John Gellibrand, and are to be sold
by A.Baldwin,* 1703   [Narratives & Tryals VII]
    2255(13)

ACCOUNT (An) of the debate in town about
peace and war. In letters to a gentleman in the
countrey.   fo.
[London, 1701]   [Consutilia X]   **1436(13)**

ACCOUNT (An) of the execution of Brigadier
Rookwood, Major Lowick and Mr.Cranburn.   brs.
London, for Richard Baldwin, 1696   [Narratives
& Tryals VI]   Wing A287.   **2254(11)**

ACCOUNT (An) of the growth of deism in England, 1696.
See STEPHENS (William).   **1435(5)**

ACCOUNT (An) of the late great victory obtained
at sea, against the French.   4to.
London, for John Rawlins, 1692   [Naval
Pamphlets]   Wing A310.   **1399(8)**

ACCOUNT (An) of the tryal of C.Bateman [and
others], 1685.
See BATEMAN (Charles).   **2253(18)**

ACCOUNT (An) of what passed at the execution
of the late Duke of Monmouth.   fo.
*London, for Robert Horne, John Baker and
Benjamin Took,* 1685   [Narratives & Tryals V]
Wing A433.   **2253(16)**

ACHMET BEN ABDALLA, *pseud.* Mohammedica:
sive dissertatio epistolaris de veritate religionis
Christianæ.   12mo.
Altdorfii, apud Ch.Wagenselium jun., 1700   **433**

ACOSTA (Joseph de). The naturall and morall
historie of the East and West Indies ... translated
into English by E.G[rimstone?].   4to.
*London, printed by Val:Sims for Edward Blount
and William Aspley,* 1604   Wants A1,4, b4.
STC 94.   **1126**

ACTA eruditorum anno (1682)-(1691).   10 vols.
4to.
Lipsiæ, prostant apud J.Grossium [etc.], 1682
(-1691)   **1611-20**

———— Supplementa. Vol.I. 4to.
Ib., 1692   1621

———— Indices generales. 4to.
Ib., 1693   1622

ACTA eruditorum anno (1692)-(1696) publicata.
5 vols.   4to.
Lipsiæ, prostant apud J.Grossii hæred. [*etc.*],
1692 (-1696)   1623-7

———— Supplementa. Vol.II. 4to.
Ib., 1696   1628

ACTA eruditorum anno (1697)-(1702) publicata.
6 vols.   4to.
Lipsiæ, prostant apud Joh.Grossii hæred. [*etc.*],
1697 (-1702)   1629-34

———— Supplementa. Vol.III. 4to.
Ib., 1702   1635

ACTA eruditorum anno (1703) publicata.   4to.
Lipsiæ, prostant apud Joh.Grossii hæred. [*etc.*],
1703   1636

ACTES et memoires des negotiations de la paix de
Nimegue, 1680.
See FRANCE. *Treaties.*   469-72

ACTS (The) and life of ... Robert Bruce King of
Scotland, 1670.
See BARBOUR (John).   528

ACTS (The) and negotiations ... of the general
peace, concluded at Ryswick, 1698.
See FRANCE. *Treaties.*   1247

ADAM Bell, Clim of the Clough, and William of
Cloudesle.   4to.
London, by A.M. for W.Thackeray [c.1685]
[Vulgaria III]   Woodcut on title-page.
Wing A473.   1192(16)

ADAMS (John). Index villaris.   fo.
*London, by A.Godbid and J.Playford, for the
Author,* 1680   Wing A479.   2886

ADDISON (Lancelot). The life and death of
Mahumed.   8vo.
London, printed for William Crooke, 1679
Wing A523.   936

ADDY (William). Stenographia or the art of short-
writing compleated.   8vo.
*London, printed for ye author, sold by Dorman
Newman and Samuel Crouch* [*etc.*], [c.1693]
[Short-hand Collection IV]   Engr. port. (Charr-
ington p.1).   Engr. title-page, 16 engr. pp.
Wing A571.   Carlton p.104.   860(3)

ADMONITION (An) to the Parliament [1572].
See FIELD (John).   209(3)

[ADRICHOMIUS (Christianus)]. A description
and explanation of two hundred sixty and eight
places in Jerusalem.   fo.
[*London,*] *pr. and sould by Iohn Overton,* 1677
10 leaves, mounted. With an engr. folding map of
Jerusalem, 49.5 x 74 cm., engr. by C.Whitwell,
with imprint: *printed and sould by peter stent.*
                                            2907(7)

ADVENTURES (The) of (Mr.T.S.) an English
merchant, 1670.
See S.(T.).   244(2)

AELFRIC. A Saxon treatise concerning the Old
and New Testament. (—A testimonie of antiquitie.
—A sermon of the paschall lambe.)   4to.
London, by Iohn Haviland for Henrie Seile, 1623.
With title-page and conjugate leaf of "Divers
ancient monuments in the Saxon tongue", 1638
(STC 15705) bound in after f4.   STC 160.
                                            1170

AESCHINES. Ὁ κατὰ Κτησιφῶντος καὶ Δημο-
σθένους ὁ περὶ στεφάνου λόγος. Interpretationem
Latinam ... adjecerunt P.Foulkes, J.Freind.   8vo.
Ἐκ Θεάτρου ἐν Ὀξονία, *excud. Johan.Crooke,*
1696   Engr. ports.   Wing A682.   1781

AESOP. Fabularum Æsopicarum delectus. [Ed.
A.Alsop.]   *Gk & Lat.*   8vo.
*Oxoniæ, e Theatro Sheldoniano, excud. Johan.
Croke,* 1698   Engr. fp.   Wing A729.   1758

———— The fables of Æsop paraphras'd in
verse ... by J.Ogilby.   fo.
London, by Thomas Roycroft, for the author,
1665   Engr. port. (Charrington p.128), 82
engr. pls.   Wing A693; Diary 5 & 18 Jan.
1660/1, 24 May 1663, 19 Feb. 1665/6.   2832

———— Æsop's fables with his life ...
Illustrated by F.Barlow.   fo.
*London, by H.Hills jun. for Francis Barlow, and
are to be sold by Chr.Wilkinson* [*etc.*], 1687
31 engr. pls, 112 engr. in text.   Wing A703.
                                            2637

———— Fables of Æsop ... with morals and
reflexions. By Sir Roger L'Estrange.   fo.
London, for R.Sare, T.Sawbridge, B.Took [*etc.*],
1692   Engr. port. (Charrington p.99).
Wing A706.   2340

———— Fables and storyes moralized.
Being a second part of the fables of Aesop.   fo.
London, for R.Sare, 1699   Wing L1247.   2341

AGARDE (Arthur). The repertorie of records,
1631.
See POWELL (Thomas), *Londino-Cambrensis.*
                                            940(1)

AGREDA (Sor María de Jesús de). Mystica ciudad
de Dios.   3 vols.   fo.
Lisboa, de Antonio Craesbeeck de Mello, 1681.
Engr. title-page, port.   Gaselee 99.   2202-4

AGRICOLA (Georgius). De re metallica libri XII ...
Ejusdem de animantibus subterraneis liber.   fo.
Basileæ Helvet., sumpt. itemque typis chalco-
graphicis Ludovici Regis, 1621   a6 missing:
oblong slip at p.97. Woodcuts.   **2357**

AGRIPPA (Heinrich Cornelius). The vanity of
arts and sciences.   8vo.
London, by J.C. for Samuel Speed, 1676
Engr. fp. (port., Charrington p.1).   Wing A790.
        1158

AGUIRTE (Francisco). Gracioso cuento, y ardid,
que tuvo vna muger para engañar à tres demonios...
al fin vn Romance, de como el Rey Don Alonso
ganò à Toledo.   4to.
(*Seuilla, por Juan Cabeças,*) [c.1680]   Gaselee 1;
Wilson p.267.   **1545(54)**

AIM. Ayme for Finsbvrie archers, 1601.
See B.(E.).   **4**

AITZEMA (Lieuwe van). Historia pacis, à foedera-
tis Belgis ab anno (1621) ad hoc usque tempus
tractatæ.   4to.
Lugduni Batavorum, ex off. Joannis & Danielis
Elsevier, 1654   **1752**

ALABASTER (William). Roxana tragædia.   8vo.
Londini, excud. Gulielmus Jones, 1632.   Engr.
title-page.   STC 250.   **218(2)**

ALARM. An allarum from heaven; or a warning to
rash wishers.   8vo.
London, for Iosiah Blare, 1683   [Penny-
Godlinesses]   Woodcut.   Wing A824A.
        365(46)

ALBANI (Giovanni Francesco).
See CLEMENT XI, Pope.

ALBERTI (Giovanni Matteo). Giuochi festivi, e
militari ... et altri sontuosi apprestamenti di
allegrezza esposti alla sodisfattione vniversale dalla
generosità d'Ernesto Augusto Duca di Brunsvich ...
nel tempo di sua dimora in Venetia.   fo.
Venetia, nella stamparia di Andrea Poletti, 1686.
15 engr. (chiefly by A.della Via).   **2567**

[ALBERUS (Erasmus)]. Alcoranus Franciscanorum
... blasphemiarum et nugarum lerna.   12mo.
Daventriæ, typis Johannis Columbii, 1651
Engr. title-page.   **52**

ALCÁZAR Y ZUÑIGA (Juan Antonio del).
Panegyrico historial, y exhortacion gratulatoria.
4to.
Seuilla, por Iuan Vejarano, 1683   Gaselee 2.
        1546(4)

ALCORANUS Franciscanorum, 1651.
See ALBERTUS (Erasmus).   **52**

ALDRETE (Bernardo José). Del origen, y principio
de la lengua Castellana.   4to.

En Roma, acerca de Carlo Wllietto, 1606.   Engr.
title-page (by P.Thomassinus).   Gaselee 3.
        1550(1)

——————— Del origen y principio de la
lengua castellana. (– Tesoro de la lengua castellana
... compuesto por ... S.de Covarruvias Orozco.)
3 vols in 1.   fo.
Madrid, por Melchor Sanchez, a costa de Gabriel
de Leon, 1674 (1673)   Gaselee 4.   **2183**

[ALDRICH (Henry)]. Artis logicæ compendium.
12mo.
Oxoniæ, e Theatro Sheldoniano excud. Johan.
Crooke, 1696   Engr. fp.   Wing A898.   **569**

——————— A narrative of the proceedings of
... Convocation, 1701.
See HOOPER (George), Bp of Bath and Wells.
        1697(4)

[ALENCÉ (Joachim d')]. Traitté de l'aiman ... Par
Mr.D*** [i.e. J.d'Alencé].   12mo.
Amsterdam, chez Henry Wetstein, 1687   Engr.
fp. and 33 pls.   **489(1)**

[———————] Traittez des baromÉtres, ther-
momÉtres, et notiomÉtres ou hygromÉtres. Par
Mr.D*** [i.e. J.d'Alencé].   12mo.
Amsterdam, chez Henry Wetstein, 1688   Engr.
& pr. title-pages, 35 pls.   **489(2)**

ALETHAEUS (Theophilus), *pseud.*
See LYSER (Johann).

ALEXANDER (Joannes). Synopsis algebraica ...
In usum Scholæ mathematicæ apud Hospitium-
Christi Londinense.   8vo.
Londini, impensis Hospitii: typis Benj. Motte,
1693   Diagrams.   Wing A913.   **961**

ALFANTEGA Y CORTÉS (Francisco). Aqui se
contienen quatro Romances famosos.   4to.
(*Sevilla, por Juan Vejarano, à costa de Lucas*
Martin de Hermosa,) [c.1680]   Gaselee 5;
Wilson p.255.   **1545(36)**

ALLESTREE (Charles). The desire of all men. A
sermon preach'd ... March 5, 1694/5 (Being the day
of the interment of our late ... Queen).   4to.
London, for Thomas Bennet, and Obediah Smith,
1695   Wing A1080.   **1528(11)**

[ALLESTREE (Richard)]. The art of contentment.
8vo.
Oxford, at the Theater, 1675   Engr. fp.
Wing A1085.   **1088**

[———————] The causes of the decay of
Christian piety.   8vo.
London, by R.Norton for Edward Pawlet, 1694
Woodcut on title-page.   Wing A1108.   Diary
5 Jan. 1667/8.   **1086**

[——————] The gentleman's calling.   8vo.
London, by R.Norton for Robert Pawlet, 1673
Engr. title-page by W.Dolle.   Wing A1123.
1084

[——————] The government of the tongue.
2nd impr.   8vo.
Oxford, at the Theater, 1674   Engr. fp.
Wing A1134.   **1087**

[——————] The ladies calling.   2nd impr.
2 pts.   8vo.
Oxford, at the Theater, 1673   Engr. fp.
Wing A1142.   **1085**

[——————] The lively oracles given to us.
8vo.
Oxford, at the Theater, 1678   Engr. fp. by Burg.
Wing A1149.   **1089**

[——————] The whole duty of man.   8vo.
London, printed by W.Norton for Edward Pawlet,
1702   Engr. & pr. title-pages, engr. fp.   **1083**

ALLIX (Pierre). Réflexions sur les cinq livres de
Moyse, pour établir la verité de la religion
chrétienne.   8vo.
Londres, chés B.Griffin, pour Jean Cailloué, 1687
Wing A1228.   **1206**

—————— Reflexions upon the books of the
Holy Scripture.   2 vols in 1.   8vo.
London, for Richard Chiswell, 1688
Wing A1227.   **1171**

—————— Remarks upon the ecclesiastical
history of the antient churches of the Albigenses.
4to.
London, for Richard Chiswell, 1692
Wing A1230.   **1549(3)**

—————— Some remarks upon the ecclesiastical history of the ancient churches of Piedmont.
4to.
London, for Richard Chiswell, 1690
Wing A1231.   **1549(2)**

ALMANAC. An almanack but for one day.   12mo.
*[London] for J.Clarke, W.Thackeray, and T.Pass-
inger*, [c.1685]   [Penny-Godlinesses]
Woodcut on title-page.   **365(14)**

—————— An almanack for two days, viz. the
day of death. And the day of judgement.   12mo.
[c.1680]   [Penny-Godlinesses]   Woodcuts on
title-page and B4v. Title cropped.   **365(44)**

ALSTED (Johann Heinrich). Encyclopædia.
7 vols in 2.   fo.
Herbornæ Nassoviorum, 1630   Diary 27 Oct.
1660.   **2523-4**

—————— Thesaurus chronologiæ.   Ed. 3a.
8vo.
Herbornæ Nassoviorum, 1637   **1136**

ALVA (Perro de).   *See* RODRIGUEZ (Pedro).

ALVAREZ SOLÍS (Antonio). Aqui se contiene un
notable caso, que sucedió â vna muger.   4to.
[Seville, c.1680]   Gaselee 169; Wilson p.229.
1545(14)

AMELOT DE LA HOUSSAYE (Abraham
Nicolas). The history of the government of Venice.
8vo.
London, printed by H.C. for John Starkey, 1677
Wing A2974.   **1220**

AMMAN (Jost). *For* Cleri totius Romanæ ecclesiæ
... *and* Gynæceum ..., *see* MODIUS (Franciscus).

AMOUR (L') marié, ou la bisarrerie de l'amour en
l'estat du mariage.   12mo.
Cologne, chez Pierre Marteau, 1681.   **83(1)**

[AMPELE ende waarachtige beschrijving ...].
A large and true discourse, wherein is set foorth ...
in what manner all the six great gallies — sent out
of Spayne ... — are destroyed ... All written aboord
the ship of G.Euertson ... 7 Oct.1602. Truly translated out of the Dutch.   4to.
London, Felix Kyngston, sold by Iohn Newberry
[1602]   [Consutilia V]   Title-page cropped.
1431(15)

AMYDENUS (Theodorus).
See MEYDEN (Theodor van).

AMYNTOR: or, a defence of Milton's life, 1699.
See TOLAND (John).   **1082(1)**

AMYRAUT (Moïse). Traitté des religions.
2e éd.   4to.
Saumur, par Iean Lesnier, 1652.   **1829**

ANACREON. Carmina ... operaque & studio
H.Foppens recusa.   *Gk & Lat.*   12mo.
Antverpiae, apud viduam J.Cnobbari, 1651
Autograph Σαμνὴλ Πῆπυς in Pepys's hand.   **17**

—————— Les poësies d'Anacreon et de
Sapho, traduites de grec en françois ... par
Mademoiselle Le Fevre.   *Gk & Fr.*   12mo.
Paris, chez Denys Thierry. Et Claude Barbin, 1681
727

ANALOGIA honorum [by J.Logan], 1677.
See GUILLIM (John). A display of heraldry.   **2576**

ANALYSE des infiniment petits, 1696.
See L'HOSPITAL (Guillaume François Antoine de),
Marquis de Sainte-Mesme.   **1939**

ANDERSON (Lionel). The tryals ... of L.Anderson
[and others], 1680.   *See* TRIALS. The tryals
and condemnation ...   **2252(6)**

ANDREWES (Lancelot), Bp of Winchester. [Form
of consecration of a church.]   12mo.
[London, sold by T.Garthwait, 1659?]   Wants
all before B1.   Wing A3126.   **428(2)**

———————— XCVI. sermons ... 4th ed.
(A sermon preached at the funerall of ... Lancelot
late Lord Bishop of Winchester ... by Iohn [Buck-
eridge] late L.Bishop of Ely.)   fo.
London, printed by Richard Badger, 1641
Engr. fp. (port., Charrington p.4).   Wing A3142.
                                                2485

———————— Preces privatæ Graecè & Latinè.
12mo.
Oxonii, e theatro Sheldoniano, 1675   Engr. fp.
(port., Charrington p.4).   Wing A3149.   141

ANDREWS (William). News from the stars: or, an
ephemeris for the year, 1688.   8vo.
*London, printed by A.G. for the Company of
Stationers*, 1688   [Almanacks for the year 1688]
Wing A1284.   **425(1)**

ANGEL (El) de la guarda. Comedia famosa: de don
Pedro Calderon.
For this work, probably not by Calderon, see
CALDERÓN DE LA BARCA (Pedro).   **1553(21)**

ANGLICA, Normannica, Hibernica, Cambrica a
veteribus scripta ... ex bibliotheca G.Camdeni. fo.
*Francofurti, impensis Claudij Marnii, & hæredum
Ioannis Aubrij*, 1603   Woodcut ports. Autograph
on title-page: 'Jo: Dauys, 24 July 1605'; with
marginal notes in same hand.   Diary 21 Nov.
1661.   **2530**

ANGLO-SAXON CHRONICLE. Chronicon Saxon-
icum. Opera & studio Edmundi Gibson.
Anglo-Saxon and Lat.   4to.
Oxonii, e theatro Sheldoniano, 1692   Engr. map.
Wing A3185.   **1856**

ANIMADVERSIONS upon a letter and paper,
1656.   *See* SEDGWICK (William).   **1185(6)**

ANNALS (The) of King James and King Charles,
1681.   *See* FRANKLAND (Thomas).   **2560**

ANNE, *Queen of England*. By the Queen, a pro-
clamation. Forasmuch as it hath pleased Almighty
God, lately to call unto his infinite mercy ...
William the Third ... 9 March [1701/2].   brs.
*London, by Charles Bill, and the executrix of
Thomas Newcomb*, 1701   [*Inserted between
nos 3790 & 3791 of the London Gazette.*]   **2090**

ANNOTATIONS upon all the books of the Old
and New Testament. [By J.Downame, etc.]
2nd ed.   2 vols.   fo.
London, by John Legatt, 1651   Wing D2063.
                                           2495-6

ANSWER (An) to a book entituled, An humble
remonstrance, 1641.   *See* MARSHALL
(Stephen).   **1429(1)**

ANSWER (An) to a book, intituled, The state of
the Protestants in Ireland under the late King
James's government, 1692.
See LESLIE (Charles).   **1591**

ANSWER (An) to a Third letter to a clergyman in
the country, 1702.   *See* TRIMNELL (Charles),
Bp of Winchester.   **1696(8)**

ANSWER (An) to Mr Langhorn's speech.   fo.
[*London*, c.1679]   [Narratives & Tryals III]
Wing A3368.   **2251(27)**

ANSWER (An) to the late exceptions made by Mr
Erasmus Warren against the theory of the earth,
1690.   *See* BURNET (Thomas).   **2271(1)**

ANSWER (An) to the late K.James's last declaration, 1693.   *See* WELLWOOD (James).
                                         1433(3)

ANSWER (An) to the paper ... by Mr Ashton,
1690.
See FOWLER (Edward), Bp of Gloucester.
                                        2253(24)

[ANTHONISZ (Cornelis)]. The safegarde of
saylers, or great rutter ... Transl. out of Dutch [i.e.
from Het Leeskaartboek van Wisbuy] ... by R.
Norman.   4to.
London, by Edward Allde, 1590
[Sea Tracts II]   Woodcut, diagrams.
STC 21547.   **1078(2)**

ANTHONY, of Padua, St. Responsorio di
S.Antonio di Padova. Con molt' altre diuotioni.
32mo.
Ronciglione, per il Menichelli, [c.1698]   Last
leaf defective.   **145(5)**

ANTIDOTUM Britannicum, 1681.
See W.(W.).   **467(1)**

ANTIQUITÉ (L') des tems rétablie et defenduë,
1687.   *See* PEZRON (Paul Yves).   **680**

APOLOGIE pour les Catholiques, 1681-2.
See ARNAULD (Antoine).   **494-5**

APOLOGY (An) for the new separation, 1691.
See HICKES (George).   **1573(2)**

APOPHTHEGMATA aurea, regia, Carolina ...
Collected out of the incomparable Εἰκὼν Βασιλική.
8vo.
*London, printed by William Du-gard for Francis
Eglesfield*, 1649.   Wing A3560A.   **721(2)**

APPENDIX (An) containing a brief account of
some other eminent fathers, 1682.
See CAVE (William).   **2355(3)**

APPIAN. The history ... in two parts ... Made Eng-
lish by J.D.   fo.
London, for John Amery, 1679   Wants a4.
Wing A3579.   **2408**

AQUI se contienen dos obras maravillosas,
[c.1680].
See SANCHEZ DE LA CRUZ (Matheo).   **1545(18)**

AQUI se contienen dos romances contemplativos.
El primero trata, como el glorioso ... San Fran-
cisco dexò la casa de su padre.   4to.
*En Sevilla, por Juan Vejarano, à costa de Lucas
Martin de Hermosa*, [c.1680]   Gaselee 156;
Wilson p.144.   **1545(4)**

AQUI se contienen quatro loas famosas, 1673.
See VALLEJO (Manuel de).   **1545(43)**

ARANDA (Emanuel d'). The history of Algiers
and it's slavery ... English'd by John Davies of
Kidwelly.   8vo.
London, printed for John Starkey, 1666
Double-page engr.   Wing A3595.   Diary
18 Dec.1667.   **754**

[ARBUTHNOT (John)]. An examination of Dr.
Woodward's account of the deluge, &c. By
J.A[rbuthnot]. M.D.   8vo.
London, for C.Bateman, 1697   Wing A3601.
                                        1242(2)

ARCANA aulica: or Walsingham's manual; of
prudential maxims, for the states-man, 1655.
See DU REFUGE (Eustace).   **43**

ARCHOMBROTUS et Theopompus, 1669.
See BUGNOT (Louis Gabriel).   **1369**

ARCONS (César d'). Du flux et reflux de la mer.
2e éd.   4to.
Bourdeaux, se vend à Paris chez Iacques Cottin,
1667.   Wants ã4.   **1814**

ARGUMENT (An) against war: in opposition to
some late pamphlets, particularly; The first and
second part of the Duke of Anjou's succession
consider'd.   4to.
London, 1701   [Consutilia X]   **1436(12)**

ARGUMENT (An) shewing, that a standing army
is inconsistent with a free government, 1697.
See TRENCHARD (John).   **1433(19)**

ARGUMENT (An) shewing, that a standing army,
with consent of Parliament, is not inconsistent
with a free government, 1698.
See DEFOE (Daniel).   **1433(21)**

ARGUMENTUM anti-Normannicum, 1682.
See COOKE (Edward).   **970**

ARISTEAS. Historia LXXII interpretum.
Gk & Lat.   8vo.
Oxonii, e Theatro Sheldoniano, 1692   Engr. fp.
(by M.Burg).   Wing A3683.   **1309**

ARISTOTLE. Τέχνης ῥητορικῆς βιβλία γ΄... Artis
rhetoricae libri tres; ab A.Riccobono Latine con-
versi.   *Gk & Lat.*   2 pts.   8vo.
*Hanoviae, typis Wechelianis, apud Claudium
Marnium & heredes Iohannis Aubrii*, 1606.   **576**

ARLINGTON (Henry Bennet, 1st Earl of). Letters
to Sir W.Temple, Bar. from July 1665 ... to Sept.

1670. Ed. by Tho.Bebington.   (Vol.2: Letters to
Sir Richard Fanshaw, [etc.] ... from 1664 to
1674.)   8vo.
London, Tho.Bennet, 1701.   Engr. fps (ports,
Charrington p.7).   **1355-6**

ARMINIUS (Jacobus). Opera theologica.
2 vols.   4to.
Lugduni Batavorum, apud Godefridum Basson,
1629.   **1176-7**

ARMSTRONG (Sir Thomas). The proceedings
against Sir Thomas Armstrong.   fo.
(*London, for Robert Horn, John Baker, and John
Redmayne*, 1684)   [Narratives & Tryals V]
Wing P3546.   **2253(12)**

[ARNAULD (Antoine)]. Apologie pour les
Catholiques, contre les faussetez & les calomnies
d'un livre intitulé: La politique du Clergé de
France.   2 pts.   12mo.
Liege, chez la veuve Bronkart, 1681-2   **494-5**

[————————] Grammaire generale, 1664.
See LANCELOT (Claude).   **509**

[————————] Nouvelle défense de la
traduction du Nouveau Testament imprimée à
Mons; contre le livre de M.Mallet.   2 vols.
12mo.
Cologne, chez Symon Schouten, 1682   **510-11**

[————————] The pernicious consequences
of the new heresie of the Jesuites against the
king and the state. [By A.Arnauld and P.Nicole.
Transl. by J.Evelyn.]   8vo.
London, by J.Flesher, for Richard Royston, 1666
Wing N1138.   **930**

[ARNOLD (Richard)]. [I]n this booke is con-
teyned the names of ye baylifs custos mairs and
sherefs of the cite of londō from the tyme of king
richard the furst.   fo.
[*Antwerp, Adrien van Berghen*, 1503?]   Wants
title-page & 6 leaves.   STC 782. Duff p.1. **1882**

ARRAIGNMEN[T] (The) of lewd, idle, froward,
and unconstant women, 1682.
See SWETNAM (Joseph).   **1192(23)**

ARROWSMITH (John). The covenant-avenging
sword ... a sermon ... Jan.25.   4to.
London, for Samuel Man, 1643   [Sermons
Polemical I]   Wing A3773.   **1179(1)**

——————————— Englands Eben-ezer ... In a sermon preached ... March 12.   4to.
London, by Robert Leyburn, for Samuel Man,
1645   [Sermons Polemical I]   Wants A4, F2.
Wing A3775.   **1179(2)**

ART (L') de naviger, 1677.
See MILLIET DE CHALES (Claude François). **1910**

ART(L') de plaire dans la conversation, 1690.
See ORTIGUE DE VAUMORIÈRE (Pierre d'). **439**

ART (The) of contentment, 1675.
See ALLESTREE (Richard). **1088**

ART (The) of courtship. 12mo.
[*London*] *Printed for J.M. by I.Back*, 1687
[Penny-Merriments II]　Wing A3789A.
363(16)

ART (The) of numbring by speaking-rods, 1667.
See LEYBOURN (William). **12(1)**

ARTICULI Lambethani ... cura & impensis F.G.
12mo.
Londini, typis G.D., veneunt apud Rob.Beaumont,
1651　Wing A3890. **374(1)**

ARTIS logicæ compendium, 1696.
See ALDRICH (Henry). **569**

ASCHAM (Anthony). A discourse: wherein is examined, what is particularly lawfull during the con-
fusions and revolutions of government.　8vo.
London, printed, anno Dom: 1648　Wing A3920.
701

ASHBY (Sir John). The account given by Sir John
Ashby Vice-Admiral, and Reere-Admiral Rooke ...
of the engagement at sea ... June the 30th. 1690.
4to.
London, for Randal Taylor, 1691　[Naval Pam-
phlets]　Wing A3937. **1399(7)**

ASHE (Simeon). The best refuge for the most
oppressed, in a sermon preached ... March 30. 4to.
London, for Edward Brewster and Iohn Burroughs,
1642　[Sermons Polemical I]　Wing A3949.
1179(3)

───────── The doctrine of zeal explained ...
in a sermon preached ... 12th of Novemb. 1654.
4to.
London, by A.M. for George Saubridge, 1655
[Sermons Polemical I]　Wing A3952. **1179(4)**

ASHMOLE (Elias). The institution, laws & ceremonies of the most noble Order of the Garter. fo.
London, by J.Macock, for Nathanael Brooke,
1672　Engr. fp. (port., Charrington p.32).
32 pls by W.Hollar.　Wing A3983. **2574**

ASHTON (John). The arraignment, trials ... of ...
John Ashton, 1691.
See PRESTON (Sir Richard Graham, Viscount).
2253(23)

───────── Mr.Ashton's paper [1690].
See FOWLER (Edward), Bp of Gloucester.
2253(24)

ASSIZE (The) of bread. Here begynnethe the boke
named the assyse of bread, what it ought to waye,
after the pryce of a quarter of wheete.　4to.
*Enprynted at the request of Mychaell Englysshe
and Johñ Rudstone aldermen, (by Rychard Bākes,)*
[c.1530]　Vellum; woodcuts.　[Consutilia
VIII]　STC 864; Duff p.1. **1434(9)**

ASSIZE (The) of bread, with sundry good and
needful ordinances.　4to.
London, for And.Crook, 1671　Woodcuts.
Wing P3059. **1340(10)**

ATHENÆ Oxonienses, 1691-2.
See WOOD (Anthony à). **2822**

ATHENIAN (The) Mercury. Nos 29-31. 5-12 July,
1692.　fo.
London, for John Dunton, 1692
[*Inserted between nos 2781 & 2782 of the London
Gazette.*] **2086**

[ATKYNS (Richard)] . The original and growth of
printing.　s.sh. 31.5 x 18 cm.
[c.1660]　Wing A4134. **1398(3)**

ATKYNS (Sir Robert). An argument in the great
case concerning election of members to Parliament.
fo.
London, for Tim.Goodwin, 1689　The final
section of Atkyns' 'A defence of the late Lord
Russel's innocency'.　Wing A4136. **2364(3)**

───────── A defence of the late Lord
Russel's innocency.　fo.
London, for Timothy Goodwin, 1689　Wants
the final section 'An argument in the great case ...'
[Narratives & Tryals V]　Wing A4136. **2253(4)**

───────── An enquiry into the power of
dispensing with penal statutes.　fo.
London, for Timothy Goodwin, 1689
Wing A4138. **2364(2)**

───────── The Lord Russel's innocency
further defended.　fo.
London, for Timothy Goodwin, 1689　[Narra-
tives & Tryals V]　Wing A4140. **2253(5)**

───────── The power, jurisdiction and
priviledge of Parliament.　fo.
London, for Timothy Goodwin, 1689
Wing A4141. **2364(1)**

[ATTERBURY (Francis), Bp of Rochester]. The
case of the schedule stated.　4to.
London, for T.Bennet, 1702　[Convocation
Pamphlets XI]　MS notes in hand of Daniel
Waterland. On title-page 'Bp Atterbury' in same
hand. **1697(13)**

[─────────] A continuation of the faithful
account of what past in Convocation.　fo.
(*London, for John Nut*, 1702)　[Convocation
Pamphlets XI] **1697(12)**

[─────────] A faithful account of some
transactions in ... Convocation.　fo.
(*London, for John Nutt*, 1702)　[Convocation
Pamphlets XI]　MS notes in hand of Daniel
Waterland. **1697(10)**

[——————] A faithful account of what past in Convocation, Feb.19, 1701/2. fo. (*London, for John Nut*, 1702) [Convocation Pamphlets XI] MS notes in hand of Daniel Waterland. **1697(11)**

[——————] A letter to a clergyman in the country concerning the choice of members ... for the ensuing Convocation. (— A second letter ...) 4to. (*London, for Thomas Bennet*, 1710) [Convocation Pamphlets XI] On p.1 MS note 'Bp Atterbury' in hand of Daniel Waterland. **1697(7)**

[——————] The parliamentary original and rights of the Lower House of Convocation cleared. 4to. *London, for T.Bennet*, 1702 Wants H4. [Convocation Pamphlets XI] MS notes in hand of Daniel Waterland. On title-page 'Atterbury' in same hand. **1697(14)**

[——————] The power of the Lower House of Convocation to adjourn itself vindicated. 4to. (*London, for Thomas Bennet*, 1701) [Convocation Pamphlets XI] On p.1 'Bp Atterbury' in hand of Daniel Waterland. **1697(3)**

[——————] The rights, powers and principles of an English convocation stated and vindicated. 2nd ed. 8vo. *London, for Tho.Bennet*, 1701 [Convocation Pamphlets VIII] Copy of 25 Hen. VIII Cap. XIX inserted after p.98; at end MS copy of proceedings in Convocation of University of Oxford, 5 May 1701, approving recommendation of the Chancellor, the Duke of Ormonde, that the degree of D.D. be conferred on Atterbury for this book. **1694**

[——————] A third letter to a clergyman in the country. fo. (*London, for Thomas Bennet*, 1702) [Convocation Pamphlets XI] On p.1 'Bp Att:' in Daniel Waterland's hand. **1697(8)**

AUBERT DE VERTOT (René). *See* VERTOT (René Aubert de).

AUBERY (Antoine). L'histoire du Cardinal Duc de Richelieu. fo. *Paris, chez Antoine Bertier*, 1660 Engr. fp. (port. by A.Rousselet, Charrington p.144). **2657**

[——————] Mémoires pour l'histoire du Cardinal Duc de Richelieu. 2 vols. fo. *Paris, chez Antoine Bertier*, 1660 **2658-9**

AUBERY DU MAURIER (Louis). Mémoires pour servir à l'histoire de Hollande et des autres Provinces-Unies. 12mo. *Paris, chez Jean Villette*, 1687 **541**

AUBREY (John). Miscellanies. 8vo. *London, for Edward Castle*, 1696 Wing A4188. **1271**

AUCTORES Latinæ linguæ in vnum redacti corpus ... Adiectis notis D.Gothofredi. Editio postrema. 4to. *Genevæ, apud Iohannem Vignon*, 1622 **1813**

AUGUSTINE, Saint, Bp of Hippo. Of the citie of God: with the learned comments of I.L.Vives. Englished first by J.H[ealey]. 2nd ed. fo. *London, by G.Eld and M.Flesher*, 1620 Wants K3-4. STC 917. **2243**

[——————] Las confessiones ... Traducidas del latin en castellano por el R.Padre P. de Ribadin-eyra. 16mo. *Brusselas, por Francisco Foppens*, 1674 Engr. fp. by R.Collin. Gaselee 6. **7**

[AULNOY (Marie-Catherine Le Jumel de Barne-ville, comtesse d')]. Memoires de la Cour d'Espagne. 2e ed. 2 vols in 1. 12mo. *La Haye, chez Adrian Moetjens*, 1691 **297**

[——————] Relation du voyage d'Espagne. 3 vols in 1. 12mo. *La Haye, chez Henri van Bulderen*, 1691 **298**

AURELIUS (Marcus), Emperor. Τῶν εἰς ἑαυτὸν βιβλία ιβ' ... De seipso & ad seipsum. *Gk & Lat.* 12mo. *Oxoniæ, e theatro Sheldoniano*, 1680 Wing A4226. **140**

[——————] Meditations. 4th ed. 8vo. *London, printed for, and are to be sold by Charles Harper*, 1673 Wing A4229. **942**

AURIGARIUS (Lucas). *See* WAGHENAER (Lucas Jansz).

AVENTURES. Les avantures de Telemaque fils d'Ulysse, 1699. *See* FÉNELON (François de Salignac de la Mothe). **229-30**

AVILER (Augustin Charles d'). Cours d'archi-tecture. 2 vols. 4to. *Paris, chez Nicolas Langlois*, 1691 I: engr. title-page by I.Langlois, 108 engr. pls. II: engr. title-page by I.B.Corneille. **1664-5**

AYME for Finsburie archers, 1601. *See* B.(E.). **4**

B

B****, Mons. Histoire des ouvrages des sçavans, 1687-1703.
See BASNAGE (Jacques), Sieur de Beauval.
109-27

B.(A.). Gloria Britannica; or, the boast of the Brittish seas.   4to.
London, for Thomas Howkins, 1689   [Naval Pamphlets]   Wing B7.   **1399(5)**

B.(A.). The life or the ecclesiasticall historie of S.Thomas Archbishope of Canterbury.   8vo.
Colloniæ, 1639   STC 1019.   **916**

B.(A.). The merry tales of the mad-men of Gotam. By A.B.   12mo.
[*London*] *for J.Clarke, W.Thackeray, and T. Passinger* [c.1680]   [Penny-Merriments II]
Woodcut on title-page.   **363(21)**

B.(A.). A vindication of the late sermon, on — Curse ye Meroz.   4to.
London, by J.Redmayne, 1680   [Sermons Polemical V]   Wing B33.   **1183(23)**

B.(E.). Ayme for Finsbvrie archers ... by E.B. and I.I.   16 mo.
London, by R.F. and are to be sold ... by F. Sergeant, 1601   MS additions in unidentified hand.   **4**

B.(J.). A compleat and true narrative of the manner of the discovery of the Popish plot.   fo.
London, printed and to be sold by Henry Million, 1679   [Narratives & Tryals III]   Wing B98.   **2251(25)**

B.(J.). Crumbs of comfort ... A sermon preached by ... Mr.J.B. ... Novemb. 30th. 1679.   8vo.
[*London*] *for W.T., sold by J.Clarke* [c.1680]
[Penny-Godlinesses]   Woodcut port.
Wing B98A.   **365(10)**

B.(J.). The description and use of the carpenters-rule. [*By* John Brown?]   12mo.
London, by W.G. for William Fisher, 1662
Engr. fp. by R.Gaywood, 3 pls.   Wing B99A.   **85**

B.(J.). The pilgrims progress to the other world; or, a dialogue between two pilgrims.   12mo.
London, by H.B. for T.Passinger, 1684   [Penny-Godlinesses]   **365(41)**

B.(L.). Remarques ou reflexions, 1692.
See BORDELON (Laurent).   **338**

B.(R.). A free enquiry into the ... notion of nature, 1685/6.   *See* BOYLE (Hon. Robert).   **887**

B.(R.). Occasional reflections, 1665.
See BOYLE (Hon. Robert).   **709(2)**

B.(R.). A school of divine meditations.   8vo.
[*London*] *for Jonah Deacon,* [c.1680]   [Penny-Godlinesses]   Wing B170B.   **365(20)**

B.(S.A.).   *See* KINCARDINE (Alexander Bruce, 4th Earl of).

B.(T.H.R.). The Christian virtuoso, 1690-1.
See BOYLE (Hon. Robert).   **759(1-3)**

B.(W.). Cupid's court of salutations.   8vo.
[*London*] *for J.Deacon, to be sold by R.Kell,* 1687   [Penny-Merriments II]   Woodcut on title-page.   Wing B207.   **363(37)**

BABINGTON (Zachary). Advice to Grand Jurors in cases of blood.   8vo.
London, for John Amery, 1680   Wing B249.
1105

BACHELOR'S. The batchellor's banquet, 1677.
See QUINZE (Les) joies de mariage.   **1193(1)**

BACILLY (Bénigne de). Remarques curieuses sur l'art de bien chanter.   12mo.
Paris, chez l'autheur, et chez Monsieur Ballard (de l'imprimerie de C.Blageart), 1668   Engr. title-page.   **570**

BACON (Francis, Viscount St Albans). Baconiana. 8vo.
London, printed by J.D. for Richard Chiswell, 1679   Engr. fp. (port., Charrington p.149).
Wing B269.   **955**

[————————] A declaration of the demeanor ... of Sir W.Raleigh, 1618.
See DECLARATION (A) of the demeanor ...
1429(14)

———————— The elements of the common lawes of England ...   4to.
London, by the assignes of Iohn More, 1639
STC 1134.   **1172**

———————— The essays, or counsels, civil & moral ... With a table of the colours of good and evil. Whereunto is added the wisdome of the ancients.   12mo.
London, printed by Thomas Ratcliffe and Tho. Daniel, for Humphrey Robinson, 1669
Engr. fp. (port., Charrington p.148).
Wing B286A.   **306**

———————— Sermones fideles ... Accedunt Faber fortunae, Colores boni et mali, &c.   12mo.
Amstelodami, ex officina Elzeviriana, 1662
Diary 18 May 1661, 20 July 1663, 5 Feb. 1663/4.
Engr. title.   **48**

——————The history of the reigns of Henry the seventh, Henry the eighth, Edward the sixth, and Queen Mary. The first written by ... Francis ... Viscount St.Alban. The other three by ... F.Godwyn.　2 pts.　fo.
London, by W.G. for R.Scot, T.Basset [etc.], 1676 (1675)　Engr. fp. (port.).　Wing B300.
2201

——————The naturall and experimentall history of winds, &c. ... Translated into English by R.G[entili].　12mo.
London, for Humphrey Moseley and Tho.Dring, 1653　Engr. fp. (port., Charrington p.149). Wing B305.　**429**

——————Resuscitatio, or, bringing into public light several pieces of the works of ... F.Bacon ...　2nd ed. (— Several letters.)　fo.
London, by S.Griffin (by F.L.) for William Lee, 1661 (1657)　Engr. fp. (port., Charrington p.149).　Wing B320.　**2134**

——————Sylva sylvarum: or a natural history. 10th ed., in which is added an epitomy of ... Novum organum.　3 pts.　fo.
London, by S.G. and B.Griffin for Thomas Lee, 1676　Engr. ports, Charrington p.149.　Wing B332 & B310; Diary 15 May 1660.　**2135**

BACON (Nathaniel). An historical and political discourse, 1689.
See SELDEN (John).　**2423**

BACON (Roger). The mirror of alchimy ...　4to.
London (by Thomas Creede) for Richard Oliue, 1597　STC 1182.　**985(3)**

——————Perspectiva ... Nunc primum in lucem edita opera & studio I. Combachii.　4to.
Francofurti, typis Wolffgangi Richteri, sumptibus Antonii Hummij, 1614　Diagrams.　**1208**

BAERLE (Kasper van). Medicea hospes, sive descriptio publicæ gratulationis, qua ... Reginam, Mariam de Medicis, excepit Senatus Populusque Amstelodamensis.　fo.
Amstelodami, typis Iohannis & Cornelii Blaeu, 1638　9 pls.　**2810**

BAGSHAW (Edward). The rights of the Crown of England.　8vo.
London, by A.M. for Simon Miller, 1660 Wing B397.　**606(3)**

BAÏF (Lazare de). Annotationes in L.II. de captiuis, & postliminio reuersis: in quibus tractatur de re nauali ... Antonii Thylesii de coloribus libellus, a coloribus vestium non alienus.
2 vols in 1.　4to.
Lutetiae, ex officina Roberti Stephani, 1549 28 engr. pls.　Adams B37; Duff p.2.　**1763**

——————De re nauali libellus ... ex Bayfii uigilijs excerptus.　8vo.
Lugduni, apud hæredes Simonis Vincentii, 1537 Adams B49; Duff p.3.　**419(1)**

——————De re vestiaria libellus ex Bayfio excerptus.　8vo.
Lugduni, apud hæredes Simonis Vincentii, (excud. Melchior et Gaspar Trechsel fratres,) 1536 Adams B42; Duff p.3.　**419(2)**

——————De re vestiaria, vascularia & nauali: Ex Bayfio. [*Abridged.*]　8vo.
Lutetiæ, apud Carolum Stephanum, 1553 Adams B47; Duff p.3.　**716(1)**

——————De vasculis libellus ... ex Bayfio. 8vo.
Lugduni, apud hæredes Simonis Vincentii, (excud. Melchior et Gaspar Trechsel fratres,) 1536 Adams B55; Duff p.4.　**419(4)**

BAILLET (Adrien). Des enfans devenus célèbres par leurs études ou par leurs écrits. Traité historique.　12mo.
Paris, chez Antoine Dezallier, 1688.　**805**

——————La vie de Mr.Des-Cartes. Réduite en abregé.　12mo.
Paris, chez la veuve Mabre Cramoysi, 1693 Engr. fp.　**430**

[BAILLIE (Robert)]. A parallel, or, briefe comparison of the Liturgie with the Masse-book ... and other Romish ritualls.　4to.
London, by Thomas Paine, 1641　[Liturgick Controversies II]　Wing B465.　**1188(5)**

BAKER (Sir Richard). A chronicle of the Kings of England ...　6th impr.　fo.
London, for George Sawbridge, and Thomas Williams, 1674　Engr. fp. & title-page (ports, Charrington p.11, 32).　Wing B507.　**2566(1)**

[BAKER (Thomas)]. Reflections upon learning ... By a Gentleman [i.e. T.Baker, B.D.].　8vo.
London, for A.Bosvile, 1700　Wing B520.　**1406**

BALCÁRCEL Y LUGO (Francisco). El premio en la tirania. Comedia famosa.　4to.
[*Seville, Juan Cabezas, c.1675*]　Gaselee 7.
1553(1)

BALE (John), Bp of Ossory. Acta Romanorum Pontificum.　8vo.
Basileæ (ex officina I.Oporini, 1558)　Wants all after Q7.　Engr. port., Charrington p.11. Adams B130.　**207**

——————The apology of Johan Bale agaynste a ranke Papyst.　8vo.
London, by Jhon Day, [1555]　STC 1275; Duff p.4.　**108(2)**

———————— The first two partes of the actes or vnchaste examples of the Englyshe votaryes. 2 pts. 8vo.
(*London, by John Tysdale*, 1560)   STC 1274.
128

———————— Scriptorum illustriū maioris Brytannie ... catalogus.   2 pts.   fo.
Basileae, apud Ioannem Oporinum, (1557-9)
Adams B136.   **2167**

BALES (Peter). The writing schoolemaster.   4to.
London, by Thomas Orwin [1590]   [Short-hand Collection V]   STC 1312; Carlton pp.7-9.
1111(1)

BALTRAN (Pedro).   *See* BELTRÁN (Pedro).

[BANCROFT (Richard), Abp of Canterbury].
Daungerous positions and proceedings.   4to.
London, by Iohn Wolfe, 1593   STC 1344.
1237

[————————] A survey of the pretended holy discipline.   4to.
London, printed by R.Hodgkinson, sold by Gab. Bedell, 1663   Wing B639A.   **1651**

BARATTI (Giacomo). The late travels of S.Giacomo Baratti into the remote countries of the Abissins, or of Ethiopia, Interior. Transl. by G.D. 8vo.
London, for Benjamin Billingsley, 1670
Wing B677.   **390**

BARBON (John). Λειτουργία θειοτέρα ἐργία: or, liturgie a most divine service.   4to.
Oxford, by A. & L.Lichfield, 1662   [Liturgick Controversies II]   Wing B703.   **1189(9)**

[BARBOUR (John)]. The acts and life of ... Robert Bruce King of Scotland.   12mo.
Edinburgh, by Andrew Anderson, 1670
Wants sig.K.   Wing B708.   **528**

BARCLAY (John). Argenis, nunc primum illustrata [by L.G.Bugnot].   8vo.
Lugd. Bat., ex officina Francisci Hackii, 1659
Engr. title-page.   Diary 24 Aug. 1660, 8 Nov. 1663.   **1368**

———————— Euphormionis Lusinini, sive Jo. Barclaii, Satyricon ... Accessit Conspiratio anglicana.   8vo.
Lugd. Batavorum, ex officina Hackiana, 1674
Engr. fp. (port., Charrington p.12).   **1367**

[BARIN (Théodore)]. Le monde naissant ou la création du monde demonstrée.   12mo.
Utrect, pour la Compagnie des Libraires, 1686
8 engr. pls.   **579**

BARKER (Matthew). Jesus Christ the great vvonder ... a sermon.   4to.

London, by R.W. for Rapha Harford, 1651
[Sermons Polemical I]   Wing B776.
1179(5)

BARLAEUS (Caspar).
See BAERLE (Kasper van).

BARLOW (William). A breife discovery of the idle animadversions of Marke Ridley ... vpon a treatise entituled, Magneticall aduertisements. 4to.
London, by Edward Griffin for Timothy Barlow, 1618   STC 1443.   **928(4)**

———————— Magneticall aduertisements.   4to.
London, by Edward Griffin for Timothy Barlow, 1616   Engr. diagrams.   STC 1442.   **928(2)**

[————————] The nauigators supply.   4to.
London, by G.Bishop, R.Newbery, and R.Barker, 1597   [Sea Tracts I]   4 engr. diagrams. Wants b4.   On title-page, MS motto 'Magnus ope minorum' in unidentified hand.   STC 1445.
1077(7)

BARNARDISTON (Sir Samuel). The tryal and conviction of Sr Sam.Bernardiston, Bart for high-misdemeanor ... Feb.14.1683.   fo.
London, for Benjamin Tooke, 1684
[Narratives & Tryals V]   Wing T2164.
2253(11)

BARNES (Joshua). The history of that most victorious monarch Edward IIId.   fo.
Cambridge, by John Hayes for the author, 1688
Engr. ports (Charrington p.53-4).   Wing B871.
2557

BARNES (Robert). [A supplicacion vnto the most gracious prynce H. the viii.]   4to.
(*London, imprinted by Johñ Byddell*, 1534)
Wants all before B1.   Port.   STC 1471; Duff p.4.
958(2)

BARNETT (Andrew). A just lamentation ... A sermon preached ... March 5.1694/5.   4to.
London, for Tho.Parkhurst, 1695
Wing B875B.   **1528(12)**

BAROZZI (Giacomo). Regola delli cinque ordini d'architettura.   fo.
Siena, Pietro Marchetti For, [1635]   45 engr. pls.   **2763(1)**

———————— Regola delli cinque ordini d'architettura.   fo.
Venetia, per Catarin Doino, [c.1640]   46 engr. pls.   **2839**

BARRI (Giacomo). The painter's voyage of Italy... Englished by W.L. [i.e. W.Lodge].   8vo.
London, for Tho.Flesher, 1679   Engr. title-page, map, ports (Charrington p.24, 43, 143, 170-1).
Wing B916.   **842**

BARROW (Isaac). Works.   2 vols.   fo.
London, by M.Flesher, for Brabazon Aylmer,
1683   Engr. fps (ports, Charrington p.13).
Wing B925.   **2338-9**

BARTHOLIN (Thomas). Anatomia.   8vo.
Hagæ-Comitis, ex typographia Adriani Vlacq, 1660
Engr. fp. (port., Charrington p.13), title-page & 42
pls.   Diary 12 Sept. 1660.   **1479**

BARTHOLOMAEUS, Anglicus. De proprietatibus
rerum.   fo.
[*W. de Worde, Westminster,* 1495]
See Appendix   **2126**

BARTOLI (Baldassare). Le glorie mæstose del
santuario di Loreto.   8vo.
Macerata, per gl'heredi del Pannelli, 1696
Tanner II, p.130.   **348**

[BASNAGE (Jacques), Sieur de Beauval]. Histoire
des ouvrages des sçavans, par Mons.B**** [i.e.
J.Basnage].   19 vols.   12mo.
Rotterdam, chez Reinier Leers, 1687-1703.
109-27

BASSET (Thomas). A catalogue of the common
and statute law-books of this realm ... Collected by
Thomas Basset.   12mo.
[*London*] *to be sold by Thomas Basset,* 1682
Wing B1044.   **445(1)**

———————— An exact catalogue of the
common and statute law books of this realm.   brs.
[*London*] *by Thomas Basset,* 1684
Wing B1047.   **445(2)**

BASSOMPIERRE (François de). Ambassade du
Mareschal de Bassompierre en Espagne l'an 1621.
12mo.
Cologne, chez Pierre du Marteau, 1668   **305(1)**

———————— Ambassade du Mareschal de
Bassompierre en Suisse l'an 1625.   2 vols.
12mo.
Cologne, chez Pierre du Marteau, 1668   **303-4**

———————— Memoires.   2 vols.   12mo.
Cologne, chez Pierre du Marteau, 1666
Engr. port.   **104-5**

———————— Negociation du Mareschal de
Bassompierre envoyé ambassadeur extraordinaire,
en Angleterre de la part du Roy tres-chrestien,
l'an 1626.   12mo.
Cologne, chez Pierre du Marteau, 1668   **305(2)**

BASTWICK (John). The severall humble petitions
of D.Bastwicke, 1641.
See SEVERAL.   **1429(9)**

BASURTO (Diego de). Vida, y milagros de la
bienaventurada Santa Teresa de Iesus.   4to.
(*Seuila, por Juan Vejarano, à costa de Lucas
Martin,*) [c.1680]   Gaselee 9; Wilson p.153.
1545(13)

BATCHELLORS.   *See* BACHELORS.

BATE (George). Elenchi motuum nuperorum in
Anglia pars prima (— secunda).   8vo.
*Londini, typis J.Flesher & prostant apud R.Roy-
ston,* 1661-3   Engr. fps (ports, Charrington
p.31, 32).   With a MS copy of letter in Latin
(10 Feb. 1662/3) from Dr Richard Owen to John
Evelyn inserted.   Wing B1078, 1081; Diary 25
Feb. 1659/60.   **1055-6**

BATEMAN (Charles). An account of the tryal of
C.Bateman ... for high-treason ... The tryals of
J.Holland and W.Davis ... and A.Wearing.   fo.
London, for D.Mallet, 1685   [Narratives &
Tryals V]   Wing A415.   **2253(18)**

BATES (William). Considerations of the existence
of God.   2nd ed., 2 vols in 1.   8vo.
London, by J.D. for Brabazon Aylmer, 1677
Wing B1102.   **1173**

———————— A sermon preached upon the ...
death of ... Queen Mary ...   2nd ed.   4to.
London, for Brabazon Aylmer, 1695
Wing B1119.   **1528(18)**

BATHE (Henry de). The charter of Romney-
Marsh.   8vo.
London, printed by S.R. for Samuel Keble, 1686
Wing B1133.   **1178**

BATTLE. The battell of Glenlivet foughten by the
Earls of Huntlie and Errol, against Argyle.   12mo.
1681   Wing B1161A.   **358(4)**

BAUDELOT DE DAIRVAL (Charles César). De
l'utilité des voyages.   2 vols.   12mo.
Paris, chez Pierre Auboüin et Pierre Émery, 1686
Engr. pls.   **1003-4**

BAUDIER (Michel). The history of the adminis-
tration of Cardinal Ximenes ... Written originally
in French ... transl. ... by W.Vaughan.   8vo.
London, for John Wilkins, 1671   Engr. fp.
(port., Charrington p.182).   Wing B1164.   **590**

[————————] The history of the imperiall
estate of the Grand Seigneurs ... (— The history of
the serrail ... — The history of the court of the
King of China ...)   2 pts.   4to.
London, William Stansby for Richard Meighen,
1635   STC 1593.   **1149**

[BAXTER (Richard)]. A breviate of the life of
Margaret ... Charlton ... wife of Richard Baxter.
4to.
London, for B.Simmons, and Brabazon Aylmer,
1681   Wing B1194.   **1240**

———————— Church-history of the government
of bishops.   4to.
London, by B.Griffin, for Thomas Simmons, 1680
1809

──────── The poor-man's help to devotion.
12mo.
[*London*] *For P.Brooksby,* [c.1680]   [Penny-
Godlinesses]   Woodcut on title-page.   **365(28)**

──────── The saints everlasting rest.
11th ed., revised.   4to.
London, for Francis Tyton, and Robert Boulter,
1677   Engr. title-page.   Wing B1394.   **1775**

──────── Two papers of proposals concerning the discipline and ceremonies of the Church
of England.   4to.
London, 1661 · [Liturgick Controversies III]
Wing B1440.   **1189(6)**

BAYLE (Pierre). Dictionaire historique et
critique.   2e éd.   3 vols.   fo.
Rotterdam, chez Reinier Leers, 1702   Engr. on
title-pages.   **2731-3**

BAYLY (Lewis), Bp of Bangor. The practice of
piety.   8vo.
London, for Edward Brewster, 1685   Engr. fp.
(port., Charrington p.30). Wants A1-2.
Wing B1497.   **1147**

BEAU (Le) Polonais nouvelle galante, 1681.
See PRECHAC (Jean), sieur de.   **83(4)**

BEAUMONT (Francis). Fifty comedies and
tragedies.   fo.
*London, by J.Macock, for John Martyn, Henry
Herringman, Richard Marriot,* 1679   Engr. fp.
(port., Charrington p.62).   Wing B1582.   **2623**

BEAUMONT DE PÉRÉFIX (Hardouin de).
See PÉRÉFIX (Hardouin de Beaumont de).

BEDE, the Venerable. Historiæ ecclesiasticæ
gentis Anglorum libri V.   fo.
*Cantabrigiæ, ex officina Rogeri Daniel, prostant
Londini apud Cornelium Bee,* 1644   Engr. map.
Wing B1662.   **2528**

──────── The history of the church of
Englande. Transl. ... by T.Stapleton.   4to.
Antwerp, by Iohn Laet, 1565   2 engr. pls.
STC 1778.   **1135(1)**

BEDFORD (Jasper Tudor, Duke of). The epitaph
of Jasper, Duke of Bedford.   4to.
R.Pynson [*London,* 1496]
See Appendix   **1254(5)**

BEDLOE (William). The examination of Captain
William Bedlow ... relating to the Popish plot.   fo.
*London, by the assigns of John Bill, Thomas New-
comb, and Harry Hills,* 1680   [Narratives &
Tryals III]   Wing E3714.   **2251(1)**

──────── A narrative and impartial discovery of the horrid Popish plot.   fo.

*London, for Robert Boulter, John Hancock, Ralph
Smith, and Benjamin Harris,* 1679   [Narratives
& Tryals I]   Engr. fp. (port., Charrington
p.14); mezzotint port., Charrington p.127; map of
London [1666] ·inserted.   Wing B1677.
   2249(2)

BEE (The) hiue of the Romish churche, 1580.
See MARNIX (Philips van).   **153**

BEKKER (Balthasar). Le monde enchanté. Traduit
du Hollandois.   4 vols.   12mo.
Amsterdam, chez Pierre Rotterdam, 1694
Vol.1: engr. fp. (port., Charrington p.14).
Vol.4: 5 engr. pls.   **223-6**

[BELLEFOREST (François de)]. L'innocence de
la tres illustre tres-chaste, et debonnaire princesse,
Madam Marie royne d'Escosse.   2 pts.   8vo.
1572   **600**

BELLINGEN (Fleury de). Les premiers essays des
proverbes.   8vo.
La Haye, chez Adrian Vlac, 1653   **88**

BELLORI (Giovanni Pietro). Veterum illustrium
philosophorum poetarum rhetorum et oratorum
imagines ex vetustis nummis ... desumptæ.   fo.
*Romæ, apud Io.Iacobum de Rubeis, (typis Ioannis
Baptistæ Bussotti)* 1685   92 engr. pls.   **2346**

BELTRÁN (Pedro). Tres romances hechos por el
que dize: entre los sueltos cavallos.   4to.
(*Seuilla, en casa de Juan Cabeças*) [c.1680]
Gaselee 8; Wilson p.239.   **1545(24)**

BELVALETI (Mondonus). Catechismus ordinis
equitum periscelidis Anglicanae; seu speculum
Anglorum. Ed. P.Bosquier.   8vo.
Coloniæ Agrippinae, apud Henricum Crithium,
1631   **490**

BENÍTEZ MONTERO (Juan). Tratados militares.
4to.
*Madrid, por Melchor Alvarez, a costa de Nicolàs de
Xamares,* 1679   Gaselee 10.   **1270(2)**

BENNET (Robert). Information for Mr.Robert
Bennet Dean of Faculty, and the other advocates
complained upon.   4to.
[*London,* 1702?]   [Consutilia XI]   **1437(15)**

BENT (James). The bloody assizes: or, a compleat
history of the life of George Lord Jefferies.   4to.
London, for J.Dunton, sold by R.Janeway, 1689
[Consutilia IV]   Wing B1905.   **1430(18)**

BENTLEY (Richard). A dissertation upon the
epistles of Phalaris. With an answer to the objections of ... Charles Boyle.   8vo.
*London, printed by J.H. for Henry Mortlock, and
John Hartley,* 1699   Wing B1929; Tanner I,
p.169.   **1256(1)**

─────────── The folly and unreasonableness of atheism.   4th ed.   4to.
London, by J.H. for H.Mortlock, 1699
Wing B1931.   **1589**

BÉRAIN (Nicolas). Les differentes moeurs et coutumes des anciens peuples, dans les actions les plus considerables de la vie.   12mo.
Paris, en la boutique de Langelier. Chez René Guignard, 1668   **240**

BERKELEY (John), 1st Baron. Memoirs.   8vo.
London, by J.Darby, for A.Baldwin, 1699
Wing B1971.   **1455**

BERNARD (Edward). Orbis eruditi literaturam à charactere Samaritico ... deduxit E.Bernardus. brs.
Oxoniae, apud Theatrum, 1689   Wing B1989.
                                                    2905(2)

[───────────] Catalogi librorum manuscriptorum Angliæ et Hiberniæ in unum collecti.
2 vols in 1.   fo.
Oxoniæ, e theatro Sheldoniano, 1697   Engr. fp. (port., Charrington p.18).   Wing C1253; Howarth pp.244, 251.   **2797**

BERNARDISTON (Sir Samuel).
See BARNARDISTON (Sir Samuel).

BERNIER (François). The history of the late revolution of the empire of the Great Mogol ... (– Particular events ... Together with a letter concerning the extent of Indostan.)   2 vols in 1. 8vo.
London, printed and sold by Moses Pitt, Simon Miller, and John Starkey (– printed by S.G. for Moses Pitt), 1671   Engr. map   Wing B2043.
                                                    748

BERNOULLI (Jacques). Conamen novi systematis cometarum.   8vo.
Amstelædami, apud Henr.Wetstenium, 1682
8 engr. diagrams, table.   **656(2)**

─────────── Dissertatio de gravitate ætheris. 8vo.
Amstelædami, apud Henr.Wetstenium, 1683
Engr. title-page, 4 diagrams.   **656(1)**

BERTISO (Felix Persio).
See PERSIO BERTISO (Felix).

BESONGNE (Nicolas). L'état de la France.. 2 vols.   12mo.
Paris, chés Guillaume de Luines (de l'imprimerie d'Etienne Chardon), 1687   Woodcuts.   **421-2**

─────────── L'état de la France.   2 vols. 12mo.
Paris, chez Charles Osmont, 1694   **464-5**

BEST (The) companion (Author of). The Word of God the best guide, 1689.
See BIBLE. *English. Selections.*   **823(1)**

BEST (George). A true discourse of the late voyages of discouerie, for the finding of a passage to Cathaya, by the northvveast, vnder ... Martin Frobisher.   4to.
London, by Henry Bynnyman, 1578   Woodcut.
STC 1972; Tanner I, p.17?   **931**

[BETHEL (Slingsby)] . The interest of princes and states.   8vo.
London, for John Wickins, 1680   Wing B2064; Naval Minutes pp.153-4.   **943**

[───────────] Ludlow no lyar. [By S.Bethel?] 4to.
Amsterdam, 1692   Wing B2068.   **1286(7)**

BÉTHUNE (Maximilien de, duc de Sully).
See SULLY (Maximilien de Béthune, duc de).

BEUGHEM (Cornelius à). Bibliographia historica, chronologica & geographica.   12mo.
Amstelædami, apud Janssonio-Waesbergios, 1685
                                               132

BEVERIDGE (William), Bp of St Asaph. Codex canonum ecclesiæ primitivæ vindicatus ac illustratus.   4to.
Londini, S.Roycroft, prostant apud Robertum Scott, 1678   Wing B2090.   **1822**

─────────── A sermon concerning the excellency, and usefulness of the Common-Prayer. Preached ... the 27th of November, 1681. 8th ed.   4to.
London, by A.Grover for Richard Northcott, 1687
[Liturgick Controversies III]   Wing B2106.
                                          1189(13)

BEYERLINCK (Laurens). Magnum theatrum vitæ humanæ.   8 vols.   fo.
Lugduni, sumpt. Joannis Antonij Huguetan, 1678   Vol.1: engr. & pr. title-pages.   **2754-61**

BEZA (Theodorus). Theodori Bezæ responsio ad defensiones & reprehensiones S. Castellionis, quibus suam Noui Testamēti interpretationem defendere ... conatus est.   8vo.
[Geneva,] excudebat Henricus Stephanus, Huldrichi Fuggeri typographus, 1563
Adams B944.   **1131**

BIBLE

BIBLE. *Polyglot.* Biblia sacra polyglotta, complectentia textus originales ... versionumque antiquarum ... quicquid comparari potest. Cum ... translationibus latinis. Edidit B.Waltonus.
6 vols.   fo.
Londini, imprimebat Thomas Roycroft, (1655-) 1657   Vol.1: engr. fp. (port., Charrington p.174), title-page, maps, pls, plan.   Wing B2797; Diary 5 Oct. 1666.   **2948-53**

[BIBLE] *Anglo-Saxon. Heptateuch.*
Heptateuchus, liber Job, et Evangelium Nicodemi
Anglo-Saxonicè. Historiæ Judith fragmentum;
Dano-Saxonicè. Ed. E.Thwaites.   8vo.
Oxoniæ, e theatro Sheldoniano, typis Junianis,
1698   Engr. fp.   Wing B2198.   **1756**

——————————*Anglo-Saxon, English. Gospels.*
The gospels of the fower euangelistes.   4to.
London, printed by Iohn Daye, 1571   STC 2961.
1317

——————————*Anglo-Saxon, Gothic. Gospels.*
Quatuor ... euangeliorum versiones perantiquæ
duæ, Gothica scil. et Anglo-Saxonica: quarum
illam ... depromsit F.Junius F.F. Hanc autem ...
recudi curavit T.Mareschallus ... Accessit &
glossarium Gothicum ... operâ ejusdem F.Junii.
2 vols.   4to.
Dordrechti, typis & sumptibus Junianis. Excude-
bant Henricus & Joannes Essæi, 1665 (1664)
Vol.1: Engr. title-page; MS notes (on flyleaf and in
margins) by Daniel Waterland.   Vol.2: MS notes
by D.Waterland.   **1830-1**

—————————*English.* The bybble in Englyshe.
fo.
[*London*] *by Rychard Grafton ↄ Edward Whit-*
church, 1539   STC 2068; Duff p.6.   **2638**

————— ——————[The holy bible.   fo.
Oxford, at the Theater, 1680]   Wing B2314.
Wants all except the index.   **2907(1)**

————— ——————Holy bible containing the old and
new testament with singing psalms in short hand,
written by W.Addy.   12mo.
(*London, printed for the author, and Peter Story.*
And sold by, Tho:Fabian [*etc.*]) 1687
Engr. fp. (port., Charrington p.1), title-page & 2
pls.   Wing B2802; Carlton, pp.105-9.   **10**

————— ——————The holy bible.   fo.
London, by Charles Bill, and the executrix of
Thomas Newcomb, 1696   Wing B2367.   **2677**

————— ——————*Selections.* The Word of God the
best guide ... a collection of scripture-texts ... by
the author of the Best companion [i.e. W.Howell].
8vo.
Oxford, at the Theater, for John Howell, 1689
823(1)

————— ——————*Job.* The book of Job paraphras'd.
By Symon Patrick. [With the text.]   8vo.
London, by E.Flesher, for R.Royston, 1679
Wing B2639.   **1040**

————— ——————*Psalms. Metrical.* Certayne psalmes
... commonlye called thee .vii. penytentiall
psalmes, drawen into Englyshe meter by Sir
Thomas Wyat.   8vo.
London, by Thomas Raynald. and John Harryng-
ton, (1549)   STC 2726; Duff p.7.   **75(3)**

[BIBLE] ——— ——— ———The whole booke
of Psalmes. Collected into English meeter by
T.Sternhold, I.Hopkins and others ... with apt
notes to sing them withall.   4to.
London, printed by Iohn Windet, for the assignes
of Richard Day, 1596   *See also* vol.IV.   **1280(2)**

——— ——— ——— ———The whole booke
of psalms: with the hymnes evangelicall, and songs
spirituall. Composed into 4. parts by sundry
authors ... Newly corrected and enlarged by Tho:
Rauenscroft.
Printed at London for the Company of Stationers,
1621   STC 2575.   *See also* vol.IV.   **612**

——— ——— ——— ———[The Psalmes of
David in metre, with the prose version.]   8vo.
(*Edinburgh, by the heires of Andrew Hart,* 1635)
Wants title-page and all before leaf B1.   With
music.   Autograph: John Haward, 1683.
See also vol.IV.   **863(2)**

——— ——— ——— ———The whole book
of psalmes ... collected into English meeter, by
T.Sternhold, J.Hopkins and others.   8vo.
London, for the Company of Stationers, 1641
Wants all except *8, containing the calendar.
Wing B2384.   **863(1)**

——— ——— ——— ———The whole book
of psalmes: collected into English meeter by
Thomas Sternhold, Iohn Hopkins, and others ...
with apt notes to sing them withall.   8vo.
London, printed by A.M. for the Companie of
Stationers, 1647   Wing B2422.
See also vol.IV.   **875(3)**

——— ——— ——— ———A paraphrase upon
the psalms of David, by S.Woodford.   4to.
London, by R.White, for Octavian Pullein, 1667
Engr. fp.   Wing B2491.   **1491**

——— ——— ——— ———The whole book of
psalms: with the usual hymns and spiritual songs;
together with ... tunes ... Compos'd in three parts
... By John Playford.   8vo.
London, pr. by W.Godbid for the Co. of Stnrs, and
are sold by John Playford, 1677   Engr. fp.
Wing B2527.   *See also* vol.IV.   **1164**

——— ——— ——— ———A new version of
the psalms of David, fitted to the tunes used in
churches. By N.Tate and N.Brady.   12mo.
London, printed by M.Clark, for the Company of
Stationers, 1696   Wing B2598.   **477**

——— ——— ——— ———The psalms of
David in metre: fitted to the tunes used in parish-
churches. By John Patrick. [*With 15 tunes at the*
end.]   2 pts.   12mo.
London, printed for L.Meredith, and sold by D.
Browne, T.Benskin, J.Walthoe and F.Coggan, 1701
See also vol.IV.   **476**

[BIBLE]——— ——— ——— A supplement to the new version of psalms by Dr.Brady and Mr.Tate ... with their tunes ... The 5th edition corrected and enlarged. 12mo.
London, printed by W.Pearson for D.Brown, 1704
478

——— ——— ——— ——— The whole book of psalms, collected into English metre, by Thomas Sternhold, John Hopkins, and others. 12mo.
London, printed for the Company of Stationers, 1704.
475

——— ———*New Testament.* The newe testament of our Sauiour Jesu Christe. [Tr. by Tyndale.] 4to.
(*London, by Rycharde Jugge*,) [1552]
STC 2867; Duff p.8. **1671**

——— ———*Gospel of Nicodemus.*
See GOSPEL of Nicodemus.

——— ———*English, Latin. New Testament.*
The newe testament both Latine and Englyshe ... Faythfully translated [by Myles Couerdale]. 4to.
Southwarke, printed by James Nicolson, 1538
STC 2816; Duff p.8. Coverdale's name erased from title-page. Wants [*]2-4, Vv 7-8. **1277**

——— ———*French.* La sainte Bible.
Vols 1 & 2. 4to.
Se vend a Charenton, par Anthoine Cellier, demeurant à Paris, 1675 Wants vol.3, containing the New Testament. **1964-5**

——— ———*Psalms. Metrical.* Les pseaumes de David, mis en rime françoyse par Cl.Marot & Th. de Beze. [*With music.*] 4to.
Rotterdam, chez Pierre d'Alphen, 1660
See also vol.IV. **1458**

——— ——— ——— ——— Les pseaumes de David, mis en rime françoise, par Clément Marot, et Théodore de Bèze. [*With music.*] 12mo.
Charenton, par Anthoine Cellier, demeurant à Paris, 1675 *See also* vol.IV. **403(2)**

——— ——— ——— ——— Paraphrase des pseaumes de David, en vers françois, par Mre. Antione Godeau. Derniere edition ... les chants corrigez ... par Me Thomas Gobert. [*With music.*] 12mo.
Paris, chez Pierre le Petit, 1676 Engr. fp. and title-page. **434**

——— ———*New Testament.* Le nouveau testament. 12mo.
Se vend à Charenton, par Antoine Cellier, demeurant à Paris, 1672 **403(1)**

——— ———*French, Latin. New Testament.*
Le nouveau testament ... en latin et en françois. 25e éd. (–8e éd.) 2 vols. 12mo.
Mons, chez Gaspard Migeot, 1684
Vol.1: engr. pl. **657-8**

[BIBLE] *Greek. New Testament.* Τη̂ς καινη̂ς διαθήκης ἀπαντα. Novi testamenti libri omnes. Accesserunt parallela scripturæ loca, nec non variantes lectiones. 12mo.
Oxonii, e theatro Sheldoniano, 1675 MS note in Pepys's hand at end of Preface. Wing B2737. **967**

——— ———*Psalms.* Ψαλτηρίον του̂ Δαβίδ, κατὰ του̂ ʻΕβδομήκοντα. 8vo.
ʼΕν Κανταβριγίᾳ, ἐτυπώθη παρʼ ʼΙωάννου του̂ Φιέλδου, ͵αχξδ [1664] Wing B2720. **875(2)**

——— ———*Greek, Latin. Psalms.* Ψαλτηριον. Psalterium. Juxta exemplar Alexandrinum editio nova. [Ed. by T.Gale.] 8vo.
Oxoniæ, e theatro Sheldoniano, 1678
Wing B2725. **1318**

——— ———*New Testament.* Τη̂ς καινη̂ς διαθηκης ἀπαντα. Nouum Iesu Christi ... testamentum latine ... nunc denuo à Theodoro Beza uersum; cum eiusdem annotationibus. fo.
Tiguri, 1559 Adams B1693. *1-2, a1 defective. **2429**

——— ———*Gospels.* Harmonia evangelica cui subjecta est historia Christi ex quatuor evangeliis concinnata. Accesserunt tres dissertationes ... auctore Joanne Clerico. fo.
Amstelodami, sumptibus Huguetanorum, 1699 **2394**

——— ———*Latin.* Biblia, interprete Sebastiano Castalione. fo.
Basileae, per Ioannem Oporinum (per Iacobum Parcum, 1551) Adams B1045. Two autographs: 'Willm Worthington Junior'. **2273**

——— ——— Biblia ad vetustissima exemplaria nunc recens castigata. fo.
Francoforti ad Moenum, 1566 Woodcuts.
Adams B1073. **2403**

——— ——— Biblia sacra vulgatæ editionis. fo.
Lutetiæ Parisiorum, (sumptibus Roberti Foüet, Nicolai Buon, Sebastiani Cramoisy,) 1618
Engr. title-page. **2726**

——— ———*Pentateuch.* Mosis prophetæ libri quatuor ... ex translatione Joannis Clerici. Cum ejusdem paraphrasi. fo.
Amstelodami, sumtibus auctoris, prostant apud Henricum Wetstenium, 1696 3 engr. maps. **2316**

——— ———*Genesis.* Genesis ... ex translatione Joannis Clerici cum ejusdem paraphrasi. fo.
Amstelodami, sumptibus auctoris, et veneunt apud Abrahamum Wolfgangum et Jansonio-Waesbergios, 1693 **2315**

——— ———*Psalms. Metrical.* Psalmorum Davidis paraphrasis poëtica G.Buchanani: argumentis ac melodiis explicata atque illustrata operâ & studio N.Chytræi. 12mo.

Londini, apud Edvv.Griffinum, 1640   MS notes in unidentified hand on verso of title-page. STC 3988.   *See also* vol.IV.   **22**

——— ———*New Testament.* Novum testamentum ... cum paraphrasi et adnotationibus H.Hammondi. Ex Anglica lingua ... transtulit ... J.Clericus.   2 vols in 1.   fo.
Amstelodami, apud Georgium Galletum, 1698 Engrs on both title-pages.   **2736**

——— ———*Gospel Harmonies.* G.I. Vossii Harmoniæ evangelicæ de passione, morte resurrectione ac adscensione Iesu Christi libri tres.   4to.
Amstelodami, apud Ludovicum et Danielem Elzevirios, 1656   **1533**

——————*Malay. Gospels.* Jang ampat evangelia ... That is, the four gospels ... and the Acts of the holy apostles, translated into the Malayan tongue.   4to.
Oxford, printed by H.Hall, 1677   Wing B2796.   **1323**

——————*Spanish. Old Testament.* Biblia en lengua espanola.   fo.
[*Amsterdam*] (5390, i.e. 1630)   Gaselee 14.   **2268**

——— ———*New Testament.* El testamento nueuo.   8vo.
'*Venecia, en casa de Iuan Philadelpho*' [*Geneva, Jean Crespin*], 1556   MS note on title-page in unidentified 17th-cent. hand.   Adams B1795.   **65**

BIBLIOTHECA exotica, 1625.
See DRAUD (Georg).   **1682(2)**

BIBLIOTHECA Norfolciana, 1681.
See P.(W.).   **1795**

BIBLIOTHÈQUE universelle et historique. [By J.Le Clerc, etc.]   22 vols.   12mo.
Amsterdam, chez Wolfgang [*etc.*], 1686-93. Vol.1: 2nd ed., engr. title-page.   Tanner II, p.106.   **315-36**

BIDDULPH (William). The travels of foure English men and a preacher into Africa, ... finished 1611. (– The preachers travels.)   2 pts.   4to.
London, Felix Kyngston, for William Aspley, 1612   [Consutilia V]   STC 3052.   **1431 (19, 21)**

BIET (Antoine). Voyage de la France equinoxiale en l'isle de Cayenne ... en l'année M.DC.LII. 4to.
Paris, chez François Clouzier, 1664   **1805**

BIGARRURES (Les), 1626.
See TABOUROT (Étienne).   **148**

[BINCKES (William), Dean of Lichfield]. An expedient propos'd: or the occasions of the late controversie in Convocation consider'd.   4to.

London, by T.Warren for Thomas Bennet, 1701 [Convocation Pamphlets XI]   MS notes by Daniel Waterland.   **1697(6)**

[————————]· An explanation of some passages in Dr.Binckes's sermon preached ... January the 30th, 1701/2. With part of a sermon [by H. Leslie] ... intituled The martyrdom of King Charles ... preached at Breda ... June 3/13 1649. 4to.
London, for R.Clavel, 1702   [Convocation Pamphlets XII]   **1698(10)**

[————————] A prefatory discourse to an examination of a late book, entituled An exposition of the thirty nine articles ... by Gilbert [Burnet], Bishop of Sarum. By a Presbyter of the Church of England.   4to.
London, for Robert Clavell, 1702   MS note 'Dr Binckes' on title-page (in Daniel Waterland's hand).   **1771**

——————— A sermon preach'd on January the 30th 1701/2 ... before ... the Lower House of Convocation.   4to.
London, for R.Clavel, 1702   [Convocation Pamphlets XII]   **1698(9)**

BINET (Étienne). Abrégé des vies des principaux fondateurs des religions de l'église.   4to.
Anuers, chez Martin Nutius, 1634   Engr. title-page, 39 engr. ports.   **1580**

BIRD (William). The magazine of honour.
See DODDRIDGE (Sir John). Judge Dodaridge, his law of nobility.   **606(1)**

BIRTH (The), life and death of John Frank. 12mo.
[*London*] *by J.M. for J.Deacon and C.Dennisson* [c.1680]   [Penny-Merriments II] Woodcut.   **363(20)**

BISHOP (The) of Armaghes direction, concerning the lyturgy, and episcopall government, 1660.
See UDALL (Ephraim).   **1188(7)**

BISHOP (The) of London his legacy, 1623.
See MUSKET (George).   **958(1)**

[BISSELIN (Olivier)]. Les tables de la declinaison ... que fait le soleil de la ligne equinoctiale chacun iour des quatre ans.   4to.
Poitiers, par Ian de Marnef (1559)
[Sea Tracts I]   On title-page MS motto 'Magnus ope minorum' in unidentified hand.
Adams B2084.   **1077(10)**

BIZOT (Pierre). Histoire metallique de la republique de Hollande ... Nouvelle ed.   2 vols.   8vo.
Amsterdam, chez Pierre Mortier, 1688 42, 60 pls.   **1485-6**

——————— Supplement.   8vo.
Id., ib., 1690   Engr. fp., 79 pls.   **1487**

BLACK (The) book of conscience [c.1680].
See HART (John). **365(5)**

BLACKALL (Offspring), Bp of Exeter. Mr.Blackall's reasons for not replying to a book ... entituled Amyntor ... 2nd ed. 8vo.
London, printed for Walter Kettilby, 1699
Wing B3049. **1082(3)**

BLACKBORROW (Peter). Navigation rectified: or, the common chart proved to be the true chart. 8vo.
London, printed by John Playford, and are to be sold by Joseph Hindmarsh, 1684 8 diagrams.
MS notes (in unidentified 17th-cent. hand) in margins, and 5 MSS concerning this book inserted at end. *See below*, vol.4. Wing B3062. **694**

BLACKWOOD (Adam). Opera omnia. 4to.
Parisiis, apud Sebastianum et Gabrielem Cramoisy, 1644 Engr. fp. (port., Charrington p.17). **1852**

BLAEU (Jan). Institutio astronomica, pt 2.
For the adaptation of this work by J.Moxon, see
MOXON (Joseph). A tutor to astronomy ... **1321**

——————— Nouveau theatre d'Italie. [*Vol.1 only, with a few plates from other vols.*] fo.
Amsterdam, par les soins de Pierre Mortier, 1704
Engr. title-page, 78 engr. pls. **2996(1)**

——————— Theatrum civitatum et admirandorum Italiæ (necnon Neapolis et Siciliæ regnorum). 3 pts. fo.
Amstelædami, typis Ioannis Blaeu, 1663
Pt 1: engr. title-page, 72 col. pls.
Pt 2: engr. title-page, 44 col. pls.
Pt 3: 32 col. pls. **2993-5**

BLAGRAVE (John). Astrolabium Vranicum generale. A necessary and pleasaunt solace and recreation for nauigators. 4to.
[*London*], *by Thomas Purfoot, for William Matts, 1596* I 1-2 *defective.* [Sea Tracts IV]
STC 3117. **1080(4)**

——————— The mathematical iewel. fo.
London, (by Thomas Dawson for) Walter Venge, 1585 With a 2-leaf table of 'fixed starres' inserted. STC 3119. **1979(2)**

BLASON. Le blazon des armes [c.1520].
See SICILE, herald. **46(2)**

[BLAXTON (John)]. A remonstrance against the non-residents. 4to.
London, by T.Badger, for Rich.Royston [1642]
[Consutilia II] Engr. on title-page. Title-page cropped. Wing B3177. **1428(2)**

BLÉGNY (Nicolas de). Le bon usage du thé du caffé et du chocolat pour la préservation. 12mo.
Paris, chez Estienne Michallet, 1687 12 engr. pls. **404**

BLOEMAERT (Abraham). Sylva anachoretica Ægypti et Palæstinæ, figuris ænis ... expressa ... Boetio à Bolswert sculptore. 4to.
Antuerpiæ, ex typographia Henrici AErtssii, sumptibus auctoris, 1619 Engr. fp., title-page & 50 pls. **1265(2)**

BLOME (Richard). The gentlemans recreation. 2 pts. fo.
London, S.Roycroft, for Richard Blome, 1686
28, 40 engr. pls. Wing B3213. **2908**

BLONDEL (David). Des Sibylles. 4to.
Se vendent à Charenton par la veuve L.Perier & N.Perier, demeurans à Paris, 1649 **1779**

BLONDEL (François). Histoire du calendrier romain. 12mo.
La Haye, chez Arnout Leers, 1684 Engr. on title-page, 6 engr. pls. **546**

BLOUNT (Charles). Anima mundi: or, an historical narration. 8vo.
London, printed for Will.Cademan, 1679
Wing B3298. **352**

[——————] Great is Diana of the Ephesians. 8vo.
London, 1680 Wing B3303. **387**

[——————] King William and Queen Mary conquerors. 4to.
London, for Richard Baldwin, 1693
[Consutilia VII] Wing B3309. **1433(1)**

——————— The oracles of reason ... in several letters to Mr.Hobbs and other persons ... By C. Blount, Mr.Gildon and others. 12mo.
London, 1693 Wing B3312. **593**

BLOUNT (Sir Henry). A voyage into the Levant. 2nd ed. 4to.
London, I.L[*eggatt*] *for Andrew Crooke, 1637*
[Consutilia V] STC 3137. **1431(2)**

[BLOUNT (Thomas)]. Boscobel: or the compleat history of his sacred majesties most miraculous preservation after the battle of Worcester. (— Boscobel ... The second part. — Claustrum regale reseratum, or the kings concealment at Trent. Published by A.W. [i.e. A.Wyndham.]) 2 pts. 3rd ed. 8vo.
London, printed by M.Clark, and are to be sold by H.Brome and C.Harper, 1680 (1681)
Engr. title-page, pls. Wing B3331. **726**

——————— Fragmenta antiquitatis. Antient tenures of land. 8vo.
London, printed by the assigns of Richard and Edward Atkins. For Abel Roper, [etc.] 1679
MS note in Pepys's hand on [A] 1 giving page-numbers for 'Tenures Maritime'. A second note (not in Pepys's hand) on M8. **1048**

BLOUNT (Sir Thomas Pope), Bart. Censura celebriorum authorum.　fo.
Londini, impensis Richardi Chiswel, 1690
Wing B3346.　　　　2422

BLUNDEVILLE (Thomas). A briefe description of vniuersal mappes and cardes.　4to.
London, by Roger Ward for Thomas Cadman,
1589　[Sea Tracts III]　Diagram.
Autographs and price on title-page: 'John Whytt';
'Rog:Goodday'; 'viiid'.　STC 3145.　1079(2)

BOCCACCIO (Giovanni). A treatise excellent and compĕdious, shewing ... the falles of sondry most notable princes and princesses ... translated ... by Dan John Lidgate.　fo.
(London,) in ædibus Richardi Tottelli (1554)
Woodcuts.　STC 3177; Duff p.37.　2272

BOCCALINI (Traiano). I ragguagli di Parnasso: or, advertisements from Parnassus ... Put into English by ... Henry Earl of Monmouth.　fo.
London, printed by and to be sold by Peter Parker, 1674　Engr. fp. (port., Charrington p.120).　Wing B3384.　2166

BOCCONE (Paolo). Museo di fisica e di esperienze. 4to.
Venetia, per Io:Baptistam Zuccato, 1697
Engr. fp. (port., Charrington p.18), 13 pls.　1815

————— Museo di piante rare della Sicilia, Malta [*etc.*].　4to.
Venetia, per Io:Baptista Zuccato, 1697
Engr. fp., 131 pls.　　　　1816

BOCHART (Samuel). Opera omnia ... Editio 3a. 3 vols.　fo.
Lugduni Batavorum, apud Cornelium Boutesteyn, & Jordanum Luchtmans; Trajecti ad Rhenum, apud Guilielmum vande Water, 1692 [Vols 1 & 2 have colophon: *Utrajecti, apud Ernestum Voskuyl,* 1690]
Vol.1: Engr. fp. (port., Charrington p.18), engr. title-page.　Vol.2: Engr. pl.　Vol.3: 13 engr. maps.　　　　2701-3

BODIN (Jean). De magorum daemonomania libri IV. In latinum translati per L.Philoponum.　4to.
Basileæ, per Thomam Guarinum, 1581
Wants sig.X.　Adams B2219 *or* 2220.　1563

————— Les six liures de la republique. fo.
Paris, chez Iacques du Puys, 1577
Adams B2234.　　　　2402

BOECKLER (Georg Andreas). Architectura curiosa nova.　4 pts.　fo.
Norimbergæ, impensis Pauli Fürsten, typis Christophori Gerhardi, [1664]　Engr. title-page, pls.　　　　2488

————— Theatrum machinarum novum ...
Ex Germaniâ in Latium recens translatum operâ R.D.Henrici Schmitz.　fo.

Coloniæ Agrippinæ, sumptibus Pauli Principis,
1662　Engr. title-page, 154 engr. pls.　2473

BOEHME (Jacob). XL. questions concerning the soule. (The clavis, or key.)　4to.
London, printed by M.S. for H.Blunden, 1647
Engr. diagram.　Wing B3408A.　1130(1)

————— The second booke. Concerning the three principles of the divine essence.　4to.
London, printed by M[atthew] S[immons] for H. Blunden, 1648　Wing B3417.　1130(2)

BOETHIUS (Anicius Manlius Severinus). Consolationis philosophiæ libri V. Anglo-Saxonice redditi ab Alfredo.　8vo.
Oxoniæ, e Theatro Sheldoniano, sumtibus editoris, typis Junianis, 1698　Engr. fp. (port., Charrington p.91).　Wing B3429.　　1773

BOETHIUS (Hector). Heir beginnis the hystory and croniklis of Scotland. (Translatit ... be J.Bellenden.)　fo.
Imprentit in Edinburgh, be me Thomas Davidson,
[1540?]　STC 3203; Duff p.9.　　2071

[BOHUN (Edmund)]. The doctrine of non-resistance.　4to.
London, for Richard Chiswell, 1689　[Consutilia I]　Wing B3451.　　1427(4)

[—————] The history of the desertion, or an account of ... publick affairs in England from ... September 1688 to the twelfth of February following.　4to.
London, for Ric.Chiswell, 1689　[Consutilia I]
Wing B3456.　　　　1427(5)

BOHUN (Ralph). A discourse concerning the origine and properties of wind.　8vo.
Oxford, by W.Hall for Tho.Bowman, 1671
Wing B3463.　　　　780

[BOILEAU (Jacques)]. Historia flagellantium. 12mo.
Parisiis, apud Joannem Anisson, 1700　799

[BOILEAU-DESPRÉAUX (Nicolas)]. Oeuvres diverses du Sieur D***, avec le traité du sublime ... Traduit du grec de Longin.　2 pts.　12mo.
Paris, chez Denys Thierry, 1675　747

[BOISSAT (Pierre de)]. Histoire des cheualiers de l'ordre de S.Iean de Hierusalem, 1659.
See BOSIO (Giacomo).　　2681

BOLRON (Robert). Narrative ... concerning the late horrid Popish plot.　fo.
London, for Thomas Simmons, and Jacob Sampson, 1680　[Narratives & Tryals III]
Wing B3501.　　　　2251(3)

BONA (Giovanni), Cardinal. Opera.　4to.
Antverpiæ, sumptibus viduæ Johannis Jac.F. Schipperi, 1677　Engr. fp. (port., Charrington p.18), title-page.　　1735

BONANNI (Filippo).
See BUONANNI (Filippo).

BONAVENTURA, St. Incipit speculum vite xp̄i.
fo.
[London,] (Emprynted by Rychard Pynson,)
[1506]   Woodcuts.   STC 3263; Duff p.10.
2051(3)

──────────── Vita Christi.   4to.
(London, by me Wynkyn de Worde, 1530)
Woodcuts.   STC 3267; Duff p.11.   **1011(2)**

BOND (Henry). The art of apparelling and fitting
of any ship. 2nd impr. [*Another ed. of* The boat
swaines art.]   4to.
[London,] for the widow Seyle, 1663
Wing B3559.   **1267(3)**

──────────── The boat swaines art.   4to.
London, by William Godbid for William Fisher,
1664   Wing B3560A.   **1267(5)**

──────────── The longitude found.   4to.
London, by W.Godbid, to be sold by the author,
Robert Greene [etc.], 1676   7 engr. diagrams.
Wing B3564.   **1153**

[────────────] A plain and easie rule to rigge
any ship.   4to.
London, for William Fisher, 1664
Wing B3565.   **1267(4)**

BOND (John). Salvation in a mystery ... a sermon
preached ... March 27.   4to.
London, by L.N. for Francis Eglesfeild, 1644
[Sermons Polemical I]   Wing B3574.   **1179(7)**

──────────── A sermon preached in Exon.   4to.
London, by T.B. for F.Eglesfeild, 1643
[Sermons Polemical I]   Wing B3575.   **1179(6)**

BONET (Juan Pablo). Reduction de las letras, y
arte para enseñar a ablar los mudos.   4to.
Madrid, por Francisco Abarca de Angulo, 1620
Engr. title-page, 9 engr. pls.   Gaselee 16.
1396(2)

BONILLA (Alonso de). Glossas a la inmaculada
concepcion de la siempre Virgen Maria.   4to.
Sevilla, por Juan Vejarano, à costa de Lucas
Martin de Hermosilla, 1682   Gaselee 17;
Wilson p.150.   **1545(10)**

BONNER (Edmund), Bp of London. A profitable
and necessarye doctryne, with certayne homelies
adioyned thervnto set forth.   2 pts.   4to.
(Londini, excusum in ædibus Iohannis Cawodi,
*1555)   Pt 1 wants Q1.   STC 3282; Duff
p.11.*   **1257**

BOOK. The boke named the royall [1507].
See LAURENT, Dominican.   **1011(1)**

BOOK. A booke of christian prayers, 1590.
See DAY (Richard).   **1280(1)**

BOOK of Common Prayer.
See LITURGIES. *Church of England.*

BOOK (The) of hawking, hunting, and heraldry.
fo.
St Albans, 1486.   See Appendix.   **1985**

BOOK (The) of hawking, hunting, and heraldry.
—The treatise of fishing.   fo.
W.de Worde, Westminster, 1496.
See Appendix.   **1984**

BOOK (The) of merry riddles.   12mo.
[London,] for W.T[hackeray], sold by John
Black, 1685   [Penny-Merriments I]
Wing B3712.   **362(24)**

BOOK (The) of oaths, 1689.
See GARNET (Richard).   **909**

BOOK (A) of the names of all parishes ... in
England and Wales.   4to.
London, printed by M.S[immons] for Tho:Jenner,
1662   Engr. maps. MS index to maps inserted in
the hand of one of Pepys's clerks.
Wing B3717A.   **1005**

BOOK. The boke of wysdome, folowynge the
auctoryties of auncyent phylosophers. [*Transl. by*
J.Larke, from 'Fiore di Virtu'.]   8vo.
[London,] (by me Robert Wyer, 1532)
STC 3357; Duff p.12.   **19(2)**

BOOKBINDERS (The) case unfolded: or, A duty
of man, 12°. Rate for binding, six pence.
[*Followed by a list of items of work and mater-*
ials needed.]
[c.1690]   s. sh.   **1398(6)**

BOORDE (Andrew). The fyrst boke of the intro-
duction of knowledge.   4to.
(London, by me william Copland,) [1548]
Woodcuts.   STC 3383; Duff p.12.   **843**

[────────────] The merry tales ... of Gotam
[c.1680]   *See* B.(A.).   **363(21)**

──────────── Scogin's jests.   4to.
London, for W.Thackeray and J.Deacon [c.1680]
[Vulgaria IV]   Wing B3750.   **1193(3)**

[BORDELON (Laurent)]. Remarques ou reflexions critiques, morales et historiques.   12mo.
Paris, chez Arnoul Seneuse, 1692   **338**

BOREL (Pierre). De vero telescopii inventore. Accessit etiam centuria observationum microcospic-
arum [*sic*].   2 vols in 1.   4to.
Hagæ-Comitum, ex typographia Adriani Vlacq,
1655-6   Engr. fps (ports, Charrington pp.88,
101), pls, diagrams.   **1162**

BORELLI (Giovanni Alfonso). De motu animalium. Pars prima (secunda). Ed. altera. 2 vols.
4to.
Lugduni in Batavis, apud Danielem à Gaesbeeck,

Cornelium Boutesteyn, Johannem de Vivie &
Petrum vander Aa. 1685   Vol.1: engr. title-
page, 18 engr. pls.   **1561-2**

[BORLASE (Edmund)]. The history of the execrable Irish rebellion. (Appx.)   fo.
London, for Robert Clavel, 1680   Wants the
map.   Wing B3768.   **2277**

BORNE (William).   *See* BOURNE (William).

BORODŻYCKI (Jerzy). The tryal and condemnation of George Borosky ... C.Vratz and J.Stern,
for the barbarous murder of Thomas Thynn.   fo.
London, for Thomas Basset, 1682   [Narratives
& Tryals IV]   Wing T2141.   **2252(29)**

BOROUGH (Sir John). The soveraignty of the
British seas ... written in the yeare 1633.   12mo.
London, for Humphrey Moseley, 1651
Wing B3774.   **71**

BOROUGH (William). A discourse of the variation of the cumpas ... by W.B.   4to.
(London, by Thomas East for Richard Ballard,)
1585   [Sea Tracts I]   STC 3390.   **1077(6)**

———————— A discourse of the variation of
the compasse ... by W.B.   4to.
London, by E.Allde for Hugh Astley, 1596
[Sea Tracts II]   STC 3391.   **1078(4)**

BOSCOBEL: or the compleat history of His ...
Majesties ... preservation, 1680.
See BLOUNT (Thomas).   **726**

[BOSIO (Giacomo)]. Histoire des cheualiers de
l'ordre de S.Iean de Hierusalem ... par le feu
S.D.B.S.D.L. [i.e. Sieur de Boissat, Sieur de
Licieux, *or rather translated by him from the
Italian of G.Bosio.*]   Derniere éd.   4 pts.
fo.
Paris, chez Iacques d'Allin, 1659   Engr. title-
page, pls (portraits & maps).   **2681**

BOSSE (Abraham). Maniere vniverselle de Mr.
Desargues pour pratiquer la perspectiue.   8vo.
Paris, de Pierre Des-Hayes, 1647   Engr. title-
page, 156 engr. pls.   **1517**

———————— Moyen vniuersel de pratiquer la
perspectiue sur les tableaux.   8vo.
Paris, chez ledit Bosse, 1653   Engr. title-page,
31 engr. diagrams.   **1537**

———————— Le peintre converty aux precises
et universelles regles de son art.   8vo.
Paris, par A.Bosse, 1667 (1668)   Engr. fp.
                                        1564

———————— Traicté des manieres de grauer en
taille douce sur l'airin.   8vo.
*Paris, chez ledit Bosse (de l'imprimerie de Pierre
Des-Hayes), 1645*   Engr. title-page (misbound).
18 engr. pls.   **1519**

BOSSUET (Jacques Bénigne), Bp of Meaux.
Discours sur l'histoire universelle à ... le Dauphin.
12mo.
*Suivant la copie imprimée à Paris, chez Sebastien,
etc., 1681*   **672**

———————— Exposition de la doctrine de
l'église catholique sur les matiéres de controverse.
Avec un avertissement sur cette nouvelle édition.
12mo.
*Suivant la copie imprimée à Paris ... Et se vend à
Bruxelles chez Eug:Henry Fricx, 1681*   **94**

———————— An exposition of the doctrine of
the Catholic church in matters of controversie.
2 pts.   4to.
London, 1685   Wing B3783.   **1544(1)**

BOTELER (Nathaniel).
See BUTLER (Nathaniel).

BOTLEY (Samuel). Maximum in minimo, or Mr
Jeremiah Rich's pens dexterity compleated.   8vo.
London, printed for John Man [1692?]
Engr. throughout. Ports, Charrington p.19, 143.
[Short-hand Collection IV]   Wing 3808;
Carlton p.92.   **860(4)**

BOULENCOURT (Le Jeune de).
See LE JEUNE DE BOULENCOURT.

BOULES (R.) The Queens royal closet newly
opened.   12mo.
[London] for T.Passenger, 1682   [Penny-
Merriments I]   Woodcut on title-page. **362(12)**

BOURDEILLE (Pierre de), seigneur de Brantôme.
See BRANTÔME (Pierre de Bourdeille, seigneur
de).

BOURNE (William). The arte of shooting in great
ordnaunce.   4to.
*London, (Thomas Dawson) for Thomas Wood-
cocke, 1587*   Engrs.   STC 3420.   **1156(2)**

———————— Inuentions or deuises. Very
necessary for all generalles and captaines.   4to.
London, for Thomas VVoodcock, 1578
STC 3421.   **1156(1)**

———————— A regiment for the sea.   4to.
London, for Thomas Hacket [1574]
Woodcuts.   STC 3422.   **1478(2)**

———————— A regiment for the sea ... corrected
and amended by T.Hood, who hath added a new
regiment and table of declination.   2 pts.   4to.
London, by T.Est, for Thomas Wight [1592]
[Sea Tracts I]   MS notes and, on title-page, MS
motto 'Magnus ope minorum', in unidentified
hands.   STC 3427.   **1077(3)**

——————— A regiment for the sea ... Whereunto is also adioyned the Mariners guide [*by T. Hood*].   2 pts.   4to.
London, by T.Este for Thomas Wight, 1596
[Sea Tracts II]   Map.   STC 3428.   **1078(5)**

BOWBER (Thomas). A sermon preached ...
March 10th 1694/5.   4to.
London, for William Rogers, 1695
Wing B3866.   **1528(14)**

BOWLES (Oliver). Zeale for Gods house quickned: or, a sermon preached ... Iuly 7.   4to.
London, by Richard Bishop for Samuel Gellibrand, 1643   [Sermons Polemical I]
Wing B3884.   **1179(8)**

BOXHORN (Marcus Zuerius). Monumenta illustrium virorum et elogia.   fo.
Amstelodami, apud Joannem Janssonium, 1638
Engr. title-page, 125 engr. pls.   **2317**

[BOYER (Abel)] . The history of King William the third. In III parts.   8vo.
London, for A.Roper, and F.Coggan, 1702
Engr. fp., ports (Charrington p.86, 178).
Vol.1 only.   **1418**

BOYLE (Hon. Robert). The aerial noctiluca.   8vo.
London, printed by Tho.Snowden, and are to be sold by Nath.Ranew, 1680   [A2] defective.
Wing B3925.   **1101(1)**

——————— Certain physiological essays.
2nd ed.   4to.
London, for Henry Herringman, 1669
Wing B3930.   **1653**

[———————] The Christian virtuoso ... To which are subjoyn'd, I. A discourse about the distinction that represents some things as above reason ... II. The first chapters of a discourse, entituled, Greatness of mind.   3 pts.   8vo.
In the Savoy, printed by Edw.Jones, for John Taylor, and John Wyat, 1690 (pt 3: Edward Jones, for John Taylor, 1691)   Wing B3931, 4019, 3983.   **759(1-3)**

——————— A continuation of new experiments physico-mechanical, touching the spring and weight of the air ... The I. part.   4to.
Oxford, Henry Hall, for Richard Davis, 1669
8 engr. pls.   Wing B3934.   **1539(1)**

——————— A continuation of new experiments ... The second part.   4to.
London, Miles Flesher, for Richard Davis, 1682
5 engr. pls.   Wing B3935.   **1539(2)**

[———————] Curiosities in chymistry.   8vo.
London, by H.C. for Stafford Anson, 1691
Wing G1877.   **601**

[———————] A discourse of things above reason ... To which are annexed ... some advices about judging of things said to transcend reason.
2 pts.   8vo.
London, printed by E[van] .T[yler] and R.H[olt] for Jonathan Robinson, 1681
Wing B3944.   **759(4)**

——————— A disquisition about the final causes of natural things ... To which are subjoyn'd ... some uncommon observations about vitiated sight.   8vo.
London, by H.C. for John Taylor, 1688
Wing B3946.   **937**

——————— An essay about the origine & virtues of gems.   8vo.
London, by William Godbid, to be sold by Moses Pitt, 1672   Wing B3947.   **938**

——————— An essay of the great effects of even languid and unheeded motion.   8vo.
London, by M.Flesher, for Richard Davis, bookseller in Oxford, 1685   Wing B3949.   **951**

——————— Essays of the strange subtilty ... of effluviums.   8vo.
London, printed by W.G[odbid]. for M.Pitt, 1673
Wing B3951.   **870**

[———————] The excellency of theology, compar'd with natural philosophy. By T.H.R.B.E. [i.e. The Hon.Robert Boyle, Esq.]   2 pts.   8vo.
London, by T.N. for Henry Herringman, 1674
Wing B3955.   **803**

——————— Experimenta & observationes physicæ ... to which is added a small collection of strange reports.   2 pts.   8vo.
London, for John Taylor, and John Wyat, 1691
Wing B3959.   **919**

——————— Experiments and considerations about the porosity of bodies, in two essays.   8vo.
London, printed for Sam.Smith, 1684
Wing B3966.   **759(6)**

——————— Experiments and considerations touching colours.   8vo.
London, for Henry Herringman, 1664
Engr. diagram.   Wing B3967; Diary 28 Apr., 26 May & 2 June 1667.   **798**

——————— Experiments, notes, &c. about the mechanical origine or production of divers particular qualities.   11 pts.   8vo.
London, by E.Flesher, for R.Davis, bookseller in Oxford, 1676 (1675)   Wing B3977 [*etc.*].   **813**

[———————] A free enquiry into the vulgarly receiv'd notion of nature ... By R.B., Fellow of the Royal Society.   8vo.
London, by H.Clark, for John Taylor, 1685/6
Wing B3979.   **887**

———— The general history of the air.
4to.
London, for Awnsham and John Churchill, 1692
Wing B3981.   **1472**

———— Hydrostatical paradoxes.   8vo.
Oxford, by William Hall, for Richard Davis, 1666
3 engr. pls (diagrams).   Wing B3985; Diary 4 &
10 June, 24 July & 25 Aug. 1667.   **790**

[————] The martyrdom of Theodora,
and of Didymus. By a person of honour.   8vo.
London, by H.Clark, for John Taylor and Chris-
topher Skegnes, 1687   Wing B3987.   **882**

———— Medicina hydrostatica.   8vo.
London, for Samuel Smith, 1690   Engr. fp.
(diagram).   Wing B3988.   **816(1)**

———— Medicinal experiments. 2nd ed.
To which is annexed a catalogue of his theologi-
cal and philosophical books.   3 vols.   12mo.
London, for Sam.Smith (for S.Smith and B.Wal-
ford), 1693   Vols 1 and 2 (in 1) only.
Wing B3990.   **375**

———— Memoirs for the natural history of
humane blood.   8vo.
London, for Samuel Smith, 1684
Wing B3994.   **524**

———— New experiments, and obser-
vations, made upon the icy noctiluca.   8vo.
London, printed by R.E. for B.Tooke, 1681/2
Wing B3995.   **1101(2)**

———— New experiments and obser-
vations touching cold.   8vo.
London, for John Crook, 1665   Engr. pls.
Wing B3996.   **818**

———— New experiments physico-
mechanical, touching the spring of the air.   (2nd
ed.)   3 pts.   4to.
Oxford, H.Hall for Tho:Robinson (London, J.G.
for Thomas Robinson), 1662   Engr. pls.
Wing B3999.   **1405**

[————] Occasional reflections upon
several subjects. (Signed:R.B.)   8vo.
London, by W.Wilson for Henry Herringman,
1665   Wing B4005.   **709(2)**

[————] Of the high veneration man's
intellect owes to God. By a Fellow of the Royal
Society.   8vo.
London, by M.F. for Richard Davis, bookseller in
Oxford, 1685   Wing B4009.   **759(5)**

———— Of the reconcileableness of
specifick medicines to the corpuscular philosophy.
8vo.
London, for Sam.Smith, 1685   Inscribed on
front paste-down a note of its presentation to
Pepys: 'For ye President of the Royal Society'
Wing B4013.   **976**

———— The origine of formes and qualities.   2nd ed.   8vo.
Oxford, by H.Hall, for Ric:Davis, 1667
Wing B4015; Diary 1 Apr. 1668; 29-30 Jan.
1668/9.   **1160**

[————] The sceptical chymist ... to
which ... are subjoyn'd divers experiments and
notes.   2 pts.   8vo.
Oxford, by Henry Hall for Ric.Davis and B.Took,
1680   Wing B4022.   **960**

———— Short memoirs for the natural ex-
perimental history of mineral waters.   8vo.
London, for Samuel Smith, 1684/5
Wing B4023.   **817**

———— Some considerations touching the
style of the H.Scriptures.   8vo.
London, for Henry Herringman, 1663
Wing B4026; Diary 15 Sept. 1667.   **832**

———— Some considerations touching the
usefulnesse of experimental natural philosophy.
2nd ed.   2 vols in 1.   [*Vol.2, 1st ed.*]   4to.
Oxford, by Henry Hall, for Ric.Davis, 1664-71
Wing B4030-1.   **1538**

———— Some motives and incentives to
the love of God.   4th ed.   8vo.
London, for Henry Herringman, 1665
Wing B4035.   **709(1)**

———— Tracts ... about the cosmicall
qualities of things [*etc.*].   8vo.
Oxford, by W.H. for Ric.Davis, 1671
Wing B4057.   **987**

———— Tracts ... A discovery of the
admirable rarefaction of the air [*etc.*].   4to.
London, T.N. for Henry Herringman, 1671
Wing B4059.   **1539(3)**

———— Tracts ... containing new experiments, touching the relation betwixt flame and
air.   8vo.
London, for Richard Davis, book-seller in Oxon.,
1672   Wing B4060.   **840**

———— Tracts containing I. Suspicions
about some hidden qualities of the air ... II. Animadversions upon Mr.Hobbes's Problemata in
vacuo. III. A discourse of the cause of attraction
by suction.   6pts.   8vo.
London, by W.G., sold by M.Pitt, 1674
Wing B4054.   **927**

———— Tracts consisting of observations
about the saltness of the sea.   9pts.   8vo.
London, by E.Flesher for R.Davis, bookseller in
Oxford, 1674   Wing B4053.   **876**

BOYS (John). An exposition of al the principall
Scriptures vsed in our English liturgie.   4to.
London, by Felix Kyngston, to be sold by

William Aspley, 1610   [Liturgick Controversies I]   STC 3456.   **1187(3)**

BOYS (William). The narrative of Mr.W.Boys ...
concerning the late horrid popish plot, and the
death of Sir Edmund-Bury Godfrey.   fo.
London, for Dorman Newman, 1680
[Narratives & Tryals III]   Wing B4067.
2251(4)

BRADDON (Laurence). The tryal of Laurence
Braddon and Hugh Speke ... 7 Feb. 1683.   fo.
London, for Benjamin Tooke, 1684
[Narratives & Tryals V]   Wing T2196.
2253(10)

BRADY (Robert). A complete history of England ... unto the end of the reign of King Henry III.
2 pts.   fo.
*In the Savoy, by Tho.Newcomb for Samuel
Lowndes*, 1685   Wing B4186.   **2625**

———————— A continuation of the complete
history of England: containing the lives ... of
Edward I. II. & III. and Richard the Second.
2 pts.   fo.
*In the Savoy, by Edward Jones, for Sam.Lowndes,
and Awnsham and John Churchil*, 1700
Engr. title-page.   Wing B4187.   **2626**

———————— An historical treatise of cities.
2 pts.   fo.
London, for Samuel Lowndes, 1690
Wing B4192.   **2324**

———————— An introduction to the old English history, comprehended in three several tracts.
3 pts.   fo.
London, by Tho.Newcomb, for Samuel Lowndes,
1684   Wing B4194.   With a copy of 'A brief
history of the succession' by John, Baron Somers
(Wing S4638) inserted.   **2565(1)**

BRANCATI (Lorenzo), Cardinal. Epitome canonum omnium ... Editio in Germania prima.   fo.
*Coloniæ Agrippinæ, sumptibus Arnoldi Metter-
nich*, 1684   **2486**

BRANT (Sebastian). Stultifera nauis ... The ship of
fooles ... Transl. ... by A.Barclay. (The mirrour of
good maners ... by D.Mancin. —Certayne egloges of
A.Barclay.)   *Engl. & Lat.*   fo.
(London, by John Cavvood,) [1570]   Woodcuts.
STC 3546; Howarth p.189.   **2032**

BRANTÔME (Pierre de Bourdeille, seigneur de).
Memoires.   2 vols.   12mo.
Leyde, chez Jean Sambix le Jeune, 1692   **210-11**

BRAVO (Cristóbal). Aqui se contienen dos obras
graciosas ... La primera, del Testamento de la
Zorra. La segunda, el llanto que hizieron sus
parientes.   4to.
*(Seuilla, por Juan Vejarano, à costa de Lucas
Martin de Hermosa*, 1682)   Gaselee 18;
Wilson p.308.   **1545(59)**

———————— Obra llamada los trabajos que
passa la triste de la bolsa.   4to.
*(Sevilla, en la imprenta de Iuan Cabeças, acosta de
Lucas Martin de Hermosilla*, 1676)
Gaselee 19; Wilson p.264.   **1545(50)**

———————— Obra muy graciosa ... la qual se
llama el Testamento del Gallo.   4to.
(Sevilla, por Juan Cabeças, 1680)   Gaselee 20;
Wilson p.309.   **1545(61)**

BRERETON (Henry). Newes of the present
miseries of Rushia: occasioned by the late warre
in that countrey.   4to.
London, for Iohn Bache, 1614   [Consutilia V]
STC 3609.   **1431(22)**

BREREWOOD (Edward). Enquiries touching the
diversity of languages, and religions.   4to.
*London, printed by Iohn Norton, for Ioyce
Norton, and Richard Whitaker*, 1635
STC 3621.   **1213**

[BRETON (Nicholas)]. Crossing of proverbs ...
Newly corrected ... By B.R.   8vo.
London, for Margaret White, 1683   [Penny-
Merriments I]   **362(53)**

———————— A poast with a pacquet of
letters.   2 pts.   4to.
London, for Thomas Fabian, 1685
[Vulgaria IV]   Woodcut on title-page.
Wing B4390.   **1193(17)**

BREVE suma de la vida y milagros de el bien aven-
turado San Ignacio.   4to.
(Sevilla, por Thomè de Dios Miranda, 1675)
Gaselee 83; Wilson p.229.   **1545(15)**

BREVIATE (A) of the life of Margaret ... Charlton,
1681.
See BAXTER (Richard).   **1240**

BREVINT (Daniel). Saul and Samuel at Endor, or
the new waies of salvation and service.   8vo.
Oxford, at the Theater, 1674
Wing B4423.   **1450**

BREVISSIMA institutio, 1662.
See LILY (William).   **886**

BREWSTER (Sir Francis). Essays on trade and
navigation ... The first part. [*No more published.*]
8vo.
London, for Tho.Cockerill, 1695
Wing B4434.   **821**

[BRICE (Germain)]. A new description of Paris ...
Transl. out of French.   2 pts.   12mo.
London, printed for Henry Bonwicke, 1687
Wing B4440.   **463**

BRIDGE (William). Babylons downfall. A sermon.
4to.
London, by I.N. for Iohn Rothwell, 1641
[Sermons Polemical I]   Wing B4448.   **1179(9)**

———————— England saved with a notwithstanding ... A sermon ... Novemb. 5. 1647. 4to.
London, for R.Dawlman, 1648 [Sermons Polemical I] Wing B4452. **1179(11)**

———————— A sermon preached unto the voluntiers of the city of Norwich and ... Great Yarmouth. 4to.
London, by J.F. for Ben.Allen, 1642 [Sermons Polemical I] Wing B4466. **1179(10)**

BRIDGES (Noah). Stenographie and crytographie [*sic*] : or the arts of short and secret writing. 8vo.
London, by J.G. for the author, 1659 24 engr. pls. Wants engr. fp. (port.). [Short-hand Collection III] Wing B4482; Carlton, p.74.
402(2)

BRIDGES (Walter). Ioabs counsell ... A sermon ... Feb.22. 4to.
London, by R.Cotes, for Andrew Crooke, 1643 [Sermons Polemical I] Wing B4484A.
1179(12)

BRIEF (A) account of the intended Bank of England, 1694.
See PATERSON (William). **1433(7)**

BRIEF (A) and perfect journal, 1655.
See S.(I.). **1431(11)**

BRIEF (A) chronology of the most remarkable passages and transactions which occurred since his late renowned Highness, Oliver Lord Protector was invested with the government ... of England. brs.
London, by T.N. for Edward Thomas, 1658 Engr. port. (Charrington p.45). Wing B4554.
2566(2)

BRIEF (A) collection out of the records of the City, touching the election of the Sheriffs ... By order of the Lord Mayor. fo.
[*London*] (*by S.Roycroft*, 1682.) Bound in after p.652. Wing B4556. **2476**

BRIEF directions shewing how a fit and perfect model of popular government may be made (1659).
See HARRINGTON (James), the elder. **1297(9)**

BRIEF. A briefe discourse of the troubles begun at Frankeford in Germany, 1642.
See WHITTINGHAM (William). **1188(11)**

BRIEF. A breif [*sic*] enquiry into the ground, authority, and rights of ecclesiastical synods. 8vo.
London, by M.B. for Richard Sare, 1699 [Convocation Pamphlets III] **1689(3)**

BRIEF (A) history of the succession [1680].
See SOMERS (John, 1st Baron). **2565(2)**

BRIEF (A) history of the Unitarians called also Socinians, 1687.
See NYE (Stephen). **635**

BRIEF instructions for making observations, 1696.
See WOODWARD (John). **1435(4)**

BRIGHT (Timothy). Characterie. An arte of shorte, swifte, and secrete writing by character. 24mo.
London, by I.Windet, the assigne of Tim.Bright, 1588 [Short-hand Collection I] STC 3743; Carlton p.1. **13**

BRIGHTMAN (Thomas). The Revelation of St John illustrated with an analysis & scholions. 4th ed. (— A most comfortable exposition of the last ... part ... of Daniel. — A commentary on the ... song of Solomon.) 4to.
'*London, for Samuel Cartwright*' [*Amsterdam, printed by Thomas Stafford?*] , 1644 Engr. fp. (port., Charrington p.21). Wing B4693. **1332**

BRINSLEY (John). The araignment of the present schism of new separation in old England. 4to.
London, by John Field for Ralph Smith, 1646 [Sermons Polemical I] Wing B4707. **1179(14)**

———————— The glorie of the latter temple greater then of the former ... a sermon preached ... 11 March 1630. 4to.
London, for Robert Bird, 1631 [Sermons Polemical I] STC 3789. **1179(13)**

[BRISCOE (John)] . A discourse of money. 8vo.
London, printed for Sam.Briscoe, 1696 Wing B4744. **1138**

BRISSON (Barnabé). De formulis et sollemnibus populi Romani verbis, libri VIII. 4to.
Francofurti, apud Ioannem Wechelum & Petrum Fischerum consortes, 1592 Adams B2848.
1817

BRITAIN'S. Brittains glory: or the history ... of K. Arthur, 1684.
See SHIRLEY (John). **1192(8)**

[BRIZUELA (Mateo Sanchez de)] . Aqui se contienen dos obras maravillosas [c.1680].
See SANCHEZ DE LA CRUZ (Matheo).
1545(18)

———————— Aqui se contiene vn traslado de vna carta ... embiada por Melchor de Padilla. 4to.
(*Seuilla, por Iuan de Ossuna*, 1680) Gaselee 21; Wilson p.317. **1545(68)**

———————— La fiera batalla que passo entre el Conde D.Roldan, y el Moro Mandricardo. 4to.
(*Sevilla, por Iuan Vejarano, a costa de Lucas Martin de Hermosa*, 1681) Gaselee 22; Wilson p.305. **1545(56)**

BROÉ (Samuel de).
See CITRI DE LA GUETTE (Samuel de Broé, seigneur de).

BROME (Richard). A joviall crew ... a comedie.
4to.
London, for Henry Brome, 1661   [Loose
Plays I]   Wing B4874.   **1075(9)**

BROMWICH (Andrew). The tryal and condem-
nation of two popish priests, A.Brommich and
W.Atkyns, for high treason at Stafford.   fo.
London, for John Amery, 1679   [Narratives
& Tryals IV]   Wing T2157.   **2252(3)**

BROOKE (Fulke Greville, 1st Baron). The life of
the renowned Sr Philip Sidney.   8vo.
London, for Henry Seile, 1652   Wing B4899;
Diary 1-2 Jan. 1668.   **214**

———————— The remains of Sir Fulk Grevill
Lord Brooke; being poems of monarchy and
religion.   8vo.
London, by T.N. for Henry Herringman, 1670
Wing B4900.   **699**

[BROOKE (Nathaniel)]. England's glory; or, an
exact catalogue of the lords of His Majesties most
honourable Privy Councel.   8vo.
London, for Nath.Brooke, and Hen.Eversden,
1660   Engr. fp.   Wing B4907.   **606(2)**

BROOKES (Thomas). The dying ministers last
sermon.   12mo.
[*London,*] *for J.Conyers*, [c.1680]   [Penny-
Godlinesses]   Woodcut on title-page.
Wing B4939A.   **365(11)**

[BROUSCON (Guillaume)]. [Tide-tables. 12
vellum leaves, printed from wood-blocks, containing diagrams, tables and maps.]
[*Conquet*, 1546]   Misbound; with a MS map on
vellum attached. Autograph: 'F.Drak'.
Duff p.35.   **1**

BROWN (John). The carpenters joynt-rule.   12mo.
London, sold by John and Thomas Browne, 1684
10 engrs.   Wing B5035.   **420**

[———————] The description and use of the
carpenters-rule, by J.B. [i.e. John Brown?], 1662.
See B.(J.).   **85**

[BROWN (Thomas)]. The reasons of Mr.Joseph
Hains ... conversion.   4to.
London, for Richard Baldwin, 1690
[Consutilia I]   Wing B5071.   **1427(15)**

BROWNE (Edward). A brief account of some
travels in divers parts of Europe.   2nd ed.   fo.
London, for Benj.Tooke, 1685   16 engr. pls.
Wing B5111.   **2653**

BROWNE (John). Myographia nova, sive muscul-
orum omnium ... descriptio.   fo.
Londini, excudebat Joannes Redmayne, 1684
Engr. fp. (port., Charrington p.22), 40 engr. pls.
Wing B5127.   **2517**

———————— Myographia nova: or, a graphical
description of all the muscles.   fo.
London, by Tho.Milbourn for the author, 1698
Engr. fp. (port., Charrington p.22), 42 engr. pls.
Wing B5129.   **2288**

BROWNE (Sir Thomas). Works.   4 pts.   fo.
*London, for Tho.Basset, Ric.Chiswell, Tho.Saw-
bridge, Charles Mearn, and Charles Brome*, 1686
Engr. fp. (port., Charrington p.22).
Wing B5150.   **2368**

BRUEYS (David Augustin de). Histoire du
fanatisme de nostre temps.   12mo.
Paris, chez François Muguet, 1692   1 engr. pl.
543

BRUIN (Cornelis de). A voyage to the Levant ...
Enrich'd with above two hundred copper-plates ...
Done into English, by W.J.   fo.
London, for Jacob Tonson, and Thomas Bennet,
1702   Engr. fp., port. (Charrington p.23), map,
pls.   **2492**

[BRUNEL (Antoine de)]. Voyage d'Espagne ...
fait en l'année 1655.   4to.
Paris, chez Charles de Sercy, 1665   **1827**

BUCHANAN (George). Rerum Scoticarum historia
... Accessit De iure regni apud Scotos dialogus.
2 pts.   fo.
'*Edimburgi, ad exemplar A.Arbuthneti editum*'
[*Antwerp, G.van den Rade.*], 1583   STC 3992.
2298

BUCK (Sir George). The history of the life and
reigne of Richard the third.   fo.
*London, by W.Wilson, to be sold by W.L., H.M.
and D.P.*, 1646   Engr. fp. (port., Charrington
p.144).   Wing B5306.   **1991**

BUCKINGHAM (George Villiers, 2nd Duke of).
Miscellaneous works. (Speeches ... spoken in both
Houses of Parliament, by several noblemen and
commoners.)   2 pts.   8vo.
London, printed for and sold by J.Nutt, 1704
1357

———————— The Duke of Buckingham's speech
in a late conference.   4to.
London, for M.I., 1668   [Consutilia I]
Wing B5331.   **1427(14)**

BUCKLER (The) of state and justice, 1667.
See LISOLA (François Paul de), Baron.   **841**

BUDÉ (Guillaume). Lucubrationes uarię.   fo.
Basileæ, apud Nicolaum Episcopium iuniorem,
1557   Adams B3150.   **2343**

[BUGNOT (Louis Gabriel)]. Archombrotus et
Theopompus, sive Argenidis secunda & tertia pars.
8vo.
Lugd. Batav. et Roterod., ex officina Hackiana,
1669   Engr. title-page.   **1369**

BULIFON (Antonio). Compedio istorico del Monte Vesuvio, in cui si ha piena notizia di ... eruzioni ... in fino a quindici di giugno del 1698. 12mo.
Nap[oli]., presso Antonio Bulifon, 1698
Engr. pl.   **345(2)**

——————— Ragionamento intorno ad un' antico marmo discoverto nella città di Pozzuoli. 12mo.
Napoli, nella stamperia di Giuseppe Roselli, 1698
Engr. pl.   **346(2)**

BULL (George). Defensio fidei Nicænæ.   Ed. 2a.
4to.
Oxonii, e Theatro Sheldoniano, 1688
Wing B5415.   **1570**

BULLET (Pierre). Plan de Paris, levé ... en l'année 1675.   fo.
Paris, se vend au logis de Monsieur Blondel (1676)
                                             1913

BULWER (John). Anthropometamorphosis ... Scripsit J.B.   4to.
London, printed by William Hunt, 1653
Engr. fp. (port., Charrington p.24), title-page, woodcuts.   **1115**

BUONANNI (Filippo). Numismata pontificum Romanorum ... ad annum M.DC.XCIX.   2 vols. fo.
Romæ, ex typographia Dominici Antonii Herculis, 1699   Vol.1: 44 engrs. Vol.2: 54 engrs.
                                             2892-3

——————— Numismata summorum pontificum templi Vaticani fabricam indicantia.   fo.
Romæ, sumptibus Felicis Cæsaretti & Paribeni, typis Dominici Antonii Herculis, 1696   87 engrs.
                                             2891

[BUONI (Tommaso)]. Della famosissima compagnia della Lesina.   8vo.
Venetia, 1647   **423**

BURATTINO.
See MISELLI (Giuseppe), called Burattino.

BURCHETT (Josiah). Memoirs of transactions at sea during the war with France, 1688-1697.   8vo.
London, by John Nutt, 1703   **1144**

——————— Mr.Burchett's justification of his naval-memoirs, in answer to reflections made by Col.Lillingston.   8vo.
London, by Edward Jones, sold by John Nutt, 1704   **1145(2)**

BURGERSDIJCK (Franco). Institutionum logicarum libri duo.   8vo.
Cantabrigiæ, apud Joann.Hayes, prostant venales apud Guil.Graves jun., 1680   Wing B5636. **356**

BURGES (Cornelius). Another sermon preached ... November the fifth.   4to.
London, by R.B. for P.Stephens and C.Meridith, 1641   [Sermons Polemical I]   MS notes in unidentified 17th-cent. hand on title-page and elsewhere.   Wing B5668.   **1179(18)**

[———————] No sacrilege nor sinne to aliene or purchase the lands of bishops. By C.B.D.D. 2nd ed.   8vo.
London, by J.C., sold by Ed.Brewster, 1659
Wing B5675.   **695**

——————— The second sermon, preached to the ... House of Commons, April 30.   4to.
London, by J.R. for Christoph.Meredith, 1645
[Sermons Polemical I]   Wing B5681. **1179(19)**

——————— A sermon preached to the ... House of Commons ... Novem.17.1640.   4to.
London, by T.Badger for P.Stephens and C.Meredith, 1641   [Sermons Polemical I]
Wing B5683.   **1179(17)**

[———————] Some of the differences and alterations in the present common-prayer-book, from the Book established by law.   4to.
[1660]   [Liturgick Controversies II]
Wing B5686.   **1188(6)**

BURGESS (Anthony). The difficulty of, and the encouragements to a reformation. A sermon preached ... Septem.27.   4to.
London, by R.Bishop for Thomas Vnderhill, 1643
[Sermons Polemical I]   Wing B5643.
                                             1179(15)

——————— The reformation of the church ... A sermon preached ... August 27.   4to.
London, by G.M. for T.Underhill, 1645
[Sermons Polemical I]   Wing B5654. **1179(16)**

[BURGHLEY (William Cecil, 1st Baron)]. Copie of a letter sent ... to Don B.Mendoza, 1588.
See LEIGH (Richard).   **1080(1)**

BURNET (Gilbert), Bp of Salisbury. A discourse of the pastoral care.   8vo.
London, by R.R. for Ric.Chiswell, 1692
Wing B5777.   **962(2)**

——————— An enquiry into the measures of submission to the supream authority.   4to.
London, for Ric.Chiswell, 1693   [Consutilia VII]   Wing B5810.   **1433(6)**

——————— An exposition of the Thirty-nine Articles.   2nd ed.   fo.
London, by R.Roberts for Ri.Chiswell, 1700
Wing B5792.   **2418**

——————— The history of the Reformation of the Church of England.   3 pts.   fo.
London, by T.H. for Richard Chiswell, 1679-1715

Pts 1 & 2 only. Pt 1: engr. title-page, 6 engr. ports.
Pt 2: engr. title-page, 8 engr. ports.   Wing B5797.
2383-4

———————— The history of the rights of
princes ... To which is added a collection of
letters.   2 pts.   8vo.
*London, by J.D. for Richard Chiswell, 1682
(1681)*   Wing B5801.   **1123**

———————— The life and death of Sir Matthew
Hale, Kt. sometime Lord Chief Justice.   8vo.
London, for William Shrowsbery, 1682
Engr. fp. (port., Charrington p.73).
Wing B5828; Tanner I, p.112.   **979**

[————————] The life of William Bedell, D.D.
8vo.
London, for John Southby, 1685
Wing B5830.   **1068**

———————— The memoires of the lives ... of
James and William, Dukes of Hamilton. (The
history of the church and state of Scotland [by
J.Spottiswoode], pt II.)   fo.
London, by J.Grover, for R.Royston, 1677
Engr. ports., Charrington p.74.   Wing B5832.
2335

———————— Reflections on a book entituled,
The rights, powers and privileges of an English
convocation stated and vindicated.   4to.
London, for Ri.Chiswell, 1700   [Convocation
Pamphlets IX]   Wing B5848.   **1695(4)**

———————— Remarks on the examination of
the exposition of the second article of our church.
4to.
(London, for Ri.Chiswell, 1702)   **1772(3)**

———————— Some letters. Containing an account of ... Switzerland, Italy, &c. ... To which is
annexed [Burnet's] answer to Mr.Varillas.
2 pts.   12mo.
Amsterdam, 1686   Wing B5914.   **679(1)**

———————— Some passages of the life and
death of ... John Earl of Rochester.   8vo.
London, for Richard Chiswel, 1680
Engr. fp. (port., Charrington p.146).
Wing B5922.   **810(3)**

[————————] Three letters concerning the
present state of Italy.   8vo.
[London,] 1688.   Wing B5931.   **679(2)**

[BURNET (Thomas)]. An answer to the late
exceptions made by Mr Erasmus Warren against
the theory of the earth.   fo.
London, by R.Norton, for Walter Kettilby, 1690
Wing B5942.   **2271(1)**

———————— Archæologiæ philosophicæ: sive
doctrina antiqua de rerum originibus.   4to.
Londini, typis R.N. impensis Gualt.Kettilby, 1692
Wing B5943.   **1525**

[————————] A short consideration of Mr
Erasmus Warren's defence of his exceptions against
the theory of the earth.   fo.
London, by R.Norton, for Walter Kettilby, 1691
Wing B5947.   **2271(2)**

———————— Telluris theoria sacra.   2 vols.
4to.
*Londini, typis R.N., impensis Gualt.Kettilby,
1681-9*   Vol.1: engr. map, illus. Vol.2: engr.
title-page.   Wing B5948-9.   **1523-4**

———————— The theory of the earth ... The first
two (two last) books.   2 vols.   fo.
*London, by R.Norton, for Walter Kettilby,
1684-90*   Vol.1: engr. title-page, maps, illus.
Vol.2: engr. title-page.   Wing B5950, 5954;
Tanner I, p.23.   **2641-2**

BURROUGHS (Jeremiah). The glorious name of
God ... in two sermons ... With a post-script ...
answering a late treatise by H.Ferne.   4to.
London, for R.Dawlman, 1643   Wing B6075.
1066

———————— A sermon preached before the ...
House of Commons ... August 26.   4to.
*London, by Matthew Simmons, for Hanna Allen,
1646*   [Sermons Polemical I]   Wing B6118.
1179(21)

———————— Sions joy. A sermon preached ...
September 7.   4to.
London, by T.P. and M.S. for R.Dawlman, 1641
[Sermons Polemical I]   **1179(20)**

BURROUGHS (Sir John).
See BOROUGH (Sir John).

BURTON (Henry). An apology of an appeale.
4to.
[London] 1636   [Sermons Polemical II]
STC 4135.   **1180(2)**

———————— Englands bondage ... A sermon
preached ... Iune 20.   4to.
London, 1641   [Sermons Polemical II]
Wing B6162.   **1180(4)**

———————— For God, and the King. The
summe of two sermons.   4to.
[London,] 1636   [Sermons Polemical II]
STC 4141.   **1180(3)**

———————— Israels fast. Or, a meditation vpon
the seuenth chapter of Joshuah ... by H.B. (H.
Burton).   4to.
Rochel, 1628   [Sermons Polemical II]
STC 4147.   **1180(1)**

[BURTON (Robert)]. The anatomy of melancholy ... By Democritus Junior [*i.e.* R.Burton].
7th ed.   fo.
*London, for John Garway (for Henry Cripps, and
are to bee sold by him, and by Elisha Wallis),
1660*   Engr. title-page.   **2113**

BURTON (William), 1575-1645. The description of Leicester Shire. fo.
London, [W.Jaggard?] for Iohn White [1622]
Engr. fp. (port., Charrington p.24), title-page, map. STC 4179. **2023**

BURTON (William), 1609-57. A commentary on Antoninus his itinerary ... so far as it concerneth Britain [*with the text*]. fo.
London, by Tho.Roycroft, sold by Henry and T. Twyford, 1658 Engr. fp. (port., Charrington p.25), map. Wing B6185. **2025**

BURY (John). A true narrative of the late design of the Papists. fo.
London, for Dorman Newman, 1679
[Narratives & Tryals III] Wing B6215. **2251(48)**

BUSBY (George). The tryal and condemnation of G.Busby, for high treason, as a Romish priest. fo.
London, for Randolph Taylor, 1681 [Narratives & Tryals IV] Wing T2142. **2252(22)**

BUSHNELL (Edmund). The compleat shipwright. 4to.
London, by W.Leybourn for George Hurlock, 1664 Engr. diagram. Wing B6252. **1267(1)**

BUSSY d'Ambois, 1641.
See CHAPMAN (George). **1075(4)**

BUSSY-RABUTIN (Roger, comte de). Mémoires. (— L'usage des adversitez ... contenant un discours du comte ... sur les divers evenements de sa vie.) 3 vols in 2. 12mo.
Paris, chez Jean Anisson, 1697 Vol.1: engr. fp. (port., Charrington p.25). **660-1**

BUTLER (Charles). The English grammar. [*In phonetic spelling*]. 4to .
Oxford, by William Turner, for the authour, 1633
STC 4190. **1100(1)**

——————— The principles of musik. [*In phonetic spelling.*] 4to.
London, by John Haviland, for the author, 1636
STC 4196. *See also* vol.IV. **1100(3)**

——————— [The feminin' monarchi', or the histori of bee's. *In phonetic spelling.* 4to.
Oxford, by William Turner, for ðe author, 1634]
Wants title-page. Substitute title-page supplied in hand of one of Pepys's clerks: 'Dr Butler's Feminine Monarchy, or History of Bees'.
STC 4194. **1100(2)**

BUTLER (John). Χριστολογία. Or a brief ... account of the certain year ... of the birth of Jesus Christ. 8vo.
London, by Joseph Moxon, sold by him, and by Hen.Broom, 1671 Table. Wing B6270. **585**

BUTLER (Nathaniel). Six dialogues about sea-services. 8vo.
London, for Moses Pitt, 1685 Dedicated to Pepys by the publisher. Wing B6288. **822**

[BUTLER (Samuel)]. Hudibras. 3 pts. 8vo.
London, for Henry Herringman, sold by Tho.Sawbridge (pt 2: for R.Chiswell, T.Sawbridge, R. Bentley and G.Wells — pt 3: for Thomas Horne), 1689 Wing B6304, 6317A; Diary 26 Dec. 1662, 6 Feb., 28 Nov. & 10 Dec.1663, 29 Aug.1683. **889**

BUXTORF (Johann). Lexicon chaldaicum talmudicum et rabbinicum. fo.
Basileæ, sumptibus et typis Ludovici König, 1639 **2687**

——————— Lexicon hebraicum et chaldaicum ... Ed. 7a. 8vo.
Basileæ, sumptibus Johannis König, 1663 **858**

——————— Synagoga judaica. 8vo.
Basileæ, impensis Ludovici König, 1641 **749**

——————— Thesaurus grammaticus linguæ sanctæ hebrææ. 8vo.
Basilea, impensis hæred. Ludovici Regis, 1651
Diary 25 Jan.1659/60. **779**

BYFIELD (Richard). Temple-defilers defiled ... Two sermons preached ... Feb.20 & 27.1644. 4to.
London, by John Field for Ralph Smith, 1645
[Sermons Polemical II] Wing B6394. **1180(5)**

C

C.(C.). Treason's master-piece. 8vo.
London, printed for Daniel Major, 1680
Wing C19. **750**

C.(E.). A full and final proof of the Plot ... by E.C. fo.
London, for Thomas Simmons and Jacob Sampson, 1680 [Narratives & Tryals IV]
Wing C23. **2252(33)**

C.(E.). The poor doubting Christian drawn unto Christ. 9th impr. 12mo.
[*London,*] *by H.B. for J.Wright, J.Clark [etc.], 1683* [Penny-Godlinesses] Woodcut.
Wing C26B. **365(30)**

C.(H.). Cupid's love-lessons. 12mo.
[*London,*] *for J.Clarke senior, 1683* [Penny-Merriments I] Woodcut. Wing C38. **362(47)**

C.(J.). Christ's voice to England ...   5th ed.
12mo.
London, by H.B. for J.Wright, J.Clark [etc.],
1683   [Penny-Godlinesses]   Woodcuts.
Wing C52A.   365(32)

C.(M.C.E.P.). Description des antiquitez ...
d'Orange, 1700.
See ESCOFFIER (Charles).   1638(3)

C.(M.D.). Le dictionnaire des arts et des sciences,
1694.
See CORNEILLE (Thomas).   2812

C.(M.L.D.). Journal ... du voyage de Siam, 1687.
See CHOISY (François Timoléon de).   685

C.(R.). The triumphant weaver: or the art of
weaving.   4to.
[London] for J.Deacon, 1682   [Vulgaria IV]
Woodcut on title-page.   Wing C116.   1193(14)

C.(S.). Mock poem, or, Whiggs supplication, 1681.
See COLVIL (Samuel).   614

C.(S.). Roman-Catholick doctrines, 1663.
See CRESSY (Hugh Paulin).   575

C.(W.). The historian's guide, 1688.
See CLARKE (Samuel), Minister of Bennet Fink.
                                      487(1)

C.(W.), *M.D.C.M.L.C.* The grand essay, 1704.
See COWARD (William).   1133

C.(W.S.F.). A most delightful history of ... Jack of
Newbery, 1684.
See DELONEY (Thomas).   363(50)

CABALA, sive scrinia sacra; mysteries of state and
government: in letters of illustrious persons and
great ministers of state.   fo.
London, for G.Bedell and T.Collins, 1663
MS copy of letter of Elizabeth I to Earl of Pembroke (2 July 1599) inserted: made by one of
Pepys's clerks (?from 2502, p.9).
Wing C185; Diary 10 Dec.1663; Naval Minutes
p.151.   2261

CABINET (Le) satyrique. Dernière éd.   2 vols in
1.   12mo.
[Leyden, officina Hackiana?] 1666   58

CADIZ. Cathedral. Letras de los villancicos que se
cantaron en la Santa Iglesia Cathedral de Cadiz, en
la kalenda ... del nacimiento ... 1683.   4to.
[Seville?] 1683   Gaselee 23; Wilson p.242.
                                      1545(26)

——————— [Another copy. Wants A2 and A3.]
Gaselee 24; Wilson p.243.   1545(27)

CADIZ. Cathedral. Letras de los villancicos, que
se cantaron en la Santa Iglesia Cathedral de Cadiz,
en los maytines solemnes ... 1683.   4to.

[Seville? 1683]   Gaselee 25, 26; Wilson p.243,
244. [Two copies.]   1545(28-9)

CÆREMONIALE ... electionis Romani pontificis,
1622.
See LITURGIES. Roman Catholic Church. 1743(1)

CÆREMONIALE episcoporum, 1633.
See LITURGIES. Roman Catholic Church.   2608

CAESAR (Gaius Julius). Quae exstant, cum
selectis variorum commentariis ... opera A.Montani.
Accedunt notitia Galliae ... ex autographo
I.Scaligeri.   8vo.
Amstelodami, ex officina Elzeviriana, 1661
Engr. title-page, map.   1326

——————— The commentaries. Transl. ... by
C.Edmonds ... Together with the life of Cæsar.
2 pts.   fo.
*London, by R.Daniel, to be sold by Henry Twy-
ford, Nathaniel Ekins and John Place*, 1655
Engr. fp. (port.), title-page, 14 engr. pls.
Wing C199; Diary 25 Dec.1668.   2221

——————— Les commentaires.   3e éd.
3 pts.   4to.
Paris, chez Augustin Courbé, 1658 (pt.2: 1657)
Engr. title-page, diagram.   1804

——————— La guerre des Suisses, traduite du
I. livre des commentaires de Iule Cesar, par Louys
XIV. Dieudonné Roy de France.   fo.
Paris, de l'Imprimerie Royale, 1651
4 engr. pls.   2685

CALDERÓN DE LA BARCA (Pedro). El angel de
la guarda. Comedia famosa. *[Probably not by
Calderón.]*   4to.
[Seville, Tomé de Dios Miranda, c.1675]
Gaselee 27.   1553(21)

——————— Las cadenas del demonio. Comedia
famosa.   4to.
[?Seville, ?Cadiz, ?1650-80]   Gaselee 28.
                                      1553(10)

——————— La gran comedia. De la exaltacion
de la Cruz.   4to.
[Seville, ?Tomé de Dios Miranda, c.1671]
Gaselee 30.   1553(9)

——————— El mejor padre de pobres. Comedia
famosa [c.1680].
See MEJOR (El) padre ...   1553(22)

CALENDARIUM Catholicum or, an almanack for
... 1689.   12mo.
London, printed by Henry Hills, 1689
[Almanacks for the year 1689]   Wing A1386A.
                                      426(3)

CALEPINUS (Ambrosius). Dictionarium. Ed.
nouissima. *Lat., Hebr., Gk, Fr., It., Ger., Span. &
Engl.* 2 pts. fo.
*Lugduni, sumptibus Philippi Borde, & Laurentii
Arnaud*, 1663 (pt 2: 1662)   Engr. on title-pages.
2753

CALL (A) to extravagant youth ... the last will
and testament of William Crook.   8vo.
[*London,*] *by J.B. for P.Brooksby* [c.1685]
[Penny-Godlinesses]   Woodcut on title-page.
365(3)

[CALLIÈRES (François de)]. Des mots à la mode
et des nouvelles façons de parler.   3e éd.
12mo.
À la Haye, chez Abraham Troyel, 1692   150

CALVIN (Jean). Institutionum Christianæ religionis libri quatuor. Ed. postrema ... Cui accesserunt
epistolæ atque responsa ... Præmissa est vita ejusdem Calvini, à T.Beza conscripta.   2 pts.   fo.
*Amstelodami, apud Joannem Jacobi Schipper,
(ex typographia Borritii Jansonii Smit,)* 1667
2737

CALVINUS (Joannes). Lexicon iuridicum iuris
Cæsarei.   fo.
[*Geneva,*] *sumptibus Samuelis Chouët*, 1669
2531

CAMBRIDGE. University. Academiæ Cantabrigiensis carmina, quibus decedenti ... Wilhelmo III
parentat; et succedenti ... Annæ gratulatur.   fo.
Cantabrigiæ, typis academicis [1702]   2282(2)

——————————Gratulatio academiæ Cantabrig-
iensis de reditu ... Gulielmi III. post pacem &
libertatem Europæ feliciter restitutam anno
MDCXCVII.   fo.
Cantabrigiæ, typis academicis [1697]
Wing C337.   2281

—————————— Illustrissimi principis ducis Cornu-
biae ... genethliacon.   4to.
Cantabrigiae, ex officinâ Joan.Hayes, 1688
Wing C339.   2279(1)

—————————— Lacrymæ Cantabrigienses in
obitum ... reginæ Mariæ.   4to.
Cantabrigiæ, ex officina Johan.Hayes, 1694/5
Wing C342.   2280(2)

—————————— Mœstissimæ ac lætissimæ
Academiæ Cantabrigiensis affectus, decedente
Carolo II.   4to.
Cantabrigiae, ex officina Joan.Hayes, 1684/5
Wing C343.   2280(1)

—————————— Musæ Cantabrigienses ... Wilhelmo
et Mariæ ... hæc officii & pietatis ergò D.D.   4to.
Cantabrigiæ, ex officina Joann.Hayes, 1689
Wing C344.   2279(2)

——————————Threnodia Academiæ Cantabrigiensis in immaturum obitum ... principis Gulielmi
ducis Glocestrensis.   fo.
Cantabrigiæ, typis academicis, 1700
Wing C357.   2282(1)

CAMDEN (William).
See ANGLICA, Normannica, Hibernica, Cambrica
a veteribus scripta ... ex bibliotheca G.Camdeni.
2530

CAMDEN (William). Britannia, newly translated
into English.   fo.
*London, by F.Collins for A.Swalle, and A. and J.
Churchil*, 1695   Engr. fp. (port., Charrington
p.26), 49 engr. maps, engr. pls.   Wing C359;
Diary 21 Nov.1661.   2807

——————————Gulielmi Camdeni, et illustrium
virorum ad G.Camdenum epistolæ ... Præmittitur
G.Camdeni vita. Scriptore T.Smitho. *Lat., Fr. &
Engl.* 2 pts.   4to.
Londini, impensis Richardi Chiswelli, 1691
Wing C361.   1956

——————————The history of the most renowned
... Elizabeth.   3rd ed.   fo.
*London, by E.Flesher for Charles Harper, and
John Amery*, 1675   Engr. fp. (port.).
Wing C362.   2229(1)

[——————————] Institutio Græcæ grammatices
compendiaria in usum regiæ scholæ Westmonasteriensis.   8vo.
Londini, excudit Rogerus Nortonus, 1692
Wing C372.   355

——————————Remains concerning Britain.
7th impr.   8vo.
*London, printed for, and sold by, Charles Harper,
and John Amery*, 1674   Engr. fp. (port.,
Charrington p.26).   Wing C375; Naval Minutes
p.22.   918

CAMPAGNE (La) du Roy [Louis XIV] en
l'année 1677, 1678.
See PRIMI VISCONTI (Giovanni Battista), conte
di San Maiole.   531

CANTERBURY (Province of). Articles to be
enquired of, within the prouince of Canterburie,
1546 [1576].
See ENGLAND. *Church of England. Visitation
Articles.*   1761(6)

——————————Articles wherupon it was agreed
by ... the Archbishop of Canterbury, & other the
bishops ... of the prouince of Canterbury.   4to.
(*London, by Richard Iugge*) [1575]
STC 4582.   1761(5)

CANTERBURY tales, rendred into familiar verse,
viz. The plain proof. The forreigner. *&c.*   8vo.
London, 1701   1411

CAPACCIO (Giulio Cesare). La vera antichità di Pozzuolo. 8vo.
Roma, appresso Filippo de' Rossi, 1652
10 engr. pls., map. **901**

CAPECE. L'état de la république de Naples sous le gouvernement de Monsieur le Duc de Guise. Traduit de l'Italien par M.Marie Turge-Loredan. 12mo.
Sur la copie à Paris, chez Fédéric Léonard, 'LXXX' [1680] **236**

CAPPEL (Louis). Critica sacra. fo.
Lutetiæ Parisiorum, sumptibus Sebastiani Cramoisy et Gabrielis Cramoisy, 1650 **2592**

CARADOC, St, of Llancarfan. The historie of Cambria, now called Wales ... transl. ... by H. Lhoyd. (A description of Cambria, drawne first by Sir Iohn Price.) 4to.
London, Rafe Newberie and Henrie Denham, 1584
Woodcuts. STC 4606. **1251**

CARDANO (Girolamo). De libris propriis. 8vo.
Lugduni, apud Gulielmum Rouillium, 1557
Adams C687. **716(2)**

CARDINALISMO (Il) di Santa Chiesa, 1670.
See LETI (Gregorio). **2176**

CARE (Henry). The triall of Henry Carr ... Also the tryal of Elizabeth Cellier. 2 pts. fo.
London, by I.G. for R.Taylor, 1681 (pt 2: 1680)
[Narratives & Tryals IV] Wing T2187, 2190. **2252(10)**

CAREW (George). Fraud and oppression detected and arraigned. fo.
[London,] 1676 Wing C546. **2198(1)**

———————— A retrospect into the Kings certain revenue annexed to the Crown. fo.
London, 1661 Wing C550. **2900**

CAREW (Thomas). Hinc illæ lacrymæ; or an epitome of the life and death of Sir W.Courten and Sir P.Pyndar. fo.
London, for the persons interested, 1681
Last 2 leaves misbound. Wing C563. **2198(2)**

CARLIERI (Jacopo). Ristretto delle cose più notabili della citta di Firenze. Seconda impressione con aggiunta della seconda parte contenente i luoghi suburbani. 12mo.
Firenze, per il Carlieri, 1698 Engr. plan. **347**

CARLILE (James). The fortune-hunters ... a comedy. 4to.
London, for James Knapton, 1689 [Loose Plays II] Wing C590. **1604(12)**

CARMARTHEN (Peregrine Osborne, Marquis of).
See LEEDS (Peregrine Osborne, 2nd Duke of).

CARMELIANUS (Petrus). [Hoc presenti libello ... cōtinentur honorifica gesta ... ʒ triūphi nuper habiti, in suscipieda [sic] legatione ... pro spōsalibus ... inter ... principem Karolum ʒ ... dominam Mariam.] 4to.
[London, Richard Pynson, 1508] First and last leaves defective. STC 4659; Duff p.14. **945**

CARMONA (Bartolomé). Oracion panegyrica ... que consagro ... la ... Hermandad de la Caridad de Sevilla. 4to.
Sevilla, por Tomas Lopez de Haro, 1683
Gaselee 32. **1546(3)**

CARO (Rodrigo). Antiguedades y principado de la ilustrissima ciudad de Sevilla. fo.
Sevilla, por Andres Grande, 1634
Gaselee 33. **2098(1)**

CARO CEJUDO (Jerónimo Martín). Refranes, y modos de hablar castellanos con latinos. 4to.
En Madrid, por Iulian Izquierdo, 1675
Gaselee 34. **1550(2)**

CARR (Henry). *See* CARE (Henry).

[CARR (William)]. An accurate description of the United Netherlands, and of ... Germany, Sweden & Denmark ... Together with an exact relation of the entertainment of ... King William at the Hague. 8vo.
London, for Timothy Childe, 1691
5 folding plates. Wing A438. **849**

CARRASCO (Juan). Obra nueua ... donde se contienen tres romances. 4to.
(Seuilla, vendese en casa de Juan Cabeças,) [c.1680] Gaselee 35; Wilson p.253. **1545(34)**

CARRASCO DEL MÁRMOL (Benito). Cuento gracioso, que sucedio a vn harriero con su muger. 4to.
(Seuilla, por Iuan Cabeças, 1680)
Gaselee 36; Wilson p.246. **1545(31A)**

CARRINGTON (Samuel). The history of the life and death of ... Oliver, late Lord Protector. 8vo.
London, printed for Nath.Brook, 1659
Engr. fp. (port., Charrington p.45). Wing C643. **793(1)**

CARROL (James). A narrative of the Popish plot in Ireland. fo.
London, for Richard Janeway, 1681
[Narratives & Tryals III] Wing C644. **2251(5)**

CARTER (William). Israels peace with God, Benjamines overthrow. A sermon ... preached ... August 31. 4to.
London, for Giles Calvert, to be sold by Christopher Meredith, 1642 [Sermons Polemical II] Wing C679A. **1180(6)**

[CARTWRIGHT (Thomas)]. A second admonition to the Parliament. 8vo.
[*Wandsworth, J.S.*, 1572] STC 4713. **209(5)**

CARYL (Joseph). The nature ... and benefits, of a sacred covenant ... Delivered in a sermon ... Octob.6.1643. 4to.
London, by E.G. for John Rothwell, and Giles Calvert, 1643 [Sermons Polemical II]
Wing C782. **1180(7)**

[CARYLL (John)]. The English princess, or the death of Richard the III. A tragedy. 4to.
London, for Thomas Dring, 1667 [Loose Plays II] Wing C744; Diary 7 March 1666/7.
1604(8)

CASALIUS (Joannes Baptista). De veteribus sacris Christianorum ritibus. fo.
Romæ, apud Bernardinum Tanum, 1647
6 engrs. **2449**

[CASAUBON (Méric)]. The use of daily publick prayers. 4to.
London, for Iohn Maynard, 1641 [Liturgick Controversies II] Wing C816. **1188(1)**

CASE (The) of a murther [of J.Norkott] in Hertfordshire. s.sh.
London, 1699 Wing C872. **2671(2)**

CASE (A) of conscience concerning flying in times of trouble, 1643.
See TORSHELL (Samuel). **1428(3)**

CASE (The) of the Church of England, briefly and truly stated, 1681.
See PARKER (Samuel), Bp of Oxford. **1053**

CASE (The) of the Praemunientes considered. [c.1702].
See KENNETT (White), Bp of Peterborough.
1696(6)

CASE (The) of the Regale ... stated, 1702.
See LESLIE (Charles). **1030**

CASE (The) of the schedule stated, 1702.
See ATTERBURY (Francis), Bp of Rochester.
1697(13)

CASE (The) of Tho.Dangerfield, 1680.
See DANGERFIELD (Thomas). **2251(8)**

CASE (The) stated concerning the judicature of the House of Peers, 1675.
See HOLLES (Denzil Holles, Baron). **731**

CASE (Thomas). Deliverance — obstruction ... A sermon ... March 25. 4to.
London, by Ruth Raworth, for Luke Fawne, 1646
[Sermons Polemical II] Wing C827. **1180(15)**

——————————Gods rising, his enemies scattering ... A sermon ... 26.Octob.1642. 4to.
London, by J.R. for Luke Fawne, 1644
[Sermons Polemical II] Wing C830. **1180(10)**

——————————Gods vvaiting to be gracious unto his people ... Delivered in certaine sermons. 4to.
London, by Felix Kingston for Luke Fawne, 1642
[Sermons Polemical II] Wing C831. **1180(9)**

——————————Jehoshaphats caveat to his judges. Delivered in a sermon ... 17th of August 1644. 4to.
London, by Felix Kingston for Luke Fawn, 1644
[Sermons Polemical II] Wing C832. **1180(12)**

——————————A model of true spiritual thankfulnesse. Delivered in a sermon ... Feb.19.1645. 4to.
London, by Ruth Raworth, for Luke Fawne, 1646
[Sermons Polemical II] Wing C833. **1180(16)**

[——————————] The morning exercise methodized. 4to.
London, by R.W. for Ralph Smith, 1676
Wing C836. **1794**

——————————The quarrell of the covenant ... Three sermons. 4to.
London, for Luke Fawne, 1644 [Sermons Polemical Il] Wing C838. **1180(13)**

——————————The root of apostacy ... Delivered in a sermon. 4to.
London, by J.R. for Luke Fawne, 1644
[Sermons Polemical II] Wing C839. **1180(11)**

——————————A sermon preached ... August 22. 1645. 4to.
London, by Ruth Raworth, for Luke Fawne, 1645
[Sermons Polemical II] Wing C842. **1180(14)**

——————————Spirituall whordome discovered in a sermon ... May 26.1647. 4to.
London, by J.Macock, for Luke Fawne, 1647
[Sermons Polemical II] Wing C843. **1180(17)**

——————————Two sermons. 4to.
London, by I.Raworth for Luke Fawne, 1641
[Sermons Polemical II] Wing C845.
1180(8)

CASTALDO (Andrea Piscara).
See PISCARA CASTALDO (Andreas).

CASTLEHAVEN (James Touchet, 3rd Earl of).
The memoir's of James Lord Audley, Earl of
Castlehaven ... in the wars of Ireland, from the
year 1642 to the year 1651. (— An appendix.)
8vo.
London, for Henry Brome (for Joanna Brome),
1680-1   Wing C1234-5.   **522**

CASTLEMAINE (Roger Palmer, Earl of). An acc-
ount of the present war between the Venetians &
Turk; with the state of Candie.   8vo.
London, printed by J.M. for H.Herringman, 1666
Engr. fp. (port., Charrington p.28), 2 engr.maps.
Wing C1239.   **220**

───────────The English globe.   4to.
London, for Joseph Moxon, 1679   13 pls.
Wing C1242.   **1555**

───────────The tryal of Roger Earl of Castle-
maine for high treason ... 23 June 1680.   fo.
*London, for S.G. and N.E., to be sold by Randal
Taylor,* 1681   [Narratives & Tryals IV]
Wing T2214.   **2252(9)**

CASWELL (John). A brief — but full — account
of the doctrine of trigonometry.   fo.
*London, by John Playford, for Richard Davis,
Oxford,* 1685   Wing C1252.   **2396(2)**

CATALOGI librorum manuscriptorum Angliæ,
1697.   *See* BERNARD (Edward).   **2797**

CATALOGUE (A) of books continued. Numb.
1-58. [Ed. by R.Clavell.]   fo.
(For the booksellers of London (for B.Tooke)
1680[-1695])   **2104(2)-2105(1)**

CATALOGUE (A) of books printed in England,
1696.   *See* CLAVELL (Robert).   **2105(2)**

CATALOGUE (The) of honor, 1610.
See MILLES (Thomas).   **2381**

CATALOGUE (A) of the philosophical books and
tracts written by the Hon.Robert Boyle.   8vo.
London, for Sam.Smith, 1690
Wing B3928A.   **816(2)**

CATÉCHISME des courtisans.   12mo.
Cologne, 1680   **99(5)**

CATHARINUS (Ambrosius).
See POLITI (Lancelotto), Abp of Conza.

CATHOLIC (A) & Protestant almanack for ...
1688.   18mo.
London, printed by Henry Hills, 1688
[Almanacks for the year 1688]   Wing A1389.
                    425(2)

CATS (Jacob). Alle de wercken.   2 vols.   fo.
Amsterdam, by Jan Jacobsz Schipper, 1658
Engr. title-pages, pls, ports (Charrington pp.29,
153).   **2706-7**

CAUS (Salomon de). La pratique et demonstration
des horloges solaires.   fo.
Paris, chez Hierosme Droüart, 1624   8 engr. pls,
engr. diagrams.   Autograph 'Edmund Chilmead'
on title-page.   **2602**

CAUSES (The) of the decay of Christian piety,
1694.   *See* ALLESTREE (Richard).   **1086**

CAUSSIN (Nicolas). La cour sainte.   2 vols in 1.
fo.
Paris, chez Denis Bechet, 1664   Vol.1: Engr.
port.   **2655**

CAVACCIO (Giacomo). Illustrium anachoretarum
elogia.   4to.
Venetiis, in typographia Pinelliana, 1625
Engr. title-page, 32 engr. pls.   **1798**

CAVALCANTI (Andrea). Esequie del serenissimo
Principe Francesco [Medici] celebrate in Fiorenza
... 30.d'Agosto 1634.   4to.
Fiorenza, per Gio:Batista Landini, 1634
Engr. pls (port., Charrington p.116).   **1750**

CAVE (William). Antiquitates apostolicæ, 1678.
See TAYLOR (Jeremy), Bp of Down and Connor.
Antiquitates Christianæ.   **2599**

───────────Apostolici; or, the history of ...
those who were contemporary with or immedi-
ately succeeded the apostles. (Vol.2: Ecclesiastici;
or, the history of the ... Fathers of the church. —
An appendix.)   2nd ed.   2 vols in 1.   fo.
London, by J.R. for Richard Chiswell, 1682-3
Vol.1: Engr. title-page, 23 engr. pls.
Vol.2: Engr. fp., 14 engr. pls.   Wing C1591, 6.
                    2355

───────────A dissertation concerning the
government of the ancient church.   8vo.
London, for R.Chiswel, 1683   Wing C1595.   **964**

───────────Primitive Christianity.   2nd ed.
8vo.
London, printed by J.M. for Richard Chiswell,
1675   Engr. title-page.   Wing C1599.   **1203**

───────────Scriptorum ecclesiasticorum
historia literaria.   2 vols.   fo.
Londini, typis T.H. & impensis Richardi Chiswell,
1688-98   Wing C1602.   **2453-4**

[CAVENDISH (George)]. The life and death of
Thomas Woolsey, cardinal ... Written by one of his
own servants.   8vo.
London, for Dorman Newman, 1667   Engr. fp.
(port., Charrington p.180).   Wing C1618; Diary
3 June 1667.   **794**

CAWDREY (Daniel). The good man a public good
... A sermon preached ... January 31.1643.   4to.
*London, by Tho.Harper, for Charles Greene &
P.W.,* 1643   [Sermons Polemical III]
Wing C1628.   **1181(1)**

CAWLEY (William). The laws of Q.Elizabeth, K.James and K.Charles the First, concerning Jesuites ... and ... the oaths of Supremacy and Allegiance, explained by divers judgments.   fo.
London, for John Wright, and Richard Chiswell,
1680   Wing C1651.   **2354**

CELLIER (Elizabeth). The tryal and sentence of Elizabeth Cellier; for ... libel.   fo.
London, for Thomas Collins, 1680   [Narratives & Tryals IV]   Wing T2171.   **2252(13)**

——————— The tryal of Elizabeth Cellier the Popish midwife.   fo.
[London,] (by A.Godbid, for L.C., 1680)
[Narratives & Tryals IV]   Wing T2187A.
2252(14)

——————— Malice defeated: or a brief relation of the accusation and deliverance of Elizabeth Cellier.   fo.
London, for Elizabeth Cellier, 1680
[Narratives & Tryals III]   Wing C1661.
2251(6)

[———————] The matchless picaro.   fo.
[London, 1680]   Pp.42-6 only.   [Narratives & Tryals III]   Wing C1661A.   **2251(6a)**

[CERDAN (Jean Paul, comte de)]. L'empereur et l'empire trahis, et par qui & comment.   12mo.
'Cologne, chez Pierre Marteau', 1680   **206(2)**

CÉRÉMONIAL (Le) françois, contenant les cérémonies ... aux sacres et couronnemens de roys ... Recueilly par T.Godefroy.   2 vols.   fo.
Paris, chez Sebastien Cramoisy et Gabriel Cramoisy, 1649   **2597-8**

CERTAIN. Certaine briefe, and speciall instructions for gentlemen, merchants ... employed in seruices abrode, 1589.
See MEIER (Albrecht).   **1431(3)**

CERTAIN. Certaine worthye manuscript poems, 1597.   *See* S.(J.).   **29(4)**

CERVANTES SAAVEDRA (Miguel de). Nouelas exemplares.   8vo.
Seuilla, por Iuan Gomez de Blas, 1664
Gaselee 37.   **1552(1)**

——————— Vida y hechos del ingenioso cavallero Don Quixote de la Mancha.   Nueva ed.
2 vols.   8vo.
Bruselas, de la emprenta de Juan Mommarte, 1662   Vol.1: engr. title-page, 7 engr. pls.
Vol.2: 7 engr. pls.   Gaselee 38.   **912-3**

——————— The history of ... Don Quixote.
[Transl. by T.Shelton.]   2 pts.   fo.
London, for R.Scot, J.Basset [etc.], 1675 (pt.2: by Richard Hodgkinson, 1672)   Wing C1777.
2029

[———————] The famous history of Don Quixote de la Mancha. [*An anonymous abridgment.*]   12mo.
London, for G.Conyers, 1686   [Penny-Merriments II]   Wing C1772.   **363(29)**

CESSOLIS (Jacobus de). The game of chess.   fo.
[Westminster] W.Caxton [c.1478]
See Appendix.   **1945**

CEVENNOLS (Les) justifiez, par le politique du temps.   8vo.
Se vend à Londres, chez Jean Cailloüe, 1704
417

CHALES (Claude François Milliet de).
See MILLIET DE CHALES (Claude François).

CHAMBERLAYNE (Edward). Angliæ notitia: or the present state of England.   2 pts.   16th ed. (pt 2: 13th ed.).   12mo.
London, for R.Chiswel, T.Sawbridge, G.Wells [etc.] (pt 2: by Thomas Hodgkin), 1687
Engr. fp. (port., Charrington p.86).
Wing C1833, 1857.   **537**

——————— 17th ed.   2 pts.   12mo.
London, by T.Hodgkin, for R.Scot, T.Sawbridge [etc.], 1692 (1691)   Engr. fp. (port.).
Wing C1834.   **910**

——————— 18th ed.   3 pts.   8vo.
London, by T.Hodgkin, for R.Scot, R.Chiswell [etc.], 1694   Engr. fp. (port., Charrington p.178).   Wing C1835.   **788**

——————— 19th ed.   3 pts.   8vo.
London, by T.Hodgkin, for R.Chiswell, M.Gillyflower [etc.], 1700   Engr. fp. (port., Charrington p.177).   Wing C1836.   **965**

——————— 20th ed.   3 pts.   8vo.
London, by T.H. for S.Smith and B.Walford [etc.], 1702   Engr. fp. (port., Charrington p.4).
Diary 30 Jan.1668/9.   **997**

CHAMBERS (Humphrey). A divine ballance ... A sermon preached ... Sept.27.1643.   4to.
London, by M.F. for Samuel Man, 1643
[Sermons Polemical III]   Wing C1915.   **1181(2)**

CHAMBRAY (Roland Fréart, Sieur de). An idea of the perfection of painting demonstrated ... Rendered English by J.E[velyn].   8vo.
In the Savoy, for Henry Herringman, 1668
Wing C1922.   **809**

——————— A parallel of the antient architecture with the modern ... With L.B.Alberti's Treatise of statues.   fo.
London, by Tho.Roycroft, for John Place, 1664
Engr. title-page (port., Charrington p.46). 39 engr. pls.   Wing C1923.   **2470**

[CHAPMAN (George)]. Bussy D'Ambois: a
tragedie.   4to.
London, by A.N. for Robert Lunne, 1641
[Loose Plays I]   Wing C1941; Diary 30 Dec.
1661 & 15 Nov.1662.   1075(4)

CHARACTER (The) of a trimmer, 1689.
See HALIFAX (George Savile, 1st Marquis of).
                                       1427(10)

CHARACTERS of the royal family ...
See NOUVEAUX caractères de la famille roïale ...
de France.   588

CHARDIN (Sir John). The travels of Sir John
Chardin into Persia and the East-Indies. The first
volume.   2 pts.   fo.
London, for Moses Pitt, 1686   Engr. fp. (port.,
Charrington p.30), engr. title-page, 16 engr. pls.
Wing C2043.   2336

CHARITABLE (The) Christian, 1682.
See HART (John).   365(27)

CHARLES I, King of England. Βασιλικα. The
workes of King Charles the Martyr: with a
collection of declarations ... and other papers.
2 vols.   fo.
London, by James Flesher for R.Royston, 1662
Engr. fps, title-page, pls (port., Charrington p.31).
MS copies of attestation by Dr Zachary Cradock
(1 Nov.1678) inserted in each volume concerning
expurgations, made by order of the Inquisition in
Lisbon, of a copy of the work afterwards presented to the Lambeth Library by Barnaby Crafford,
English merchant at Lisbon. With a note that the
expurgations had been entered in Pepys's copy by
himself and his clerk Thomas Henderson, with
signatures of both, 7 Oct.1700.   Wing C2075;
Diary 10 June 1662, 13 May & 27 Aug.1665;
Tanner II, pp.77, 80-1.   2577-8

——————— A true copy of the journal of the
High Court of Justice, for the tryal of K.Charles I.
Taken by J.Nalson.   fo.
London, H.C. for Thomas Dring, 1684
Engr. pls (ports, Charrington p.31).   Wing N116.
                                       2319

CHARLES II, King of England. His Majesties declaration to all his loving subjects, touching the
causes & reasons that moved him to dissolve the
two last Parliaments.   fo.
*London, by the assigns of John Bill, Thomas New-
comb, and Henry Hills, 1681*   [Parliamentary
votes and papers, 1679, 1681]   Wing C3000.
                                       2137(33)

——————— His Majesties gracious speech to
both Houses of Parliament ... 21st of October,
1680.   fo.
*London, by the assigns of John Bill, Thomas
Newcomb, and Henry Hills, 1680*
[Parliamentary votes and papers 1679, 1681]
Wing C3066.   2137(2)

——————— His Majesties most gracious speech
to both Houses of Parliament ... 15th of December,
1680.   fo.
*London, by the assigns of John Bill, Thomas
Newcomb, and Henry Hills, 1680*
[Parliamentary votes and papers 1679, 1681]
Wing C3159.   2137(9)

——————— His Majesties most gracious
speech to both Houses of Parliament, ... 21st of
March, 1680/1.   fo.
*(London, by the assigns of John Bill, Thomas
Newcomb, and Henry Hills, 1680/1)*
[Parliamentary votes and papers 1679, 1681]
Wing C3162.   2137(28)

——————— A letter from K.Charls the
second ... to Mr Cawton, late Minister of the
English church in Roterdam.   4to.
*London, William Wilson for Richard Lownds,
1660*   [Consutilia V]   Wing C3097A.
                                       1431(26)

——————— By the King. A proclamation pro-
hibiting his Majesties subjects to ... serve at sea,
against any foreign prince ... in amity with his
Majesty. 26 May, 1676.   brs.
*London, by the assigns of John Bill and Christo-
pher Barker, 1676*   [Inserted between nos
1098 & 1099 of the London Gazette.]
Wing C3528.   2081

——————— By the King. A proclamation
commanding all masters and owners of ships to
stay for their convoy before they put to sea. 23
June, 1681.   brs.
*London, by the assigns of John Bill, Thomas
Newcomb, and Henry Hills, 1681*   [Inserted
between nos 1627 & 1628 of the London
Gazette.]   Wing C3238.   2083

——————— The royal charter [1680].
See LONDON.   953

CHARLES II, King of Spain. Copia de las cedulas
reales, que su Magestad ... el Rey Don Carlos
segundo ... mandó expedir para la fundacion del
Colegio, y Seminario ... en la ciudad de Seuilla ...
en la arte maritima, y reglas de marineria.   fo.
En Seuilla, por Juan Cabeças, 1681
Gaselee 39.   2140(2)

CHARLETON (Walter). Onomasticon zoicon ...
Cui accedunt Mantissa anatomica; et quaedam de
variis fossilium generibus.   4to.
Londini, apud Jacobum Allestry, 1668
12 engr. pls.   Wing C3688.   1510

CHARNOCK (Robert). The tryals and condemnation of R.Charnock, E.King and T.Keyes for the
... conspiracy to assasinate ... King William.   fo.
London, for Samuel Heyrick & Isaac Cleave, 1696
[Narratives & Tryals VI]   Wing T2255.
                                       2254(4)

CHARPENTIER (François). Relation de l'établissement de la Compagnie Françoise pour le commerce des Indes Orientales.   12mo.
Paris, chez Sébastien Cramoisy, & Sébastien Mabre-Cramoisy, 1666   **106**

CHASSEPOL (François de). The history of the Grand Visiers, Mahomet, and Achmet Coprogli ... Englished by John Evelyn, junior.   8vo.
London, printed for H.Brome, 1677
Wing C3728.   **1039**

CHASTEIGNER DE LA ROCHEPOSAY (Henri Louis), Bp of Poitiers. Celebriorum distinctionum philosophicarum synopsis. Editio nova.   8vo.
Lugduni Batavorum, apud Adrianum Wyngaerden & Franciscum Moiardum, 1645   **758**

[CHASTELET (Paul Hay, Marquis du)]. The politicks of France. By Monsieur P.H., Marquis of C.   2 pts.   12mo.
London, printed and sold by Thomas Sharpe, 1680   Wing H1202.   **578**

[————————] Testament politique ... [of] Cardinal duc de Richelieu.   12mo.
Amsterdam, chez Henry Desbordes, 1688   **80**

CHASTISING (The) of God's children.   fo.
[*W.de Worde, Westminster, c.1494.*]
See Appendix.   **2051(1)**

CHAUCER (Geoffrey). The Canterbury tales.   fo.
W.Caxton [Westminster, c.1484].
See Appendix.   **2053**

————————————— The workes ... newly printed.   fo.
London, by Adam Islip, 1602
Woodcut title-page; woodcut inserted (port., Charrington p.36).   At end, MS notes (3 leaves) in hand of one of Pepys's clerks: (1) publisher's advertisement from 1687 edition giving additions to the conclusions of the Cook's Tale and the Squire's Tale, and (2) a collation of 2006 ('MSS Fragments of Chaucer') with this volume. Cf. below, vol.IV. STC 5080; Diary 8, 9 July 1664.
2365

CHAUCER JUNIOR, *pseud.* Canterbury tales ... by Chaucer junior.   12mo.
[*London*] *for J.Back*, 1687   [Penny-Merriments II]   Wing C3737.   **363(12)**

CHAUMONT (Alexandre de). Relation de l'ambassade de Mr. le chevalier de Chaumont à la cour du roy de Siam.   2 pts.   12mo.
Paris, chez Arnoult Seneuse et Daniel Horthemels, 1686   9 engr. pls.   **587**

CHAUNCY (Sir Henry). The historical antiquities of Hertfordshire.   fo.
London, for Ben.Griffin, Sam.Keble, Dan.Browne [*etc.*] 1700   Engr. fp. (port., Charrington p.36), map, 44 engr. pls.   Wing C3741.   **2738**

CHEATS (The). A comedy, 1664.
See WILSON (John).   **1604(4)**

CHETWIND (Charles). A narrative of the depositions of Robert Jenison Esq; ... that Mr.William Ireland ... was in London the nineteenth of August, 1678.   fo.
London, for Henry Hills, Thomas Parkhurst, John Starkey [*etc.*], 1679   [Narratives & Tryals I]
Wing C3792.   **2249(11)**

————————————— [Another copy.]   [Narratives & Tryals III]   **2251(22)**

CHEVALIER (Nicolas). Remarques sur la pièce antique de bronze, trouvée depuis quelques années aux environs de Rome.   12mo.
Amsterdam, chez Abraham Wolfgang, 1694
Engr. fp., pls.   **508**

[CHEVALIER (Pierre)]. A discourse of the ... Cossacks.   8vo.
London, printed by T.N. for Hobart Kemp, 1672
Wing C3800.   **808**

CHEVREAU (Urbain). Chevræana.   12mo.
Suivant la copie de Paris. A Amsterdam, chez Thomas Lombrail, 1700   Engr. fp. (port., Charrington p.36).   **771**

CHEYNELL (Francis). The man of honour, described in a sermon, preached ... March 26.1645.   4to.
London, by J.R. for Samuel Gellibrand, 1645
[Sermons Polemical III]   MS quotation from Aristotle on last leaf.   Wing C3812.   **1181(4)**

————————————— Sions memento, and Gods alarum.
In a sermon ... on the 31 of May, 1643.   4to.
London, for Samuel Gellibrand, 1643
[Sermons Polemical III]   Wing C3816.   **1181(3)**

CHILD (Sir Josiah). A new discourse of trade.   8vo.
London, printed, and sold by Sam.Crouch, Tho. Horne, and Jos.Hindmarsh, 1694
Wing C3861; Naval Minutes p.319.   **820**

CHILDREY (Joshua). Britannia Baconica: or, the natural rarities of England, Scotland, & Wales.   8vo.
London, for the author, sold by H.E., 1662
Wing C3872.   **615**

CHILLINGWORTH (William). The religion of Protestants a safe way to salvation.   4th ed.   fo.
London, by Andrew Clark, for Richard Chiswell, 1674   Wing C3891.   **2326**

CHINESE calendars.
See HUNG (Chih-ang), [1685?], *and* TA-MING (1670?).

[CHOISY (François Timoléon de)] . Journal ou suite du voyage de Siam.   12mo.
Suivant la copie de Paris imprimée, A Amsterdam, chez Pierre Mortier, 1687   **685**

CHRIST in the clouds: or, God's coming to judgment. A short treatise.   12mo.
London, by T.H. for J.Wright, J.Clarke, W.Thackeray, and T.Passenger, 1682
[Penny-Godlinesses]   Wing C3931A.   **365(18)**

CHRISTIAN (A) indeed; or, Heaven's assurance. 12mo.
London, by A.P. and T.H. for J.Wright, 1677
[Penny-Godlinesses]   Wing C3945A.   **365(22)**

CHRISTIAN religious meetings ... no seditious conventicles [1664].
See FARNWORTH (Richard).   **1189(12)**

CHRISTIAN (The) virtuoso, 1690-1.
See BOYLE (Hon. Robert).   **759(1-3)**

CHRISTIANITY not mysterious, 1696.
See TOLAND (John).   **1082(5)**

CHRISTIANS (The) triumph over temptation. 12mo.
[London] for J.Deacon [c.1680]
[Penny-Godlinesses]   Wing C3961.   **365(13)**

CHRISTINE, de Pisan. The book of the feat of arms and chivalry.   fo.
W.Caxton [Westminster] , 14 July 1489.
See Appendix   **1938(1)**

CHRIST'S kirk on the green [c.1700].
See JAMES V, King of Scotland.   **358(11)**

CHRIST'S voice to England, 1683.
See C.(J.).   **365(32)**

CHRONICA. Cronica cronicarum abbrege.   fo.
(Paris, pour Iehan Petit ʒ Francoys Regnault. Et par Jaques Ferrebouc, 1521)   Adams C1494;
Duff p.18.   **2992**

CHRONICLES of England.   fo.
[W. de Machlinia, London, 1486.]
See Appendix.   **1997**

CHRONICLES of England.   fo.
W.Caxton, Westminster, 8 October 1482
See Appendix   **1997**

CHRONICON Saxonicum, 1692.
See ANGLO-SAXON CHRONICLE.   **1856**

CHRONOLOGICAL tables, [1689] .
See MARCEL (Guillaume).   **9**

CHURCH OF ENGLAND.
See ENGLAND. *Church of England.*

CHURCHILL (Sir Winston). Divi Britannici: being a remark upon the lives of all the kings of this isle. fo.
London, by Tho.Roycroft, to be sold by Francis Eglesfield, 1675   Wing C4275.   **2239**

CHURCHYARD (Thomas). The [mi] rror and manners of men.   4to.
London, by Arnold Hatfield for W.Holme, 1594
[Consutilia VIII]   Two MS verses, in 16th-cent. hand, signed Paull(?) Balliden on verso of title-page.   STC 5242.   **1434(2)**

CICERO (Marcus Tullius). M.Tullius Cicero Mannucciorum commentariis illustratus.   10 vols in 4.   fo.
Venetiis, apud Aldum, (1581-)1583   Engr. title-page.   Adams C1660.   **2290-3**

——————— Les Œuvres de Ciceron de la traduction de M. du Ryer.   12 vols.   12mo.
Paris, par la compagnie des libraires (Guillaume de Luyne, Jean Cochart, Estienne Loyson [etc.]), 1670   **639-50**

——————— De officiis.   8vo.
Oxoniæ, e theatro Sheldoniano, 1695
Engr. fp.   Wing C4297.   Presentation copy from Dr A.Charlett, with MS inscription dated 1 Jan.1695/6 on front flyleaf.   **856**

——————— Tully's three books of offices in English.   12mo.
London, (by W.Onley) for Sam.Buckley, 1699
Wing C4322; Diary 5 Jan.1660/1.   **795**

——————— Epistolarum selectarum libri tres. 8vo.
Londini, pro Societate Stationariorum venales prostant apud Obadiam Blagrave, 1689
Wing C4305.   **603**

CINQUE PORTS. The great and ancient charter of the Cinque-ports.   12mo.
London, by T.N. for the Mayor and Jurats of Hasting, 1682   Wing G1632.   **468**

CIRUELO (Pedro). Reprouacion de las supersticiones y hechizerias.   4to.
(Salamanca, por Pedro de Castro, a costa de Guillermo de Milis, 1539)   Woodcut.
Adams C2042; Gaselee 41.   **1395(2)**

[CITRI DE LA GUETTE (Samuel de Broé, Seigneur de)] . The history of the triumvirates ... made English by T.Otway.   8vo.
London, for Charles Brome, 1686
Wing C4345.   **1027**

CITY (The) and countrey chapmans almanack for ... 1688.   8vo.
London, printed by Tho.James for the Company of Stationers, 1687   [Almanacks for the year 1688]   Wing A1405A.   **425(3)**

CITY (The) and countrey chapmans almanack for ... 1689. 8vo.
London, printed by Tho.James for the Company of Stationers, 1689 [Almanacks for the year 1689] Wing A1406. **426(12)**

CIVILE (La) honestete pour les enfans. Auec la maniere d'aprendre à bien lire. 8vo.
Paris, de l'imprimerie de Philippe Danfrie, et Richard Breton, 1559 **941(2)**

CIVILITY. The ciuilitie of childehode, 1560.
See ERASMUS (Desiderius). **46(3)**

[CLAIN (Johann Theodor)]. Historia Britannica, 1640. *See* HISTORIA Britannica. **28**

CLARENDON (Edward Hyde, 1st Earl of). A brief view and survey of the ... errors to Church and State, in Mr.Hobbes's book, entitled Leviathan. 4to.
[Oxford,] printed at the Theater, 1676 Engr. fp. Wing C4420. **1596**

———————The history of the rebellion and civil wars in England. 3 vols. fo.
Oxford, at the Theater, 1702-4 Engr. fp. in each vol. (ports, Charrington p.38).
Tanner II, pp.266, 319. **2944-6**

CLARKE (Sir Edward). By the Mayor. [Instructions to aldermen about preparations for the King's passage.] brs.
[London] Samuel Roycroft, 1697
Bound in after p.78. **2476**

CLARKE (Samuel), of Grendon-Underwood. Christian good-fellowship ... a sermon. 4to.
London, for Thomas Underhill, 1655 [Sermons Polemical III] Wing C4505. **1181(5)**

[CLARKE (Samuel), Minister of Bennet Fink]. The historian's guide: or, Britains remembrancer ... from the year 1600, to 1688 ... 3rd impr. 12mo.
London, printed by W.Horton, for W.Crooke, 1688 Wing C4521. **487(1)**

[———————] Some modern passages towards a continuation of a book, called the Historian's guide [1689].
See SMITHURST (Benjamin). Britain's glory. **487(2)**

[CLARKE (Samuel), of St James's, Westminster]. Some reflections on that part of a book called Amyntor [by J.Toland] ... which relates to the writings of the Primitive Fathers and the canon of the New Testament. 8vo.
London, printed for James Knapton, 1699 Wing C4498. **1082(4)**

CLAVELL (Robert). A catalogue of books continued. [Ed. by R.Clavell.] 1680-95.
See CATALOGUE (A) of books continued. **2104(2)-2105(1)**

[———————] A catalogue of books printed in England since the ... Fire of London in 1666. To the end of Michalmas Term, 1695. 4th ed. fo.
London, for R.Clavel, and Benj.Tooke, 1696 Wing C4599. **2105(2)**

———————The general catalogue of books, printed in England ... 1666-1680. (3rd ed.) fo.
London, by S.Roycroft for Robert Clavell, 1680 Wing C4601. **2104(1)**

[CLEIRAC (Estienne)]. Les us, et coûtumes de la mer. 4to.
Rouen, chez Jean Berthelin, 1671 **1849**

CLEMENT IX, Pope. Conclave de Clement IX, 1669.
See CONCLAVE de Clement IX. **92**

CLEMENT X, Pope. Bulla de Indulgencia plenaria, concedida por la Santidad de Clemente Dezimo ... y mandada publicar por ... Inocencio Undezimo. brs.
Madrid, (1684) Gaselee 42. **1363(4)**

———————Bulla de la Sata Cruzada, cocedida por la Santidad de Clemente Dezimo, de seltze recordacion, y mandada publicar por ... Santo Padre Inocencio Undezimo. brs.
Madrid, (1684) Gaselee 43. **1363(3)**

CLEMENT XI, Pope. Discorso ... della maestà di Cristina Regina di Svezia in lode di Giacomo II. Re della Gran Bretagna. fo.
Roma, per il Tinassi stampatore Cam., 1687 **2721(2)**

CLENDON (Thomas). Justification justified ... A sermon preached ... the eleventh of December. 1652. 4to.
London, by Robert Ibbitson, 1653 [Sermons Polemical III] Wing C4641. **1181(6)**

CLERICUS (Joannes). *See* LE CLERC (Jean).

CLEVELAND (John). Poems. 8vo.
London, for W.Shears, 1662 Engr. fp. (port., Charrington p.38) Wing C4696. **388**

[CLIFFORD (Martin)]. A treatise of humane reason. 12mo.
London, for Hen.Brome, 1674 Wing C4707. **51**

CLIMSELL (Richard). *See* CRIMSAL (Richard).

CLOCKMAKERS' COMPANY. The Clock-makers bill, as it lyes before the Common Council ... November, 1697. (With notes thereon.) brs.
[London, 1697]
Bound in after p.646. **2476**

CLÜVER (Philipp). Introductio in universam geographiam. 4to.
Guelferbyti, impensis viduæ Conradi Bunonis,

typis Caspari Johannis Bismarci, 1686
Engr. fp. (port., Charrington p.39), title-page,
maps, diagrams.   1737

COCQUIUS (Adrianus). Observationes critico-
sacrae in sacrum N.Testamenti codicem. Qui agit
de philosophia & doctrina morum.   4to.
Lugduni Batavorum, apud Arnoldum Doude, 1678
                                                  1120

CODEX juris gentium diplomaticus ... ed. G.G.
Leibnitius. (— Mantissa codicis ...)   2 vols.   fo.
*Hannoveræ, literis & impensis Samuelis Amonii
(— sumptibus Gotfridi Freytagii)*, 1693-1700
                                                  2404-5

COKE (Sir Edward). Certain select cases in law.
2nd ed.   fo.
*London, by the Assigns of R. and E.Atkins, for
H.Twyford [etc.]*, 1677
Wing C4910.   2526(3)

——————————— The first part of the institutes
[i.e. Sir T.Littleton's Tenores novelli].   6th ed.
fo.
London, for the Company of Stationers, 1664
Engr. fp. (port., Charrington p.39), title-page.
Table.   Wing C4925.   2150

——————————— The second part of the institutes.
fo.
London, by J.Flesher, for W.L., D.P., and G.B.,
1662   Engr. fp. (port., Charrington p.39),
title-page.   Wing C4949.   2151

——————————— The third part of the institutes.
fo.
London, by J.Flesher, for W.Lee, and D.Pakeman,
1660   Engr. fp. (port., Charrington p.39), title-
page.   Wing C4962.   2152(1)

——————————— The fourth part of the institutes.
fo.
London, by M.Flesher, for W.Lee, and D.Pakeman,
1648   Engr. fp. (port., Charrington p.39), title-
page.   Wing C4930.   2152(2)

——————————— The reports ... 2nd ed.   fo.
London, for H.Twyford, T.Collins, T.Basset [etc.],
1680   Wing C4946.   2526(1)

——————————— The twelfth part of the reports.
2nd ed.   fo.
*London, by the assigns of Richard and Edward
Atkins, for Hen.Twyford and Tho.Basset*, 1677
Wing C4971.   2526(2)

COKE (Roger). A detection of the court and state
of England during the four last reigns, and the
interregnum.   2 vols.   8vo.
London, 1694   Wing C4973.   947-8

COLEMAN (Edward). The tryal of Edward Coleman, Gent. for conspiring the death of the King.
fo.

London, for Robert Pawlet, 1678   [Narratives
& Tryals I]   Wing T2185.   2249(9)

COLEMAN (Thomas). The hearts ingagement: a
sermon preached ... Septem.29 ... 1643.   4to.
London, for Christopher Meredith, 1643
[Consutilia II]   Wing C5052.   1428(4)

COLES (Elisha). The newest, plainest, and the
shortest short-hand.   8vo.
London, printed for Peter Parker, 1674
[Short-hand collection IV]   14 engr. leaves
Wing C5078; Carlton p.87.   860(5)

COLET (John). Æditio, vna cum quibusdam
G.Lilii grammatices rudimentis. (— Thomas Cardi-
nalis Eboracen. &c. Gypsuychianæ scholæ præ-
ceptoribus S.D.)   8vo.
[*Antwerp, J.Grapheus?*]   (1534)   Leaf E6 defective.   [Cardinal Wolsey's Rules, which should
precede Colet's Æditio, have been bound out of
order.]   Duff pp.16 & 73.   424(1), (4)

——————————— Paules accidence. I. Coleti ...
Æditio. Vna cum quibusdam G.Lilii grammatices
rudimentis.   8vo.
[*London, W.Rastell*, 1534?]   STC 5546; Duff
p.17; Diary 4 Feb.1662/3, 9 Mar.1664/5.
                                                  424(5)

——————————— A sermon of conforming and re-
forming ... To which is now added an Appendix of
Bp.Andrews, and Dr.Hammonds ... advice to the
Convocation. (The life of Dr Colet by Erasmus.)
8vo.
[*Cambridge*] *by J.Field, for William Morden*, 1661
Cropped.   Wing C5096.   75(4)

COLEY (Henry). Merlinus Anglicus junior: or, an
ephemeris for the year 1688.   8vo.
*London, printed by J.Macock for the Company of
Stationers*, 1688   [Almanacks for the year
1688]   Wing A1439.   425(16)

——————————— Merlinus Anglicus junior: or, an
ephemeris for the year 1689. According to the
method of Mr.W.Lilly.   8vo.
*London, printed by J.Macock for the Company of
Stationers*, 1689   [Almanacks for the year
1689]   Engr. port., Charrington p.101.
Wing A1440.   426(1)

——————————— Nuncius sydereus: or, the starry
messenger for ... 1688.   17th impr.   8vo.
*London, printed by A.G. for the Company of
Stationers*, 1688   [Almanacks for the year
1688]   Wing A1465.   425(4)

——————————— Nuncius sydereus ... for ... 1689.
18th impr.   8vo.
*London, printed by E.W. for the Company of
Stationers*, [1689]   [Almanacks for the year
1689]   Wing A1466.   426(4)

COLLECTION (A) of English proverbs. By J. Ray. 2nd ed. 8vo.
Cambridge, by John Hayes, for W.Morden, 1678
Wing R387. **619**

COLLECTION (A) of letters and other writings relating to the horrid Popish plot. [Ed. by Sir George Treby.] fo.
London, for Samuel Heyrick, Thomas Dring, and John Wickins, 1681 [Narratives & Tryals III] Wing T2102. **2251(43)**

COLLECTION (A) of original voyages ... publ. by W.Hacke. 8vo.
London, for James Knapton, 1699 Engr. fp. (map), maps. Wing H168. **1426**

COLLECTION (A) of several treaties, &c., since the late Revolution. Viz. I. The Grand Alliance between the Emperor, the King of England, and States General. [Etc.] 4to.
London, 1701 [Consutilia X] **1436(14)**

COLLECTION (A) of the brave exploits ... of several famous generals, 1686.
See D'ASSIGNY (Samuel). **376(2)**

COLLECTION (A) of the substance of several speeches ... made in the ... Commons, 1681.
See ENGLAND. *Parliament. Commons.* **2251(37)**

COLLEGE (Stephen). The arraignment, tryal and condemnation of Stephen College ... 17th and 18th 18th of August 1681. fo.
London, for Thomas Basset, and John Fish, 1681 [Narratives & Tryals IV] Wing A3761. **2252(23)**

——————————— The speech and carriage of Stephen College at Oxford, 31 Aug.1681. fo.
London, for Thomas Basset, and John Fish, 1681 [Narratives & Tryals IV] Wing C5229. **2252(24)**

——————————— A true copy of the dying words of Mr Stephen Colledge. fo.
(*London, for Edith Colledge*, 1681) [Narratives & Tryals IV] Wing C5231. **2252(25)**

COLLEGE OF PHYSICIANS.
See ROYAL COLLEGE OF PHYSICIANS.

COLLIER (Jeremy). A defence of the absolution given to Sr.William Perkins. 4to.
[*London*] (1696) [Consutilia IX] Wing C5247. **1435(7)**

——————————— Essays upon several moral subjects. 3rd ed. 2 pts. 8vo.
London, for R.Sare, and H.Hindmarsh, 1698 Wing C5254. **1401**

——————————— The great historical ... dictionary (— Supplement.), 1701-5.
See GREAT (The) historical ... dictionary. **2750-2**

——————————— A short view of the immorality, and profaneness of the English stage. 8vo.
London, for S.Keble, R.Sare, and H.Hindmarsh, 1698 Wing C5263. **1325**

COLLINS (John). Salt and fishery, a discourse. 4to.
London, by A.Godbid, and J.Playford, to be sold by Robert Horne [etc.], 1682 Wing C5380. **1287**

[COLONNE (Guido delle)]. The hystorye, sege and dystruccyon of Troye (translated by Johñ Lydgate). fo.
[*London,*] (*Richard Pynson*, 1513) Woodcuts. On vellum. STC 5579; Duff p.37. **2257**

COLUMNA (Petrus), Galatinus. De arcanis catholicæ veritatis ... Item, I. Reuchlini De cabala. fo.
Francofurti, apud Claudium Marnium, et hæredes Joannis Aubrii, 1602 **2348**

[COLVIL (Samuel)]. Mock poem, or, Whiggs supplication. 2 pts. 8vo.
London, 1681 Wing C5426. **614**

COMIERS (Claude de). L'art d'écrire et de parler occultement. 12mo.
Paris, chez Michel Guerout, se vend à Bruxelles, chez J.Leonard, 1690 Engr. pl. **86**

COMINES (Philippe de). The history of Philip de Commines. 3rd ed. fo.
London, by S.G. for Joshua Kirton, 1665 Engr. fp. **2110**

COMMERCE (Le) honorable, 1646.
See EON (Jean). **1674**

COMMON prayer-book no divine service, 1660.
See POWELL (Vavasor). **1188(18)**

COMMON (The) prayer-book the best companion, 1689. *See* HOWELL (William). **823(2)**

COMPENDIOUS (A) history of the taxes of France, and of the oppressive methods of raising them.
London, J.M. and B.B. for Richard Baldwin, 1694 [Consutilia VII] Wing C5608. **1433(10)**

[COMPENDIOUS (A) or briefe account.] (1581).
See STAFFORD (William). **1431**

COMPLETE. A compleat and true narrative ... of the Popish plot, 1679. *See* B.(J.). **2251(25)**

COMPLETE. A compleat collection of farewel sermons, preached by Mr.Calamy [and 27 others]. 4to.
London, 1663 Wants sigs 4C, 4D.
Wing C5638. **1168**

COMPLETE. The compleat cook: or, the accomplished servant-maids necessary companion.
12mo.
London, for J.Deacon [c.1685] [Penny-Merriments I] **362(39)**

COMPLETE. The compleat cookmaid. 12mo.
London, for P.Brooksby, 1684 [Penny-Merriments II] **363(11)**

COMPLETE. The compleat gamester, 1674.
See COTTON (Charles). **714**

COMPLETE. A compleat history of Europe,
1702-5. *See* JONES (David). **1385-91**

COMPLETE. A compleat history of the pretended Prince of Wales. 8vo.
London, 1696 Wing C5640. **980(2)**

COMPOST et kalendrier des bergiers.
See SHEPHERDS. The shepheards kalender. **2127**

COMPTON (Henry), Bp of London. A true narrative of all the proceedings against the Lord Bishop of London. fo.
London, printed and to be sold by Randal Taylor, 1689 [Narratives & Tryals V]
Wing T2774. **2253(21)**

CONANT (John). The woe and weale of Gods people. Displayed in a sermon preached ... Iuly 26. 1643. 4to.
London, by G.M. for Christopher Meredith, 1643 [Sermons Polemical III] Wing C5689. **1181(7)**

CONCILIA ... in re ecclesiarum orbis Britannici, 1639-64.
See ENGLAND. *Church of England.* **2818-9**

CONCIONES et orationes ex Latinis historicis excerptæ. Opus recognitum recensitumque in vsum scholarum Hollandiæ & Westfrisiæ. 8vo.
Amstelodami, sumptibus Henrici Laurentii, 1636 **102**

CONCLAVE de Clement IX. ou iournal de ce qui s'est passé pendant le siege vaccant. 12mo.
Paris, chez Charles de Sercy, 1669 **92**

CONDENADO (El) por desconfiado [c.1680].
See TÉLLEZ (Gabriel). **1553(15)**

CONFERENCE (A) about the next succession to the crowne of Ingland ... Published by R.Doleman [i.e. R.Parsons], 1594.
See PARSONS (Robert). **518**

CONFESSION (The) of faith: together with the larger and lesser catechisms, 1688.
See WESTMINSTER ASSEMBLY. **636**

CONFUCIUS. Confucius Sinarum philosophus, sive scientia Sinensis Latinè exposita. 4 pts. fo.
Parisiis, apud Danielem Horthemels, 1687
Engr. port., map. **2452**

CONFUTATION (A) of M.Lewis Hewes his dialogue. 4to.
London, for I.M., 1641 [Liturgick Controversies II] Wing C5811. **1188(9)**

CONSET (Henry). The practice of the spiritual or ecclesiastical courts. 8vo.
London, for T.Basset, to be sold by Will.Hensman, 1685 Wing C5901. **1590**

CONSIDERATIONS upon corrupt elections, 1701.
See DEFOE (Daniel). **1437(6)**

CONSILIA et methodi aureæ studiorum optime instituendorum. 4to.
Rotterodami, apud Petrum vander Slaart, 1692 **1522**

CONSTANTINI (Angelo). La vie de Scaramouche.
12mo.
Paris, chez Claude Barbin, 1695 Engr. fp. (port., Charrington p.152). **82**

[CONSULADO de mar.] Libro llamado Cõsulado de mar. 4to.
(*Valencia, por Francisco Diaz,*) 1539
Adams C2539; Gaselee 45. **1577**

CONTEMPLACION de la estacion de la Via-Sacra. 4to.
(*En Seuilla, por Juan Vejarano, à costa de Lucas Martin de Hermosa,* 1682) Gaselee 46;
Wilson p.146. **1545(5)**

CONTINUATION (A) of the faithful account of what past in Convocation, 1702.
See ATTERBURY (Francis), Bp of Rochester. **1697(12)**

CONTINUATION (A) of the history of passive obedience since the Reformation, 1690.
See SELLER (Abednego). **1516(2)**

CONVOCATION. *See* ENGLAND. *Church of England. Convocation.*

CONYERS (J.). A hundred notabe [sic] things, 1680. *See* CROYNES (Joshua). **362(52)**

COOK (John). The vindication of the professors & profession of the law. 4to.
London, for Matthew Walbancke, 1646 [Consutilia III] Wing C6029. **1429(15)**

[COOKE (Edward)]. Argumentum anti-Normannicum. 8vo.
London, printed by John Darby, 1682
Engr. fp. Wing C4907A. **970**

——————————The history of the successions of the kings of England. fo.
London, for Thomas Simmons, and John Kidgel, 1682 Engr. pls. Wing C6000. **2310**

COOKE (John). [Greenes tu quoque: or, the cittie gallant.] 4to.

[*London, M.Flesher*] [1628?] [Old Plays II]
Wants title-page. STC 5675. **1102(9)**

[COOKE (Sir John)]. A summary view of the articles exhibited against the late Bishop of St. David's. 8vo.
London, printed and are to be sold by A.Baldwin,
1701 **1231**

COOKE (Peter). The arraignment, tryal, and condemnation of P.Cooke, 13 May 1696. fo.
London, for Benjamin Tooke, 1696
[Narratives & Tryals VII] Wing A3757.
2255(1)

COPIES of the informations and original papers relating to the ... conspiracy against the late King, 1685.
See SPRAT (Thomas), Bp of Rochester. A true account ... of the horrid conspiracy. **1137(2)**

COPY. The copie of a letter sent ... to Don B.Mendoza, 1588. *See* LEIGH (Richard). **1080(1)**

COPY. A copie of the proceedings of some divines, appointed by the Lords ... touching innovations in the doctrine and discipline of the Church of England. 4to.
London, 1641 [Liturgick Controversies II]
Wing C4103D. **1188(4)**

CORBETT (Edward). Gods providence, a sermon preached ... Decemb.28.1642. 4to.
London, by F:Neile, for Robert Bostock, 1647
[Sermons Polemical III] Wing C6242.
1181(8)

CORDEIRO (Jacinto). El juramento ante Dios, y lealtad contra el amor. Comedia famosa. 4to.
[*Seville, widow of Nicolás Rodríguez,* 1671-4]
Gaselee 47. **1553(11)**

CORDEMOY (Géraud de). A philosophicall discourse concerning speech. 12mo.
In the Savoy, printed for John Martin, 1668
Wing C6282. **385**

[CORNEILLE (Pierre)]. Polyeuctes, or the martyr. A tragedy. By Sr.W.Lower. [*Transl. from Corneille's Polyeucte.*] 4to.
London, by Tho.Roycroft for G.Bedell and T. Collins, 1655 [Loose Plays I] Wing C6316.
1075(5)

[————————] Pompey the great. A tragedy.
4to.
London, for Henry Herringman, 1664
[Loose Plays II] Wing C6319. **1604(2)**

[CORNEILLE (Thomas)]. Le dictionnaire des arts et des sciences. 2 vols in 1. [*Vols 3-4 of the* Dictionnaire de l'Académie Françoise.] fo.
Paris, chez la veuve de Jean Baptiste Coignard, et chez Jean Baptiste Coignard, 1694
Vol.1: engr. fp. Vol.2: engr. fp. (port., Charrington p.103). **2812**

CORNELIANUM dolium, 1638.
See RANDOLPH (Thomas). **218(1)**

CORNISH (Henry). The tryals of Henry Cornish ... J.Fernley, W.Ring and E.Gaunt ... Octob.19. 1685. fo.
London, George Croom, to be sold by William Miller, 1685 [Narratives & Tryals V]
Wing T2250. **2253(17)**

CORONELLI (Vincenzo Maria). Guida de' forestieri sacro-profana ... nella città di Venezia ... estratta dal tomo I. de' Viaggi d'Inghilterra ... Aggiuntovi in questa quarta edizione il protogiornale perpetuo. 16mo.
[*Venice,*] *pubblicata da N.N.,* 1700 Plan. **3**

CORRARO (Angelo). A relation of the state of the court of Rome, 1664.
See ROME exactly describ'd ... **383(1)**

CORTÉS (Martin). The arte of nauigation ... transl. out of Spanyshe ... newly corrected and amended. 4to.
(*London, by Richarde Iugge*) 1572
Map, diagrams, volvelles. STC 5799. **1478(1)**

————————— The arte of nauigation. 4to.
(*London, by the widowe of Richarde Iugge*)
1584 [Sea Tracts I] Map, diagrams, volvelles.
MS notes and, on title-page, MS motto 'Magnus ope minorum', in unidentified hands. Autograph 'Wm Andrew 1664' at H2. STC 5801. **1077(2)**

————————— The arte of nauigation. Corrected and augmented, with a regiment or table of declination. 4to.
London, by Edw.Allde for Hugh Astley, by the assignes of Richard Watkins, 1596 [Sea Tracts II]
Diagrams, volvelles. STC 5803. **1078(1)**

CORYATE (Thomas). Three crude veines are presented in this booke following — besides the foresaid Crudities —. 4to.
London, by W.S[*tansby*], 1611 Wants engr. title-page. STC 5808. **1728**

COSAS (Las) maravillosas ... de Roma, 1651.
See FRANZINI (Girolamo). **592**

COSIN (John), Bp of Durham. A collection of private devotions. 7th ed. 12mo.
London, J.Grover for R.Royston, 1676
Engr. fp., title-page. Wing C6355. **517**

————————— A scholastical history of the canon of the Holy Scripture. 4to.
London, by E.Tyler and R.Holt for Robert Pawlett, 1672 Engr. title-page. Wing C6362.
1850

COSTER (François). Augmentum Enchiridij controuersiarum præcipuarum nostri temporis de religione. 8vo.
Coloniæ Agrippinæ in officina Birckmannica, sumptibus Arnoldi Mylij Birckmanni, 1605 **400(2)**

———————— Enchiridion controuersiarum præcipuarum nostri temporis de religione.   8vo.
Coloniæ Agrippinæ in officina Birckmannica, sumptibus Arnoldi Mylij, 1599
Adams C2745.   **400(1)**

COTTA (John). A short discouerie of severall sorts of ignorant and unconsiderate practisers of physicke in England.   4to.
London, by W.I[ones], to be sold by Iohn Barnes, 1619   STC 5835.   **985(4)**

[COTTON (Charles)]. The compleat gamester. 8vo.
London, by A.M. for R.Cutler, sold by Henry Brome, 1674   Engr. fp.   Wing C6382.   **714**

———————— The wonders of the Peake.   8vo.
London, for Joanna Brome, 1681
Wing C6400.   **1200**

COTTON (Clement). A large and complete concordance to the Bible in English, according to the last translation ... Now much enlarged ... by S. Newman.   fo.
London, for Thomas Downes and James Young, 1643   On title-page, Pepys's note of price (£1.7s.0d).   Wing C6404; Diary 5 & 8 June 1663.   **2535**

COTTON (John). The covenant of Gods free grace. 4to.
London, by M.S. for Iohn Hancock, 1645   [Sermons Polemical III]   Wing C6424.   **1181(10)**

———————— Gods promise to his plantation ... A sermon.   4to.
London, by William Iones, 1630   [Sermons Polemical III]   **1181(9)**

COTTON (Sir Robert Bruce). An answer to such motives as were offer'd ... to Prince Henry... 2nd ed. ... To which is annexed The French charity, or an essay.   8vo.
London, for Henry Mortlock, 1675
A1 missing.   Wing C6480.   **956(2)**

———————— Cottoni posthuma: divers choice pieces.   8vo.
London, M.C[lark] for C.Harper, sold by W.Hensman [etc.], 1679   Wing C6487.   **956(1)**

COUNTER (The) scuffle, 1693.
See SPEED (Robert).   **1193(19)**

COUNTRY (The) garland.   12mo.
[*London*] *for P.Brooksby,* 1687   [Penny-Merriments II]   Woodcut.   Wing C6530A.   **363(41)**

COUNTRY (The) mouse, and the city mouse, 1683.   *See* SALTONSTALL (Wye).   **362(8)**

COUNTRY-MANS (The) counsellor: or, every man made his own lawyer.   12mo.
[*London*] *for J.Clark,* [c.1680]   [Penny-Merriments II]   Wing C6549A.   **363(33)**

COURT (The) and character of King James, 1650.
See WELDON (Sir Anthony).   **62(1)**

COURT (The) of curiosities.   8vo.
[*London*], *for J.Brooksby* [c.1683]   [Penny-Merriments II]   Woodcut.   Wing C6588.   **363(30)**

[COURTILZ DE SANDRAS (Gatien)]. La vie de Gaspard de Coligny.   12mo.
'*Cologne, chez Pierre Marteau,*' 1686   **530**

[COURTIN (Antoine de)]. Suite de la civilité françoise, ou traité du point-d'honneur.   12mo.
Iouxte la copie imprimée à Paris, chez Helie Josset, 1680   **135**

COVARRUBIAS DE OROZCO (Sebastián de). Tesoro de la lengua castellana, 1673-4.
See ALDRETE (Bernardo José).   **2183**

COVENTRY (Hon. Sir William). The character of a trimmer, 1689.
See HALIFAX (George Savile, 1st Marquis of).   **1427(10)**

[COWARD (William)]. Second thoughts concerning human soul.   8vo.
London, [*by David Edwards*] *for R.Basset,* 1702 Inserted at front: MS note (in hand of one of Pepys's clerks) of proceedings in House of Commons (10, 17 March 1703/4) against this book and another by the same author (*The grand essay,* q.v.), which led to their being burnt.   **1132**

[————————] The grand essay: or, a vindication of reason, and religion.   8vo.
London, printed for P.G. and sold by John Chantry, 1704   Inserted at front: a MS note similar to that in the same author's *Second thoughts* (q.v.).   **1133**

COWELL (John). Νομοθετης. The interpreter ... of ... obscure words and terms ... in the common or statute lawes.   2nd ed.   fo.
London, by the assigns of Richard Atkins, and Sir Edward Atkins for H.Twyford [etc.], 1684
Wing C6646.   **2309**

COWLEY (Abraham). The works.   4th ed.   fo.
London, by J.M[acock] for Henry Herringman, 1674   Engr. fp. (port., Charrington p.44).
Wing C6652.   **2428**

———————— Cutter of Coleman-street. A comedy.   4to.
London, for Henry Herringman, 1663   [Loose Plays I]   Wing C6669.   **1075(12)**

———————— Naufragium ioculare, comœdia ... acta in collegio SS. et individuæ Trinitatis.   8vo.
Londini, impensis Henrici Seile, 1638
STC 5905; Diary 19 Feb.1660/1.   **217(2)**

COWPER (Spencer). The tryal of Spencer Cowper, J.Marson, E.Stevens and W.Rogers ... for ...

murther.   fo.
London, for Isaac Cleave, Matt.Wotton and John Bullord, 1669   [Narratives & Tryals VII]
Wing T2224.   **2255(2)**

COWPER (William). The anatomy of humane bodies.   fo.
Oxford, at the Theater, for Sam.Smith and Benj. Walford, 1698   Engr. title-page, 114 engr. pls. Mezzotint port. (Charrington p.44) inserted.
Wing C6698.   **3000**

COX (Sir Richard). Hibernia Anglicana: or, the history of Ireland.   2 vols.   fo.
London, H.Clark for Joseph Watts (Vol.2: Edward Jones for Joseph Watts [etc.]), 1689-90
Engr. fps (ports, Charrington p.178), engr. map.
Wing C6722.   **2215-6**

[CRADOCK (Francis)]. Wealth discovered.   4to.
London, E.C. for A.Seile, 1661
Last 2 leaves cropped.   Wing C6743.   **1174(2)**

CRADOCK (Walter). The saints fulnesse of joy ... A sermon preached July 21.1646.   4to.
London, by Matthew Simmons, to be sold by George Whittington, 1646   [Sermons Polemical III]   Wing C6765.   **1181(11)**

CRANBURNE (Charles). The arraignments, tryals and condemnations of C.Cranburne and R.Lowick, for ... conspiracy.   fo.
London, for Samuel Heyrick, and Isaac Cleave, 1696   [Narratives & Tryals VI]
Wing A3767.   **2254(9)**

CRANFORD (James). Hæreseo-machia: or, the mischiefe which heresies doe ... A sermon ... Feb. 1st, M.DC.XLV.   4to.
London, James Young for Charles Green, 1646
[Sermons Polemical III]   Wing C6823.   **1181(12)**

CRANTZ (Albertus).   *See* KRANTZ (Albertus).

CRECCELIUS (Joannes). Collectanea ex historijs de origine et fundatione omnium ferè monasticorum ordinum.   4to.
Francofurti, per Ioh.Th.de Bry, 1614
Engr. title-page, 11 engr. pls.   Bookplate: Jean Jobert.   **1412(2)**

CRESS (William). A true copy of the papers that were delivered by Mr.William Cress, and Edward Robinson ... at their execution ... the 22d. instant Decemb.1699.   brs.
London, by Jer.Wilkins, [1699]
Wing C6884.   **2671(3)**

CRESSY (Hugh Paulin). The church-history of Brittany from the beginning of Christianity to the Norman conquest.   fo.
[Rouen] 1668   Wing C6890.   **2734**

[————————] Roman-Catholick doctrines no novelties.   8vo.
1663   Wing C6902.   **575**

CRIMSAL (Richard). Cupid's soliciter of love. 12mo.
[London] by I.M. for W.T., to be sold by J.Back, [c.1640]   [Penny-Merriments I]
STC 5419.   **362(46)**

[CROCKAT (Gilbert)]. The Scotch Presbyterian eloquence.   2nd ed., with additions.   4to.
London, for Randal Taylor, 1693
[Consutilia VI]   Wing C6962.   **1432(20)**

CROESE (Gerard). The general history of the Quakers.   3 pts.   8vo.
London, printed for John Dunton, 1696
Wing C6965.   **1219**

CROFT (Herbert), Bp of Hereford. Some animadversions upon a book intituled The theory of the earth.   8vo.
London, for Charles Harper, 1685
Wing C6979.   **1113**

CROMWELL (Oliver), Lord Protector. His Highnesse the Lord Protector's speeches to the Parliament ... The one on ... the 4th of September; the other on ... the 12. of September, 1654.   4to.
London, by T.R. and E.M. for G.Sawbridge, 1654
[Consutilia III]   Wing C7175.   **1429(11-12)**

CRONICA.   *See* CHRONICA.

CROSSING of proverbs, 1683.
See BRETON (Nicholas).   **362(53)**

[CROUCH (Humphrey)]. The second part of Tom Tram.   12mo.
[London] for J.Dacon [c.1680]   [Penny-Merriments I]   Woodcut.   **362(42)**

[————————] Tom Tram of the west.   12mo.
[London] for W.T., sold by J.Deacon [c.1680]
[Penny-Merriments I]   Woodcut.   **362(41)**

————————— The Welch traveller.   12mo.
[London] by H.B. for J.Clark, W.Thackeray, and T.Passinger, [1685]   [Penny-Merriments I]
Woodcut.   **362(40)**

CROWNE (William). A true relation of all the remarkable places ... observed in the travels of ... Thomas Lord Howard, Earle of Arundell and Surrey.   4to.
London, for Henry Seile, 1637   [Consutilia V]
STC 6097.   **1431(1)**

CROYNES (Joshua). A hundred notabe [*sic*] things, and merry conceits for a penny. By J. Croynes [i.e. J.Conyers?].   8vo.
London, for J.Conyers, 1680   [Penny-Merriments I]   Woodcut.   Wing C7414A. **362(52)**

CRUMBS of comfort [c.1680].
See B.(J.).   **365(10)**

CRUMPTON (Hugh). The distressed Welshman. 12mo.

45

[*London*] *for W.T., to be sold by J.Conyers,*
[c.1680]   [Penny-Merriments I]
Woodcut.   362(30)

CRUZ (Diego de la). Aqui se contienen unas pre-
guntas, ó enigmas.   4to.
(*Seuilla, por Iuan Vejarano, à costa de Lucas
Martin de Hermosilla*, 1683)
Gaselee 48; Wilson p.310.   1545(62)

——————————— Siguense siete Romances à lo
Divino.   4to.
*Sevilla, por Tomè de Dios Miranda, à costa de la
viuda de Nicolas Rodriguez*, [c.1675]
Gaselee 49; Wilson p.230.   1545(17)

CRUZ (Jerónimo de la). Defensa de los estatutos
y noblezas españolas.   fo.
Zaragoça, en el Hospital Real, 1637   Engr. fp.
Gaselee 50.   2139(2)

CRUZ (Matheo Sanchez de la).
See SANCHEZ DE LA CRUZ (Matheo).

CUATRO. Quatro romances de la historia de
Fernando de Pulgar, y de Garcilaso de la Vega,
estando sobre Granada.   4to.
(*Seuilla, por Juan Vejarano, à costa de Lucas
Martin de Hermosa*, 1682)   Gaselee 140;
Wilson p.262.   1545(47)

CUATRO. Quatro romances, el primero de la
batalla naval, que el señor Don Juan de Austria
tuvo con el Armada de el Gran Turco.   4to.
(*Sevilla, por Iuan Vejarano, à costa de Lucas
Martin de Hermosa*, 1682)   Gaselee 87; Wilson
p.319.   [*For pt 2 of the 'Batalla naval', see
SEGUNDA ...*]   1545(70)

CUBILLO DE ARAGÓN (Alvaro). El mejor rey
del mundo, y templo de Salomon. Comedia
famosa.   4to.
[*Seville, Juan Francisco de Blas, c.1673*]
Gaselee 51.   1553(14)

CUDWORTH (Ralph). A discourse concerning the
true notion of the Lord's Supper.   3rd ed.   fo.
London, for R.Royston, 1676
Wing C7468.   2234

——————————— The true intellectual system of the
universe: the first part. [*No more published.*]   fo.
London, for Richard Royston, 1678   Engr. fp.
Wing C7471.   2308

CULPEPPER (Nathaniel). Culpepper revived.
Being an almanack for ... 1688.   8vo.
Cambridge, printed by John Hayes, 1688
[Almanacks for the year 1688]
Wing A1509.   425(5)

CUMBERLAND (Richard), Bp of Peterborough.
De legibus naturæ disquisitio philosophica.   4to.
*Londini, typis E.Flesher, prostat vero apud
Nathanaelem Hooke*, 1672
Wing C7580.   1808

——————————— An essay towards the recovery of
the Jewish measures and weights.   8vo.
London, by Richard Chiswell, 1686   Engr. table.
Wing C7581.   988

CUNINGHAM (William). The cosmographical
glasse, conteinyng the pleasant principles of cosmo-
graphie.   fo.
Londini, in officina Ioan.Daij, 1559
Woodcuts.   STC 6119.   2049(2)

CUPERUS (Franciscus). Arcana atheismi reve-
lata.   4to.
Roterodami, apud Isaacum Næranum, 1676
                                       1566

CUPID'S court of salutations, 1687.
See B.(W.).   363(37)

CUPIDS garland, set round about with guilded
roses.   12mo.
[*London*] *for John Clark, William Thackeray, and
Thomas Passinger* [c.1685]   [Penny-Merriments
II]   Woodcut.   Wing C7602A.   363(38)

CUPID'S love lessons, 1683.
See C.(H.).   362(47)

CUPID'S master-piece.   12mo.
[*London*] *by H.B. for J.Clark, W.Thackeray and
T.Passinger*, 1685   [Penny-Merriments I]
Woodcuts.   Wing C7606.   362(33)

CUPIDS posies.   8vo.
*London, for J.Wright, J.Clarke, W.Thackeray, &
T.Passenger*, 1683   [Penny-Merriments I]
Wing C7609A.   362(21)

CURATE (Jacob), *pseud.* [i.e. G.Crockat and J.
Monroe].   *See* CROCKAT (Gilbert).

CUREAU DE LA CHAMBRE (Marin). Traité de
la connoissance des animaux.   4to.
Paris, chez Iacques d'Allin, 1662 (*de l'imprim. de
Iacques Langlois*, 1648)   1821

[CURIO (Caelius Secundus)]. Pasquine in a
traunce. A Christian and learned dialogue ...
Turned ... out of the Italian ... by W.P.   4to.
London, by William Seres [1566]
STC 6130.   1264

CURIOSITIES in chymistry, 1691.
See BOYLE (Hon. Robert).   601

CURIOSOS romances del Rey D.Fernando, sobre
Granada.   4to.
*Sevilla, por Iuan Vejarano, a costa de Lucas Martin
de Hermosa*, 1681   Gaselee 61; Wilson p.245.
                                       1545(31)

CURRIEHILL (Sir John Skene, Lord).
See SKENE (Sir John).

CURTIS (Martin).   *See* CORTÉS (Martin).

CURTIUS RUFUS (Quintus). De rebus gestis Alexandri Magni cum supplementis Freinshemii. Interpretatione et notis illustravit M. Le Tellier ... In usum Delphini.   4to.
Parisiis, apud Fredericum Leonard, 1678
Engr. title-page.   **1951**

D

D*** (Mr).   *See* ALENCÉ (Joachim d').

D*** (Sieur).   *See* BOILEAU DESPRÉAUX (Nicolas).

D.(A.). De l'ame des bêtes, 1676.
See DILLY (Antoine).   **414**

D.(C.B.D.). No sacrilege nor sinne to aliene ... the lands of bishops, 1659.
See BURGES (Cornelius).   **695**

D.(R.). A booke of Christian prayers, 1590.
See DAY (Richard).   **1280(1)**

D.(T.). The first part of ... the gentle-craft [c.1685].
See DELONEY (Thomas).   **1193(12)**

D.(T.). The garland of good-will, 1688.
See DELONEY (Thomas).   **364(2)**

D.(T.). The pleasant history of John Winchcomb ... corrected ... by T.D. [c.1680].
See DELONEY (Thomas).   **1192(19)**

D.(T.). The pleasant history of Thomas of Reading ... corrected ... by T.D., 1672.
See DELONEY (Thomas).   **1192(17)**

D.(T.). A suruey of Fraunce, 1618.
See DANETT (Thomas).   **1429(7)**

D'A.(M.). A collection of the brave exploits ... of several famous generals, 1686.
See D'ASSIGNY (Samuel).   **376(2)**

DADE (William). Dade, 1688. The country-man's kalender, for ... 1688. (A prognostication.)   8vo.
[*London*] *printed by J.Millet, for the Company of Stationers*, 1688   [Almanacks for the year 1688]
Wing A1531.   **425(6)**

DAILLÉ (Jean). A treatise concerning the right use of the Fathers.   4to.
London, for John Martin, to be sold by Robert Boulter, 1675   Wing D119; Howarth pp.363, 365.   **1419**

DALE (Anthony van). Dissertationes de origine ac progressu idololatriæ et superstitionum.   fo.

Amstelodami, apud Henricum et viduam Theodori Boom, 1696   **1606**

DALICOURT (Pierre). La campagne royale, ou le triomphe des armes de Sa Maiesté [Louis XIV] és années 1667 & 1668.   12mo.
Paris, chez la veuve Gervais Alliot, & Gilles Alliot son fils, 1668   Engr. ports, Charrington pp.104, 121.   **559**

DALLINGTON (Sir Robert). A suruey of the great dukes state of Tuscany ... 1596.   4to.
London, for Edward Blount, 1605   [Consutilia V]
STC 6200.   **1431(9)**

DALTON (Michael). The countrey justice.   fo.
London, by G.Sawbridge, T.Roycroft, W.Rawlins [*etc.*], 1677   Wing D147.   **2369**

DAMPIER (William). A new voyage round the world.   2nd ed.   8vo.
London, for James Knapton, 1697   Engr. fp. (map), 4 engr. maps.   Wing D162.   **1351**

———————— A voyage to New Holland, &c. in the year 1699.   8vo.
London, for James Knapton, 1703   Engr. fp. (map), engr. maps & pls.   **1353**

———————— Voyages and descriptions.   8vo.
London, for James Knapton, 1699   Engr. maps.
Wing D165.   **1352**

DANET (Pierre). A complete dictionary of the Greek and Roman antiquities.   4to.
London, for John Nicholson, Tho.Newborough, John Bullord [*etc.*], 1700   Engr. maps inserted.
Wing D171.   **1845**

[DANETT (Thomas)]. A suruey of Fraunce.   4to.
London, for Leonard Becket, 1618
[Consutilia III]   **1429(7)**

DANGER (The) of dispair, arising from a guilty conscience.   12mo.
[*London*] *for J.Back*, 1686   [Penny-Godlinesses]   Woodcut.   **365(24)**

DANGER (The) of mercenary Parliaments [c.1700].
See TOLAND (John).   **1437(5)**

DANGERFIELD (Thomas). Tho.Dangerfield's answer to a certain scandalous lying pamphlet entituled Malice defeated.   fo.
London, for the author, to be sold at Randal Taylor's, 1680   [Narratives & Tryals III]
Wing D183.   **2251(7)**

———————— The case of Tho.Dangerfield.
[Written by himself?]   fo.
London, for the author, 1680   [Narratives & Tryals III]   Wing C1181.   **2251(8)**

——————— The information of T.Dangerfield, delivered at the bar of the House of Commons ... the twentieth day of October ... 1680.   fo.
London, by the assigns of John Bill, Thomas Newcomb, and Henry Hills, 1680   [Narratives & Tryals III]   Wing D187.   **2251(9)**

——————— Mr.Tho.Dangerfeilds particular narrative of the late Popish design.   fo.
London, for Henry Hills, John Starkey, Thomas Basset [etc.], 1679   [Narratives & Tryals III]   Wing D192.   **2251(11)**

——————— Mr.Tho.Dangerfield's second narrative.   fo.
London, for Thomas Cockerill, 1680
[Narratives & Tryals III]   Wing D193.
2251(10)

DANGEROUS. Daungerous positions and proceedings, 1593.
See BANCROFT (Richard), Abp of Canterbury.
1237

[DANIEL (Gabriel)]. Voiage du monde de Descartes.   12mo.
Paris, chez la veuve de Simon Bénard, 1691   **577**

DANIEL (Samuel). The collection of the history of England. 5th ed. ... With a continuation unto ... Henry the Seventh, by J.Trussel.   2 pts.   fo.
London, printed by F.Leach, for Benj.Tooke, and Tho.Hodgkin (by Tho.Hodgkin, for Richard Chiswell), 1685   Wing D208; T3146.   **2230**

DANIEL (William). A journal or account of William Daniel, his late expedition ... from London to Surrat. In India.   8vo.
London, 1702   **1310**

DARELL (John). Strange news from th' Indies. Or, East-India passages further discovered.   4to.
London, for Stephen Bowtel, 1652
[Consutilia V]   Wing D251.   **1431(24)**

DARLING (John). The carpenters rule made easie.   8vo.
London, printed by R. & W.Leybourn, for John Jones, bookseller in Worcester, 1658   Tables.
MS note on title-page in Pepys's hand: 'Whereto I have annex'd ye use of the Universall Ring-Diall' [by Henry Wynne, q.v.].   Wing D260.   **232(1)**

DASSIÉ (F.). L'architecture navale. (— Le routier des Indes orientales et occidentales.)   2 pts.   4to.
Paris, chez Jean de la Caille, 1677   Engr. plans & diagrams.   **1842(2)**

[D'ASSIGNY (Samuel)]. A collection of the brave exploits and subtil strategems of several famous generals since the Roman Empire.   12mo.
London, for S.Heyrick, J.Place and R.Sare, 1686
Wing D287.   **376(2)**

DAVENANT (Charles). Circe, a tragedy.   2nd ed.   4to.
London, for Richard Tonson, 1685   [Loose Plays II]   Sig.I mis-bound.   Wing D303.
1604(13)

[———————] A discourse upon grants and resumptions.   8vo.
London, for James Knapton, 1700
Wing D305.   **1379**

[———————] Discourses on the publick revenues, and on the trade of England.   2 pts.   8vo.
London, for James Knapton, 1698   Tables.
Wing D306.   **1288-9**

[———————] An essay on the East-India-trade.   8vo.
London, 1696   Wing D307.   **1459**

[———————] An essay upon the probable methods of making a people gainers in the ballance of trade.   8vo.
London, for James Knapton, 1699   Tables, plans.   Wing D309.   **1492**

[———————] An essay upon ways and means of supplying the war.   8vo.
London, for Jacob Tonson, 1695   Engr. table; MS table (in hand of one of Pepys's clerks) inserted.   Wing D311.   **1324**

[———————] Essays upon I. The ballance of power. II. The right of making war, peace, and alliances. III. Universal monarchy.   2 pts.   8vo.
London, for James Knapton, 1701   **1378**

——————— Essays upon peace at home, and war abroad. Part I. [*No more published.*]   2nd ed.   8vo.
London, for James Knapton, 1704   **1381**

[———————] The true picture of a modern Whig set forth in a dialogue.   8vo.
London, 1701   **1380(1)**

[———————] Tom Double return'd out of the country: or, the true picture of a modern Whig, set forth in a second dialogue.   8vo.
London, 1702   **1380(2)**

DAVENANT (Sir William). Works.   3 pts.   fo.
London, by T.N. for Henry Herringman, 1673
Engr. fp. (port., Charrington p.47).
Wing D320.   **2347**

DAVIES (John).   *See* RHYS (John David).

DAVIES (John), of Kidwelly. The ancient rites, and monuments of the monastical, & cathedral church of Durham.   8vo.
London, for W.Hensman, 1672   Wing D392.
457

D'AVILA (Enrico Caterino). The history of the civil wars of France. 2nd impr. fo.
In the Savoy, printed by T.N. for Henry Herring-man, 1678 Wing D414. 2430

DÁVILA OREJON GASTÓN (Francisco). Excelencias del arte militar. 4to.
Madrid, por Julian de Paredes, 1683 Engr. pl. inserted. Gaselee 52. 1473(2)

DAVIS (John). The seamans secrets ... The eighth time reprinted. 2 pts. 4to.
London, by Gartrude Dawson, 1657
[Sea Tracts IV] Diagrams, volvelles.
Wing D446. 1080(6)

DAVIS (William). News out of the west from the stars: or, a new ephemeris made in Wiltshire ... for ... 1688. 8vo.
London, printed by R.R. for the Company of Stationers [1688] [Almanacks for the year 1688] Wing A1587. 425(7)

DAWBENY (Henry). Historie & policie re-viewed, in the heroick transactions of ... Oliver, late Lord Protector. 8vo.
London, printed for Nathaniel Brook, 1659
Wing D448. 793(2)

[————————] A sober and temperate discourse, concerning the interest of words in prayer. 4to.
London, printed for W.A., 1661 [Liturgick Controversies III] Title-page cropped.
Wing D449. 1189(5)

[DAY (Richard)]. A booke of christian prayers. 4to.
London, printed by Richard Yardley, and Peter Short, for the assigns of Richard Day, 1590
STC 6431. 1280(1)

DE antiquitate Britannicæ ecclesiæ, 1605.
See PARKER (Matthew), Abp of Canterbury. 2547

DE diluvii universalitate dissertatio prolusoria, 1667.
See KIRCHMAIER (Georg Caspar). 373(2)

DE divinis Catholicæ Ecclesiæ officiis et mysteriis varii vetustorum aliquot ecclesiæ patrum ac scriptorum ecclesiasticorum libri. Ed. M.Hittorp. fo.
Parisiis, 1624 2837

DE imitatione Christi, 1640.
See THOMAS, à Kempis. 2690

DE imperio maris variorum dissertationes ... cum præfatione J.Hagemeieri. 12mo.
Francofurti ad Moenum, 1663 Engr. title-page.
Naval Minutes p.118. 208

DE l'ame des bêtes, 1676.
See DILLY (Antoine). 414

DE l'art de parler, 1676.
See LAMY (Père Bernard). 70

DE la meilleure maniere de prêcher, 1700.
See DESBORDS DES DOIRES (Olivier). 453

DE la sainteté et des devoirs de la vie monastique, 1683.
See LE BOUTHILLIER DE RANCÉ (Armand Jean). 1897-8

DE la théorie de la manœuvre des vaisseaux, 1689.
See RENAU D'ELIÇAGARAY (Bernard). 1415

DE poematum cantu. Et viribus rythmi, 1673.
See VOSSIUS (Isaac). 1565

DEATH (The) and burial of Mistress Money. 12mo.
London, by A.Clark, to be sold by T.Vere and J. Clark, 1678 [Penny-Merriments II]
Woodcut. Wing D501. 363(24)

DEATH (The) of Robert, Earle of Huntington, 1601.
See MUNDAY (Anthony). 1103(7)

DEATH triumphant [c.1680]
See HART (John). 365(19)

DEBES (Lucas Jacobson). Færoæ, & Fœroa reserata ... Englished by J.S. 12mo.
[*London*] *printed by F.L. for William Iles,* 1676
Engr. map, diagram. Wing D511. 392

DECLARATION (A) of the demeanor and cariage of Sir Walter Raleigh. 4to.
London, by Bonham Norton and Iohn Bill, 1618
[Consutilia III] Woodcut. STC 20652.5. 1429(14)

DECLARATION (A) of the faith and order owned and practised in the Congregational Churches in England, 1659.
See NYE (Philip). 1188(20)

DECLARATION (A) of the sense of the Archbishops and Bishops, 1696.
See WILLIAMS (John), Bp of Chichester. 1435(6)

DECLARATION (A) of the state ... of Virginia, 1620.
See VIRGINIA, colony. 1429(5)

DEE (John). [General and rare memorials pertayning to the perfecte art of nauigation.]
(— Georgii Gemisti Plethonis ... de rebus Peloponnes: oratio posterior.) fo.
(*London, by Iohn Daye,* 1577)
Running title: The Brytish monarchie. Wants all before A1; wants last leaf. MS title ('The Brytish monarchie 1576') on flyleaf. Inserted at end, a letter to Pepys, from W.Croune, 8 Dec. 1674, presenting the book; and a MS list (2 leaves)

of Dee's other works on navigation. Title and list in hand of one of Pepys's clerks.
STC 6459.   **2158**

———————— A letter containing a most briefe discourse apologeticall.   4to.
(*London, by Peter Short,* 1599)   Woodcut.
STC 6460.   **1080(2)**

———————— A true & faithful relation of what passed ... between Dr.John Dee ... and some spirits.   fo.
London, by D.Maxwell, for T.Garthwait, 1659
Engr. fp. (port., Charrington p.47).
Wing D811.   **2382**

DEFENCE (A) and continuation of the ecclesiastical politie, 1671.
See PARKER (Samuel), Bp of Oxford.   **1051**

DEFENCE (A) of pluralities, 1692.
See WHARTON (Henry).   **962(1)**

DEFENCE (A) of the Arch-bishop's sermon, 1695.
See WILLIAMS (John), Bp of Chichester.
                                                 1528(10)

DEFENCE (A) of the ministers reasons, 1607.
See HIERON (Samuel).   **1187(1)**

DEFENCE (A) of the vindication of K.Charles the martyr, 1699.
See WAGSTAFFE (Thomas).   **1082(2)**

DEFENSIO regia, 1649.
See SALMASIUS (Claudius).   **2519**

[DEFOE (Daniel)] . An argument shewing, that a standing army, with consent of Parliament, is not inconsistent with a free government, &c.   4to.
London, for E.Whitlock, 1698   [Consutilia VII]
Wing D828.   **1433(21)**

[————————] Considerations upon corrupt elections of members to serve in Parliament.   4to.
London, printed in the year 1701
[Consutilia XI]   **1437(6)**

[————————] The free-holders plea against stock-jobbing elections of Parliament men.   4to.
London, 1701   [Consutilia XI]   **1437(7)**

[————————] A new test of the Church of England's loyalty.   4to.
[*London*] 1702   [Consutilia X]   **1436(7)**

[————————] Original right ... an answer to the first chapter in Dr.D'Avenant's essays.   4to.
London, printed and sold by A.Baldwin, 1704
                                                 1382(1)

[————————] The pretences of the French invasion examined, 1692.
See LLOYD (William), Bp of St Asaph.   **1432(21)**

[————————] The succession to the crown of England, considered.   4to.
London, 1701   [Consutilia X]   **1436(4)**

[————————] The two great questions consider'd. I. What the French king will do, with respect to the Spanish monarchy. II. What measures the English ought to take.   4to.
London, printed by R.T. for A.Baldwin, 1700
[Consutilia X]   Wing D850.   **1436(9)**

[DEKKER (Thomas)] . The batchellor's banquet, 1677.
See QUINZE (Les) joies de mariage.   **1193(1)**

DE LA GUARD (Theodore), *pseud.*
See WARD (Nathaniel).

DE LA MARCH (John). A complaint of the false prophets mariners upon the drying up of their hierarchicall Euphrates.   4to.
[*London, by Thomas Payne, to be sold by Humphry Blunden,* 1641]   [Sermons Polemical III]   Engr. map on title-page; title-page cropped; table inserted.   Wing D868; L202.   **1181(13)**

DELAMER (Henry Booth, 2nd Baron).
See WARRINGTON (Henry Booth, 1st Earl of).

DELAUNE (Thomas). The present state of London.   12mo.
London, printed by George Larkin, for Enoch Prosser and John How, 1681   Engr. fp., 7 engr. pls.   Wing D894.   **507**

———————— Τροπολογία: a key to open scripture metaphors. ([By] T.Delaune & B.Keach.)
3 pts.   fo.
London, by J.R. and J.D. for Enoch Prosser, 1682
(1681)   Wing D896.   **2433(1)**

DELECTABLE (The) history of poor Robin [c.1680].
See WINSTANLEY (William).   **362(19)**

DÉLICES (Les) de la Hollande, 1678.
See PARIVAL (Jean-Nicolas de).   **147**

DELIGHTFUL (The) history of Dorastus and Fawnia [c.1680].
See GREENE (Robert).   **362(17)**

DELL (William). Right reformation ... A sermon preached ... November 25.1646.   4to.
London, by R.White, for Giles Calvert, 1646
[Sermons Polemical III]   Wing D927.
                                                 1181(14)

DELLA famosissima compagnia della Lesina, 1647.
See BUONI (Tommaso).   **423**

[DELLON (Charles)] . Relation de l'Inquisition de Goa.   12mo.
A Leyde, chez Daniel Gaasbeek, 1687   **78**

[DELONEY (Thomas)]. The first part of the pleasant and princely history of the gentle-craft ... shewing; what famous men have been shooe-makers ... [By] T.D.   4to.
London, by J.Millet, for W.T., and are to be sold by J.Gilbertson [c.1685]   [Vulgaria IV]
Woodcuts.   Wing D945.   **1193(12)**

——————————The garland of delight. 30th ed.
[*An edition of the* Garland of good-will.]   8vo.
London, by T.H. for William Thackeray, and Thomas Passenger, 1681   [Penny-Merriments III]   Woodcuts.   Wing D945A.   **364(1)**

[——————————] The garland of good-will ...
Written by T.D.   8vo.
[*London*] *By Fr.Clark for George Conyers*, 1688   [Penny-Merriments III]   Woodcut.
Wing D948.   **364(2)**

[——————————] A most delightful history of the famous clothier of England, called Jack of New-bery ... Written by W.S.F.C. [i.e. T.Deloney]   12mo.
[*London*], *by H.B. for W.Thackeray*, 1684   [Penny-Merriments III]   Wing D958.   **363(50)**

[——————————] The pleasant history of John Winchcomb ... the fourteenth time imprinted ... corrected ... by T.D.   4to.
London, by W.Wilde, for Thomas Passenger, and William Thackeray, [c.1680]   [Vulgaria III]
Wing D964.   **1192(19)**

[——————————] The pleasant history of Thomas of Reading ... corrected ... by T.D.   4to.
London, for William Thackeray, 1672
[Vulgaria III]   Wing D966.   **1192(17)**

[——————————] The royal garland, of love and delight.   12mo.
[*London*] *by T.H. for W.Thackeray, T.Passenger, J.Clark, and P.Brooksby*, 1681   [Penny-Merriments II]   Woodcut.   **363(39)**

DEMERY (Antoine).   *See* EMERY (Antoine d').

DEMOCRITUS JUNIOR, *pseud.*
See BURTON (Robert).

DEMOSTHENES. Traduction des Philippiques de Demosthene, d'une des Verrines de Ciceron [*etc.*]. Des Srs de Maucroy, et de La Fontaine.   2 vols in 1.   [*Vol.2 has title:* Ouvrages de prose et de poësie des SSrs de Maucroy et de La Fontaine.]
12mo.
Amsterdam, chez Pierre Mortier, 1688   **432**

DENHAM (Sir John). Poems and translations, with The Sophy.   2 pts.   8vo.
London, for H.Herringman, 1668 (1667)
Wing D1005; Diary, 10 Aug.1667.   **824**

DES mots à la mode et des nouvelles façons de parler, 1692.
See CALLIÈRES (François de).   **150**

DES principes de l'architecture, 1690.
See FÉLIBIEN (André).   **1957**

DES ACCORDS (Seigneur), *pseud.*
See TABOUROT (Étienne).

[DESBORDS DES DOIRES (Olivier)]. De la meilleure maniere de prêcher.   12mo.
Paris, chez Jean Boudot, 1700   **453**

DESCARTES (René). Opera philosophica. (Principia philosophiæ; Specimina philosophiæ; Passiones animæ.)   Ed.3a.   3pts.   4to.
Amstelodami, apud Ludovicum & Danielem Elzevirios, 1656   Engr. port. (Charrington p.48).
1402

DESCRIPTION (A) and explanation of two hundred sixty and eight places in Jerusalem, 1677.
See ADRICHOMIUS (Christianus).   **2907(7)**

DESCRIPTION (The) and use of the carpenters-rule, 1662.
See B.(J.).   **85**

DESCRIPTION de l'abbaye de la Trappe, 1682.
See FÉLIBIEN (André).   **95**

DESCRIPTION des antiquitez ... d'Orange, 1700.
See ESCOFFIER (Charles).   **1638(3)**

DESCRIPTION exacte de tout ce qui s'est passé dans les guerres entre le roy d'Angleterre, le roy de France, les Estats des provinces unies du Pays-Bas & l'evesque de Munster. ... 1664 [—] 1667.   4to.
Amsterdam, chez Jacques Benjamin, 1668
Engrs.   **1169**

DESCRIPTION generalle et particulliere d'une gallaire.   brs.
Paris, chez Antoine de Fer et Nicolas Berey, 1667
Engr.   **1842(3)**

DESCRIZIONE di Roma antica (— moderna), 1697.
See ROSSI (Filippo).   **800-801**

DESGODETZ (Antoine). Les edifices antiques de Rome.   fo.
Paris, chez Iean Baptiste Coignard, 1682
Engr. pls.   **2913**

DESJEANS (J.B.L.), Sieur de Pointis.
See POINTIS (Jean Bernard Louis Desjean, Sieur de).

DESMARETS DE SAINT SORLIN (Jean). La verité des fables, ou l'histoire des dieux de l'antiquité.   2 vols.   8vo.
Paris, chez Henry le Gras, 1648   **1057-8**

DESROCHES ( ), Officier des vaisseaux du roi.
Dictionaire des termes propres de marine ... Avec
les enseignes. 8vo.
*Paris, chez Amable Auroy (de l'imprimerie de la
veuve D. Langlois)*, 1687   Engr. pls.   **1205**

DESTRUCTION (The) of Troy, 1684.
See LEFEVRE (Raoul).   **1190(4)**

DEVOUT. Deuout psalmes and collectes ... for
daylye meditacions. 8vo.
(London, by Edward Whitchurche) [1550]
STC 2999.5; Duff p.40.   **75(1)**

DEYRON (Jacques). Des antiquites de la ville de
Nismes. 4to.
Nismes, par Iean Plasses, 1663
Tanner II, p.130.   **1638(1)**

DIALOGUE (A) betwene a knyght and a clerke
[1532?].
See WILLIAM, of Occam.   **368(2)**

DIALOGUE (A) between a young divine, and an
old beggar. 8vo.
[London] for J.Deacon, 1683   [Penny-Godli-
nesses]   Wing D1300A.   **365(33)**

DIALOGUE (A) concerning the strife of our
Churche. 8vo.
London, by Robert Walde-graue, 1584
STC 6801.   **209(1)**

DIALOGUES. [The dialoges of creatures moral-
ysed.] 4to.
[Antwerp, M.de Keyser, 1535]   Wants :: 1, TT4.
Woodcuts.   STC 6815; Duff p.19.   **1246**

DÍAZ DEL CASTILLO (Bernal). Historia verdad-
era de la conquista de la Nueva-España.   fo.
Madrid, en la imprenta del Reyno, 1632
Gaselee 53.   **2118(2)**

DICKINSON (Edmund). Epistola ... ad T.Mundan-
um ... De quintessentia philosophorum et de vera
physiologia ... His accedunt Mundani responsa.
8vo.
Oxoniæ, e theatro Sheldoniano, 1686
Wing D 1386.   **1494**

————————— Physica vetus & vera: siue tractatus
de naturali veritate hexaëmeri Mosaici. 4to.
*Londini, typis Ilivianis, vænales prostant apud
Henricum Ribotteau*, 1702   Engr. title-page,
diagrams.   **1862**

DICTA poetarum, quæ apud J.Stobæum extant
emendata ... ab H.Grotio. [*Gk. & Lat.*]   2pts.
4to.
Parisiis, apud Nicolaum Buon, 1623   **1833**

DICTIONNAIRE (Le) des arts et des sciences,
1694.
See CORNEILLE (Thomas).   **2812**

DIFFICILES nugæ: or, observations touching the
Torricellian experiment, 1674.
See HALE (Sir Matthew).   **935**

DIGBY (Everard). De arte natandi.   4to.
Londini, excudebat Thomas Dawson, 1587
44 engr. pls.   STC 6839.   **985(1)**

DIGBY (Sir Kenelm). A discourse concerning the
vegetation of plants.   12mo.
London, by J.G. for John Dakins, 1661
Wing D1432.   **11**

————————— Two treatises. In the one of which,
the nature of bodies; in the other, the nature of
mans soule; is looked into.   fo.
Paris, by Gilles Blaizot, 1644   Wing D1448.
   2828

DIGGES (Sir Dudley). The compleat ambassador.
fo.
*London, by Tho:Newcomb, for Gabriel Bedell
and Thomas Collins*, 1655   Engr. title-page.
Wing D1453.   **2236**

DIGGES (Leonard). A geometrical practical trea-
tize named Pantometria ... First published by
Thomas Digges.   fo.
London, by Abell Jeffes, 1591   STC 6859.
   1979(1)

[DILLY (Antoine)]. De l'ame des bêtes.   12mo.
Lyon, chez Anisson & Posuel, 1676   **414**

DIODATI (Giovanni). Pious and learned annotations upon the Holy Bible.   4th ed.   2 pts.
fo.
*London, printed by Tho.Roycroft, for Nicholas
Fussell*, 1664   Engr. fp. (port., Charrington
p.48), title-page.   Wing D1508.   **2199**

DIOGENES. His search through Athens.   12mo.
*[London] for J.Wright, J.Clarke, W.Thackeray,
and T.Passinger*, [c.1683]   [Penny-Merriments
I]   Woodcut.   **362(55)**

DIRECTIONS propounded ... concerning the
Booke of Common Prayer, 1641.
See UDALL (Ephraim).   **1188(3)**

DIRECTORY (A) for the publique worship of
God, 1644.
See WESTMINSTER ASSEMBLY.   **1188(14)**

DISCOURS sur les anciens, 1687
See LONGEPIERRE (Hilaire Bernard Requeleyne, baron de).   **450**

DISCOURSE (A) concerning banks. [By Sir T.
Janssen?]   4to.
(London, for James Knapton, 1697)
[Consutilia VII]   Wing D1577.   **1433(9)**

DISCOURSE (A) concerning liturgies, 1662.
See OWEN (John), D.D.   **1189(8)**

DISCOURSE (A) concerning prayer ex tempore, 1646.
See TAYLOR (Jeremy), Bp of Down and Connor.
1188(13)

DISCOURSE (A) of ecclesiastical politie, 1670.
See PARKER (Samuel), Bp of Oxford. **1050**

DISCOURSE (A) of money, 1696.
See BRISCOE (John). **1138**

DISCOURSE (A) of the empire, 1658.
See HOWELL (James). **606(4)**

DISCOURSE (A) of the original ... of the Cossacks, 1672.
See CHEVALIER (Pierre). **808**

DISCOURSE (A) of the variation of the cumpas, 1585.
See BOROUGH (William). **1077(6)**

DISCOURSE (A) of the variation of the compasse, 1596.
See BOROUGH (William). **1078(4)**

DISCOURSE (A) of things above reason, 1681.
See BOYLE (Hon. Robert). **759(4)**

DISCOURSE (A) touching Tanger, 1680.
See SHEERES (Sir Henry). **558**

DISCOURSE (A) upon grants and resumptions, 1700.
See DAVENANT (Charles). **1379**

DISCOURSES on the publick revenues, and on the trade of England, 1698.
See DAVENANT (Charles). **1288-9**

DISPENSARY (The): a poem, 1699.
See GARTH (Sir Samuel). **1424**

DISQUISITIONES criticæ, 1684.
See SIMON (Richard). **1560**

DISTINTA relazione della celebre machina, candelabri, fiaccole, & altro, fatta fare dalla ven. archiconfraternita de i Santi Bartolomeo, et Alessandro di Roma della nazione Bergamasca. 4to.
(*Roma, per Gio:Francesco Buagni*, 1700)
1743(3)

DISTINTA relatione delle cerimonie fatte in Roma nell' aprire le porte sante delle quattro principali basiliche per l'anno corrente del Giubileo. 4to.
Roma, pe'l Buagni, 1700 **1743(2)**

DISTINTA relazione della famosissima machina rappresentante tutti i misterij della Passione di ... Giesu Cristo. 4to.
Roma, per Gio:Francesco Buagni, 1700 **1743(4)**

DISTINTA relazione della machina, luminari, fanali, & altro di più solenne fatto dalla vener. Archiconfr. del SS.Crocifisso in S.Marcello di Roma. 4to.
(*Roma, per Gio:Francesco Buagni*, 1700)
1743(5)

DIVERS voyages de la Chine, et autres royaumes de l'Orient, 1682.
See RHODES (Alexandre de). **1915**

DIVERS voyages touching the discouerie of America, 1582.
See HAKLUYT (Richard). **1077(8)**

DIVINE (The) history of the genesis of the world explicated, 1670.
See GOTT (Samuel). **1575**

DIVINE (The) right of convocations examined. 4to.
London, for A.Baldwin, 1701 [Convocation Pamphlets IX] **1695(3)**

DIX (Henry). The art of brachygraphy. 3rd ed. 8vo.
London, printed for T.B., sold by the author, 1641 [Short-hand Collection III]
Wing D1744; Carlton p.46. **402(5)**

DOCTRINE (The) of non-resistance, 1689.
See BOHUN (Edmund). **1427(4)**

DODDRIDGE (Sir John). Judge Dodaridge, his law of nobility and peerage. [*Another issue of W.Bird's Magazine of honour.*] 8vo.
London, for L.Chapman, 1658
Wing D1794. **606(1)**

DODWELL (Henry). Annales Velleiani, Quintiliani, Statiani, seu vitæ. (Appendix dissertationum duarum.) 2 pts. 8vo.
Oxonii, e Theatro Sheldoniano, 1698
Wing D1802A. **1371**

————————De nupero schismate Anglicano parænesis ad exteros. 8vo.
Londini, impensis Richardi Smith, 1704 **1372**

————————A treatise concerning the lawfulness of instrumental musick in holy offices. 2nd ed. 8vo.
London, for William Haws, 1700
Wing D1821. **1354**

[————————] A vindication of the deprived bishops. 2 pts. 4to.
London, 1692 [Consutilia X]
Wing D1827. **1436(2)**

DOLEMAN (R.) *pseud.* See PARSONS (Robert).

DONATUS (Aelius). Ars minor (Donatus pro pueris). 4to.
R.Pynson [*London*, 1500]
See Appendix **1305(1)**

───────── Accidence.   4to.
W. de Worde, Westminster [1499]
See Appendix   **1305(2)**

DONNE (John). Βιαθανατος.   4to.
London, printed for Humphrey Moseley, 1648
Wing D1859.   **1059**

───────── Poems ... with elegies on the
author's death.   8vo.
In the Savoy, by T.N. for Henry Herringman, 1669
Wing D1871.   **722**

DOOR (The) of salvation opened [c.1680].
See PASSINGER (Thomas).   **365(8)**

DOS romances contemplativos [c.1680].
See AQUI se contienen dos romances ...   **1545(4)**

DOVE (Jonathan). Dove. Speculum anni or an
almanack for ... 1688 ... Calculated properly for
... Cambridge.   8vo.
[*Cambridge*] *printed by John Hayes*, 1688
[Almanacks for the year 1688]
Wing A1633.   **425(8)**

───────── Dove. Speculum anni or an
almanack for ... 1689 ... Calculated properly for
... Cambridge.   8vo.
Cambridge, printed by John Hayes, 1689
[Almanacks for the year 1689]
Wing A1634.   **426(9)**

[DOWNAME (John)]. Annotations upon ... the
Old and New Testament, 1651.
See ANNOTATIONS upon ... the Old and New
Testament.   **2495-6**

DOWNFALL (The) of Robert Earle of Huntington,
1601.
See MUNDAY (Anthony).   **1103(6)**

DOWNING (Calybute). A sermon preached ...
1 September 1640.   4to.
London, by E.G. for Iohn Rothwell, 1641
[Sermons Polemical III]   Wing D2105.
                                         1181(15)

DRAKE (Sir Francis). Sir Francis Drake revived,
1653.
See SIR Francis Drake revived.   **1253**

[DRAKE (James)]. The history of the last Parlia-
ment began at Westminster, the tenth day of
February ... 1700.   8vo.
*London, for Fra.Coggan; Robert Gibson, and
Tho.Hodgson*, 1702   On flyleaf, a note in hand
of one of Pepys's clerks drawing attention to the
*Proceedings and resolution of the ... Lords ... 9th
of May, 1702* (959(2)) inserted at end of book.
This censures part of the Preface.   **959(1)**

[─────────] Some necessary considerations
relating to all future elections of members to serve
in Parliament ... By a true English-man [i.e. J.

Drake.]   4to.
London, printed in the year 1702
[Consutilia XI]   **1437(8)**

[DRAKE (Sir William)]. The Long Parliament
revived. By Tho.Philips [i.e. Sir W.Drake].   4to.
*London, printed for the author, and are to be sold
at the Castle and Lyon in St.Pauls Church-yard*,
1661   [Consutilia IV]   Wing D2137.
                                         1430(14)

DRAKESTEIN (H.A. van R. tot).
See REEDE TOT DRAKESTEIN (Hendrik
Adriaan van).

DRAUD (Georg). Bibliotheca classica.   4to.
*Francofurti ad Moenum, impensis Balthasaris
Ostern*, 1625   **1680-1682(1)**

[─────────] Bibliotheca exotica ... La biblio-
theque universail.   4to.
Frankfourt, par Balthasar Ostern, 1625   **1682(2)**

───────── Bibliotheca librorum Germanic-
orum classica.   4to.
*Frankfurt am Mayn, bey Egenolff Emmeln, in
Verlegung Balthasaris Ostern*, 1625   **1683**

DRAYTON (Michael). Poly-olbion. Or a choro-
graphicall description of ... Great Britaine.   fo.
*London, by H.L. for Matthew Lownes, I.Browne,
[etc.]*, 1613   Engr. fp. (port., Charrington p.79),
title-page, 18 engr. maps.   STC 7227.   **2022(1)**

DREADFUL (The) character of a drunkard, 1686.
See HART (John).   **365(1)**

DRUMMOND (William). The history of Scotland,
1423-1542.   2nd ed.   8vo.
London, printed for Tho.Fabian, 1681
Engr. fp. (port., Charrington p.50), engr. pls.
(ports, Charrington pp.86-7).
Wing D2198.   **1109**

DRYDEN (John). Fables ancient and modern;
translated into verse, from Homer, Ovid, Boccace
& Chaucer: with original poems.   fo.
London, for Jacob Tonson, 1700   MS letter from
Dryden to Pepys, 14 July 1699, with Pepys's draft
reply, same date (in Pepys's hand), inserted at
p.530. Both printed in Howarth pp.280-1.
Wing D2278.   **2442**

───────── The rival ladies. A tragi-comedy.
4to.
London, by W.W. for Henry Herringman, 1644
[Loose Plays II]   Wing D2346; Diary 4 Aug.
1664, 18 July & 2 Aug.1666.   **1604(3)**

DU BARTAS (Guillaume de Saluste). Divine
weekes and workes.   fo.
*London, by Robert Young, to be sold by William
Hope*, 1641   Wants engr. title-page and port.
Wing D2405; Diary 2 Nov.1662.   **2417**

DU CANGE (Charles du Fresne, sieur). Glossarium ad scriptores mediæ et infimæ Latinitatis. 3 vols. fo.
Lutetiæ Parisiorum, typis Gabrielis Martini. Prostat apud Ludovicum Billaine, 1678
Engr. title-page, pls. **2716-8**

DU CHESNE (André). Histoire d'Angleterre, d'Escosse, et d'Irlande ... Nouvelle ed. ... par le Sr Du Verdier. 2 vols. fo.
Paris, chez Louys Billaine (chez Thomas Iolly), 1666 **2632-3**

———————— Histoire des papes et souverains chefs de l'Église. 2 vols in 1. fo.
Paris, chez Iacques Villery, 1645 Engr. title-page. **2606**

DU CHOUL (Guillaume). Discours de la religion des anciens Romains, de la castramétation et discipline militaire. 2 pts.
Lyon, par Guillaume Roville, 1581 Engr. pls. Adams D1026. **1912**

DUCK (Sir Arthur). De usu & authoritate juris civilis, per dominia principum Christianorum. 12mo.
Londini, impensis Thomæ Dring, & venales prostant apud Johannem Dunmore, 1679
Wing D2428. **532**

DU FRESNOY (Charles Alphonse). De arte graphica. The art of painting ... with remarks. [*Lat. & Engl.*] 2 pts. 4to.
London, by J.Heptinstall for W.Rogers, 1695
Wing D2458. **1844**

DUGDALE (Stephen). The further information of S.Dugdale ... delivered ... 30 Oct.1680. fo.
London, for Thomas Parkhurst and Thomas Simmons, 1680 [Narratives & Tryals III]
Wing D2474. **2251(14)**

———————— The information of S.Dugdale ... delivered ... the first day of November ... 1680. fo.
London, by the assigns of John Bill, Thomas Newcomb, and Henry Hills, 1680 [Narratives & Tryals III] Wing D2475. **2251(13)**

DUGDALE (Sir William). The antient usage in bearing ... arms. 2nd ed. 8vo.
Oxford, printed at the Theater for Moses Pitt, and sold by Samuel Smith, London, 1682
Wing D2478. **466**

———————— The antiquities of Warwickshire illustrated. fo.
London, by Thomas Warren, 1656 Engr. fp. (port., Charrington p.51), engr. pls and maps.
Wing D2479. **2497**

———————— The baronage of England. 2 vols in 1. fo.
London, by Tho.Newcomb, for Abel Roper, John

Martin, Henry Herringman, 1675-6
Wing D2480. **2669**

———————— The history of St Paul's Cathedral in London. fò.
London, by Thomas Warren, 1658
Engr. fp. (port., Charrington p.51), pls.
Wing D2482; Diary 10 Dec.1663. **2444**

———————— Monasticon Anglicanum. Ed.2a. 3 vols. [*Vols 2-3 are the first edition.*] fo.
Londini, impensis Christopheri Wilkinson [etc.] (vol.2: *typis Aliciæ Warren*, vol.3: *excudebat Tho: Newcomb*), 1682 (1661, 1673)
Engr. title-page, 110 engr. pls. Wing D2485, 2486, 2483. **2478-80**

———————— Origines juridiciales; or, historical memorials of the English laws. 3rd ed. 2pts. fo.
London, for Christop.Wilkinson, Tho.Dring, and Charles Harper, 1680 Engr. ports, Charrington pp.21, 38, 39, 44, 75, 154, 169; and engr. pls.
Wing D2490; Diary 15 & 17-18 Apr.1667. **2552**

———————— A perfect copy of all summons, 1685.
See ENGLAND. *Parliament.* **2572**

[————————] A short view of the late troubles in England. fo.
Oxford, at the Theater for Moses Pitt, London, 1681 Wing D2492. **2605**

[DU HAMEL (Jean Baptiste)]. Philosophia vetus et nova. Ed.4a. 2 vols. 12mo.
Londini, impensis Georgii Wells & Abel Swalle, 1685 Engr. pls, diagrams. Wing D2499. **712-3**

———————— Regiæ scientiarum Academiæ historia. 4to.
Parisiis, apud Stephanum Michallet, 1698
Tanner II, p.107. **1899**

DU JONQUIER ( ). Le secretaire critique. Du sieur B.P. dit Du Jonquier, dedié à moy-meme. 12mo.
Amsterdam, chez Waesberg, & à Leyden, chez Gaasbeek, 1680 **99(2)**

DUKE (The) of Anjou's succession [to the throne of Spain] considered. 2nd ed. 2 pts. 4to.
London, printed and sold by A.Baldwin, 1701 [Consutilia X] **1436(10-11)**

DU MAURIER (Louis Aubery).
See AUBERY DU MAURIER (Louis).

DU MOLINET (Claude). Le cabinet de la bibliothèque de Sainte Genevieve. 2 pts. fo.
Paris, chez Antoine Dezallier, 1692 Engr. title-pages. 46 engr. pls (port., Charrington p.119). **2930**

[DU MONT (Jean)]. Nouveau voyage du Levant.
12mo.
La Haye, chez Étienne Foulque, 1694   Engr.
title-page, 8 engr. pls.   **633**

DU MOULIN (Pierre). The accomplishment of the
prophecies; or, the third booke in defense of the
Catholicke faith.   8vo.
*Oxford, by Ioseph Barnes and are to be sold by
Iohn Barnes*, 1613   STC 7306.   **243**

DUNTON (John). A true iournall of the Sally
fleet, with the proceedings of the voyage.   4to.
*London, printed by Iohn Dawson for Thomas
Nicholes*, 1637   [Naval Pamphlets; Consutilia
V]   STC 7357.   **1399(1); 1431(25)**

DUPIN (Louis Ellies). A compleat history of the
canon and writers, of the books of the Old and
New Testament.   2 vols in 1.   fo.
London, for H.Rhodes, T.Bennet, A.Bell [etc.]
1699-1700   Wing D2640.   **2211**

───────────── Nouvelle bibliothèque des auteurs
ecclesiastiques.   2e (− dernière) éd.   14 vols.
4to.
Paris (Mons) chez André Pralard [etc.], 1690-
1703   **1918-31**

DUPORT (Gilles). L'art de prêcher.   2e éd.
12mo.
Paris, chez Charles de Sercy, 1684
ã12 signed E1 (cancellans).   **568**

DURANTI (Jean Étienne). De ritibus Ecclesiæ
Catholicæ, ed. novissima.   4to.
Lugduni, apud Joannem Certe, 1675   **1828**

[DU REFUGE (Eustace)]. Arcana aulica: or,
Walsingham's manual; of prudential maxims, for
the states-man. [*A translation of Pt 2 of* Traicté de
la cour.]   12mo.
London, printed by T.C., sold by Iohn Wright,
1655   Wing D2685; Diary 9 Jan.1663/4; 11 June
1666.   **43**

DURET (Claude). Thresor de l'histoire des langues
de cest vniuers.   2e éd.   4to.
*Yverdon, de l'imprimerie de la Société Helvetiale
Caldoresque*, 1619   Table.   **1793**

DURHAM, Bishop of.
See COSIN (John), Bp of Durham.

DUTCH-TUTOR (The): or, a new-book of Dutch
and English.   8vo.
London, printed for William Fisher [1660]
Wing D2907.   **295**

DU TILLET (Jean), Sieur de la Bussière. Recueil
des guerres et traictez d'entre les roys de France et
d'Angleterre.   fo.
Paris, chez Iaques du Puys, 1588   Adams D1207.
2522(2)

───────────── Recueil des roys de France.
2 pts.   fo.
Paris, chez Iaques Du Puys, 1587   Engrs.
Adams D1209.   **2522(1)**

DUVAL (Pierre). La France sous le roy Louis XIV.
[*Pt 2*, Acquisitions de la France, *only*.]   12mo.
Paris, chez l'auteur, 1667   Engr. title-page, half-
title, table & maps.   **382**

DYCK (Christoffel van). Proeven van letteren, die
gesneden zijn door wylen Christoffel van Dyck,
welke gegoten werden by Jan Bus ten huyse van
Sr.Joseph Athias ... tot Amsterdam.   brs.
[*Amsterdam, c.1690?*]   **1398(1)**

DYING (The) Christians pious exhortations ... to
his wife, children & friends.   8vo.
[*London*] *by H.Brugis for J.Wright, J.Clark* [etc.]
[c.1685]   [Penny-Godlinesses]   Woodcut.
365(7)

DYING (The) man's last sermon [c.1685].
See HART (John).   **365(34)**

E

E.(G.d'). Observations on a journy to Naples,
1691.
See GAVIN (Antonio).   **880**

E.(J.). Publick employment and an active life,
1667.
See EVELYN (John).   **461**

E.(T.). The lawes resolutions of womens rights,
1632.
See LAW'S.   **1127**

E.(T.), a layman. Some considerations about the
reconcileableness of reason and religion ... To
which is annex'd ... A discourse of Mr.Boyle,
about the possibility of the Resurrection.
2 pts.   8vo.
London, by T.N. for H.Herringman, 1675
Wing B4024.   **791**

E. (T.H.R.B.). The excellency of theology, 1674.
See BOYLE (Hon. Robert).   **803**

EACHARD (John). Good newes for all Christian
souldiers ... A sermon.   4to.
London, by Matthew Simmons, 1645
[Sermons Polemical III]   Wing E48.
1181(16)

EADMER. Historiæ novorum siue sui sæculi libri
VI ... In lucem ... emisit I. Seldenus, & notas porro
adjecit & spicilegium.   fo.

Londini, typis & impensis Guilielmi Stanesbeij, ex officinis Richardi Meighen & Thomæ Dew, 1623
STC 7438. **2440**

EAST INDIA COMPANY. A true relation of the ... proceedings ... at Amboyna, 1651.
See TRUE (A) relation ... **79**

ECCLESIASTICAL (The) politie (*Author of*).
See PARKER (Samuel), Bp of Oxford. **1052**

ECKIUS (Johann). *See* JOHANN, von Eck.

ÉCOLE. L'eschole de Salerne en vers burlesques, 1651.
See MARTIN (Louis). **50**

ÉCOLE. L'escole parfaite des officiers de bouche ... 3e éd., augmentée. 12mo.
Paris, chez Jean Ribou, 1676 Engrs. **634**

EDGEWORTH (Roger). Sermons very fruitfull, godly, and learned. 4to.
Londini, in ædibus Roberti Caly, 1557
STC 7482; Duff p.20. **1285**

[EDWARDS (Jonathan)]. The exposition given by my Lord Bishop of Sarum, of the second article of our religion, examined. 4to.
London, for Tho.Bennet, 1702 On title-page 'Dr Jonathan Edwards' in Daniel Waterland's hand. **1772(1)**

EGAN (Anthony). The book of rates, now used in the sin custom-house of the church and court of Rome. 4to.
London, for Benjamin Southwood, 1674
[Consutilia II] Wing E246. **1428(15)**

EIKON BASILIKE. Εἰκὼν Βασιλική. The pourtraicture of his sacred majesty. 8vo.
Reprinted in R.M. [London, W.Dugard for F. Eglesfield], 1648 Engr. fp. (port., Charrington p.31), engr. port., Charrington p.32.
Wing E277. **721(1)**

EIRENOPHILALETHES (J.A.), *pseud.*
See JENNINGS (Abraham).

ELLIES DUPIN (Louis).
See DUPIN (Louis Ellies).

ELLIS (John). The sole path to a sound peace ... A sermon. 4to.
London, by John Raworth, for George Latham, and John Rothwell, 1643 [Sermons Polemical III] Wing E592. **1181(17)**

ELSYNGE (Henry). The ancient method and manner of holding Parliaments. 3rd ed. 12mo.
London, for S.S. and to be sold by Tho.Dring, 1675 Wing E645A. **354**

ELYOT (Sir Thomas). [Bibliotheca Elyotæ.] fo.
(*Londini, in officina Thomæ Bertheleti, 1542*)
Nn6 only. STC 7660; Duff p.21. **1978(2)**

[————————] Pasquil the playne. 8vo.
Londini, in ædibus Thomæ Bertheleti, 1533
STC 7672; Duff p.21. **368(4)**

EMERY (Antoine d'). Nouveau recueil de curiositez ... Dernière éd. 2 vols. 12mo.
Leyde, chez Pierre van der Aa, 1688
Vol.1: Engr. fp., title-page, 7 engr. pls. **398-9**

EMILIANE (Gabriel de), *pseud.*
See GAVIN (Antonio).

EMPEREUR (L') et l'empire trahis, 1680.
See CERDAN (Jean Paul, comte de). **206(2)**

ENDERBIE (Percy). Cambria triumphans, or Brittain in its perfect lustre. fo.
London, for Andrew Crooke, 1661 Engr. pls.
Wing E728. **2477**

ENGHIEN (Jacques d').
See SICILE, herald.

ENGLAND
Admiralty

———————— James Duke of York ... Instructions for the better ordering His Majesties fleet in sayling. fo.
[London, c.1662] Engrs. **2801(1)**

———————— James Duke of York ... Instructions for the better ordering His Majesties fleet in fighting. (— Encouragement for the captains and companies of fire-ships.) fo.
[London, c.1662] **2801(3)**

———————— James Duke of York ... Instructions to be observed by all masters, pilots, ketches, hoys & smacks, attending the fleet. fo.
[London, c.1662] **2801(2)**

[————————] [Instructions to be observed at sea. *No title-page.*] fo.
[c.1700] Forms for muster-book, pay-book, officers' journal. At front: MS guide (1 leaf) to contents, in hand of one of Pepys's clerks. **2173**

Church of England

———————— *For the Book of Common Prayer, and other special forms of prayer, see* LITURGIES. *Church of England.*

———————— Articles to be enquired of, within the prouince of Canterburie, in the metropoliticall visitation of Edmonde [Grindal], Archbishop ... in the xviij. yeare of ... Elizabeth. 4to.
London, by Willyam Seres, 1546 [or rather 1576]
STC 10155. **1761(6)**

———————— A booke of certaine canons, concernyng some parte of the discipline of the Churche of England. 1571. 4to.
London, by Iohn Daye [1571] In MS. on title-page, 'Muberia'. STC 10063. **1761(4)**

57

———————Certain sermons or homilies appointed to be read in churches.   fo.
London, by T.R. for Andrew Crooke, Samuel Mearne, and Robert Pawlet, 1673
Wing C4091K.   **2376**

———————A collection of articles, injunctions, canons ... of the Church of England ... published ... (by A.Sparrow). 3rd impr., with additions. 4to.
London, for Robert Pawlet, 1675   Engr. fp.
Wing C4092 & S4825.
MS note on title-page in Pepys's hand: 'With more annex'd by SP. 1689.' List of 4 annexed items (in fact there are 5) in hand of one of Pepys's clerks on A2v.   **1761(1)**

———————Concilia, decreta, leges, constitutiones, in re ecclesiarum orbis Britannici. 2 vols. fo.
Londini, excudebat Richardus Badger, impensis Ph.Stephani, & Ch.Meredith (– apud Aliciam Warren) 1639-64   STC 23066; Wing S4920;
Naval Minutes p.341.   **2818-9**

———————The confession of faith, 1688.
See WESTMINSTER ASSEMBLY.   **636**

———————Constitutions and canons ecclesiastical.   fo.
Oxford, at the Theater, 1683   [Part of Wing B3671.]   **2604(2)**

———————Iniunctions giuen by ... John [Jewel], ... Bishop of Salisburie.   4to.
London, by Henry Denham for Richard Jackson, 1569   **1761(3)**

———————A necessary doctrine and erudition for any Christen man, sette furthe by the Kynges maiestie of England &c.   4to.
(*London, by Thomas Barthelet*, 1543)
STC 5168; Duff p.29.   **1757**

———————Orders taken the x. day of October, in the thirde yere of the raigne of ... Elizabeth.   4to.
(*London, by Richarde Jugge*,) [1561]
STC 9186.   **1761(2)**

———————A true and exact list of the members of both Houses of ... Convocation.   brs.
London, for Richard Wilkin, 1701   **1698(2)**

———————   brs.
Ib., Id., 1702   [Convocation Pamphlets XII]   **1698(5)**

Commissioners appointed to enquire into the forfeited estates of Ireland

———————The report made to the honourable House of Commons, Decemb.15.1699. By the Commissioners appointed to enquire into the forfeited estates of Ireland.   4to.
London, 1700   [Consutilia XI]   **1437(2)**

Miscellaneous Public Documents

———————At the Court at Whitehall, 10 March 1675/6. [Rules for granting passes to ships, with a blank certificate and form, both on vellum.] fo.   **2456**

———————At the court of Whitehall the 29th day of December 1694. [Order in Council relating to certain alterations in the form of common prayers.]   fo.
[*London, by Charles Bill and the executrix of Thomas Newcomb*, 1694]   Imprint cut off.
Wing E2921.   **1528(2)**

———————By his Grace the Duke of Norfolke, Earl-Marshal of England. In pursuance of an order of the ... Privy-Council ... the third day of January 1694. [Giving notice as to mourning.]   4to.
Single leaf.   Imprint cut off.   **1528(3)**

———————Letters of State, written by Mr. John Milton, 1694.
See MILTON (John).   **519**

———————A note of the head-lands of England, as they beare one from another. [A proclamation.]   brs.
London, by Robert Barker [1605]   1 leaf with engr. map.   STC 8371.   **2131(3)**

Parliament

———————A collection of some memorable and weighty transactions in Parliament, in the year 1678, and afterwards; in relation to the impeachment of Thomas Earl of Danby.   4to.
London, 1695   [Consutilia VII]
Wing E1280.   **1433(14)**

———————The debate at large, between the House of Lords and House of Commons ... 1688. Relating to the word, Abdicated, and the vacancy of the throne in the Common's vote. 8vo.
[*London*] *for J.Wickens*, 1695
Wing D506.   **617**

———————The declaration of the Lords spiritual and temporal, and Commons ... presented to the King and Queen ... with His Majesties ... answer thereunto.   fo.
London, for James Partridge, Matthew Gillyflower, and Samuel Heyrick, 1689
Wing E1489.   **1967(3)**

———————Ephemeris parliamentaria; or, a faithfull register of the transactions in Parliament, in the third and fourth years of ... King Charles. [Ed. by T.Fuller.]   fo.
London, for John Williams and Francis Eglesfield, 1654   Wing F2422; Diary 9 Jan.1666/7.   **2115**

[ENGLAND]
———————— [*Ephemeris parliamentaria.*] The Parliament of the third and fourth years of ... King Charles the first. [Ed. by T.F., i.e. Thomas Fuller. *A reissue of* Ephemeris Parliamentaria 1654.] fo.
London, for John Williams and Francis Eglesfield, 1660   Wing F63.   **2024**

———————— A exact abridgement of the records in the Tower of London ... of all the Parliaments ... Collected by Sir R.Cotton. Revised ... by William Prynne.   fo.
London, for William Leake, 1657
Wing C6489.   **2130**

———————— The journals of all the parliaments during the reign of Queen Elizabeth ... Collected by Sir S.D'Ewes.   fo.
London, for John Starkey, 1682   Engr. fp. (port., Charrington p.55).   Wing D1250.   **2670**

———————— A perfect copy of all summons of the nobility to the great councils and parliaments. fo.
London, by S.R. for Robert Clavell, 1685
Wing D2491.   **2572**

———————— Placita Parlamentaria ... Authore G.Ryley. [*Known as the 'Vetus Codex'.*]   fo.
Londini, impensis Hen.Twiford & Thomæ Dring, 1661   Wing R2422.   **2121**

———————— A Proclamation. Whereas it hath pleased Almighty God ... to vouchsafe us a miraculous deliverance from Popery.   brs.
London, for James Partridge, Matthew Gillyflower, and Samuel Heyrick, 1689
Wing E2200.   **1967(4)**

———————— The severall humble petitions of D.Bastwicke, 1641.
See SEVERAL.   **1429(9)**

———————— A supplement to the collection of the debates and proceedings in Parliament, in 1694, and 1695. Upon the inquiry into the late briberies and corrupt practices.   4to.
London, 1695   [Consutilia VII]
Wing E2317 (part of E1281).   **1433(15)**

Parliament. Lords

———————— The humble address of the ... Lords ... presented to His Majesty ... the eighth day of December, 1697.   fo.
London, by Charles Bill, and the executrix of Thomas Newcomb, 1697   **2156(6)**

———————— Proceedings and resolution of the ... Lords ... 9th of May, 1702. Upon part of the preface to the book intituled 'The history of the last Parliament ... 1700'.   fo.
London, by Charles Bill, and the executrix of Thomas Newcomb, 1702   **959(2)**

———————— The vote, or resolution and orders made by the Lords relating to William Fuller and the books published by him.   fo.
London, by Charles Bill and the executrix of Thomas Newcomb, 1701   [Narratives & Tryals VII]   **2255(6)**

———————— The whole series of all that hath been transacted in the House of Peers, concerning the Popish plot.   2 pts.   8vo.
London, by J.Redmayne, 1681
Wing E2876.   **1249**

Parliament. Commons

———————— A collection of the substance of several speeches and debates made in the ... House of Commons relating to the horrid Popish plot. fo.
London, for Francis Smith, 1681   [Narratives & Tryals III]   Wing E2538.   **2251(37)**

———————— A coppy of the journal-book of the House of Commons for the sessions ... begun ... the 21 day of October 1678.   8vo.
London, 1680   Wing E2544.   **1013**

———————— The humble address of the House of Commons to the King. No.4.   brs.
By John Leake for Timothy Goodwin, and Thomas Cockerill, 1697   **2156(7)**

———————— A list of the knights, citizens, burgesses, and barons of the Cinque-Ports ... return'd to serve in the Parliament ... 1679.   brs.
London, for Nathaniel Ponder, and Nathaniel Thompson, 1679   [Parliamentary votes and papers 1679, 1681]   Wing C2452.   **2137(1)**

———————— The Oxford list of the names of the knights, citizens, burgesses, and barons of the Cinque Ports, that are returned to serve in the Parliament assembled at Oxford the twenty first of March, 1680/1   brs.
Oxford, by L.Lichfield, for John Starkey, London, 1681   [Parliamentary votes and papers 1679, 1681]   Wing O857.   **2137(27)**

———————— The several debates of the House of Commons, in the reign of the late King James II ... relating to the establishment of the militia. 4to.
London, 1697   [Consutilia VII]
Wing E2725.   **1433(22)**

———————— A true copy of the journal-book of the last Parliament, begun ... the 6th day of March, 1678/9.   8vo.
London, 1680   Wing E2748.   **1250**

———————— Votes of the House of Commons. 21 Oct.1680 – 10 Jan.1680 [1681]. Nos 1-58. fo.

London, by the assignes of John Bill, Thomas
Newcomb, and Henry Hills [etc.], 1680 [1681]
[Parliamentary votes and papers 1679, 1681]
Wing E2764.   2137(3-21)

———————— Votes of the House of Commons,
at Oxford. 21-28 die Martii, 1680/1. Nos 1-5.   fo.
London, for Gabriel Kunholt, published by Langley Curtis, 1681   [Parliamentary votes and
papers 1679, 1681]   Wing E2765.   2137(30)

Statutes, Collections

———————— A collection of acts and ordinances
of general use, made ... 1640 ... unto ... 1656. By
H.Scobell. 2 pts. fo.
London, printed by Henry Hills and John Field,
1658(1657)   Wing E873; Diary 23, 30 Nov.
1663.   2520

———————— An exact abridgment of publick
acts and ordinances ... 1640 to ... 1656 ... By W.
Hughes. 4to.
London, by T.R. for H.Twyford, T.Dring and J.
Place, 1657   Wing E915.   1654

———————— The great boke of statutes ...
from ... Edwarde the Thyrde tyll ... Henry the
.viii. fo.
(London, by Wyllyam Meddelton) [1545]
STC 9288; Duff p.58.   1992(1)

———————— The second volume, conteyninge
those statutes, whiche haue ben made in the tyme
of ... Henry the Eyght. fo.
Londini, in ædibus Thomæ Bertheleti, 1543
(– 1546)   STC 9301; Duff p.59-64.   1993

———————— The statutes at large in paragraphs
... by J.Keble. 2 vols. fo.
London, by the assigns of John Bill, Thomas Newcomb, and Henry Hills [etc.], 1681
Wing K118.   2765-6

———————— A table to al the statutes made
from ... Edwarde the .vi. unto this present .xii.
yeare of ... Queene Elizabeth.   fo.
[London] in ædibus Richardi Tottelli [1570]
STC 9546; Duff p.64.   1994(1)

Statutes, Chronological

———————— Anno decimonono Henrici
septimi. Statuta.   fo.
(London, by me Rycharde Pynson) [1505?]
STC 9356; Duff p.59.   1992(2)

———————— Anno primo Edwardi Sexti.
Statutes.   fo.
(Londini, in ædibus Richardi Graftoni, 1548)
STC 9418; Duff p.64.   1994(1A)

———————— Anno secundo et tertio Eduardi
Sexti. Actes.   fo.
[London] (Richardus Graftonus excudebat, 1552)
STC 9427; Duff p.64.   1994(2)

———————— Anno III. et IIII. Eduuardi Sexti.
Actes.   fo.
(London, by Richard Grafton, 1553)
STC 9431; Duff p.65.   1994(3)

———————— Anno quinto et sexto Eduuardi
Sexti. Actes.   fo.
[London] (Richardus Graftonus excudebat, 1552)
STC 9435; Duff p.65.   1994(4)

———————— Anno septimo Eduuardi Sexti.
Actes.   fo.
(Londini, in ædibus Richardi Graftoni excusum,
1553)   STC 9440; Duff p.65.   1994(5)

———————— Anno Mariæ primo. Actes made
in the Parliament ... the second day of Aprill.   fo.
(Londini, excusum in ædibus Iohannis Cawodi,
1554)   STC 9441; Duff p.65.   1994(6)

———————— Anno Maria [sic] primo. Actes
made ... the .v. day of October.   fo.
(Londini, excusum in ædibus Iohannis Cawoodi,
1554)   STC 9446; Duff p.66.   1994(6A)

———————— Anno secundo & tertio Philippi &
Mariæ. Actes.   fo.
(Londini, excusum in ædibus Iohannis Cawodi,
1555)   STC 9454; Duff p.66.   1994(7)

———————— Anno quarto et quinto, Philippi
& Mariæ. Actes.   fo.
(Londini, excusum in ædibus Iohannis Cawodi,
1558)   STC 9457.   1994(8)

———————— Anno primo Reginæ Elizabethe.
fo.
(London, by Richarde Iugge) 1559
STC 9461.   1994(9)

———————— Anno quinto Reginæ Elizabethe.
fo.
(London, by Richarde Iugge) 1563
STC 9467.   1994(10)

———————— Anno octauo Reginæ Elizabethe.
fo.
(London, by Rycharde Jugge) 1566
STC 9470.   1994(11)

———————— Anno .xiij. Reginæ Elizabethe.
fo.
(London, by Richarde Jugge and John Cawod)
1571   STC 9475.   1995(1)

———————— Anno .xiiij. Reginæ Elizabethe.
fo.
(London, by Richarde Jugge) 1572
STC 9478.   1995(2)

———————— Anno .xviii. Reginæ Elizabethe.
fo.
[London, R.Jugge] 1575   Wants sigs ²A-C, ³A.
STC 9483.   1995(3)

[ENGLAND]

——————— Anno xxiii. Reginæ Elizabethæ.
(– A table of certayne actes.)   fo.
London, by Christopher Barker, 1581
STC 9484.   **1995(4)**

——————— Anno xxvii. Reginæ Elizabethæ.
fo.
London, by Christopher Barker, 1585
STC 9485.   **1995(5)**

——————— Anno xxix. Reginæ Elizabethæ.
fo.
London, by Christopher Barker, 1587
STC 9487.   **1995(6)**

——————— Anno xxxj. Reginæ Elizabethæ.
fo.
London, by the deputies of Christopher Barker,
1589   STC 9488.   **1995(7)**

——————— Anno xxxv. Reginæ Elizabethæ.
fo.
London, by the deputies of Christopher Barker,
1593   STC 9491.   **1995(8)**

——————— Anno xxxix. Reginæ Elizabethæ.
fo.
London, by the deputies of Christopher Barker
[1597]   STC 9493.   **1995(9)**

——————— Anno xliij. Reginæ Elizabethæ.
fo.
London, by Robert Barker (1601)
STC 9496.   **1995(10)**

——————— Anᵒ reg. Iacobi, Regis ... primo.
fo.
London, by Robert Barker, 1604
STC 9500.   **1995(11)**

——————— Anᵒ regni Iacobi ... 3ᵒ.   fo.
London, by Robert Barker, 1606
STC 9502.   **1995(12)**

——————— Anᵒ regni Iacobi, Regis ... 4ᵒ. fo.
London, by Robert Barker, 1607
STC 9505.   **1995(13)**

——————— The Act of tonnage and poundage,
and book of rates.   12mo.
London, by the assigns of John Bill and Christo-
pher Barker, 1675   Wing E1147A.   **572**

——————— Anno regni Caroli II ... tricesimo
secundo.   fo.
London, by the assigns of John Bill, Thomas New-
comb, and Henry Hills, 1680/1   [Parliamentary
votes and papers, 1679, 1681]   **2137(22)**

——————— Anno regni Jacobi II. Regis ...
primo. At the Parliament begun at Westminster
the nineteenth day of May, A.D. 1685.   fo.

London, by the assigns of John Bill deceas'd:
and by Henry Hills, and Thomas Newcomb,
1685   Without 'An Act for erecting a new
parish ... within the Liberty of Westminster'.
                                            1966

——————— Anno regni Willielmi et Mariæ ...
primo. [Acts of Session 1.]   fo.
London, by Charles Bill and Thomas Newcomb,
1688 (1689)   Wing E1237.   **1967(1)**

——————— Anno regni Gulielmi et Mariæ ...
primo. [Acts of Session 2.]   fo.
London, by Charles Bill and Thomas Newcomb,
1689   **1967(5)**

——————— Anno regni Gulielmi III ... octavo.
(An Act to attaint Sir John Fenwick, Baronet, of
high treason.)   fo.
London, by Charles Bill, and the executrix of
Thomas Newcomb, 1696
Wing E1251.   **2180(3)**

——————— Anno regni Gulielmi III ... decimo.
(An Act for granting an aid to His Majesty, for
disbanding the army.)   fo.
London, by Charles Bill, and the executrix of
Thomas Newcomb, 1699
Wing E1252.   **2179(2)**

——————— Anno regni Gulielmi III ... XII. &
XIII. (An Act for the better settling and preserv-
ing the Library kept in the house at Westminster,
called Cotton-house.)   4to.
London, by Charles Bill, and the executrix of
Thomas Newcomb, deceas'd, 1701   **2730(2)**

Treaties

——————— Several treaties of peace and
commerce concluded between the late King [i.e.
Charles II] ... and other princes and states.   4to.
London, by the assigns of John Bill, and by Henry
Hills and Thomas Newcomb, 1685
Wing C3604A.   **1440(1)**

——————— Articles of peace and commerce
between ... James II ... and ... the Douletli Basha,
Aga and governours of ... Algiers.   4to.
[*London*] *by Thomas Newcomb in the Savoy*,
1687   Wing J153.   **1440(2)**

——————— Traitté d'alliance defensive, entre
l'Angleterre et les Estats Generaux, conclu le 3.
Mars 1678.   4to.
'*Cologne, chez Pierre Marteau*', 1680
MS note (undated) by W.Bridgeman: 'I find this
agrees with the Copy I have by mee'.   **1440(4)**

——————— Treaty of Ryswick, 1697.
See FRANCE. *Treaties.*

ENGLAND'S fair garland.   8vo.
[*London*] *for R.Kell*, 1687   [Penny-Merri-
ments II]   Woodcut.   **363(48)**

ENGLAND'S glory, or, an exact catalogue of the lords of His Majesties ... Privy Councel, 1660.
See BROOKE (Nathaniel). **606(2)**

ENGLAND'S great concern. In the perpetual settlement of a commission of accounts.   4to.
London, printed for D.Brown, and sold by J.Nutt,
1702   [Consutilia XI]   **1437(4)**

ENGLISH (The) princess, 1667.
See CARYLL (John).   **1604(8)**

ENQUIRY (An) into the measures of submission to the supream authority, 1693.
See BURNET (Gilbert), Bp of Salisbury.   **1433(6)**

ENYEDI (György). Explicationes locorum Veteris et Novi Testamenti, ex quibus Trinitatis doctrina stabiliri solet.   4to.
[Groningen, c.1670]   **1404**

[EON (Jean)]. Le commerce honorable, ou considerations politiques.   4to.
Nantes, par Guillaume Le Monnier, 1646 (1647)
1674

EPICTETUS. Enchiridion, unà cum Cebetis Thebani Tabula. Accessêre Arriani Commentariorum ... libri IV. Omnia Hieronymo Wolfio interprete. *Gk & Lat.*   8vo.
Cantabrigiæ, ex Academiæ typographeo, impensis
G.Morden, 1655   Wing E3144.   **696**

——————— Enchiridion, 1640.
See SIMPLICIUS. Commentarius in Enchiridion Epicteti [*with the text*].   **1548**

——————— Epicteti Enchiridion, made English in a poetical paraphrase, by E.Walker.   8vo.
London, by Ben.Griffin, for Sam.Keble, 1692
Engr. fp., port.   Wing W3149.   **829**

——————— [*Enchiridion.*] Epictetus his Morals, with Simplicius his comment. Made English ... By G.Stanhope.   8vo.
London, for Richard Sare, and Joseph Hindmarsh,
1694   Wing E3153.   **969**

ERASMUS (Desiderius). Colloquia ... accurante C.Schrevelio.   8vo.
Lugd.Batavorum, apud Franciscum Hackium,
1655   Engr. title-page.   **1117**

——————— [De civilitate morum puerilium.]
Lat. & Engl.   8vo.
(*London, by John Wallye, 1554*)   Wants A1.
STC 10469; Duff p.21.   **209(4)**

[———————] [*De civilitate morum puerilium.*]
The ciuilitie of childehode ... translated oute of French into Englysh, by Thomas Paynell.   8vo.
(*London, by John Tisdale*) 1560   MS addition on frontispiece: 'John Hawll oner hereoff'.   **46(3)**

——————— De conscribendis epistolis ...
Ed. nova.   12mo.
Lugduni Batavorum, ex officina Ioannis Maire,
1645   **27**

——————— [*De morte declamatio.*] A treatise perswadynge a man patientlye to suffre the deth of his frende.   8vo.
[*London*] (*Thomas Berthelet excudebat*) [1532]
STC 10510; Duff p.22.   **368(3)**

——————— De octo orationis partium constructione libellus (1534). [*Written by W.Lily and revised by Erasmus.*]
See LILY (William).   **424(2)**

——————— Enchiridion militis christiani ...
Ejusdem de præparatione ad mortem liber, cum aliis nonnullis.   12mo.
Cantabrigiæ, ex officinâ Joh.Hayes, impensis Guil.
Graves, 1685   Engr. fp.   Wing E3200.   **56**

——————— Epistolarum libri XXXI, et P. Melancthonis libri IV. Quibus adjiciuntur Th.Mori & Lud. Vivis epistolæ.   2 vols.   fo.
Londini, excudebant M.Flesher & R.Young,
sumptibus Adriani Vlacq, 1642
Engr. fp. (port., Charrington p.57).
Wing M1635.   **2545-6**

——————— Μωριας ἐγκωμιον. Stultitiæ laus. D.Erasmi declamatio cum commentariis G.Listrii, et figuris J.Holbenii.   8vo.
Basileæ, typis Genathianis, 1676
Engr. title-page, ports (Charrington pp.57, 81), pls.   **1258**

——————— [*Moriæ encomium.*] The praise of folie ... Englished by Sir T.Chaloner.   4to.
(*London, Thomas Berthelet, MDLXIX* [*sic*]) 1549
STC 10500.   **1276**

ERBERY (William). The Lord of Hosts: or, God guarding the camp.   4to.
London, by Tho.Newcomb for Giles Calvert, 1648
[Sermons Polemical III]
Wing E3229.   **1181(18)**

ERCKER (Lazarus). Fleta minor ... In two parts. The first contains assays of L.Erckern ... transl. into English. The second contains essays on metallick words ... By Sir J.Pettus.   fo.
London, for the Author, by Thomas Dawks, 1683
Engr. fp. (port., Charrington p.135), pls.
Wing P1906.   **2559**

ERRA PATER. Pronostication for euer.   8vo.
[*London*] (*by me Robert Wyer*) [1538?]
STC 10516; Duff p.22.   MS notes in unidentified 16th-century hands on title-page and elsewhere.
209(6)

——————— Lilly's new Erra Pater [1683].
See LILLY (William).   **363(19)**

ESCLAVO (El) de Maria. Comedia famosa. De don Pedro Calderon. [*Authorship denied by Calderón.*] [*Seville, Tomé de Dios Miranda, c.1678*] Gaselee 29. **1553(6)**

ESCOBAR (Juan de). Cinco romances famosos. El primero, del Cosario Barba Roxa. 4to. *Madrid, por Andres Garcia de la Iglesia, vendese en casa de Iuan Calatayu*, 1671 Gaselee 54; Wilson p.318. **1545(69)**

[ESCOFFIER (Charles)]. Description des antiquitez de la ville et cité d'Orange. Par M.C.E.P.C. 8vo. *Orange, par Claude Marchy*, 1700 **1638(3)**

ESPAGNE (Jean d'). Nouvelles observations sur le symbole de la foy. 8vo. *Londres, chez R.R. pour Thomas Whitaker*, 1647 Wing E3265. **413(2)**

———————— Shibbóleth, ou, reformation de quelques passages ... de la Bible. 8vo. *Londres, chez Thomas Maxey, pour Antoine Wiliamson*, 1653 Wing E3269; Diary 24 Feb. 1663/4. **413(1)**

ESPINOSA (Andrés de). Consideraciones para la conversion de vn pecador, en tres romances. 4to. (*Seuilla, por Juan Vejarano, à costa de Lucas Martin de Hermosa*, 1682) Gaselee 55; Wilson p.236. **1545(22)**

ESPRIT (L') de la France et les maximes de Louis XIV. Découvertes à l'Europe. Reveu corrigez & augmentez. 12mo. 'Cologne, chez Pierre Marteau', 1688 **98**

ESPRIT (L') de Mr Arnaud, 1684. *See* JURIEU (Pierre). **525-6**

ESSAY (An) for a new translation of the Bible, 1702. *See* LE CÈNE (Charles). **1299(1)**

ESSAY (An) of the profits incident to the Mayoralty of London, yearly. brs. [*London, c.1690*] Bound in at end. **2476**

ESSAY (An) on the certainty and causes of the earth's motion, 1698. *See* SHEERES (Sir Henry). **1139**

ESSAY (An) on the East India trade, 1696. *See* DAVENANT (Charles). **1459**

ESSAY (An) on the usefulness of mathematical learning, 1701. *See* STRONG (Martin). **1090**

ESSAY on ways and means (*Author of*) *See* DAVENANT (Charles).

ESSAY (An) touching the gravitation ... of fluid bodies, 1673. *See* HALE (Sir Matthew). **366**

ESSAY (An) upon the probable methods of making a people gainers in the ballance of trade, 1699. *See* DAVENANT (Charles). **1492**

ESSAY (An) upon ways and means of supplying the war, 1695. *See* DAVENANT (Charles). **1324**

ESSAYS upon I. The ballance of power. II. The right of making war, peace, and alliances. III. Universal monarchy, 1701. *See* DAVENANT (Charles). **1378**

ESSEX (Arthur Capel, 1st Earl of). The Earl of Essex's speech at the delivery of the petition to the King, Jan.25.1680. brs. *London, for Francis Smith*, 1681 [Parliamentary votes and papers 1679, 1681] Wing E3305. **2137(23)**

ESTA obra contiene dos letras famosas ... La primera, del bayle de las damas de Madrid orillas de Mançanares. La segunda, los sueltos cauallos, glossado. 4to. (*Sevilla*) *a costa de Lucas Martin de Hermosa* (*por Iuan Vejarano*, 1681) Gaselee 96; Wilson p.316. **1545(67)**

ESTIBIUS PSYCHALETHES, *pseud.* *See* COWARD (William).

ESTIENNE (Charles). De re hortensi libellus. 8vo. *Lugduni, apud hæredes Simonis Vincentii* (*excudebant Melchior et Gaspar Trechsel*), 1536 Adams S1731. **419(3)**

ESTIENNE (Henri). L'introduction au traité de la conformité des merueilles anciennes auec les modernes. Ou, traité preparatif à l'Apologie pour Herodote. 8vo. *Anuers, par Henrich Wandellin*, 1568 Adams S1772. **707**

———————— [*L'introduction au traité.*] A world of wonders; or an introduction to a treatise ... Translated ... by R.C[arew]. fo. *London*, [*R.Field*] *for Iohn Norton*, 1607 STC 10553. **2034**

ESTRADA Y BOCA NEGRA (Matias de). Aqui se contiene vna graciosa contienda que en la ciudad de Ualencia tuvieren vn sastre, y vn zapatero en materia de su oficio. 4to. *Madrid, impresso por la viuda de Melehor Clegre* [*sic*] (*vendese en casa de la viuda de Iuan de Valdes*), 1672 Gaselee 56; Wilson p.312. **1545(63)**

ESTWICK (Nicolas). Christ's submission to His Fathers will ... A sermon. 4to. *London, by George Miller*, 1644 [Sermons Polemical III] Wing E3358. **1181(19)**

ETERNAL (The) gospel once more testified unto
and vindicated.   8vo.
London, for Allen Banks, 1681
Wing E3365.   **442**

ETHEREGE (Sir George). The comical revenge;
or, love in a tub.   4to.
London, for Henry Herringman, 1664   [Loose
Plays II]   Wing E3368.   **1604(5)**

———————— She wou'd if she cou'd, a comedy.
4to.
London, for H.Herringman, 1668
[Loose Plays II]   Wing E3378.   **1604(9)**

ETTEN (Hendrik van), *pseud.*
See LEURECHON (Jean).

EUCLID. The elements of Euclid [bks I, VI, XI
and XII], explained and demonstrated ... By C.F.
Milliet de Chales ... Done out of French ... by
R.Williams.   12mo.
London, for Philip Lea, 1685   Engr. fp. (port.),
diagrams.   Wing E3399.   **692**

EUSEBIUS, Pamphili. The history of the Church,
... to ... 594 ... By Eusebius Pamphilus ... Socrates
Scholasticus ... and Evagrius Scholasticus.   fo.
*Cambridge, by John Hayes, for Han.Sawbridge,
London*, 1683   Wing E3423.   **2660**

EUSEBIUS, Romanus, *pseud.*
See MABILLON (Jean).

EVANCE (Daniel). The noble order; or the honour
which God confers on them that honour him ...
a sermon ... January 28.1645.   4to.
London, by T.W. for Abel Roper, 1646
[Sermons Polemical III]   Wing E3443.
                                      1181(20)

EVELYN (John). Acetaria. A discourse of sallets.
8vo.
London, printed for B.Tooke, 1699
Wing E3480.   **613**

———————— Kalendarium hortense; or, the
gard'ners almanac ... (— The garden, by A.Cowley.)
9th ed.
*London, printed for Rob.Scott, Ri.Chiswell, Geo.
Sawbridge, and Benj.Tooke*, 1699   Engr. fp.
Wing E3500.   **666**

———————— Navigation and commerce, their
original and progress.   8vo.
London, printed by T.R. for Benj.Tooke, 1674
Wing E3504.   **1060**

———————— Numismata. A discourse of medals
antient and modern ... To which is added a
digression concerning physiognomy.   fo.
London, for Benj.Tooke, 1697   99 engrs.
Wing E3505.   **2323**

———————— A philosophical discourse of earth,
relating to the culture and improvement of it.
London, printed for John Martyn, 1676
Wing E3507.   **708**

———————— Publick employment and an active
life with all its appanages ... prefer'd to solitude.
By J.E.Esq; S.R.S.   8vo.
London, printed by J.M. for H.Herringman, 1667
Wing E3511; Diary 26 May 1667.   **461**

———————— Sculptura; or the history and art
of chalcography ... To which is annexed a new
manner of engraving or mezzo tinto, communi-
cated by ... Prince Rupert.   8vo.
*London, by J.C. for G.Beedle, and T.Collins, and
J.Crook*, 1662   Engr. title-page, engr. pl.,
mezzotint pl.   Wing E3513.   **868**

———————— Sylva, or, a discourse of forest-
trees ... Terra, a philosophical essay of earth ... To
which is annexed Pomona ... also Kalendarium
hortense.   3rd ed.   fo.
London, for John Martyn, 1679(1678)
Engr. pls. Inscribed by the author: 'For my most
honour'd Friend Samuell Pepys Esqr from his
most humble Servant'.   Wing E3518.   **2371**

EVERARD (Edmund). The depositions and
examination of Mr.Edmund Everard ... concerning
the horrid Popish plot.   fo.
London, for Dorman Newman, 1679
[Narratives & Tryals I]   Engr. pl. inserted.
Wing E3527.   **2249(5)**

———————— Discourses on the present state of
the Protestant princes of Europe.   fo.
London, for Dorman Newman, 1679
3 engr. pls inserted (port., Charrington p.107).
[Narratives & Tryals I]   Wing E3528.   **2249(6)**

EVERARDT (Job). An epitome of stenographie.
8vo.
[*London*] printed by M.S. for Lodowick Lloyd,
1658   [Short-hand Collection III]   Engr.
title-page, 25 engr. leaves.   Wing E3545;
Carlton p.72.   **402(12)**

EVERETT (George). Encouragement for seamen
and mariners: being a proposed method for ...
furnishing ... able seamen and mariners.   4to.
London, 1695   [Naval Pamphlets]
Wing E3546.   **1399(14)**

———————— The path-way to peace and profit
... a sure and certain way for ... building and
repairing [the] ... Navy.   4to.
London, for the author, sold by Randal Taylor,
1694   [Naval Pamphlets]   Wing E3548.
                                      1399(10)

EVERTSON (Gerrit).
See LARGE (A) and true discourse ... All written
aboord the ship of Captaine Gerrit Euertson
[1602?].   **1431(15)**

EXACT (An) abridgment of all the trials ...
published since the year 1678; relating to the
Popish, and pretended Protestant plots.   8vo.
London, by J.D. for Jonathan Robinson, 1690
MS index in hand of one of Pepys's clerks.
Wing N64.   **933**

EXACT (An) abridgment of all the tryals ...
relating to high treasons, piracies, &c. in the reigns
of ... William the III ... and ... Queen Anne.   8vo.
London, for Jonathan Robinson, and John Wyat,
1703.   **934**

EXACT (An) and most impartial accompt of the
... trial, and judgment ... of nine and twenty
regicides, 1660.
See NOTTINGHAM (Heneage Finch, Earl of).
1430(1)

EXACT (An) narrative and relation of His Most
Sacred Majesties escape from Worcester on the
third of September, 1651.   4to.
London, for G.Colborn, 1660   **2141(2)**

EXACT (An) relation of the several engagements
and actions of His Majesties fleet, under the
command of ... Prince Rupert.   4to.
London, for J.B., 1673   [Naval Pamphlets]
Wing E3696.   **1399(4)**

EXAMINATION (An) of Dr.Woodward's account
of the deluge, 1697.
See ARBUTHNOT (John).   **1242(2)**

EXCELLENCY (The) of theology, 1674.
See BOYLE (Hon. Robert).   **803**

EXCELLENT (The) and renowned history of the
famous Sir Richard Whittington.   12mo.
[*London?* c.1680]   [Penny-Merriments II]
Woodcut.   Title-page cropped.   **363(31)**

EXCERPTA ex tragœdiis et comœdiis Græcis ...
Emendata et Latinis versibus reddita ab H.Grotio.
4to.
Parisiis, apud Nicolaum Buon, 1626   **1787**

EXPEDIENT (An) propos'd: or the occasions of
the late controversie in Convocation consider'd,
1701.
See BINCKES (William), Dean of Lichfield.
1697(6)

EXPLANATION (An) of some passages in Dr.
Binckes's sermon, 1702.
See BINCKES (William), Dean of Lichfield.
1698(10)

EXPOSITION (The) given by my Lord Bishop of
Sarum ... examined, 1702.
See EDWARDS (Jonathan).   **1772(1)**

EXPOSITION (An) of the doctrine of the Church
of England, 1686.
See WAKE (William) Abp of Canterbury.
1544(2)

EXPOSITION (An) on the church-catechism, 1685.
See KEN (Thomas), Bp of Bath and Wells.   **1228**

EXQUEMELIN (Alexander Olivier). Bucaniers of
America; or, a true account of the ... assaults
committed ... upon ... the West Indies ... especially,
the ... exploits of Sir H.Morgan. (Vol.2: Containing
the ... voyage ... of Captain B.Sharp ... from the
original journal ... by ... B.Ringrose.)   2 vols.
4to.
London, for William Crooke, 1684-5   Engr. pls
& woodcuts.   Wing E3894, 3897.   **1875-6**

EXTON (John). The maritime dicæologie, or sea-
jurisdiction of England.   fo.
London, by Richard Hodgkinson, 1664
Wing E3902; Naval Minutes pp.59, 61, 66-7.
2439

EXTRAORDINARY (The) case of the Bp. of St.
David's, further clear'd and made plain.   4to.
[*London?*] 1703   [Consutilia XII]   **1438(2)**

EYQUEM (Mathurin), Sieur du Martineau. Le
pilote de l'onde vive, ou le secret du flux et reflux
de la mer.   12mo.
Paris, chez Jean Dhoury et chez l'autheur, 1678
Engr. pls.   **462**

F

F.(E.). The history ... of Edward II, 1680.
See FALKLAND (Henry Cary, Viscount).   **2260**

F.(R.). Christian religious meetings ... no seditious
conventicles [1664].
See FARNWORTH (Richard).   **1189(12)**

FABLES ancient and modern, 1700.
See DRYDEN (John).   **2442**

FABRETTI (Raffaello). De aquis et aquæductibus
veteris Romæ dissertationes tres.   4to.
Romæ, typis Ioannis Baptistæ Bussotti, 1680
Engr. pls, 3 engr. maps.   **1865**

FABRICIUS (Wilhelm). Lithotomia vesicæ; that is,
an accurate description of the stone in the bladder
... Done into English by N.C.   8vo.
London, by John Norton, to be sold by William
Harris, 1640   Engrs (diagrams).   STC 10658.
792

FABRO BREMUNDAN (Francisco). Viage del
rey ... Carlos II. al reyno de Aragon. Entrada de su
Magestad en Zaragoça.   4to.
Madrid, de Bernardo de Villa-Diego, 1680 (1677)
Engr. title-page.   Gaselee 57.   **1542(2)**

FABYAN (Robert). The chronicle ... newly
perused. And continued ... to thende of Queene
Mary.   2 pts.   fo.
London, by Jhon Kyngston, 1559
Wants a5, g5-6, h1.   STC 10664.   **2055**

FAIRCLOUGH (Samuel). The troublers troubled
... A sermon preached ... April, 4.1641.   4to.
London, by R.Cotes, for Henry Overton, 1641
[Sermons Polemical IV]   Wing F109.   **1182(1)**

FAIRFAX (Nathaniel). A treatise of the bulk and
selvedge of the world ... With an answer to
Tentamina de Deo, by S.P[arker].   8vo.
London, for Robert Boulter, 1674   Wing F131.
850

FAIRFAX (Thomas, 3rd Baron). Short memorials
of Thomas Lord Fairfax. Written by himself.   8vo.
London, printed for Ri.Chiswell, 1699
Wing F235.   **756**

FAITHFUL (A) account of some transactions in
... Convocation, 1702.
See ATTERBURY (Francis), Bp of Rochester.
1697(10)

FAITHFUL (A) account of what past in Convocation, 1702.
See ATTERBURY (Francis), Bp of Rochester.
1697(11)

[FAJARDO Y ACEVEDO (Antonio)]. El mejor
padre de pobres [c.1680].
See MEJOR (El) padre ...   **1553(22)**

FALCÓN (Felipe). Relacion que embio un sacer-
dote à su padre á Gibraltar.   4to.
(Sevilla, por Iuan Cabeças, 1679)
Gaselee 58; Wilson p.149.   **1545(9)**

FALCÓN (Lope). Curioso tratado de las orden-
anzas del tabaco.   4to.
*(Seuilla, por Juan Vejarano, à costa de Lucas
Martin de Hermosa)* [c.1680]
Gaselee 59; Wilson p.248.   **1545(32)**

——————— Exhortacion Christiana.   4to.
*Seuilla, por Juan Vejarano, à costa de Lucas
Martin de Hermosilla, 1682*
Gaselee 60; Wilson p.153.   **1545(12)**

FALDA (Giovanni Battista). Li giardini di Roma.
fo.
Romæ, Gio:Giacomo de Rossi [c.1670]
Engr. title-page, pls.   **2959(3)**

——————— Nuovi disegni dell'architettura
[1655].
See FERRERIO (Pietro). Palazzi di Roma.
2959(2)

[FALKLAND (Henry Cary, Viscount)]. The
history of the life, reign, and death of Edward II.
fo.

*London, by J.C. for Charles Harper, Samuel
Crouch, etc., 1680*   Engr. fp. (port., Charrington
p.52).   Wing F313.   **2260**

FAMILY. The familie of loue, 1608.
See MIDDLETON (Thomas).   **939(8)**

FAMOUS (The) and remarkable history of Sir
Richard Whittington [c.1680].
See HEYWOOD (Thomas).   **1192(12)**

FAMOUS (The) history of Aurelius, 1686.
See S.(J.).   **362(14)**

FAMOUS (The) history of Don Quixote, 1686.
See CERVANTES SAAVEDRA (Miguel de).
363(29)

FAMOUS (The) history of Frier Bacon.   4to.
*London, by M.Clark, to be sold by T.Passinger,
1679*   [Vulgaria III]   Woodcut.
Wing F373.   **1192(13)**

FAMOUS (The) history of Montelion, 1687.
See FORDE (Emanuel).   **1192(1)**

FAMOUS (The) history of ... Prince Palmerin of
England, 1685.
See HURTADO (Luís).   **1190(1)**

FAMOUS (The) history of the seven champions of
Christendom, 1686-7.
See JOHNSON (Richard).   **1191(1)**

FANNANT (Thomas). An historicall narration of
the manner and forme of that ... Parliament ...
begun ... 1386.   4to.
[*London*] 1641   [Consutilia III]
Wing F415.   **1429(13)**

FARDOIL (Nicolas). Harangues discours et lettres.
3 pts.   4to.
*Paris, chez Sebastien Cramoisy, & Sebastien Mabre-
Cramoisy, 1665*   **1893**

FARIA (Francisco de). The information of
Francisco de Faria, delivered at the ... House of
Commons, Nov.1, 1680.   fo.
*London, by the assigns of John Bill, Thomas New-
comb, and Henry Hills, 1680*   [Narratives &
Tryals III]   Wing F425.   **2251(15)**

FARIN (François). Histoire de la ville de Rouen.
3 vols.   12mo.
Rouen, chez Iacques Herault, 1668   **342-4**

——————— La Normandie chrestienne, ou
l'histoire des archevesques de Rouen qui sont au
catalogue des saints.   4to.
Roüen, chez Louys du Mesnil, 1659   **1785**

FARNABY (Thomas). Index rhetoricus et orat-
orius ... Ed. novissima.   12mo.
Amstelodami, apud Ioannem Ianssonium, 1648
Diary 15 May 1660.   **81**

[FARNWORTH (Richard)]. Christian religious meetings, allowed by the liturgie, are no seditious conventicles.   4to.
[*London*, 1664]   [Liturgick Controversies III]
Wing F476.   **1189(12)**

FARTHING (John). Short-writing shortned.   8vo.
London, printed for Tho.Parkhurst, 1684
[Short-hand Collection IV]   10 engr. ll.
Wing F533; Carlton p.69.   **860(9)**

FASTI magistratuum et triumphorum Romanorum, 1617-18.
See GOLTZ (Hubert).   **2665**

FEBVRE (Michel), *pseud*. Theatre de la Turquie.
4to.
Paris, chez Edmé Couterot, 1682   **1960**

FEDERICI (Cesare). The voyage and trauaile: of M.C.Frederick ... into the East India ... Out of Italian, by T.H(ickock).   4to.
London, Richard Jones and Edward White, 1588
[Consutilia V]   STC 10746.   **1431(17)**

FÉLIBIEN (André). Des principes de l'architecture, de la sculpture, de la peinture et des autres arts.
2e éd.   4to.
Paris, chez la veuve de Jean Baptiste Coignard et Jean Baptiste Coignard fils, 1690
65 engr. pls.   **1957**

[——————] Description de l'abbaye de la Trappe.   2e éd.   12mo.
Paris, chez Christophe Jornel, 1682   **95**

[FELL (John), Bp of Oxford]. Grammatica rationis.   12mo.
Oxonii, e theatro Sheldoniano, 1697   Engr. title-page, diagrams.   Wing F611.   **410**

—————— A specimen of the several sorts of letter given to the University by Dr.J.Fell. To which is added the letter given by Mr.F.Junius. (— An account of the matrices, punchions, &c.)
8vo.
Oxford, printed at the Theatre, 1693
Wing F622.   **1398(5)**

FEMALE (The) ramblers; or, a fairing for cuckolds.   8vo.
[*London*] for *J.Wright, J.Clarke, W.Thackeray* [*etc.*], 1683   [Penny-Merriments I]
Woodcut.   **362(26)**

FÉNELON (François de Salignac de La Mothe), Abp of Cambrai. Les avantures de Telemaque, fils d'Ulysse. (— Les avantures d'Aristonoüs.)
3 vols in 2. [*Various eds*]   12mo.
La Haye, chez Adrian Moetjens, 1699   **229-30**

—————— Explication des maximes des saints sur la vie intérieure ... éd. nouvelle.   12mo.
Amsterdam, chez Henri Wetstein, 1698   **454**

FENWICK (Sir John). The tryal, attainder, or condemnation of Sir John Fenwick.   fo.
The Hague, 1697   Wing T2172.   **2180(1)**

—————— [Another copy.]
[Narratives & Tryals VI]   **2254(12)**

FER (Nicolas de). Les forces de l'Europe, ou description des principales villes; avec leurs fortifications.   2 vols (vol.1 in 6 pts).   fo.
Paris, chez l'auteur, 1693-5   Engr. title-page, engr. pls.   [Vol.2 consists of a collection of engr. plates, of which some may belong to 'Les forces de l'Europe'.]   **2709-10**

FERGUSON (Robert). A large review of the summary view, of the Articles exhibited against the Bp. of St.David's.   4to.
[*London*?] 1702   [Consutilia XII]   **1438(1)**

[FERNÁNDEZ (Jerónimo)]. The honour of chivalry. Or, the famous and delectable history of Don Bellianis of Greece. [*A translation of part of Book 1, based on an Italian version of the Spanish original.*] (The second and third part. Written by J.S. [i.e. John Shirley].)   4to.
London, for Tho.Passinger, 1683
[Vulgaria I]   Wing F780, S3507.   **1190(2)**

FERNÁNDEZ DE NAVARRETE (Pedro). Conservacion de monarquias. Discursos politicos sobre le gran consulta que el Consejo hizo a Felipe Tercero.   fo.
Madrid, en la Imprenta Real, 1626   Engr. title-page.   Gaselee 62.   **2108(1)**

FERNÁNDEZ DE QUIRÓS (Pedro). Terra Australis incognita, or a new southerne discoverie.
4to.
London, for Iohn Hodgetts, 1617
[Consutilia V]   STC 10822.   **1431(20)**

FERRERIO (Pietro). Palazzi di Roma de' piu celebri architetti disegnati da P.Ferrerio. (Libro secondo: Nuovi disegni dell'architetture, e piante de' palazzi ... disegnati ... da G.B.Falda.)
2 vols in 1.   fo.
(*Romæ, Gio.Jacomo Rossi*)[1655]   Engr. title-pages, 100 engr. pls.   **2959(1-2)**

FEUILLET (Raoul Auger). Choregraphie ou l'art de décrire la dance.   4to.
Paris, chez l'auteur, et chez Michel Brunet (*de l'imprimerie de Gilles Paulus Du Mesnil*), 1700
24 engr. pls (diagrams).   **1871(1)**

—————— Recueil de dances.   4to.
Paris, chez l'auteur, et chez Michel Brunet, 1700
Engr.   **1871(2)**

—————— *For dances composed by L.G. Pécour and published by Feuillet.* see PÉCOUR (Louis Guillaume).

[FIELD (John)]. An admonition to the Parliament. 8vo.
[*Wandsworth*, 1572]   STC 10848.   **209(3)**

FIESTAS que celebro de S.Maria la blanca, Capilla de la Sta. iglesia metropolitana ... de Sevilla ... En favor del purissimo mysterio de la Concepcion sin culpa original de Maria Santissima nuestra Señora.   4to.
(*Sevilla, por Iuan Gomez de Blas*, 1666)
Gaselee 63.   **1543(2)**

FIGURE (The) of seaven [1686].
See POOR ROBIN.   **362(34)**

[FILMER (Sir Robert), Bart]. The free-holders grand inquest touching ... the King and his Parliament.   4to.
[*London*] *printed in the three and twentieth year of the raign of* ... *King Charles* [1648]
[Consutilia IV]   Wing F912.   **1430(16)**

————————— The free-holders grand inquest ... To which are added observations on forms of government.   8vo.
London, 1679   Engr. fp. (port., Charrington p.32).   Wing F913.   **1098**

————————— Patriarcha: or the natural power of kings.   8vo.
London, printed, and are to be sold by Walter Davis, 1680   Engr. fp. (port.).   Wing F922.   **1073**

FINCH (Leopold William). A sermon preach'd ... May 29th 1701.   4to.
London, for Thomas Bennet, 1701
[Convocation Pamphlets XII].   **1698(8)**

FINETT (Sir John). Finetti Philoxenis: som choice observations ... touching the reception, and precedence ... of forren ambassadors in England. 8vo.
London, by T.R. for H.Twyford and G.Bedell, 1656   Wing F947.   **556**

FIORE di virtu.
See BOOK. The boke of wysdome.   **19(2)**

FIORI (Giacomo).   *See* FLORUS (Jacobus).

FIRMIN (Giles). Stablishing against shaking ... Being the substance of one sermon preached Feb.17.1655.   4to.
London, by J.G. for Nathaniel Webb and William Grantham, 1656
[Sermons Polemical IV]   Wing F967.   **1182(2)**

FIRST (The) part of Dr Faustus, abbreviated and brought into verse.   12mo.
[*London*] *by J.M. for J.Deacon, and C.Dennisson* [c.1680]   [Penny-Merriments I]   Woodcut.   **362(54)**

FIRST (The) part of the pleasant and princely history of the gentle-craft [c.1685].
See DELONEY (Thomas).   **1193(12)**

FIRST (The) search: after one grand cause of the wrath of God ... in the use of the ... liturgie.   4to.
London, by Robert White [1644]   [Liturgick Controversies II]   Fore-edge cropped.
Wing F981.   **1188(17)**

FISHER (Ambrose). A defence of the liturgie of the Church of England.   4to.
London, by W.S[tansby] for Robert Milbourne, 1630   [Liturgick Controversies I]
STC 10885.   **1187(5)**

FISHER (John), St, Cardinal. This treatyse concernynge the fruytful saynges of Dauyd ... in the seuen penytencyall psalmes.
(*London, by Wynkyn de Worde*, 1509) [1515?]
STC 10903a; Duff p.23.   **1036(1)**

FITZGERALD (   ). A short narrative of Mr Fitz-Gerald, 1680.
See PHILALETHES.   **2251(7)**

FITZGERALD (David). A narrative of the Irish Popish plot.   fo.
London, for Tho.Cockerill, 1680   [Narratives & Tryals III]   Wing F1072.   **2251(18)**

FITZGERALD (John). The narrative of Mr.J.Fitz-Gerrald. [*Preface signed* H.P.]   fo.
London, for Richard Janeway, 1681
[Narratives & Tryals III]   Wing F1074; P31.   **2251(19)**

FITZHARRIS (Edward). The arraignment and plea of Edw.Fitz-Harris ... Kings-Bench ... Easter term, 1681.   fo.
London, for Fr.Tyton, and Tho.Basset, 1681
[Narratives & Tryals IV]   Wing A3746.   **2252(16)**

————————— The confession of E.Fitz-Harys ... July 1, 1681 ... together with his last speech.   fo.
London, for S.Carr, 1681   [Narratives & Tryals IV]   Wing F1092.   **2252(18)**

————————— The examination of Edw.Fitzharris, relating to the Popish plot ... 10 March, 1680/1. fo.
London, for Thomas Fox, 1681   [Parliamentary votes and papers 1679, 1681]
Wing E3717.   **2137(31)**

————————— [Another copy.]
[Narratives & Tryals III]   **2251(20)**

————————— The tryal and condemnation of E.Fitz-Harris, for high treason ... Also the tryal ... of Dr O.Plunket.   fo.
London, for Francis Tyton and Thomas Basset, 1681   [Narratives & Tryals IV]
Wing T2140.   **2252(17)**

FIVE cases of conscience, 1666.
See SANDERSON (Robert), Bp of Lincoln.   **529**

FIVE letters concerning the inspiration of the
Holy Scriptures, 1690.
See LE CLERC (Jean).   **481**

FIVE (The) strange wonders of the world, 1683.
See PRICE (Lawrence).   **363(2)**

FLÉCHIER (Valentin Esprit), Bp of Nîmes.
Histoire du Cardinal Ximenés.   2 vols in 1.
12mo.
Amsterdam, chez Henry Desbordes, 1693   Engr.
fp. (port., Charrington p.182).   **503**

FLEETWOOD (William), Bp of Ely. Inscriptionum
antiquarum sylloge, 1691.
See INSCRIPTIONUM antiquarum sylloge ...
1230

FLETCHER (John). Fifty comedies and tragedies,
1679.   *See* BEAUMONT (Francis).

[FLEUR (La) des commandements de Dieu ...]
Ihesus. The floure of the commaundementes of
god. [Transl. from the French.]   fo.
(*London, by Wynkyn de Worde*, 1510)
STC 23876; Duff p.24.   **2001**

FLORES historiarum per Matthæum Westmonas-
teriensem collecti ... Et Chronicon ex chronicis ...
auctore Florentio Wigorniensi.   fo.
*Francofurti, typis Wechelianis apud Claudium
Marnium & heredes Ioannis Aubrij*, 1601.   **2549**

FLORES (Lázaro). Arte de navegar, navegacion
astronomica, theorica y practica.   4to.
Madrid (por Iulian de Paredes, 1673)   Engrs,
diagrams.   Title-page cropped.   Gaselee 64.
1473(1)

FLORIO (John). Vocabolario italiano, 1659.
See TORRIANO (Giovanni).   **2445**

FLORUS (Jacobus). Aduersus impia & pestifera
Martini Lutheri dogmata.
[*Rome*] (*apud Antonium Bladū de [Asula]*, 1525)
Leaves A4-d4 defective.   Adams F639.   **1481(4)**

FLOWER. The floure of the commaundementes
of god, 1510.
See FLEUR (La) des commandements de Dieu.
2001

FLY: an almanack for ... 1688 ... Calculated for
the meridian of Kings-Lynn. (A prognostication,
for ... 1688.)   8vo.
Cambridge, printed by John Hayes, 1688
[Almanacks for the year 1688]   **425(9)**

FLY: an almanack for ... 1689 ... Calculated for
the meridian of Kings-Lynn. (A prognostication.)
8vo.

*London, printed by Ben.Griffin (J.Millet), for the
Company of Stationers*, 1689   [Almanacks for
the year 1689]   Wing A1692.   **426(11)**

[FOCQUEMBERGUES (Jean de)]. Le voyage de
Beth-el ... avec des prières et meditations de
Messieurs Drelincour, Dumolin.   12mo.
*Paris, et se vendent à Montpelier, chez Paul
Marret*, 1678   **6**

FOLKINGHAM (William). Brachygraphie, post-
writt. Or, the art of short-writing.   2nd ed.
8vo.
London, printed by Thomas Snodham, 1622
Folding tables.   [Short-hand Collection III]
Carlton p.26.   **402(8)**

FONTAINE (Nicolas). The history of the Old
(-New) Testament ... illustrated with sculptures ...
translated from the works of ... Le Sieur de
Royaumont [i.e. N.Fontaine].   2 vols.   fo.
*London, by Samuel Roycroft, for Richard Blome,
Mr.Nott [etc.]*, (1688-) 1690   Engr. pls.
Wing F1408, 1406.   **2935-6**

FORDE (Emanuel). The famous history of
Montelion, knight of the oracle.   4to.
*London, by J.R. and W.W. for W.Thackeray and
T.Passenger*, 1687   [Vulgaria III]   Woodcut.
Wing F1529.   **1192(1)**

————— The most famous, delectable,
and pleasant history of Parismus ... Prince of
Bohemia.   9th impr.   2 pts.   4to.
*London, by A.P. (by E.Crouch) for F.Coles,
T.Vere [etc.]*, 1671-2   [Vulgaria II]
Woodcut fp.   Wing F1534.   **1191(3)**

[—————] The most pleasant history of
Ornatus and Artesia.   8th impr.   4to.
London, by M.White, for J.Wright, J.Clark [etc.],
1683   [Vulgaria III]   Wing F1543.   **1192(4)**

FORMAN (Simon). The groundes of the longitude.
4to.
London, by Thomas Dawson, 1591
[Sea Tracts I]   STC 11185.   **1077(9)**

FORTESCUE (Sir John). De laudibus legum
Angliæ ... Hereto are added the two sums of Sir
R.de Hengham, L. Ch. Justice to K. Edward I
commonly called Hengham magna & Hengham
parva. With notes ... by ... J.Selden.   8vo.
*London, by John Streater, Eliz.Flesher and H.Twy-
ford [etc.]*, 1672   Wing F1613.   **418**

FOUQUET (Nicolas). Recueil des defenses de
M.Fouquet.   11 vols in 10.   12mo.
1665-8
1: A nosseigneurs de la Chambre de justice.
   (— Defenses de M.Fouquet sur tous les points.)
2: Réponse à la réplique de M.Talon.
3: Production de M.Fouquet. (Suite du recueil
   des defenses, 1.)

4: Continuation de la production. (Suite du recueil, 2.)

5: Suite de la continuation. (Suite du recueil, 3.)

6: Continuation de la production. (Suite du recueil, 4.)

7: Suite de la continuation. (Suite du recueil, 5.)

8-9: Inventaire des pieces baillées à la Chambre de justice. (Suite du recueil, 6-7.)

10: Conclusion des defenses de M.Fouquet.

This set lacks 'De la production de M.Fouquet', in 3 pts.　**31-40**

FOURNIER (Georges). Hydrographie, contenant la theorie et la pratique de toutes les parties de la navigation.　2e ed.　fo.
Paris, chez Jean Du Puis, 1667　Engr. pl.
Diary 10 Jan.1667/8.　**2678**

———————— [Another copy of the plate, with printed material added.]
Paris, chez Nicolas Beray et Antoine de Fer.
1842(1)

FOURTH (A) collection of papers relating to the present juncture of affairs in England.　4to.
London, printed and are to be sold by Rich. Janeway, 1688　[Consutilia I]
Wing F1686.　**1427(16)**

FOWLE (Thomas). Speculum uranicum; or, an almanack and prognostication for ... 1688. (— An appendix to the precedent almanack.)　8vo.
London, printed by R.E. (by M.C.) for the Company of Stationers, 1688　[Almanacks for the year 1688]　Wing A1722.　**425(10)**

[FOWLER (Edward), Bp of Gloucester]. [An answer to the paper delivered by Mr Ashton at his execution ... Together with the paper it self.　4to.
London, for Robert Clavell, 1690]
[Narratives & Tryals V]　Pp.5-8 only, containing Mr.Ashton's paper.　Wing F1695.
2253(24)

FOX (George). A journal, or historical account of the life ... of G.Fox ... Vol.1. (— The preface, being a summary account of the divers dispensations of God to men, [by] W.Penn.)　fo.
London, for Thomas Northcott (by T.Sowle),
1694　Wing F1854; P1341.　**2471(1)**

FOX (Luke). North-west Fox, or, Fox from the North-west Passage.　4to.
London, by B.Alsop and Tho.Fawcet, 1635
Engr. map. Wants ¹A1.　STC 11221.　**1252**

FOXCROFT (John). The good of a good government ... A sermon preached ... December 31.1645.
4to.
London, for Tho.Badger, to be sold by G.Badger,
1645　[Sermons Polemical IV]
Wing F2034.　**1182(3)**

FOXE (John). Acts and monuments of matters ... happening in the Church ... With ... the ... great persecutions against the true martyrs ... The eight time newly imprinted. 3 vols. [*Vols 2-3 entitled:* The ecclesiasticall historie ...]　fo.
London, for the Company of Stationers, 1641
Engr. fp. (port., Charrington p.63), woodcuts.
Wing F2035; Diary 21 Aug. & 12 Oct.1668.
2536-8

FRANCE. *Laws.* Le code du roy Henry III, roy de France et de Pologne, redigé en ordre par B.Brisson.
fo.
Paris, chez la veufue de Sebastien Niuelle, 1605
2563

———————— Grand conference des ordonnances et edits royaux, 1679.
See GRANDE conference ...　**2673-5**

———————— Recueil des edits, declarations, arrests, et autres pieces concernant les duels et rencontres.　12mo.
Paris, par Sebastien Mabre-Cramoisy, 1669　**783**

———————— Reglemens et ordonnances du roy pour les gens de guerre: depuis le traité de paix conclu le 7.Novembre 1659 ... jusques à l'année 1668 inclusivement.　12mo.
Paris, par Sebastien Mabre-Cramoisy, 1669　**605**

———————— Reglement des droits et salaires des officiers des admirautez (fait & arresté au Conseil d'Estat du Roy).　4to.
Paris, par Sebastien Mabre-Cramoisy, 1673
1907(2)

FRANCE. *Treaties.* Actes et memoires des negotiations de la paix de Nimegue. [Ed. by A.Moetjens.]　2e éd.　4 vols.　12mo.
Amsterdam, chez Abraham Wolfgangk. Et à La Haye, chez Adriaen Moetjens, 1680
Engr. pl.　**469-72**

———————— Articles de la paix accordée ... au nom du Roy, au Bacha, Dey, Divan et Milice d'Alger.　4to.
Paris, imprimerie de François Muguet, 1684
1440(3)

———————— Articles of peace between ... William the Third, King of Great Britain, and ... Lewis the Fourteenth ... concluded ... at Ryswicke the 10/20 day of September, 1697.　fo.
London, by Charles Bill, and the executrix of Thomas Newcomb, 1697
Wing W2309.　**2156(1)**

———————— The acts and negotiations ... of the general peace concluded at Ryswick. [Ed. by J.Bernard.]　8vo.
London, for Robert Clavel, and Tim.Childe, 1698
2 engr. pls inserted.　Wing B1994.　**1247**

———————— Recueil des traitez de paix ... faits par les rois de France ... Assemblé ... & imprimé par F.Leonard. (Observations historiques et politiques par A. de la Houssaie.)   6 vols.   4to.
Paris, 1693   MS leaves inserted in vol.1: a collation of the trade treaty of 1475 with the original in Paris, by Dr John Shadwell, 1699 (3 leaves; after p.176 of the Recueil); transcripts in two different hands of the paragraph in which English place-names are 'ill-spelt', with an extract from a letter from Shadwell to Pepys, 27 March 1700 (4 leaves; after p.181 of the Recueil); and at the end (2 leaves; in the hand of one of Pepys's clerks), a list of the names of English ports and sea-roads as printed in this volume, with Pepys's 'Conjecture' of their names in current English usage.   **1884-9**

———————— The treaty betwixt the Most Christian King [Louis XIV], the King of Great Britain [William III], and the States General of the United Provinces, for settling the succession of the Crown of Spain ... In English and French.   4to.
London, for A.Baldwin, 1700   [Consutilia X]
Wing L3139.   **1436(8)**

FRANCISCANS. Riaghuil threas uird S.Froinsias.   12mo.
Lobhain, 1641.   **26(2)**

FRANCISCO, de los Santos.
See SANTOS (Francisco).

[FRANKLAND (Thomas)]. The annals of King James and King Charles the first.   fo.
London, by Tho.Braddyl, for Robert Clavel, 1681
Wing F2078.   **2560**

[FRANZINI (Girolamo)]. Las cosas maravillosas dela sancta ciudad de Roma.   8vo.
Roma, por Francisco Moneda, a istancia de los Delfines, 1651   Woodcuts.   Gaselee 157;
Diary 11 Feb. 1659/60.   **592**

[————————] Les merveilles de la ville de Rome.   8vo.
Rome, chez Iean François de Buagni, elles se vendent chez François Leon, 1690
Engr. fp., woodcuts.   **655**

FRAUDS (The) of Romish monks and priests, 1691.   *See* GAVIN (Antonio).   **879**

FREE (A) enquiry into the vulgarly receiv'd notion of nature, 1685/6.
See BOYLE (Hon. Robert).   **887**

FREE (The) state of Noland: or, the frame and constitution of that happy ... state.   4to.
London, for D.Brown, and sold by A.Baldwin, 1701   [Consutilia XI]   **1437(11)**

FREE-HOLDERS (The) grand inquest [1648].
See FILMER (Sir Robert).   **1430(16)**

FREE-HOLDERS (The) plea against stock-jobbing elections of Parliament men, 1701.
See DEFOE (Daniel).   **1437(7)**

FREEMAN (John). A sermon preached without a text at the Inner-Temple, March the 12. ... 1643.   4to.
London, 1643   [Sermons Polemical IV]
Wing F2134.   **1182(4)**

FREIND (Sir John).   *See* FRIEND (Sir John).

FREJUS (Roland). The relation of a voyage made into Mauritania in Africk.   2 pts.   8vo.
London, by W.Godbid, to be sold by Moses Pitt, 1671   Wing F2161.   **244(1)**

FRÉMONT D'ABLANCOURT (Jean Jacobé de). Memoires ... contenant l'histoire de Portugal ... de 1659 jusqu' à 1668.   12mo.
Paris, chez les heritiers de la veuve de Marbré [sic] Cramoisi, 1701   **596**

FRÉMONT D'ABLANCOURT (Nicolas). Nouveau dictionnaire de rimes, 1667.
See NOUVEAU dictionnaire ...   **479**

FRIAR. The frier and the boy. [c.1690]   12mo.   **358(5)**

[FRIAR (The) and the boy.] Here beginneth the second part of the Fryer and the boy.   12mo.
London, by A.M. and R.R. for Edward Brewster [etc.], 1680   [Penny-Merriments II]
Woodcuts.   **363(23)**

FRIEND (Sir John). The arraignment, tryal and condemnation of Sir John Friend for high treason ... March 23.1695/6.   fo.
London, for Samuel Heyrick and Isaac Cleve, 1696   [Narratives & Tryals VI]
Wing A3759.   **2254(5)**

———————— The tryal and condemnation of Sir John Friend for conspiring to raise rebellion ... March 23.1695/6.   fo.
London, for Brabazon Aylmer, 1696
[Narratives & Tryals VI]   Wing T2152.   **2254(6)**

FROIDMONT (Libert). Meteorologicorum libri sex. Cui accessit ... T.Fieni, & L.Fromondi Dissertationes de cometa anni 1618.   8vo.
Londini, typis & impensis J.Redmayne, pro Georgio West, apud quem prostant Oxonii, 1670
Wing F2236.   **837**

FROISSART (Jean). [H]ere begynneth the fyrst volum of Syr Iohan Froyssart: of the Cronycles of Englande ... Translated ... by Johan Bouchier knyght Lorde Berners.   fo.
(London, by Wyllyam Myddylton) [1545]
STC 11398; Duff p.25.   **2412(1)**

———————— Here begynneth the thirde and fourthe boke of Sir Johñ Froissart of the Cronycles of Englande ... translated ... by Johan Bourchier knyght Lorde Berners.   fo.
(*London, by Rycharde Pynson*, 1525 [*or rather by W.Powell & T.Marsh, c.1560*])
STC 11397a; Duff p.25.   **2412(2)**

FRONTINUS (Sextus Julius). The stratagems of war.   12mo.
London, for S.Heyrick, J.Place, and R.Sare, 1686
Wing F2244A.   **376(1)**

FRYER (John). A new account of East-India and Persia ... travels begun 1672, and finished 1681. fo.
London, by R.R. for Ric.Chiswell, 1698
Engr. fp. (port., Charrington p.65), pls, maps.
Wing F2257.   **2358**

FUEIL (V.). La terrible et merveilleuse vie de Robert le Diable.   4to.
Rouen, chez Louys Costé, 1628
[Consutilia II]   Woodcut.   **1428(12)**

FULL (A) and final proof of the Plot, 1680.
See C.(E.).   **2252(33)**

FULL (A) declaration of the true state of the secluded members case, 1660.
See PRYNNE (William).   **1430(13)**

FULLER (Thomas). The church-history of Britain. (– History of the University of Cambridge. – History of Waltham Abbey.)   6 pts.   fo.
London, for J.Williams, 1656   Engr. pls.
Wing F2417; Diary 15 Feb.1659/60 [*etc.*].   **2437**

———————— The historie of the holy warre.
4th ed.   fo.
[*Cambridge*] *by Thomas Buck, to be sold by Philemon Stephens*, 1651   Engr. title-page, map.   Wing F2439; Diary 3 Nov.1661.
                    2095(1)

———————— The history of the worthies of England.   fo.
London, by J.G., W.L. and W.G., 1662
Wants engr. fp. (port.).   Wing F2440; Diary 10 Dec.1663.   **2438**

———————— The holy state.   3rd ed.   fo.
London, by R.D. for John Williams, 1652 (1648)
Engr. title-page, 21 engr. ports.   Wing F2445.
                    2095(2)

FULLER (William). A brief discovery of the true mother of the pretended Prince of Wales.   8vo.
London, for the author, 1696   Wing F2479.
                    980(1)

———————— A full demonstration that the pretended Prince of Wales was the son of Mrs Mary Grey.   8vo.
London, for the author, and sold by A.Baldwin, 1702   **980(5)**

———————— Fullers non-recantation to the Jacobites.   8vo.
London, for the author, 1701   **981(3)**

———————— A further confirmation that Mary Grey was the true mother of the pretended Prince of Wales.   8vo.
London, for the author, 1696   Wing F2482.
                    980(3)

———————— The life of William Fuller ... Written by his own hand.   2 pts.   8vo.
London, printed and published by A.Baldwin, 1701   **981(2)**

———————— Mr.William Fuller's trip to Bridewell ... written by his own hand.   8vo.
London, 1703   **982(1)**

———————— Original letters of the late King's, 1702.
See JAMES II, King of England.   **980(7)**

———————— A plain proof of the true father and mother of the pretended Prince of Wales. 8vo.
London, for the author, 1700
Wing F2485.   **980(4)**

———————— The proceedings and sentence against William Fuller ... at the King's-Bench-Bar, Westminster ... 23d of July 1702   brs.
London, for A.Banks, 1702   [Narratives & Tryals VII]   Cf. below, vol.4. 2255(5): Parliament-Censures & Formal Trial of William Fuller.
                    2255(7)

———————— The sincere and hearty confession of Mr.William Fuller.   8vo.
London, 1704   Engr. fp. (port., Charrington p.65).   **982(3)**

———————— The tryal of William Fuller ... May 20.1702.   fo.
London, for Isaac Cleave, 1702   [Narratives & Tryals VII]   **2255(11)**

———————— A true account of the sentence and judgment against William Fuller ... June 23. 1702.   brs.
(*London, for John Nutt*, 1702)
[Narratives & Tryals VII]   **2255(9)**

———————— A true and full account of the examination and sentence of William Fuller ... 23rd June, 1702.   brs.
(*London, for R.G.*, 1702)   [Narratives & Tryals VII]   **2255(8)**

———————— Twenty six depositions of persons of quality ... Proving the whole management of the supposititious birth of the pretended Prince of Wales.   3rd ed.   8vo.
London, for the author, sold by A.Baldwin, 1702
                    980(6)

———————— The whole life of Mr.William Fuller ... writ by himself during his confinement in the Queen's-Bench.　8vo.
London, 1703　Engr. fp. (port., Charrington p.65).　　　　**982(2)**

[FULMAN (William)] . Notitia Oxoniensis Academiæ.　4to.
Londini, typis T.R. impensis Ric.Davis, 1675 Wing F2524.　　　　**1535**

———————— Rerum Anglicarum scriptorum veterum tomus I, 1684.
See RERUM Anglicarum ...　　　　**2628**

FUMBLERS-HALL, kept and holden in Feeble-Court, at the sign of the Labour-in-vain, in Doolittle Lane.　12mo.
[*London*] *for J.Clarke, W.Thackeray, and T. Passinger* [c.1680]　[Penny-Merriments I] Woodcut.　　　　**362(7)**

FUR prædestinatus: sive, Dialogismus, 1651.
See SLATIUS (Henricus).　　　　**374(2)**

FURETIÈRE (Antoine). Dictionaire universel, contenant ... les mots françois.　3 vols.　fo.
A la Haye, et à Rotterdam, chez Arnout & Reinier Leers, 1690　Engr. fp. (port., Charrington p.65).　　　　**2691-3**

G

G.(G.). The history of the Church of Great Britain, 1674.
See GEAVES (William).　　　　**1759**

G.(H.). Curiosities in chymistry ... published by ... H.G. [i.e. Hugh Gregg] , 1691.
See BOYLE (Hon. Robert).　　　　**601**

G.(John). The myrrour or lokynge glasse of lyfe [1532].
See GOODALE (John).　　　　**19(1)**

G.(M.L.). Le tresor des harangues, 1668.
See GILBAULT (L.).　　　　**547-8**

G.(W.). Status ecclesiæ Gallicanæ, 1676.
See GEAVES (William).　　　　**1782**

GADBURY (John). Εφημερις: or, a diary ... for ... 1688.　8vo.
London, printed by J.D. for the Company of Stationers, 1688　[Almanacks for the year 1688]　Wing A1767.　　　　**425(11)**

———————— Εφημερις: or, a diary ... for ... 1689.　8vo.

London, printed by J.D. for the Company of Stationers, 1689　[Almanacks for the year 1689]　Wing A1768.　　　　**426(2)**

———————— Festum festorum: or, a discourse touching the holy feast of Easter.　8vo.
London, by N.Thompson, for the Company of Stationers, 1687　Wing G83.　　　　**833(1)**

GAILHARD (Jean). The present state of the princes and republicks of Italy.　2nd ed. 12mo.
London, printed for John Starkey, 1671 Wing G125.　　　　**379(1)**

GALATINUS (Petrus).
See COLUMNA (Petrus), Galatinus.

GALE (Theophilus). The court of the gentiles. 2nd ed.　4 pts in 2 vols.　4to.
Oxford, London, for Tho.Gilbert, T.Cockeril, John Hill and Samuel Tidmarsh (1671-8) Wing G137, 139, 141-3.　　　　**1501-2**

GALE (Thomas). Historiæ Britannicæ (– Anglicanæ) ... scriptores, 1691.
See RERUM Anglicarum scriptorum veterum tom.I.　　　　**2629-30**

———————— Sermons preached on several holydays.　8vo.
London, by Tho.Warren, for Thomas Bennet, 1704 Inscribed on flyleaf in John Jackson's hand: 'Ex dono Car. amici et consobrini Sam. Gale. Jul.21. 1704. JJ.'　　　　**1407**

GALILEI (Vincentio). Dialogo della musica antica, et della moderna.　fo.
Fiorenza, Giorgio Marescotti, 1581　Diagrams. Adams G139.　*See also below*, vol.IV.　　　　**2247**

GALLANT (The) history of ... Sir Bevis of Southampton.　4to.
[*London*] *by A.M. for J.Deacon* [1690?] [Vulgaria III]　Woodcuts.　Wing G170.
　　　　1192(10)

GALLEN (William). Gallen. 1688. A complete pocket almanack for ... 1688.　12mo.
London, printed by M.F. for the Company of Stationers, 1688　[Almanacks for the year 1688] Wing A1791B.　　　　**425(12)**

GAMMER Gurton's needle, 1661.
See STEVENSON (William).　　　　**1103(3)**

GARCÍA (Juan Pablo). Vespertinas sagradas que explican los mandamientos de la ley de Dios ... y sermones.　4to.
Alcalà, por Francisco Garcia Fernandez, 1682 Gaselee 66.　　　　**1546(1)**

GARCÍA DE CÉSPEDES (Andrés). Regimiento de navegacion que mando hazer el Rei.　2 pts.　fo.
(*Madrid, en casa de Iuan de la Cuesta*, 1606) Engr. title-page, map.　Gaselee 67.　　　　**2140(1)**

[GARCIE (Pierre)]. The rutter of the sea, w^t the hauõs, rodes, soundinges ... With a rutter of the Northe added to the same. (Transl. by R.Copland.) 8vo.
(*London, Wyllyam Copland* [1555?])
Pepys adds MS note at end recording that the only other extant copy known to him was Selden's in the Bodleian.   STC 11551; Duff p.56.   **96(1)**

GARCILASO DE LA VEGA.
See VEGA (Garcilaso de la).

GARDINER (Ralph). Englands grievance dis-covered in relation to the coal-trade.   4to.
London, for R.Ibbitson and P.Stent, 1655
[Consutilia III]   Engr. map, ports.
Wing G230.   **1429(8)**

GARLAND (The) of good-will, 1688.
See DELONEY (Thomas).   **364(2)**

[GARNET (Richard)]. The book of oaths.   8vo.
London, printed for H.Twyford, T.Basset, B.Griffin [etc.], 1689   Wing G265.   **909**

[GARTH (Sir Samuel)]. The dispensary: a poem ... 2nd ed., corrected by the author.   8vo.
London, printed and sold by John Nutt, 1699
Engr. fp. Corrections added in MS in hand of one of Pepys's clerks. A key to the characters inserted at end, in same hand.   Wing G274.   **1424**

GARUFFI (Giuseppe Malatesta). L'Italia accad-emica; o sia le Accademie aperte a pompa, e decoro delle lettere più amene nelle città italiane. Parte prima.   8vo.
Rimino (per Gio:Felice Dandi), 1688   **378**

GASCOIGNE (George). The whole woorkes of George Gascoigne ... Newlye compyled into one volume.   4to.
London, by Abell Ieffes, 1587
STC 11638.   **1235**

────────────── The glasse of gouernment. A tragicall comedie.   4to.
(*London, by A.M. for Christopher Barker*, 1575)
Wants πA1.4.   [Old Plays III]   STC 11643.   **1103(4)**

GASCOYNE (Sir Thomas). The tryal of Sir Tho. Gascoyne ... 11th of Feb., 1679.   fo.
London, for Tho.Basset and Sam.Heyrick, 1680
[Narratives & Tryals IV]   Wing T2219.   **2252(8)**

GASSENDI (Pierre). Institutio astronomica ... Cui accesserunt Galilei Galilei Nuncius sidereus et Johannis Kepleri Dioptrice.   3a ed.   8vo.
Londini, impensis Hen.Dickinson, 1683 (1682)
Engr. pls, diagrams.   Wing G293; Diary 12 Sept. 1660.   **1224**

────────────── The mirrour of true nobility & gentility. Being the life of N.C.Fabricius Lord of Peiresk ... Englished by W.Rand.   8vo.
London, printed by John Streater for Humphrey Moseley, 1657   Engr. fp. (port., Charrington p.133).   Wing G295.   **812**

GATAKER (Thomas). Adversaria miscellanea. fo.
Londini, apud Sa.Gellibrand, 1659
Wing G309.   **2128**

────────────── Gods eye on his Israel.   4to.
London, by E.G. for Foulke Clifton, 1645
[Sermons Polemical IV]   Wing G321.   **1182(5)**

────────────── A iust defence of certaine passages in a former treatise concerning the nature and vse of lots.   4to.
London, printed by Iohn Haviland for Robert Bird, 1623   STC 11666.   **1125(2)**

────────────── Of the nature and use of lots. 4to.
London, printed by Edward Griffin and are to be sold by William Bladen, 1619   STC 11670.   **1125(1)**

GAUDEN (John), Bp of Worcester. Considerations touching the liturgy of the Church of England. 4to.
London, by J.G. for John Playford, 1661
[Liturgick Controversies III]   Wing G348.   **1189(4)**

────────────── The religious & loyal protestation ... against the ... proceedings of the army and others.   4to.
London, for Richard Royston, 1648
[Consutilia IV]   Wing G367.   **1430(9)**

GAUTRUCHE (Pierre). The poetical history: being a ... collection of all the stories ... of the Greek and Latine poets ... Written originally in French.
4th ed., corrected and amended by M.D'Assigny. 8vo.
London, by W.G., and are to be sold by M.Pitt, 1678   Wing G387A.   **923**

GAVANTI (Bartolommeo). Theasurus sacrorum rituum seu commentaria in rubricas missalis et breviarii Romani ... vltimâ ed. (Enchiridion, seu manuale episcoporum.)   4 pts.   4to.
Lugduni, sumptibus Hor.Boissat, & Georg.Remeus, 1664   **1812**

[GAVIN (Antonio)]. The frauds of Romish monks and priests set forth in eight letters.   8vo.
London, printed by Samuel Roycroft, for Robert Clavell, 1691   Wing G390.   **879**

[──────────────] Observations on a journy to Naples. Wherein the frauds of Romish monks and priests are farther discover'd.   8vo.
London, printed by Samuel Roycroft, for Robert Clavell, 1691   Wing G393.   **880**

GAYA (Louis de). L'art de la guerre.   2e éd.
12mo.
Paris, chez Estienne Michallet, 1679
Engr. diagrams.   372

———————— Ceremonies nuptiales de toutes
les nations.   12mo.
A la Haye, chez Adrian Moetjens, 1681   83(5)

GAZET (Angelin). Pia hilaria.   2 vols in 1.
12mo.
Londini, impensis Guil:Morden, 1657
Wing G425.   542

GAZETTE (La) d'Amsterdam. 9 May, 1675.   4to.
Amsterdam, chez Corneille Jansz.Zwol, 1675
[*Inserted between nos 987 & 988 of the London
Gazette.*]   Heath p.130.   2081

GEARING (William). *For the* History of the
church of Great Britain, *and* Status ecclesiæ
Gallicanæ, *sometimes ascribed to W.Gearing, see*
GEAVES (William).

[GEAVES (William)] . The history of the church
of Great Britain.   4to.
London, for Philip Chetwin, 1674
Wing G440.   1759

[————————] Status ecclesiæ Gallicanæ: or
the ecclesiastical history of France.   4to.
*London, for Thomas Passenger, and Ralph Smith,
1676*   Wing G442.   1782

GEDDE (Walter). [A booke of sundry draughtes,
principaly serving for glasiers ... whereunto is
annexed the manner how to anniel in glas.]
4 pts.   4to.
[*London, by Walter Dight, 1615*] (1616)
Wants sig.A; sig.R misbound at front. Woodcut
diagrams.   STC 11695.   1375

GELL (Robert). An essay toward the amendment
of the last English-translation of the Bible ... The
first part on the Pentateuch.   fo.
London, by R.Norton for Andrew Crook, 1659
Wing G470.   2004

GENERAL. A generall bill for this present year,
ending the 19 of December 1665.   brs
[*London, 1665*]   Wing G491.   1595(2)

GENERAL (A) index ... to all the Philosophical
transactions, 1678.
See PHILOSOPHICAL transactions.   1712(3)

GENTILIS (Albericus). Hispanicæ advocationis
libri duo.   Ed. 2a.   8vo.
*Amstelredami, apud Joannem Ravesteinium,
1661*   516

GENTLEMAN'S (The) calling, 1673.
See ALLESTREE (Richard).   1084

GENTLEMANS (The) recreation, 1686.
See BLOME (Richard).   2908

GENTLEWOMANS (The) cabinet unlocked ...
Receipts for neat dressing of divers sorts of meats.
12mo.
[*London*] *for W.Thackeray and T.Passinger*
[c.1680]   [Penny-Merriments II]   363(5)

GENTLEWOMAN'S (The) delight in cookery.
12mo.
London, for J.Back [c.1685]   [Penny-Merri-
ments II]   Woodcut.   363(32)

GENUINE (The) epistles of the Apostolical
Fathers S.Barnabas, S.Clement, S.Ignatius,
S.Polycarp. The Shepherd of Hermas ... Transl.
and publish'd ... by W.Wake.   2 pts.   8vo.
London, for Ric.Sare, 1693   n4-6 misbound
after A2; wants A3-8.   Wing G523A.   1025

GEOFFREY, of Monmouth, Bp of St Asaph.
Britānie utriusꝙ regū ꝫ p̄cipū origo ꝫ gesta
insignia.   4to.
[*Paris, Io.Badius Ascensius*] (1508)
Adams G444; Duff p.26.   1511

GEOGRAPHIAE veteris scriptores Graeci minores.
[Ed. by J.Hudson.]   Vols 1 & 2.   8vo.
Oxoniæ, e Theatro Sheldoniano, 1698-[1712]
Engr. fp. Wants vols 3-4.   Wing H3260; Tanner I,
p.131.   1765-6

GEORGIRENES (Joseph), Abp of Samos.
A description of the present state of Samos, Nic-
aria, Patmos, and Mount Athos.   8vo.
*London, printed by W.G. and sold by Moses Pitt,
1678*   Wing G536.   890

[GERBERON (Gabriel)] . Memorial historique de
ce qui s'est passé depuis ... 1647, jusques à ...
1653. Touchant les cinq propositions [of Jansen-
ius] .   12mo.
'*Cologne, chez Pierre Marteau*' [*Holland?*] , 1676
77(2)

GERHARD (Johann). Locorum theologicorum ...
copiosè explicatorum tomus primus (— nonus),
quartùm editus.   9 vols in 4.   fo.
Genevæ, ex typographia Philippi Gamoneti, 1639
Vol.9, PL2465(1), misplaced before vols.7-8.
2463-6

———————— Exegesis ... articulorum de
scriptura sacra ... in tomo primo ... concisiùs
pertractorum.   fo.
Ib., id., 1639   2465(2)

GESNER (Konrad). The history of four-footed
beasts, 1658.
See TOPSELL (Edward).   2521

[GIBSON (Edmund), Bp of London]. A letter to a friend in the country, concerning the proceedings of the present Convocation.   4to.
[*London, A. & J.Churchill*, 1701]
[Convocation Pamphlets IX]   **1695(6)**

[——————] The marks of a defenceless cause in the proceedings ... of Convocation.   4to.
London, for A. and J.Churchill, 1703
[Convocation Pamphlets X]   Notes in Daniel Waterland's hand; 'Bp Gibson' on title-page in same hand.   **1696(21)**

[——————] The parallel continu'd, between a Presbyterian assembly and the new model of an English provincial synod.   4to.
[*London*, 1702]   [Convocation Pamphlets X]
                    1696(16)

[——————] The pretended independence of the Lower-House upon the Upper a groundless notion.   4to.
London, for A. and J.Churchill, 1703
[Convocation Pamphlets X]   MS notes in Daniel Waterland's hand; 'Bp Gibson' on title-page in same hand.   **1696(18)**

[——————] Reflexions upon a late paper entitl'd An expedient propos'd.   4to.
London, for A. and J.Churchil, 1702
[Convocation Pamphlets X]   MS notes in Daniel Waterland's hand; 'Bp Gibson' on title-page in same hand.   **1696(1)**

[——————] The right of the Archbishop to continue or prorogue the whole Convocation. 4to.
London, for Awnsham and John Churchill, 1701
[Convocation Pamphlets IX]   MS notes in Daniel Waterland's hand; 'Bp Gibson' on title-page in same hand.   **1695(7)**

[——————] The Schedule review'd, or the right of the Archbishop to continue or prorogue the whole Convocation.   4to.
London, for A. and J.Churchill, 1702
[Convocation Pamphlets X]   MS notes in Daniel Waterland's hand; 'Bp Gibson' on title-page in same hand.   **1696(17)**

[——————] A short state of some present questions in Convocation.   4to.
London, for A. and J.Churchill, 1703
[Convocation Pamphlets X]   MS notes in Daniel Waterland's hand; 'Bp Gibson' on title-page in same hand.   **1696(19)**

[——————] A summary of the arguments for the Archbishop's right to continue the whole Convocation.   4to.
[*London*, 1701]   [Convocation Pamphlets IX]
                    1695(8)

[——————] Synodus Anglicana: or, the constitution and proceedings of an English Convocation shown ... to be agreeable to the principles of an episcopal church.   8vo.
London, for A. and J.Churchill, 1702
[Convocation Pamphlets VI]   **1692**

[——————] A vindication of the author of the Right of the Archbishop to continue, &c. from some little exceptions taken by the writer of two letters concerning the choice of members, &c. 4to.
(*London, for Richard Sare*, 1702)   [Convocation Pamphlets X]   Pp.25-7. A fragment of a larger work.   On title-page: 'Bp Gibson' in Daniel Waterland's hand.   **1696(9)**

GIBSON (Thomas). The anatomy of human bodies epitomiz'd.   3rd ed.   8vo.
London, for Awnsham Churchil, 1688
Engr. pls.   MS notes on front flyleaf, Q5 and S5 in unidentified hand.   Wing G674.   **1301**

GIFFENIUS (Hermannus). Paradoxus philosophus enervatus.   12mo.
Groningæ, apud Dominicum Lens, 1673   **69**

[GILBAULT (L.)] Le tresor des harangues. Par (– Recueilles par) M.L.G.   2 vols.   12mo.
Paris, chez Michel Bobin & Nicolas Le Gras, 1668
                    547-8

GILBERT (William). De magnete, magneticisque corporibus, et de magno magnete tellure.   fo.
Londini, excudebat Petrus Short, 1600
Engr. pl., diagrams.   STC 11883; Naval Minutes p.420.   **2045**

GILLESPIE (George). A sermon preached ... 27th of August, 1645.   4to.
London, for Robert Bostock, 1645   [Sermons Polemical IV]   Wing G758.   **1182(6)**

GILES (John). The tryal of John Giles ... July, 1680 ... for a barbarous ... attempt to assassinate ... J.Arnold.   fo.
London, by Thomas James for Randal Taylor, 1681   [Narratives & Tryals IV]
Wing T2192.   **2252(11)**

GIOCHI. I giuochi circensi, 1700.
See MODENA. Collegio de' Nobili.   **1451(4)**

GIRAFFI (Alessandro). An exact history of the late revolutions in Naples ... rendred to English by J.Howell. (– The second part of Massaniello, by J.Howell.)   2 pts.   8vo.
London, for R.Lowndes (by J.M. for A.Roper and T.Dring), 1664 (1663)   Engr. fps (port., Charrington pp.115-16).   Wing G786.   **717**

GIRALDI (Lilio Gregorio). Operum ... tomi duo. (Dialogismus unicus L.Frizzolii de Lilii operibus deque ejus vita.)   2 vols.   fo.
Basileae, per Thomam Guarinum, 1580
Adams G716.   **2245-6**

GIUSTINIANO, of Tours.
See FEBVRE (Michele), *pseud.*

GLANVILL (Joseph). Essays on several important subjects in philosophy and religion.   4to.
London, by J.D. for John Baker, and Henry Mortlock, 1676   Wing G809.   **1449**

———————Saducismus triumphatus: or ... evidence concerning witches and apparitions. In two parts ... with a letter of Dr H.More on the same subject.   8vo.
London, for J.Collins and S.Lownds, 1681
Engr. fps.   Wing G822; Diary 24 Nov.1666.
1211

———————Two choice and useful treatises: the one Lux orientalis (by J.Glanvill) ... The other, A discourse of truth, by the late Dr.Rust, Lord Bishop of Dromore.   2 pts.   8vo.
London, for James Collins, and Sam.Lowndes, 1682   Engr. fp.   Wing G833.   **1248**

GLAUBER (Johann Rudolph). Works ... containing ... choice secrets in medicine and alchymy ... Transl. ... by C.Packe.   3 pts.   fo.
London, by Thomas Milbourn, for the author, sold by D.Newman and W.Cooper, 1689
Engr. pls.   MS index (4 leaves, in unidentified secretarial hand) at front; unbound.
Wing G845.   **2631**

GLORIA Britannica, 1689.   *See* B.(A.).
1399(5)

GODEAU (Antoine), Bp of Grasse. Histoire de l'Église.   4e éd.   5 vols in 3.   fo.
Paris, chez Thomas Jolly (— François Muguet), 1672-8   Engr. fp. (port., Charrington p.68).
2569-71

GODEFROY (Théodore). Le cérémonial françois, 1649.
See CÉRÉMONIAL (Le) françois.   **2597-8**

GODLY (A) sermon of Peter's repentance, 1682.
See HART (John).   **365(26)**

GODOLPHIN (John). Συνηγορος Θαλασσιος.
A view of the Admiral jurisdiction ... Whereunto is added ... an extract of the ancient laws of Oleron.   8vo.
London, by W.Godbid for Edmund Paxton and John Sherley, 1661   Wing G952; Tangier Papers 11 (5 Sept.1683).   **846**

GODOY (Juan de). Testamento, y codicilo, y maravilloso discurso de la platica que hizo el Rey Don Felipe Segundo.   4to.
(Seuilla, por Juan Vejarano, à costa de Lucas Martin de Hermosa, 1682)   Gaselee 69; Wilson p.244.   **1545(30)**

GODWIN (Francis), Bp of Hereford. A catalogue of the bishops of England.   4to.
London, for Thomas Adams, 1615
Autograph on verso of title-page: 'Robt Sprakeling, 20mo Decembris Anno 1617mo.'
STC 11938.   **1163**

GODWIN (Thomas). Romanæ historiæ anthologia ... Moses and Aaron ... Seven books of the Attick antiquities (by F.Rous).   4to.
London, printed, and sold by Awnsham Churchill, 1686   Wing G997.   **1343**

GOLDEN drops of Christian comfort, 1687.
See M.(S.).   **365(25)**

GOLDEN (The) garland of ... mirth and merriment.   12mo.
[London] for J.Blare [1690]   [Penny-Merriments II]   Woodcut.   Wing G1017.   **363(43)**

GOLDSMITH (John). Goldsmith, 1688. An almanack for ... 1688.   24to.
London, printed by Mary Clark, for the Company of Stationers, 1688   [Almanacks for the year 1688]   Wing A1796A.   **425(13)**

GOLTZ (Hubert). *For works by Goltz with commentaries by L.Nonnius, see* NONNIUS (Ludovicus).

———————Fasti magistratuum et triumphorum Romanorum ... ad Augusti obitum ex antiquis ... monumentis. Thesaurus item rei antiquariae ... Fastiq.Siculi denuo restituti a P.A. Schotto.   2 pts.   fo.
Antuerpiae, apud Iacobum Biaeum (ex officina Gerardi Wolfsschati), 1617-18   Engr. title-page, pls.   **2665**

———————Icones imperatorum Romanorum, ex priscis numismatibus ... delineatæ ... Accessit modò impp. Romano-Austriacorum series ... opera C.Geuartii.   fo.
Antuerpiæ, ex officina Plantiniana Balthasaris Moreti, 1645   Engr. title-page, ports.   **2662**

———————Sicilia et Magna Græcia siue Historiæ vrbium et populorum Græciæ ex antiquis nomismatibus liber primus. (— Siciliæ historia posterior.)   fo.
Antuerpiæ, in officina Plantiniana, 1644
Engr. title-page, pls, maps.   **2663**

GOMBAULD (Jean Ogier de). A discourse of Christianity ... Now done into English by P.Lorrain.   12mo.
London, printed for S.Lowndes, 1693
Wing G1023.   **436**

GÓMEZ DE QUEVEDO VILLEGAS (Francisco).
See QUEVEDO VILLEGAS (Francisco).

GÓNGORA Y ARGOTE (Luís de). Relacion nueua, y verdadera de vna industria que diò vna muger en la ciudad de Jaen. 4to.
(Seuilla, en casa de Juan Cabeças) [c.1680]
Gaselee 71; Wilson p.265. **1545(52)**

GONZÁLEZ DE AVILA (Gil). Teatro de las grandezas de la villa de Madrid, corte de los reyes catolicos de España. fo.
(Madrid, por Tomas Iunti, 1623)
Gaselee 72. **2143**

GONZÁLEZ DE FIGUEROA (Francisco). Obra nueuamente compuesta ... La qual trata de la vida ... de Santa Tais. 4to.
(Sevilla, por Juan Cabeças) [c.1680]
Gaselee 73; Wilson p.230. **1545(16)**

GONZÁLEZ DE LEGARIA (Juan). Aqui se contiene vna obra graciosa ... de vn cuento que le passó à vn soldado con vn gato. 4to.
(Seuilla, por Iuan Cabeças, 1680)
Gaselee 74; Wilson p.308. **1545(60)**

[GONZÁLEZ DE MENDOZA (Juan)]. The historie of the great and mightie kingdome of China ... Translated out of Spanish by R.Parke. 4to.
London, by I.Wolfe for Edward White, 1588
STC 12003. **1216(1)**

GOOD work for a good magistrate, 1651.
See PETERS (Hugh). **129**

[GOODALE (John)]. Here begynneth a lytell treatyse called, or named the (Myrrour or lokynge glasse of lyfe). 8vo.
[London, Robert Wyer, 1532?] Woodcut.
Wants all after m4. STC 11499; Duff p.26. **19(1)**

GOODLY. The goodli history of the moste noble ... Lady Lucres, 1567.
See PIUS II, Pope. **29(3)**

GOODWIN (John). Θεομαχια ... the substance of two sermons ... upon occasion of the late disaster ... in the West. 4to.
London, for Henry Overton, 1644 [Sermons Polemical IV] MS notes in unidentified hand.
Wing G1206. **1182(7)**

GOODWIN (Meg). Old Meg of Herefordshire, 1609. *See* OLD Meg ... **1434(3)**

GOODWIN (Thomas), D.D. Christ the universall peace-maker. 4to.
London, by J.G. for R.Dawlman, 1651
[Consutilia II] Wing G1237. **1428(7)**

———————— A sermon of the Fifth Monarchy. 4to.
London, for Livewel Chapman, 1654
[Sermons Polemical IV] Wing G1256. **1182(9)**

———————— Zerubbabels encouragement to finish the Temple. A sermon preached ... Apr.27, 1642. 4to.
London, for R.D[awlman], and are to be sold by Francis Eglesfield, 1642 [Sermons Polemical IV]
Wing G1267. **1182(8)**

GOODWIN (Thomas), of Pinner. Of the happiness of princes ... A sermon occasioned by the death of ... Queen Mary. 4to.
London, by J.D. for Jonathan Robinson, 1695
Wing G1269. **1528(19)**

GORIN DE SAINT AMOUR (Louis).
See SAINT AMOUR (Louis Gorin de).

[GOSPEL of Nicodemus.] Nichodemus his gospel. [Transl. & ed. by J.Warren.] 8vo.
[Rouen] by Iohn Cousturier [1635?]
STC 18571. **753**

[GOTT (Samuel)]. The divine history of the genesis of the world explicated. 4to.
London, by E.C[otes]. & A.C[lark]. for Henry Eversden, 1670 Wing G1353. **1575**

GOUGE (William). Mercies memoriall. Set out in a sermon preached ... Novemb.17, 1644. 4to.
London, by George Miller for Joshua Kirton, 1645 [Sermons Polemical IV] Wing G1392. **1182(10)**

[GOULART (Simon)]. Histoire de la miraculeuse delivrance envoyée de Dieu à la ville de Geneve, le XII. jour de Decembre 1602. *[Variously attributed to S.Goulart and J.Sarasin.]*
[c.1603] 8vo.
On title-page: 'James Paris 1700 . SP'.
Tanner II, p.19. **506**

GOULD (Robert). The corruption of the times by money. A satyr. 4to.
London, for Matthew Wotton, 1693
[Consutilia IX] Wing G1417. **1435(3)**

GOVERNMENT (The) of the tongue, 1674.
See ALLESTREE (Richard). **1087**

GOWER (John). De confessione amantis. fo.
London, by Thomas Berthelette, 1554
STC 12144. **2093**

GOWER (Stanley). Things now-a-doing ... A sermon preached ... Iuly 31, 1644. 4to.
London, by G.M. for Philemon Stephens, 1644 [Sermons Polemical IV] Wing G1462. **1182(11)**

GRACIÁN (Lorenzo).
See GRACIÁN Y MORALES (Baltasar).

GRACIÁN Y MORALES (Baltasar). Obras de Lorenzo Gracian. 2 vols in 1. 4to.
Madrid, en la Imprenta Real de la Santa Cruzada, a costa de Santiago Martin Redondo, 1674
Gaselee 75. **1541**

———————— The critick ... Transl. into English
by P.Rycaut.   8vo.
London, by T.N. for Henry Brome, 1681
Engr. fp. (port., Charrington p.148).
Wing G1470.   **1106**

GRAFTON (Richard). A chronicle at large and
meere history of the affayres of Englande.   2 pts.
fo.
(*London, by Henry Denham, for Richarde Tottle
and Humffrey Toye*) 1569   STC 12147.   **2074**

GRAMMAIRE generale, 1664.
See LANCELOT (Claude).   **509**

GRAMMATICA rationis, 1697.
See FELL (John), Bp of Oxford.   **410**

GRANADA (Luís de). Primera (— quinta) parte de
la introduccion del simbolo de la fè.   fo.
*Madrid, en la Imprenta Real, por Juan Garcia
Infançon, a costa de Gabriel de Leon*, 1676
Engr. fp. (port., Charrington p.107).
Gaselee 92.   **2146**

GRAND (The) essay, 1704.
See COWARD (William).   **1133**

GRAND (The) question, concerning the Bishops
right to vote in Parlament in cases capital, 1680.
See STILLINGFLEET (Edward), Bp of Worcester.
    874

GRAND (The) question concerning the judicature
of the House of Peers stated, 1669.
See HOLLES (Denzil Holles, Baron).   **498**

GRANDE (La) conference des ordonnances et
edits royaux, [compiled by] P.Guenois.   3 vols.
fo.
Paris, chez Antoine Dezallier, 1679   **2673-5**

GRASWINCKEL (Dirk). Maris liberi vindiciæ:
adversus Petrum Baptistam Burgum.   4to.
Hagae-Comitum, ex typographiâ Adriani Vlac,
1652   **1023**

———————— Maris liberi vindiciæ; adversus
Gulielmum Welwodum.   4to.
Hagæ-Comitum, ex typographiâ Adriani Vlac,
1653   **1024(1)**

GRAUNT (John). Natural and political observations ... upon the bills of mortality.   5th ed.
8vo.
London, by John Martyn, 1676   2 tables, one
with MS additions on verso.   Wing G1602;
Diary 24 March 1661/2, 25 July 1665.   **891(1)**

GREAT Britain's groans, 1695.
See HODGES (William).   **1399(15)**

GREAT (The) historical ... dictionary. [Ed.] by
J.Collier.   2nd ed.   2 vols.   fo.

*London, for Henry Rhodes, Thomas Newborough,
assigns of L.Meredith [etc.]*, 1701   Engr. fp.
(port., Charrington p.40).   **2750-1**

———————— A supplement ... With a continuation from the year 1688 ... by another hand.
fo.
*London, for Henry Rhodes and Thomas New-
borough*, 1705   **2752**

GREAT is Diana of the Ephesians, 1680.
See BLOUNT (Charles).   **387**

GREAVES (John). A discourse of the Romane
foot, and denarius.   8vo.
London, printed by M.F. for William Lee, 1647
Engr. pl.   Wing G1800.   **814**

GREEK (The) and Roman history illustrated by
coins & medals, 1692.
See WALKER (Obadiah).   **811**

GREEN (Robert). The tryals of Robert Green,
Henry Berry, & Lawrence Hill, for the murder of
Sr.Edmond-bury Godfrey.   fo.
London, for Robert Pawlet, 1679   [Narratives
& Tryals I]   Wing T2256.   **2249(12)**

GREEN (Theophilus). A narrative of some
passages in the life of T.Green ... both before and
after he received the truth, as professed by the ...
Quakers.   8vo.
London, by T.Sowle, 1702   At end: a MS note
(2 pp., in clerical hand, signed 'S.P. Xmas 1702'),
casting doubt on Green's story of a vision which
he alleged had appeared to him on the Thames.
    444

GREENE (John). Nehemiahs teares and prayers
for Judah's affliction ... in a sermon ... April 24,
1644.   4to.
London, by G.M. for Philemon Stephens, 1644
[Sermons Polemical IV]   Wing G1822.
    1182(12)

[GREENE (Robert)]. The delightful history of
Dorastus and Fawnia.   12mo.
[*London*] *for C.Dennisson* [c.1680]
[Penny-Merriments I]   Woodcut. Title-page
cropped.   **362(17)**

[————————] The historie of Orlando
Furioso.   4to.
London, by Simon Stafford, for Cuthbert Burby,
1599   [Old Plays II]   STC 12266.   **1102(5)**

———————— The pleasant history of Dorastus
and Fawnia.   4to.
London, for Geo.Conyers, 1688   [Vulgaria III]
Wing G1837.   **1192(2)**

———————— Theeves falling out, true-men
come by their goods.   4to.
London, for Henry and Moses Bell, 1637
[Vulgaria III]   Woodcut.   STC 12238.
    1192(22)

GREENHILL (William). Ἀξίνη πρὸς τὴν Ῥίζαν.
The axe at the root. A sermon preached ...
April 26, 1643.   4to.
London, by R.O. & G.D. for Benjamin Allen,
1643   [Sermons Polemical IV]   Wing G1848.
1182(13)

GREGG (Hugh). Curiosities in chymistry ...
published by ... H.G. [i.e. Hugh Gregg] , 1691.
See BOYLE (Hon. Robert).   **601**

GREGORIANA ACADEMIA.
See ROME. Collegium Romanum Societatis Jesu.

GREGORY XIII, Pope. The holy Bull and
Crusado of Rome: first published by Gregory the
xiii ... Compared with the testimony of the Holy
Scriptures.   4to.
London, reprinted by Iohn Wolfe, 1588
[Consutilia II]   STC 12354.   **1428(20)**

GREGORY (David). Catoptricae et dioptricae
sphaericae elementa.   8vo.
Oxonii, e theatro Sheldoniano, 1695
Wing 1883.   **1684**

GREGORY (John). Works ... in two parts.
4th ed.   4to.
London, by M.Clark, for Rich.Royston, Benj.
Tooke and Tho.Sawbridge, 1684 (1683)
Woodcuts.   Wing G1915.   **1037**

[GRELOT (Guillaume Joseph)] . Rélation nouvelle
d'un voyage de Constantinople.   12mo.
Paris, en la boutique de Pierre Rocolet, chez la
veuve de Damien Foucault, 1681   Engr. pls.
512

GREVILLE (Sir Fulke).
See BROOKE (Fulke Greville, 1st Baron).

GREW (Nehemiah). The anatomy of plants.   fo.
[*London*] *by W.Rawlins, for the author, 1682*
Engr. pls. Wants pl.43.   Wing G1945.   **2618**

——————— Cosmologia sacra.   fo.
London, for W.Rogers, S.Smith, and B.Walford,
1701   Engr. fp. (port., Charrington p.70).
2304

——————— A discourse made before the
Royal Society, Decemb.10.1674. Concerning the
nature, causes, and power of mixture.   12mo.
London, for John Martyn, 1675
Wing G1948.   **97(2)**

——————— Musæum Regalis Societatis.
2 pts.   fo.
London, by W.Rawlins, for the author, 1681
Engr. fp. (port., Charrington p.4l), pls.
Wing G1952.   **2400**

GRIMSTONE (Edward). A generall historie of the
Netherlands ... Continued from ... 1608 till ... 1627
by W.Crosse.   2nd impr.   fo.
London, by Adam Islip, 1627   Engr. title-page,
pls.   STC 12376.   **2331**

GRINDAL (Edmund), Abp of Canterbury.
Articles ... in the ... visitation of Edmonde, Arch-
bishop, 1546 [1576] .
See ENGLAND. *Church of England.*   **1761(6)**

GROENEVELT (Joannes). Dissertatio lithologica.
Ed. 2a.   8vo.
Londini, typis M.Flesher, impensis Abeli Swalle,
1687   Engr. pls.   Wing G2062.   **1194**

———————Λιθολογια. A treatise of the stone
& gravel.   8vo.
London, printed by H.C. for J.T., sold by Rob.
Clavel, 1677   Wing G2063.   **371**

GRONOVIUS (Jacobus). Thesaurus Græcarum
antiquitatum.   13 vols.   fo.
Lugduni Batavorum, excudebant Petrus et Balduin-
us vander Aa, cælabat Hildebrandus vander Aa,
fratres, 1697-1702   Engr. title-pages, pls.
Vol.1: engr. fp. (port., Charrington p.71).
Vol.4: engr. maps.
Tanner II, p.319.   **2767-79**

GROTIUS (Hugo). Opera omnia theologica.
3 vols in 4.   fo.
Londini, apud Mosem Pitt, 1679   Vol.1: engr.
fp. (port., Charrington p.71).   Wing G2081.
2722-5

———————De jure belli ac pacis.   8vo.
Amstelædami, apud Janssonio-Wæsbergios, 1680
Engr. fp. (port.), engr. title-page.   **1507**

——————— [De jure belli ac pacis.] The most
excellent Hugo Grotius his three books treating of
the rights of war and peace ... Transl. by W.Evats.
fo.
London, by M.W. for Thomas Basset and Ralph
Smith, 1682   Engr. fp. (ports, Charrington
pp.58, 71).   Wing G2126.   **2353**

——————— Via ad pacem ecclesiasticam, 1642.
See VIA ad pacem ecclesiasticam ...   **1012**

GUALDI, Abbot, *pseud.*   *See* LETI (Gregorio).

[GUALDO PRIORATO (Galeazzo)] . Histoire de
la paix concluë sur la frontière de France et
d'Espagne ... l'an M.DC.LIX. [Transl. by H.
Courtin.]   12mo.
Cologne, chez Pierre de la Place, 1667
Engr. pl.   **460**

[GUARINI (Giovanni Battista)] . Il pastor fido.
The faithfull shepheard. With ... other poems [by
Sir R.Fanshawe] .   8vo.

London, for A.Moseley, 1664   Engr. fp. (port.,
Charrington p.71), pl.   Wing G2176; Diary
25 Feb.1667/8.   **926**

GUEVARA (Antonio de), Bp of Mondoñedo.
A booke of the inuention of the art of nauigation.
4to.
London, for Ralph Newberrie, 1578   [Sea
Tracts I]   Wants Bb1, 8, D1-4, & G4.
On title-page MS motto 'Magnus ope minorum' in
unidentified hand.   STC 12425.   **1077(1)**

GUGLIELMINI (Domenico). Della natura de'
fiumi.   4to.
Bologna, per gl'eredi d'Antonio Pisarri, 1697
    1666(1)

——————— Epistolæ duæ hydrostaticæ.
Bononiæ, apud HH.Antonij Pisarij, 1692
Engr. diagram.   **1666(2)**

GUICHENON (Samuel). Histoire généalogique de
la royale maison de Savoye.   2 vols.   fo.
Lyon, chez Guillaume Barbier, 1660   Engr.
title-page, pls (inc. ports, Charrington pp.37, 71).
    2897-8

[GUILFORD (Francis North, Baron)] . A philo-
sophical essay of musick.   4to.
London, for John Martyn, 1677
Wing G2216.   **1712(2)**

[GUILLET DE SAINT-GEORGE (Georges)] . An
account of a late voyage to Athens. By M.de La
Guilletiere.   8vo.
London, by J.M. for H.Herringman, 1676
Wing G2218.   **896**

——————— Les arts de l'homme d'epée, ou le
dictionaire du gentilhomme.   12mo.
A la Haye, chez Adrian Moetjens, 1680
Engr. pls.   **459**

GUILLIM (John). A display of heraldry ... 5th ed.,
to which is added a treatise of honour ... by J.
Logan.   2 pts.   [*Pt 2 entitled* Analogia
honorum ...]   fo.
*London, by S.Roycroft (— by Tho.Roycroft) for
R.Blome* [*etc.*] , 1679 (1677)   Engrs, some col.;
engr. ports. 2 insertions: in Guillim, after p.312,
drawing of naval coronet ('from Mr King, Lancaster
Herald', 25 May 1699); in Analogia, after p.32,
engraving of achievements of the 1st Duke of
Marlborough (1702?; titled in French).
Wing G2222; L2834; Diary 6 Sept.1667.   **2576**

GUISE (Henri II de Lorraine, Duc de). Les
mémoires de feu Monsieur le Duc de Guise.   4to.
*Paris, chez Edme Martin, et Sebastien Mabre-
Cramoisy*, 1668   **1969**

GULIELMUS, Abp of Tyre.
See WILLIAM, Abp of Tyre.

GULIELMUS, de Occam.
See WILLIAM, of Occam.

GUMBLE (Thomas). The life of General Monck,
Duke of Albemarle.   8vo.
London, by J.S. for Thomas Basset, 1671
Engr. fp. (port., Charrington p.1).   Wing G2230;
Naval Minutes p.9.   **1000**

GUNTON (Simon). The history of the church of
Peterburgh ... Set forth by Symon Patrick.   fo.
London, for Richard Chiswell, 1686   Engrs.
Wing G2246.   **2548**

GUTHRIE (Henry), Bp of Dunkeld. Memoirs of
Henry Guthry.   8vo.
London, printed for W.B. and sold by J.Nutt,
1702   **1308**

GWINNE (Matthew). Nero, tragœdia nova.   12mo.
Londini, typis M.F., prostant apud R.Mynne, 1639
STC 12553.   **217(3)**

GYRARDUS (L.G.).   *See* GIRALDI (Lilio
Gregorio).

H

H.(C.). A pleasant discourse between conscience
and plain-dealing.   12mo.
*London, for Iohn Wright, Iohn Clarke, William
Thackeray, and Thomas Passinger* [c.1680]
[Penny-Merriments I]   **362(29)**

H.(J.), minister. Jehojadahs justice, 1645.
See HOYLE (Joshua).   **1183(3)**

H.(M.). Historia Britannica, 1640.
See HISTORIA Britannica.   **28**

H.(M.). A narrative of the proceedings of the fleet.
4to.
London, printed by John Streater, 1659
[Naval Pamphlets]   Wing H93.   **1399(2)**

H.(P.). The politicks of France, 1680.
See CHASTELET (Paul Hay, Marquis du).   **578**

H.(R.). Divers voyages, 1582.
See HAKLUYT (Richard).   **1077(8)**

H.(R.). The life and death of Mother Shipton,
1684.
See HEAD (Richard).   **1193(7)**

H.(Sir R.). The young clerks guide, 1690.
See HUTTON (Sir Richard).   **966**

H.(T.). An account of several new inventions,
1691.
See HALE (Thomas).   **396**

H.(T.). The famous and remarkable history of Sir Richard Whittington, by T.H. [c.1680].
See HEYWOOD (Thomas).　　　　**1192(12)**

HABINGTON (William). The historie of Edward the fourth.　fo.
London, by Tho.Cotes for William Cooke, 1640
MS notes on p.37 in unidentified hand.
STC 12586.　　　　**2003**

[HACKET (John), Bp of Lichfield]. Loiola [*a comedy in verse*]. (— Stoicus vapulans [by J.Barret]. — Cancer, comoedia. — Paria ... authore T.Vincent.)　12mo.
Londini, typis R.C., sumptibus Andr.Crooke, 1648　Wing H170.　　　　**216**

————————— Scrinia reserata: a memorial ... of John Williams ... Archbishop of York.　2 pts.　fo.
In the Savoy, by Edw.Jones, for Samuel Lowndes, 1693　Engr. fp. (port., Charrington p.179); MS notes on end flyleaf in Daniel Waterland's hand.
Wing H171.　　　　**2306**

HAKEWILL (George). An apologie or declaration of the power and providence of God.　3rd ed. 2 pts.　fo.
Oxford, by William Turner (— London, for Robert Allott), 1635　Engr. title-page.
STC 12613; Diary 3 Feb.1666/7.　　　　**2016**

[HAKLUYT (Richard)]. Diuers voyages touching the discouerie of America ... with two mappes annexed.　4to.
London, (by Thomas Dawson) for Thomas Woodcocke, 1582　[Sea Tracts I]　Wants the maps.
MS notes and, on title-page, MS motto 'Magnus ope minorum' in unidentified hands.
STC 12624.　　　　**1077(8)**

————————— The principal navigations, voyages, traffiques and discoveries of the English nation. 3 vols in 2.　fo.
London, by George Bishop, Ralph Newberie and Robert Barker, 1599-1600　Without the map.
STC 12626, 12626a; Tangier Papers p.51 (29 Oct. 1683).　　　　**2111-2**

[HALE (Sir Matthew)]. Difficiles nugæ: or, observations touching the Torricellian experiment.　8vo.
London, printed by W.Godbid, for William Shrowsbury, 1674　Diagrams.　Wing H238.　　　　**935**

————————— A discourse of the knowledge of God, and of ourselves.　8vo.
London, printed by B.W. for William Shrowsbery, 1688　Engr. fp. (port., Charrington p.73).
Wing H240.　　　　**1175**

[—————————] An essay touching the gravitation, or non-gravitation of fluid bodies.　8vo.
London, printed by W.Godbid, for William Shrewsbury, 1673　Wing H244.　　　　**366**

————— —————Pleas of the Crown.　8vo.
London, by the assigns of Richard Atkins, and Edward Atkins Esq; for William Shrewsbury, and John Leigh, 1685　Wing H256.　　　　**1114**

————————— The primitive origination of mankind considered and examined.　fo.
London, by William Godbid, for William Shrowsbery, 1677　Engr. fp. (port., Charrington p.73).
Wing H258.　　　　**2380**

————————— A short treatise touching sheriffs accompts ... To which is added, a tryal of witches. ... March 1664, before ... Sir Matthew Hale. 2 pts.　8vo.
London, printed, and are to be sold by Will. Shrowsbery, 1683 (1682)　Wing H260; T2240.
　　　　904

[HALE (Thomas)]. An account of several new inventions ... relating to building ... shipping. Also a treatise of naval philosophy ... by Sir W.Petty. 12mo.
London, for James Astwood, and are to be sold by Ralph Simpson, 1691　2 printed leaves inserted at end, entitled 'A survey of the buildings and encroachments on the Thames ... Navy Office, 30th Oct.1684'.　Wing H265; Tanner I, p.66.
　　　　396

HALES (John). Golden remains.　2nd impr., with additions.　4 pts.　4to.
London, by Tho.Newcomb, for Robert Pawlet, 1673　Engr. title-page.　Wing H271.　　　　**1789**

[HALIFAX (George Savile, 1st Marquis of)]. The character of a trimmer. By Sir W.Coventry [*or rather by the Marquis of Halifax*].　2nd ed. 4to.
London, for Richard Baldwin, 1689
[Consutilia I]　Wing H297.　　　　**1427(10)**

————————— Miscellanies.　7 pts.　8vo.
London, for Matt.Gillyflower, (1699-)1700
Wing H315; Diary 22 Dec.1662.　　　　**1447**

[—————————] A rough draught of a new model at sea.　4to.
London, for A.Banks, 1694　[Naval Pamphlets]
Wing H319.　　　　**1399(11)**

[—————————] Some cautions offered to the consideration of those who are to chuse members to serve in the ensuing Parliament.　4to.
London, 1695　[Consutilia VII]　Wing H322.
　　　　1433(12)

HALL (Henry). Heaven ravished ... A sermon ... May 29.1644.　4to.
[*London*] *by J.Raworth, for Samuel Gellibrand*, 1644　[Sermons Polemical IV]　Wing H340.
　　　　1182(14)

[HALL (Thomas)] . The pulpit guarded with XX arguments.   The 4 ed.   4to.
London, by J.Cottrel, for E.Blackmore, 1652
[Liturgick Controversies II]   Wing H439.
1188(19)

HALLE (Edward). [The vnion of the twoo noble and illustre famelies of Lancastre ℒ Yorke.]   fo.
[*Londō, by Rychard Grafton, 1550*]   Wants πA⁴, A2, Y6, Z⁶. A7 supplied from another copy. Title, preface, dedication and table supplied in MS.   STC 12723; Duff p.27; Howarth p.189.
1978(1)

HALLEY (Edmund). [*Begins*] May it please the King's Most Excellent Majesty. [A paper on the tides, printed to accompany Newton's Principia.] 4to.
[*London, 1687*]   **1866(2)**

HALLIFAX (William). A sermon preach'd ... January 30.1701.   4to.
London, printed and sold by M.Wotton, 1702
[Convocation Pamphlets X]   **1696(10)**

HALLIMAN (Peter). The square and cube root compleated.   8vo.
London, by J.Leake for the author, and [*sold*] *by Edward Poole, 1686*   **602**

HAMBDEN (John). [The tryal and conviction of J.Hambden ... 6 Feb.1683.]   fo.
[*London, for Benjamin Tooke, 1684*]
Wants title-page.   [Narratives & Tryals V]
Wing T2160.   **2253(9)**

——————— The tryal of John Hambden. 30 Dec.1685.   fo.
London, by E.Mallet for D.Mallet, 1685
[Narratives & Tryals V]   Wing T2193.
2253(19)

HAMILTON (William), Archdeacon of Armagh. The exemplary life and character of James Bonnell ... The sermon preached at his funeral.   8vo.
London, printed and sold by J.Downing, 1704
Engr. fp. (port., Charrington p.18).   MS note on flyleaf 'Ex dono ... Jo.Millington ... 1704'.   **1006**

HAMMOND (Henry). A paraphrase and annotations upon ... the New Testament.   3rd ed.
[*With the text.*]   fo.
London, by J.F. and E.T. for Richard Davis bookseller in Oxford, 1671   **2720**

——————— Supplement, 1699.
See LE CLERC (Jean).   **1574**

[———————] A view of the new directory and a vindication of the ancient liturgy of the Church of England.   4to.
Oxford, by Leonard Lichfield, 1645   [Liturgick Controversies II]   Wing H612.   **1188(15)**

HAMPDEN (John).   *See* HAMBDEN (John).

HANMER (Meredith). The historie of Ireland, collected by ... M.Hanmer, E.Campion ... and E.Spenser. (Published by Sir J.Ware.)   fo.
Dublin, by the Societie of Stationers, 1633
STC 25067a; Howarth p.189.   **2000**

HAPPY (The) future state of England, 1688.
See PETT (Sir Peter).   **2413**

HARANGUES sur toutes sortes de sujets, 1688.
See ORTIGUE DE VAUMORIÈRE (Pierre d').
1883

HARDWICK (Humphrey). The difficulty of Sions deliverance and reformation ... a sermon ... June 26.1644.   4to.
London, by I.L. for Christopher Meredith, 1644
[Sermons Polemical IV]   Wing H704.   **1182(15)**

HARDYNG (John). The chronicle of Jhon Hardyng, from the firste begynnyng of Englande. 2 pts.   8vo.
Londini, ex officina Richardi Graftoni, 1543
STC 12767; Duff p.28; Howarth p.189.   **1442**

HARMER (Anthony), *pseud.*   *See* WHARTON (Henry).

HARPSFIELD (Nicholas). Historia Anglicana ecclesiastica ... adjecta brevi narratione de divortio Henrici VIII ... ab E.Campiano.   fo.
Duaci, sumptibus Marci Wyon, 1622   **2489**

HARRINGTON (James), the elder. Aphorisms political.   2nd ed.   4to.
London, by J.C. for Henry Fletcher, 1659
Wing H805.   **1297(6)**

——————— The art of law-giving: in III books ... To which is added an appendix concerning an House of Peers.   8vo.
London, by J.C. for Henry Fletcher, 1659
Wing H806.   **533(1)**

[———————] Brief directions shewing how a fit and perfect model of popular government may be made.   4to.
(*London, for Daniel Pakeman, 1659*)
At end: two final half-lines obliterated.
Wing H807.   **1297(9)**

——————— The commonwealth of Oceana. fo.
London, for D.Pakeman, 1656   Wing H809A;
Diary 26 Dec.1667.   **2114**

——————— A discourse shewing that the spirit of parliaments ... is not to be trusted for a settlement: lest it introduce monarchy.   4to.
London, by J.C. for Henry Fletcher, 1659
Wing H812.   **1297(13)**

——————— A discourse upon this saying: The spirit of the nation is not yet to be trusted with liberty.   4to.
London, by J.C. for Henry Fletcher [1659]
Wing H813.   **1297(12)**

[———————] A letter unto Mr Stubs in answer to his Oceana weighed.   4to.
(*London, for J.S.*, 1660)   Wing L1756.   **1297(4)**

——————— A parallel of the spirit of the people, with the spirit of Mr.Rogers.   4to.
London, by J.C. for Henry Fletcher [1659]
Wing H817.   **1297(11)**

——————— Political discourses.   7 pts.
4to.
London, by J.C. for Henry Fletcher, 1660
Title-page misbound between (8) and (9).
Wing H818.   **1297(6-13)**

——————— Pour enclouer le canon. [*Engl.*]
4to.
(*London, for Henry Fletcher*, 1659)
Wing H819.   **1297(10)**

——————— The prerogative of popular government ... in 2 books.   4to.
London, (by G.Dawson) for Tho.Brewster,
1658 (1657)   Engr. fp. (port., Charrington
p.74).   Wing H820.   **1297(1)**

[———————] The rota: or, a model of a free-state.   4to.
London, for John Starkey, 1660   Wing H821.
                                         1297(2)

——————— The stumbling-block of dis-obedience & rebellion ... removed.   4to.
(*London, for D.Pakeman*, 1658)   Wing H822.
                                         1297(8)

[———————] The use and manner of the ballot.   brs.
[1660]   Engr.   Wing H823.   **1297(3)**

——————— Valerius and Publicola, or the true form of a popular common-wealth.   4to.
London, by J.C. for Henry Fletcher, 1659
Wing H824.   **1297(7)**

[———————] The wayes and meanes whereby an equal & lasting commonwealth may be suddenly introduced.
London, for J.S., 1660   Wing H825.   **1297(2A)**

[HARRINGTON (James), the younger]. Some reflexions upon a treatise [*by T.Carre*] call'd Pietas Romana & Parisiensis.   4to.
Oxford, printed at the Theater, 1688
MS note on title-page (in hand of one of Pepys's clerks): 'By Mr Harrington of Christ-Church, Oxford'.   Wing H834.   **1873**

HARRIS (John). The destruction of Sodome: a sermon preached ... Feb.18.1628.   4to.
London, by H.L. and R.Y. for G.Lathum [1628]
[Sermons Polemical IV]   STC 12806.   **1182(16)**

HARRIS (John), D.D. Remarks on some late papers relating to the universal deluge.   8vo.
London, for R.Wilkin, 1697   Wing H856.   **1243**

HARRIS (Robert). Hezekiah's recovery. A sermon.
4to.
London, by R.Y. for Iohn Bartlet, 1626
[Sermons Polemical IV]   STC 12836.   **1182(17)**

HARRISON (Henry). The arraignment, tryal, conviction and condemnation of Henry Harrison, for the barbarous murther of Andrew Clenche.
2 pts.   fo.
London, printed by Thomas Braddyll, and are to be sold by William Battersby, and R.Baldwin,
1692   [Consutilia VI]   Wing A3765.   **1432(5)**

——————— The last dying words, behaviour, and confession of Henry Harrison.   brs.
London, printed, and are to be sold by Richard Baldwin, 1692   [Consutilia VI]
Wing H891.   **1432(4)**

——————— The last words of a dying penitent ... written with his own hand.   4to.
London, printed, and are to be sold by Randal Taylor, 1692   [Consutilia VI]   Wing H892.
                                         1432(1)

——————— A true copy of a letter, writen by Mr.Harrison ... after his condemnation.   brs.
London, printed for Randal Taylor [1692]
[Consutilia VI]   Wing H893.   **1432(2)**

HARRISON (John). The tragicall life and death of Muley Abdala Melek the late King of Barbarie.
4to.
Delph, 1633   [Consutilia V]   STC 12860.
                                         1431(16)

HARRISON (Thomas). The speeches and prayers, 1660.
See SPEECHES (The) and prayers of Major General Harison [and 9 others].   **1430(2)**

HARRISSON (John). Syderum secreta: or an astrological ... diary, for ... 1688.   8vo.
London, printed by John Richardson, for the Company of Stationers, 1688   [Almanacks for the year 1688]   Wing A1814.   **425(14)**

——————— Syderum secreta, or an astrologi-cal ... diary, for ... 1689.   8vo.
London, printed by John Richardson for the Company of Stationers, 1689   [Almanacks for the year 1689]   Wing A1814A.   **426(7)**

[HART (John)]. The black book of conscience ... by A.Jones [*or rather by J.Hart*].   42nd ed.
12mo.

[*London*] *for J.Clark, W.Thackery, & T.Passing*[*er*] [c.1680] [Penny-Godlinesses] **365(5)**

[――――――――] The charitable Christian. 12mo. [*London*] *by T.H., to be sold by J.Wright, J.Clarke* [*etc.*], 1682 [Penny-Godlinesses] Woodcut fp. (port., Charrington p.75). **365(27)**

[――――――――] Death triumphant ... By A. Jones [i.e. J.Hart?]. 6th ed. 12mo. *London, for I.Clarke, W.Thackeray, and T.Passinger* [c.1680] [Penny-Godlinesses] Woodcuts. **365(19)**

[――――――――] The dreadful character of a drunkard. 12mo. [*London*] *by J.M. for J.Clarke, W.Thackeray, and T.Passinger*, 1686 [Penny-Godlinesses] Woodcut. **365(1)**

[――――――――] The dying man's last sermon. By A.Jones [i.e. J.Hart?]. 12mo. [*London*] *for J.Wright, J.Clarke, W.Thackeray, and T.Passinger* [c.1685] [Penny-Godlinesses] Woodcut fp. (port., Charrington p.75). **365(34)**

[――――――――] A godly sermon of Peter's repentance. 14th ed. 12mo. *London, for J.Wright, J.Clarke, W.Thackeray, and T.Passenger*, 1682 [Penny-Godlinesses] Woodcut fp. (port., Charrington p.75). **365(26)**

HARTSOEKER (Nicolaas). Principes de physique. 4to. *Paris, chez Jean Anisson*, 1696 **1983**

[HARVEY (Christopher)]. The synagogue: or the shadow of the temple ... In imitation of George Herbert. 7th ed. 12mo. *London, by S.Roycroft, for R.S., and are to be sold by John Williams junior*, 1679 Wing H1050. **480(2)**

HATHAWAY (Richard). The tryal of Richard Hathaway ... March the 24th, 1702. fo. *London, for Isaac Cleave*, 1702 [Narratives & Tryals VII] **2255(12)**

HAUSTED (Peter). Senile odium, comoedia. 12mo. *Cantabrigiæ, ex academiæ typographeo*, 1633 STC 12936. **218(3)**

HAWES (Stephen). Here begynneth the boke called the example of vertu. [*London, Wynkyn de Worde*, 1510] MS verse in unidentified 16th-cent. hand at cc2. STC 12945; Duff p.28. **1254(2)**

HAWKINS (Francis). A narrative, being a true relation of what discourse passed between Dr. Hawkins and Edward Fitz-Harys. *London, for Samuel Carr*, 1681 Wing H1173. **2052(19)**

HAWKINS (Sir Richard). The observations of Sir Richard Hawkins in his vojage into the South Sea, A.D. 1593. fo. *London, by I.D*[*awson*] *for Iohn Iaggard*, 1622 STC 12962. **2020**

HAY (Paul), Marquis du Chastelet. *See* CHASTELET (Paul Hay, Marquis du).

HAYLEY (William), Dean of Chichester. Concio ad synodum ... habita. 4to. *Londini, excudebat T.Hodgkin, impensis Jacobi Tonson*, 1701 [Convocation Pamphlets XII] **1698(3)**

HAYWARD (Edward). The sizes and lengths of riggings for all His Majesties ships and frigates. fo. *London, by Peter Cole*, 1660 With an extra leaf containing 'A list of ships whose names have been changed'. Wing H1230. **2056**

[HEAD (Richard)]. The life and death of Mother Shipton. 4to. *London, for Benj.Harris*, 1684 [Vulgaria IV] Woodcuts. Wing H1258. **1193(7)**

[――――――――] The life and death of the English rogue. 4to. *London, for Charles Passinger*, 1679 [Vulgaria III] Woodcut. Wing H1262. **1192(20)**

HEADS (The) of reasons for which a generall councell of Protestants ought to be called. 4to. *London, by E.P. for Nicolas Bourne*, 1641 [Consutilia II] Wing H1287. **1428(11)**

HEATH (James). A chronicle of the late intestine war ... 2nd ed. To which is added A continuation to ... 1675 (by J.Philips). fo. *London, printed by J.C. for Thomas Basset*, 1676 Engr. fp. Wing H1321. **2160**

HEATH (Thomas). Stenographie: or, the art of short-writing. 8vo. *London*, 1644 [Short-hand collection III] Wing H1342; Carlton pp.67-8. **402(7)**

HEAVENLY (An) acte concernynge howe man shall lyue. 8vo. [*London*] (*by me Robert Wyer*,) [1550?] STC 97; Duff p.28. **75(2)**

HEAVEN'S messengers. 8vo. *London, for J.Clarke* [c.1680] [Penny-Godlinesses] Woodcut. **365(21)**

HEEREBOORD (Adrian). Ἑρμηνεια logica, seu synopseos logicæ Burgersdicianæ explicatio ... Ed. nova. Accedit Praxis logica. 8vo. *Cantabrigiæ, ex officina Joan.Hayes*, 1680 U4 missing, supplied in pen-facsimile. Wing H1361. **357**

[HEGG (Robert)]. The legend of St.Cuthbert.
With the antiquities of the Church of Durham.
By B.R.   8vo.
London, for Christopher Eccleston, 1663
Engr. fp.   Wing H1370.   **131**

HELMOLDUS. Chronica Slavorum Helmoldi ...
et Arnoldi Abbatis Lubecensis ... H.Bangertus ...
notis illustravit.   4to.
*Lubecæ, sumptibus Statii Wesselii, literis Jacobi
Hinderlingii,* 1659   Engr. title-page, pl.   **1466**

[HELMONT (Franciscus Mercurius van)]. Two
hundred queries ... concerning the doctrine of the
revolution of humane souls.   8vo.
London, printed for Rob.Kettlewell, 1684
Wing H1396.   **415**

HELWICH (Christoph). The historical and chrono-
logical theatre.   fo.
*London, by M.Flesher, for George West and John
Crosley, in Oxford,* 1687   Wing H1411.   **2238**

HENDERSON (Alexander). A sermon preached ...
December 27.1643.   4to.
London, for Robert Bostock, 1644   [Sermons
Polemical IV]   Wing H1439.   **1182(18)**

————————— A sermon preached ... 28 of May,
1645.   4to.
London, by F.N. for Robert Bostock, 1645
[Sermons Polemical IV]   Wing H1443.
                                        1182(19)

HENNEPIN (Louis). A new discovery of a vast
country in America.   2 pts.   8vo.
*London, for M.Bentley, J.Tonson, H.Bonwick
[etc.],* 1698   Engr. pls, maps.   Wing H1450.
                                          1360

HENRY VIII, King of England. A necessary
doctrine ... sette furthe by the Kynges maiestie,
1543.
See ENGLAND. Church of England.   **1757**

————————— (Assertio septē sacramēto 4
aduersus Marti. Luthe ꝝ.)   4to.
(Romæ, opera Stephani Guillireti, 1521)
The 'Assertio' is preceded by four leaves contain-
ing the letter of Leo X to Henry VIII.
Adams H246; Duff p.29.   **1481(1)**

HENRY III, King of France. Le code du roy
Henry III, 1605.
See FRANCE. *Laws.*   **2563**

[HENRY, the Minstrel]. The life and acts of ...
Sir William Wallace.   12mo.
Edinburgh, printed by Andrew Anderson, 1673
Wing L1987.   **358(1)**

HENSHAW (Nathaniel). Aero-chalinos: or, a
register for the air.   2nd ed.   12mo.
London, for Benj.Tooke, 1677   Wing H1482.
                                              72

HERBELOT (Barthélemy d'). Bibliothèque orient-
ale, ou dictionaire universel.   fo.
Paris, par la compagnie des libraires, 1697   **2793**

HERBERAY (Nicholas de), Sieur des Essars. The
most excellent history of the valiant & renowned
knight Don Flores of Greece.   3rd ed.   4to.
London, for R.I., 1664   [Vulgaria I]
Wing H1493.   **1190(3)**

HERBERT (George). The temple ... Together with
[the author's] life [by I.Walton].   11th ed.
2 pts.   12mo.
*London, by S.Roycroft, for R.S., to be sold by
John Williams junior,* 1679   Engr. pls.
Wing H1522.   **480(1)**

HERBERT (Sir Thomas), Bart. Some years travels
into divers parts of Africa, and Asia.   4th impr.
fo.
*London, by R.Everingham, for R.Scot, T.Basset
[etc.],* 1677   Engr. title-page, pls.
Wing H1536.   **2352**

HERBERT OF CHERBURY (Edward, Baron).
De religione gentilium, errorumque apud eos
causis.   4to.
Amstelædami, typis Blæviorum, 1663   **1457**

————————— The life and raigne of King Henry
the eighth.   fo.
London, by E.G. for Thomas Whitaker, 1649
Engr. fp. (port., Charrington p.78).
Wing H1504.   **2068**

HERBINIUS (Joannes). Dissertationes de admir-
andis mundi cataractis.   4to.
Amstelodami, apud Janssonio-Waesbergios, 1678
Engr. title-page, map, pls.   **1540**

HERING (Theodore). The triumph of the Church
over water and fire ... in a sermon preached on the
fifth day of November.1625.   4to.
London, by I.D. for Nicholas Bourne, 1625
[Sermons Polemical V]   STC 13204.   **1183(2)**

HERLE (Charles). Davids song of three parts ...
A sermon preached the 15.day of June, 1643.
4to.
London, by T.Brudenell for N.A., 1643
[Sermons Polemical V]   Wing H1556.   **1183(1)**

HERMANN (Paul). Paradisus Batavus ... cui
accessit Catalogus plantarum.   4to.
*Lugduni Batavorum, impensis viduæ (Anna-
Geertruda Stomphius), apud Abrahamum Elzevier,*
1698   110 engr. pls.   **1908**

HERNE (Samuel). Domus Carthusiana; or, an
account ... of the Charterhouse.   8vo.
*London, printed by T.R. for Richard Marriott and
Henry Brome,* 1677   Engr. pls. (port.).
Wing H1578.   **1063**

HERODIANUS. Ἱστοριων Βιβλια ἡ. [With a Latin translation by A.Politianus.] 8vo.
Oxoniæ, e Theatro Sheldoniano, 1699
Wing H1580. **1754**

HERODOTUS. Ἱστοριῶν λόγοι θ' ... τοῦ αὐτοῦ ἐξήγησις περὶ τῆς Ὁμήρου βιωτῆς ... Cum Vallæ interpret. Latina ... Excerpta è Ctesiæ libris. fo.
[Geneva] Oliva Pauli Stephani, 1618 Woodcuts.
2487

———————— Les histoires. Mises en François, par P.Du-Ryer. 2e éd. fo.
Paris, chez Augustin Courbé, 1658 Engr. title-page. **2562**

HEROLDT (Johann), Basilius. De bello sacro continuatæ historiæ, libri VI. Commentarijs rerum Syriacarum Guilhelmi Tyrensis Archiepiscopi, additi. fo.
Basileæ [N.Brylinger & J.Oporinus, 1549]
On title-page, autograph: 'Rob:Burtons', with MS note in Latin in unidentified 16th-cent. hand. Marginal MS notes in text. Adams H416.
2270(2)

HERRERO (Simón). Aqui se contienen quatro romances ... de algunos hurtos que hizo vn famoso ladron, llamado Moro Hueco. 4to.
Seville, impressos a costa de Iuan de Yllanes, 1670
Gaselee 77; Wilson p.314. **1545(65)**

HEVELIUS (Joannes). Annus climactericus. fo.
Gedani, sumptibus Auctoris, typis Dav.-Frid.
Rhetii, 1685 Engr. pls. Sig.Q misbound.
2715(1)

HEVIA BOLAÑOS (Juan de). Curia Filipica.
2 pts. 4to.
Madrid, por Melchor Sanchez (1657-69)
Gaselee 78, and p.13. **2117**

HEXAMERON rustique, 1671.
See LA MOTHE LE VAYER (François de).
307(2)

HEXHAM (Henry). A copious Englisg [sic] and Netherduytch dictionarie ... Het groot Woorden-Boeck. 2 pts. 4to.
Rotterdam, by Arnout Leers, 1660 (1658)
Wing H1650. **1420**

HEYLYN (Peter). Aërius redivivus: or the history of the Presbyterians. 2nd ed. fo.
London, by Robert Battersby for Christopher Wilkinson and Thomas Archer [etc.], 1672
Wing H1682. **2162**

———————— Cosmography. (6th ed.) fo.
London, for P.C., T.Passenger, B.Tooke [etc.], 1682 Engr. title-page, maps. Wing H1696.
2541

———————— Cyprianus Anglicus: or, the history of the life and death of ... William ... Archbishop of Canterbury. fo.
London, for A.Seile, 1668 Wing H1699; Diary 28 Aug., 16 Sept., 23 & 29 Nov.1668. **2222**

———————— Ecclesia restaurata. The history of the Reformation. 3rd ed. fo.
London, by R.B. for H.Twyford, J.Place [etc.], 1674 Wing H1703. **2209**

———————— A help to English history containing a succession of all the kings of England. 12mo.
London, for Tho.Basset, and C.Wilkinson (1674-) 1675 Woodcuts. Wing H1719; Tanner I, p.106. **440**

———————— The historie of ... St.George ... The institution of the ... Order of ... the Garter. 4to.
London, (by B.A. and T.F.) for Henry Seile, 1631 Engr. title-page. A3, 4 misbound. STC 13272.
1010

———————— The history of the Sabbath.
2 pts. 2nd ed. 4to.
London, for Henry Seile (by T.Cotes, for Henry Seyle), 1636 STC 13275. **1558**

HEYWOOD (John). A fourth hundred of epygrams. 8vo.
Londini, 1560 STC 13297a. **412(2)**

———————— An hundred epigrammes. 8vo.
(London, by Thomas Powell) 1556
STC 13295. **412(1)**

[————————] A mery play betwene Johan Johan the husbande, Tyb his wyfe, ℧ syr Jhān the preest. fo.
[London] (by Wyllyam Rastell, 1533)
STC 13298; Duff p.31. **1977(3)**

[————————] A mery play betwene the pardoner and the frere, the curate and neybour Pratte. fo.
[London] (by Wyllyam Rastell, 1533)
STC 13299; Duff p.30. **1977(4)**

[————————] Of gentylnes ℧ nobylyte [1525?].
See RASTELL (John). **1977(5)**

———————— The play called the foure P. 4to.
London, by John Allde, 1569 Woodcut.
STC 13302. **1977(6)**

———————— A play of loue. fo.
[London] (by W.Rastell, 1534) On title-page, in MS, Greek motto and autograph 'Thomas Skeffington'. STC 13303; Duff p.31. **1977(1)**

———————— The play of the wether. fo.
[London] (by W.Rastell, 1533) STC 13305; Duff p.31. **1977(2)**

——————The spider and the flie. 4to.
London, by Tho.Powell, 1556   MS notes in unidentified hand.   STC 13308; Duff p.32.
1099

[HEYWOOD (Thomas)]. The famous and remarkable history of Sir Richard Whittington ... Written by T.H. 4to.
[London] for W.Thackeray and T.Passinger [c.1680]   [Vulgaria III]   Woodcuts.
Wing H1782.   **1192(12)**

[——————] The life of Merlin, sirnamed Ambrosius. 4to.
London, printed by J.Okes, and are to be sold by Jasper Emery, 1641   Engr. fp.   Wing H1786.
1112(1)

HICKERINGILL (Edmund). Curse ye Meroz ... A sermon preached ... May the 9th, 1680.   4to.
London, by J.R. for J.Williams, 1680
[Sermons Polemical V]   Wing H1803.
1183(22)

HICKES (Gaspar). The glory and beauty of Gods portion: set forth in a sermon preached ... Iune 26. 1644. 4to.
London, by G.M. for Christopher Meredith, 1644
[Sermons Polemical V]   Wing H1838.   **1183(4)**

[HICKES (George)]. An apology for the new separation in a letter to Dr John Sharpe, Archbishop of York. 4to.
London, 1691   Wing H1841.   **1573(2)**

——————Institutiones grammaticæ Anglo-Saxonicæ et Moeso-Gothicæ. 3 pts. 4to.
Oxoniæ, e Theatro Sheldoniano, (1688-) 1689
Wing H1851.   **1802**

[——————] Jovian. Or, an answer to Julian the Apostate. 8vo.
London, by Sam.Roycroft for Walter Kettilby, 1683   Wing H1852.   **1026**

——————Linguarum vett. septentrionalium thesaurus grammatico-criticus et archæologicus. 2 vols. fo.
Oxoniæ, e theatro Sheldoniano, 1705 (1703)
Engr. fp. (port., Charrington p.80).
Tanner I, p.172.   **2937-8**

[——————] A vindication of some among our selves against the false principles of Dr.Sherlock. 4to.
London, 1692   [Consutilia X]
Wing H1878.   **1436(3)**

HIEROCLES, of Alexandria. Upon the golden verses of the Pythagoreans. Transl. immediately out of the Greek into English. 8vo.
London, by M.Flesher, for Thomas Fickus, bookseller in Oxford, 1682   Wing H1939.   **1017**

[HIERON (Samuel)]. A defence of the ministers reasons for refusall of subscription to the Booke of Common Prayer. Pts 1, 2. 4to.
1607-8   [Liturgick Controversies I]   Wants pt 3.   STC 13395.   **1187(1-2)**

HIGDEN (Ranulph). Polycronicon.   fo.
W.Caxton [*Westminster, after 2 July 1482*].
See Appendix.   **2063**

——————Polycronicon.   fo.
W. de Worde, Westminster, 13 April 1495.
See Appendix.   **2063**

HIGH (The) Court of Justice. Or Cromwells new slaughter-house in England, 1651.
See WALKER (Clement).   **1148(3)**

HIGHMORE (Nathaniel). The history of generation ... To which is joyned a discourse of the cure of wounds by sympathy. 8vo.
London, by R.N. for John Martin [1651]
Engr. pls.   π1-7 & A1-3 cropped.
Wing H1969.   **76**

HILL (Joseph). Historical dissertations. I. Concerning the antiquity of temples under the Old Testament ... II. Concerning the antiquity of churches under the New Testament. 4to.
London, for Tho.Parkhurst, 1698
Wing H1998-9.   **1361**

[——————] The interest of these United Provinces. Being a defence of the Zeelanders choice. 4to.
Middleburg, printed by Thomas Berry, 1673
Wing H2000; Naval Minutes p.48.   **1643**

[HILL (Samuel), Archdeacon of Wells]. Municipium ecclesiasticum; or, the rights, liberties and authorities of the Christian church asserted. 8vo.
London, printed and to be sold by the booksellers of London and Westminster, 1697   [Convocation Pamphlets VII]   Wing H2009.   **1693(1)**

——————The rights, liberties and authorities, of the Christian church asserted. 2 pts. 8vo.
London, for the author, and sold by the booksellers of London and Westminster, 1701
[Convocation Pamphlets VII]   **1693(2-3)**

HILL (Thomas). The militant Church triumphant ... presented in a sermon preached ... the 21. of July, 1643. 4to.
London, for John Bellamie and Ralph Smith, 1643   [Sermons Polemical V]   Wing H2024.
1183(6)

——————The strength of the saints ... Prescribed in a morning exercise in Westminster Abbey, the XIXth of April, 1648. 4to.
London, for Peter Cole, 1648   [Liturgick Controversies II]   Wing H2030.   **1188(7)**

—————The trade of truth advanced. In a sermon preached ... Iuly 27.1642.   4to.
London, by I.L. for Iohn Bellamie, Philemon Stephens [etc.], 1642   [Sermons Polemical V]
Wing H2031.   **1183(5)**

HISTOIRE d'Emeric Comte de Tekeli, 1693.
See LECLERC (Jean).   **715**

HISTOIRE de l'Academie Françoise, 1688.
See PELLISSON-FONTANIER (Paul).   **215**

HISTOIRE de la miraculeuse delivrance ... de Geneve [c.1603].
See GOULART (Simon).   **506**

HISTOIRE de la paix concluë ... l'an M.DC.LIX, 1667.
See GUALDO PRIORATO (Galeazzo).   **460**

HISTOIRE de la Papesse Jeanne, 1694.
See LENFANT (Jacques).   **580**

HISTOIRE de la Ste Écriture, 1678.
See PAGIT (Eusebius).   **2742(2)**

HISTOIRE des cheualiers de l'ordre de S.Iean de Hierusalem, 1659.
See BOSIO (Giacomo).   **2681**

HISTOIRE des conclaves depuis Clement V, 1694.
See LETI (Gregorio).   **535-6**

HISTOIRE des ouvrages des scavans, 1687-1703.
See BASNAGE (Jacques), Sieur de Beauval.
                                               109-27

HISTOIRE des revolutions de Suede, 1695.
See VERTOT (René Aubert de).   **670**

HISTOIRE naturelle ... des Iles Antilles, 1665.
See ROCHEFORT (César de).   **1855**

HISTORIA Britannica; hoc est, de rebus gestis Britanniæ seu Angliæ. Commentarioli tres. [By E.S., i.e. J.T.Clain? *Preface signed* M.H.]   12mo.
Oxoniæ, excudebat Leonard. Lichfield, impensis Matthiæ Hunt, 1640   STC 10013.   **28**

HISTORIA flagellantium, 1700.
See BOILEAU (Jacques).   **799**

HISTORIA histrionica: an historical account of the English-stage, 1699.
See WRIGHT (James).   **1293**

HISTORIA pontifical y catolica ... por ... G.de Illescas [*etc.*].   Vols 1-5. (Vols 1-2, 5a impr.)   fo.
Madrid, por Melchor Sanchez, a costa de Gabriel de Leon, 1652   Wants vol.6.   Gaselee 84.
                                               2186-90

HISTORIÆ Anglicanæ scriptores X ... ex vetustis manuscriptis. [Ed. by R.Twysden.]   2 vols.   fo.
Londini, typis Jacobi Flesher, sumptibus Cornelii Bee, prostant Lugd. Batav. apud Johannem et Danielem Elsevier, 1652   Wing H2094.   **2532-3**

HISTORIÆ Anglicanæ scriptores quinque, 1691.
See RERUM Anglicarum ...   **2629-30**

HISTORIAE Britannicae ... scriptores XV, 1691.
See RERUM Anglicarum ...   **2629-30**

HISTORIÆ poeticæ scriptores antiqui ... Græcè & Latinè. Accessêre breves notæ. [Ed. by T.Gale.]   8vo.
Parisiis, typis F.Muguet, prostant apud R.Scott bibliopolam Londinensem, 1675   **1110**

HISTORIÆ sacræ Veteris et Novi Testamenti. Biblische Figuren.   fo.
Amstelædami, ex officina Nicolai Vischer [c.1640]   Engr. title-page, 130 engr. pls.   **2925**

HISTORIAN'S (The) guide, 1688.
See CLARKE (Samuel), Minister of Bennet Fink.
                                               487(1)

HISTORICAL collections ... concerning the changes of religion, 1674.
See TOUCHET (George).   **848**

HISTORICAL (An) narration of ... Jesus Christ, 1685.
See WOODHEAD (Abraham).   **1854**

HISTORY (The) of Barbados, 1666.
See ROCHEFORT (César de).   **2102**

HISTORY (The) of Frier Bacon.   12mo.
London, for M.W. and are to be sold by D.Newman and B.Alsop, 1683   [Penny-Merriments I]
Woodcuts.   **362(1)**

HISTORY (The) of Independency, 1660.
See WALKER (Clement).   **1148(4)**

HISTORY (The) of King William the third, 1702.
See BOYER (Abel).   **1418**

HISTORY (The) of Mrs Jane Shore.   12mo.
[*London*] *for F.Coles, T.Vere and J.Wright* [c.1665]   [Penny-Merriments I]   Woodcuts.
                                               362(11)

HISTORY. The historie of Orlando Furioso, 1599.
See GREENE (Robert).   **1102(5)**

HISTORY (The) of passive obedience since the Reformation, 1690.
See SELLER (Abednego).   **1516(1)**

HISTORY (The) of the Apostles Creed, 1702.
See KING OF OCKHAM (Peter, 1st Baron).   **1416**

HISTORY (The) of the birth, travels, strange adventures, and death of Fortunatus. 4to.
London, printed by and for, T.Haly, 1682
[*Vulgaria III*]   Wing H2145.   **1192(3)**

HISTORY (The) of the blind beggar of Bednal-green. 12mo.
[*London*] *printed for Charles Dennisson*, 1686
[*Penny-Merriments I*]   Woodcut.
Wing H2146.   **362(15)**

HISTORY (The) of the Church of Great Britain, 1674.
See GEAVES (William).   **1759**

HISTORY (The) of the Convocation, 1702.
See KENNETT (White), Bp of Peterborough.   **1695(10)**

HISTORY (The) of the Council of Trent, 1676.
See SARPI (Paolo).   **2401**

HISTORY (The) of the damnable life and deserved death of Dr John Faustus. 4to.
London, for William Whitwood, 1674
[*Vulgaria III*]   Woodcuts.   Wing H2152.   **1192(14)**

HISTORY (The) of the desertion, 1689.
See BOHUN (Edmund).   **1427(5)**

HISTORY (The) of the execrable Irish rebellion, 1680.
See BORLASE (Edmund).   **2277**

HISTORY (The) of the goluen-eagle. 4to.
London, for William Thackeray, 1677
[*Vulgaria IV*]   Wing H2162.   **1193(11)**

HISTORY. The historie of the great and mightie Kingdome of China, 1588.
See GONZÁLEZ DE MENDOZA (Juan). **1216(1)**

HISTORY (The) of the imperiall estate of the Grand Seigneur, 1635.
See BAUDIER (Michel).   **1149**

HISTORY (The) of the last Parliament, 1702.
See DRAKE (James).   **959(1)**

HISTORY (The) of the life, reign and death of Edward II, 1680.
See FALKLAND (Henry Cary, Viscount).   **2260**

HISTORY (The) of the plot, 1679.
See L'ESTRANGE (Sir Roger).   **2249(17)**

HISTORY (The) of the quarrels of Pope Paul.V., 1626.
See SARPI (Paolo).   **1141**

HISTORY (The) of the Seven Wise Masters, 1687.
See SEVEN Wise Masters of Rome.   **364(5)**

HISTORY (The) of the seven wise mistresses of Rome, 1686.
See HOWARD (Thomas).   **364(6)**

HISTORY (The) of the triumvirates, 1686.
See CITRI DE LA GUETTE (Samuel de Broé, Seigneur de).   **1027**

HISTORY. The hystorye, sege and dystruccion of Troye, 1513.
See COLONNE (Guido delle).   **2257**

HITA (G.Pérez de).
See PÉREZ DE HITA (Ginés).

HOBBES (Thomas). A letter about liberty and necessity ... With observations [by B.Laney]. 12mo.
London, printed by J.Grover, for W.Crooke, 1676
Wing H2245A; Diary 20 Nov.1661.   **47**

———————— Leviathan, or the matter, forme, & power of a Common-wealth, ecclesiasticall and civill. fo.
London, for Andrew Crooke, 1651   Engr. title-page. Note in Pepys's hand on flyleaf: 'Sept.1668 – 30s.'   Wing H2246; Diary 3 Sept.1668. **2037**

———————— Tracts. 3 pts. 8vo.
London, for W.Crooke, 1682   Engr. fp. (port., Charrington p.80).   Wing H2265.   **1161**

HOCES (Bernardo de).
See HOZES (Bernardo de).

HOCUS pocus junior. The anatomy of legerdemain. 11th ed.   4to.
[*London*] *by J.M. for J.Deacon, to be sold by J.Gilbertson*, 1686   [*Vulgaria III*]   Woodcuts.   **1192(21)**

HODGES (Thomas). The growth and spreading of hæresie ... A sermon preached ... 10th day of March. 4to.
London, by T.R. and E.M. for Abel Roper, 1647
[*Sermons Polemical V*]   Wing H2315. **1183(8)**

HODGES (William). Great Britain's groans ... the oppression ... of the ... seamen of England. 4to.
[*London*] 1695   [*Naval Pamphlets*]
Inserted at end: MS copy (4pp., in hand of one of Pepys's clerks) of petition to parliament (1694) on behalf of seamen's widows & relations.
Wing H2327.   **1399(15)**

HODY (Humfrey). A history of English councils and convocations. 3 pts. 8vo.
London, for Rob.Clavell, 1701   [*Convocation Pamphlets IV*]   **1690**

[————————] Some thoughts on a convoc-ation. 4to.
London, for Tim.Childe, 1699   [*Convocation Pamphlets IX*]   Wing H2346.   **1695(2)**

HOFMANN (Johann Jacob). Lexicon universale.
2 vols.   fo.
*Basileæ, impensis Johan.Herman.Widerhold, typis
Jacobi Bertschii & Joh.Rodolphi Genathii*, 1677
Engr. title-page.   **2579-80**

HOGERS (Theophilus). Binæ orationes habitæ Bello
Anglico secundo ad Senatum Populumque Daven-
triensem.   12mo.
Amstelodami, apud Jodocum Pluymer, 1669
Title-page misbound before 63(1).   **63(2)**

[HOLBEIN (Hans)]. The images of the Old
Testament, lately expressed [by H.Holbein], set
forthe in Ynglishe and Frenche, with a playn and
brief exposition.   4to.
Lyons, Johan Frellon, 1549   Woodcuts.
Autograph 'Jacob Bell 1605' on title-page.
STC 3045.   **946**

HOLDEN (Mary). The womans almanack for ...
1688.   8vo.
*London, printed by J.Millet, for the Company of
Stationers*, 1688   [Almanacks for the year
1688]   Wing A1827.   **425(15)**

HOLDER (William). A discourse concerning time.
8vo.
London, printed by J.Heptinstall, for L.Meredith,
1694   Wing H2385.   **1202**

————————Elements of speech.   8vo.
London, by T.N. for J.Martyn, 1669
Wing H2386.   **831(1)**

————————A treatise of the natural grounds,
and principles of harmony.   8vo.
*London, printed by J.Heptinstall, for the author,
and sold by John Carr*, 1694   Engrs.
Wing H2389.   *See also below*, vol.IV.   **1225**

HOLDSWORTH (Richard). A sermon preached in
St.Maries in Cambridge ... 27 of March.   4to.
Cambridge, by Roger Daniel, 1642   [Sermons
Polemical V]   Wing H2401.   **1183(9)**

HOLINSHED (Raphael). The first and second
(— the third) volumes of chronicles.   3 vols in 2.
fo.
*London, at the expenses of Iohn Harison, George
Bishop, Rafe Newberie [etc.]*, 1587
STC 13569.   **2585-6**

HOLLANDERS (The) declaration of the affaires
of the East Indies.   4to.
Amsterdam [London], 1622   [Consutilia III]
STC 13598.   **1429(6)**

[HOLLES (Denzil Holles, Baron)]. The case
stated concerning the judicature of the House of
Peers.   8vo.
[London?] 1675   Wing H2452.   **731**

[————————] The grand question concerning
the judicature of the House of Peers stated.   8vo.
London, for Richard Chiswel, 1669
Wing H2459.   **498**

————————Memoirs ... 1641 to 1648.   8vo.
London, for Tim.Goodwin, 1699   Engr. fp.
(port., Charrington p.81).   Wing H2464.   **1383**

HOLLINGWORTH (Richard). The character of
King Charles I,.from the declaration of Mr.Alex-
ander Henderson.   4to.
London, printed, and are to be sold by R.Tayler,
1692   Wing H2500.   **1286(8)**

————————The death of King Charles I.
proved a down-right murder ... in a sermon.   4to.
London, printed by R.Norton for Walter Kettilby,
1693   Wing H2501.   **1286(10)**

————————A defence of King Charles I.
4to.
London, printed for Samuel Eddowes, 1692
Wing H2502.   **1286(2)**

————————A second defence of King Charles
I. By way of reply to ... Ludlow's letter to Dr.
Hollingworth.   4to.
London, for S.Eddowes, sold by Randal Taylor,
1692   Wing H2504.   **1286(4)**

————————Dr.Hollingworth's defence of
K.Charles the first's ... book, called Εικων Βασι-
λικη.   4to.
London, printed for Samuel Eddowes, 1692
Wing H2503.   **1286(6)**

HOLLOWAY (James). The free and voluntary confession and narrative of J.Holloway ... as also the
proceedings ... in ... Kings-Bench Court.   fo.
(London, for R.H., J.B. and J.R., 1684)
[Narratives & Tryals III]   **2251(21)**

[HOLYOKE (Francis)]. A large dictionary in 3
parts ... [*Engl. & Lat.*] Performed by ... T.Holyoke.
[*or rather by F.Holyoke, revised by T.Holyoke*].
fo.
*London, by W.Rawlins, for G.Sawbridge, W.Place
[etc.]* 1677 (1676)   Wing H2535.   **2688**

HOMER. Ἰλιας και Ὀδυσσεια, και εις αὐτας
σχολια ... (— Βατραχομυομαχια. — Ὑμνοι.)
Accurante C.Schrevelio. [*Gk & Lat.*]
2 vols in 1.   4to.
Lugd.Batauorum, apud Franciscum Hackium,
1656 (1655)   Engr. title-page.   **1780**

————————L'Iliade. Nouvelle traduction.
[By Le Sieur de La Valterie.]   2 vols.   12mo.
Paris, chez Claude Barbin, 1681   **851-2**

————————L'Odyssée. Nouvelle traduction.
[By Le Sieur de La Valterie.]   2 vols.   12mo.
Paris, chez Claude Barbin, 1681   **853-4**

HOMES (Nathaniel). A sermon preached ... Octob. the 6th, A.D.1659.   4to.
London, by J.B. for Edward Brewster, 1660
[Sermons Polemical V]   Wing H2577.   **1183(10)**

HONEY out of the rock, 1644.
See PRICE (John), of London.   **1184(13)**

HONOUR (The) of chivalry, 1683.
See FERNÁNDEZ (Jerónimo).   **1190(2)**

HONOUR (The) of the gentle craft.   12mo.
London, by H.B. for J.Clark, W.Thackeray, and T.Passinger, 1685   [Penny-Merriments I]
Woodcut.   **362(36)**

HOOD (Thomas). The marriners guide ... a dialogue.   4to.
London, by Thomas Est, for Thomas Wight, 1592
[Sea Tracts I]   MS notes in unidentified early 17th-cent. hand.   STC 13696.   **1077(4)**

————— The vse of the celestial globe in plano.   4to.
London, (by Iohn Windet) for Thobie Cooke, 1590   [Sea Tracts III]   MS notes in unidentified hand.   STC 13697.   **1079(3)**

————— The vse of the two mathematicall instruments, the crosse staffe ... And the Iacobs staffe ... the second time imprinted.   2 pts. 4to.
London, by Richard Field for Robert Dexter, 1596   [Sea Tracts IV]   Woodcut.
STC 13701.   **1080(3)**

HOOKE (Robert). Animadversions on the first part of the Machina coelestis of ... Johannes Hevelius.   4to.
London, by T.R. for John Martyn, 1674
Wing H2611.   **1727(2)**

————— A description of helioscopes. 4to.
London, by T.R. for John Martyn, 1676
Wing H2614.   **1727(3)**

————— Lampas: or descriptions of some mechanical improvements of lamps and water-poises.   4to.
London, for John Martyn, 1677
Wing H2616.   **1727(6)**

————— Lectures and collections made by Robert Hooke ... Cometa ... Microscopium.   4to.
London, for J.Martyn, 1678   Engr. pls.
Wing H2618.   **1712(4)**

————— [Another copy.]   **1727(5)**

————— Lectures de potentia restitutiva; or, of spring.   4to.
London, for John Martyn, 1678   Wing H2619.
1727(4)

————— Micrographia.   fo.
London, by Jo.Martyn, and Ja.Allestry, 1665
Engr. fp., diagrams.   Wing H2620; Diary 2, 20 & 21 Jan.1664/5.   **2116**

HOOKE (William). New Englands teares, for old Englands feares ... a sermon ... July 23, 1640. 4to.
London, by E.G. for Iohn Rothwell and Henry Overton, 1641   [Sermons Polemical V]
Wing H2624.   **1183(11)**

HOOKER (Richard). The Works ... With an account of his life and death [by I.Walton].   [*Engr. title-page has title:* Of the lawes of ecclesiastical politie.]   fo.
London, by Thomas Newcomb for Andrew Crook, 1666   Engr. fp. (port., Charrington p.82), engr. title-page.   Wing H2631; Diary 18 Aug.1661; 15 Apr.1667; 19 May 1667.   **2499**

HOOKER (Thomas). The danger of desertion: or, a farewell sermon.   2nd ed.   4to.
London, by G.M. for George Edwards, 1641
[Sermons Polemical V]   Wing H2645. **1183(12)**

[HOOPER (George), Bp of Bath and Wells]. A narrative of the proceedings of the Lower House of Convocation, relating to prorogations and adjournments. [*Also attributed to H.Aldrich.*] 4to.
London, for Tho.Bennet, 1701   [Convocation Pamphlets XI]   MS notes in hand of Daniel Waterland. On title-page 'Bp Hooper' in same hand.   **1697(4)**

[—————] The narrative of the Lower House of Convocation, as to the point of adjournments, vindicated.   4to.
[*London*, 1701]   [Convocation Pamphlets XI]
1697(5)

[—————] A summary defence of the Lower House of Convocation.   4to.
London, 1703   [Convocation Pamphlets XI]
MS notes in hand of Daniel Waterland. On title-page 'Bp Hooper' in same hand.   **1697(15)**

HOOPER (John), Bp of Gloucester. An oversight, and deliberacion vpon the holy Prophete Jonas. 8vo.
[*London, J.Daye and W.Seres*, 1550]
Wants Z8.   STC 13763; Duff p.33.   **55**

HOPE (Sir William). The compleat fencing master. [*A re-issue of* The Scots fencing master.]   8vo.
London, for Dorman Newman, 1691   Engr. pls.
Wing H2711.   **486**

HÔPITAL DE LA TRINITÉ, Paris. Institution, reglemens, statuts et privileges de la Maison et Hospital de la Trinité. Avec la forme du gouvernement.   4to.
Paris, de l'imprimerie de M.Le Prest, 1682   **1872**

HOPTON (Arthur). Hoptons concordancy enlarged ... Exactly computed by Iohn Penkethman.   2 pts. 8vo.
London, printed by Anne Griffin for Andrew Hebb, 1635   STC 13781.   755

HORACE. Q.Horatius Flaccus cum commentariis ... J.Bond. Accedunt indices ... accurante C. Schrevelio.   8vo.
Lugd.Batavorum, ex officina Hackiana, 1663
Engr. title-page.   1370

———————— The poems of Horace ... rendred in English verse by several persons. [Ed. by A.Brome.] 8vo.
London, by E.C. for W.Lee, G.Bedell, etc., 1666
Engr. fp. (port., Charrington p.21), title-page.
Wing H2782.   857

———————— Les oeuvres d'Horace, traduites en françois ... Par M.Dacier [i.e. A.Lefèvre]. Derniere ed. [*Lat. & Fr.*]   10 vols.   12mo.
Paris, chez Denys Thierry et Claude Barbin, 1691
Engr. fps.   761-70

HORMAN (William). Introductorium linguae latinae.   4to.
W. de Worde [*Westminster*, 1495]
See Appendix.   1305(5)

HORNIUS (Georgius). Accuratissima orbis delineatio. Sive Geographia vetus, sacra & profana. fo.
Amstelodami, apud Janssonio Wæsbergianos, 1677
52 engr. maps. MS index inserted.   2971

HORTA (Melchor). Obra ... sobre que vn gentilhombre tenia vna muger braua, y mal acondicionada.   4to.
(*Senilla* [sic] *por Juan Vejarano, à costa de Lucas Martin de Hermosa*) [c.1680]   Gaselee 80; Wilson p.256.   1545(37)

———————— [Another copy.]   1545(44)

HOSTE (Paul). L'art des armées navales. (— Théorie de la construction des vaisseaux.) 2 pts.   fo.
Lyon, chez Anisson et Posuel (de l'imprimerie de la veuve de Jacques Faeton), 1697   145 engr. pls, diagrams.   2697

———————— Recueil des traités de mathematique.   3 vols.   12mo.
Lyon, & se vend à Paris chez J.Anisson, 1692
1: 13 engr. pls.   2: 31 engr. pls.   3: 23 engr. pls.   620-2

HOUGH (Roger). Gods hatred against sin and wickedness.   12mo.
[*London*] *by H.B. for T.Passinger*, 1683
[Penny-Godlinesses]   365(39)

———————— Saints blessed for ever.   12mo.
[*London*] *by A.M. for J.Deacon* [c.1700]
[Penny-Godlinesses]   365(2)

HOW the members of the Church of England ought to behave themselves under a Roman Catholic king, with reference to the Test and Penal laws.   8vo.
London, printed·and are to be sold by Randal Taylor, 1687   Wing H2961.   1062

HOWARD (Sir Robert). Four new plays. The surprisal, The committee, The Indian-queen, The Vestal-virgin.   fo.
London, for Henry Herringman, 1665
Wing H2995.   2070

———————— The great favourite, or, the Duke of Lerma.   4to.
In the Savoy, for Henry Herringman, 1668
Includes errata leaf.   [Loose Plays II]
Wing H2996.   1604(11)

[————————] The life and reign of King Richard the second.   8vo.
London, for M.L. and L.C. and sold by Langly Curtis, 1681   Wing H3001; Naval Minutes p.48.
                                          877

[HOWARD (Thomas)]. The history of the seven wise mistresses of Rome.   8vo.
London, for M.Wotton, and G.Conyers, 1686
[Penny-Merriments III]   Woodcuts.
Wing H3009.   364(6)

[HOWELL (James)]. A discours of the Empire, and of the election of a King of the Romans. 8vo.
London, by F.L. for Charles Webb, 1658
Engr. fp.   Wing H3065.   606(4)

———————— Epistolæ Ho-elianæ.   3rd ed. 4 pts.   8vo.
London, printed for Humphrey Moseley, and are to be sold by Joseph Nevill, 1655
Engr. title-page.   Autograph: John Pepys [Pepys's brother]. MS notes in same hand on front endpaper.   Wing H3073.   806

———————— Londinopolis; an historical discourse.   fo.
London, by J.Streater, for Henry Twiford, George Sawbridge, [*etc.*], 1657   Engr. fp., pl.
Wing H3090.   2005

———————— Προεδρια-βασιλικη: a discourse concerning the precedency of kings.   fo.
London, by Ja.Cottrel, for Sam.Speed, and Chr. Eccleston, 1664   Engr. fp. (port., Charrington p.33), pls (ports, Charrington pp.83, 104, 136).
Wing H3109.   2038

———————— S.P.Q.V. A survay of the Signorie of Venice.   fo.
London, for Richard Lowndes, 1651
Engr. fp., pl. (port.).   Wing H3112.   1980

————————The second part of Massaniello, 1663.
See GIRAFFI (Alessandro). An exact history of the late revolutions in Naples. **717**

HOWELL (William), of Magdalene College, Cambridge. An institution of general history, or the history of the world. 2nd ed. 4 vols in 3. fo.
London, for Henry Herringman, Thomas Bassett, William Crook [etc.], 1680-85
Wing H3138. **2727-9**

————————An institution of general history, or the history of the ecclesiastical affairs of the world. Contemporary with the second part [*of the author's* History of the world]. fo.
London, for the authors widdow, by Miles Flesher, 1685 Wing H3139. **2728(2)**

[HOWELL (William), of Wadham College, Oxford] The common-prayer-book the best companion ... A collection of prayers. 4th ed. 8vo.
Oxford, at the theater, for John Howell, 1689
Wing H3132. **823(2)**

[————————] The Word of God the best guide, 1689.
See BIBLE. *English. Selections.* **823(1)**

[HOYLE (Joshua)] . Jehojadahs justice against Mattan, Baal's priest ... A sermon preacht ... by J.H. 4to.
London, by M.Simmons for Henry Overton, 1645
[Sermons Polemical V] Wing H3203. **1183(3)**

HOZES (Bernardo de). Zelo pastoral con que nuestro santissimo padre Innocencio XI ha prohibido sesenta y cinco proposiciones. 4to.
Sevilla, en la oficina de Thomas Lopez de Haro, 1683 Gaselee 79. **1363(1)**

HUARTE NAVARRO (Juan de Dios de). Examen de ingenios para las ciencias. 4to.
Madrid, por Melchor Sanchez, acosta de Gabriel de Leon, 1668 Gaselee 81. **1396(1)**

HUDIBRAS, 1689. *See* BUTLER (Samuel). **889**

[HUDSON (John)] . Geographiae veteris scriptores Graeci minores [ed. by J.Hudson], 1698-1703.
See GEOGRAPHIAE veteris scriptores ... **1765-6**

HUERTA (Antonio de). Triunfos gloriosos, epitalamios sacros ... que se celebraron año de M.DC.LXIX. en ... Madrid ... a la canonizacion solemne del ... San Pedro de Alcantara. 4to.
Madrid, por Bernardo de Villa-Diego, a costa de Gabriel de Leon, 1670 Gaselee 82. **1543(1)**

HUET (Pierre Daniel), Bp of Soissons. Demonstratio evangelica. fo.
Parisiis, apud Stephanum Michallet, 1679 **2686**

94

————————A treatise of romances and their original; transl. out of French. 8vo.
London, printed by R.Battersby, for S.Heyrick, 1672 Wing H3301. **238**

————————A treatise of the situation of Paradise ... Transl. from the French. 12mo.
London, for James Knapton, 1694 Engr. map.
Wing H3302. Cf. Tanner II, 143-4. **700**

HUGHES (George). Væ-euge-tuba, or the wo-joy-trumpet ... A sermon ... May 26.1647. 4to.
London, by E.G. for Iohn Rothwell, 1647
[Sermons Polemical V] Wing H3310. **1183(13)**

HUGHES (Lewis). Certain grievances, or, the popish errors ... of the service-book; plainly laid open ... The fifth time imprinted. 4to.
London, by T.P., 1642 [Liturgick Controversies II] Wing H3315. **1188(8)**

————————Signes from heaven of the wrath ... of God. 4to.
London, by T.P. and M.S., 1642 [Consutilia II]
Wing H3318. **1428(5)**

HUGHES (William). An exact abridgment of publick acts, 1657.
See ENGLAND. *Statutes.* **1654**

————————Parsons law: or a view of advowsons. 3rd ed. 8vo.
London, by John Streater, 1663
Wing H3327A. **894**

HUGO (Hermann). De prima scribendi origine. 8vo.
Antuerpiæ, ex officina Plantiniana, apud Balthasarem & Ioannem Moretos, 1617 **864**

————————The siege of Breda ... Transl. into English by C.H.G[age]. fo.
[Ghent] (typis Iudoci Dooms) 1627 Engr. title-page, 15 engr. maps. STC 13926. **2192**

HUNG (Chih-ang). K'ang-hsi êrh-shih wu nien ping-yin li-fa hsüan-chi t'ung-shu. [Almanac for the 25th year of K'ang-hsi, 1686.]
Wu Ch'i-hsiang. Changchow [1685?] **1914(1)**

[HUNT (Thomas)] . The rights of the Bishops to judge in capital cases in Parliament, cleared, being an answer to two books. 8vo.
London, by Tho.Braddyll, for Robert Clavel, 1680 Wing H3759. **839**

HUNT (William). The gaugers magazine. 8vo.
London, by Mary Clark, for the Author, 1687
Engr. pls (diagrams). Wing H3763. **1221**

HUNTINGTON (Robert), Bp of Raphoe.
R.Huntingtoni epistolæ: et veterum mathematicorum ... synopsis, collectore E.Bernardo. Præmittitur D.Huntingtoni & D.Bernardi vitæ. 8vo.
Londini, typis Gul.Bowyer, impensis A. et J. Churchill, 1704 **1348**

[HURTADO (Luís)]. The famous history of the life of the renowned Prince Palmerin of England ... In three parts.   4to.
London, for William Thackeray, and Thomas Passinger, 1685   [Vulgaria I]   Woodcuts.
Wing H3796.   **1190(1)**

HURTADO DE MENDOZA (Antonio). El premio de la virtud, y sucessos prodigiosos de don Pedro Guerrero. Comedia famosa.   4to.
[*Seville, Tomás López de Haro*, c.1679-83]
Gaselee 106.   **1553(7)**

[HUTTON (Sir Richard)]. The young clerks guide. 16th ed.   4 pts.   8vo.
London, for T.B., S.H., R.C. [etc.], 1690   **966**

HUYGENS (Christiaan). Traité de la lumiere. Avec un discours de la cause de la pesanteur.   4to.
Leide, chez Pierre van der Aa, 1690   **1373**

HYDE (Thomas). Catalogus impressorum librorum Bibliothecæ Bodleianæ.   fo.
Oxonii, e Theatro Sheldoniano, 1674
Wing O864.   **2672**

——————————Historia religionis veterum Persarum.   4to.
Oxonii, e Theatro Sheldoniano, 1700
18 engr. pls.   Wing H3876.   **1736**

I

I.(H.). The interest of these United Provinces, 1673.
See HILL (Joseph).   **1643**

IAMBLICHUS, of Chalcis. Περι μυστηριων λογος ... De mysteriis liber ... T.Gale ... Græce nunc primum edidit, Latine vertit, et notas adjecit.   fo.
Oxonii, e Theatro Sheldoniano, 1678
Wing I26.   **2639**

IHESUS. The floure of the commaundementes, 1510.
See FLEUR (La) des commandements ...   **2001**

ILLESCAS (Gonzalo de). Historia pontificial, 1652.
See HISTORIA pontificial ...   **2186-90**

ILLUSTRIUM. Inlustrium viror vt. exstant. in vrbe expressi, vultus.   fo.
Romæ, 1569   52 engr. pls.   Adams R702.
2345

IMAGE du Monde. The mirror of the world.   fo.
W.Caxton [Westminster, 1490]
See Appendix.   **1941(1)**

IMAGE du Monde. The myrrour ⁊ dyscrypcyon of the worlde. [Transl. by W.Caxton.]
[*London*] (*by me Laurence Andrewe*) [1527?]
STC 24764; Duff p.70.   **1941(2)**

IMAGES (The) of the Old Testament, 1549.
See HOLBEIN (Hans).   **946**

IMHOF (Jacob Wilhelm). Regum pariumque Magnæ Britanniæ historia genealogica.   fo.
Norimbergæ, sumptibus Johannis Andreæ Endteri filiorum, 1690   Engr. fp., pls.   **2373**

IN stemma gentilitium Serenissimi Joannis III Regis Poloniarum. [Verses by J.Hevelius, J.E. Schmieden, &c.]   fo.
[*Gedani*, 1684]   **2715(2)**

[INDEX librorum prohibitorum.] [Index auctorum dānatæ memoriæ, tum etiam librorum ... editus auctoritate F.M.Mascaregnas ... De consilio Inquisitionis Lusitaniæ.]   fo.
(*Vlyssipone, ex officina Petri Craesbeeck*, 1624)
Leaf ¶1 signed by the Inquisitor General.
Wants engr. title-page.   **2050**

INDUSTRIA spiritualis sive praeparatio ad confessionem. Index peccatorum.   12mo.
[*Rome?* 16—]   MS title and, inserted at end, MS table of contents, in hand of one of Pepys's clerks. Pages printed on one side only, and cut horizontally into strips, one for each sin.   Wants all before G1.   **5**

INFORMATIO puerorum.   4to.
R.Pynson [London, c.1500]
See Appendix.   **1305(3)**

INFORMATIONE per i forastieri curiosi di vedere le cose più notabili di Bologna.   12mo.
Bologna, per gli eredi del Sarti. Per la direttione di Petronio Ruuinetti, 1700   **2(1)**

INLUSTRIUM ...   *See* ILLUSTRIUM ...

INNOCENCE (L') de la ... Royne d'Escosse, 1572.
See BELLEFOREST (François).   **600**

INQUISITIO Anglicana, 1654.
See SADLER (Anthony).   **1428(16)**

INQUISITION, Portugal. Index, 1624.
See INDEX librorum prohibitorum.   **2050**

INSCRIPTIONES Græcæ Palmyrenorum, cum scholiis & annotationibus E.Bernardi et T.Smithi. 8vo.
Trajecti ad Rhenum, apud Franciscum Halmam, 1698   **1233(1)**

INSCRIPTIONUM antiquarum sylloge in duas partes distributa ... Edita ... a G.Fleetwood.   8vo.
Londini, impensis Guil.Graves, & prostant apud Tim.Childe, 1691   Wing F1247.   **1230**

INSIGNIUM Romæ templorum prospectus exteriores interioresque.   fo.
[Rome] a Jo.Jacobo de Rubeis, 1684   Engr. pls.
2960

INSTITUTIO Graecae grammatices compendaria, 1692.
See CAMDEN (William).   **355**

INTELLIGENCER (The); published for the satisfaction ... of the people. (— The newes ...)
[Ed. by Sir R.L'Estrange. *The 'Intelligencer' and the 'Newes' were published alternately.*] 31 Aug. 1663 – 28 Dec.1665.   4to.
London, Richard Hodgkinson, 1663-5
[News-pamphlets 1660-66 II-IV]   Wants nos 83 & 94 of 1665.   Diary 4 Sept.1663.
1745(2)-1747

INTEREST (The) of princes and states, 1680.
See BETHEL (Slingsby).   **943**

INTEREST (The) of these United Provinces. Being a defence of the Zeelanders choice, 1673.
See HILL (Joseph).   **1643**

IRELAND. *Parliament.* An account of the sessions of Parliament in Ireland, 1692.   4to.
London, for J.T., 1693   [Consutilia VI]
Wing I297.   **1432(16)**

——————— A true and compleat list ... of the present Parliament of Ireland ... the Fourth of October, 1692.   brs.
Printed by Edward Jones in the Savoy, 1692
[Consutilia VI]   Wing T2425.   **1432(15)**

——————— *Statutes.* A collection of all the statutes now in use in ... Ireland.   fo.
Dublin, by Benjamin Tooke, 1678
Wing I356.   **2299**

IRELAND (William). The tryals of William Ireland, Thomas Pickering, and John Grove; for conspiring to murder the King.   fo.
London, for Robert Pawlet, 1678   [Narratives & Tryals I]   Wing T2268.   **2249(10)**

ISAACSON (Henry). Saturni ephemerides, sive tabula historico-chronologica.   fo.
London, by B.A [lsop] & T.F[awcet] for Henry Seile [etc.], 1633   Engr. title-page.
STC 14269.   See also below, vol.V: Adversaria Navalia Chronologica (2919-22).   **2923**

ISHAM (Zacheus). A sermon preach'd ... April the 4th 1701.   4to.
London, by J.L. for Robert Clavel and Walter Kettilby, 1701   [Convocation Pamphlets XII]
1698(7)

ISLE (The) of pines, or a late discouery by H.C. van Sloetten, 1668.
See NEVILLE (Henry).   **1399(3)**

ISRAELS fast. Or, a meditation vpon the seuenth chapter of Joshuah, 1628.
See BURTON (Henry).   **1180(1)**

IZACKE (Richard). Antiquities of the city of Exeter.   8vo.
London, printed by E.Tyler and R.Holt, for Richard Marriott [etc.], 1677   Engr. map, woodcuts. Sig 2* misbound.   Wing I1110.   **1217**

J

J.(A.). Miraculum basilicon, 1664.
See JENNINGS (Abraham).   **359**

J.(R.). A letter of advice to a friend about the currency of clipt-money.   2nd ed.   8vo.
London, printed for Edw.Castle, 1696   **796(5)**

JACK. Jacke Drums entertainment: or the comedie of Pasquill and Katherine. [By J.Marston?]   4to.
London, [T.Creed] for Richard Oliue, 1601
[Old Plays II]   STC 7243.   **1102(8)**

JACOBUS, de Voragine.
See VORAGINE (Jacobus), Abp of Genoa.

JAMES I, King of England. The workes.   fo.
London, by Robert Barker and Iohn Bill, 1616
Engr. fp. (port., Charrington p.85), title-page.
STC 14344.   **2370**

——————— A true transcript and publication of His Maiesties letters pattent. For an office to bee erected, and called the Publike Register.
2nd ed., enlarged.   4to.
[London, W.Stansby] for Iohn Budge, 1612
[Consutilia VIII]   STC 9227.   **1434(5)**

JAMES II, King of England. *For instructions issued by James II as Lord High Admiral, see* ENGLAND. *Admiralty.*

——————— James the Second, by the grace of God ... Whereas it is the highest prerogative ...
[*Letters patent authorising collections for the relief of French Protestant refugees.*]   brs.
In the Savoy, by Thomas Newcomb, 1685
Wing J407.   **1549(1)**

——————— By the King. An establishment touching salutes by guns to be henceforth observed in his Majesties Royal Navy.
[London, 1688]   **2174**

——————— Original letters of the late King's [i.e. James II's] and others ... proving the corruption lately practised to ruin this nation.

Published by command of W.Fuller.   8vo.
London, for the author, sold by Mrs.Baldwin,
1702   **980(7)**

———————— The royal charter ... [of] the
Trinity-House, 1685.
See TRINITY HOUSE, Deptford.   **1377**

JAMES (Thomas). An apologie for Iohn Wickliffe.
4to.
Oxford, by Ioseph Barnes, 1608
STC 14445.   **958(4)**

———————— Bellum Papale.   12mo.
Londini, impensis Joh.Dunmore, 1678
Wing J434.   **446**

JANSSEN (Sir Theodore). A discourse concerning
banks (1697). [Sometimes attributed to Sir
Theodore Janssen.]
See DISCOURSE (A) concerning banks.   **1433(9)**

JAQUELOT (Isaac). Dissertations sur l'existence
de Dieu.   4to.
La Haye, chez Etienne Foulque, 1697   Engr. fp.
                                         1905

JEHOJADAHS justice ... A sermon, 1645.
See HOYLE (Joshua).   **1183(3)**

JENISON (Robert). The information of R.Jenni-
son ... delivered at the ... House of Commons,
9th Nov., 1680.   fo.
*London, by the assigns of John Bill, Thomas New-
comb and Henry Hills,* 1680   [Narratives &
Tryals III]   Wing J559.   **2251(23)**

———————— The narrative of R.Jenison ...
containing ... A further discovery ... of the late ...
Popish plot.   fo.
London, for F.Smith, T.Basset, J.Wright, [etc.],
1679   [Narratives & Tryals I]   Engr. port.
(Charrington p.155) inserted.   Wing J561.
                                         2249(4)

JENKINS (David). Jenkinsius redivivus: or the
works of ... Judge Jenkins whilst a prisoner in the
Tower.   12mo.
London, for Jo.Hindmarsh, 1681   Engr. fp.
(port., Charrington p.88).   Wing J592.   **467(2)**

JENKYN (William). A sermon, preached ... the
fifth day of November, 1651.   4to.
London, by T.R. for W.R., 1652   [Sermons
Polemical V]   Wing J652.   **1183(14)**

[JENNINGS (Abraham)]. Miraculum basilicon:
or the ... wonderful preservation of His Sacred
Majesty ... after the battel of Worcester. By A.J.,
Eirenophilalethes.   8vo.
London, 1664   Wing J669.   **359**

JERÓNIMO, de la Cruz.
See CRUZ (Jerónimo de la).

JESUS. Ihesus. The floure of the commaundementes of god, 1510.
See FLEUR (La) des commandements de Dieu.
                                         2001

JÉSUS MARÍA (José de). Historia de la vida y
excelencias de la ... Virgen Maria.   2a impr.   fo.
Madrid, en la Imprenta Real, 1657   Gaselee 89.
                                         2182

JEWEL (John), Bp of Salisbury. Iniunctions given
by ... John, Bishop of Salisbury, 1569.
See ENGLAND. *Church of England.*   **1761(3)**

JIMENEZ SEDEÑO (Francisco). La aurora del sol
divino. Comedia famosa.   4to.
[Seville, Juan Francisco de Blas, c.1673]
Gaselee 184.   **1553(8)**

JOANNES, Scotus, Erigena. De divisione naturæ
libri quinque ... Accedit Appendix ex ambiguis
S.Maximi. (— Maximi Scholia in Gregorium
Theologum.)   fo.
Oxonii, e theatro Sheldoniano, 1681
Wing J747.   **2227**

[JOBERT (Louis)]. La science des medailles.
12mo.
Paris, chez la veuve Marbre Cramoisy, 1693
Engr. fp.   **219**

[————————] The knowledge of medals ...
From the French.   8vo.
London, for William Rogers, 1697
Wing J755.   **1333**

JOHANN, von Eck. Asseritur hic inuictissimi
Angliæ regis liber de sacramentis, a calumniis &
impietatibus Ludderi.   4to.
(Rhoma, typis Marcelli Franck, 1523)
Adams E29; Duff p.20.   **1481(3)**

JOHANNES, Stobaeus.
See STOBAEUS (Johannes).

JOHN and his mistris.   12mo.
[London] printed for J.Deacon [c.1680]
[Penny-Merriments I]   Woodcut.   **362(35)**

JOHNSON (Francis). A narrative of the ... tryal of
F.Johnson, a Franciscan, at Worcester ... To which
is annexed his speech at his execution.   fo.
[London, 1679]   [Narratives & Tryals IV]
Wing J773.   **2252(1)**

———————— Mr Johnson's speech (at the place
of execution).   fo.
[London, 1679]   [Narratives & Tryals IV]
Wing J774.   **2252(2)**

JOHNSON (Richard). The crown garland of
golden roses.   8vo.
*London, for M.W., and are to be sold by Dorman
Newman, and Ben Alsop*, 1683
[Penny-Merriments III]   Woodcut.
Wing J794.   **364(3)**

[————————] The famous history of the
Seven Champions of Christendom.   Pts 1-2.
4to.
*London, for R.Scot, Tho.Basset, Ric.Chiswell,
[etc.]*, 1687   [Vulgaria II]   Wing J799.
                                              1191(1)

[————————] The famous history of the
Seven Champions of Christendom.   Pt 3.   4to.
London, by J.R. for Benj.Harris, 1686
[Vulgaria II]   Wing J806.   **1191(1a)**

[————————] The most pleasant history of
Tom A Lincoln ... The Red-Rose Knight.
12th impr.   4to.
London, by H.Brugis for W.Thackery, 1682
[Vulgaria III]   Woodcut. With an additional
title-page.   Wing J808-9.   **1192(18)**

JOHNSON (Samuel), Rector of Corringham. An
argument proving, that the abrogation of King
James ... was according to the Constitution.   4to.
London, printed for the author, 1692
[Consutilia VI]   Wing J821.   **1432(12)**

———————— An essay concerning Parliaments
at a certainty.   4to.
London, for the author, 1693   [Consutilia VII]
Wing J826.   **1433(4)**

[————————] Julian the Apostate: being a
short account of his life.   8vo.
London, for Langley Curtis, 1682
Wing J830.   **998**

———————— Notes upon the Phoenix edition of
the pastoral letter [of Bishop Burnet]. Pt 1. [*No
more published.*]   4to.
London, for the author, 1694   [Consutilia VII]
Wing J835.   **1433(5)**

JOHNSTON (Nathaniel). The excellency of
monarchical government.   fo.
London, by T.B. for Robert Clavel, 1686
Wing J877.   **2305**

———————— The King's visitatorial power
asserted. Being an impartial relation of the late
visitation of St.Mary Magdalen College in Oxford.
4to.
London, printed by Henry Hills, 1688
Wing J879.   **1366**

JONES (Andrew), *pseud.*
See HART (John).

[JONES (David)] . A compleat history of Europe
... from the year, 1600, to the Treaty of Nimeguen.
4 vols.   8vo.
*London, printed by T.Mead (Vols 2-3: By R.Jane-
way), for H.Rhodes [etc.]*, 1705   **1385-8**

[————————] A compleat history of Europe
... from the beginning of the Treaty of Nimeguen,
1676. To ... 1700.   4th ed.   8vo.
*For Henry Rhodes, Tho.Newborough, John
Nicholson [etc.]*, 1705   **1389**

[————————] A compleat history of Europe
... for the year 1701.   8vo.
*Printed and sold by the booksellers of London
and Westminster*, 1702   **1390**

[————————] A compleat history of Europe
... for the year, 1702.   8vo.
*London, printed for H.Rhodes, J.Nicholson, and
Andr.Bell*, 1701 [*or rather* 1703]   **1391**

[————————] A compleat history of Europe
... for the year, 1703.   8vo.
*London, printed for H.Rhodes, J.Nicholson, and
Andr.Bell*, 1704   **1392**

[————————] The life of James II, late King
of England.   8vo.
*London, for J.Knapton, J.Nicholson, J.Sprint, and
T.Ballard*, 1702   Engr. fp. (port., Charrington
p.86).   **1417**

JONES (Inigo). The most notable antiquity of
Great Britain, vulgarly called Stone-Heng ...
restored. [Ed. by J.Webb.]   fo.
*London, by James Flesher for Daniel Pakeman,
and Laurence Chapman*, 1655   Engr. pls.
Wing J954.   **2010**

JONES (Robert), D.D., *pseud.*
See LUSHINGTON (Thomas).

JONES (Thomas). Y Gymraeg yn ei disgleirdeb ...
The British language in its lustre, or a copious
dictionary. [*Welsh & Engl.*]   8vo.
*London, printed and sold by Mr.Lawrence
Baskervile, and Mr.John Marsh*, 1688
Wing J997.   **502**

JONSON (Ben). Works. (— Leges convivales.)   fo.
*London, by Thomas Hodgkin, for H.Herringman,
E.Brewster [etc.]*, 1692   Engr. fp. (port.,
Charrington p.90).   Wing J1006.   **2645**

JOSÉ, de Jesús María.
See JESÚS MARÍA (José de).

JOSEPHUS (Flavius). Works, transl. by Sir Roger
L'Estrange.
London, for Richard Sare, 1702   Engr. title-
page, plates, map.   **2796**

JOSSELYN (John). New-Englands rarities discovered.   8vo.
London, printed for G.Widdowes, 1672
Wing J1093.   **405**

JOURNAL (Le) des scavans.   Vols 1-31.   12mo.
Amsterdam, chez Pierre Le Grand (– G.P. & J. Blaeu [etc.]), 1679-1704   Tanner II p.106.
154-84

JOURNAL du voyage du roy [i.e. Louis XIV] en Flandre. Avec une relation de ce qui s'est passé sur le vaisseau l'Entreprenant.   12mo.
Paris, du Bureau d'Adresse, 1680   **99(1)**

JOURNAL fidelle de tout ce qui s'est passé au siege de Mastricht, attaqué par Louis XIV ... Et defendu par Mr.de Fariaux, Baron de Maude.   8vo.
Amsterdam, chés P.Warnaer & F.Lamminga, 1674
Engr. map.   **830**

JOURNAL ou suite du voyage de Siam, 1687.
See CHOISY (François Timoléon de).   **685**

JOUSTS. Here begynneth the iustes of the moneth of Maye parfurnysshed ⁊ done by Charles Brandon [etc.] (The iustes ... of yᵉ moneth of June ... by Rycharde Graye [etc.]).   4to.
[*London, W. de Worde, 1507?*]
In unidentified 16th-century hands on B4: a note; a fragment of verse; and accounts.   STC 3543;
Duff p.34.   **1254(1)**

JOVIAN. Or, an answer to Julian the Apostate, 1683.
See HICKES (George).   **1026**

JUDGEMENT. The judgment of foraign divines ... touching the discipline, liturgie, and ceremonies of the Church of England.   4to.
London, 1660   [Liturgick Controversies III]
Wing J1176.   **1189(3)**

JULIAN, the Apostate, 1682.
See JOHNSON (Samuel), Rector of Corringham.
998

JURA populi Anglicani, 1701.
See SOMERS (John Somers, 1st Baron).   **1437(10)**

[JURIEU (Pierre)]. L'esprit de Mr.Arnaud.
2 vols.   12mo.
Deventer, chez les héritiers de Jean Colombius,
1684   **525-6**

————————— The history of the Council of Trent ... done into English.   8vo.
London, by J.Heptinstall, for Edward Evets, Henry Faithorne [etc.], 1684   Engr. fp.
Wing J1203.   **1275**

[—————————] La politique du clergé de France. 2e éd. Augmentée de plusieurs lettres sur le mesme sujet & principalement de celle de Mr.Spon. au P. la Chéze.   12mo.
A la Haye, chez Abraham Arondeus, 1681   **206(1)**

[—————————] Présages de la décadence des empires.   12mo.
Mekelbourg, chez Rodolphe Makelckauw, 1688
632

IUST (A) narrative of the hellish new counter-plots of the Papists.   fo.
London, for Dorman Newman, 1679
[Narratives & Tryals III]   Wing J1235.   **2251(2)**

JUSTES.   *See* JOUSTS.

JUSTIFICATION (A) of the present war, 1672.
See STUBBE (Henry).   **1226(1)**

JUSTINIAN I, Emperor of Rome. Institutionum, sive Elementorum libri quatuor ... Cura & studio Arnoldi Vinnii.   Ed. 2a.   12mo.
Amstelodami, apud Ludovicum Elzevirium, 1652
Engr. title-page.   **137**

JUSTINUS. De historiis Philippicis, et totius mundi originibus, 1677.
See TROGUS POMPEIUS.   **1950**

JUVENAL. D.J.Juvenalis et A.Persii Flacci satyræ, cum veteris scholiastæ ... commentariis. Ed. nova.   2 pts.   8vo.
Amstelædami, apud Henricum Wetstenium, 1684
Engr. title-page.   **1423**

K

K.(R.B.). A parallel, or, briefe comparison, 1641.
See BAILLIE (Robert).   **1188(5)**

K.(T.). The royal sufferer, 1699.
See KEN (Thomas), Bp of Bath and Wells.   **1002**

KAHL (Johann).   *See* CALVINUS (Joannes).

K'ANG-HSI êrh-shih-wu nien ... [1686].
See HUNG (Chih-ang).   **1914(1)**

[KAYLL (Robert)]. The trades increase.   4to.
London, by Nicholas Okes, and are to be sold by Walter Burre, 1615   [Sea Tracts III]
STC 14894.7; Naval Minutes, p.424.   **1079(5)**

KEACH (Benjamin). Τροπολογία: a key to open scripture metaphors. ([By] T.Delaune and B.Keach.) 1682 (1681).
See DELAUNE (Thomas).   **2433(1)**

──────── Τροποσχημαλογια: tropes and figures ... Philologia sacra, the second part.   fo. *London, by J.D. for John Hancock, and Benj. Alsop*, 1682   Wing K101.   **2433(2)**

KEBLE (Joseph). An assistance to justices of the peace.   fo. *London, by W.Rawlins, S.Roycroft, and H.Sawbridge [etc.]*, 1683   Wing K113.   **2459**

──────── The statutes, 1681. *See* ENGLAND. *Statutes.*   **2765-6**

KEILL (John). An examination of Dr.Burnet's theory of the earth. Together with some remarks on Mr.Whiston's new theory of the earth.   8vo. *Oxford, printed at the Theater*, 1698 Wing K132.   **1245**

──────── Introductio ad veram physicam. 8vo. *Oxoniæ, e Theatro Sheldoniano, impensis Thomæ Bennet, Londini*, 1702   Diagrams. Tanner II, p.258 [?] .   **1167**

[KEN (Thomas), Bp of Bath and Wells] . An exposition on the church-catechism.   8vo. *London, printed for Charles Brome, and William Clarke in Winchester*, 1685 Wing K261.   **1228**

[────────] The royal sufferer. A manual of meditations and devotions. By T– K–, D.D.   8vo. 1699   Wing K278.   **1002**

KENNET (Basil). The lives and characters of the ancient Grecian poets.   2 pts.   8vo. *London, for Abel Swall*, 1697   Engr. fp., ports. Wing K297.   **1331**

──────── Romæ antiquæ notitia.   8vo. *London, printed for A.Swall and T.Child*, 1696 10 engr. pls.   Wing K298.   **1362**

[KENNETT (White), Bp of Peterborough] . The case of the Præmunientes considered.   4to. (*London, for Richard Sare*, 1702) [Convocation Pamphlets X]   **1696(6)**

──────── Ecclesiastical synods, and Parliamentary convocations ... justly vindicated.   Pt 1. 8vo. *London, for A. and J.Churchill*, 1701 [Convocation Pamphlets V]   **1691(1)**

[────────] The history of the Convocation of the prelates and clergy of the Province of Canterbury, summon'd to meet ... February 6, 1700.   4to. *London, for A. and J.Churchill*, 1702 [Convocation Pamphlets IX]   On title-page, in Daniel Waterland's hand, 'Bp Kennett'.   **1695(10)**

[────────] An occasional letter on the subject of English convocations.   8vo. *London, for A. and J.Churchill*, 1701 [Convocation Pamphlets V]   **1691(2)**

──────── Parochial antiquities attempted in the history of Ambrosden, Burcester ... in the counties of Oxford and Bucks.   4to. *Oxford, at the Theater*, 1695   9 engr. pls. Wing K302.   **1943**

[────────] The present state of Convocation, in a letter giving the full relation of proceedings in several of the late sessions.   4to. *London, for A. and J.Churchill*, 1702 [Convocation Pamphlets X]   **1696(14)**

[────────] A reconciling letter upon the late differences about convocational rights and proceedings.   4to. [*London, for Richard Sare*, 1702] [Convocation Pamphlets IX]   **1695(9)**

KHUNRATH (Henricus). *See* KUNRAT (Heinrich).

KIDD (William), Captain. The arraignment, tryal, and condemnation of Captain William Kidd, for murther and piracy ... May, 1701.   fo. *London, for J.Nutt*, 1701   [Narratives & Tryals VII]   **2255(4)**

KIDDER (Richard), Bp of Bath and Wells. A commentary on the five books of Moses. [*With the text.*]   2 vols.   8vo. *London, by J.Heptinstall, for William Rogers*, 1694   Vol.1 contains two copies of sig.f. Wing K399.   **1345-6**

KILLIGREW (Henry). The conspiracy. A tragedy. 4to. *London, by Iohn Norton, for Andrew Crooke*, 1638   [Loose Plays I]   Wants N2-4. STC 14958.   **1075(2)**

KILLIGREW (Thomas). Comedies and tragedies. fo. *London, for Henry Herringman*, 1664 (1663) Engr. fp. (port., Charrington p.92). Wing K450.   **2157**

KIMBERLEY (Jonathan). A sermon preach'd ... November the fifth, 1702.   4to. *London, for Thomas Bennet, and sold by T.Hart*, 1702   [Convocation Pamphlets XII]   **1698(11)**

KINCARDINE (Alexander Bruce, 4th Earl of). A speech made in the Parliament of Scotland, in relation to Presbyterian government.   4to. [*London*, 1702?]   [Consutilia XI]   **1437(14)**

KING William and Queen Mary conquerors, 1693. *See* BLOUNT (Charles).   **1433(1)**

KING (Daniel). The cathedrall and conventuall churches of England and Wales orthographically delineated.   fo.
[London] 1656   Engr. title-page, engr. pls.
Wing K484.   2624

——————— The vale-royall of England, or the county-palatine of Chester illustrated. Published by D.King.   4 pts.   fo.
London, by John Streater, 1656   Engr. title-page, pls. Wants sigs Bbb and Ccc.   Wing K488.
   2094

KING (John), Bp of London. Vitis Palatina. A sermon ... preached ... after the mariage of the Ladie Elizabeth.   4to.
London, for John Bill, 1614   [Consutilia II]
STC 14989.5.   1428(19)

[KING (William), Abp of Dublin]. The state of the Protestants of Ireland under the late King James's government.   4to.
London, for Robert Clavell, 1691
Wing K538.   1729

[KING OF OCKHAM, (Peter, 1st Baron)]. The history of the Apostles Creed.   8vo.
London, by W.B. for Jonathan Robinson, and John Wyat, 1702   1416

KIRCHER (Athanasius). Arca Noë in tres libros. fo.
Amstelodami, apud Joannem Janssonium à Wæsberge, 1675   Engr. fp. (port., Charrington p.34), title-page, pls, maps.   2667(1)

——————— China monumentis, qua sacris, qua profanis ... illustrata.   fo.
Amstelodami, apud Joannem Janssonium, 1664
Engr. fp. (port., Charrington p.92), title-page, pls, maps.   Diary 10, 14 Jan.1667/8 [?].   2683

——————— Magneticum naturæ regnum. 12mo.
Amstelodami, ex officina Johannis Janssonii à Wæsberge & viduæ Elizei Weyerstraet, 1667   133

——————— Musurgia uniuersalis.   2 vols. fo.
Romæ, ex typographia hæredum Francisci Corbelletti (– typis Ludouici Grignani), 1650
Engr. fp., engr. port. (Charrington p.98), pls, woodcut diagrams, music. Vol.2 misbound.
Diary 22, 24 & 29 Feb., 4 Mar.1667/8.   See also vol.IV.   2467-8

——————— Sphinx mystagoga, sive Diatribe hieroglyphica.   fo.
Amstelodami, ex officina Janssonio-Wæsbergiana, 1676   Engr. pls.   2667(2)

[KIRCHMAIER (Georg Caspar)]. De diluvii universalitate dissertatio prolusoria.   12mo.
Genevæ, apud Petrum Columesium, 1667   373(2)

KLOCK (Caspar). Tractatus juridico-politico-polemico-historicus de ærario ... 2a ed ... operâ ... C.Pelleri.   fo.
Norimbergæ, sumptibus Johannis Andreæ, & Wolfgangi Endteri junioris, hæredum, 1671
Engr. fp.   2483

KNIGHT (Francis). A relation of seaven yeares slaverie under the Turkes of Argeire.   4to.
London, by T.Cotes, for Michael Sparke junior, 1640   [Consutilia III]   Woodcut fp., woodcut pl.   STC 15048.   1429(2)

KNOCK (A) at the door of Christless ones.   12mo.
London, for T.Passenger, 1683   [Penny-Godlinesses]   365(38)

KNOLLES (Richard). The Turkish history ... With a continuation ... by Sir Paul Rycaut.
3 pts.   6th ed.   fo.
London, for Tho.Basset, 1687 (Pt 2: by J.D. for Tho.Basset, R.Clavell [etc.] , 1687)
20 engr. pls.   Wing K702.   2739

KNOWLEDGE (The) of medals, 1697.
See JOBERT (Louis).   1333

KNOWLES (William). The great assizes: or general day of judgment.   12mo.
London, by H.Brugis for W.Thackery, 1681
[Penny-Godlinesses]   365(17)

——————— A serious call to obstinate sinners. 12mo.
London, by H.B. for W.Thackeray, 1684
[Penny-Godlinesses]   365(29)

KNOX (Robert). An historical relation of the island Ceylon.   fo.
London, by Richard Chiswell, 1681   Engr. map, 15 engr. pls.   Wing K742.   2322

KNOX (Thomas). The tryal and conviction of Thomas Knox and John Lane ... about the horrid Popish plot ... 25th of Novemb., 1679.   fo.
London, for Robert Pawlett, 1680   [Narratives & Tryals IV]   Wing T2165.   2252(5)

KORAN. The Alcoran of Mahomet ... newly Englished.   4to.
London, 1649   Wing K747.   1096

KORNMANN (Heinrich). Sibylla Trig-Andriana seu de virginitate, virginum statu et jure. Ed. ultima.   3 pts.   12mo.
Hagæ-Comitum, ex typographia Adriani Vlacq, 1654   25

KORTHOLT (Christian). De vita et moribus.   4to.
Kilonii, literis Joachimi Reumanni, 1683
Tanner I, pp.180, 198; Howarth p.284.   1410

KRANTZ (Albertus). Chronica regnorum Aquilon-
arium.   fo.
Argent (orati), apud Ioannem Schottum (1548)
On title-page: 'Herm.Theod.Caesar', followed by
monogram.   Adams C2871.   **2213**

———————— Saxonia.   fo.
Francofurti ad Moenum, apud A.Wechelum, 1575
Adams C2886.   **2263(1)**

———————— Wandalia. (Poloniæ descriptionis,
libri duo.)   fo.
*Francofurti, ex officina typographica Andreæ
Wecheli,* 1575   Adams C2890.   **2263(2)**

KUNRAT (Heinrich). Amphitheatrum sapientiæ
æternæ, solius veræ, Christiano-Kabalisticum.
2 pts.   fo.
(Hanoviæ, excudebat Guilielmus Antonius, 1609)
Engr. title-page, 20 engr. ll.   **2267**

KURICKE (Reinold). Jus maritimum Hanseaticum.
[*Germ. & Lat.*]   2 pts.   4to.
Hamburgi, sumptibus Zachariæ Hertelii, 1667
1475

L

L.(I.). The lawes resolutions of womens rights,
1632.
See LAW'S.   **1127**

L.(S.). A letter from a gentleman of the Lord
Ambassador Howard's retinue ... Dated at Fez,
Nov.1.1669.   4to.
London, by W.G. for Moses Pitt, 1670
[*Consutilia V*]   Wing L61.   **1431(7)**

L. (S.D.B.S.D.). Histoire des cheualiers de l'ordre
de S.Iean de Hierusalem, 1659.
See BOSIO (Giacomo).   **2681**

L.(W.). The art of numbring, 1667.
See LEYBOURN (William).   **12(1)**

LA BARBE (Le Febvre de).
See LE FEBVRE DE LA BARBE (   ).

LA BRUYÈRE (Jean de). The characters, or the
manners of the age. With the Characters of
Theophrastus.   2 pts.   8vo.
*London, printed for John Bullord, and sold by
Matt.Gilliflower, Ben.Tooke* [*etc.*], 1699
Wing L104.   **1327**

LA CHAMBRE, le Sieur de.
See CUREAU DE LA CHAMBRE (Marin).

LACTANTIUS (Lucius Coelius). A relation of
the death of the primitive persecutors ... Englished
by Gilbert Burnet D.D.   12mo.
Amsterdam, for J.S., 1687   Wing L142.   **369**

LADIES (The) calling, 1673.
See ALLESTREE (Richard).   **1085**

LA FONTAINE (Jean de). Fables choisies mises
en vers.   2 pts.   12mo.
Paris, chez Claude Barbin, 1669   Engrs.   **604**

———————— Ouvrages de prose et de poësie,
1688.
See DEMOSTHENES. Traduction des Philippiques.
432

LA GUILLATIÈRE (de). An account of a
late voyage to Athens, 1676.
See GUILLET DE SAINT-GEORGE (Georges).
896

LA HAYE (   ), Sieur de. The policy and
government of the Venetians.   12mo.
London, printed for John Starkey, 1671   **379(2)**

LA HIRE (Philippe de). Mémoires de mathémat-
ique et de physique.   4to.
*Paris, de l'Imprimerie Royale (par les soins de
Jean Anisson),* 1694   Engr. diagrams.   **1959**

LA HOUSSAYE (A.N.A.de).
See AMELOT DE LA HOUSSAYE (Abraham
Nicolas).

LA LOUBÈRE (Simon de). A new historical
relation of the Kingdom of Siam.   2 vols in 1.
fo.
*London, by F.L. for Tho.Horne, Francis Saunders
and Tho.Bennet,* 1693   Engr. maps, pls.
Wing L201.   **2296**

LA MARTINIÈRE (Pierre Martin de). A new
voyage into the northern countries.   12mo.
London, printed for John Starkey, 1674
Wing L204.   **296**

LAMBARD (William). A perambulation of Kent
... Now increased and altered.   4to.
London, by Edm.Bollifant, 1596   Woodcut
maps.   STC 15176.   **1046**

LAMBETH articles.
See ARTICULI Lambethani ...   **374(1)**

[LA MOTHE LE VAYER (François de)]. Cincq
dialogues faits à l'imitation des anciens, par
Oratius Tubero.   12mo.
Mons, chez Paul de la Fleche, 1671   **307(1)**

[————————] Hexameron rustique.   12mo.
Amsterdam, chez Jaques le Jeune [*Daniel
Elzevier*], 1671   **307(2)**

LAMPLUGH (Thomas), Abp of York. A sermon preached before the House of Lords on the fifth of November.   4to.
In the Savoy, by Tho.Newcomb, and are to be sold by Henry Brome, 1678   Wing L305.
1413(2)

[LAMY (Bernard)]. De l'art de parler.   12mo.
Suivant la copie imprimée à Paris, chez André Pralard, 1676   **70**

[LANCELOT (Claude)]. Grammaire generale. (Par le Sieur D.T. [i.e. C.Lancelot, and by A. Arnauld].)   2e ed.   12mo.
Paris, chez Pierre le Petit, 1664   **509**

LANFIERE (Thomas). The garland of love and mirth.   8vo.
[London] for I.Deacon, and are to be sold by R.Kell [c.1685]   [Penny-Merriments II]
Woodcut.   **363(45)**

LANGBAINE (Gerard). An account of the English dramatick poets.   8vo.
Oxford, by L.L[ichfield] for George West, and Henry Clements, 1691   Wing L373.   **881**

———————— Momus triumphans: or, the plagiaries of the English stage expos'd in a catalogue.   4to.
London, for N.C. and are to be sold by Sam. Holford, 1688   [Loose Plays II]
Wing L377.   **1604(14)**

LANGENES (Bernardt). The description of a voyage made by certaine ships of Holland into the East Indies.   4to.
London, Iohn Wolfe, 1598   [Consutilia V]
Woodcut maps.   STC 15193.   **1431(4)**

LANGHORNE (Richard). The petition and declaration of Richard Langhorne.   fo.
[London, c.1679]   [Narratives & Tryals III]
Wing L398.   **2251(28)**

———————— The speech of Richard Langhorne ... at his execution July 14, 1679.   fo.
[London, c.1679]   [Narratives & Tryals III]
Wing L399.   **2251(26)**

———————— The tryall of Richard Langhorn ... for conspiring the death of the King.   fo.
London, for H.Hills, T.Parkhurst, J.Starkey [etc.], 1679   [Narratives & Tryals I]   Wing T2212.
2249(14)

[LANGLAND (William)]. The vision of Pierce Plowman, now fyrste imprynted.   4to.
(London) by Robert Crowley (1550)
With a later title-page, 'nowe the seconde tyme imprinted', 1550.   STC 19906; Duff p.35.
1302

LANGLEY (John). Gemitus columbæ ... A sermon preached ... Decemb.25, 1644.   4to.
London, by Joh.Raworth for Philemon Stephens, 1644   [Sermons Polemical V]   Wing L404.
1183(15)

[LA PEYRÈRE (Isaac de)]. Men before Adam. (— A theological systeme upon that presupposition.)   8vo.
London, 1656 (1655)   Engr. map.
Wing L427, 428.   **669**

LA POPELINIÈRE (Henri Lancelot-Voisin, sieur de). L'amiral de France.   4to.
Paris, chez Thomas Perier, 1585   Title-page hand-ruled in red; MS notes in French in unidentified hand; at end MS note on author in hand of one of Pepys's clerks.   Adams L201.   **1790**

[LA PORTE (— de)]. Description ... de l'Hostel Royal des Invalides, 1683.
See LE JEUNE DE BOULENCOURT.   **2909**

LARA (Tomás de). Tres Romances nueuos. El primero de las virtudes de la noche. El segundo, y tercero de las grandezas de Cordoua, y Madrid.   4to.
(Sevilla, en casa de Juan Cabeças,) [c.1680]
Gaselee 90; Wilson p.266.   **1545(53)**

LA RAMÉE (Pierre de). Dialecticæ libri duo. Exemplis ... illustrati ... Per Rolandum Makilmenæum Scotum.   8vo.
Londini, excudebat Thomas Vautrollerius, 1574
STC 15241.7.   **716(3)**

LARGE (A) and true discourse [1602].
See AMPELE ende waarachtige beschrijving ...
1431(15)

LARGE (A) review of the summary view, 1702.
See FERGUSON (Robert).   **1438(1)**

LA ROQUE (Gilles André de). Traité de la noblesse.   4to.
Paris, chez Estienne Michallet, 1678   **1942**

LARROQUE (Matthieu de). Histoire de l'Eucharistie.   2e éd.   8vo.
Amsterdam, chez Daniel Elsevier, 1671   **501**

LARTIGUE (Jean de). La politique des conquerans.   2e éd.   8vo.
Paris, chez Claude Barbin, 1663   **1199**

[LA SALE (Antoine de)]. Les quinze joies de mariage.
See QUINZE (Les) joies de mariage.   **1193(1)**

LA SERRE (Jean de).   *See* PUGET DE LA SERRE (Jean).

LAST (The) speeches of the five notorious traitors and Jesuits ... executed at Tyburn. fo.
[*London*, 1679] [*Narratives & Tryals* III]
Wing L506. **2251(24)**

LAST (The) will of George Fox. brs.
London, for and sold by W.Haws, 1701 **2471(2)**

LATE (The) King James's manifesto answer'd. [*With the text.*] 4to.
London, sold by Richard Baldwin, 1697
[*Consutilia* VII] Wing L550. **1433(17)**

LATE (The) King James's second manifesto ... answered. [*With the text.*] 4to.
London, for Richard Baldwin, 1697
[*Consutilia* VII] Wing L552. **1433(18)**

LATE (The) pretence of a constant practice to enter the Parliament [c.1702].
See TRIMNELL (Charles), Bp of Winchester.
1696(5)

LATE (The) pretence of a constant practice to enter the Parliament ... in a second letter [1702].
See TRIMNELL (Charles), Bp of Winchester.
1696(7)

LATIMER (Hugh), Bp of Worcester. Frutefull sermons. 4to.
London, by Iohn Daye, 1578 Engr. pl.
STC 15279. **1336(1)**

LAUD (William), Abp of Canterbury. The history of the troubles and tryal of W.Laud ... Wrote by himself. fo.
London, for Ri.Chiswell, 1695 Engr. fp.
(port., Charrington p.95). Wing L586. **2764**

[LAURENT, Dominican]. The boke named the royall. [Translated from Laurent's La somme des vices et vertues by W.Caxton.] 4to.
(*London, by Rycharde Pynson*) [1507]
Woodcuts. STC 21430a; Duff p.55. **1011(1)**

LAWMIND (John), *pseud.*
See WILDMAN (John).

LAWRENCE (Thomas). Mercurius centralis: or, a discourse of subterraneal ... oyster-shels, found ... in Norfolk. 12mo.
London, printed by J.G. for J.Collins, 1664
Wing L687. **42**

LAW'S. The lawes resolutions of womens rights: or, the lawes provision for wooemen. [*Prefaces signed I.L. and T.E.*] 4to.
London, by the assignes of Iohn More, Esq. and are to be sold by Iohn Grove, 1632
STC 7437. **1127**

LEARNED (A) discourse on ... the rise and power of Parliaments, 1685.
See SHERIDAN (Thomas). **416**

LE BLANC (François). Traité historique des monnoyes de France ... Augmenté d'une dissertation historique sur quelques monnoyes de Charlemagne. 4to.
Sur l'imprimé à Paris, à Amsterdam, chez Pierre Mortier, 1692 52 engr. pls.
Tanner II, p.106 [?]. **1874**

LE BLANC (Vincent). The world surveyed ... voyages and travailes. fo.
London, for John Starkey, 1660 Engr. fp.
(port., Charrington p.96). Wing L801. **2013**

[LE BOUTHILLIER DE RANCÉ (Armand Jean)]. De la sainteté et des devoirs de la vie monastique. 2 vols. 4to.
Paris, chez François Muguet, 1683 **1897-8**

LE BRUN (Charles). Conference ... upon expression, general and particular ... with 43 copperplates. Transl. 12mo.
London, for John Smith, Edward Cooper, and David Mortier, 1701 **589**

LE BRUYN (Corneille).
See BRUIN (Cornelis de).

[LE CÈNE (Charles)]. An essay for a new translation of the Bible. [Translated] by H.R[oss]. 2 pts. 8vo.
London, for John Nutt, 1702 On front flyleaf an undated and unsigned note (in hand of Daniel Waterland, Master of Magdalene, 1713-40) on the book and the author. Inserted at end a letter from Humphrey Wanley to Pepys (12 Oct.1702) on the authorship. Howarth p.366 (Pepys's reply to Wanley, 20 Oct.1702). **1299(1)**

LE CLERC (Jean), of Amsterdam. Ars critica, in qua ad studia linguarum ... munitur. 2 vols. 8vo.
Amstelædami, apud Georgium Gallet, 1697
Engr. fp. **551-2**

[——————] Five letters concerning the inspiration of the Holy Scriptures. Translated out of French. [*Part of works by J.Le Clerc and R.Simon.*] 8vo.
1690 Wing L815. **481**

[——————] Histoire d'Emeric Comte de Tekeli ... Par ****. 12mo.
Cologne, chez Jaques de la Verité, 1693
Engr. fp. (port., Charrington p.164). **715**

——————Parrhasiana, ou pensées diverses ... Par T.Parrhase [i.e. J.Le Clerc]. 8vo.
Amsterdam, chez les heritiers d'Antoine Schelte, 1699 **819**

——————A supplement to Dr.Hammond's paraphrase and annotations on the New Testament. 4to.
London, for Sam.Buckley, 1699
Wing L826. **1574**

LE CLERC (Sébastien). Pratique de la geometrie, sur le papier et sur le terrain. 12mo.
Paris, chez Thomas Jolly, 1669 (*de l'imprimerie de Jean Cusson, 1668*)   Engr. fp., diagrams. **237**

LE COMTE (Florent). Cabinet des singularitez d'architecture, peinture, sculpture et graveure. Vols 1 & 2.   12mo.
Paris, chez Estienne Picart, Nicolas Le Clerc, 1699
Vol.2: engr. fp., pls. Wants vol.3.   **777-8**

LE COMTE (Louis Daniel). Nouveaux memoires sur l'etat present de la Chine.   2 vols.   12mo.
Suivant la copie de Paris, Amsterdam, chez J.L. de Lorme et Est.Roger, 1697   Vol.1: engr. fp.
(port., Charrington p.26), 18 engr. pls.
Vol.2: engr. fp. (as in vol.1), engr. pls (port., Charrington p.102).   **637-8**

LEDERER (John). The discoveries ... in three several marches from Virginia, to the west of Carolina ... Collected and transl. ... by Sir William Talbot.   4to.
London, J.C. for Samuel Heyrick, 1672
[Consutilia V]   Engr. map.
Wing L835.   **1431(6)**

LEEDS (Peregrine Osborne, 2nd Duke of). A journal of the Brest-expedition.   4to.
London, for Randal Taylor, 1694   Engr. map.
[Naval Pamphlets]   Wing C197.   **1399(13)**

LEEUWENHOEK (Anthony van). Anatomia. 2 pts.   4to.
Lugduni Batavorum, apud Cornelium Boutesteyn, 1687   Engr. title-page, reading 'Epistolæ A.a Leeuwenhoek, 1685', engr. pls.   **1578(1)**

———————Arcana naturæ.   4to.
Delphis Batavorum, apud Henricum a Krooneveld, 1695   27 engr. pls (port., Charrington p.97).   **1579**

———————Continuatio epistolarum, datarum ad ... Regiam Societatem Londinensem. 4to.
Lugduni Batavorum, apud Cornelium Boutestein, 1689   9 engr. pls.   **1578(2)**

LE FEBVRE DE LA BARRE (   ).
Description de la France équinoctiale, ci-devant appelée Guyanne.   4to.
Paris, chez Jean Ribou, 1666   Engr. map.
1531(2)

LE FÉRON (Jean). Histoire des connestables: chanceliers ... mareschaux: admiraux ...
Augmenté ... par D.Godefroy.   6 pts.   fo.
Paris, de l'Imprimerie Royale, 1658   **2916**

[LE FÈVRE (Raoul)]. The destruction of Troy. In three books ... [Transl. by W.Caxton.]
11th ed.   4to.
London, for T.Passinger, 1684   [Vulgaria I]
Wing L933.   **1190(4)**

——————— [T]he recuyles or gaderige to gyder of ye hystoryes of Troye.   fo.
(*London, by Wynken de Worde*, 1502)
Wants D2, P4, Q2, Ee1.   STC 15376; Duff p.36.
1996

LE GALLOIS (Pierre). Traitté des plus belles bibliothèques de l'Europe.   12mo.
Paris, chez Estienne Michallet, 1680   **554**

LEGEND (The) of Captain Jones, 1671.
See LLOYD (David), Dean of St Asaph.   **411**

LEGEND (The) of St.Cuthbert, 1663.
See HEGG (Robert).   **131**

LEGENDA aurea, 1527.
See VORAGINE (Jacobus de), Abp of Genoa.
2040

LE GRAND (Antoine). Historia naturæ.   Ed. 2a.
4to.
Londini, apud J.Martin, 1680   Wing L952.
1676

———————Institutio philosophiæ, secundum principia D.R.Descartes. Ed. 4a ... auctior.   4to.
Londini, typis M.Clark, impensis J.Martyn, 1680
Wing L957.   **1675**

———————[*Institutio philosophiæ*...] An entire body of philosophy, according to the principles of the famous R.Des Cartes. [Ed.] by Richard Blome.   fo.
London, by Samuel Roycroft, and sold by the undertaker Richard Blome, 1694   84 engr. pls.
Wing L950.   **2484**

LE GRAND (Joachim). Histoire du divorce de Henry VIII roy d'Angleterre et de Catherine d'Arragon.   3 vols.   12mo.
Paris, chez la veuve de Edme Martin, Jean Boudot [etc.] (*de l'imprimerie de Jean Baptiste Coignard*), 1688   **732-4**

LEIBNITZ (Gottfried Wilhelm von), Baron. Codex juris gentium diplomaticus ... (Mantissa codicis ...), 1693-1700.
See CODEX juris ...   **2404-5**

LEICESTER (Sir Peter), Bart.
See LEYCESTER (Sir Peter), Bart.

LEICESTER'S. Leycesters common-wealth: conceived, spoken, and published.   8vo.
[*London*] 1641   Engr. fp. (port., Charrington p.97).   Wing L968.   **386**

LEICKHER (Georg Jacob). De jure maritimo. 12mo.
Dresdæ, sumptibus Michaëlis Güntheri, 1685   **308**

LEIGH (Charles). The natural history of Lancashire, Cheshire, and the Peak.   3 pts.   fo.
*Oxford, for the author, and to be had at Mr.George
West's, and Mr.Henry Clement's, there [etc.],*
1700   Engr. fp. (port., Charrington p.97), 24
engr. pls, map.   Wing L975.   **2564**

LEIGH (Edward). Critica sacra ... 4th ed.   4 pts.
fo.
London, by Abraham Miller and Roger Daniel,
1662   Engr. port., Charrington p.97.
Wing L992.   **2207**

[LEIGH (Richard)]. The copie of a letter sent ...
to Don Bernadin Mendoza, ambassadour in France
for ... Spain ... Whereunto are adioyned certaine
late aduertisements. [*Variously attributed to
R.Leigh and W.Cecil, Baron Burghley.*]   4to.
London, by I.Vautrollier for Richard Field, 1588
[Sea Tracts IV]   STC 15412.   **1080(1)**

LE JEUNE DE BOULENCOURT. Description
générale de l'Hostel Royal des Invalides. [*Also
attributed to De La Porte.*]   fo.
*Paris, chez l'Auteur, (de l'imprimerie de Gabriel
Martin,)* 1683   Engr. fp., 17 engr. pls.   **2909**

LELAND (John). The laboryouse journey ʒ serche
... for Englandes antiquitees.   8vo.
[*London,by Johan Bale,* 1549]   Wants H8.
STC 15445; Duff p.36-7.   **108(1)**

LELLIS (Carlo de). Discorsi delle famiglie nobili
del regno di Napoli.   3 vols.   fo.
*Napoli, nella stampa di Honofrio Savio (di Gio:
Francesco Paci, appresso Ignatio Rispoli [etc.]),*
1654-71   **2153-5**

LE LORRAIN DE VALLEMONT (Pierre).
Description de l'aimant ... à ... N.Dame de
Chartres.   12mo.
Paris, chez Laurent d'Houry, Edmé Couterot,
1692   Engr. diagram.   **677**

LE MAIRE (C.). Paris ancien et nouveau.   3 vols.
12mo.
Paris, chez Théodore Girard, 1685   **702-4**

LE MAISTRE (Antoine). Les plaidoyez, et
harangues de M.Le Maistre ... Donnez au public
par M.Iean Issali.   5e éd.   4to.
Paris, chez Pierre le Petit, 1660   **1936**

LEMÉE (François). Traité des statuës.   2 pts.
12mo.
*Paris, chez Arnould Seneuze (de l'imprimerie
d'Antoine Lambin),* 1688 (1687)
Engr. title-page.   **786**

LÉMERY (Nicolas). Cours de chymie.   9e éd.
8vo.
Paris, chez Estienne Michallet, 1697
Engr. diagrams.   **1532**

———————— [*Cours de chymie ...*] A course of
chymistry ... 2nd ed. ... from the 5th ed. in the
French.   8vo.
London, by R.N. for Walter Kettilby, 1686
Engr. pls.   Wing L1039.   **1212**

[LE NOIR (Jean)]. Les nouvelles lumieres
politiques pour le gouvernement de l'Eglise, ou
l'évangile nouveau du Cardinal Palavicin.   12mo.
*Suivant la copie imprimée à Paris, chez Jean
Martel,* 1676   **77(1)**

LEO (Johannes), Africanus. A geographical
historie of Africa, written in Arabicke and Italian
... Translated and collected by Iohn Pory.   fo.
Londini, impensis Georg.Bishop, 1600
STC 15481.   **1894**

LÉONARD (Jean). Journal du voyage de la Reine
[Anne Marie of Spain] depuis Neubourg jusqu'à
Madrid.   8vo.
Bruxelles, chez Jean Léonard, 1691   **757**

LE PETIT (Claude). La chronique scandaleuse, ou
Paris ridicule.   12mo.
'*Cologne, chez Pierre de la Place*' [*Amsterdam*],
1668   **99(6)**

[LESLIE (Charles)]. An answer to a book,
intituled, The state of the Protestants in Ireland
under the late King James's government.   4to.
London, 1692   Wing L1120.   **1591**

[————————] The case of the Regale and of
the Pontificat stated, in a conference concerning
the independency of the church.   2nd ed.   8vo.
London, for C.Brome, G.Strahan, &c., 1702 **1030**

[————————] The snake in the grass: or,
Satan transform'd ... discovering the ... subtilty ...
of those people call'd Quakers.   3rd ed.   8vo.
London, printed for Charles Brome, 1698
Wing L1158.   **1269**

L'ESTRANGE (Hamon). The alliance of divine
offices exhibiting all the Liturgies of the Church
of England since the Reformation.   fo.
London, for Henry Broom, 1659
Wing L1183.   **2076**

L'ESTRANGE (Sir Roger). The dissenter's say-
ings.   2nd ed.   4to.
London, for Henry Brome, 1681   [Consutilia I]
Wing L1241.   **1427(3)**

[————————] The history of the plot.   fo.
London, for Richard Tonson, 1679
[Narratives & Tryals I]   Wing L1258. **2249(17)**

————————The observator, 1681-7.
See OBSERVATOR (The) ...   **2450-1**

[LETI (Gregorio)]. Il cardinalismo di Santa
Chiesa ... by the author of the Nipotismo di
Roma. and faithfully Englished by G.H.   fo.

London, for John Starkey, 1670   Engr. fp.
(port., Charrington p.38).   Wing L1330.   **2176**

──────── Dialogues politiques, ou bien la
politique. Traduite d'Italien.   2 vols.   12mo.
Paris, chez Claude Garnier, 1681   **100-1**

[────────] Histoire des conclaves depuis
Clement V.   2 vols.   12mo.
Cologne, 1694   Engr. title-page, pl.   **535-6**

[────────] The life of Donna Olimpia
Maldachini ... Written in Italian by Abbot Gualdi
[i.e. G.Leti].   8vo.
*London, printed by W.G., sold by Robert Little-
bury*, 1667   Wing L1334.   **383(3)**

[────────] Il nipotismo di Roma: or, the
history of the Popes' nephews.   2 pts.   8vo.
London, for John Starkey, 1669   Engr. fp.
(port., Charrington p.99).   Wing L1335; Diary
27 Apr.1669.   **986**

──────── The present state of Geneva. With
a brief discription of that city ... untill ... 1681.
8vo.
London, printed for William Cademan, 1681
Wing L1338.   **505**

[────────] Le syndicat du pape Alexandre
VII, avec son voyage en l'autre monde. Traduit de
l'italien.   12mo.
1669   **41**

LETRAS de los villancicos, 1683.
See CADIZ. Cathedral.   **1545(26-9)**

LETTER (A) concerning toleration, 1690.
See LOCKE (John).   **152**

LETTER (A) containing a most briefe discourse
apologeticall, 1599.
See DEE (John).   **1080(2)**

LETTER (A) from a clergy-man in the diocese of
Bath and Wells.   brs.
[c.1702]   [Convocation Pamphlets X]   **1696(3)**

LETTER (A) from a country clergyman, 1702.
See WAKE (William), Abp of Canterbury.   **1696(4)**

LETTER (A) from a Member of the Parliament of
Scotland ... containing his reasons, for with-
drawing from that Assembly.   4to.
[*London*] 1702   [Consutilia XI]   **1437(13)**

LETTER (A) from General Ludlow to Dr.Holling-
worth ... defending his former letter to Sir E.
S[eymour].   [*Not written by Ludlow.*]   4to.
Amsterdam, 1692   Wing L1469.   **1286(3)**

LETTER (A) from Major General Ludlow to Sir
E.S[eymour].   [*Not written by Ludlow.*]   4to.
Amsterdam, 1691   Wing L1489.   **1286(1)**

LETTER (A) from Oxford, 1693.
See N.(N.).   **1432(13)**

LETTER (A) from the borders of Scotland, con-
cerning ... agreement between a Scotch General
Assembly and an English provincial convocation.
By an Episcopal divine.   4to.
(*London, for A.Baldwin*, 1702)   [Convocation
Pamphlets X]   **1696(15)**

LETTER (A) to a clergyman in the city concerning
the instructions lately given to the Proctors for
the clergy of the diocese of Worcester.   4to.
(*London, for John Nutt*, 1702)   [Convocation
Pamphlets XI]   **1697(9)**

LETTER (A) to a clergyman in the country, 1701.
See ATTERBURY (Francis), Bp of Rochester.
1697(7)

LETTER (A) to a friend concerning the Bank of
England, 1696.
See P.(S.).   **796(4)**

LETTER (A) to a friend, giving an account of all
the treatises, 1692.
See MONRO (Alexander).   **1437(12)**

LETTER (A) to a friend in the country, concerning the proceedings of the present Convocation
[1701].
See GIBSON (Edmund), Bp of London.   **1695(6)**

LETTER (A) to a Member of Parliament;
occasioned by a letter to a Convocation-man,
1697.
See WRIGHT (William).   **1695(1)**

LETTER (A) to a Member of Parliament,
occasion'd by the votes of the House of Commons
against their late Speaker, and others.   4to.
London, 1695   [Consutilia VII]
Wing L1678.   **1433(13)**

LETTER (A) to a member of the late Parliament,
concerning the debts of the nation.   4to.
London, for Edward Poole, 1701
[Consutilia XI]   **1437(1)**

LETTER (A) to a peer concerning the power and
authority of metropolitans over their com-
provincial bishops.   4to.
London, for A.Baldwin, 1701   [Convocation
Pamphlets XI]   **1697(2)**

LETTER (A) unto Mr Stubs, 1660.
See HARRINGTON (James), the elder.   **1297(4)**

LETTERS writ by a Turkish spy, 1637-82.
See MARANA (Giovanni Paolo).   **607-10**

LETTRES et memoires d'estat, des roys, princes,
ambassadeurs ... de François I. Henry II. &
François II.   2 vols.   fo.
*Blois, chez I.Hotot, et se vendent à Paris, chez
François Clousier, et la vefue Aubouin*, 1666   **2621-2**

[LEURECHON (Jean)]. Mathematicall recreations ... lately compiled in French by H.van Etten [i.e. J.Leurechon] and now in English [by W. Oughtred] ... The description ... of the ... horo-logicall ring. 2 pts. 8vo.
London, for William Leake, 1653 (1652)
Engr. title-page, diagrams. Wing L1790; O578.
618

LE VASSOR (Michel). Histoire du règne de Louis XIII. 2e éd. 3 vols. 12mo.
Amsterdam, chez Pierre Brunel (– chez Estienne Le Jeune) 1701 1: Engr. fp. 2: Engr. title-page. 16 engr. ports. **662-4**

LEWIS (David). The last speech of David Lewis ... at Uske ... 27 Aug., 1679. fo.
[*London*, 1679] [Narratives & Tryals IV]
Wing L1836. **2252(4)**

LEWIS (William). The information of William Lewis. fo.
London, for Randal Taylor, 1680 [Narratives & Tryals III] Wing L1851. **2251(32)**

[LEYBOURN (William)]. The art of numbring by speaking-rods: vulgarly termed Nepeirs Bones. Published by W.L. 12mo.
London, for G.Sawbridge, 1667 Engr. tables.
Wing L1904. **12(1)**

———————— The compleat surveyor. 4th ed. fo.
London, by E.Flesher, for George Sawbridge, 1679 Engr. fp. (port., Charrington p.100), pls, diagrams. Wing L1910. **2175**

———————— Dialling ... shewing how to make all ... dials. fo.
London, for Awnsham Churchill, 1682
Engr. fp. (port., Charrington p.100), diagrams.
Wing L1912. **2264**

———————— The line of proportion or numbers, commonly called Gunters line, made easie. 12mo.
London, printed by J.S. for G.Sawbridge, 1667
Engr. diagram. Wing L1916. **12(2)**

LEYCESTER (Sir Peter), Bart. Historical antiquities, in two books. The first ... of Great-Brettain and Ireland. The second ... concerning Cheshire. fo.
London, by W.L. for Robert Clavell, 1673
Woodcuts. Engr. of Hugh Lupus, Earl of Chester, sitting in his parliament inserted after p.106 (Charrington p.36). Wing L964, L1943.
2436

LEYCESTERS commonwealth, 1641.
See LEICESTER'S ... **386**

[L'HOSPITAL (Guillaume François Antoine de), Marquis de Sainte-Mesme]. Analyse des infiniment petits. 4to.
Paris, de l'imprimerie royale (par les soins de Jean Anisson,) 1696 11 folding pls. **1939**

LHUYD (Edward). Ichnographia. Sive lapidum aliorumque fossilium Britannicorum ... distributio classica. 8vo.
Londini, ex officina M.C., 1699 23 engr. pls.
Wing L1946. **1587**

LICETUS (Fortunius). De his, qui diu vivunt sine alimento libri quatuor. 2 pts. fo.
Patavii, apud Petrum Bertellium (Vicetiæ, typis Francisci Grossi duo libri priores, Patavii, prælo Gasparis Crivellarij duo posteriores), 1612 **2225**

———————— De lucernis antiquorum reconditis libb. sex. fo.
Vtini, ex typographia Nicolai Schiratti, prostant Patavij apud Franciscum Bolzettam, 1653 (1652)
Engr. pls. **2475**

———————— De monstrorum caussis, natura, & differentijs. 4to.
Patavii, apud Gasparem Crivellarium, 1616 **1393**

LICHTENDE (Die) columne, 1663.
See SHORT (A) compendium ... **1079(7)**

LIFE (The) and acts of ... Sir William Wallace, 1673.
See HENRY, the Minstrel. **358(1)**

LIFE (The) and death of Mother Shipton, 1684.
See HEAD (Richard). **1193(7)**

LIFE (The) and death of Rosamond. 12mo.
[*London*] *for F.Coles, T.Vere, J.Wright [etc.]* [c.1675] [Penny-Merriments I] Woodcuts.
362(2)

LIFE (The) and death of Sheffery ap Morgan. 12mo.
[*London*] *for J.Deacon* [c.1680] [Penny-Merriments I] Woodcut. **362(45)**

LIFE (The) and death of the English rogue, 1679.
See HEAD (Richard). **1192(20)**

LIFE (The) and death of the famous champion of England, St.George. 12mo.
[*London*] *by J.M. for J.Clake [sic], W.Thackeray, T.Passinger* [c.1685] [Penny-Merriments II] Woodcuts. **363(6)**

LIFE (The) and death of Thomas Woolsey, 1667.
See CAVENDISH (George). **794**

LIFE (The) and reign of King Richard the second, 1681.
See HOWARD (Sir Robert). **877**

LIFE (The) of Donna Olimpia Maldachini, 1667.
See LETI (Gregorio). **383(3)**

LIFE (The) of James II., late King of England, 1702.
See JONES (David). **1417**

LIFE (The) of Long Meg of Westminster.   12mo.
London, by J.M. for G.Convers, [c.1690]
[Penny-Merriments II]   Woodcut.   **363(26)**

LIFE (The) of Merlin, surnamed Ambrosius, 1641.
See HEYWOOD (Thomas).   **1112(1)**

LIFE (The) of Mr.Thomas Firmin, 1698.
See NYE (Stephen).   **1009**

LIFE (The) of the valiant ... Sir Walter Raleigh,
1677.
See SHIRLEY (John).   **892**

LIFE (The) of William Bedell, D.D., 1685.
See BURNET (Gilbert), Bp of Salisbury.   **1068**

LIFE (The) of William Fuller, 1692.
See ROPER (Abel).   **1432(8)**

LIFE (The) of Wm Fuller, alias Fullee, alias
Ellison ... Printed to prevent his further imposing
upon the publick.   2 pts.   8vo.
London, 1701   Wants sig.C of pt 2.   **981(1)**

LIFE (The) or the ecclesiasticall historie of
S.Thomas Archbishope of Canterbury, 1639.
See B.(A.).   **916**

LIGHT (The) appearing more and more, 1651.
See MAYHEW (Thomas).   **1428(1)**

LIGHTFOOT (John). Elias redivivus: a sermon
preached ... March 29, 1643.   4to.
London, by R.Cotes, for Andrew Crooke, 1643
[Sermons Polemical V]   Wing L2053.   **1183(16)**

———————— Works.   2 vols.   fo.
*London, by W.R. (William Rawlins) for Robert
Scot, Thomas Basset* [etc.], 1684
1: engr. fp. (port., Charrington p.100), map.
2: engr. map.   Wing L2051.   **2711-2**

LIGON (Richard). A true & exact history of the
island of Barbadoes.   fo.
London, sold by Peter Parker, and Thomas Guy,
1673   Engr. map, 9 engr. pls.
Wing L2076.   **2228**

LILBURNE (John). An agreement of the free
people of England. By I.Lilburne, W.Walwyn,
T.Prince, and R.Overton.   4to.
(*London, for Gyles Calvert*) [1649]
[Consutilia IV]   Wing L2079.   **1430(5)**

———————— A discourse betwixt Lieutenant
Colonel Iohn Lilburn ... and Mr Hugh Peter.   4to.
London, 1649   [Consutilia IV]   Wing L2100.
1430(4)

———————— The picture of the Councel of
State, held forth ... by J.Lilburn, T.Prince, and
R.Overton.   4to.
[*London*] 1649   [Consutilia IV]
Wing L2154.   **1430(3)**

———————— The triall of Lieut. Collonell
John Lilburne ... Publ. by Theodorus Verax
[i.e. C.Walker].   4to.
Southwark, by Hen.Hils [1649]   [Consutilia IV]
Wing W338.   **1430(6)**

LILLINGSTON (Luke). Reflections on Mr.
Burchet's memoirs. Or, remarks on ... Captain
Wilmot's expedition.   8vo.
London, 1704   **1145(1)**

LILLY (William). A groatsworth of wit for a
penny.   8vo.
[*London*] *for W.T. and sold by Jonah Deacon*
[c.1680]   [Penny-Merriments I]   Woodcut.
Wing L2224.   **362(49)**

———————— The mirror of natural astrology.
8vo.
[*London*] *for W.T. and sold by J.Deacon,*
[c.1680]   [Penny-Merriments II]   Woodcut.
363(10)

———————— Monarchy or no monarchy in
England.   2 pts.   4to.
London, printed for Humfrey Blunden, 1651
Woodcuts.   Wing L2228.   **1112(2)**

———————— Lilly's new Erra pater. Or, a
prognostication for ever.   12mo.
[*London*] *for J.Conyers* [c.1683]   [Penny-
Merriments II]   Woodcut. Title-page cropped.
363(19)

LILY (William). De generibus nominum, ac
uerborum præteritis & supinis.   8vo.
(*Antuerpiæ, excudebat Martinus Cæsar,* 1535)
MS note in 16th-cent. schoolboy hand at end.
Adams L679; Duff p.38.   **424(3)**

———————— De generibus nominum, ac
uerborum præteritis & supinis.   8vo.
(*Londini, per me Henricum Pepuuel*) 1539
On title-page, MS note in unidentified 17th-cent.
hand, of 8vo. edition of 1533 (Antwerp). At end,
in same hand: 'Opus recognitum ... per Jo.
Ritwissum ...' [Ritwyse, High Master of St Paul's
School, 1522-32].   STC 15609; Duff p.39.
424(8)

———————— De octo orationis partium
constructione libellus. [*Written by W.Lily and
revised by Erasmus.*]   8vo.
(*Friburgi Brisgoiæ, excudebat Ioannes Faber
Emmeus,* 1534)   MS marginal notes, some
cropped, in Latin and English, with autographs,
in several 16th-cent. schoolboy hands. At E6:
'Thomas Hoy (?) is a knave So sayth Jo Carwell'.
At E5: (cropped) extract from collect for Third
Sunday after Epiphany ('... to looke upon my
infirmities').   Adams E609; Duff p.22.   **424(2)**

———————— Libellus de constructione octo partium orationis.   8vo.
Londini, diligentia Henrici Pepuuel, 1539
On title-page, MS note in unidentified 17th-cent. hand, of 8vo edition of 1536 (Antwerp).
STC 15603; Duff p.38.   **424(7)**

[————————] A short introduction of grammar. (— Brevissima institutio.)   8vo.
London, by Roger Norton, 1662   Engr. title-page; woodcut.   Wing L2283.   **886**

LIMBORCH (Philippus van). De veritate religionis Christianæ, amica collatio cum erudito Judæo. 4to.
Goudæ, apud Justum ab Hoeve, 1687   **1786**

LIMITATIONS for the next foreign successor, or new Saxon race.   4to.
London, 1701   [Consutilia X]   **1436(5)**

LINSCHOTEN (Jan Huygen van). Discours of voyages into ye Easte & West Indies.   fo.
London, by Iohn Wolfe [1598]   Engr. title-page, maps.   STC 15691.   **2100**

LINTON (Anthony). Newes of the complement of the art of nauigation.   4to.
London, by Felix Kyngston, 1609
[Sea Tracts III]   STC 15692.   **1079(4)**

LIPENIUS (Martinus). Navigatio Salomonis Ophiritica illustrata.   12mo.
Witteb., impensis Andrea' Hartmanni, 166[0]
Engr. title-page. Sig Q wrongly imposed, title-page defective.   **59**

LISET (Abraham). Amphithalami, or, the accomptants closet.   fo.
London, by James Flesher, for Nicholas Bourne, 1660   Wing L2367.   **2447(2)**

LISOLA (François Paul de), Baron. Bouclier d'estat et de justice, contre le dessein de la France. 12mo.
1701   **340**

[————————] The buckler of state and justice. 8vo.
London, printed by James Flesher, for Richard Royston, 1667   Wing L2370.   **841**

LIST (A) of the knights [*etc.*] of the Cinque-Ports ... in the Parliament, 1679.
See ENGLAND. *Parliament. Commons.*   **2137(1)**

LIST (A) of their names who were taken out of the House [of Commons], and others (being forty-three in number) that sate in the Other House.   fo.
[*London*, 1657?]   [Consutilia VIII]   **1434(7)**

LISTER (Martin). A journey to Paris in the year 1698.   3rd ed.   8vo.
London, for Jacob Tonson, 1699   6 engr. pls.
Wing L2527.   **1316**

LITTLETON (Adam). Linguæ Latinæ liber dictionarius quadripartitus.   2 vols.   4to.
London, for T.Basset, J.Wright, R.Chiswell, 1678
Engr. fps; engr. maps.   Wing L2563.   **1895-6**

LITTLETON (Sir Thomas). Tenores novelli.
See COKE (Sir Edward). The first part of the institutes.   **2150**

LITURGIES. Church of England. The Booke of the Common Praier.   fo.
Londini, in officina Richardi Graftoni, 1549
STC 16275; Duff p.39.   **1976(1)**

LITURGIES . Church of England. The Book of Common Prayer ... With ye Psalter.   fo.
Oxford, for M.Pitt [*London*, 1683?]
Engr. title-page.   Wing B3671.   **2604(1)**

LITURGIES. Church of England. [*Book of Common Prayer.*] Βίβλος τῆς δημοσίας εὐχῆς. Ἐν τῇ Κανταβριγίᾳ, ἐξετυπώθη παρ' Ἰωάννου Φιέλδου, αχξέ [1665]   Wing B3632.   **875(1)**

LITURGIES. Church of England. [*Book of Common Prayer.*] Liturgia inglesa, o libro del rezado publico. [Transl. by T.Carrascon.]   4to.
Augustæ Trinobantum [*R.Barker*], CIↃ.IↃI. IXIIV [misprint for 1623]   On front-flyleaf, (in hand of one of Pepys's clerks) taken from *Cabala, sive scrinia sacra* (1654) [2261, p.309] extract from letter from Lord Keeper Williams to Duke of Buckingham, 26 July 1623, about the translation.   STC 16434; Gaselee 91.   **1734**

LITURGIES. Church of England. [*Book of Common Prayer.*] Liturgia, seu liber precum communium ... una cum psalterio.   12mo.
Londini, apud Car.Mearne, 1685   Engr. title-page.   Wing C4188C.   **553**

LITURGIES. Church of England. [*Book of Common Prayer.*] Llyfr Gweddi Gyffredin ... A'r Psallwyr.   2 pts.   8vo.
Haerlûdd, dros Thomas Jones, ag ar werth drosto ef Charles Beard, a John Marsh, yn Llundain, 1687   **972**

LITURGIES. Church of England. A form of prayer and thanksgiving ... to be used ... on Thursday the 27th ... October ... for the signal victory.   4to.
London, printed by Charles Bill, and the executrix of Thomas Newcomb, 1692   [Consutilia VI]
Wing C4128.   **1432(18)**

LITURGIES. Church of England. A form of prayer to be used ... during the time of Their Majesties fleets being at sea.   4to.
London, by Charles Bill and the executrix of Thomas Newcomb, 1691   [Consutilia I & VI]
Wing C4138.   **1427(11), 1432(17)**

LITURGIES. Church of England. Forma precum in utrâque domo Convocationis.   4to.

Londini, typis Car.Bill & executricis Tho.New-comb, defuncti, 1700   [Convocation Pamphlets XII]   Wing C4184.   **1698(1)**

LITURGIES. Church of England. A prayer for victorie and peace.   8vo.
(*Londini, excusum in ædibus Richardi Graftoni*, 1548)   On title-page, in Pepys's hand: 'Upon a Marriage then in viewe betweene K.Edwd. 6th. & the Princesse ye young Queen of Scotland. 1548' [1547]. Cf. Cal.State Papers Dom., 1547-80, p.4. STC 16503; Duff p.41.   **1976(2)**

LITURGIES. Church of England. Prayers to be used during the Queens sickness.   4to.
London, by Charles Bill and executrix of Thomas Newcomb, 1694   **1528(1)**

LITURGIES. Church of England. A thankes geuing to God vsed in Christes churche on the Monday, Wednisday and Friday, 1551.   12mo.
[*London*] *Richardus Grafton excudebat* [1551] MS notes by Pepys (in hand of one of his clerks) on front and end flyleaves explaining that this service-book (meant for use during the sweating sickness) has been bound up with a volume of Skelton's poems so that it may be made clear how well the Psalms (in the metrical version of the unjustly neglected Sternhold and Hopkins) stand comparison with the 'highest of the Secular Poetry' at that time.   STC 16504; Duff p.41.
228(2)

LITURGIES. Church of Scotland. [*Book of Common Order.*] [The psalmes of David in prose and meeter. With their whole tunes.]   8vo.
(*Edinburgh, by the heires of Andrew Hart*, 1635) Wants all before B1.   STC 16599.
See also below, vol.IV.   **863(2)**

LITURGIES. Church of Scotland. The service, discipline, and forme, of the common prayers ... used in the English Church of Geneva ... Approved by ... J.Calvin, and the Church of Scotland.   4to.
London, for William Cooke, 1641
[Liturgick Controversies II]   Wing S2646.
1188(2)

LITURGIES. Roman Catholic Church. [*Breviarium* [*Breviarium.*] Portiforiū seu Breuiarium ad vsum ecclesie Sarisburiensis ... Pars estiualis.
Londini, R.C[*aly*] ('*in vniuersitate Parisieñ., p Franciscū Regnault'*), 1555 ('1535') STC 15840; Duff p.42.   **1749**

LITURGIES. Roman Catholic Church. [*Breviarium.*] Portiforium seu Breuiarium, ad insignis sarisburiensis, ecclesie vsum ... Pars hyemalis.   4to.
Londini (*per Johannes Kyngston. et Henricus Sutton*) 1555   Wants P4; a6, 7; i7, 8; p4. STC 15839; Duff p.42.   **1748**

LITURGIES. Roman Catholic Church. [*Breviarium.*] Officium Beatæ Mariæ Virginis, nuper reformatum ... ad instar Breviarij Romani sub Vrbano VIII. recogniti.   8vo.
Antuerpiæ, ex officina Plantiniana Balthasaris Moreti, 1685   17 engr. pls.   **1602**

LITURGIES. Roman Catholic Church. Breviarium Romanum ... Urbani PP.VIII. auctoritate recognitum. Pars verna.   8vo.
Antuerpiæ, ex officina Plantiniana Balthasaris Moreti, 1685   Engr. title-page, 5 engr. pls. **1667**

LITURGIES. Roman Catholic Church. Breviarium Romanum ... Urbani PP.VIII. auctoritate recognitum. Pars æstiva.   8vo.
Antuerpiæ, ex officina Plantiniana Balthasaris Moreti, 1685   Engr. title-page, 4 engr. pls. **1668**

LITURGIES. Roman Catholic Church. Breviarium Romanum ... Urbani PP.VIII. auctoritate recognitum. Pars autumnalis.   8vo.
Antuerpiæ, ex officina Plantiniana Balthasaris Moreti, 1685   Engr. title-page, 3 engr. pls. **1669**

LITURGIES. Roman Catholic Church. Breviarium Romanum ... Urbani PP.VIII. auctoritate recognitum. Pars hiemalis.   8vo.
Antuerpiæ, ex officina Plantiniana Balthasaris Moreti, 1685   Engr. title-page, 4 engr. pls. **1670**

LITURGIES. Roman Catholic Church. Cæremoniale, continens ritus electionis Romani Pontificis. Gregorii Papæ XV. iussu editum.   4to.
Romæ, ex typographia Cameræ Apostolicæ, 1622
1743(1)

LITURGIES. Roman Catholic Church. Cæremoniale episcoporum iussu Clementis VIII ... reformatum.   fo.
Parisiis, impensis Societatis Typographicæ Officij Ecclesiastici, 1633   Engr. title-page, engrs.
2608

LITURGIES. Roman Catholic Church. [*Horae.*] Ces presentes heures a lusaige du Mans toutes au long sans reqrir.   8vo.
Paris, pour Symō Vostre [1516]   Vellum; 18 woodcut pls.   Adams L1075; Duff p.41.
993

LITURGIES. Roman Catholic Church. [Hore Beatissime Virginis Marie ad legitimum Sarisburiensis ecclesie ritum.   4to.
Parisijs, venundantur a Francisco Regnault, 1530] Wants ✠1-3, 5-6, Z8, ᴢ1-10; supplied in illuminated MS.   STC 15968; Adams L1106; Duff p.43.
1848

LITURGIES. Roman Catholic Church. [*Horae.*] This prymer of Salysbury vse is set out a long wout ony serchyng. (— An inuocacyon gloryous named the Psalter of Jesus.)   16mo.

Parys (impensis Joannis Growte, opera Yolande Bonhomme vidue defuncti Thielmanni Keruer), 1532   Woodcut pls.   STC 15978; Adams L1114; Duff pp.43, 47.   **23**

LITURGIES. Roman Catholic Church. [*Horae.*]
[A goodly prymer in Englyshe, newly corrected.]
(— A goodly exposition vpon the .xxx. psalme ...
of Hierome of Ferrarie [i.e. G.Savonarola].)
4to.
(*London, by Johñ Byddell, for Wylliam Marshall,*
1535)   Wants title-page.   STC 15988;
Duff pp.44, 57.   **1374**

LITURGIES. Roman Catholic Church. [*Horae.*]
The manual of prayers or the prymer in Englysh ꝛ
Laten.   4to.
(*Lōdō, by me Johñ Wayland, 1539*)
Wants X1, Ii4, Tt2-3.   STC 16009.5; Duff p.44.
                                                        1403

LITURGIES. Roman Catholic Church. Hore Beate
Marie Virginis, secundum vsum insignis ecclesie
Eboriensis. De nouo impres.   8vo.
London, for Jhon Wight [1557]   STC 16109;
Duff p.47.   **136**

LITURGIES. Roman Catholic Church. Martyrologium romanum Gregorii XIII Pont. Max. jussu
editum et Urbani VIII authoritate recognitum.
Authore A.Lubin.   4to.
Lutetiæ Parisiorum, apud Renatum Guignard,
1679   **1843**

LITURGIES. Roman Catholic Church. Missale
ad vsum insignis ac preclare ecclesie Sarum.   fo.
(*London, per Richardum Pynson,* 1520)
Vellum; on end flyleaf, in a 16th-cent. hand, 3
MS Latin prayers for the reconciliation of the
Kingdom with the Catholic Church [1554].
STC 16202; Duff p.45; Diary 2 Nov.1660.   **2795**

LITURGIES. Roman Catholic Church. Missale
Romanum ex decreto sacrosancti Concilii Tridentini
restitutum ... nunc denuo Vrbani Papæ
Octavi auctoritate recognitum.   4to.
Antuerpiæ, ex officina Plantiniana Balthasaris
Moreti, 1683   6 engr. pls.   **2047**

LITURGIES. Roman Catholic Church. Ordinale
Sarum (1503).
See MAYDESTON (Clement).   **1700**

LITURGIES. Roman Catholic Church. Pontificale
Romanum Clementis VIII. primum; nunc denuo
Vrbani VIII. auctoritate recognitum.   4 pts.   fo.
Parisiis, impensis Societatis Typographicæ
Librorum Officij Ecclesiastici (sumptibus
Sebastiani [&] Gabrielis Cramoisy [etc.]) 1664
Engrs.   **2814**

LITURGIES. Roman Catholic Church.
Processionale ad vsum insignis eccl'ie Saꝝ.   4to.
Lond. [*J.Kingston and H.Sutton*] , 1554
STC 16244; Duff p.46.   **1238**

LITURGIES. Roman Catholic Church. Psalterium
Dauidicum, ad vsum ecclesie Sarisburiensis.   8vo.
Londini, per Ioannem Kyngston, & Henricum
Sutton, 1555   STC 16266; Duff p.47.   **301**

LITURGIES. Roman Catholic Church. [*Rituale.*]
[A]d laudem Dei ... ecce manuale quoddam
secunduȝ vsū matris eccl'ie Eboraceñ.   4to.
(*Impressum per Wynandū de Worde cōmorāte*
Londoñ — pro Johāne Gaschet et Jacobo Ferre-
bouc sociis —, 1509)   STC 16160; Duff p.48.
                                                        1823

LITURGIES. Roman Catholic Church. [*Rituale.*]
Manuale ad vsum percelebris ecclesie Sarisburiensis.
4to.
Londini [*J.Kingston and H.Sutton*] , 1554
STC 16154; Duff p.45.   **1699**

LITURGIES. Roman Catholic Church. Rituale
Romanum, Pauli V ... jussu editum. Ed. novissima.
8vo.
Parisiis, apud Joannem de la Caille, 1679   **1648**

LIVELY (The) oracles given to us, 1678.
See ALLESTREE (Richard).   **1089**

LIVERIES and fees anciently given, and paid
annually by the City of London, to persons of
honour, &c.   brs.
[*London, 1692?*]   Bound in at end.   **2476**

LIVY. Historiarum quod extat, cum C.Sigonii et
J.F.Gronovii notis.   3 vols.   8vo.
Amstelodami, apud Danielem Elsevirium, (1678-)
1679   Engr. title-page.   **1504-6**

LIVY. The Roman history ... With the supple-
ments of ... J.Freindshemius, and J.Dujatius.   fo.
London, for Awnsham Churchill, 1686
Engr. fp., maps.   Wing L2615.   **2420**

[LLEWELLYN (Martin)] . The legend of Captain
Jones, 1671.
See LLOYD (David), Dean of St Asaph.   **411**

LLOYD (David), Canon of St Asaph. The states-
men and favourites of England since the Reformation.   8vo.
London, printed by J.C. for Samuel Speed, 1665
Engr. fp., title-page.   Wing L2648.   **859**

[LLOYD (David), Dean of St Asaph]. The legend
of Captain Jones. [*Variously attributed to D.Lloyd*
& M.Llewellyn.]   8vo.
London, for E.Okes, and Francis Haley, 1671
Engr. fp.   Wing L2633.   **411**

LLOYD (John). A treatise of the episcopacy, liturgies, and ecclesiastical ceremonies of the primitive times. 4to.
London, by W.G. for John Sherley, and Robert Littlebury, 1660 [Liturgick Controversies III] Wing L2659. **1189(1)**

LLOYD (William), Bp of St Asaph. An historical account of church-government as it was in Great Britain and Ireland. 2nd ed. 8vo.
London, printed by M.Flesher, for Charles Brome, 1684 Wing L2682. **1054**

[———————] The pretences of the French invasion examined. [*Variously ascribed to W. Lloyd and D.Defoe.*] 4to.
London, for R.Clavel, 1692 [Consutilia VI] Wing L2690. **1432(21)**

[———————] A sermon at the funeral of Sir Edmund-Bury Godfrey ... preached on ... the last day of Octob.1678. 4to.
London, by M.Clark, for Henry Brome, 1678 Wing L2699. **1413(1)**

LOCCENIUS (Joannes). De iure maritimo & navali. 12mo.
Holmiæ, ex officinâ Joannis Janssonii, 1650 Engr. title-page. **68**

LOCKE (John). An essay concerning humane understanding. 2nd ed., with large additions. fo.
London, for Awnsham and John Churchil, and Samuel Manship, 1694 Engr. fp., (port., Charrington p.102); MS letter from J.Evelyn (26 Feb. 1689/90) inserted. Wing L2740; Tanner I, pp.95, 99. **2421(1)**

[———————] A letter concerning toleration. 2nd ed., corrected. 12mo.
London, for Awnsham Churchill, 1690 Wing L2748. **152**

[———————] A letter to the ... Bishop of Worcester [E.Stillingfleet] concerning some passages relating to Mr.Locke's Essay of humane understanding. 8vo.
London, by H.Clark for A. and J.Churchill [etc.], 1697 Wing L2749. **1262(1)**

[———————] Reason and religion, 1694.
See REASON and religion ... **474**

[———————] Mr Locke's Reply to the Bishop of Worcester's [E.Stillingfleet's] Answer to his Letter. 8vo.
London, by H.Clark for A. and J.Churchill [etc.], 1697 Wing L2753. **1262(2)**

[———————] Mr.Locke's Reply to the ... Bishop of Worcester's [E.Stillingfleet's] Answer to his Second letter. 8vo.
London, by H.C. for A. and J.Churchill [etc.], 1699 Wing L2754. **1263**

[———————] The reasonableness of Christianity. 8vo.
London, for Awnsham and John Churchil, 1695 On p.287 MS correction (in unidentified hand) of misprint. Wing L2751. **807**

[———————] Several papers relating to money, interest and trade. 3 pts. 8vo.
London, printed for A. and J.Churchill, 1696 Wing L2757. **796(1)**

[———————] Some thoughts concerning education. 3rd ed., enlarged. 8vo.
London, printed for A. and J.Churchill, 1695 Wing L2763. **883**

LOCKE (Matthew). Observations upon a late book entituled, An essay to the advancement of musick, &c. written by T.Salmon. 8vo.
London, by W.G[odbid], sold by John Playford, 1672 Wing L2776.
See also below, vol.IV. **893(2)**

LOCKYER (Nicholas). A sermon preached ... Octob.28.1646. 4to.
London, by Matthew Simmons, for John Rothwell, and Han.Allen, 1646 [Sermons Polemical V] Wing L2800. **1183(17)**

LODGE (Thomas). A looking glasse for London and England. By T.Lodge and R.Greene. 4to.
London, by Barnard Alsop, 1617 STC 16682. **939(5)**

[LOGAN (John)]. Analogia honorum, 1677.
See GUILLIM (John). A display of heraldry. **2576**

LOGGAN (David). Cantabrigia illustrata. fo.
Cantabrigiæ [1676-90] Mezzotint fp. (port.); engr. title-page, 29 engr. pls. Wing L2837. **2933**

[———————] Oxonia illustrata. fo.
Oxoniæ, e Theatro Sheldoniano, 1675 Engr. title-page, 40 engr. pls; 4 additional pls inserted. Wing L2838; Tanner I, p.71. **2912**

LOIOLA, 1648.
See HACKET (John), Bp of Lichfield. **216**

LONDON. The royal charter of confirmation granted by King Charles II. to the City of London ... Translated into English by S.G.Gent. 8vo.
London, printed for Samuel Lee and Benjamin Alsop [1680?] Wing C3604A; L2888. **953**

LONDON. Clockmakers' Company.
See CLOCKMAKERS' COMPANY.

LONDON. Common Council. An act of the Common Council for regulating the election of Sheriffs. fo.
London, by Samuel Roycroft, 1683 Bound in at end. Wing L2858. **2476**

LONDON. Common Council. The order of the
hospitalls ... [c.1680].
See ORDER (The) of the hospitalls ...   **394**

LONDON. Lord Mayor, 1655.
See PACK (Sir Christopher).

———————— 1697.
See CLARKE (Sir Edward).

LONDON. Royal College of Physicians.
See ROYAL COLLEGE OF PHYSICIANS.

LONDON. St Bartholomew's Hospital.
See SAINT BARTHOLOMEWS HOSPITAL.

LONDON. Sessions. The proceedings on the King
and Queens commissions of the peace ... held for
the city of London ... in the Old Bayly.   fo.
*London, for Richard Baldwin, 1662 [or rather
1692]*   [Inserted between nos 2830 & 2831 of
the London Gazette.]   Wing P3609.   **2086**

LONDON. Shipwrights' Company.
See SHIPWRIGHTS' COMPANY.

LONDON (The) gazette. Nos 1-3980. (Nos 1-23
entitled The Oxford gazette.) [Nov.1665]-3 Jan.
1703/4. 13 vols. fo.
*Oxford, London, by T.Newcomb (– Edw:Jones),
1665-1703*   Nos 85, 2586 not publ. Two
variant copies of no.206. Wants nos.158, 212,
326, 1898, 2042-3, 2047, 2049, 2051, 2085, 2354
& 2396. Several proclamations, etc. inserted.
Diary 22 Nov.1665.   **2078-90**

———————— [Another copy of no.3821,
22 June, 1702.]   **2255(10)**

LONDON'S dreadful visitation: or, a collection of
all the bills of mortality for this present year:
beginning the 20th. of December, 1664.   4to.
*London, printed and are to be sold by E.Cotes,
1665*   Wing L2926.   **1595(1)**

LONDON'S liberties.   4to.
London, Ja.Cottrel for Gyles Calvert, 1651
[Consutilia IV]   Wing L2936A.   **1430(12)**

LONG (The) Parliament revived, 1661.
See DRAKE (Sir William).   **1430(14)**

[LONGEPIERRE (Hilaire Bernard Requeleyne,
baron de)]. Discours sur les anciens.   12mo.
*Paris, chez Pierre Aubouin, Pierre Emery et
Charles Clousier, 1687*   **450**

LORD'S Prayer. Oratio Dominica ... plus centum
linguis ... reddita & expressa. [Compiled by
B.Motte.] Ed. novissima.   4to.
*Londini, apud Dan.Brown, et W.Keblewhite,
1700*   Wing M2944.   **1569**

LORRAIN (Paul). The dying man's assistant.
12mo.
London, printed for John Lawrence, 1702   **377**

LOUIS XIV, King of France. Edits, déclarations,
réglements et ordonnances du Roy sur le fait de la
marine.   4to.
Paris, de l'Imprimerie Royale, 1677   **1907(1)**

———————— Ordonnance donnée ... Aoust,
1681, touchant la marine.   4to.
*Paris, chez Denys Thierry et Christophle Ballard,
1681*   **1958**

———————— Ordonnance ... Pour les armées
navales et arcenaux de marine.   12mo.
Paris, chez Estienne Michallet, 1689   **693**

———————— Ordonnance ... sur le fait des
Eaux & Forests.   12mo.
Paris, par Sebastien Mabre-Cramoisy, 1683   **921**

LOVE a la mode. A comedy, 1663.
See SOUTHLAND (Thomas).   **1075(11)**

LOVE tricks, 1667.
See SHIRLEY (James).   **1075(14)**

LOVE (Christopher). Englands distemper ...
A sermon preacht ... January 30th.   4to.
*London, by John Macock, for Michael Spark
junior, 1645*   [Sermons Polemical V]
Wing L3152.   **1183(18)**

———————— Short and plaine animadversions
on some passages in Mr.Dels sermon first preached
... Novemb.25.1646.   4to.
London, by M.Bell for Iohn Bellamy, 1646
[Sermons Polemical V]   Wing L3174. **1183(19)**

LOVE (Richard). The watchmans watchword.
A sermon preached ... upon the 30 of March last.
4to.
Cambridge, by Roger Daniel, 1642
[Sermons Polemical V]   Wing L3193. **1183(20)**

LOVERS (The) academy.   12mo.
[London] for T.Passinger [c.1680]
[Penny-Merriments II]   Woodcut.   **363(35)**

LOVERS (The) quarrel.   12mo.
*London, by J.M., sold by W.T. and T.Passinger
[c.1685]*   [Penny-Merriments I]   Woodcuts.
362(9)

LOVES masterpeice.   12mo.
[London] by H.B. for P.Brooksby, 1683
[Penny-Merriments II]   Woodcut.   **363(18)**

LOVES school: or, a new merry book of
complements.   12mo.
*[London] for W.Thackeray, T.Passenger, P.
Brooksby [etc.], 1682*   [Penny-Merriments II]
Woodcuts.   **363(15)**

LOWER (Sir William). Polyeuctes, or the martyr.
A tragedy, 1655.
See CORNEILLE (Pierre).   **1075(5)**

LOWNDES (William). A report containing an essay for the amendment of the silver coins. 8vo.
London, by Charles Bill, and the executrix of Thomas Newcomb, 1695
Wing L3323.   **1559**

LOYAL (A) garland, 1685.
See M.(S.).   **363(44)**

LUBIN (Augustin). Martyrologium Romanum ... Authore A.Lubin, 1679.
See LITURGIES. Roman Catholic Church.   **1843**

LUCAN. [*Pharsalia*.] De bello civili, cum H.Grotii, Farnabii notis integris & variorum selectiss.   8vo.
Amsteldami, ex officina Elzeviriana, 1669
Engr. fp. (map).   **1439**

───────── Pharsalia ... Englished by T.May. 3rd ed., corrected.   8vo.
London, by A.M. and are to be sold by Will. Sheares (– for Tho:Jones), 1635   Engr. title-page.   STC 16889.   **367(1)**

LUCAS (Franciscus). In sacrosancta quatuor Iesu Christi euangelia ... commentarius. [*With the text in Gk and Lat.*]   4 vols in 3.   fo.
Antuerpiæ, ex officina Plantiniana apud Ioannem Moretum (– apud viduam et filios Ioannis Moreti), 1606-16   Engr. title-page.   **2397-9**

LUCRETIUS. An essay on the first book of T.Lucretius Carus De rerum natura. Interpreted and made English by J.Evelyn. [*Lat. and Engl.*]   8vo.
London, for Gabriel Bedle, and Thomas Collins, 1656   Engr. title-page. Corrections in Evelyn's hand. In same hand: below frontispiece, 'This Frontispiece was of my Wifes invention and designing: but engrav'd by Hollar'; below title-page, 'For my honor'd friend Sam:ll Pepys Esqr; from his humble servant [Greek motto added] JE:'.   Wing L3446.   **1001**

───────── T.Lucretius Carus, the Epicurean philosopher, his six books De rerum natura done into English verse (by T.Creech). 2nd ed., corrected and enlarged.   8vo.
Oxford, by L.Lichfield, for Anthony Stephens, 1683   Engr. fp.   Wing L3448.   **922**

LUDLOW no lyar, 1692.
See BETHEL (Slingsby).   **1286(7)**

LUDLOW (Edmund). A letter from Major General (– from General) Ludlow, 1691-2.
See LETTER ...   **1286(1), (3)**

───────── Memoirs. In two [*or rather* three] vols.   8vo.
Vivay, 1698-9   Engr. fp. (port., Charrington p.106).   Wing L3460-2.   **1282-4**

───────── Truth brought to light, 1693.
See TRUTH brought to light ...   **1286(9)**

LUDOLF (Heinrich Wilhelm). Grammatica Russica.   8vo.
Oxonii, e Theatro Sheldoniano, 1696   Engr. pl.
Wing L3463.   **1649**

LUDOLF (Hiob). A new history of Ethiopia ... Made English by J.P.   fo.
London, for Samuel Smith, 1682   9 engr. pls, table.   Wing L3468,   **2415**

LUIDIUS (Edward).   *See* LHUYD (Edward).

LUÍS, de Granada.   *See* GRANADA (Luís de).

LUNA (Alvaro de). Primera (– quarta) parte de los romances de Don Aluaro de Luna.   4to.
(Sevilla, por Iuan Cabeças, 1677)   Gaselee 93;
Wilson p.249.   **1545(33)**

LUNA (Miguel). Historia verdadera del rey don Rodrigo. Por A.Tarif Abentarique ... traducida [or rather written by] M.de Luna.   6a impr. 2 pts.   4to.
Madrid, por Melchor Sanchez, y a su costa, 1676 (1675)   Gaselee 94.   **1514**

LUNADORO (Girolamo). Relazione della corte di Roma. Con l'aggiunta del Moderno maestro di camera (di F.Sestini da Bibbiena).   2 pts. 12mo.
Roma, presso Michel' Angelo, e Pier Vincenzo Rossi, 1697-8   **145(1)**

LUQUE (Cristóbal Francisco de). Vejamen con que se celebro el grado que de doctor en sagrada theologia recibio ... F.L.Garcia ... En ... Sevilla ... 1682.   4to.
Sevilla, por Juan Francico [sic] de Blas, a costa de Pedro de Santiago [1682]   Gaselee 95.
                                            1553(28)

[LUSHINGTON (Thomas)]. The Resurrection rescued from the soldiers calumnies, in two sermons ... by R.Jones [i.e. T.Lushington].   12mo.
London, for Richard Lowndes, 1659
Wing L3503.   **57**

LYCOPHRON. Λυκοφρονος ... Ἀλεξανδρα ... cum Græcis J.Tzetzis commentariis ... Cura ... J.Potteri. [*Gk & Lat.*]   2 pts.   fo.
Oxonii, e Theatro Sheldoniano, 1697
Wing L3523.   **2682**

[LYDGATE (John)]. The serpent of deuision ... Whereunto is annexed the tragedye of Gorboduc (by T.Norton and T.Sackuyle).   2 pts.   4to.
London, by Edward Allde for Iohn Perrin, 1590
[Old Plays I]   STC 17029.   **939(7)**

LYLY (John). Loues metamorphosis. A wittie and courtly pastorall.   4to.
London, for William Wood, 1601   [Old Plays II]
G2 missing.   STC 17082.   **1102(7)**

[——————] Mother Bombie.   4to.
London, by Thomas Creede, for Cuthbert Burby,
1598   [Old Plays I]   STC 17085.   **939(1)**

[LYSER (Johann)]. Discursus politicus de
polygamia, authore T.Alethæo [i.e. J.Lyser].
Ed. altera.   8vo.
Friburgi, apud Henricum Cunrath, 1676   **504**

M

M.(A.), Philopatris.   *See* MUDIE (Alexander).

M.(D.), le sieur. Nouveau voyage du Levant, 1694.
See DUMONT (Jean).   **633**

M.(E.). St Cecily: or, the converted twins, 1666.
See MEDBOURNE (Matthew).   **1604(7)**

M.(G.). The new state of England, 1693.
See MIÈGE (Guy).   **787**

M.(I.). The abridgement or summarie of the Scots
chronicles, 1671.
See MONIPENNIE (John).   **337**

M.(I.). New conceited letters, newly laid open.
4to.
London, for John Stafford, 1662   [Vulgaria IV]
Woodcuts.   **1193(18)**

M.(J.). Sports and pastimes.   4to.
[London] by A.M. for W.Thackeray, and J.
Deacon [c.1680]   [Vulgaria IV]   Woodcuts.
1193(6)

M.(J.). The tenure of kings and magistrates, 1649.
See MILTON (John).   **1430(8)**

M.(S.). The golden drops of Christian comfort.
8vo.
(London, by J.M.) for J.Blare, 1687   [Penny-
Godlinesses]   Engr. title-page.   **365(25)**

M.(S.). A loyal garland.   8vo.
[London] by J.M. for J.Deacon, 1685
[Penny-Merriments II]   Woodcut.   **363(44)**

M.(S.). The true tryal of understanding ... a book
of ... riddles.   12mo.
[London] by J.M. for J.Deacon, 1687
[Penny-Merriments I]   Woodcuts.
Wing M92.2.   **362(23)**

M.(T.). The history of Independency. The fourth
and last part, 1660.
See WALKER (Clement).   **1148(4)**

MABILLON (Jean), Cardinal. De liturgia
Gallicana libri III ... Accedit Disquisitio de cursu
Gallicano.   4to.
Luteciæ Parisiorum, apud viduam Edmundi
Martin, et Johannem Boudot, 1685   **1961**

——————————De re diplomatica libri VI.
[*Without pt 2.*]   fo.
Luteciæ Parisiorum, (excud. Johannes Baptista
Coignard) sumtibus Ludovici Billaine, 1681
Engr. title-page, pls.   **2905(1)**

[——————————] Traduction [by A.Le Roy] de
la lettre d'Eusèbe Romain [i.e. J.Mabillon], à
Theophile François, sur le culte des saints inconnus.
12mo.
Paris, chez Jean Musier (de l'imprimerie de Jean de
Saint Aubin), 1698   **370**

——————————Traité des études monastiques.
12mo.
Suivant la copie imprimée à Paris, chez Charles
Robustel, se vend à Bruxelles, chez Eug.Henry
Fricx, 1691   **781**

MACHIAVELLI (Niccolò). The works.   fo.
London, for John Starkey, 1675   **2385**

MACKENZIE (Sir George). A defence of the
antiquity of the Royal-Line of Scotland.   8vo.
London, printed for R.C. and are to be sold by
Abell Swalle, 1685   Wing M155.   **1065**

——————————Jus regium: or, the just and solid
foundations of monarchy.   8vo.
London, for R.Chiswel, 1684   Engr. fp. (port.,
Charrington p.32).   Wing M163.   **1014**

——————————The laws and customes of Scotland
in matters criminal.   4to.
Edinburgh, by George Swintoun, 1678
Wing M165.   **1513**

——————————A moral essay, preferring solitude
to publick employment.   8vo.
London, by W.W. and to be sold by H.Sawbridge,
1685   Wing M173.   **380(1)**

——————————Moral gallantry. (– A moral para-
dox. – A consolation against calumnies.)   3 pts.
12mo.
London, (by T.B.) for Hanna Sawbridge, 1685
Wing M178.   **380(2)**

——————————The moral history of frugality.
8vo.
London, for J.Hindmarsh, 1691   Wing M179.
838

——————————Observations upon the laws and
customes of nations as to precedency.   fo.
Edinburgh, by the heir of Andrew Anderson, 1680
Engr. fp.(port., Charrington p.107).
Wing M186.   **2054(1)**

———————— Reason. An essay.　12mo.
London, for Joseph Hindmarsh, and Rich.Sare,
1695　Wing M194.　　　　　　**381**

———————— The science of herauldry.　fo.
Edinburgh, by the heir of Andrew Anderson, 1680
Engr. title-page, 27 engr. pls.　Wing M204.
　　　　　　　　　　　　　　　2054(2)

MACNAMARA (John). The several informations
of J.Macnamara, M.Fitzgerrald, and J.Nash,
relating to the horrid Popish plot in Ireland.　fo.
London, for John Wright, and Richard Chiswell,
1680　[Narratives & Tryals III]
Wing S2766.　　　　　　　　**2251(16)**

MAFFEI (Giovanni Pietro). Historiarum Indic-
arum libri XVI ... Accessit Ignatii Loiolæ vita.　fo.
Coloniæ Agrippinæ, in officina Birckmannica,
sumptibus Arnoldi Mylij, 1589　Adams M92.
　　　　　　　　　　　　　　　2206

MAGNETICALL aduertisements, 1616.
See BARLOW (William).　　　**928(2)**

MAIDENS (The) garland.　8vo.
[*London*] for *J.Back* [c.1685]　[Penny-Merri-
ments II]　Woodcuts.　　　**363(47)**

MAIMBOURG (Louis). Histoire de l'Arianisme.
3e éd.　3 vols.　12mo.
Paris, chez Sebastien Mabre-Cramoisy, 1678　**673-5**

———————— Histoire de l'hérésie des icon-
oclastes.　3e éd.　2 vols in 1.　12mo.
Paris, chez Sebastien Mabre-Cramoisy, 1679　**738**

———————— Histoire de la décadence de
l'Empire après Charlemagne.　3e éd.
2 vols in 1.　12mo.
Paris, chez Sebastien Mabre-Cramoisy, 1682　**739**

———————— Histoire des croisades.　3e éd.
4 vols in 2.　12mo.
Paris, chez Sebastien Mabre-Cramoisy, 1680　**742-3**

———————— Histoire du Calvinisme.　2e éd.
2 vols in 1.　12mo.
Paris, chez Sebastien Mabre-Cramoisy, 1682　**744**

———————— Histoire du grand schisme d'Occid-
ent.　2e éd.　2 vols in 1.　12mo.
Paris, chez Sebastien Mabre-Cramoisy, 1679
Vol.1 wants all after T12.　　　**737**

———————— Histoire du Lutheranisme.　2e éd.
2 vols in 1.　12mo.
Paris, chez Sebastien Mabre-Cramoisy, 1680　**740**

———————— Histoire du schisme des Grecs.
3e éd.　2 vols in 1.　12mo.
Paris, chez Sebastien Mabre-Cramoisy, 1680
Aa 2-3 misbound.　　　　　　**741**

———————— The history of the League ...
Transl. by Mr.Dryden.　8vo.

London, printed by M.Flesher, for Jacob Tonson,
1684　Engr fp.　Wing M292.　　**983**

———————— Traité historique de l'établissement et des prérogatives de l'église de Rome.　4to.
Paris, chez Sebastien Mabre-Cramoisy, 1685　**1940**

MAIMONIDES. Liber מורה נבוכ׳ם doctor
perplexorum ... in linguam Latinam ... conversus,
à J.Buxtorfio.　4to.
Basileæ, sumptibus & impensis Ludovici König,
excudebat Jo.Jacob Genath, 1629　　**1568**

MALATESTA GARUFFI (Giuseppe).
See GARUFFI (Giuseppe Malatesta).

[MALORY (Sir Thomas)]. Brittains glory, 1684.
See SHIRLEY (John), fl.1680-1702.　**1192(8)**

———————— [The story of the moste noble and
worthy kynge Arthur newly imprynted.]　fo.
(*Imprynted at Londō, by Wyllyam Copland*)
[1557]　Wants title-page and O8. MS notes in
various unidentified 16th-century hands; the name
Helen Houghton occurring twice.
STC 804; Duff p.48.　　　　**1982**

MALPIGHI (Marcello). Opera omnia. 2 vols in 1.
fo.
Londini, (typis M.F.) apud Thomam Sawbridge
(*R.Littlebury* [*etc.*]), 1686　Engr. pls.
Wing M342B, 344.　　　　　**2601**

———————— Dissertationes epistolicæ duæ,
una de formatione pulli in ovo. Altera de bombyce.
4to.
Londini, impensis Joannis Martyn, 1673 (1669)
Engr. pls.　Wing M351.　　　**1770**

MALYNES (Gerard de). Consuetudo; vel, lex
mercatoria, or the ancient law-merchant ... Also,
advice concerning bils of exchange ... The merchants mirrour ... An introduction to merchants
accounts.　4 pts.　fo.
London, by William Hunt, for Nicholas Bourne,
1656　Parts dated 1655-1664.
Wing M364; Diary 15 Dec.1667.　　**2447(1)**

MANDEVILLE (Sir John). The voyages and
travels.　4to.
London, for R.Scott, T.Basset, J.Wright [*etc.*],
1677　Woodcuts.　Wing M415.　**1244**

MANESSON MALLET (Alain). Description de
l'univers.　5 vols.　8vo.
Paris, chez Denys Thierry, 1683　Engr. fp.
(port., Charrington p.104), title-page, pls (port.,
Charrington p.109), maps.　　**1655-9**

MANILIUS (Marcus). [*Astronomicon* I.] The
sphere ... made an English poem: with annotations
and an astronomical appendix. By E.Sherburne.
London, for Nathanael Brooke, 1675　Engr. pls.
Wing M432.　　　　　　　**2885**

MANLEY (Sir Roger). Commentariorum de rebellione Anglicana ab anno 1640 usque ad annum 1685 pars prima (– liber secundus).   8vo.
Londini, impensis L.Meredith & T.Newborough,
1686   Wing M437.   **1279**

————————The history of the late warres in Denmark.   fo.
London, for Thomas Basset, 1670   Engr. maps.
Wing M439.   **2148**

MANNERS (The) of the Israelites.   12mo.
London, printed for William Freeman, 1683   **393**

MANNINGHAM (Thomas), Bp of Chichester.
A sermon preach'd ... the 30th of December 1694.
4to.
London, for Sam.Smith, Benj.Walford, and Eliz. Crooke, 1695   Wing M504.   **1528(6)**

MANRIQUE (Gerónimo). Relacion verdadera, donde se dà cuenta del desastrado sucesso que aconteciò en la ciudad de Logroño.   4to.
Seuilla, impresso por Iuan de Ossuna, 1681
Gaselee 97; Wilson p.263.   **1545(49)**

MANRIQUE (Jorge). Coplas que hizo Don J. Manrique à la muerte del Maestre de Santiago, D.Rodrigo Manrique su padre.   4to.
(Sevilla, por Juan Cabeças, 1678)
Gaselee 98; Wilson p.265.   **1545(51)**

MANSELL (Roderick). An exact and true narrative of the late Popish intrigue.   fo.
London, for Tho.Cockerill and Benj.Alsop,
1680   [Narratives & Tryals III]   Bound in two parts.   Wing M514.   **2251(33), (47)**

MANSVELT (Regnerus à). Adversus anonymum theologo-politicum [i.e. B.de Spinoza] liber.   4to.
Amstelædami, apud Abrahamum Wolfgang, 1674
1582

MANWARING (Sir Henry). The sea-man's dictionary.   4to.
London, by W.Godbid for G.Hurlock, 1667
1142(2)

[MARANA (Giovanni Paolo)]. Letters writ by a Turkish spy. 8 vols in 4. [Var. eds.]   12mo.
London, for Joseph Hindmarsh, Richard Sare,
(and Henry Rhodes) (1692-)1694
Engr. fps (ports, Charrington p.108).
Wing M565A-E.   **607-10**

[MARCEL (Guillaume)]. Chronological tables; containing the successions of all ye popes, emperours, & kings ... in Europe ... to ye year 1688. [*Translated by W.P. (i.e. William Parsons) from the French of G.Marcel.*]
London, printed & sold by I.Knight; and W.Rogers, Phillip Lea [etc.] [1689]   22 engr. ll.
Wing P576.   **9**

MARCORT (Antoine). A declaration of the masse.
8vo.

(Wyttenberge, by Hans Luft [London?], 1547)
STC 17314a; Duff p.49.   **209(2)**

MARCULFUS, Monachus. Marculfi monachi aliorumque auctorum formulæ veteres, ed. ab ... H.Bignonio ... Accessit liber legis Salicæ.   2 pts.
4to.
Parisiis, apud Sebastianum Cramoisy, et Sebastianum Mabre-Cramoisy, 1665   Engr. fp.
(port., Charrington p.16).   Tanner I, pp.181, 197, 198.   **1937**

MARÍA, de Jesús de Agreda.
See AGREDA (Sor María de Jesús de).

MARIANA (Juan de). Historia general de España.
2 vols in 1.   fo.
Madrid, por Andrès Garcia de la Iglesia, a costa de Gabriel de Leon, 1678   Gaselee 100; Diary 28 Apr.1669.   **2147**

MARKS (The) of a defenceless cause, 1703.
See GIBSON (Edmund), Bp of London.   **1696(21)**

MARLBOROUGH (John Churchill, Duke of).
The speech of ... the Earl of Marlborough ... to ... the States-General of the United Provinces ...
20/31 March 1701/2.   brs.
[London] by Edward Jones, 1701   [Inserted between nos 3794 & 3795 of the London Gazette.]
2090

MARLOW (Jeremiah). A book of cyphers.   8vo.
London, printed for W:Rogers, 1683
68 engr. pls.   Wing M698.   **1129**

MARLOWE (Christopher). The massacre at Paris with the death of the Duke of Guise.   8vo.
London, by E.A [llde], for Edward Whit[e]
[1600?]   [Old Plays I]   Title-page defective.
STC 17423.   **939(10)**

[————————] Tamburlaine the greate.   4to.
London, for Edward White, 1605
[Old Plays II]   STC 17428.   **1102(4)**

[————————] Tamburlaine the greate ... The second part.   4to.
London, by E.A [llde] for Ed.White, 1606
[Old Plays II]   STC 17428a.   **1102(4a)**

[MARNIX (Philips van)]. The bee hiue of the Romishe churche ([by] I.Rabbotenu [i.e. P.van Marnix]). Transl. by G.Gilpin. Newly imprinted, with a table.   8vo.
(Lōdon, by Thomas Dawson for Iohn Stell) 1580
Woodcut.   STC 17446.   **153**

MARPRELATE (Martin), *pseud.* Oh read over D.John Bridges, for it is a worthy work: Or an epitome of the fyrste booke of that ... volume, written against the Puritans.   4to.
'Printed oversea in Europe, within two furlongs of a bounsing priest, at the cost and charges of M. Marprelate' [East Molesey, R.Waldegrave, 1588?]
[Consutilia II]   STC 17453.   **1428(17)**

[MARSHALL (Stephen)]. An answer to a book [by J.Hall] entituled An humble remonstrance ... By Smectymnuus [i.e. S.Marshall and others]. 4to.
[*London*] 1641   [Consutilia III]
Wing M748A.   **1429(1)**

──────── A divine proiect to save a Kingdome: opened in a sermon ... Apr.22.1644.   4to.
London, by Richard Cotes, for Stephen Bowtell, 1644   [Sermons Polemical V]   Wing M752.
                                      1183(25)

──────── Meroz cursed, or, A sermon preached ... Febr.23, 1641.   4to.
London, by R.Badger, for Samuel Gellibrand, 1641   [Sermons Polemical V]
Wing M762.   **1183(21)**

──────── Reformation and desolation: or, a sermon ... preached ... Decemb.22, 1641.   4to.
London, for Samuel Gellibrand, 1642 [Sermons Polemical V]   Wing M770. **1183(24)**

MARSHAM (Sir John). Chronicus canon Ægyptiacus, Ebraicus, Græcus, et disquisitiones. fo.
Londini, excudebat Tho.Roycroft, prostant apud Guliel.Wells & Rob.Scott, 1672   Wing M810.
                                      2361

[MARSTON (John)]. Jacke Drums entertainment [by J.Marston?], 1601.
See JACK. Jacke Drums entertainment.   **1102(8)**

MARTIAL. Epigrammatum libros XV. Interpretatione et notis illustravit V.Collesso ... Ad usum ... Delphini.   2 pts.   4to.
Parisiis, apud Antonium Cellier, 1680   Engr. fp.
                                      1947

[MARTIN (Louis)]. L'eschole de Salerne en vers burlesques, & duo poemata macaronica.   12mo.
Suivant la copie imprimée à Paris [*Leyden, J. & D. Elsevier*], 1651   **50**

MARTIN (Martin). A late voyage to St.Kilda. 8vo.
London, for D.Brown, and T.Goodwin, 1698
Engr. map.   Wing M847.   **1227**

MARTÍNEZ DE LLAMO (Juan). Sermones para las festividades de Cristo.   fo.
Madrid, de Andres Garcia de la Iglesia, 1676
Gaselee 101.   **2119(1)**

──────── Sermones para los miercoles.
2 pts.   fo.
Madrid, 1679   Gaselee 102.   **2119(2)**

MARTYRDOM (The) of Theodora, and of Didymus, 1687.
See BOYLE (Hon. Robert).   **882**

MARTYROLOGIUM Romanum, 1679.
See LITURGIES. Roman Catholic Church.   **1843**

[MARVELL (Andrew)]. The rehearsal transpros'd: or, animadversions upon a late book [by S.Parker]. 2 vols.   8vo.
London (for Nathaniel Ponder), 1672-3
Wing M880, 882:   **710-11**

──────── A short historical essay touching general councils, creeds, and impositions.   4to.
London, for R.Baldwin, 1687   [Consutilia X]
Wing M889.   **1436(1)**

MARY II, Queen of England.
For proclamations, etc., by William and Mary, see WILLIAM III, King of England.

MASON (William). Arts advancement or the most exact ... method of short-hand-writing.   8vo.
London, sold by Benj:Alsop, Mr Wilkins, Mr Jacob Sampson [*etc.*], 1682   [Short-hand Collection III]   Engr. fp. (port., Charrington p.113); 24 engr. ll.   Wing M941; Carlton pp.79-87.   **402(9)**

──────── A pen pluck'd from an eagles wing. Or, the most swift ... method of short-writing.   8vo.
London, printed by J.Darby, for the author, 1672 [Short-hand Collection IV]   Wing M945; Carlton p.77.   **860(1)**

MASSINGER (Philip). The bond-man.   4to.
London, by Iohn Raworth for Iohn Harrison, 1638   [Loose Plays I]   STC 17633; Diary 25 May 1661, 2 Nov.1666.   **1075(3)**

MATCHLESS (The) picaro [1680].
See CELLIER (Elizabeth).   **2251(6a)**

MATHEMATICALL recreations, 1653.
See LEURECHON (Jean).   **618**

MATTHEW, of Westminster, *pseud.* Flores historiarum, 1601.
See FLORES historiarum ...   **2549**

MAUCROIX (François de). Ouvrages de prose et de poësie, 1688.
See DEMOSTHENES. Traduction des Philippiques ...   **432**

MAUNSELL (Andrew). The first part (seconde parte) of the catalogue of English printed bookes. fo.
London, by Iohn VVindet (by Iames Roberts) for Andrew Maunsell, 1595   MS additions in unidentified early 17th-century hand.
STC 17669.   **2039**

MAVELOT (Charles). Nouueau liure de chiffres, qui contient en general tous les noms et surnoms entrelassez par alphabet.   2 pts.   4to.
Se vend à Paris chez l'autheur, 1680   Engr. titlepages, 78 engr. pls.   **1585**

MAY (Thomas). A continuation of the subiect of Lucan's historicall poem.   2nd ed.   8vo.

London, for James Boler, 1633   Engr. title-page.   STC 17712.   **2107**

———————— The history of the Parliament of England: which began November the third 1640. 3 pts.   fo.
London, by Moses Bell, for George Thomason, 1647   Wing M1410.   **2107**

MAYDESTON (Clement). Ordinale Sarum.   4to.
(*Londoñ, exaratum per me Ricardum Pynson*, 1503)   STC 17728; Duff p.46.   **1700**

MAYDMAN (Henry). Naval speculations and maritime politicks ... a ... discourse of the Royal Navy.   8vo.
London, by William Bonny, and sold by Sam.Manship, J.Fisher [etc.], 1691   Engr. fp. (port., Charrington p.115).   Wing M1420.   **932**

MAYERNE TURQUET (Louis de). The generall historie of Spaine ... vnto the yeare 1583: transl. ... and continued ... by E.Grimeston.   fo.
London, by A.Islip, and G.Eld, 1612
STC 17747.   **2333**

[MAYHEW (Thomas)]. The light appearing more and more ... or a farther discovery of ... the Indians in New-England ... by letters [of T.Mayhew and J.Eliot] ... Published by H.Whitfeld.   4to.
London, by T.R. and E.M. for John Bartlet, 1651 [Consutilia II]   Wing W1999.   **1428(1)**

MAYNARD (John). A sermon preach'd ... Feb.26, 1644.   4to.
London, by George Bishop, for Samuel Gellibrand, 1645   [Sermons Polemical VI]
Wing M1452.   **1184(1)**

MAYNERIIS (Maynus de). Dialogus creaturarum moralisatus.   fo.
G.Leeu, Gouda, 6 June 1481
See Appendix.   **2002(2)**

MEADOWS (Sir Philip). A narrative of the principal actions occurring in the wars betwixt Sueden and Denmark.   12mo.
London, printed by A.C[lark] for H.Brome, 1677
Wing M1566.   **443**

———————— Observations concerning the dominion and sovereignty of the seas.   4to.
In the Savoy, printed by Edw.Jones, and sold by Samuel Lowndes and by Edward Jones, 1689
Wing M1567.   **1474**

[MEDBOURNE (Matthew)]. St.Cecily: or, the converted twins.   4to.
London, by J.Streater, 1666   [Loose Plays II]
Wing M1583B.   **1604(7)**

MEDE (Joseph). Works. [3rd ed.]   fo.
London, by Roger Norton, for Richard Royston, 1672   Engr. pls.   Wing M1588.   **2656**

MEDINA (Pedro de). L'art de nauiguer ... Traduict de Castillan ... par N.de Nicolai.   fo.
Lyon, chez Guillaume Rouille, 1554   Engr. map. Adams M1027.   **2455**

———————— The arte of nauigation ... Transl. ... by J.Frampton.   fo.
London, by Thomas Dawson, 1581   Diagrams.
In MS on title-page: one autograph obliterated and illegible; Greek motto; second autograph, Lib: T. Barlow è Coll: Reg: Oxōn. Ann: C̅I̅Ɔ. I̅Ɔ̅C̅. X̅L̅I̅I̅I̅.'
STC 17771.   **2059**

MEIBOMIUS (Marcus). De fabrica triremium liber. 4to.
Amsterdami, 1671   Engr. pl.   **1359**

[MEIER (Albrecht)]. Certaine briefe, and speciall instructions for gentlemen ... employed in seruices abrode. [Transl. by P.Jones.]   4to.
London, Iohn Woolfe, 1589   [Consutilia V]
STC 17784.   **1431(3)**

MEJOR (El) padre de pobres. Comedia famosa, de don P.Calderon. [*Not by Calderón; variously attributed to J.Peréz de Montalván and A.Fajardo y Acevedo.*]   4to.
[Seville, Juan Cabezas, c.1678]   Gaselee 31.
1553(22)

MELVILLE (Sir James). Memoires ... published ... by G.Scott.   fo.
London, by E.H. for Robert Boulter, 1683
Wing M1654.   **2200**

MEMOIRES de la cour d'Espagne, 1691.
See AULNOY (Marie-Catherine Le Jumel de Barneville, comtesse d').   **297**

MEMOIRES of what past in Christendom, 1692.
See TEMPLE (Sir William), Bart.   **1071**

MEMORIAL historique de ce qui s'est passé, 1676.
See GERBERON (Gabriel).   **77(2)**

MEMORIALS of the English affairs, 1682.
See WHITELOCK (Sir Bulstrode).   **2679**

MEN before Adam, 1656.
See LA PEYRÈRE (Isaac de).   **669**

MÉNAGE (Gilles). Menagiana, ou bon mots. 12mo.
Suivant la copie de Paris, Amsterdam, chez Adrian Braakman, 1693   Engr. title-page.   **212**

MÉNDES PINTO (Fernão). The voyages and adventures ... Done into English by H.C[ogan]. [2nd ed.]   fo.
London, by J.Macock, and are to be sold by Henry Herringman, 1663   Wing M1706.   **2212**

MÉNDEZ DE SAN JUAN (Joseph). Theologia moralis de triplici bulla, scilicet, cruciatæ, compositionis, et defunctorum.   4to.

[*Madrid*] *ex typographia Andreæ de la Iglesia, a costa de Iuan Martin Merinero*, 1666
Gaselee 104. **1363(2)**

MÉNDEZ SILVA (Rodrigo). Poblacion general de España. Añadida y enmendada. fo.
Madrid, por Roque Rico de Miranda, a costa de Iuan Martin Merinero, 1675 Gaselee 105.
2120

MENDOZA (Antonio de).
See HURTADO DE MENDOZA (Antonio).

MENESTRIER (Claude François). Histoire du roy Louis le Grand par les médailles, emblêmes, deuises. fo.
Paris, chez I.B.Nolin, 1691 Engr. title-page, pls.
2294

MENOCHIO (Giovanni Stefano). Commentaria ... sensus litteralis totius S.Scripturæ. 2 pts. fo.
Antverpiae, apud Hieronymum Verdussen, 1678
Engr. title-page. **2534**

——————Stuore ... tessute di varie eruditioni sacre, morali, e profane. Noua impr. 3 vols. 4to.
Roma, a spese di Felice Cesaretti, appresso Gio. Battista Bussotti, 1689 **1799-1801**

MENTEL (Jacob). De vera typographiæ origine paraenesis. 4to.
Parisiis, ex officina Roberti Ballard, 1650 **1303**

MERBECKE (John). The booke of Common praier noted, 1550.
See LITURGIES. Church of England. **1118(1)**

MERCURE historique et politique, contenant l'état present de l'Europe. 35 vols. 12mo.
'*Parme, chez Juan Batanar*', 1686-8; *La Haye, chez Henri van Bulderen*, 1688-1703 **258-92**

MERCURE (Le) Hollandois. 13 vols. 12mo.
Amsterdam, chez Henry & Théodore Boom (— & la veuve Théodore Boom), 1673-86 Engr. title-pages, pls. **245-57**

MERCURIUS publicus. [By H.Muddiman.]
29 Dec.1659 – 20 Aug.1663. 4to.
London, 1659-63 [News-pamphlets 1660-66 I & II] Wants nos 8 & 36 of 1659/60.
1744-1745(1)

MERCURY, or the secret ... messenger, 1641.
See WILKINS (John), Bp of Chester. **784**

MERITON (George). The parson's monitor.
12mo.
London, by the assigns of Richard and Edw.Atkins, for Richard Tonson, 1681 Wing M1808. **594**

MERRY (A) dialogue between Andrew and his sweet heart Joan [c.1680].
See W.(L.). **362(5)**

MERRY (A) dialogue, between Tom the taylor, and his maid Jone. 8vo.
[*London*] *printed for J.Clarke*, 1684
[Penny-Merriments II] Woodcuts. **363(4)**

MERRY (The) Oxford knight. 12mo.
[*London*] *by A.M. for James Bissel* [c.1680]
[Penny-Merriments II] Woodcut. **363(25)**

MERRY. A mery play betwene Johan Johan the husbande, Tyb his wyfe, ꝛ Syr Jhān the preest, 1533.
See HEYWOOD (John). **1977(3)**

MERRY. A mery play betwene the pardoner and the frere, 1533.
See HEYWOOD (John). **1977(4)**

MERRY (The) tales ... of Gotam [c.1680].
See B.(A.). **363(21)**

MERSENNE (Marin). Harmonie universelle contenant la theorie et la pratique de la musique. (— Traité de mechanique ...) 2 vols in 1. fo.
Paris [*S.Cramoisy*, 1636] Diagrams, engr. pl., port. Title-page defective. Diary 28 May 1668. *See also below*, vol.IV. **2494**

MERVAULT (Pierre de). The last famous siege of the city of Rochel ... with the edict of Nantes.
8vo.
London, for John Wickins, 1680
Wing M1879. **984**

MERVEILLES (Les) de la ville de Rome, 1690.
See FRANZINI (Girolamo). **655**

METCALFE (Theophilus). Short-writing. The last ed. 8vo.
London, printed for, and are to be sold by, J.Hancock, 1690 [Short-hand Collection IV]
Engr. fp. (port., Charrington p.117), title-page, 20 engr. ll. Wing M1935; Carlton p.48.
860(2), (6)

METFORD (James). A discourse of licenses to preach. 4to.
London, for H.Hindmarsh, 1698
[Consutilia IX] Wing M1937. **1435(9)**

MEUNG (Jean de). Le miroir d'alquimie ... avec la table d'emeraude d'Hermes Trismegiste ... Traduict de Latin en François. 8vo.
Paris, chez Charles Sevestre, 1612 **862(2)**

MEYDEN (Theodor van). Pietas Romana et Parisiensis ... The one taken out of ... T.Amydenus. The other out of ... Mr.Carr. [Abridged by A.Woodhead.] 8vo.
Oxford, 1687 Wing W3450. **665**

MEYER (Cornelio). L'arte di restituire à Roma la tralasciata navigazione del suo Tevere. fo.
Roma, nella stamperia del Lazzari Varese, 1685
(— *di Nicol'Angelo Tinassi*, 1681) 56 engr. pls.
2887(1)

MÉZERAY (François Eudes, sieur de). Histoire de France.   Nouvelle ed.   3 vols.   fo.
Paris, chez Denys Thierry, Jean Guignard, et Claude Barbin, 1685   Engr. fp. (ports, Charrington pp.5, 103), title-page.   **2694-6**

——————— A general chronological history of France ... Transl. by J.Bulteel.   fo.
London, by T.N. for Thomas Basset, Samuel Lowndes, Christopher Wilkinson [etc.], 1683
Engr. title-page.   Wing M1958.   **2416**

[MIDDLETON (Thomas)]. The familie of loue.   4to.
London, for Iohn Helmes, 1608   [Old Plays I]
STC 17879a.   **939(8)**

——————— The mayor of Quinborough: a comedy.   4to.
London, for Henry Herringman, 1661
[Loose Plays I]   Wing M1984.   **1075(8)**

[———————] The phoenix.   4to.
London, by E.A [llde], for A.I[ohnson], 1607
[Old Plays II]   STC 17892.   **1102(3)**

[MIDGLEY (Robert)]. A new treatise of natural philosophy.   12mo.
London, printed by R.E. for J.Hindmarsh, 1687
Wing M1995.   **431**

MIÈGE (Guy). The great French dictionary.   fo.
London, for Tho.Basset, 1688
Wing M2012.   **2689**

[———————] The new state of England.   2nd ed.   12mo.
London, for R.Clavell, H.Mortlock and J.Robinson, 1693   Engr. title-page (port., Charrington p.178).   Wing M2020.   **787**

MIJL (Abraham van der). De origine animalium, et migratione populorum.   12mo.
Genevæ, apud Petrum Columesium, 1667   **373(1)**

MILLER (Thomas). The compleat modellist: shewing the ... way of raising the model of any ship.   2nd ed.   4to.
London, by W.Leybourn, for George Hurlock, 1664   Engr. diagrams.   **1267(2)**

[MILLES (Thomas)]. The catalogue of honor or tresury of true nobility peculiar ... to ... Great Britaine. [Transl. from works by R.Glover and others, by T.Milles.]   fo.
London, printed by William Iaggard, 1610
Engr. title-page, pls.   Part of p.493 cut out. MS amendments added (in hand of one of Pepys's clerks) naming the three bastards which Charles Blount, Earl of Devonshire (d.1606) had by Lady Rich.   STC 17926.   **2381**

[MILLIET DE CHALES (Claude François)].
L'art de naviger demonstré par principes.   4to.
Paris, chez Estienne Michallet, 1677
Diagrams.   **1910**

——————— Traitté du mouvement local, et du ressort.   12mo.
Lyon, chez Anisson, et Posuel, 1682   **659**

MILTON (John). A complete collection of the historical, political, and miscellaneous works.
3 vols.   fo.
Amsterdam, 1698   Engr. port., Charrington p.118.   Wing M2087.   **2377-9**

——————— Letters of state, written by Mr. John Milton ... from ... 1649. Till ... 1659.
12mo.
London, 1694   Wing M2126.   **519**

——————— Paradise lost.   4th ed.   fo.
London, by Miles Flesher, for Jacob Tonson, 1688   Engr. fp. (port., Charrington p.118), engr. pls.   Wing M2146.   **2699(1)**

——————— Paradise regain'd ... To which is added Samson Agonistes.   2 pts.   fo.
London, by R.E. and to be sold by Randal Taylor (pt 2: printed and to be sold by Randal Taylor), 1688   Wing M2154, 2177.   **2699(2)**

[———————] The tenure of kings and magistrates.   4to.
London, by Matthew Simmons, 1649
[Consutilia IV]   Wing M2181.   **1430(8)**

MILWARD (Matthias). The souldiers triumph: and the preachers glory ... a sermon preached ... 31 of August 1641.   4to.
London, by W.E. and I.G. for Iohn Clark, 1641
[Sermons Polemical VI]   Wing M2186.
                              1184(2)

MINUCIUS FELIX (Marcus). Marcus Minucius Felix his Octavius; or, a vindication of Christianity against paganism. Transl. by P.Lorrain.   8vo.
London, by J.M. for R.Royston, 1682
Wing M2201.   **581**

MIRACULUM basilicon, 1664.
See JENNINGS (Abraham).   **359**

MIRK (John). Liber festivalis. — Quattuor sermones. (2 pts).   fo.
R.Pynson [London, 1493]
See Appendix.   **1944**

MIRROR. The myrrour or lokynge glasse of lyfe [1532].
See GOODALE (John).   **19(1)**

MISCELLANEA, 1680.
See TEMPLE (Sir William), Bart.   **973**

MISELLI (Giuseppe), called Burattino. Il Burattino veridico, o'vero instruzzione generale per chi viaggia con la descrizzione dell' Europa.   12mo.
Roma, ad instanza di Nicolò L'hulliè, 1684
Engr. fp., pl.   **349**

MISSON (François Maximilien). Nouveau voyage d'Italie, fait en l'année 1688. 2 vols. 12mo.
La Haye, chez Henri van Bulderen, 1691
Engr. title-page, 56 engr. pls. **681-2**

MOCK poem, or, Whiggs supplication, 1681.
See COLVIL (Samuel). **614**

MODENA. Collegio de' Nobili. I giuochi circensi rinnouati nel giorno natalizio del Serenissimo Principe di Modona Francesco Maria d'Este. Vmilmente offerto da Signori Convittori del Collegio de' Nobili. 4to.
Modona, per Bartolomeo Soliani, 1700
Tanner II, p.19. **1451(4)**

MODIUS (Franciscus). Cleri totius Romanæ ecclesiæ subiecti, seu, pontificiorum ordinum ... utriusque sexus, habitus. 2 pts. 4to.
Francoforti, sumptibus Sigismundi Feyrabendi (ex officina Martini Lechleri), 1585
104 woodcuts. Adams A966; M1535. **1265(1)**

————————Gynæceum, siue theatrum mulierum. 4to.
Francoforti, impensis Sigismundi Feyrabendij, 1586 Woodcuts; bookplate of Janus Jobertus. Adams A968. **1412(1)**

MOHUN (Charles, 5th Baron). The tryal of Charles Lord Mohun. fo.
In the Savoy, printed by Edward Jones, published by him and Randal Taylor, 1693
[Narratives & Tryals VI] Wing T2181. **2254(3)**

[MOLESWORTH (Robert, Viscount)]. An account of Denmark, as it was in ... 1692. 3rd ed., corrected. 8vo.
London, printed for Timothy Goodwin, 1694
Wing M2383. **1209**

MOLIERE (Jean Baptiste de). Les œuvres de M.de Molière reveuës, corrigées et augmentées. 8 vols. 12mo.
Paris, chez Denis Thierry, Claude Barbin, et Pierre Trabouillet, 1682 Engr. pls. **624-31**

MOLINA (Tirso de), *pseud.*
See TÉLLEZ (Gabriel).

MOLINOS (Miguel de). The spiritual guide ... With a short treatise concerning daily communion ... Translated from the Italian copy. 2 pts. 12mo.
[*London*] 1688 Wing M2387. **485**

MOLLOY (Charles). De jure maritimo et navali ... 3rd ed., much enlarged. 8vo.
London, for John Bellinger, and George Dawes, 1682 Engr. fp., title-page. Wing M2397. **1597**

MOLLOY (Franciscus).
See O'MOLLOY (Franciscus).

MOLYNEUX (William). The case of Ireland's being bound by Acts of Parliament in England, stated. 8vo.
Dublin, by Joseph Ray, 1698 Wing M2402. **978**

————————Dioptrica nova. A treatise of dioptricks. 4to.
London, for Benj.Tooke, 1692 43 diagrams. Inserted at end: MS letter from J.Flamsteed to Sir Littleton Powys, 2 May 1692, confuting the treatise. Wing M2405. **1906**

————————Sciothericum telescopicum; or a new contrivance of adapting a telescope. 4to.
Dublin, Andrew Crook and Samuel Helsham, sold by W.Norman [etc.], 1686
[Consutilia IX] Engr. pl.
Wing M2406. **1435(2)**

MONDE (Le) naissant ou la creation du monde demonstrée, 1686.
See BARIN (Théodore). **579**

MONIER (Pierre). The history of painting. [Transl. from the French.] 8vo.
London, for T.Bennet, D.Midwinter and T.Leigh, [etc.], 1699 Engr. fp. Wing M2419. **1409**

[MONIPENNIE (John)]. The abridgement or summarie of the Scots chronicles. 12mo.
Edinburgh, printed by George Swintoun and James Glen, and are to be sold by them, and by Thomas Brown [etc.], 1671 Table.
Wing M2422. **337**

[MONRO (Alexander)]. A letter to a friend, giving an account of all the treatises that have been publish'd, with relation to the present persecution against the Church of Scotland. 4to.
London, for Joseph Hindmarsh, 1692
[Consutilia XI] Wing M2440. **1437(12)**

MONROY, Doctor. Aqui se contienen tres obras de mucha deuocion. 4to.
(Seuilla, por Iuan de Ossuna, 1671)
Gaselee 110; Wilson p.233. **1545(19)**

MONROY Y SILVA (Christobal). Aqui se contienen dos famosos romances. El primero, del Horror de las Montañas ... El segundo, de los amantes de Teruel, del Doctor Iuan Perez de Montaluan. 4to.
Seuilla, por Iuan de Ossuna, 1681
Gaselee 113; Wilson p.261. **1545(45), (48)**

————————El gigante Cananeo. Comedia famosa. 4to.
[*Seville, Tomé de Dios Miranda,* c.1678]
Gaselee 111. **1553(17)**

————————La sirena del Iordan, San Juan Baptista. Comedia famosa. 4to.
[*Seville, Tomé de Dios Miranda,* c.1678]
Gaselee 112. **1553(4)**

MONSON (Sir William). A true and exact account of the wars with Spain in the reign of Q.Elizabeth. fo.
London, for W.Crooke, and sold by W.Davis, 1682
Wing M2466.   **2301**

MONT. PRISACCHI RETTO (B.del). A new yeeres gift, 1577.
See ROBSON (Simon).   **941(3)**

MONTAGU (Richard), Bp of Norwich. De originibus ecclesiasticis. [*With a second title-page after ¶4, reading* 'Θεανθρωπικὸν: seu de vita Jesu Christi ... 1640'.]   fo.
Londini, impressum per Milonem Fletcher, & Robertum Young, 1636   STC 18034.   **2109(1)**

———————— Θεανθρωπικὸν seu de vita Jesu Christi ... pars posterior.   fo.
Londini, typis R.Olton & Eliz.Purslow, & prostant venales apud Jos.Kirton & Tho.Warren, 1640
STC 18036.   **2109(2)**

MONTAIGNE (Michel de). Essays ... Made English by C.Cotton.   2nd ed.   3 vols.   8vo.
London, for M.Gilliflower, W.Hensman, R.Bently [*etc.*] 1693   Engr. fp. (port., Charrington p.120).
Wing M2480; Diary 18 Mar.1667/8.   **1018-20**

MONTALTE (Louis de), *pseud.*
See PASCAL (Blaise).

MONTANO (Giovanni Battista). Tabernacoli diversi novamente inventati.   fo.
Roma, 1628   Engr. title-page, port., 26 engr. pls.   **2763(2)**

MONTANUS (Arnoldus). Atlas Japannensis: being remarkable addresses by way of embassy from the East-India Company of the United Provinces to the Emperor of Japan ... English'd ... by J.Ogilby.   fo.
London, by Tho.Johnson for the author, 1670
25 engr. pls.   Wing M2485.   **2914**

MONTEMAYOR (Jorge de). Los siete libros de la Diana. Traduicts ... par I.D.Bertranet. [*Span. & Fr.*]   8vo.
Paris, pour Toussaints du Bray, 1611
Gaselee 114.   **745**

MONTGOMERIE (Alexander). The cherry and the slae.   12mo.
Edinburgh, printed by the heir of Andrew Anderson, 1680   **358(2)**

MOORE (Sir Jonas). A new systeme of the mathematicks.   2 vols.   4to.
London, by A.Godbid and J.Playford for Robert Scott, 1681   Engr. title-page, pls, diagrams, maps.   Wing M2579.   **1846-7**

MORAL (A) essay concerning the nature and unreasonableness of pride.   8vo.
London, printed for Joseph Hindmarsh, 1689
Wing M2614.   **954**

MORANTE (Pedro Díaz).
See DÍAZ MORANTE (Pedro).

MORE (Alexandre). Fragmens des sermons de Monsieur Morus; avec ses dernieres heures.   12mo.
La Haye, chez Abraham Troyel, 1685   **534**

MORE (Henry). An antidote against atheism. 2nd ed., corrected and enlarged.   8vo.
London, by J.Flesher, and are to be sold by William Morden in Cambridge, 1655
Wing M2640; Diary 12 Jan.1666/7.   **867(1)**

———————— Apocalypsis apocalypseos; or the revelation of St.John the Divine unveiled.   4to.
London, by J.M. for J.Martyn, and W.Kettilby, 1680   Engr. table.   Wing M2641.   **1520**

———————— Conjectura cabbalistica.   8vo.
London, by James Flesher, and are to be sold by William Morden in Cambridge, 1653   On front flyleaf: autograph, 'Samuel Pepys AB Magd.Coll. Camb.1654'.   Wing M2647.   **884**

———————— An exposition of the seven epistles to the seven churches. Together with A brief discourse of idolatry.   8vo.
London, by James Flesher, 1669
Wing M2660.   **437**

———————— Remarks upon two late ingenious discourses [by Sir M.Hale].   8vo.
London, for Walter Kettilby, 1676
Wing M2675.   **574**

MORE (Sir Thomas), St. The vvorkes ... wrytten ... in the Englysh tonge.   2 vols.   fo.
London, at the costs and charges of Iohn Cawod, Iohn VValy, and Richarde Tottell, 1557
STC 18076; Duff p.50.   **2008-9**

———————— The common-wealth of Vtopia. [Transl. by R.Robinson.]   12mo.
London, by B.Alsop & T.Fawcet, and are to be sold by Wil:Sheares, 1639   Engr. title-page (port., Charrington p.122).   STC 18098.
                                                       222(1)

———————— The debellacyon of Salem and Bizance.   2 pts.   8vo.
([*London*] *by W.Rastell*, 1533)   STC 18081; Duff p.50.   **752(2)**

MORENO DE VARGAS (Bernabé). [Discursos de la nobleza de España.]   4to.
[*Madrid, por la biuda de Alonso Martin*, 1622?]
Gaselee 115.   Wants title-page.   **1268**

MORÉRI (Louis). Le grand dictionaire historique. 3e éd., corrigée.   2 vols.   fo.
Lyon, chez Jean Girin et Barthélémy Rivière, se vend à Paris chez Denys Thierry, 1683
Engr. fp. (port.), engr. title-page.   **2748-9**

MORETO Y CABANA (Agustín). San Franco de Sena. Comedia famosa.   4to.
[*Seville, Tomé de Dios Miranda, c.1675*]
Gaselee 116.   **1553(2)**

MORISOT (Claude Barthélemy). Orbis maritimi sive rerum in mari et littoribus gestarum generalis historia.   fo.
Divione, apud Petrum Palliot, 1643
Engr. title-page, pls.   **2446**

MORLAND (Sir Samuel). The description and use of two arithmetick instruments.   4 pts. 8vo.
London, printed, and sold by Moses Pitt, 1673
Engrs, tables. Wants fp. (port.).   Wing M2777.
293(1)

MORLEY (Thomas). A plaine and easie introduction to practicall musicke.   fo.
London, by Peter Short, 1597   Engr. title-page.
STC 18133; Diary 10 Mar.1666/7.
See also below, vol.IV.   **2031**

MORNAY (Philippe de), Sieur du Plessis-Marly. De la verité de la religion chrestienne.   8vo.
Leyde, chez Bonaventure & Abraham Elsevier, 1651   **1154**

MORNING (The) exercise methodized, 1676.
See CASE (Thomas).   **1794**

MORTON (Thomas), Bp of Chester. A defence of the innocencie of the three ceremonies of the Church of England.   2nd impr.   4to.
London, [W.Stansby] for William Barret, 1619
STC 18180.   **1197**

MORYSON (Fynes). An itinerary ... containing his ten yeeres travell through the twelve dominions of Germany [*etc.*].   3 pts.   fo.
London, by John Beale, 1617   Woodcuts.
STC 18205.   **2312**

MOST (The) delectable history of Reynard the fox, 1681.
See SHIRLEY (John).   **1193(8)**

MOST (A) delightful history of ... Jack of Newbery, 1684.
See DELONEY (Thomas).   **363(50)**

MOST (The) excellent and delightful history of Fortunatus.   12mo.
London, by A.M. for J.Conyers and J.Blare
[*c.*1680]   [Penny-Merriments I]   Woodcut.
362(18)

MOST (The) excellent history of Antonius and Aurelia.   4to.
London, by T.Haley, and are to be sold by J.Wright, J.Clarke [*etc.*], 1682   [Vulgaria III]
Wing M2882.   **1192(5)**

MOST (The) famouse and worthie historie of ... Pandauola, 1566.
See PARTRIDGE (John).   **29(2)**

MOST (The) pleasant and delightful art of palmistry.   8vo.
[*London*] by A.M. for J.Deacon and C.Dennisson
[*c.*1680]   [Penny-Merriments II]   Woodcuts.
Title-page cropped.   **363(8)**

MOST (The) pleasant history of Ornatus & Artesia, 1683.
See FORDE (Emanuel).   **1192(4)**

MOST (The) pleasant history of Tom A Lincoln, 1682.
See JOHNSON (Richard).   **1192(18)**

MOTHER Bombie, 1598.
See LYLY (John).   **939(1)**

MOTHER Bunch's closet newly broke open. 12mo.
[*London*] by A.M. for P.Brooksby, 1685
[Penny-Merriments II]   Woodcut.   **363(13)**

MOTHERS (The) blessing: being several godly admonitions.   12mo.
[*London*] by I.M. for I.Clarke, W.Thackeray
[*etc.*], 1685   [Penny-Godlinesses]   Woodcuts.
365(31)

MOTTE (Benjamin). Oratio Dominica, 1700.
See LORD'S Prayer.   **1569**

MOWBRAY (Lawrence). The narrative of Lawrence Mowbray.   fo.
London, for Thomas Simmons, and Jacob Sampson, 1680   [Narratives & Tryals III]
Wing M2994.   **2251(35)**

MOXON (Joseph). [A brief discourse of a passage by the North-Pole to Japan, China, &c.]   4to.
[*London, printed for Joseph Moxon, 1674*]
Wants title-page & engr. map.   Wing M2999.
2542(2)

———————— A catalogue of globes ... maps ... instruments and books, made and sold by J.Moxon.   8vo.
[*London, c.1678*]   **1482(2)**

———————— Mathematicks made easie, or a mathematical dictionary.   3rd ed.   8vo.
London, for J.Moxon and John Tuttell, 1700
Engr. title-page, pls, diagrams.
Wing M3008.   **898**

———————— Mechanick exercises, or, the doctrine of handy-works. Nos 1-14.   4to.
London, for Joseph Moxon, 1677   18 engr. pls.
Wing M3013.   **1397**

———————— Mechanick exercises: or, the doctrine of handy-works. Applied to the art of printing.   4to.

London, for Joseph Moxon, 1683   2 engr. fps
(ports, Charrington pp.43, 73), 33 engr. pls.
Wing M3014.   1398(2)

——————— Practical perspective; or, perspective made easie.   fo.
London, by Joseph Moxon, 1670   43 engr. pls
(diagrams).   Wing M3018.   2419

——————— Proves of several sorts of letters
cast by Joseph Moxon.   brs.
Westminster, printed by Joseph Moxon, 1669
                                           1398(4)

——————— A tutor to astronomy & geography.
[Adapted from J.Blaeu.]   4to.
London, for Joseph Moxon, 1665   Diagrams.
Wing M3022.   1321

——————— A tutor to astronomy and geography. 3rd ed., corrected and enlarged.   4to.
London, printed by Tho.Roycroft, for Joseph
Moxon, 1674   Engr. title-page, diagrams.
Wing M3024.   1482(1)

MOYENS (Les) de se guerir de l'amour. Conversations galantes.   12mo.
Suivant la copie imprimée. A Paris, en la boutique
de G.Quinet, 1681   83(2)

MOYNET (Simon). L'eschole de Salerne.
[Dedication signed: S.Moynet.] 1651.
See MARTIN (Louis).   50

[MUDIE (Alexander)]. Scotiæ indiculum: or the
present state of Scotland. By A.M.Philopatris.
12mo.
London, printed for Jonathan Wilkins, 1682
Engr. fp.   Wing M3038.   435

MUN (Thomas). England's treasure by forraign
trade.   8vo.
London, by J.G. for Thomas Clark, 1664
Wing M3073.   706

[MUNDAY (Anthony)]. The death of Robert,
Earle of Huntington.   4to.
London, for William Leake, 1601
[Old Plays III]   STC 18269.   1103(7)

[———————] The downfall of Robert, Earle
of Huntington.   4to.
London, for William Leake, 1601
[Old Plays III]   STC 18271.   1103(6)

——————— The English Romayne lyfe.   4to.
London, by John Charlewoode, for Nicholas Ling,
1582   [Consutilia II]   Woodcut.
STC 18272.   1428(14)

——————— The paine of pleasure.   4to.
London, for Henrie Car, 1580   [Consutilia VIII]
STC 18277.   1434(1)

MUNICIPIUM ecclesiasticum, 1697.
See HILL (Samuel).   1693(1)

MURDER'S. Murthers reward.   8vo.
[London] by A.M. for W.Thackery, and T.Passinger [c.1685]   [Penny-Godlinesses]
Woodcut.   365(45)

MURET (Pierre). Rites of funeral ... Transl. by
P.Lorrain.   8vo.
London, printed for Rich.Royston, 1683
Wing M3098.   582

[MUSKET (George)]. The Bishop of London
[i.e. John King] his legacy.   4to.
[St Omer] 1623   STC 18305.   958(1)

MYRROUR.   See MIRROR.

N

N.(I.). Opticks, 1704.
See NEWTON (Sir Isaac).   1867

N.(N.). A letter from Oxford concerning Mr.
Samuel Johnson's late book [on the abrogation
of King James].   4to.
Oxford, 1693   [Consutilia VI]
Wing N40.   1432(13)

N.(P.). An exact abridgment of all the trials, 1690.
See EXACT.   933

NALSON (John). An impartial collection of the
great affairs of state, from ... 1639, to the murther
of King Charles I.   2 vols.   fo.
London, for S.Mearne, T.Dring, B.Tooke [etc.],
1682-3   Engr. fps, port.   Wing N106-7.
                                        2409-10

——————— A true copy of the journal ... for
the tryal of K.Charles I, 1684.
See CHARLES I, King of England.   2319

NALTON (James). Delay of reformation ... A sermon preached ... April 29.1646.   4to.
London, for Samuel Gellibrand, 1646
[Sermons Polemical VI]   Wing N122.   1184(3)

NAMES (The) of ye baylifs custos mairs of ...
Londō [1503?].
See ARNOLD (Richard).   1882

NAMUR. [News of the surrender of Namur,
1695.]
See THIS morning arrived here an express ...
                                           2087

NANI (Giovanni Battista). The history of the
affairs of Europe in this present age, but more
particularly ... of Venice ... Englished by Sir
R.Honywood.   fo.

London, printed by J.M. for John Starkey, 1673
Wing N151.   **2226**

NARBOROUGH (Sir John). An account of
several late voyages & discoveries to the South
and North.   2 pts.   8vo.
London, for Sam.Smith and Benj.Walford, 1694
Engr. pls, maps.   Wing N154; Howarth p.240.
                                                   1365

NARRATIVE (The) history of King James for the
first fourteen years.   4 pts.   (*Engr. title-page:*
Truth brought to light.)   4to.
London, (by Richard Cotes) for Michael Sparke,
1651   Wing S4818.   **1259**

NARRATIVE (A) of the ... Lower House of
Convocation, 1701.
See HOOPER (George), Bp of Bath and Wells.
                                                 1697(4)

NARRATIVE (The) of the Lower House of
Convocation ... vindicated [1701].
See HOOPER (George), Bp of Bath and Wells.
                                                 1697(5)

NASH (Thomas). Haue vvith you to Saffron-
VValden.   4to.
London, by Iohn Danter, 1596   [Old Plays III]
STC 18369.   **1103(8)**

———————— Nashes lenten stuffe.   4to.
London, [T.Judson and V.Sims] for N.L[ing].
and C.B[urbie]., 1599   [Old Plays II]
STC 18370.   **1102(6)**

———————— A pleasant comedie, called
Summers last will and testament.   4to.
London, by Simon Stafford, for Walter Burre,
1600   [Old Plays III]   MS notes in unidentified early 17th-cent. hand.   STC 18376.
                                                 1103(1)

NAUDÉ (Gabriel). Instructions concerning erecting of a library ... interpreted by J.Evelyn.   8vo.
London, for G.Bedle, and T.Collins, and J.Crook,
1661   On front flyleaf, undated note by John
Evelyn recording his gift of 'this trifle'; MS
corrections in Evelyn's hand.   Wing N247;
Diary 5 Oct.1665.   **789**

NAVIGATORS (The) supply, 1597.
See BARLOW (William).   **1077(7)**

NAYLER (James). A discovery of the first wisdom.
4to.
London, for Giles Calvert, 1653. And now re-
printed for Thomas Simmons, 1656
[Consutilia II]   Wing N273.   **1428(10)**

NECK (Jacob Corneliszen). The iournall ... of the
voyage ... which sayled from Amsterdam the
first day of March, 1598 (to the East Indies).   4to.
London, for Cuthbert Burby & Iohn Flasket, 1601
[Consutilia V]   STC 18417.   **1431(10)**

NEGRI (Cesare de). Nuove inventioni di balli.   fo.
Milano, appresso Girolamo Bordone, 160[4]
Engr. port. (Charrington p.124), 58 engrs, music.
Title-page defective.   *See also below*, vol.IV.
                                                   2248

NELSON (Robert). A companion for the festivals
and fasts of the Church of England.   2nd ed.
8vo.
London, by W.Bowyer for A. and J.Churchil, 1704
                                                   1358

NEPOS (Cornelius).Vitæ excellentium Impera-
torum.   8vo.
Lugd.Batavorum, ex officina Hackiana, 1675
Engr. title-page.   **1344**

——————————The life & death of Pomponius
Atticus. Transl. [by Sir M.Hale].   8vo.
London, by W.Godbid, for W.Shrowsbury, 1677
Wing N427.   **903**

NEPTUNE (Le) françois, 1693.
See PENE (Charles).   **2999**

NEPTUNES fair garland.   12mo.
[London] by J.M. for J.Deacon, 1676
[Penny-Merriments II]   Woodcut.   **363(49)**

NETHERLAND-HISTORIAN (The), containing
a ... relation of what hath passed in the late warrs.
8vo.
Amsterdam, by Stephen Swart, 1675
29 engr. pls (ports, Charrington pp.104, 120 [2],
177).   Wing N471.   **540**

NEVILLE (Alexander). De furoribus Norfolci-
ensium Ketto dùce, liber vnus. Eiusdem Noruicus.
2 pts.   4to.
Londini, ex officina Henrici Binnemani, 1575
Engr. table.   STC 18478a.   **1521**

[NEVILLE (Henry)]. The isle of pines, or a late
discovery by H.C. van Sloetten.   4to.
London, printed for Allen Banks and Charles
Harper, 1668   [Naval Pamphlets]   Engr. fp.
Wing N506.   **1399(3)**

[——————————] Plato redivivus: or, a dialogue
concerning government.   8vo.
London, for S.I., 1681   Wing N513.   **583**

NEW (A) academy of complements.   8vo.
[London, J.Conyers, c.1680]   [Penny-Merri-
ments I]   Woodcut.   Title-page defective.
                                                   362(31)

NEW conceited letters, 1662.
See M.(I.).   **1193(18)**

NEW (The) danger of Presbytery; or, the claims
and practises of some in the Lower House of
Convocation.   4to.
London, for W.Rogers, 1703   [Convocation
Pamphlets X]   **1696(20)**

NEW (A) description of Paris, 1687.
See BRICE (Germain). 463

NEW (A) garland, composed of fifteen ... songs
and catches alamode now in request. 8vo.
[*London*, c.1680] [Penny-Merriments I]
A1-2, 7-8 cropped. Woodcut. 362(32)

NEW (A) list of the offices and officers of
England, both civil & military in church and state.
12mo.
London, for Edward Castle, 1697 Interleaved.
Wing N654. 723

NEW (The) London drollery. 12mo.
London, by A.M. for P.Brooksby, 1687
[Penny-Merriments II] Woodcut. 363(42)

NEW (A) relation of Rome, 1664.
See ROME exactly describ'd ... 383(1)

NEW (The) school of education, for the behaviour
of children. 12mo.
[*London*] *by J.M. for T.Passinger* [c.1680]
[Penny-Godlinesses] Woodcuts. 365(9)

NEW (A) shining light, or discovery of the north-
ernmost and westernmost parts navigated. 2 pts.
4to.
Rotterdam, to besouled [sic] *by Pieter van Alphen*,
1662 [Sea Tracts III] Diagrams, 4 engr.
maps. 1079(6)

NEW (The) state of England, 1693.
See MIÈGE (Guy). 787

NEW (A) test of the Church of England's loyalty,
1702.
See DEFOE (Daniel). 1436(7)

NEW (A) treatise of natural philosophy, 1687.
See MIDGLEY (Robert). 431

NEW (A) yeeres gift, 1577.
See ROBSON (Simon). 941(3)

NEWBURY (Nathaniel). The yeomans preroga-
tive ... A sermon preached ... May 27.1652. 4to.
London, by J.Moxon, for J.N., 1652
[Sermons Polemical VI] Wing N847. 1184(4)

NEWCOMEN (Matthew). The craft and cruelty of
the churches adversaries ... A sermon preached ...
Novemb.5.1642. 4to.
London, for Peter Cole, 1643 [Sermons
Polemical VI] Sigs F-G cropped.
Wing N908B. 1184(5)

NEWHOUSE (Daniel). The whole art of
navigation. 4to.
London, for the Author, 1685 Engr. fp., pl.,
diagrams. Wing N920. 1863

NEWMAN (Samuel). A large ... concordance to
the Bible, 1643.
See COTTON (Clement). 2535

NEWS. Newes of the complement of the art of
nauigation, 1609.
See LINTON (Anthony). 1079(4)

NEWS. The newes, published for satisfaction ...
of the people, 1663-5.
See INTELLIGENCER (The) ... 1745(2)-1747

[NEWTON (Sir Isaac)]. Opticks. (By I.N.) 4to.
London, for Sam.Smith and Benj.Walford, 1704
18 engr. pls. 1867

——————— Philosophiæ naturalis principia
mathematica. 4to.
*Londini, jussu Societatis Regiæ ac typis Josephi
Streater*, 1687 Engr. diagrams. Imprimatur
signed by Pepys as President of the Royal Society,
5 July 1686. Wing N1048. 1866(1)

NEWTON (Samuel). An idea of geography and
navigation. 2 pts. 8vo.
*London, for Christopher Hussey, sold likewise by
M.Marlo, W.Court* [etc.], 1695 Engr. pls.
Wing N1074. 1067(1)

NICHODEMUS his gospel [1620].
See GOSPEL of Nicodemus. 753

NICHOLAS (Abraham). Thoographia, or, a new
art of shorthand ... Enlarged ... by T.Slater. 8vo
*London, printed and sold by Henry Mortlock,
W.Freeman, S.Manship* [etc.], 1692
[Short-hand Collection III] Engr. title-page,
17 engr. ll. Wing N1077; Carlton pp.121-4.
402(4)

[NICOLE (Pierre)]. The pernicious consequences,
1666.
See ARNAULD (Antoine). 930

NICOLS (Thomas). Gemmarius fidelius, or the
faithful lapidary. 4to.
London, printed for Henry Marsh, 1659
With the Cambridge, 1652 title-page inserted.
Wing N1144. 1072

NICOLSON (William), Abp of Cashel. The English
historical library. 3 vols. 8vo.
London, for Abel Swall and T.Child, 1696-9
Wing N1146-8; Tanner I, p.134. 1443-5

——————— A letter to the Reverend Dr.
White Kennet, in defence of the English historical
library. 4to.
London, for Timothy Childe, 1702
[Convocation Pamphlets X] 1696(11)

——————— The Scottish historical library.
8vo.
London, for T.Childe, 1702 1446

NIEUHOF (Jan). An embassy from the East-
India Company of the United Provinces, to the ...
Emperor of China ... Englished ... by J.Ogilby. fo.

London, by John Macock for the Author, 1669
Engr. fp. (port., Charrington p.127), title-page,
map, pls. **2830**

NIJMEGEN (*Treaty of*).
See FRANCE. *Treaties.*

NIPOTISMO (Il) di Roma: or, the history of the
Popes nephews, 1669.
See LETI (Gregorio). **986**

NO jest like a true jest: being a compendious
record of the merry life ... of Capt.James Hind,
the great robber of England. 12mo.
London, for J.Deacon [c.1660] [Penny-Merri-
ments II] Woodcut fp. (port.).
Wing N1177. **363(3)**

NO præexistence, 1667.
See WARREN (Edward). **1428(18)**

NO sacrilege nor sinne, 1659.
See BURGES (Cornelius). **695**

NOBLE (The) birth and gallant atchievements of
... Robin Hood. 4to.
London, by J.M. and are to be sold by J.Deacon
[c.1685] [Vulgaria III] Woodcut. **1192(15)**

NONNIUS (Ludovicus). Commentarius in Huberti
GoltzI Græciam, Insulas, et Asiam Minorem. fo.
(*Lugduni Batavorum, typis Isaaci ElzevirI*)
Antuerpiæ, apud Iacobum Bieum (– *apud Hier-
onymum Verdussium*) 1620 Engr. title-page.
2664

———————— Commentarius in nomismata imp.
IulI, Augusti et TiberI, Huberto Goltzio scalptore.
fo.
*Antuerpiæ, in officina Plantiniana Balthasaris
Moreti*, 1644 **2661**

NORFOLK (Henry Howard, 6th Duke of).
Bibliotheca Norfolciana, 1681.
See P.(W.). **1795**

NORFOLK (Henry Howard, 7th Duke of). A true
account of the proceedings before the House of
Lords (from Jan.7.1691 to Feb.17 following)
between the Duke and Dutchess of Norfolk. fo.
London, 1692 [Narratives & Tryals VI]
Wing T2393A. **2254(1)**

———————— The tryal between Henry Duke of
Norfolk plaintiff and John Jermaine defendant ...
24 Nov.1692. fo.
London, by H.Hills, 1692 [Narratives &
Tryals VI] Wing T2173. **2254(2)**

NORMAN (Robert). The new attractiue ... Newly
corrected ... by M.W.B[orough]. 4to.
London, by T.East, for Richard Ballard, 1585
[Sea Tracts I] Woodcuts (diagrams).
STC 18648. **1077(5)**

———————— [Another ed.] 4to.
London, by E.Allde, for Hugh Astley, 1596
[Sea Tracts II] Woodcuts (diagrams).
On title-page, MS motto 'Magnus ope minorum' in
unidentified hand. STC 18650. **1078(3)**

NORMANDY. Le grāt coustumier du pays ⁊ duche
de Normendie. fo.
*Caen, par Laurens Hostingue, pour Michel Angier,
et pour Jehan Mace a Renes*, 1510
Adams N337; Duff p.17. **1954**

[NORTH (Dudley, 4th Baron)]. Observations
and advices œconomical. 8vo.
London, by T.R. for John Martyn, 1669
Wing N1286. **350**

NORTHERN. The northren mothers blessing,
1597.
See S.(J.). Certaine worthye manuscript poems.
29(4)

NORTON (Thomas). The tragedye of Gorboduc,
1590.
See LYDGATE (John). The serpent of deuision.
939(7)

NORWOOD (Richard). The sea-man's practice.
15th ed. 4to.
*London, by A.Godbid and J.Playford, for
William Fisher* [etc.], 1682 [Sea Tracts IV]
Diagrams, tables. **1080(8)**

[———————] A triangular canon logarith-
mical. 8vo.
By J.Orme, for Christopher Hussey, 1695
Wing N1369.1. **1067(2)**

NOSTRADAME (Michel de). Les vrayes centuries
et propheties. Avec la vie de l'Autheur. 12mo.
*Amsterdam, chez Jean Jansson à Waesberge & la
vefue de fu Elizée Weyerstraet*, 1668
Engr. title-page, port., Charrington p.126. **134**

NOTE (A) of the head-lands of England [1605].
See ENGLAND. *Miscellaneous Public Documents.*
2131(3)

NOTITIA Oxoniensis Academiae, 1675.
See FULMAN (William). **1535**

NOTITIA vtraque, dignitatum, cum orientis, tum
occidentis, vltra Arcadii Honoriique tempora. Et
in eam G.Pancirolli commentarium ... Vltima ed.
fo.
*Lugduni, (ex typographia Iacobi du Creux dit
Molliard) ex offi [sic] Q.H. à Porta: apud Io.
de Gabiano*, 1608 **2457**

NOTORIOUS (The) impostor, 1692.
See SETTLE (Elkanah). **1427(13); 1432(7)**

[NOTTINGHAM (Heneage Finch, Earl of)]. An
exact and most impartial accompt of the ...
trial ... of nine and twenty regicides. 4to.

London, for Andrew Crook, and Edward Powel, 1660   [Consutilia IV]
Wing N1403.   **1430(1)**

NOUVEAU dictionnaire de rimes. [*Sometimes attributed to N.Frémont d'Ablancourt.*]   12mo.
Paris, chez Thomas Joly, 1667   **479**

NOUVEAU voyage du Levant, 1694.
See DU MONT (Jean).   **633**

NOUVEAUX caractères de la famille roïale ... de la cour de France. [*Transl. from the English* Characters of the royal family ...]   12mo.
Ville Franche, chez Paul Pinceau, 1703   **588**

NOUVELLE défense de la traduction du Nouveau Testament, 1682.
See ARNAULD (Antoine).   **510-11**

NOUVELLE methode ou l'art d'écrire aussi vîte qu' on parle, 1690.
See RAMSAY (Charles Aloys).   **401**

NOUVELLE relation du voyage et description exacte de l'isle de Malthe ... Par un gentil' homme françois.   12mo.
Paris, chez Gervais Clouzier, 1679   **456**

NOUVELLES de la republique des lettres. [By P.Bayle and others.] Mars 1684 – Dec.1703. [*The issues for March – April, 1684 are of the 2nd ed.*]   21 vols.   12mo.
Amsterdam, chez Henry Desbordes (– Daniel Pain), 1684-1703   **185-205**

NOUVELLES (Les) lumieres politiques, 1676.
See LE NOIR (Jean).   **77(1)**

NOW or never [c.1685].
See R.(B.).   **365(42)**

NÚÑEZ (Luis).   *See* NONNIUS (Ludovicus).

NÚÑEZ DE CASTRO (Alfonso). Libro historico politico. Tercera impr.   4to.
Madrid, por Roque Rico de Miranda, a costa de Antonio Riero y Texada, 1675   Gaselee 117.
                                             1542(1)

NUNS. The nunns complaint, 1676.
See VARET (Alexandre Louis).   **599**

[NYE (Philip)]. A declaration of the faith ... practised in the Congregational churches.   4to.
London, by John Field, and are to be sold by John Allen, 1659   [Liturgick Controversies II]
Wing N1487.   **1188(20)**

———————— A sermon preached ... September 29.1659.   4to.
London, by Peter Cole and Edward Cole, 1661
[Sermons Polemical VI]   Wing N1500. **1184(6)**

[NYE (Stephen)]. A brief history of the Unitarians called also Socinians.   8vo.
[*London*] 1687   Wing N1505.   **635**

[————————] The life of Mr.Thomas Firmin ... With a sermon ... [and] an account of his religion.   2 pts.   8vo.
London, printed, and sold by A.Baldwin, 1698
Wing N1508.   **1009**

O

OATES (Titus). An exact and faithful narrative of the horrid conspiracy of Thomas Knox [*etc.*].   fo.
London, for Tho.Parkhurst, Tho.Cockerill, and Benj.Alsop, 1680   [Narratives & Tryals III]
Wing O41.   **2251(36)**

————————A true narrative of the horrid plot and conspiracy.   fo.
London, for Thomas Parkhurst, and Thomas Cockerill, 1679   [Narratives & Tryals I]
Engr. fp. (port., Charrington p.127), pl. Engr. port. inserted (Charrington p.33).
Wing O59.   **2249(1)**

————————The tryals, convictions & sentence of Titus Otes ... May ... 1685.   2 pts.   fo.
London, for R.Sare, and are to be sold by Randall Taylor, 1685   [Narratives & Tryals V]
Wing T2249.   **2253(14-15)**

OBLIGATION (The) resulting from the oath of supremacy, 1688.
See PETT (Sir Peter). The happy future state of England.   **2413**

OBRA nueua y muy curiosa de como el Emperador Carlos Quinto hizo retirar al Gran Turco, estando sobre Viena.   4to.
Sevilla, por Thomè de Dios Mirāda, acosta de la viuda de Nicolas Rodriguez, 1675
Gaselee 40; Wilson p.313.   **1545(64)**

OBSERVATIONS and advices oeconomical, 1669.
See NORTH (Dudley, 4th Baron).   **350**

OBSERVATIONS on a journy to Naples, 1691.
See GAVIN (Antonio).   **880**

OBSERVATIONS upon the Dublin-bills of mortality, 1683.
See PETTY (Sir William).   **891(2)**

OBSERVATOR (The), in dialogue ... By Sir R. L'Estrange.   3 vols in 2.   fo.
London, by J.Bennet, for William Abington (– for Charles Brome), 1681-7   Wants no.399.
Engr. fps (port., Charrington p.99).   **2450-1**

OCCAM (William of).   *See* WILLIAM, of Occam.

OCCASIONAL (An) letter on ... Convocation, 1701.
See KENNETT (White), Bp of Peterborough.
1691(2)

OCCASIONAL reflections upon several subjects, 1665.
See BOYLE (Hon. Robert).   **709(2)**

OEUVRES diverses du Sieur D***, 1675.
See BOILEAU-DESPRÉAUX (Nicolas).   **747**

OF education, 1687.
See WALKER (Obadiah).   **678**

OF gentylnes ʒ nobylyte [1525?].
See RASTELL (John).   **1977(5)**

OF the high veneration man's intellect owes to God, 1685.
See BOYLE (Hon. Robert).   **759(5)**

OF ye olde god ʒ the newe, 1534.
See WATT (Joachim von).   **60**

OGILBY (John). Britannia, volume the first: or, an illustration of the kingdom of England and dominion of Wales. [*No more published.*]   fo.
London, printed by the Author, 1675
Engr. fp., map, 95 engr. diagrams. With the title-page of the variant issue 'Itinerarium Angliæ: or, a book of roads ...'.   Wing O168.   **2924**

————— The entertainment of ... Charles II, in his passage through the city of London to his coronation.   fo.
London, by Tho:Roycroft, 1662   11 engr. pls.
Wing O171; Diary 19 Feb.1665/6.   **2903**

————— Mr.Ogilby's tables of his measur'd roads.   4to.
London, printed by the Author, and sold at his house, 1676   Engr. map.   Wing O182.
1493(1)

————— The traveller's guide: or, a most exact description of the roads of England.   8vo.
London, printed by T.Ilive for Abel Swall, sold by Tim.Child [etc.], 1699   Engr. map.
Wing O184.   **1468**

OH read ouer D.Iohn Bridges [1588].
See MARPRELATE (Martin), *pseud.*   **1428(17)**

OLD Meg of Hereford-shire, for a Mayd-Marian: and Hereford towne for a morris-daunce.   4to.
London, [T.Creed] for Iohn Budge, 1609
[Consutilia VIII]   STC 12032.   **1434(3)**

OLDENBURGER (Philippus Andreas). Thesauri rerum publicarum pars prima (-quarta).   8vo.
Genevæ, apud Samuelem de Tournes, 1675
1041-4

OLEARIUS (Adam). The voyages & travels of the ambassadors ... to ... Muscovy, and ... Persia ... Rendred into English by J.Davies.   2 pts.   fo.
London, for Thomas Dring, and John Starkey, 1662   Engr. fp. (ports, Charrington pp.22, 46, 82, 109, 128), 4 engr. maps.   Wing O269; Diary 17 Dec.1663.   **2161**

OLIVA (Giovanni Paolo). Prediche dette nel Palazzo Apostolico.   2 pts.   fo.
Roma, (per Francesco Moneta)(— typis Vitalis Mascardi) a p Gio.Casoni (1659)   Engr. title-page.
2300

OLIVARES (Sebastián de). Guardar palabra a los santos. Comedia famosa.   4to.
[Seville, Tomé de Dios Miranda (?), Juan Francisco de Blas (?), c.1670-4]   Gaselee 118.   **1553(16)**

OLMO (José del). Relacion historica del auto general de fe, que se celebro en Madrid ... 1680.
4to.
[Madrid] impresso por Roque Rico de Miranda, vendese en casa de Marcos de Ondatigni, 1680
Engr. title-page, pl.   Gaselee 119.   **1395(1)**

O'MOLLOY (Franciscus). Grammatica Latino-Hibernica.   12mo.
Romæ, ex typographia S.Cong. de Prop.Fide, 1677   Wants §1, F1, 12, G1, 12; M11 defective.
26(1)

OPERA posthuma [of] B.D.S., 1677.
See SPINOZA (Benedict de).   **1376**

OPINION (The) of the Roman judges touching imprisonment, 1643.
See VICARS (John).   **1186(2)**

OPTICS. Opticks, 1704.
See NEWTON (Sir Isaac).   **1867**

OPUSCULA mythologica physica et ethica. Græce et Latine. [Ed. by T.Gale.]   8vo.
Amstelædami, apud Henricum Wetstenium, 1688
Engr. title-page.   **1557**

ORATIO dominica, 1700.
See MOTTE (Benjamin).   **1569**

ORAZIONI. Orationi divote che si possano recitare in occasione di visitare le quattro basiliche destinate da N.S. per il Giubileo dell' Anno Santo.
12mo.
Roma, pegli [sic] eredi del Corbelletti, 1700
Woodcuts.   **145(3)**

ORDER (The) and solemnitie of the creation of ... Prince Henry ... Prince of Wales ... Whereunto is annexed the royall maske (Tethys festival).   4to.
London, for John Budge, 1610
[Consutilia VIII]   STC 13161.   **1434(4)**

ORDER (The) of the hospitalls of K.Henry the viijth and K.Edward the vith.   12mo.
[London] '1557' *[c.1680.]*   Wing O389.   **394**

ORDINARY. [Thordynary of Crysten men.] 4to.
(*London, by Wynkyn de Worde,* 1506)
Woodcuts; wants Aa1-4, A2-5.   STC 5199;
Duff p.52.   **1273**

ORIGINAL (The) and growth of printing [c.1660].
See ATKYNS (Richard).   **1398(3)**

ORIGINAL right ... an answer to ... Dr.D'Avenant's essays, 1704.
See DEFOE (Daniel).   **1382(1)**

ORLÉANS (Pierre Joseph d'). Histoire de
Monsieur Constance [i.e. C.Phaulkon], premier
ministre du roy de Siam.   12mo.
Paris, chez Daniel Horthemals, 1692   **227**

———————— Histoire des revolutions d'Angleterre. 3 vols. 4to.
Paris, (Antoine Lambin) chez Claude Barbin,
1693-4   **1890-2**

ORRERY (Charles Boyle, Earl of). Dr. Bentley's
dissertations on the Epistles of Phalaris, and the
Fables of Aesop, examin'd.   8vo.
London, printed for Tho.Bennet, 1698
Wing O469.   **1255**

ORTELIUS (Abraham). Deorum dearumque
capita ex vetustis numismatibus.
*Antuerpiæ, ex museo Abrahami Ortelii (Philippus
Gallæus excudebat),* 1573   Engr. title-page,
54 engr. pls.   Adams O325.   **1556**

[ORTIGUE DE VAUMORIÈRE (Pierre d')].
L'art de plaire dans la conversation.   12mo.
Paris, chez Jean Guignard, 1690   **439**

[————————] Harangues sur toutes sortes de
sujets.   4to.
Paris, chez Jean Guignard, 1688   Engr. fp.
(port., Charrington p.19).   **1883**

ORTIZ (Lorenzo). El principe del Mar S.Francisco
Xavier.   8vo.
Brusselas, por Francisco Foppens, 1682
Engr. fp. (port.).   Gaselee 120.   **314**

ORTIZ DE ZUÑIGA (Diego). Annales ecclesias-
ticos, y seculares de la ... ciudad de Sevilla ... desde
el año de 1246 ... hasta el de 1671.   fo.
*Madrid, en la imprenta real, por Iuan Garcia
Infançon, acosta de Florian Anisson,* 1677
Engr. title-page, pl. ·   Gaselee 121.   **2145**

OSBORNE (Francis). Works ... In four several
tracts. 7th ed.   8vo.
*London, for R.D., and are to be sold by Allen
Bancks,* 1673   Wing O505; Diary 23 Jan.
1660/61, 19 Oct.1661, 5 Apr.1663.   **941(1)**

OSSAT (Arnaud d'), Cardinal. Lettres ... au roy
Henry le Grand, & à Monseigneur de Villeroy ...
(1594-1604). Dernière ed.   fo.

Paris, chez Michel Blageart, 1641   Engr. fp.
(port., Charrington p.129).   Wants leaves L3, 4.
MS notes in unidentified hand.   **2575**

OSSUNA Y RUS (Martín de). Memorias, y
recuerdos de lo sagrado, y real de la republica de
Dios. (— Memorias sagradas. 2a parte.)   4to.
Sevilla, por Juan Cabeças, (1678-) 1679
Gaselee 122-3.   **1551**

[OSTERWALD (Jean Frédéric)]. Traité des
sources de la corruption ... parmi les Chrestiens.
2 vols.   8vo.
Amsterdam, chez Henry Desbordes, 1700   **667-8**

OUDIN (César). Refranes o proverbios Castellanos,
1659.
See REFRANES o proverbios ...   **493**

———————— Tesoro de las dos lenguas española
y francesa ... Corregido y aumentado.   2 vols.
8vo.
Leon de Francia, a costa de Miguel Mayer, 1675
826-7

OUGHTRED (William). The description and use
of the general horologicall ring, 1652.
See LEURECHON (Jean). Mathematicall recreations ...   **618**

OVERALL (John), Bp of Norwich. Bishop
Overall's convocation book.   4to.
London, for Walter Kettilby, 1690   Engr. fp.
(port., Charrington p.150), engr. port. (Charrington p.130).   Wing O607.   **1826**

OVID. Opera omnia ... cum integris N.Heinsii
notis. 3 vols. 8vo.
Amstelodami, ex typographia Blaviana, 1683
Engr. title-pages, pls (port.).   **1469-71**

———————— Ovid's Metamorphosis Englished
... by G.S[andys].   fo.
London, by J.L. for Andrew Hebb, 1640
Engr. fp., title-page, 15 engr. pls.   STC 18968;
Diary 22 Dec.1662.   **2481**

OVIDE (L') bouffon, ou les Metamorphoses
travesties en vers burlesques, 1665.
See RICHER (L.).   **427**

[OWEN (John), D.D.]. A discourse concerning
liturgies.   4to.
London, 1662   [Liturgick Controversies III]
Wing O737.   **1189(8)**

———————— God's work in founding Zion ...
A sermon preached ... Septemb.17th, 1656.   4to.
Oxford, by Leon:Lichfield, for Tho:Robinson,
1656   [Sermons Polemical VI]
Wing O758.   **1184(7)**

OWEN (John), epigrammatist. Agudezas.
Traducidas en metro Castellano ... por F.de la
Torre.   4to.

Madrid, por Francisco Sanz, 1674
Gaselee 126.   **1448**

OXFORD. University. Comitia philologica in
honorem ... Annæ ... Reginæ.   fo.
*Oxonii, e Theatro Sheldoniano, venales prostant
apud Hen.Clements*, 1702   **2286(1)**

———————— Epinicion Oxoniense ... gratulatio
ob res feliciter ... gestas a copiis ... Reginæ Annæ.
fo.
Oxonii, e Theatro Sheldoniano, 1702   **2286(2)**

———————— Exequiæ desideratissimo principi
Gulielmo Glocestriæ Duci.   fo.
Oxonii, e Theatro Sheldoniano, 1700
Wing O855.   **2285(1)**

———————— Academiæ Oxoniensis gratulatio
pro exoptato ... Regis Guilielmi ex Hibernia
reditu.   fo.
Oxoniæ, e Theatro Sheldoniano, 1690
Wing O858.   **2283(3)**

———————— Pietas Oxoniensis in obitum ...
Regis Caroli secundi.   2 pts.   fo.
Oxonii, e Theatro Sheldoniano, 1685
Wing O936.   **2284(1)**

———————— Pietas Universitatis Oxoniensis in
obitum ... Reginæ Mariæ.   fo.
Oxonii, e Theatro Sheldoniano, 1695   Engr. fp.
Wing O937.   **2284(2)**

———————— Pietas Universitatis Oxoniensis in
obitum ... Regis Gulielmi III.   fo.
Oxonii, e Theatro Sheldoniano, 1702   Engr. fp.
                                        2285(2)

———————— Strenæ natalitiæ Academiæ
Oxoniensis in celsissimum Principem.   fo.
Oxonii, e Theatro Sheldoniano, 1688
Wing O969.   **2283(1)**

———————— Vota Oxoniensia pro ... Guilhelmo
Rege et Maria Regina.   fo.
*Oxonii, e Theatro Sheldoniano, prostant venales
apud Th.Bennet*, 1689   Wing O992.   **2283(2)**

OXFORD (The) gazette. Nos 1-23, 1665-6.
See LONDON (The) gazette.   **2078**

OXFORD (The) list of the names of the knights,
citizens, burgesses, and barons of the Cinque
Ports, 1681.
See ENGLAND. *Parliament. Commons.* **2137(27)**

OZANAM (Jacques). Dictionaire mathématique.
4to.
Amsterdam, aux dépens des Huguetan, 1691
Engr. fp., pl., diagrams.   **1877**

———————— Récréations mathématiques et
physiques.   2 vols.   8vo.
Paris, chez Jean Jombert, 1696   Engr. fp.,
83 engr. pls.   **1488-9**

P

P.(B.). Le secretaire critique, 1680.
See DU JONQUIER (   ).   **99(2)**

P.(H.). Good work for a good magistrate, 1651.
See PETERS (Hugh).   **129**

P.(H.). The narrative of Mr.J.Fitz-Gerrald, 1681.
See FITZGERALD (John).   **2251(19)**

P.(H.). The true portraiture of the kings of England, 1688.
See PARKER (Henry).   **1430(17)**

P.(H.). Wit and mirth, 1699.
See PLAYFORD (Henry).   **654**

P.(J.). Honey out of the rock, 1644.
See PRICE (John), of London.   **1184(13)**

P.(J.). The merry conceits and passages of Simon
and Cisley. Two Lancashire lovers.   12mo.
London, by H.B. for J.Clark, W.Thackery [etc.]
[c.1685]   [Penny-Merriments I]
Woodcut fp.   **362(57)**

P.(L.). The five strange wonders of the world,
1683.
See PRICE (Lawrence).   **363(2)**

P.(L.). Two essays sent in a letter from Oxford to
a nobleman in London.   8vo.
London, printed and are to be sold by R.Baldwin,
1695   Wing P77.   **1242(1)**

P.(L.d.). Histoire ... des Iles Antilles, 1665.
See ROCHEFORT (César de).   **1855**

P.(P.). The happy future state of England, 1688.
See PETT (Sir Peter).   **2413**

P.(S.). The case of the Church of England, 1681.
See PARKER (Samuel), Bp of Oxford.   **1053**

P.(S.). A letter to a friend concerning the Bank of
England, with some reflections on a late pamphlet
[i.e. A review of the universal remedy ...].   brs.
London, printed and sold by R.Baldwin, 1696
                                       796(4)

P.(S.). The Portugal history ... In the years 1667
and 1668 ... By S.P.Esq.   8vo.
London, printed for Richard Tonson, 1677
Sometimes, wrongly, attributed to Pepys.
Wing P1452.   **991**

P.(T.). The door of salvation opened [c.1680].
See PASSINGER (Thomas).   **365(8)**

P.(W.). Bibliotheca Norfolciana: sive catalogus
libb. ... quos ... Henricus Dux Norfolciæ, &c.

Regiæ Societati Londinensi ... donavit.   4to.
Londini, excudebat Ric.Chiswel, 1681
Wing N1230.   **1795**

P.(W.). Chronological tables, [1689].
See MARCEL (Guillaume).   **9**

P.(W.). A flying post ...   2nd ed.   4to.
[*London*] *for Edw.Thomas*, 1680   [Vulgaria IV]
Woodcut. Title-page cropped.   **1193(15)**

P.(W.). The pleasant and most delightful history
of Argalus and Parthenia newly reviv'd. [*Sometimes attributed to F.Quarles.*]   4to.
London, by T.H. for T.Passinger, 1683
[Vulgaria III]   Woodcuts.   Wing Q112.
                                              1192(7)

PACIFICO (Pietro Antonio). Cronica Veneta.
12mo.
Venetia, per Domenico Lovisa, 1697   Engr.
half-title, engr. pl.   **391**

PACK (Sir Christopher). By the Mayor. Whereas
by neglect of executing the ... statutes against
rogues ...   brs.
[*London*] *by James Flesher* [1655]   Bound in
after p.938.   **2476**

[PAGIT (Eusebius)]. Histoire de la Ste Ecriture
... en forme de catéchisme. Traduit de l'anglois.
fo.
Charenton, par Louis Vendosme pere, 1678
                                           2742(2)

PAGITT (Ephraim). Christianography.   3rd ed.
fo.
London, by J.Okes, for Matthew Costerden, 1640
3 engr. maps.   STC 19112.   **2092**

PAGNINUS (Santes). Thesaurus linguæ sanctæ,
siue lexicon Hebraicum.   fo.
Coloniæ Allobrogum, typis Petri de la Rouiere,
1614   **2740**

PALAZZI (Giovanni). De dominio maris.   12mo.
Venetiis, apud Combi & La Nou, 1663
Engr. title-page.   **64**

PALLAVICINO (Sforza), Cardinal. Les nouvelles
lumieres politiques, 1676.
See LE NOIR (Jean).   **77(1)**

PALMER (Herbert). The glasse of Gods providence
towards his faithfull ones ... A sermon ... Aug.13,
1644.   4to.
London, by G.M. for Th.Underhill, 1644
[Sermons Polemical VI]   Autograph: Elizabeth
Dewes.   Wing P235.   **1184(9)**

——————— The necessity and encouragement,
of utmost venturing for the churches help ... A
sermon preached 28.June, 1643.   4to.
London, for Sam:Gellibrand, 1643   [Sermons
Polemical VI]   Wing P242.   **1184(8)**

PALMER (Thomas). Bristolls military garden.
A sermon.   4to.
London, by Felix Kyngston, 1635   [Sermons
Polemical VI]   STC 19155.   **1184(10)**

PALMER (Sir Thomas). An essay of the meanes
how to make our trauailes, into forraine
countries, the more profitable.   4to.
London, H.L[ownes].for Mathew Lownes, 1606
[Consutilia V]   STC 19156.   **1431(13)**

PANCIROLI (Guido). Rerum memorabilium sive
deperditarum pars prior (– liber secundus).   4to.
*Francofurti, sumptibus Godefridi Schonwetteri
viduæ et hæred:*, 1660   Engr. title-page.   **1600**

PAOLO, Servita.   *See* SARPI (Paolo).

PAPIN (Denis). A continuation of the new
digester of bones. (– Experiments tried in Mr.
Sarotti's Academy at Venice.)   4to.
London, by Joseph Streater, 1687   2 engr. pls.
Sheet inserted loosely in Pepys's hand; headed
'Bottle & Furniture-weight'.   Wing P308.
                                           1725(2)

——————— A new digester or engine for
softning bones.   4to.
London, J.M. for Henry Bonwicke, 1681
Engr. pl.   Wing P309.   **1725(1)**

PARALLEL (The) continu'd [1702].
See GIBSON (Edmund), Bp of London.   **1696(16)**

PARALLEL (A) or brief comparison of the
Liturgie with the Masse-book, 1641.
See BAILLIE (Robert).   **1188(5)**

PARDIES (Ignace Gaston). Deux machines propres à faire les quadrans.   2e éd.   12mo.
Paris, chez Sebastien Mabre-Cramoisy, 1676
7 engr. pls.   **493(3)**

——————— Discours de la connoissance des
bestes.   2e éd.   12mo.
Paris, chez Sebastien Mabre-Cramoisy, 1678   **438**

——————— Elémens de géometrie ...   3e éd.
12mo.
Paris, chez Sebastien Mabre-Cramoisy, 1678
Diagrams.   **493(1)**

——————— La statique ou la science des
forces mouvantes.   2e éd.   12mo.
Paris, chez Sebast.Mabre-Cramoisy, 1674
2 engr. pls, diagrams.   **493(2)**

PARDO (Francisco). Sermon predicado ... en
accion de gracias por la feliz victoria ... en el sitio
de Viena.   4to.
Sevilla, Iuā Antonio Tarazona [1683]
Gaselee 127.   **1546(2)**

PARIS. Hôpital de la Trinité.
See HÔPITAL DE LA TRINITÉ.

PARIS (Matthew). Historia major ... Editore W.Wats. 2 pts. fo.
Londini, excudebat Richardus Hodgkinson, sumptibus Cornelii Bee & Laurentii Sadler [etc.], (1639-) 1640 Engr. fp. (port., Charrington p.131). STC 19210. **2518**

[PARIVAL (Jean Nicolas de)] . Les delices de la Hollande ... Derniere ed. 12mo.
Amsterdam, chez Jean Bouman, 1678
Engr. title-page, 17 engr. maps, 2 engr. pls.
Diary 10 Dec.1663. **147**

PARKER (George). A treatise of japaning, 1688.
See STALKER (John). **2719**

[PARKER (Henry)] . The true portraiture of the kings of England ... To which is added the political catechism. 4to.
London, 1688 [Consutilia IV]
Wing P430. **1430(17)**

PARKER (Martin). A brief sum of certain worm-wood lectures. 12mo.
London, for J.Wright, W.Thackeray, T.Passenger, 1682 [Penny-Merriments I] Woodcut.
362(16)

———————— A true tale of Robin Hood. 12mo.
[London] for J.Clark, W.Thackeray, T.Passinger, 1686 [Penny-Merriments II] Woodcut.
Title-page cropped. Wing P447. **363(36)**

[PARKER (Matthew), Abp of Canterbury]. De antiquitate Britannicæ ecclesiæ. fo.
Hanouiæ, typis Wechelianis, apud Claud.Marnium et hæredes Ioannis Aubrii, 1605 **2547**

PARKER (Samuel), Bp of Oxford. An account of the government of the Christian church, for the first six hundred years. 8vo.
London, for John Baker, 1683 Wing P453.
1104

[————————] The case of the Church of England, briefly and truly stated. 8vo.
London, for Henry Faithorne and John Kersey, sold by Walter Davis, 1681 Wing P455. **1053**

[————————] A defence and continuation of the ecclesiastical politie. 8vo.
London, by A.Clark for J.Martyn, 1671
Wing P457. **1051**

———————— A demonstration of the divine authority of the law of nature, and of the Christ-ian religion. 4to.
London, by M.Flesher, for R.Royston and R.Chis-well, 1681 Wing P458. **1572**

[————————] A discourse of ecclesiastical politie. 8vo.
London, for John Martyn, 1670 Wing P459.
1050

———————— Disputationes de Deo, et provi-dentia divina. 4to.
Londini, typis M.Clark, impensis Jo.Martyn, 1678
Wing P462. **1835**

———————— Religion and loyalty. 2 vols. 8vo.
London, for John Baker, 1684-5 Wing P470-1.
1150-1

[————————] A reproof to the Rehearsal transprosed [of A.Marvell] ... by the Authour of the Ecclesiastical politie. 8vo.
London, for James Collins, 1673 Wing P473.
1052

PARKINS (Sir William). The arraignment, tryal and condemnation of Sir William Parkins ... March 24, 1695/6. fo.
London, for Samuel Heyrick, and Isaac Cleve, 1696 [Narratives & Tryals VI]
Wing A3760. **2254(7)**

———————— The tryal and condemnation of Sir William Parkyns ... March 24. 1695/6. fo.
London, for Brabazon Aylmer, 1696
[Narratives & Tryals VI] Wing T2153.
2254(8)

PARKINSON (John). Theatrum botanicum. fo.
London, by Tho.Cotes, 1640 Engr. title-page (port., Charrington p.131), woodcuts.
STC 19302. **2551**

PARLIAMENT. *See* ENGLAND. *Parliament.*

PARLIAMENT (The) of women; with the merry laws. 12mo.
[London] for T.Passinger, J.Deacon, G.Conyers [c.1685] [Penny-Merriments II] Woodcut.
363(34)

PARLIAMENTARY (The) original and rights of the lower House of Convocation cleared, 1702.
See ATTERBURY (Francis), Bp of Rochester.
1697(14)

PARMA. Collegio de' Nobili. Nomenclatura convictorum Ducalis Collegii nobilium Parmae, ab initio Januarii anni 1699. Ad primam diem Januarii anni 1700. 4to.
Parmae, typis Joseph Rosati [1700]
Tanner II, p.19. **1451(2)**

———————— Il teatro d'onore, aperto li 10. Agosto ... 1699. Nel Ducale Collegio de' Nobili di Parma. 4to.
Parma, per Giuseppe Rosati, 1699
Tanner II, p.19. **1451(1)**

PARR (Richard). The life of ... James Usher late Lord Arch-bishop of Armagh. 5 pts. fo.
London, for Nathaniel Ranew, 1686
Engr. fp. (port., Charrington p.169).
Wing P548. **2395**

PARRHASE (Théodore), *pseud.*
See LE CLERC (Jean).

PARSONS (Robert), S.J. A Christian directory.
8vo.
London, printed by Henry Hills, printer to the
King's ... Majesty for his houshold and Chappel,
and for him and Matt.Turner, 1687   Title-page
defective.   **1218**

[————————] A conference about the next
succession to the Crowne of Ingland ... Published
by R.Doleman [i.e. R.Parsons].   8vo.
Imprinted at N.[Antwerp?], 1594
STC 19398.   **518**

————————— A treatise concerning the broken
succession of the Crown of England.   4to.
London, 1655   Wing P574.   **1755**

[PARSONS (William)]. Chronological tables
[1689].
See MARCEL (Guillaume).   **9**

PARTICULAR (A) relation of the sickness and
death of ... William the Third.   brs.
[London] for A.Roper, 1702   *[Inserted between*
nos 3790 & 3791 of the London Gazette.]   **2090**

[PARTRIDGE (John)]. The most famouse and
worthie historie, of the worthy lady Pandauola.
8vo.
London, by Thomas Purfoote, 1566
STC 19424.   **29(2)**

————————— The worthie hystorie of the
moste noble and valiaunt knight Plasidas.   8vo.
London, by Henrye Denham, for Thomas Hacket
[1566]   STC 19438.   **29(1)**

PARTRIDGE (John), M.D. Annus mirabilis:
being an almanack for ... 1688.   8vo.
London, printed by R.R. for the Company of
Stationers [1688]   [Almanacks for the year
1688]   Wing A2017.   **425(17)**

[PASCAL (Blaise)]. Les provinciales ou les
lettres ecrites par Louis de Montalte. Septiéme éd.
12mo.
Cologne, chez Nicolas Schoute, 1669   **103**

PASQUIL the playne, 1533.
See ELYOT (Sir Thomas).   **368(4)**

PASQUILS jests.   4to.
London, by I.F. and are to be sold by F.Coles,
T.Vere, and J.Wright, 1669   [Vulgaria IV]
                                            1193(5)

PASQUINE in a traunce [1566?].
See CURIO (Caelius Secundus).   **1264**

[PASSINGER (Thomas)]. The door of salvation
opened ... By T.P.   12mo.
[London] by J.M. for T.Passinger [c.1680]
[Penny-Godlinesses]   **365(8)**

PASTOR (Il) fido, 1664.
See GUARINI (Giovanni Battista).   **926**

[PATERSON (William)]. A brief account of the
intended Bank of England.   4to.
London, sold by Randal Taylor, 1694
[Consutilia VII]   Wing P710.   **1433(7)**

[PATHOMACHIA: or, the battell of affections.]
4to.
[London, by Thomas and Richard Coats for
Francis Constable, 1630]   [Loose Plays I]
Wants leaves A1-3.   STC 19462.   **1075(1)**

PATIN (Gui). Lettres choisies ... Dernière éd.
3 vols.   12mo.
Cologne, chez Pierre du Laurens, 1691
Engr. fp. (port., Charrington p.132).   **406-8**

[PATRICK (John)]. Reflexions upon the
devotions of the Roman Church.   8vo.
London, for Richard Royston, 1674   Engr. fp.
Wing P732.   **1081**

PATTERN (A) of a well-constituted and well-
governed hospital: or, a brief description of ...
the Royal Hospital of the Invalids. Near Paris.
8vo.
London, printed for Richard Baldwin, 1695
Plan.   Wing P871.   **698**

PAULDEN (Thomas). Pontefract castle. An
account how it was taken.   4to.
In the Savoy, printed by Edward Jones, 1702
                                            1776

PAYNE (William). A sermon upon the death of
the Queen ...   2nd ed.   4to.
London, by J.R. for B.Aylmer, S.Smith, and
B.Walford, 1695   Wing P910.   **1528(16)**

PEACHAM (Henry). The worth of a penny: or a
caution to keep money.   4to.
London, by S. and B.G. for Thomas Lee, 1677
[Consutilia I]   Wing P954.   **1427(12)**

PEAD (Deuel). A practical discourse upon the
death of our late glorious Queen ... A sermon.
4to.
London, for Abel Roper, E.Wilkinson, and Roger
Clavel [etc.], 1695   Wing P962.   **1528(13)**

PEARSON (John), Bp of Chester. An exposition
of the Creed ... 4th ed., revised.   fo.
London, by J.M. for John Williams, 1676
Engr. fp.(port., Charrington p.133).
Wing P998.   **2374**

PECK (Peter van). In titt. Dig. & Cod. ad rem
nauticam pertinentes, commentarii.   8vo.
Amstelodami, apud viduam Joannis Henrici Boom,
1668   **871**

PÉCOUR (Louis Guillaume). La nouvelle mariée. Dance nouvelle.   8vo.
Paris, chez le sieur Feuillet, 1700   6 engr. ll.
See also below, vol.IV.   **1871(4)**

———————— La pavanne des saisons. Dance nouvelle.   8vo.
Paris, chez le sieur Feüillet, et chez Michel Brunet, 1700   4 engr. ll.
See also below, vol.IV.   **1871(5)**

———————— Recueil de dances ... Mises en papier par M.Feuillet.   4to.
Paris, chez l'auteur, et chez Michel Brunet, 1700
Engr.   *See also below*, vol.IV   **1871(3)**

PEDLAR'S. The pedlers prophecie, 1595.
See WILSON (Robert).   **939(3)**

PEELE (George). The loue of king Dauid and fair Bethsabe. With the tragedie of Absalon.   4to.
London, by Adam Islip, 1599   [Old Plays II]
STC 19540.   **1102(1)**

———————— Merrie conceited jests.   4to.
London, for William Whitwood, 1671
[Vulgaria IV]   Wing P1054.   **1193(4)**

[PELLISSON-FONTANIER (Paul)]. Histoire de l'Academie Françoise ... Derniere ed.   12mo.
La Haye, 1688   **215**

[PENE (Charles)]. Le Neptune françois, ou recueil des cartes maritimes.   fo.
Paris, Imprimerie Royale, 1693   29 engr. maps.
Engr. title-page.   **2999**

PENINGTON (Isaac). The axe laid to the root of the old corrupt-tree.   4to.
London, printed and are to be sold by Lodowick Lloyd, 1659   [Consutilia II]   Wing P1152.
1428(9)

PENN (William). The peoples ancient and just liberties asserted in the tryal of W.Penn, and W.Mead.   4to.
[*London*] 1670   [Consutilia I]
Wing P1336A.   **1427(9)**

———————— The preface, being a summary account of the ... dispensations of God, 1694.
See FOX (George). A journal.   **2471(1)**

[————————] Some fruits of solitude ...
2nd ed.   12mo.
London, for Thomas Northcott, 1693
Wing P1369.   **61**

[PENRY (John)]. Oh read over D.John Bridges [1588].
See MARPRELATE (Martin), *pseud.*   **1428(17)**

PEOPLES (The) ancient and just liberties asserted, 1670.
See PENN (William).   **1427(9)**

PEPYS (Samuel). Memoires relating to the state of the Royal Navy ... determin'd December 1688. 8vo.
[*London*] 1690   On title-page, in unidentified hand: 'Licens'd Decemb.1 1690 / James Fraser / Henry Mortlocke Warden'.   MS corrections in clerical hand.   Wing P1449; Tanner I, p.31.
1143

PERCYVALL (Richard). A dictionary in Spanish and English ... Now enlarged ... by Iohn Minsheu. fo.
London, by Iohn Haviland for Matthew Lownes, 1623   STC 19621b.5.   **2012**

PÉRÉFIXE (Hardouin de Beaumont de), Abp of Paris. Histoire du roy Henri le grand.   12mo.
Amsterdam, chez Louys & Daniel Elzevier, 1661
Engr. & pr. title-pages.   **87**

PÉREZ (Martin). Relacion verdadera que trata de todos los sucessos, y tratos de la Carcel Real de la Ciudad de Seuilla.   4to.
(*Seuilla, por Iuan Cabeças*) [c.1680]
Gaselee 128; Wilson p.259.   **1545(42)**

PÉREZ DE HITA (Ginés). Historia de los Vandos de los Zegries, y Abencerrages ... de vn libro arabigo, cuyo autor de vista fue ... Abenhomin ... Traducida [or rather written] por G.Perez de Hita.   8vo.
Sevilla, por Pedro de Segura [1670]
Gaselee 129.   **311**

PÉREZ DE MONTALVÁN (Juan). El divino portugues san Antonio de Padua. Comedia famosa. 4to.
[*Seville, Juan Cabeças, c.1676*]   Gaselee 132.
1553(19)

———————— Dos romances famosos.   4to.
(*Seuilla, en casa de Juan Cabeças*) [c.1680]
Gaselee 131; Wilson p.262.   **1545(46)**

[————————] El mejor padre de pobres [c.1680].
See MEJOR (El) padre ...   **1553(22)**

———————— Santa Maria Egipciaca, y gitana de Menfis. Comedia famosa.   4to.
[*Seville, Tomé de Dios Miranda*, c.1675]
Gaselee 133.   **1553(26)**

———————— Sucessos, y prodigios de amor ...
Dezima impr.   8vo.
Cadiz, por el Alferez Bartolomè Nuñez de Castro [c.1682]   Gaselee 134.   **312**

———————— Vida, y muerte de Sanson.   4to.
(*Sevilla, en casa de Juan Cabeças*) [c.1680]
Gaselee 135; Wilson p.148.   **1545(8)**

PÉREZ DEL BARRIO ANGULO (Gabriel).
Secretario y conseiero de señores, y ministros.
4to.
Madrid, por Mateo de Espinosa, 1667
Gaselee 130.   **1593(1)**

PERFECT (A) copy of all summons, 1685.
See ENGLAND. *Parliament.*   **2572**

PERKINS (Francis). Perkins. A new almanack,
for ... 1688.   8vo.
*London, (R.Everingham) for the Company of
Stationers*, 1688   [Almanacks for the year 1688]
Wing A2092.   **425(18)**

PERKINS (William). Catholico reformado ...
Trasladado ... por G.Massan.   8vo.
[*London*] *en casa de Ricardo del Campo* [i.e. *R.
Field*], 1599   STC 19741; Gaselee 136.   **313**

PERNE (Andrew). Gospell courage ... A sermon
preached ... 31. of May, 1643.   4to.
London, by G.Dexter, for Stephen Bowtell, 1643
[Sermons Polemical VI]   Wing P1577.
                                              1184(11)

PERNICIOUS (The) consequences of the new
heresie of the Jesuites, 1666.
See ARNAULD (Antoine).   q   **930**

PEROTTUS (Nicolaus). Grammatica.
N. de la Barre, Paris, 1 June 1498.   4to.
See Appendix.   **1305(7)**

PERQUINO (Guillermo).
See PERKINS (William).

PERRAULT (Charles). Les hommes illustres qui
ont paru en France pendant ce siecle: avec leurs
portraits au naturel.   2 vols.   fo.
Paris, chez Antoine Dezallier, 1696-1700
103 engr. pls (ports).   Tanner II, p.106.   **2926-7**

———————— Paralelle des anciens et des
modernes en ce qui regarde les arts et les sciences.
Nouvelle éd.   2 vols.   12mo.
Paris, chez Jean Baptiste Coignard, 1693   **689-90**

PERRAULT (Claude). Ordonnance des cinq
espèces de colonnes selon la méthode des anciens.
fo.
Paris, chez Jean Baptiste Coignard, 1683
Engr. pls.   **2644**

PERRAULT (François). The divell of Mascon.
5th ed.
Oxford, by Hen.Hall, for Ric.Davis, 1679
Wing P1588.   **867(2)**

PERRY (John). A regulation for seamen.   4to.
*London (printed, and are to be sold by John
Whitlock)* 1695   [Naval Pamphlets]
Wing P1649.   **1399(16)**

PERSIO BERTISO (Felix). Curiosa obra que dec-
lara la vida del Picaro.   4to.
(*Seuilla, por Juan Vejarano, à costa de Lucas
Martin de Hermosa*, 1682)   Gaselee 11;
Wilson p.258.   **1545(40)**

———————— La harpa de Belen.   4to.
Seuilla, por Iuā de Ossuna, 1677
Gaselee 13; Wilson p.140.   **1545(1)**

———————— Segunda parte de la vida del
Picaro.   4to.
Seuilla, por Iuan de Ossuna, 1674
Gaselee 12; Wilson p.259.   **1545(41)**

PETER (John). A relation or diary of the siege of
Vienna.   4to.
London, for William Nott, and George Wells, 1684
Engr. plans.   Wing P1690.   **1878**

PETERS (Hugh). Gods doings, and mans duty,
opened in a sermon ... April 2 ... 1645.   4to.
London, by R.Raworth for G.Calvert, 1646
[Sermons Polemical VI]   Wing P1703.
                                              1184(12)

[————————] Good work for a good
magistrate.   12mo.
London, by William Du-Gard, 1651
Wing P1706.   **129**

PETOWE (Henry). Elizabetha quasi viuens, Eliza's
funerall.   4to.
London, by E.Allde for M.Lawe, 1603
STC 19804.   **2229(2)**

PETRONIUS ARBITER (Titus). Satyricon ...
Accedunt ... Lusus in Priapum, Pervigilium
Veneris ... Concinnante M.Hadrianide. 2 vols in 1.
Vol.2, ed. 2a.   8vo.
Amstelodami, typis Ioannis Blaeu, 1669-71
Engr. title-page.   **1462**

[PETT (Sir Peter)]. The happy future state of
England. (— The obligation resulting from the
oath of supremacy.)   2 pts.   fo.
London, 1688   Wing P1883, 1885.   **2413**

PETTUS (Sir John). The constitution of parlia-
ments in England.   8vo.
London, for Thomas Basset, 1680
Wing P1905.   **1122**

———————— Fleta minor, 1683.
See ERCKER (Lazarus).   **2559**

PETTY (Sir William). Another essay in political
arithmetick, concerning the growth of the city of
London.   8vo.
London, by H.H. for Mark Pardoe, 1683
Wing P1915.   **891(4)**

————— The discourse made before the Royal Society the 26. of November 1674. concerning the use of duplicate proportion. 12mo.
London, for John Martyn, 1674
Wing P1919. **97(1)**

————— Further observation upon the Dublin-bills. 2nd ed. 8vo.
Lonon [sic], for Mark Pardoe, 1686
Wing P1926. **891(3)**

[—————] Observations upon the Dublin-bills of mortality, MDCLXXI. And the state of that city. 8vo.
London, for Mark Pardoe, 1683 Tables.
Wing P1929. **891(2)**

————— The political anatomy of Ireland. 2 pts. 8vo.
London, for D.Brown, and W.Rogers, 1691
Wing P1931. **906**

————— Political arithmetick. 8vo.
London, printed for Robert Clavel, and Hen.Mortlock, 1691 Wing P1933. **897(1)**

————— Sir William Petty's Quantulum-cunque concerning money. 4to.
London, 1695 Wing P1935. **796(6)**

————— Reflections upon some persons and things in Ireland. 8vo.
London, for John Martin, James Allestreye, and Thomas Dicas, 1660 Wing P1936. **221**

————— A treatise of naval philosophy.
See HALE (Thomas). An account of several new inventions, 1691. **396**

[—————] A treatise of taxes & contributions. 4to.
London, printed for N.Brooke, 1662
Wing P1938. **1174(1)**

————— Two essays in political arithmetick, concerning the people, housing, hospitals, &c. of London and Paris. 8vo.
London, printed for J.Lloyd, 1687
Wing P1942. **897(2)**

PETYT (William). The antient right of the Commons of England asserted. 8vo.
London, for F.Smith, T.Bassett, J.Wright [etc.], 1680 Wing P1945. **1107**

————— Miscellanea Parliamentaria. 8vo.
London, by N.Thompson, for T.Basset, and J.Wickins, 1680 Wing P1948. **623**

PEYTON (Sir Edward). The divine catastrophe ... of the House of Stuarts. 8vo.
London, for Giles Calvert, 1652
Wing P1952; Diary 10 Feb.1664/5. **62(2)**

[PEZRON (Paul Yves)]. L'antiquité des tems rétablie et defenduë contre les Juifs. 12mo.
A Amsterdam, chez Henry Desbordes, 1687 **680**

PFEIFFER (August). Dubia vexata Scripturæ Sacræ. 4to.
Dresdæ, impensis Martini Gabrielis Hübeneri, ex offic. elect. typis vid. & hæred. Melch.Bergeni, 1679 Engr. fp. (port., Charrington p.135), plans, diagrams. **1778**

PHARMACOPOEIA Londinensis, 1691.
See ROYAL COLLEGE OF PHYSICIANS. **1076**

PHILALETHES, *pseud.* A short narrative of Mr Fitz-Gerald. fo.
[London?] 1680 [Narratives & Tryals III]
Wing F1075. **2251(7)**

PHILIPOTT (Thomas). Villare Cantianum: or Kent surveyed and illustrated. fo.
London, by William Godbid, 1659 Engr. map, engrs. With sig.K as cancel and cancelland. Inserted at end: 11 MS leaves of notes, in hand of one of Pepys's clerks, about watch and ward in Kent, 1585-8; with a note by Dr Plot; a map of beacons in Kent and a map of the county (engraved by Charles Whitwell, printed by P.Stent, 1659). Wing P1989; Naval Minutes p.393.
2052

PHILIPPS (Fabian). The established government of England, vindicated from all ... mistakes. fo.
London, for the Author, 1687
With an additional title-page, reading 'Investigatio jurium antiquorum et rationalium regni'.
Wing P2006. **2337**

PHILIPPS (Henry). The grandeur of the law. 2nd ed. 8vo.
London, printed for Arthur Jones, 1685
Engr. fp. (port., Charrington p.72).
Wing P2022B. **691**

PHILIPPSON (Joannes), Sleidanus.
See SLEIDAN (Joannes).

PHILIPS (Thomas), *pseud.*
See DRAKE (Sir William).

PHILLIPPS (William). The principles of law reduced to practice. 12mo.
London, for Henry Twyford, Thomas Dring, Iohn Place, 1661 Wing P2059. **14**

PHILOPATRIS (M.A.), *pseud.*
See MUDIE (Alexander).

PHILOSOPHIA vetus et nova, 1685.
See DU HAMEL (Jean Baptiste). **712-3**

PHILOSOPHICAL collections. Numb.1-7. 4to.
(London, for John Martyn, – Moses Pitt, – Richard Chiswel) 1679-82 Engr. pls.
1713(2-4)

PHILOSOPHICAL (A) essay of musick, 1677.
See GUILFORD (Francis North, Baron). **1712(2)**

PHILOSOPHICAL transactions [of the Royal
Society]. Vols 1-23. 4to.
In the Savoy (– London)(vols 13-15: Oxford)
(1667-) 1704 Engr. pls. Wants sig.Ttt of
vol.21. **1701-1712(1), 1713(1)**

––––––––––– A general index ... from the
beginning to July 1677. 4to.
London, by J.M. for John Martyn, 1678
Wing G500. **1712(3)**

PHILOSTRATUS. The two first books ...
concerning the life of Apollonius Tyaneus ... now
published in English: together with philological
notes ... by C.Blount. fo.
London, for Nathaniel Thompson, 1680
Wing P2132. **2218**

PHOENIX (The), 1607.
See MIDDLETON (Thomas). **1102(3)**

[PIÉLAT (Barthélemy)]. La vie et les actions
memorables du Sr.Michel de Ruyter. 2 pts.
12mo.
Amsterdam, chez Henry & Theodore Boom, 1677
Engr. title-page, port. **74**

PIETAS Romana et Parisiensis, 1687.
See WOODHEAD (Abraham). **665**

[PILES (Roger de)]. Abregé de la vie des peintres
avec des réflexions sur leurs ouvrages. 12mo.
Paris, chez François Muguet, 1699 **804**

PILGRIMS (The) progress to the other world,
1684.
See B.(J.). **365(41)**

PILKINGTON (Sir Thomas). The tryal of
T.Pilkington [etc.], 1683.
See TRIAL. **2252(32)**

PINAROLO (Giacomo). Trattato delle cose piu
memorabili di Roma, tanto antiche, come
moderne. 2 pts. 12mo.
Roma, per Antonio de Rossi, 1700 **146**

PINDAR. Ὀλύμπια, Νέμεα, Πύθια, Ἴσθμια ...
Una cum Latina omnium versione carmine lyrico
per N.Sudorium. 2 pts. fo.
Oxonii, e Theatro Sheldoniano, 1697 Engr. fp.
Wing P2245. **2704**

PINEL Y MONROY (Francisco). Retrado del
buen vassallo, copiado de la vida, y hechos de
D.Andres de Cabrera, primero Marques de Moya.
fo.
*Madrid, en la Imprenta Imperial, por Ioseph
Fernandez de Buendia*, 1677 Engr. title-page,
pls (ports). Gaselee 137. **2108(2)**

PISCARA CASTALDO (Andreas). Praxis
cæremoniarum seu sacrorum Romanæ Ecc:
rituum accurata tractatio. fo.
Neapoli, excudebat Lazarus Scoriggius, 1625
(1631) Engr. title-page. **2205**

PITTON DE TOURNEFORT (Joseph). Elemens
de botanique. 3 vols. 8vo.
Paris, de l'Imprimerie Royale, 1694 Engr. title-
pages, pls. **1640-2**

[PIUS II, Pope]. The goodli history of the
moste noble and beautifull ladye Lucres of Scene
in Tuskan, and of her louer Eurialus. 8vo.
(London, by me Wyllyam Copland) 1567
STC 19972. **29(3)**

PLACITA Parlamentaria, 1661.
See ENGLAND. *Parliament.* **2121**

PLAIN (A) and easie rule to rigge any ship, 1664.
See BOND (Henry). **1267(4)**

PLATINA (Bartolomeo). The lives of the Popes ...
to the reign of Sixtus IV ... Transl. ... by P.
Rycaut. fo.
London, for Christopher Wilkinson, 1685
Engr. fp. (port., Charrington p.148).
Wing P2403. **2327**

PLATO. De rebus divinis dialogi selecti Græce &
Latine. Ed.2., auctior. 8vo.
*Cantabrigiæ, ex officina Joann.Hayes, impensis
Joann.Creed*, 1683 Wing P2407. **1146**

––––––––––The works of Plato abridg'd. With
an account of his life ... Together with a translation of his choicest dialogues ... By M.Dacier
[i.e. A.Lefevre]. Transl. from the French.
2 vols. 8vo.
London, printed for A.Bell, 1701 **1452-3**

PLATO redivivus, 1681.
See NEVILLE (Henry). **583**

PLATONISME (Le) devoilé, 1700.
See SOUVERAIN (Matthieu). **595**

PLAUTUS. Comœdiæ viginti et fragmenta ... notis
illustravit J.Operarius. 2 vols. 4to.
Parisiis, apud Fredericum Leonard, 1679 (1678)
Engr. title-page. **1948-9**

PLAYFORD (Henry). Harmonia sacra. fo.
*In the Savoy, printed by Edward Jones, for Henry
Playford*, 1688 Engr. fp., title-page.
Wing P2436. *See also below, vol.IV.* **2018(1)**

––––––––––– Harmonia sacra ... the second
book. fo.
*In the Savoy, printed by Edward Jones, for
Henry Playford*, 1693 Wants sig.B.
Wing P2437. *See also below, vol.IV.* **2018(2)**

[——————] Two divine hymns: being a Supplement to the second book of Harmoniae sacra [sic]. fo.
London, printed by W.Pearson, for Henry Playford, 1700   Wing P2442.
See also below, vol.IV.   **2018(3)**

[——————] Wit and mirth: or, Pills to purge melancholy; being a collection of the best merry ballads and songs ... having each there [sic] proper tune.   12mo.
London, by Will.Pearson, for Henry Playford, 1699   Pt 1 only.   Wing W3134A.
See also below, vol.IV.   **654**

PLAYFORD (John). Psalms & hymns in solemn musick of four parts ... Also six hymns for one voyce to the organ.   fo.
London, W.Godbid for J.Playford, 1671   Wing P2498.   See also below, vol.IV.   **2278**

——————— Vade mecum, or the necessary companion. Containing I. Sir S.Morland's Perpetual almanack [etc.].   8vo.
London, by A.G. and J.P., and are to be sold by R.Northcot [etc.], 1679
Wing P2505.   **293(2)**

PLEADINGS (The) and arguments ... upon the Quo Warranto, touching the Charter of the City of London.   4 pts.   fo.
London, by the assigns of Richard and Edward Atkins Esquires, for Tho.Dring and Benj.Tooke, 1690   Wing P2527.   **2342(1)**

PLEADINGS in Parliament, 1661.
See ENGLAND. Parliament. Placita Parlamentaria.   **2121**

PLEASANT (The) and delightful history of King Henry the 8th and a cobler.   12mo.
London, for C.Dennisson [c.1680]   [Penny-Merriments I]   Woodcut.   **362(38)**

PLEASANT (The) and delightful history of King Henry the 8th: and the Abbot of Reading.   8vo.
London, by J.M. for Charles Dennisson [c.1680]   [Penny-Merriments I]   Woodcut.   **362(37)**

PLEASANT (The) and most delightful history of Argalus and Parthenia, 1683.
See P.(W.).   **1192(7)**

PLEASANT (A) dialogue betwixt honest John and loving Kate.   12mo.
London, for J.Clarke, T.Thackery and T.Passinger, 1685   [Penny-Merriments I]   Woodcut.
Wing P2543.   **362(10)**

PLEASANT (A) discourse between conscience and plain-dealing [c.1680].
See H.(C.).   **362(29)**

PLEASANT (The) history of Cawwood the rook.   4to.
[London] for I.Wright, I.Clarke, W.Thackeray [etc.], 1683   [Vulgaria IV]   Woodcuts.
Wing P2549.   **1193(10)**

PLEASANT (The) history of John Winchcomb [c.1680].
See DELONEY (Thomas).   **1192(19)**

PLEASANT (The) history of the miller: of Mansfield in Sherwood, and Henry the Second.   12mo.
[London] for J.Clarke, W.Thackeray, and T.Passinger [c.1680]   [Penny-Merriments II]   Woodcuts.   **363(7)**

PLEASANT (The) history of Thomas Hic-ka-thrift.   12mo.
[London] by J.M. for W.Thackeray, and T.Passinger [c.1665]   [Penny-Merriments I]   Woodcuts.   **362(3)**

PLEASANT (The) history of Thomas of Reading, 1672.
See DELONEY (Thomas).   **1192(17)**

PLEASANT (The) history of Tom Ladle.   12mo.
[London] for J.Blare [c.1680]   [Penny-Merriments I]   Woodcut.   **362(58)**

PLINY, the elder. The historie of the world: commonly called, The naturall historie. Transl. ... by P.Holland.   2nd ed.   fo.
London, by Adam Islip, 1634   STC 20030.   **2424**

PLINY, the younger. C.Plinii Caecilii Secundi epistolæ et panegyricus.   8vo.
Oxonii, e Theatro Sheldoniano, 1677
Wing P2577.   **1518**

PLOT (Robert). The natural history of Oxfordshire.   fo.
Oxford, printed at the Theater, and are to be had there, and in London at Mr.S.Millers, 1677
Engr. map, pls.   Wing P2586.   **2375**

——————— The natural history of Staffordshire.   fo.
Oxford, at the Theater, 1686   Engr. map, pls.
Wing P2588.   **2529**

PLUNKET (Oliver). The last speech of Mr.Oliver Plunket. ... Executed at Tyburn ... 1st July 1681.   fo.
(London, by N.Thompson, 1681)
[Narratives & Tryals IV]   Wing P2626.   **2252(20)**

PLUTARCH. Βιβλίον πῶς δεῖ τὸν νέον ποιημάτων ἀκούειν. Καὶ Βασιλείου μεγάλου ὁμιλία πρὸς νέους ... Cum interpretatione H.Grotii.   8vo.
Ἐν Ὀξονία, ἐκ Θεάτρου. αχ𝟜δ [1694]
Engr. fp.   Wing P2632.   **1239**

——————— The lives of the noble Grecians & Romans ... Transl. out of Greek into French, by J.Amiot ... and ... into English, by Sir T.North. fo.
London, by Abraham Miller, and are to be sold by William Lee, 1657 (1656)   Engr. title-page.
Wing P2633.   **2493**

——————— Plutarch's lives. Transl. ... by several hands.   5 vols. (Vols 1-3, 2nd ed.)   8vo.
London, printed by T.Hodgkin for Jacob Tonson, (1685-) 1688   Engr. fps, pls.
Wing P2639-40.   **1091-5**

POEMS on several occasions, 1680.
See ROCHESTER (John Wilmot, Earl of).   **810(1)**

[POINCY (Louis de)]. Histoire ... des Iles Antilles, 1665.
See ROCHEFORT (César de).   **1855**

[———————] The history of Barbados, 1666.
See ROCHEFORT (César de).   **2102**

[POINTIS (Jean Bernard Louis Desjean), Sieur de]. Relation de l'expedition de Carthagene faite par les François en M.DC.XCVII.   12mo.
Amsterdam, chez les héritiers d'Antoine Schelte, 1698   2 engr. plans.   **539**

POLANO (Pietro Soave), *pseud.*
See SARPI (Paolo).

POLITI (Lancelotto), Abp of Conza. Excusatio disputationis contra Martinū [Luther] ad vniuersas ecclesias.   4to.
(*Florentiæ, per hæred. Philippi Iuntae*, 1521) Adams C1087.   **1481(2)**

POLITICS. The politicks of France, 1680.
See CHASTELET (Paul Hay, Marquis du).   **578**

POLITIQUE (La) du clergé de France, 1681.
See JURIEU (Pierre).   **206(1)**

POLYBIUS. The history ... Translated by Sir H.S. To which is added, a character of Polybius and his writings: by Mr.Dryden.   2 vols.   8vo.
London, for Samuel Briscoe, 1693   Engr. maps.
Wing P2786.   **1609-10**

——————— Les histoires ... De la traduction de P.du Ryer.   fo.
Paris, chez Augustin Courbé, 1655   **2550**

POMEY (François Antoine). Pantheum mythicum seu fabulosa deorum historia.   Ed. 5.   12mo.
Utrajecti, apud Guiljelmum van de Water, 1697 Engr. title-page, pls.   **686**

POMPA funeral. Honras y exequias en la muerte de ... Doña Isabel de Borbon, reyna de las Españas.   4to.
Madrid, por Diego Diaz de la Carrera, 1645 Engr. title-page, 12 engr. pls.   Gaselee 86.
1777(1)

POMPEY the great. A tragedy, 1664.
See CORNEILLE (Pierre).   **1604(2)**

POMPONATIUS (Petrus). Tractatus de immortalitate animæ.   12mo.
[*Paris*?] 1534 [1634?]   Adams P1829.   **302**

POND (Edward). Pond; an almanack for ... 1688 ... for the meridian of Saffron-Walden in Essex. 8vo.
Cambridge, printed by John Hayes, 1688 [Almanacks for the year 1688]
Wing A2168.   **425(19)**

——————— Pond; an almanack for ... 1689 ... for the meridian of Saffron-Walden in Essex. 8vo.
Cambridge, printed by John Hayes, 1689 [Almanacks for the year 1689]
Wing A2169.   **426(6)**

PONTANUS (Joannes). Discussionum historicarum libri duo ... Accedit ... C.Varrerii de Ophyra regione. (– B.Keckermanni Problemata nautica.) 8vo.
Hardervici Gelrorum, excudebat Nicolaus à Wieringen, 1637   **441**

POOLE (Matthew). Synopsis criticorum aliorumque Sacræ Scripturæ interpretum ... ex recensione J.Leusden.   5 vols.   fo.
Ultrajecti, sumtibus Johannis Ribbii, Johannis van de Water, Francisci Halma sociorum [*etc.*], 1684-6   **2743-7**

POOR (The) doubting Christian, 1683.
See C.(E.).   **365(30)**

POOR ROBIN. The figure of seaven ... by Poor Robin.   8vo.
[*London*] *for J.Conyers* [1686]   [Penny-Merriments I]   **362(34)**

POOR Robin. 1688. An almanack ... 26th impr. 8vo.
London, printed for the Company of Stationers, 1688   [Almanacks for the year 1688]
Wing A2207.   **425(20)**

——————— 1689. An almanack ... (– A prognostication.)   27th impr.   8vo.
London, printed for the Company of Stationers, 1689   [Almanacks for the year 1689]
Wing A2208.   **426(13)**

POST (The) man. No.410. 14 Dec.1697.   8vo.
London, printed for R.Baldwin, 1697 Inserted in Sir P.Rycaut, *The present state of the Ottoman Empire*, after p.160. It contains a translation of the Sultan's order for a day of fasting, prayer and repentance following his defeat at Zenta.   **2372(2)**

PORPHYRIUS, the philosopher. De abstinentia ab animalibus necandis ... L.Holstenius Latine vertit. [*Gk & Lat.*]   2 pts.   8vo.

Cantabrigiæ, impensis Guil.Morden, 1655
Wing P2978.   **751**

PORREÑO (Baltasar). Dichos, y hechos del
Señor Rey Don Felipe Segundo, Monarca de las
Españas, y de las Indias.   8vo.
*Madrid, por Melchor Sanchez, a costa de Mateo de
la Bastida,* 1663   Gaselee 138.   **149**

PORTER (Henry). The pleasant history of the two
angry women of Abington.   4to.
London, for William Ferbrand, 1599
[Old Plays I]   Cropped; MS corrections in
unidentified hand.   STC 20122.   **939(2)**

PORTER (Thomas), dramatist. The carnival: a
comedy.   4to.
London, for Henry Herringman, 1664
[Loose Plays I]   Wing P2988.   **1075(13)**

─────────────── The villain, a tragedy.   8vo.
*London, for Henry Herringman, and Samuel
Speed,* 1663   [Loose Plays I]
Wing P2995; Diary 20 Oct.1662, 7 Sept.1665.
                                          1075(10)

PORTER (Thomas), minister at Whitchurch.
A serious exercitation upon ... 1 John v.20.
4to.
London, by T.R. and E.M. for Ralph Smith,
1651   [Sermons Polemical VI]
Wing P2992.   **1184(14)**

PORTRAITURE. The pourtraiture of His Royal
Highness, Oliver late Lord Protector.   12mo.
London, printed by T.N. for Edward Thomas,
1659   Wing P3004.   **45**

PORTUGAL (The) history ... By S.P., 1677.
See P.(S.).   **991**

POSTE per diuerse parti del mondo ... Con tutte
le fiere notabili ... per il mondo.   12mo.
*(Roma, per il Buagni) si vendono da Francesco
Leone,* 1693   **2(2)**

POTTER (Francis). An interpretation of the
number 666.   4to.
Oxford, by Leonard Lichfield, 1642   Engr. title-
page.   Wing P3028; Diary 18 Feb.1665/6, 4 &
10 Nov.1666.   **1769**

POWELL (Joseph). The death of good Josiah
lamented. A sermon ... preach'd ... March 3.1695.
4to.
London, for Thomas Speed, 1695
Wing P3063.   **1528(8)**

POWELL (Thomas), Londino-Cambrensis.
Direction for search of records remaining in the
Chancerie. Tower. Exchequer.   4to.
London, printed by B.A[lsop]. for Paul Man
[1622]   ¶2, 3 defective.
STC 20166.   **940(2)**

[───────────] The repertorie of records:
remaining in the 4. Treasuries ... at Westminster.
[Based on the work of A.Agarde.]   4to.
*London, printed by B.Alsop and T.Fawcet, for
B.Fisher,* 1631 · STC 194.   **940(1)**

POWELL (Vavasor). [Common-prayer-book no
divine service.]   4to.
[*London, for Livewell Chapman,* 1660]
[Liturgick Controversies II]   Wants sig.A.
Wing P3082.   **1188(18)**

─────────────── God the Father glorified ... A
sermon ... [2nd Dec., 1649].   4to.
London, by Charles Sumptner, for Hannah Allen,
1649   [Sermons Polemical VI]
Wing P3087.   **1184(15)**

POWELL (Walter). Newes for newters: or, the
check, cause, cure of halting ... A sermon,
November 27.1644.   4to.
*London, by Matthew Simmons, and are to be
sold by John Hancock,* 1648   [Sermons
Polemical VI]   Wing P3097.   **1184(16)**

POWER (The) of the Lower House of Convocation
... vindicated, 1701.
See ATTERBURY (Francis), Bp of Rochester.
                                          1697(3)

POWER (Henry). Experimental philosophy, in
three books, containing new experiments.   4to.
*London, by T.Roycroft, for John Martin, and
James Allestry,* 1664 (1663)   Engr. diagrams.
Inserted at end: MS index (4 leaves; in hand of
one of Pepys's clerks) of 'the several minute
Bodies micrographically illustrated' in the book.
Wing P3099; Diary 13, 14 & 16 Aug.1664.   **1422**

POZZO (Andrea). Perspectiva pictorum et
architectorum pars prima. [*Lat. & Ital.*]   fo.
Romæ, typis Joannis Jacobi Komarek, 1693
Engr. fp., 100 engr. pls.   Tanner I, p.316.   **2889**

PRADA (Francisco de). Vejamen con que se afectó
el regozijo del cumplimiento de años de ...
D.Carlos II. en el grado que de doct. en sagrada
theologia recibio Diego de Castel-Blanco.   4to.
[*Seville, Juan Cabezas,* 1676]
Gaselee 139.   **1553(27)**

PRANCE (Miles). A true narrative and discovery
of several ... passages relating to the horrid popish
plot.   fo.
London, for Dorman Newman, 1679
[Narratives & Tryals I]   Engr. fp. (port.,
Charrington p.140). Engr. pl. inserted.
Wing P3177.   **2249(3)**

─────────────── The additional narrative of Miles
Prance.   fo.
*London, for Francis Smith, Thomas Basset, John
Wright* [*etc.*], 1679   [Narratives & Tryals III]
Wing P3170.   **2251(38)**

[PRÉCHAC (Jean de)]. Le beau polonois, nouvelle galante. 12mo.
Paris, 1681   **83(4)**

[————————] La valize ouverte. 12mo.
Suivant la copie imprimée à Paris, chez la veuve d'Olivier de Varennes, 1680   **83(3)**

PREFATORY (A) discourse to an examination of a late book, 1702.
See BINCKES (William), Dean of Lichfield.   **1771**

PRÉSAGES de la décadence des empires, 1688.
See JURIEU (Pierre).   **632**

PRESENT (The) state of Convocation, 1702.
See KENNETT (White), Bp of Peterborough.
                                                1696(14)

PRESENT (The) state of Germany. 8vo.
London, printed for Richard Chiswel, 1690
Wing P3265.   **1201**

PRESENT (The) state of Ireland ... With a map of the kingdome. 12mo.
London, printed by M.D. for Chr.Wilkinson, and T.Burrell, 1673   Engr. map.
Wing P3267.   **361**

PRESTON (Sir Richard Graham, Viscount). The arraignment, trials, conviction and condemnation of Sir Rich.Grahme ... and John Ashton for high-treason. fo.
London, for Samuel Heyrick and Thomas Cockerill, 1691 (1690)   [Narratives & Tryals V]
Wing A3768.   **2253(23)**

PRETENCES (The) of the French invasion examined, 1692.
See LLOYD (William), Bp of St Asaph.   **1432(21)**

PRETENDED (The) expedient, 1702.
See SHERLOCK (William), Dean of St.Paul's.
                                                1696(2)

PRETENDED (The) independence of the Lower House upon the Upper a groundless notion, 1703.
See GIBSON (Edmund), Bp of London.   **1696(18)**

PRETTY. A pretie new enterlude, both pythie and pleasaunt, of the story of King Darius. 4to.
London, by Thomas Colwell, 1565
[Old Plays II]   STC 6277.   **1102(10)**

[PRICE (John), of London]. Honey out of the rock. 4to.
London, by Francis Neile for Henry Overton, 1644   [Sermons Polemical VI]
Wing P3343.   **1184(13)**

PRICE (Sir John). Historiae Brytannicae defensio. 2 pts. 4to.
Londini, impressum in aedibus H.Binneman, impensis Humfredi Toy, 1573   STC 20309;
Howarth p.189.   **1165**

[PRICE (Lawrence)]. The five strange wonders of the world ... By L.P. 8vo.
London, for Margaret White, 1683   [Penny-Merriments II]   **363(2)**

—— ——————— Make room for Christmas. 8vo.
[London] for W.Thackeray, and T.Passinger [c.1680]   [Penny-Merriments I]   Woodcuts.
                                                362(22)

——————————— Variety of new merry riddles. 12mo.
[London] for W.Thackeray, 1684
[Penny-Merriments I]   **362(25)**

PRIDEAUX (Mathias). An easy and compendious introduction for reading all sorts of histories. 4th ed.   2 pts.   4to.
Oxford, for A. & L.Lichfield, to be sold by Joh. Wilmot, & Joh.Crosley, 1664 (1661)
Wing P3443.   **1210**

PRIERES pour l'Hospital Royal des enfans de Dieu. 12mo.
[Paris] de l'imprimerie de François le Cointe, 1688   **24**

[PRIMI VISCONTI (Giovanni Battista), conte di San Maiole]. La campagne du Roy [Louis XIV] en l'année 1677.   12mo.
Paris, chez Estienne Michallet, 1678   Plan.   **531**

PRINCIPLES (The) of Mr.Atterbury's book ... consider'd, 1701.
See WEST (Richard).   **1695(5)**

PRIOLO (Benjamin). The history of France under ... Cardinal Mazarine. Done into English by C.Wase.   8vo.
London, printed for J.Starkey, 1671
Wing P3506A.   **888**

PRITCHARD (Sir William). An exact account of the trial between Sr.William Pritchard ... and Thomas Papillon ... 1684.   fo.
London, by Richard Janeway, 1689
[Narratives & Tryals V]   Wing E3587.
                                                2253(13)

PROCEEDINGS (The) and tryal in the case of ... William [Sancroft] Lord Archbishop of Canterbury [and six other bishops].   fo.
London, for Thomas Basset, and Thomas Fox, 1689   [Narratives & Tryals V]
Engr. fp. (port., Charrington p.17).
Wing S564.   **2253(22)**

PROCEEDINGS (The) at the Assizes holden at York 24 July 1680 ... against several prisoners ... indicted for the horrid popish plot.   fo.
London, for Thomas Simmons, 1681
[Narratives & Tryals IV]   Wing P3557.
                                                2252(12)

PROCLUS, Diadochus. The descripcion of the sphere, or frame of the worlde. (Englysshed by W.Salysburye.)   8vo.
[London] (by me Robert Wier) [1550]
Woodcuts.   STC 20399.   **46(1)**

PROCOPIUS, of Caesarea. The secret history of the Court of the Emperor Justinian.   8vo.
London, printed for John Barkesdale book-binder, 1674   Wing P3641.   **873**

PROFFET (Nicholas). Englands impenitencie under smiting ... A sermon preached ... Sept.25. 1644.   4to.
London, by George Miller for Christopher Meredith, 1645   [Sermons Polemical VI]
Wing P3647.   **1184(17)**

PROPOSAL (A) humbly offered to the consider-ation of the Lord Mayor.   brs.
[London, c.1694]   Bound in at end.   **2476**

PRUDENTIUS CLEMENS (Aurelius). Quæ exstant. N.Heinsius recensuit.   12mo.
Amstelodami, apud Danielem Elzevirium, 1667   **139**

PRYNNE (William). A breviate of the life of William Laud.   fo.
London, by F.L. for Michaell Sparke senior, 1644
Wing P3904.   **2136(1)**

———————— Brief animadversions on, amend-ments of, additional explanatory records to ... the Institutes of the lawes of England.   fo.
London, by Thomas Ratcliffe and Thomas Daniel, for A.Crooke [etc.], 1669
Wing P3905.   **2129**

———————— The first part of a brief register, kalendar and survey of ... Parliamentary writs. 4to.
London, for the author, and sold by Edward Thomas, and Henry Brome, 1659
Wing P3956.   **1319(1)**

———————— The second part of a brief register and survey.   4to.
London, by T.Childe and L.Parry, and are to be sold by Edward Thomas, 1660
Wing P4071.   **1319(2)**

———————— Brevia Parliamentaria rediviva. [Pt.3 of A brief register.]   4to.
London, for the author, and are to be sold by Edward Thomas, 1662
Wing P3902.   **1319(3)**

———————— The fourth part of a brief register, kalender and survey.   4to.
London, by T.Ratcliffe, for the author, and sold by George Thomason, and Edward Thomas, 1664   Wing P3961.   **1320**

———————— Canterburies doome. Or the first part of a compleat history of the commitment, charge, tryall, condemnation, execution of William Laud.   fo.
London, by John Macock, for Michael Spark, 1646   Engr. fp.   Wing P3917.   **2136(2)**

———————— The doome of cowardize and treachery.   4to.
London, for Michael Spark senior, 1643
Wing P3947.   **1660(4)**

[————————] A full declaration of the true state of the secluded members case.   4to.
London, printed, and are to be sold by Edward Thomas, 1660   [Consutilia IV]
Wing P3965.   **1430(13)**

———————— The history of King John, King Henry III. And ... King Edward the I.   fo.
London, printed by Tho.Ratcliff, and Tho.Daniel, for Philip Chetwind [etc.], 1670
Wing P3980.   **2620**

———————— Histrio-mastix.   4to.
London, printed by E.A[llde]. and W.I[ones]. for Michael Sparke, 1633
STC 20464a.   **1195**

———————— A plea for the Lords.   4to.
London, for the author, 1658
Wants last leaf.   Wing P4034.   **1330**

———————— The popish royall favourite.   4to.
London, for Michael Spark senior, 1643
Wing P4039.   **1660(2)**

———————— Romes masterpeece; or, the grand conspiracy of the Pope.   4to.
London, for Michael Sparke senior, 1643
Wing P4055.   **1660(3)**

———————— A short sober pacific examination of some exuberances in, and ceremonial appurt-enances to the Common Prayer.   4to.
London, by T.C. and L.P., and to be sold by Edward Thomas, 1661   [Liturgick Con-troversies III]   Wing P4081.   **1189(7)**

———————— The soveraigne power of parlia-ments and kingdomes ... With an appendix. 5 pts.   4to.
London, (J.D.) for Michael Sparke senior, 1643
Wing P4089.   **1660(1)**

[PSALTER of Jesus]. An inuocacyon gloryous named the psalter of Jesus [1532].
See LITURGIES. Roman Catholic Church. [Horae.] This prymer ...   **23(2)**

PUBLIC. Publick employment and an active life with all its appanages ... prefer'd to solitude, 1667.
See EVELYN (John).   **461**

PUFENDORF (Samuel von), Baron. Commentariorum de rebus Suecicis libri XXVI. Ab expeditione Gustavi Adolfi Regis in Germaniam ad abdicationem usque Christinae.   fo.
Ultrajecti, apud Johannem Ribbium, 1686
Engr. port. (Charrington p.141).   **2836**

———————— De officio hominis et civis juxta legem naturalem libri duo.   8vo.
Londini Scanorum, sumtibus Adami Junghans imprimebat Vitus Haberegger, 1673   **907**

PUGET DE LA SERRE (Jean). Histoire de l'entree de la Reyne Mere ... dans la Grande-Bretaigne.   fo.
Londre, par Jean Raworth, pour George Thomason, & Octauian Pullen, 1639   Engr. title-page, ports (Charrington pp.31, 77).   STC 20488.   **2817**

———————— Histoire de l'entree de la Reyne Mere dans les Provinces Unies des Pays-Bas.   fo.
Londre, par Jean Raworth, pour George Thomason, & Octavian Pullen, 1639   Engr. title-page (port., Charrington p.111), engr. pls, ports (Charrington pp.3, 65).   STC 20489.   **2816**

———————— Le panegyrique de la paix.   fo.
Paris, chez Nicolas Pepingue, 1660
Engr. fp. (port., Charrington p.141), engr. title-page, ports (Charrington pp.74, 116).   **2448**

PUGH (Thomas). Brittish and out-landish prophesies.   4to.
London, printed, and are to be sold by Lodowick Lloyd, 1658   Wing P4188.   **836**

PULPIT (The) guarded with XX arguments, 1652.
See HALL (Thomas).   **1188(19)**

PURCHAS (Samuel). Purchas his pilgrimage, or relations of the world. 4th ed., much enlarged. fo.
London, by William Stansby for Henrie Fetherstone, 1626   Engr. maps.
STC 20508.5.   **2511**

———————— Purchas his pilgrimes.   4 vols. fo.
London, by William Stansby for Henrie Fetherstone, 1625   Engr. title-page, maps.
STC 20509.   **2512-5**

PUTEUS (Andreas).   *See* POZZO (Andrea).

PYRARD (François). Voyage de F.Pyrard ... Contenant sa navigation aux Indes Orientales. Nouvelle ed.   3 pts.   4to.
Paris, chez Louis Billaine, 1679   Engr. fp. (map).
Naval Minutes p.8.   **1853**

Q

[QUARLES (Francis)] . The pleasant ... history of Argalus and Parthenia, 1683.
See P.(W.).   **1192(7)**

QUATRO romances ...
See CUATRO. Quatro romances ...

QUEVEDO VILLEGAS (Francisco de). The life and adventures of Buscon. (— The provident knight.)   2nd ed.   8vo.
London, for Henry Herringman, 1670
Wing Q191A.   **730(3)**

———————— The novels, 1671.
See SALAS BARBADILLO (Alonso Jerónimo de).   **730(2)**

———————— Satiras graciosas.   4to.
(Seuilla, por Iuan de Ossuna, 1676)
Gaselee 70; Wilson p.254.   **1545(35)**

———————— The visions ... Made English by R.L['Estrange] .   3rd ed.   8vo.
London, for H.Herringman, 1668
Wing Q197; Diary 9 June 1667.   **730(1)**

QUINTANADUEÑAS (Antonio). Casos ocurrentes en los jubileos de dos semanas.   12mo.
En Seuilla, por Simon Faiardo, 1641
Gaselee 141.   **20**

QUINTILIAN. Declamationum liber. Cum ejusdem — vt nonnullis visum — dialogo de causis corruptæ eloquentiæ.   8vo.
Oxonii, e Theatro Sheldoniano, 1675
Wing Q222.   **1515**

[QUINZE (Les) joies de mariage.] The batchellor's banquet. [*A translation, ascribed to T.Dekker and R.Tofte, of Les quinze joies de mariage, attributed to A.de La Sale.*]   4to.
London, for Edward Thomas, 1677
[Vulgaria IV]   Woodcut.   Wing B259.   **1193(1)**

QUIROGA (Francisco de).
See JESÚS MARÍA (José de).

R

R.(Rt Hon. the E. of). Poems, 1680.
See ROCHESTER (John Wilmot, Earl of). **810(1)**

R.(B.). Crossing of proverbs, 1683.
See BRETON (Nicholas). **362(53)**

R.(B.). The legend of St.Cuthbert, 1663.
See HEGG (Robert). **131**

R.(B.). Now or never. Work out your salvation.
12mo.
London, for J.Back [c.1685] [Penny-Godli-
nesses] Woodcut. **365(42)**

R.(H.). An essay for a new translation of the
Bible, 1702.
See LE CÈNE (Charles). **1299(1)**

R.(I.). The trades increase, 1615.
See KAYLL (Robert). **1079(5)**

R.(T.). Cornelianum dolium, 1638.
See RANDOLPH (Thomas). **218(1)**

R.(W.). The whole art of palmestry. 8vo.
[*London*] *for P.Brooksby* [c.1685]
[Penny-Merriments II] Woodcut. **363(9)**

RABBOTENU (I.), *pseud.*
See MARNIX (Philips van).

RACINE (Jean). Oeuvres. 2 vols. 12mo.
Paris, chez Claude Barbin, 1676 Engr. pls.
718, 719(1)

———————— Phèdre & Hippolyte. Tragédie.
12mo.
Paris, chez Claude Barbin, 1677 Engr. pl.
719(2)

RALEIGH (Sir Walter). The history of the world.
fo.
London, for Robert White, T.Basset, J.Wright
[*etc.*], 1677 Engr. fp. (port., Charrington
p.142), engr. title-page, maps.
Wing R167. **2649**

———————— An introduction to a breviary of
the history of England. 8vo.
London, for Sam.Keble. And Dan.Brown, 1693
Engr. fp. (port., Charrington p.142).
Wing R169. **611**

———————— Judicious and select essayes and
observations upon the first invention of shipping.
4 pts. 8vo.
London, by T.W. for Humphrey Moseley, 1650
Engr. fp. (port., Charrington p.142).
Wing R170; Naval Minutes pp.6-7. **294**

———————— Remains. 12mo.
London, for Henry Mortlock, 1681
Engr. port., Charrington p.142. Wing R185. **44**

[————————] A report of the truth of the
fight about the Iles of Açores ... Betwixt the
Reuenge ... and an Armada of the King of Spaine.
4to.
London, for William Ponsonbie, 1591
[Consutilia V] STC 20651. **1431(14)**

[RAMSAY (Charles Aloys)]. Nouvelle methode
ou l'art d'écrire aussi vîte qu'on parle.
(Tacheographie.) 12mo.
Paris, chez Louys Pralard, 1690 [Short-hand
Collection II] Engr. pl. Carlton p.115. **401**

RAMUS (Petrus). *See* LA RAMÉE (Pierre de).

RAMUSIO (Giovanni Battista). Nauigationi et
viaggi. 3a ed. 3 vols in 2. fo.
Venetia, nella stamperia de Giunti, 1563-74
Engr. plans, maps. Adams R136, 138, 140.
2231-2

RANCÉ (A.J.Le Bouthillier de).
See LE BOUTHILLIER DE RANCÉ (Armand
Jean).

[RANCHIN (Guillaume)]. A review of the
Councell of Trent ... First writ in French. fo.
*Oxford, by William Turner, for W.T., Edw:
Forrest, and Will:Web*, 1638 STC 20667. **2033**

RANCONNET (Aimar de). Thresor de la langue
françoyse, tant ancienne que moderne ... Reveu et
augmenté ... par J.Nicot. 4 pts.
Paris, chez David Douceur, 1606 **2539**

RANDOLPH (Bernard). The present state of the
islands in the Archipelago. 4to.
Oxford, at the Theater, 1687 Engr. map.
Wing R234. **1742(1)**

———————— The present state of the Morea.
4to.
Oxford, 1686 Engr. map.
Wing R236. **1742(2)**

[RANDOLPH (Thomas)]. Cornelianum dolium.
12mo.
*Londini, apud Tho.Harperum. Et væneunt per
Tho.Slaterum, & Laurentium Chapman*, 1638
Engr. title-page. STC 20691; Diary 14 Nov.,
3 Dec.1660. **218(1)**

RAPHAEL SANZIO. Imagines Veteris ac Novi
Testamenti. [Engr. by C.Fontettus & P.Aquila.]
fo.
Romæ, Io.Iacob de Rubeis, 1675
Engr. title-page, 52 engr. pls. **2961**

RAPIN (René). Of gardens. Four books, first
written in Latine verse. 8vo.
London, T.R. & N.T. for Thomas Collins [*etc.*],
1673 Wing R269A. **1049**

————— Reflections on Aristotle's treatise of poesie. 8vo.
London, by T.N. for H.Herringman, 1674
Wing R270. **861**

[—————] Reflections upon the eloquence of these times; particularly of the barr and pulpit. 8vo.
London, for Richard Preston, 1672
Wing R274. **571**

RASIBUS (Le), ou le procès fait à la barbe des Capucins. Par un moine défroqué. 12mo.
'Cologne, chez Pasquin Resuscité' [*Amsterdam?*], 1680 **99(4)**

[RASTELL (John)]. Of gentylnes ʒ nobylyte. A dyaloge. [Also attributed to J.Heywood.] fo.
[*London*] (*Johēs rastell me fieri fecit*) [1525?]
STC 20723; Duff p.31. **1977(5)**

[—————] Les termes de la ley: or, ... words and terms of the common lawes and statutes ... explained. 8vo.
London, by J.Streater, for the Company of Stationers, 1659 Wing R289. **900**

RAY (John). A collection of curious travels and voyages. 2 pts. 8vo.
London, for S.Smith, and B.Walford, 1693
Wing R385. **1364**

————— A collection of English proverbs, 1678.
See COLLECTION (A) of English proverbs. **619**

————— A collection of English words not generally used. 2nd ed. 12mo.
London, for Christopher Wilkinson, 1691
Wing R389. **397**

————— Three physico-theological discourses. 2nd ed. 8vo.
London, printed for Sam.Smith, 1693
4 engr. pls. Wing R409. **869**

————— The wisdom of God manifested in the works of the creation. 2nd ed. 2 pts. 8vo.
London, printed for Samuel Smith, 1692
Wing R411. **952**

READING (Nathaniel). The tryal of Nathaniel Reading Esq; for attempting to stifle the Kings evidence as to the horrid plot. fo.
London, for Robert Pawlet, 1679
[Narratives & Tryals I] Wing T2205. **2249(13)**

REASON and religion. [Sometimes attributed to J.Locke.] 12mo.
London, for W.Rogers, 1694 Wing L2750;
Tanner I, pp.96, 99. **474**

REASONABLENESS (The) of Christianity, 1695.
See LOCKE (John). **807**

REASONS humbly offer'd, for placing his Highness the Prince of Orange, singly, in the Throne during life. s.sh.fo.
[*London?* 1689] Wing R538. **2441(3)**

REASONS (The) of Mr Joseph Hains ... conversion, 1690.
See BROWN (Thomas). **1427(15)**

REASONS showing that there is no need of such a reformation of the publique Doctrine, &c. as is pretended, 1660.
See SAVAGE (Henry). **1189(2)**

RECONCILING (A) letter upon the late differences [1702].
See KENNETT (White), Bp of Peterborough.
1695(9)

RECORD (Robert). The castle of knowledge. fo.
(*London, by Reginalde Wolfe*, 1556)
Woodcuts. On title-page, autographs 'Marcus Baldin' and 'Edw Shepley. March 16— pro 4^s 6^d'; in margins notes ? by Baldin (in Italian), and by Shepley. STC 20796; Duff p.54. **2049(1)**

RECUEIL d'observations faites en plusieurs voyages ... Par Messieurs de l'Academie Royale des Sciences. 8 pts. fo.
Paris, de l'Imprimerie royale, 1693
Engr. map, plan. **2617**

RECUEIL de divers voyages faits en Afrique et en l'Amerique. [Ed. by H.Justel.] 4to.
Paris, chez la veuve Ant.Cellier, à l'Imprimerie des Roziers, 1684 Engr. pls, maps. **1900**

RECUEIL de diverses relations remarquables des principales cours de l'Europe. Traduites d'un manuscrit Italien. 12mo.
'Cologne, chez Pierre du Marteau', 1681 **233**

RECUEIL des edits ... concernant les duels, 1669.
See FRANCE. *Laws.* **783**

RECUEIL des histoires galantes. 12mo.
Cologne, [c.1665] Wants pp.491-524. **90**

REEDE TOT DRAKESTEIN (Hendrik Adriaan van). Hortus Indicus Malabaricus ... adornatus per H.van Rheede van Draakenstein [*etc.*].
Pts 1-2 only. fo.
Amstelodami, sumptibus Joannis van Someren et Joannis van Dyck, 1678-9 Engr. title-page, 113 engr. pls. **2794**

REFLECTIONS on the paper deliver'd to the Sheriffs of London and Middlesex, by Sir John Fenwick, Bart, at his execution. 4to.
London, printed, and are to be sold by Richard Baldwin, 1697 [Consutilia IX]
Wing R707. **1435(8)**

REFLECTIONS. Reflexions upon a late paper, 1702.
See GIBSON (Edmund), Bp of London. **1696(1)**

REFLECTIONS upon learning ... By a Gentleman,
1700.
See BAKER (Thomas). **1406**

REFLECTIONS. Reflexions upon the devotions
of the Roman Church, 1674.
See PATRICK (John). **1081**

REFLECTIONS upon the eloquence of these
times, 1672.
See RAPIN (René). **571**

REFLECTIONS upon the late King James's
declaration [of 20 Apr.1692], lately dispersed by
the Jacobites. 4to.
London, for Richard Baldwin, 1692
[Consutilia VI] Wing R730. **1432(22)**

REFORMED (The) common-wealth of bees.
Presented in severall letters ... to S.Hartlib [*and ed.
by him*]. With the reform'd Virginian silk-worm.
2 pts. 4to.
London, (by John Streater) for Giles Calvert, 1655
Engr. pls. Wing H997, 1000. **1031**

REFRANES o Proverbios Castellanos, traduzidos
en lengua Francesca ... Par C.Oudin. Reueus ... en
cette derniere edition. 12mo.
Paris, chez Augustin Courbé, 1659
Gaselee 124. **473**

REGIAM majestatem, 1609.
See SCOTLAND. *Laws.* **2043**

REGIS (Pierre Sylvain). Cours entier de philos-
ophie. Dernière éd. 3 vols. 4to.
*Sur l'imprimé de Paris. Amsterdam, aux depens
des Huguetans*, 1691 Engr. fp. (port.), map,
engr. & woodcut diagrams. **1858-60**

REHEARSAL (The) transpros'd, 1672-3.
See MARVELL (Andrew). **710-11**

RELACION verdadera de los hechos de Mateo
Venet, natural de Valencia. 4to.
*(Seuilla, por Juan Vejarano, à costa de Lucas
Martin de Hermosa)* [c.1680] Gaselee 182;
Wilson p.257. **1545(39)**

RELACION verdadera que da cuenta de vn
grandioso milagro, que obro la Virgen del Rosario
con vn Cauallero ... de Barcelona. 4to.
*Seuilla, por Juan Vejarano, à costa de Lucas
Martin de Hermosa*, 1682 Gaselee 142;
Wilson p.146. **1545(6)**

RELATION de l'expedition de Carthagene faite
par les François en M.DC.XCVII., 1698.
See POINTIS (Jean Bernard Louis Desjean),
Sieur de. **539**

RELATION de l'Inquisition de Goa, 1687.
See DELLON (Charles). **78**

[RELATION des différends arrivés en Espagne.]
The Spanish history: or, a relation of the differ-
ences ... between Don John of Austria, and
Cardinal Nitard. [Transl.] 8vo.
*London, printed for Will.Cademan, and Simon
Neale*, 1678 Wing S4804. **1035**

RELATION du voyage d'Espagne, 1691.
See AULNOY (Marie-Catherine Le Jumel de
Barneville, comtesse d'). **298**

RELATION (A) in form of Journal, of the voiage
and residence which ... Charles the II King of
Great Britain, &c. hath made in Holland. Rendered
... out of the original French. fo.
Hague, by Adrian Vlack, 1660 Engr. port.
(Charrington p.33), pls. Wing R781. **2821**

RÉLATION nouvelle d'un voyage de Constantinople, 1681.
See GRELOT (Guillaume Joseph). **512**

RELATION (A) of the defeating Card.Mazarine &
Oliv.Cromwel's design to have taken Ostend by
treachery, in the year, 1658. Written in Spanish ...
now translated into English. 12mo.
London, for Hen.Herringman, 1666
Wing R821. **142**

RELATIONS and observations ... upon the
Parliament begun Anno Dom.1640, 1648.
See WALKER (Clement). **1148(1)**

RELIGION (La) ancienne et moderne des Moscovites, 1698.
See SCHLEISSING (Georg Adam). **527**

REMARKS. Remarques relating to the state of
the church of the first centuries, 1680.
See SELLER (Abednego). **1140**

REMARQUES ou reflexions critiques, morales et
historiques, 1692.
See BORDELON (Laurent). **338**

REMONSTRANCE (A) against the nonresidents,
1642.
See BLAXTON (John). **1428(2)**

[RENAU D'ELIÇAGARAY (Bernard)]. De la
theorie de la manœuvre des vaisseaux. 8vo.
Paris, chez Estienne Michallet, 1689
Engr. title-page, 25 engr. diagrams. **1415**

REPERTORY. The repertorie of records, 1631.
See POWELL (Thomas), Londino-Cambrensis.
940(1)

REPORT (A) of the truth of the fight about the
Iles of Açores, 1591.
See RALEIGH (Sir Walter). **1431(14)**

REPROOF (A) to the Rehearsal transprosed,
1673.
See PARKER (Samuel), Bp of Oxford. **1052**

RERUM Anglicarum scriptores post Bedam
præcipui. [Ed. by Sir H.Savile.]   fo.
*Francofurti, typis Wechelianis, apud Claudium
Marnium & heredes Ioannis Aubrij*, 1601   **2561**

RERUM Anglicarum scriptorum veterum tom.I.
[Ed. by W.Fulman.]   fo.
Oxoniæ, e theatro Sheldoniano, 1684
Wing F2525.   **2628**

Continued as:

Historiæ Britannicæ ... scriptores XV. Opera T.
Gale. 2 vols. (*Vol.2 entitled:* Historiæ Anglicanæ
scriptores quinque.)   fo.
Oxoniae, e theatro Sheldoniano, 1691
Wing G154.   **2629-30**

RESTITUTION of decayed intelligence in
antiquities, 1673.
See ROWLANDS (Richard).   **834**

RESURRECTION (The) rescued from the soldiers
calumnies, 1659.
See LUSHINGTON (Thomas).   **57**

REVIEW (A) of the Councell of Trent, 1638.
See RANCHIN (Guillaume).   **2033**

REVIEW (A) of the universal remedy for all
diseases incident to coin ... In a letter to Mr.Locke.
8vo.
London, printed for A. and J.Churchill, 1696
Wing R1200.   **796(2)**

REYES (Félix de los). Historia sagrada, de la vida
de Christo ... en vn romance.   4to.
Seuilla, por Iuan Cabeças, 1679   Gaselee 143;
Wilson p.148.   **1545(7)**

REYNARD the fox.   fo.
[*W.Caxton, Westminster*, 1489]
See Appendix.   **1796**

REYNER (Edward). Orders from the Lord of
Hostes ... a sermon ... preached ... 27th of March,
1646.   4to.
London, by R.W. for Giles Calvert, 1646
[Sermons Polemical VI]   Wing R1222.
1184(18)

REYNOLDS (Edward), Bp of Norwich. Self-
deniall: opened and applied in a sermon.   4to.
London, for Robert Bostock, 1646
[Sermons Polemical VI]   Wing R1278.
1184(20)

REYNOR (William). Babylons ruining-earthquake
and the restauration of Zion. Delivered in a sermon
... August 28.1644.   4to.
London, by T.B. for Samuel Enderby, 1644
[Sermons Polemical VI]   Wing R1324.
1184(19)

RHAESUS (Joannes David).
See RHYS (John David).

RHETORES selecti. Demetrius Phalereus, Tiberius
Rhetor, Anonymus Sophista, Severus Alexan-
drinus. Græcè & Latinè. (Edidit T.Gale.)   8vo.
Oxonii, e Theatro Sheldoniano, 1676
Wing G157.   **1650**

[RHODES (Alexandre de)]. Divers voyages de la
Chine, et autres royaumes de l'Orient.   4to.
Paris, chez Christophe Iournel, 1682   **1915**

RHYS (John David). Cambrobrytannicæ
Cymraecæue linguæ institutiones et rudimenta.
fo.
Londini, excudebat Thomas Orwinus, 1592
On title-page, in Jonson's hand: 'Sū Ben:Jonsonij
ex Dono. Amicissimi.D.Jacobij.Howell.Kal.Jan
CIƆ IƆ C XXXIV.', with motto, 'tanquam ex-
plorator'; and autograph Gill(?) Bomell(?). On
front flyleaf, in Howell's hand, recording the gift,
a Latin inscription and a poem in English (the
latter printed in Howell, Epistolae Ho-Elianae
(1655 ed.), p.224.   STC 20966.   **2044**

RIBADENEYRA (Pedro de). Flos sanctorum o
libro de las vidas de los santos.   3 pts.   fo.
*Madrid, en la Imprenta real, acosta de Iuan de San
Vicente*, 1675   Gaselee 144.   **2138**

——————— Les fleurs des vies des saints et
festes de toute l'année.   2 vols in 1.   fo.
Rouen, chez la vefue de Louis Costé, 1659
Engr. title-page, pls.   **2619**

——————— Historia eclesiastica del scisma del
reyno de Inglaterra.   3a ed.   4to.
*Madrid, en la Imprenta real, a costa de Florian
Anisson*, 1674   Gaselee 145.   **1547**

RICCI (Olimpio). De' giubilei universali celebrati
negli anni santi incominciando da Bonifazio VIII.
fino al presente.   8vo.
Roma, per il Mascardi, 1675   **720**

RICCIUS (Bartholomaeus). Triumphus Iesu Christi
crucifixi ... A.Collaert figuras sculpsit.   8vo.
(*Antverpiæ, ex officina Plantiniana, apud Ioannem
Moretum*, 1608)   Engr. title-page, pls. Wants
pls 69, 70.   **1070**

RICH (Jeremiah). The penns dexterity ... By I.Rich.
brs.
[*London*] *sould at his house*, 1659
Engr. port., Charrington p.143.   [Short-hand
Collection V]   Inserted at end, in hand of one
of Pepys's clerks, a guide to the contents of all five
volumes of the Short-hand Collection, 25 March
1695.   Wing R1346; Carlton p.55.   **1111(3)**

RICHARDSON (John). The canon of the New
Testament vindicated; in answer to the objections
of J.T[oland]. in his Amyntor.   8vo.
London, for Richard Sare, 1700
Wing R1384.   **1306**

RICHELIEU (Armand Jean du Plessis, Cardinal Duc de). Testament politique, 1688.
See CHASTELET (Paul Hay, Marquis du).   **80**

[RICHER (L.)]. L'Ovide bouffon, ou les Metamorphoses travesties en vers burlesques.   4e éd.
12mo.
Paris, chez Estienne Loyson, 1665   Engr. title-page.   **427**

RIDER (Cardanus). Riders — 1688.— British Merlin.   12mo.
London, printed by Tho.Newcomb, for the Company of Stationers, 1688   [Almanacks for the year 1688]   Wing A2258B.   **425(21)**

RIDER (William). The twins. A tragi-comedy.
4to.
London, for Robert Pollard, and John Sweeting, 1655   [Loose Plays I]   Wing R1446.
                                                1075(7)

RIDLEY (Mark). Magneticall animadversions ... upon certaine magneticall advertisements, lately published, from Maister William Barlow.   4to.
London, by Nicholas Okes, 1617
STC 21044.   **928(3)**

——————————— A short treatise of magneticall bodies and motions.   4to.
London, by Nicholas Okes, 1613   Engr. title-page, port., diagrams.   STC 21045.5.   **928(1)**

RIDLEY (Sir Thomas). A view of the civile and ecclesiasticall law. 3rd ed., by J.G[regory].   8vo.
Oxford, by W.Hall for Edw.Forrest, 1662
Diary 29 Apr.1666.   **899**

RIDPATH (George). Short-hand yet shorter.   8vo.
London, printed by J.D. for the author, 1687
[Short-hand Collection IV]   Engrs.
Wing R1466; Carlton p.109.   **860(7)**

RIGHT (The) of the Archbishop to continue or .prorogue the whole Convocation, 1701.
See GIBSON (Edmund), Bp of London.   **1695(7)**

RIGHT (A) pithy, pleasant, and merry comedy, entituled, Gammer Gurtons needle, 1661.
See STEVENSON (William).   **1103(3)**

RIGHTS (The) and liberties of Englishmen asserted, 1701.
See WAGSTAFFE (Thomas).   **1437(9)**

RIGHTS (The) of the Bishops to judge in capital cases in Parliament, cleared, 1680.
See HUNT (Thomas).   **839**

RIGHTS of the Kingdom: or, customs of our ancestors, 1682.
See SADLER (John).   **1588**

RINGROSE (Basil). The dangerous voyage ... of Captain B.Sharp, 1685.
See EXQUEMELIN (Alexander Olivier). Bucaniers of America, vol.2.   **1876**

RIPA (Cesare). Iconologie ou la science des emblemes, devises, &c. ... tirées la pluspart de C.Ripa. Par J.B[audoin].   2 vols.   12mo.
Amsterdam, chez Adrian Braakman, 1698
Engr. title-pages, 79 pls.   **728-9**

RIPIA (Juan de la). Practica de testamentos, y modos de suceder.   4to.
Pamplona, 1692   Gaselee 147.   **1593(2)**

RIPLEY (George). The compound of alchymy.
4to.
London, by Thomas Orwin, 1591   Engr. pl.
STC 21057.   **985(2)**

ROBERT II, King of Scotland. Charta authentica ... cum observationibus historicis, quibus regiæ Stuartorum stirpis natales ab inusta labe vindicantur.   4to.
(Parisiis, ex typographia Francisci Muguet, 1695)
Woodcuts.   **2072**

ROBERTS (A.). The adventures of (Mr T.S.) an English merchant, 1670.
See S.(T.).   **244(2)**

ROBERTS (Francis). A broken spirit ... A sermon ... Decemb.9.1646.   4to.
London, for George Calvert, 1647
[Sermons Polemical VI]   Wing R1580.
                                                1184(21)

ROBERTS (Lewes). The merchants map of commerce.   2nd ed.   fo.
London, for R.Horn, and are to be sold by G. Saubridge, J.Martyn [etc.], 1671   4 engr. maps, dated 1668.   Wing R1599[?].   **2367**

ROBIN Hoods garland.   8vo.
[*London*] *by J.M. for J.Clarke, W.Thackeray, T.Passinger* [c.1685]   [Penny-Merriments III]
Woodcut.   **364(4)**

ROBINS (Thomas). The arraigning and indicting of Sir John Barley-Corn.   12mo.
[*London*] *for Thomas Passinger, and are to be sold by J.Deacon* [c.1680]   [Penny-Merriments I]   Woodcut.   **362(4)**

ROBINSON (John). Endoxa seu quæstionum quarundam miscellanearum examen probabile.
8vo.
Londini, typis T.N., impensis Sa.Thomson, 1656
Wing R1702.   **724**

ROBLES (Eugenio de). Compendio de la vida y hazañas del Cardenal F.Ximenez de Cisneros.
4to.
(Toledo, por Pedro Rodriguez) 1604   Engr. port.
Gaselee 148.   **1460**

ROBLES CORVALAN (Juan). El misterioso aparecimiento de la Santissima Cruz de Caravaca. 4to.
En Sevilla, por Juan Vejarano, à costa de Lucas Martin de Hermosa [c.1680]
Gaselee 149; Wilson p.141.   **1545(2)**

[ROBSON (Simon)]. A new yeeres gift. The courte of ciuill courtesie ... Out of Italian by S.R. [Purporting to be a translation from B.del Mont. Prisacchi Retto, but in fact written by Robson.] 4to.
London, Richard Jhones, 1577
Autograph obliterated and illegible on title-page.
STC 21134.5.   **941(3)**

ROCCA (Angelo), Bp of Tagasti. De canon-izatione sanctorum commentarius.   2. ed.   4to.
Romæ, ex typographia Reu.Cam.Apost., 1610
MS addition on p.135 (St Charles Borromeo, 1610) in unidentified hand.   **1726**

[ROCHEFORT (César de)]. Histoire naturelle et morale des Iles Antilles de l'Amerique.   2e ed.
[*Also attributed to L.de Poincy.*]   4to.
Roterdam, chez Arnout Leers, 1665   Engr. pls.
1855

[—————] The history of Barbados ... Englished by J.Davies. [*Also attributed to L.de Poincy.*]   fo.
*London, for John Starkey, and Thomas Dring jun*ʳ, 1666   Engr. pls.   Wing R1739.   **2102**

[ROCHESTER (John Wilmot, Earl of)]. Poems on several occasions.   8vo.
'*Antwerp*' [*London?*], 1680   Engr. fp. (port., Charrington p.146); 10 MS poems inserted, (q.v. below, vol.V).   Wing R1753; Howarth p.105.
810(1)

RODOMONTADES (Les) et emblemes espagnolles. Traduit de castillien. (— Rodomuntadas castellanas ... Rodomontades espagnolles.) ([Ed. by] I.Gaul-tier.)   2 pts.   12mo.
Rouen, chez Claude le Villain, 1637   Woodcuts.
Gaselee 68.   **46(4)**

RODRIGUEZ (Pedro). Coplas del Perro de Alva [i.e. P.Rodriguez], en las quales se trata, como los Judios le procuraron matar, y de como el Perro se librò dellos.   4to.
(*Sevilla, por Iuan Cabeças, a costa de Lucas Martin de Hermosilla,* 1676)
Gaselee 150; Wilson p.268.   **1545(55)**

—————— La tragedia del Conde Alarcos, y de la Infanta.   4to.
(*Seuilla, vendese en casa de Juan Cabeças*)
[c.1680]   Gaselee 151; Wilson p.306.
1545(58)

RODRIGUEZ DE MONFORTE (Pedro). Des-cripcion de las honras que se hicieron ala Cath-olica Magd. de D.Phelippe quarto Rey de las

Españas.   4to.
(*Madrid, por Francisco Nieto,* 1666)
Engr. title-page, 49 engr. pls.   Gaselee 152.
1777(2)

[ROE (Sir Thomas)]. A true and faithfull relation ... of what hath lately happened in Constantinople concerning the death of Sultan Osman.   4to.
London, [*F.Kingston*] *for Bartholomew Downes, to be sold at his house, and by William Sheffard,* 1622   [Consutilia V]   STC 18507.71A.
1431(12)

ROHAN (Henri, Duc de). De l'interest des princes et estats de la chrestienté. Derniere ed. 12mo.
[*Amsterdam?*] *iouxte la copie imprimée à Paris,* 1639   **18**

ROHAULT (Jacques). Tractatus physicus ... Latinitate donatus per Th.Bonetum.   2 pts. 8vo.
Londini, impensis G.Wells & A.Swalle, 1682
Diagrams.   Wing R1871.   **1278**

ROJAS ZORRILLA (Francisco de). La segunda Magdalena, y sirena de Napoles. Comedia famosa. 4to.
[*Seville, Tomé de Dios Miranda,* c.1675]
Gaselee 154.   **1553(12)**

—————— Los trabajos de Tobias. La nueua. Comedia famosa.
[*Seville, Tomé de Dios Miranda,* c.1675]
Gaselee 155.   **1553(25)**

—————— No ay dicha, ni desdicha hasta la muerte. Comedia famosa.
[*Seville, Juan Cabezas,* c.1678]
Gaselee 153.   **1553(24)**

ROMAN. Roman-Catholick doctrines no novelties, 1663.
See CRESSY (Hugh Paulin).   **575**

[ROMÁN (Comendador)]. La passion de ... Iesu Christo ... Compuesta por D.de San Pedro [or rather by C.Román].   4to.
Seuilla, por Iuan de Ossuna, 1677
Gaselee 162; Wilson p.240.   **1545(25)**

ROMAN CATHOLIC CHURCH.
For liturgical books, see LITURGIES. *Roman Catholic Church.*

ROMAN CATHOLIC CHURCH. Epitome canonum, 1684.
See BRANCATI (Lorenzo), Cardinal.   **2486**

ROMAN CATHOLIC CHURCH. *Congregatio Riparum Tyberi.* Remunerationis pro illustriss. D.Cornelio Meyer memoriale.   fo.
(*Romæ, ex typographia Reu.Cam.Apost.,* 1685)
2887

ROMANA (Lucretia). Ornamento nobile, per ogni gentil matrona, dove si contiene bavari.   fo.
Venetia, appresso Lessandro de'Vecchi, 1620
2097

ROMANCE del noble ... Don Reynaldos de Montalvan trata, como Carlo-Magno lo tenia preso para lo ahorcar, por los falsos consejos de Galalon. (*Sevilla, por Juan Vejarano, à costa de Lucas Martin de Hermosa*) [c.1680]
Gaselee 146; Wilson p.305.   **1545(57)**

ROME. Notitia ... dignitatum, 1608.
See NOTITIA ...   **2457**

ROME. *Collegium Romanum Societatis Jesu.* Gregorianæ Academiæ obsequium Iacobo II. Magnæ Britanniæ regi ... præstitum.   fo.
Romæ, sumptibus Nicolai Angeli Tinassij, 1687
Engr. fp., engr. pls.   **2721(1)**

ROME exactly describ'd ... under Pope Alexandre the seventh. In two curious discourses. (A new relation of Rome, *and* A relation of the state of the court of Rome, made in ... 1661 ... by ... A.Corraro.)   2 pts.   8vo.
London, by T.Mabb, for Mich. Young, and J.Starkey [etc.], 1664   Engr. fp. (port., Charrington p.2).   Wing C6345; Diary 18 Dec. 1663.   **383(1)**

ROOKWOOD (Ambrose). The arraignment, tryal, and condemnation of Ambrose Rookwood.   fo.
London, for Samuel Heyrick; and Isaac Cleave, 1696   [Narratives & Tryals VI]
Wing A3755.   **2254(10)**

ROOMS and offices bought and sold in the City of London.   brs.
[*London*, c.1696]   Bound in at end.   **2476**

[ROPER (Abel)]. The life of William Fuller, the late pretended evidence now a prisoner in the King's Bench. [By A.Roper?]   4to.
London, for Abel Roper, 1692   [Consutilia VI]
Wing L2039.   **1432(8)**

ROSE (George). Rose 1688. A new almanack for ... 1688.   8vo.
London, printed by Thomas Hodgkin, for the Company of Stationers, 1688   [Almanacks for the year 1688]   Wing A2294A.   **425(22)**

ROSINUS (Joannes). Antiquitatum Romanarum corpus absolutissimum.   4to.
Amstelodami, ex typographia Blaviana, 1685
Engr. title-page, pls, plan.   Diary 12 Sept.1660.
1869

ROSS (Alexander). Πανσεβεια: or, a view of all religions in the world.   4th ed.   2 pts.   8vo.
[*London*] *for John Williams*, 1672 (1671)
Engr. fp. (port., Charrington p.147), ports.
Wing R1975.   **885**

ROSSETTO (Pietro). Breve descrittione delle cose più notabili di Gaeta ... spiegata in otto discorsi. 12mo.
Nap[*oli*], *nella stampa del Mutio* [1699]   **346(3)**

ROSSFELD (Johann).   *See* ROSINUS (Joannes).

[ROSSI (Filippo)]. Descrizione di Roma antica formata nuovamente. (— Descrizione di Roma moderna.)   2 vols.   8vo.
Roma, nella libreria di Michel'Angelo e Pier Vincenzo Rossi, 1697   Engrs, woodcuts.   **800-801**

ROSSI (Giovanni Giacomo de'). Indice delle stampe intagliate in rame, al bulino, ed all' acqua forte ... Esistenti nella stamperia di G.G.de Rossi. 12mo.
Roma (*nella stamperia di Antonio de Rossi*), 1696
491(1)

———————— Altro indice delle carte ... che si ritrovano nella stamperia di G.G.de Rossi in Roma. 12mo.
Roma (*nella stamparia di Antonio de Rossi*), 1699
491(2)

———————— Insignium Romæ templorum prospectus ... a J.J.de Rubeis ... in lucem editi, 1684.
See INSIGNIUM Romæ templorum ...   **2960**

ROTA (The): or, a model of a Free-State, 1660.
See HARRINGTON (James), the elder.   **1297(2)**

ROTE (The) or mirror of consolation.   4to.
W.de Worde, Westminster [1499]
See Appendix.   **1254(4)**

ROUGH (A) draft of a new model at sea, 1694.
See HALIFAX (George Savile, 1st Marquis of).
1399(11)

ROWE (Robert). Mr.Harrison proved the murtherer.   4to.
London, for Randal Taylor, 1692
[Consutilia VI]   Wing R2069.   **1432(6)**

ROWLANDS (Richard).
See VERSTEGAN (Richard).

ROXAS (Francisco de).
See ROJAS ZORRILLA (Francisco de).

ROYAL (The) book [1507].
See LAURENT, Dominican.   **1011(1)**

ROYAL (The) Family described.   4to.
London, printed and sold by Benj.Bragg, 1702
[Consutilia X]   **1436(6)**

ROYAL (The) garland, 1681.
See DELONEY (Thomas).   **363(39)**

ROYAL (The) sufferer. A manual of meditations and devotions, 1699.
See KEN (Thomas), Bp of Bath and Wells.   **1002**

ROYAL COLLEGE OF PHYSICIANS.
Pharmacopœia Londinensis. Or, the new London
dispensatory ... transl. ... by W.Salmon.   4th ed.
8vo.
London, printed for T.Bassett, R.Chiswell,
M.Wotton [etc.], 1691
Wing S440.   **1076**

ROYAL COLLEGE OF PHYSICIANS. The
Statutes.   12mo.
[London] 1693   Some leaves cropped.
Wing S5340.   **341**

ROYAL SOCIETY. Philosophical transactions,
1667-1704.
See PHILOSOPHICAL transactions.
1701-1712(1), 1713(1)

ROYAUMONT, Le Sieur de.
See FONTAINE (Nicolas).

RUFO GUTIERREZ (Juan). Romance de la
muerte de los comendadores, que matô Fernando
Veintiquatro de la Ciudad de Cordova, y de su
muger.   4to.
(Sevilla, por Thome de Dios Miranda, à costa de la
viuda de Nicolas Rodrigues, 1675)
Gaselee 158; Wilson p.257.   **1545(38)**

RUGGLE (George). Ignoramus. Comœdia.
Ed.4.   12mo.
Londini, ex officina I.R [edmayne]., 1659
Engr. fp.   Wing R2214.   **53**

RUMP: or an exact collection of the choycest
poems and songs relating to the late times. ... From
... 1639 to ... 1661. *[Ed. by A.Brome?]*   8vo.
London, for Henry Brome, and Henry Marsh,
1662   Engr. title-page.   Wing B4851.   **866**

RUSDEN (Moses). A further discovery of bees.
8vo.
London, printed for the author, sold at his house,
and by Henry Million, 1679   Engr. fp., pls.
Wing R2313.   **865**

RUSHWORTH (John). Historical collections.
Pts 1-4 in 7 vols.   fo.
London, by Tho.Newcomb [etc.], 1659-1701
Engr. fps (ports, Charrington pp.31, 85, 148), pls.
Wing R2316, 2318, 2319; Diary 23, 30 Nov.,
6, 10 Dec.1663; 15 Jan.1664/5.   **2386-93**

RUSSELL (William, Lord). The speech of the late
Lord Russel ... at the place of execution.   fo.
(London, by John Darby, by direction of the
Lady Russel, 1683)   [Narratives & Tryals V]
Wing R2356.   **2253(2)**

RUTHERFORD (Samuel). A sermon preached ...
Janu.31., 1643.   4to.
London, by Richard Cotes, for Richard Whit-
takers & Andrew Crooke, 1644
[Sermons Polemical VI]   MS notes in un-
identified 17th-cent. hand.
Wing R2391.   **1184(22)**

RUTHVEN (Patrick Ruthven, 3rd Baron). A relation of the death of David Rizzi.   8vo.
London, for A.Baldwin, 1699   **1454**

RUTTER (The) of the Sea [1555?].
See GARCIE (Pierre).   **96(1)**

RYCAUT (Sir Paul). The history of the Turkish
Empire from the year 1623 to ... 1677.   4to.
London, by J.M. for John Starkey, 1680
Engr. fp. (port., Charrington p.148), pl., ports.
Wing R2406.   **2302**

——————————The present state of the Greek and
Armenian churches.   8vo.
London, for John Starkey, 1679
Wing R2411.   **1022**

——————————The present state of the Ottoman
Empire.   fo.
London, for John Starkey and Henry Brome, 1667
Engr. pls (col.).   MS note in Pepys's hand on
verso of title-page, comparing prices of the volume
before & after the Fire.   Wing R2412; Diary
15 Oct.1666; 20 March, 8, 14, 21 April & 3 May
1667.   **2372(1)**

RYLEY (William). Placita Parlamentaria, 1661.
See ENGLAND. *Parliament.*   **2121**

RYSWICK, *Peace of.*   *See* FRANCE. *Treaties.*

RYVES (Sir Thomas). Historia naualis antiqua,
libris quatuor.   8vo.
Londini, apud Robertum Barker: et hæred. Io.
Billii, 1633   Engr. pl.
STC 21475; Naval Minutes p.101.   **760(1)**

——————————Historiæ naualis mediæ libri tres.
8vo.
Londini, apud Richardum Hodgkinsonne, 1640
STC 21476.   **760(2)**

S

S.(   ), M.A. Gammer Gurtons needle, 1661.
See STEVENSON (William).   **1103(3)**

S.(A.). Remarques relating to the state of the
church, 1680.
See SELLER (Abednego).   **1140**

S.(B.D.). Opera posthuma, 1677.
See SPINOZA (Benedict de).   **1376**

[S.(E.).]. Historia Britannica, 1640.
See HISTORIA Britannica.   **28**

S.(H.), D.D. Reasons shewing that there is no need of such a reformation, 1660.
See SAVAGE (Henry). **1189(2)**

S.(I.). A brief and perfect journal of the late proceedings and success of the English army in the West-Indies. 4to.
London, 1655 Wing S35. **1431(11)**

[S.(J.). Certaine worthye manuscript poems ... now first published by J.S. [i.e. J.Stow?]. 3 pts. 8vo.
London, for R.D., 1597] Wants all except pt 2, entitled 'The northren mothers blessing. *By Robert Robinson for Robert Dexter*, 1597'.
STC 21499. **29(4)**

S.(J.). The famous history of Aurelius, the valiant London-prentice.
[*London*] *printed for J.Back*, 1686 [Penny-Merriments I] Woodcut. **362(14)**

S.(J.). The honour of chivalry. The second and third part, 1683.
See FERNÁNDEZ (Jerónimo). **1190(2)**

S.(R.). The counter scuffle, 1693.
See SPEED (Robert). **1193(19)**

S.(T.). The adventures of (Mr T.S.) an English merchant, taken prisoner by the Turks ... Written first by the author, and fitted for the publick view by A.Roberts. 8vo.
London, printed, and are to be sold by Moses Pitt, 1670 Wing S152. **244(2)**

S.(T.). Love a la mode, 1663.
See SOUTHLAND (Thomas). **1075(11)**

S.(W.). [A compendious or briefe examination.] (1581).
See STAFFORD (William). **1431**

SAAVEDRA FAJARDO (Diego de). Idea principis Christiano-politici 101 symbolis expressa. 12mo.
Amstelodami, apud Joannem Jacobi fil:Schipper, 1659 Engr. title-page, pls. **91**

SACCHI (Bartolomeo), de Platina.
See PLATINA (Bartolomeo).

SACK-FUL (The) of news. 12mo.
[*London*] *by H.B. for J.Clark, W.Thackeray, and T.Passinger*, 1685 [Penny-Merriments I] Woodcut. **362(6)**

SADELER (Aegidius). Vestigi delle antichita di Roma, Tivoli, Pozzuolo et altri luochi. fo.
Roma, Gio Iacomo de Rossi, 1660 50 engr. pls. **2955**

[SADLER (Anthony)]. Inquisitio Anglicana: or the disguise discovered ... in the examinations of Anthony Sadler. 4to.

London, by J.Grismond, for Richard Royston, 1654 [Consutilia II] Wing S265. **1428(16)**

[SADLER (John)]. Rights of the kingdom: or, customs of our ancestors. 4to.
London, printed for J.Kidgell, 1682 On title-page, in Pepys's hand: 'By one Sadler'.
Wing S279. **1588**

SAFEGUARD. The safegarde of saylers, 1590.
See ANTHONISZ (Cornelis). **1078(2)**

SAINT AMANT (Marc Antoine de Gérard, Sieur de). Moyse sauvé, idyle heroïque. 12mo.
Leyde, chez Jean Sambix, 1654 **30**

SAINT AMOUR (Louis Gorin de). The Journal. fo.
London, by T.Ratcliff, for H.Robinson and G.Thomason, 1664 Wing S296. **2458**

SAINT BARTHOLOMEW'S HOSPITAL. The ordre of the Hospital of.S.Bartholomewes in west-smythfielde in London. 8vo.
Londini (by Rycharde Grafton), 1552 STC 21557; Duff p.40. **138**

SAINT. St Cecily: or, the converted twins, 1666.
See MEDBOURNE (Matthew). **1604(7)**

SAINT-EVREMOND (Charles de Marguetel de Saint-Denis), Seigneur de. Oeuvres meslées. Nouvelle impr. 4 vols in 2. 8vo.
Paris, chez Claude Barbin, 1693 **483-4**

———————— Saint-Evremoniana, ou Dialogues des nouveaux dieux. 12mo.
Paris, chez Michel Brunet, 1700 **855**

[SAINT GERMAN (Christopher)]. Salem and Bizance. 8vo.
(*Londini, in ædibus Thomæ Bertheleti*, 1533) STC 21584; Duff p.57. **752(1)**

[————————] A treatise concernynge the diuision betwene the spiritualtie and temporaltie. 8vo.
(*Londini, in edibus Thome Bertheleti*) [1532?] STC 21587.5; Duff p.56. **368(1)**

SAINT JULIEN (Pierre de). De l'origine des Bourgongnons. fo.
Paris, chez Nicolas Chesneau (achevé d'imprimer par Henry Thierry), 1581 Woodcut plans.
Adams S90. **2435**

SAINT LO (George). England's interest; or, a discipline for seamen. 4to.
London, for Richard Baldwin, 1694 [Naval Pamphlets] **1399(12)**

———————— England's safety: or, a bridle to the French King. 4to.

London, for W.Miller, 1693   [Naval Pamphlets]
At end, MS additions (2 leaves) from second
edition ('Reasons ... for bringing down the
exorbitant Rates of Seamens Wages ...'), in hand
of one of Pepys's clerks.   Wing S341.   **1399(9)**

SAINT MARTIN (Michel de), Abbé. Le gouverne-
ment de Rome.   2e ed.   8vo.
Caen, chez Claude Le Blanc, 1659
Sig. [ò] misbound.   **725**

SALAS BARBADILLO (Alonso Jerónimo de). El
cauallero puntual ... Año 1616.   12mo.
*Madrid, per Iuã de la Cuesta, a costa de Miguel
Martinez*, 1616 (1615)   Gaselee 159.   **54**

[————————] The novels of Dom Francisco de
Quevedo Villegas. [Or rather, an adaptation of
A.J. de Salas Barbadillo's Don Diego de noche.]
Faithfully Englished ... The marriage of Belphegor
... from Machiavel.   8vo.
London, for John Starkey, 1671
Wing Q192.   **730(2)**

SALAZAR (Simon de). Promptuario de materias
morales.   8vo.
Barcelona, por Antonio Lacaualleria, 1680
Gaselee 160.   **353**

SALEM and Bizance, 1533.
See SAINT GERMAN (Christopher).   **752(1)**

SALISBURY (*Diocese of*). Iniunctions, 1569.
See ENGLAND. *Church of England. Visitation
Articles.*   **1761(3)**

SALLUST. C.Salustii Crispi quae extant. In usum
... Delphini, diligenter recensuit ... D.Crispinus.
4to.
Parisiis, apud Fredericum Leonard, 1674
Engr. fp.   **1952**

[SALMASIUS (Claudius)]. Defensio regia, pro
Carolo I.   fo.
[*Leiden, B. & A.Elzevir*] *Sumptibus regiis*, 1649
   2519

————————— Plinianæ exercitationes in C.J.
Solini Polyhistora. Item C.J.Solini Polyhistor.
2 vols in 1.   fo.
*Trajecti ad Rhenum, apud Johannem vande Water,
Johannem Ribbium, Franciscum Halma* [*etc.*],
1689 (1688)   **2896**

SALMON (Thomas). An essay to the advancement
of musick.   8vo.
London, by J.Macock, sold by John Car, 1672
Engr. title-page, 5 engr. pls (music).
Wing S417.   *See also below*, vol.IV.   **893(1)**

————————— A proposal to perform musick, in
perfect and mathematical proportions.   4to.
London, for John Lawrence, 1688   4 engr. pls.
Wing S418.   *See also below*, vol.IV.   **1730(1)**

————————— A vindication of an essay to the
advancement of musick, from Mr.Matthew Lock's
Observations.   8vo.
London, by A.Maxwell, sold by John Car, 1672
Engr. pl. (music).   Wing S419.
See also below, vol.IV.   **893(3)**

SALMON (William). Pharmacopoeia Londinensis,
1691.
See ROYAL COLLEGE OF PHYSICIANS.   **1076**

————————— Polygraphice: or the arts of drawing, engraving, etching [*etc.*].   4th ed.   8vo.
London, by Robert White, for John Crumpe,
1678 (1675)   Engr. fp. (port., Charrington
p.150), title-page, pls (ports, Charrington pp.29,
33).   **1204**

SALTMARSH (John). The smoke in the Temple ...
A designe for peace and reconciliation of
believers.   2 pts.   4to.
London, by Ruth Raworth for G.Calvert, 1646
[Consutilia II]   Wing S498.   **1428(8)**

[SALTONSTALL (Wye)]. The country mouse,
and the city mouse.   12th ed.   12mo.
London, for J.Clarke, senior, 1683   [Penny-
Merriments I]   Woodcut.   **362(8)**

SALVADOR (Christobal). Letras contra el abuso
de los juramentos, y maldiciones, y contra la
vanidad del mundo. &*c.*   4to.
(*Seuilla, por Iuan Cabeças*) [c.1680]
Gaselee 161; Wilson p.234.   **1545(20)**

SALVIANUS, of Marseille. Opera. Cum libro
commentario C.Rittershusii ... Et Vincentii Lirin-
ensis Commonitorium.   4to.
Bremæ, sumptibus Hermanni Braueri, 1688   **1592**

SALWEY (Arthur). Halting stigmatiz'd in a ser-
mon ... Octob.25.1643.   4to.
London, for Christopher Meredith, 1644
[Sermons Polemical VI]
Wing S522.   **1184(23)**

SAMMES (Aylett). Britannia antiqua illustrata.
Vol.1. [*No more published.*]   fo.
London, by Tho.Roycroft, for the author, 1676
Engr. pls (ports).   Wing S535.   **2558**

SAMSON (Thomas). A narrative of the late Popish
plot in Ireland.   fo.
London, for Sam.Lee, and Dan Major, 1680
[Narratives & Tryals III]   Wing S542.   **2251(39)**

SAMUELLIUS (Franciscus Maria), O.P.
Praxis noua obseruanda, in ecclesiasticis
sepulturis ... Disputationum controversiæ.   4to.
Taurini, sumptibus Iosephi Vernonis, 1678   **1753**

SANCHEZ DE LA CRUZ (Matheo). Aqui se contiene vn gustoso tratado, de como' vna muger natural de Valladolid, siendo cautiva quando lo de Buxia, negò la ley de nuestro Señor, y se caso con vn rico Moro. 4to.
(Seuilla, en casa de Juan Cabeças) [1680]
Gaselee 163; Wilson p.237. **1545(23)**

[―――――――――] Aqui se contienen dos obras maravillosas.
(Seuilla, por Juan Vejarano, à costa de Lucas Martin de Hermosa) [c.1680]
Gaselee 164; Wilson p.232. **1545(18)**

SANCROFT (William), Abp of Canterbury. A sermon preach'd ... Novemb.13th.1678. 4to.
In the Savoy, by Tho.Newcomb, for Robert Beaumont, 1678 Wing S568. **1413(4)**

SANCTORIUS (Santorius). Medicina statica: or, Rules of health ... English'd by J.D[avies]. 12mo.
London, printed for John Starkey, 1676
Engr. fp. Wing S571. **389**

SANDERS (Nicholas). De origine ac progressu schismatis Anglicani. (P.Ribadeneiræ ... Appendix.) 2 pts. 8vo.
Coloniæ Agrippinæ, sumptibus Petri Henningi, 1610 **500**

SANDERSON (Robert), Bp of Lincoln. De juramento. Seven lectures. 8vo.
London, printed by E.C. for Humphrey Moseley, Octavian Pulleyn, and Andrew Crook, 1655
Wing S589. **241**

[―――――――――] Five cases of conscience. 8vo.
London, by E.C. for Henry Brome, 1666
Engr. title-page. Wing S603. **529**

―――――――――― XXXIV. sermons. 5th ed., corrected. fo.
London, for A.Seil, and are to be sold by G.Sawbridge, J.Martyn [etc.], 1671 Engr. fp. (port., Charrington p.150). Wing S635. **2360**

SANDFORD (Francis). A genealogical history of the Kings of England. fo.
In the Savoy, by Tho.Newcomb, for the author, 1677 Engr. pls. Wing S651. **2634**

―――――――――― The history of the coronation of ... James II. fo.
In the Savoy, by Thomas Newcomb, 1687
Engr. pls. Wing S652. **2929**

SANDIUS (Christophorus). Interpretationes paradoxæ quatuor evangeliorum. 8vo.
'Cosmopoli, apud Libertum Pacificum' [Amsterdam], 1670 **697**

―――――――――― Tractatus de origine animæ. 8vo.
'Cosmopoli, apud Libertum Pacificum' [Amsterdam], 1671 **616**

SANDYS (Sir Edwin). Europæ speculum; or a view ... of the state of religion in the western parts of the world. 8vo.
London, for Thomas Basset, 1673
Wing S666. **1015**

SANDYS (George). A paraphrase upon the divine poems. fo.
London (Iohn Legatt)[for A.Hebb], 1638 (1637)
STC 21725. *See also below,* vol.IV. **2469**

―――――――――― Sandys travells. 6th ed. fo.
London, for Rob.Clavel, Tho.Passinger, Will.Cadman [etc.], 1670 Engr. title-page, pls, map.
Wing S679. **2194**

SAN PEDRO (Diego de). La passion de ... Iesu Christo, 1677.
See ROMÁN (Comendador). **1545(25)**

SANTA CRUZ DE DUEÑAS (Melchor de). Floresta española de apoctemas o sentencias. 12mo.
Madrid, por Andrés García de la Iglesia. Acosta de Alonso Nuñiz Montenegro, 1665
Gaselee 165. **49**

SANTOS (Francisco). Descripcion breve del monasterio de S.Lorenzo el real del Escorial. fo.
Madrid, por Ioseph Fernandez de Buendia, 1667
8 engrs. Gaselee 65; Diary 6 Nov.1668. **2123**

[SARASIN (Jean)]. Histoire de la miraculeuse delivrance ... de Geneve [c.1603].
See GOULART (Simon). **506**

SARNELLI (Pompeo), Bp of Bisceglie. Guida de' forestieri, curiosi di vedere, e d'intendere le cose più notabili della regal città di Napoli ... In questa nuova edizione ... ampliata, e da A.Bulifon di vaghe figure abbellita. 12mo.
Napoli, presso Giuseppe Roselli, 1697
Engr. fp., pls. **345(1)**

―――――――――― Guida de' forestieri, curiosi di vedere, e d'intendere le cose più notabili di Pozzoli, Baja, Miseno, Cuma ... Tradotta in Francese accresciuta, e di vaghe figure abbellita da A.Bulifon. [*Ital. & French.*] 12mo.
Napoli, per Giuseppe Roselli, 1697 Engr. title-page, pls (port.). **346(1)**

SARPI (Paolo). The history of the Council of Trent ... by P.Soave Polano [i.e. P.Sarpi]. fo.
London, printed by J.Macock, for Samuel Mearne, John Martyn [etc.], 1676
Wing S696. **2401**

[―――――――――] The history of the quarrels of Pope Paul.V. with ... Venice. 4to.
London, printed by John Bill, 1626
STC 21766. **1141**

———————— The opinion of Padre Paolo ... in what manner the Republick of Venice ought to govern themselves. [Transl. by W.Aglionby.] 12mo.
London, printed for R.Bentley, 1689
Wing S699.   **499**

SARRIÁ (Luís).   *See* GRANADA (Luís de).

SAUMAISE (Claude de).
See SALMASIUS (Claudius).

SAUNDERS (Richard). 1688. Apollo Anglicanus. 8vo.
London, printed by M.Clark for the Company of Stationers, 1688   [Almanacks for the year 1688]   Wing A2358.   **425(23)**

———————— 1689. Apollo Anglicanus.   8vo.
London, printed by M.Clark for the Company of Stationers, 1689   [Almanacks for the year 1689]   Wing A2359.   **426(5)**

———————— Two groats-worth of wit for a penny [c.1680].
See TWO groats-worth of wit ...   **362(50)**

[SAVAGE (Henry)]. Reasons shewing that there is no need of such a reformation of the publique 1. Doctrine. 2. Worship [*etc.*].   4to.
London, for Humphrey Robinson, 1660
[Liturgick Controversies III]   Wing S762.
                                          1189(2)

SAVAGE (John). A select collection of letters, 1703.
See SELECT (A) collection of letters ...   **1464**

SAVARY (Jacques). Le parfait negociant. 2e ed.   2 vols.   4to.
Paris, chez Louis Billaine, 1679   Engr. title-page, diagrams.   Naval Minutes pp.47, 222.   **1903-4**

SAVILE (Sir Henry). Rerum Anglicarum scriptores, 1601.
See RERUM Anglicarum scriptores ...   **2561**

SAVONAROLA (Girolamo). A goodly exposition vpon the.XXX. psalm, 1535.
See LITURGIES. *Roman Catholic Church.*
[*Horae.*] [A goodly prymer ...]   **1374**

SAXTON (Christopher). The shires of England and Wales ... being the best and original mapps with many additions and corrections by P.Lea.   fo.
[*London*] *sold by Phillip Lea* [c.1695]
Engr. title-page, 46 engr. maps.   **2987**

SBONSKI DE PASSEBON (Henri). Plan de plusieurs bâtimens de mer avec leurs proportions. fo.
[*Paris?*]   Engr. pls.   **2968**

SCALA (Giovanni). Delle fortificationi ... nuouamente ristampate con agiunta d'diuerse piante é fortezze.   fo.

Roma, appresso Calisto Ferrante, 1642
Engr. title-page, pls.   **2474**

SCALBERGE (Charles). Traité des causes naturelles du flux et du reflux de la mer.   4to.
Chartres, chez Claude Peigne & Estienne Massot, 1680   Diagrams.   **1909**

SCALIGER (Joseph Juste). Prima Scaligerana. 8vo.
Ultrajecti, apud Petrum Elzevirium, 1670   **573(2)**

———————— Scaligeriana.   Ed. 2.   8vo.
Lugduni Batavorum, ex officina Cornelii Driehuysen, 1668   **573(1)**

SCAPULA (Joannes). Lexicon Græco-Latinum. Ed. nova.   fo.
Amstelædami, (typis Bonaventuræ et Abrahami Elseviriorum) apud Ioannem Blaeuw, et Ludovicum Elzevirium, 1652   Diary 7 July 1664.   **2668**

SCEPTICAL (The) chymist, 1680.
See BOYLE (Hon. Robert).   **960**

SCHEDIUS (Elias). De diis Germanis.   8vo.
Amsterodami, apud Ludovicum Elzevirium, 1648
Engr. title-page.   On title-page, in Pepys's hand:
'È musaeo Samuelis Pepys. Magd.Coll.Cantabr. 1653'.   **520**

SCHEDULE (The) review'd, 1702.
See GIBSON (Edmund), Bp of London.   **1696(17)**

SCHEFFER (Joannes). De militia navali veterum libri quatuor.   4to.
Ubsaliæ, excudebat Johannes Janssonius, 1654
Engr. title-page, pls (diagrams).   **1792**

———————— De natura & constitutione philosophiæ Italicæ seu Pythagoricæ liber singularis.   8vo.
Upsaliæ, excudit Henricus Curio, 'MCDLXIV' [1664]   **452**

———————— The history of Lapland.   fo.
Oxford, at the Theater, and are to be sold by George West and Amos Curtein, 1674
Engr. fp., map.   Wing S851.   **2077**

SCHELIUS (Rabodus Hermannus). De pace et de causis belli Anglici primi ... Liber posthumus. 12mo.
Amstelodami, apud Jodocum Pluymer, 1669
The title-pages of 63(1) and 63(2) have been interchanged.   **63(1)**

[SCHLEISSING (Georg Adam)]. La religion ancienne et moderne des Moscovites. [Transl.] 8vo.
'*Cologne, chez Pierre Marteau*', 1698
Engr. fp., pls.   **527**

SCHOOL (A) of divine meditations [c.1680].
See B.(R.).   **365(20)**

SCHOOL (The) of holiness.   12mo.
[London] for I.Back, 1686   [Penny-Godlinesses]
Woodcut.   **365(23)**

SCHOOL (The) of piety.   4th ed.   12mo.
London, for J.Back, 1687   [Penny-Godlinesses]
Woodcut.   **365(43)**

SCHOONEBEEK (Adriaan). Courte & solide
histoire des ordres religieux. Avec les figures de
leurs habits.   8vo.
Amsterdam, chez Adrien Schoonebeek, 1688
Engr. fp., 73 engr. col. pls.   MS index in hand of
one of Pepys's clerks inserted at end.   **555**

SCHOTT (Gaspar). Physica curiosa. Ed. altera,
auctior.   1 vol. in 2.   4to.
Herbipoli, excudebat Jobus Hertz, sumptibus
Johannis Andreæ Endteri & Wolfgangi jun. hæredum, 1667   Engr. title-page, engr. pls.   **1685-6**

——————— Technica curiosa.   1 vol. in 2.
4to.
[Würzburg] excudebat Jobus Hertz; Norimbergæ,
prostant apud dictos Endteros, sumptibus Johannis
Andreæ Endteri [etc.], 1664   Engr. title-page,
pls (port.).   **1598-9**

SCHOUTEN (Willem). Diarium vel descriptio ...
itineris, facti ... annis 1615. 1616. & 1617.   4to.
Amsterdami, apud Petrum Kærium, 1619
Engr. pls, maps.   Inserted at end: MS transcript (8pp., in hand of one of Pepys's clerks) of
passages from Dutch edition about double-keeled
vessels.   **1045**

SCIENCE (La) des medailles, 1693.
See JOBERT (Louis).   **219**

SCLATER (William). Papisto-Mastix, or Deborah's
prayer against Gods enemies ... Explicated and
applyed ... November the fist [sic], 1641.   4to.
London, by Ric.Hodgkinsonne for Daniel Frere,
1642   [Sermons Polemical VII]   MS notes in
unidentified hand.   Wing S919.   **1185(1)**

SCOT (Reginald). The discovery of witchcraft ...
Whereunto is added ... Discourse of the nature and
substance of devils and spirits.   3rd ed.   fo.
London, for A.Clark, and are to be sold by Dixy
Page, 1665   Wing S945; Diary 12 Aug.1667.
2046

SCOTCH (The) Presbyterian eloquence, 1693.
See CROCKAT (Gilbert).   **1432(20)**

SCOTIÆ indiculum, 1682.
See MUDIE (Alexander).   **435**

SCOTLAND
Church of Scotland

——————— For service-books see LITURGIES.
Church of Scotland.

——————— The first and second Booke of
Discipline.   4to.
[Amsterdam, G.Thorp] 1621   [Liturgick
Controversies I]   STC 22015.   **1187(4)**

—————— ——————— General Assembly. A true copy of
the ... Acts of the Generall Assemblies of the
Church of Scotland ... 1638-1649.   8vo.
[Edinburgh?] 1682   Wing C4272.   **847**

——————— Laws. Regiam majestatem. The
auld lawes and constitutions of Scotland ...
Transl. be Sir J.Skene.   fo.
Edinburgh, by Thomas Finlason, 1609
STC 22626.   **2043**

——————— The laws and acts of Parliament
made by King James the first [etc.] ... of Scotland.
(— The laws and acts of ... Charles the second.
— De verborum significatione ... be J.Skene.)
3 pts.   fo.
Edinburgh, by David Lindsay, 1681
Engr. title-page, engr. ports (Charrington pp.30,
33, 85, 86, 87, 113).   Wing S1265.   **2708(1)**

——————— Act for a Company trading to
Africa and the Indies. June 26, 1695.   fo.
(Edinburgh, by the heirs ... of Andrew Anderson,
1695)   Wing S1418.   **2708(2)**

SCUDDER (Henry). Gods warning to England ...
A sermon ... Octob.30.1644.   4to.
London, by J.R. for Philemon Stephens and
Edward Blackmore, 1644   [Sermons Polemical
VII]   On flyleaf 'Scudder' in unidentified hand.
Wing S2139.   **1185(2)**

SCUDÉRY (Madelène de). Conversations nouvelles
sur divers sujets.   2 vols in 1.   12mo.
La Haye, chez Abraham Arondeus, 1685   **93**

SCULTETUS (Johannes). The chyrurgeons store-
house ... Englished by E.B.   8vo.
London, for John Starkey, 1674   43 engr. pls.
Wing S2166.   **1639**

SEAMAN (William). Grammatica linguæ Turcicæ.
4to.
Oxoniæ, excudebat Hen:Hall, prostant apud
Edvardum Millington, 1670
Wing S2179.   **990**

SEASONABLE (A) speech made by a worthy
member of Parliament [1659].
See TITUS (Silius).   **1430(15)**

SECOND (A) letter to a friend, concerning the
French invasion, 1692.
See SHERLOCK (William).   **1432(23)**

SECOND (A) modest enquiry into the causes of
the present disasters in England ... Being a farther
discovery of the Jacobite plot.   4to.
London, for John Dunton, and John Harris, 1690
[Naval Pamphlets]   Wing S2292.   **1399(6)**

SECOND (The) parte of the defence of the
ministers reasons, 1608.
See HIERON (Samuel). 1187(2)

SECOND (The) part of Tom Tram [c.1680].
See CROUCH (Humphrey). 362(42)

SECOND (The) part of Unfortunate Jack. 12mo.
[*London*] *by M.W. and are to be sold by J.Clark*,
1681 [Penny-Merriments I] Woodcut.
362(28)

SECOND thoughts concerning human soul, 1702.
See COWARD (William). 1132

SECRET (The) sinners. 8vo.
[*London*] *for P.Brooksby* [c.1680]
[Penny-Merriments I] Woodcut. 362(51)

SECRETAIRE (Le) critique, 1680.
See DU JONQUIER ( ). 99(2)

SECURITY (The) of English-mens lives, 1682.
See SOMERS (John Somers, 1st Baron). 395

SEDEÑO (Francisco Jiménez).
See JIMÉNEZ SEDEÑO.

SEDEÑO (Juan). Summa de varones illustres. fo.
Toledo, officina de Iuan Rodriguez, 1590
Adams S843; Gaselee 166; Diary 24 Apr.1668.
2149

SEDGWICK (Obadiah). England's preservation ...
a sermon ... preached ... May, 25.1642. 4to.
London, by R.B. for Samuel Gellibrand, 1642
[Sermons Polemical VII] On flyleaf 'O.Sedg-
wick' in unidentified hand. Wing S2372.
1185(3)

———————— Hamans vanity ... a sermon ...
preached ... June 15.1643. 4to.
London, by R.Bishop, for Samuel Gellibrand,
1643 [Sermons Polemical VII]
Wing S2374. 1185(4)

[SEDGWICK (William)]. Animadversions upon a
letter and paper, first sent to His Highness by
certain gentlemen and others in Wales. 4to.
[*London*] 1656 [Sermons Polemical VII]
Name of author written on title-page in unidentified hand. Wing S2383. 1185(6)

———————— Zions deliverance ... A sermon.
2nd ed. 4to.
London, for John Bellamy, and Ralph Smith,
1643 [Sermons Polemical VII]
Wing S2393. 1185(5)

SEDLEY (Sir Charles). The mulberry-garden, a
comedy. 4to.
London, for H.Herringman, 1668 [Loose
Plays II] Wing S2402. 1604(10)

SEGUIN (Joseph). Les antiquitez d'Arles.
2 pts. 4to.
Arles, chez Claude Mesnier, 1687 Engr. pls.
1638(2)

SEGUNDA parte de la batalla naval ... con el
Armada de el Gran Turco. 4to.
(*Sevilla, por Juan Vejarano, à costa de Lucas
Martin de Hermosa*) [1682]
Gaselee 88; Wilson p.320. [*For pt.1 of the
'Batalla naval', see* CUATRO *romances* ...]
1545(71)

SELDEN (John). De successionibus in bona
defuncti. Ed. altera. fo.
Londini, excudebat Richardus Bishop, 1636
STC 22170. 2035

———————— An historical and political dis-
course of the laws & government of England ...
Collected from some manuscript notes of J.Selden,
by N.Bacon. 2 pts. fo.
*London, for John Starkey, sold by J.Robinson,
R.Bentley* [*etc.*], 1689 Wing S2428. 2423

———————— Mare clausum. fo.
*Londini, excudebat Will.Stanesbeius pro Richardo
Meighen*, 1635 Engr. maps, woodcut.
STC 22175; Diary 29 Nov.1661; Naval Minutes
p.53. 2048

———————— Mare clausum. 2 pts. [*Engl.*]
fo.
London, for Andrew Kembe and Edward Thomas,
1663 [The 1652 translation, with frontispiece & title-page from 1663 edition and dedication & advertisement to reader from 1635
edition.] Engr. fp. Wing S2431; Diary
17, 21 Apr.1663. 2131(1)

———————— Of the judicature in Parliaments.
8vo.
London, for Joseph Lawson bookseller in Lincoln
[1681?] Wing S2433. 1097

———————— The priviledges of the baronage of
England ... in Parliament. 8vo.
London, by T.Badger, for Matthew Wallbanck,
1642 Wing S2434. 447

———————— Θεανθρωπος: or, God made man.
8vo.
London, by J.G. for Nathaniel Brooks, 1661
Engr. fp. (port., Charrington p.154).
Wing S2439. 671

———————— Titles of honor. 3rd ed. fo.
*London, by E.Tyler and R.Holt, for Thomas
Dring*, 1672 Engr. fp. (port., Charrington
p.154), engrs. Wing S2440; Naval Minutes,
p.9. 2297

———————— Tracts. 3 pts. fo.
*London, for Thomas Basset and Richard Chis-
well, and to be sold by Robert Clavell*, 1683

Engr. fp. (port., Charrington p.154).
Wing S2441A. **2303**

SELECT (A) collection of letters of the antients.
By Mr.Savage.   8vo.
London, for J.Hartley, F.Coggan, W.Davis, R.Gibson, and T.Hodgson, 1703   **1464**

SELLER (Abednego). The antiquities of Palmyra.
8vo.
London, printed for S.Smith and B.Walford, 1696
Engr. pls.   Wing S2448.   **1166**

[————————] A continuation of the history of
passive obedience since the Reformation.   2 pts.
4to.
Amsterdam, for Theodore Johnson, 1690
Wing S2449.   **1516(2)**

[————————] The history of passive obedience
since the Reformation.   4to.
Amsterdam, for Theodore Johnson, 1689
Wing S2453.   **1516(1)**

[————————] Remarques relating to the
state of the church of the first centuries.   8vo.
London, for Ric.Chiswell, 1680
Wing S2460.   **1140**

SEMPER eadem: or a reference of the debate at
the Savoy 1661. To the conference at Hampton-
court in 1603/4.   4to.
London, for W.Gilbertson, 1662   [Liturgick
Controversies III]   Wing S2491.   **1189(10)**

SEMPER iidem: or a parallel betwixt the ancient
and modern phanatics.   4to.
London, for Richard Lownds, 1661   [Liturgick
Controversies III]   Wing S2493.   **1189(11)**

SENECA (Lucius Annaeus). Opera.   3 vols.
8vo.
Amstelodami, apud Danielem Elsevirium, 1672
1496-8

———————— Tragœdiæ cum notis J.F.Gronovii.
8vo.
*Amstelodami, ex officina Henrici et viduæ
Theodori Boom,* 1682   Engr. title-page.   **1467**

SERGEANT (John). The informations of J.Ser-
geant and D.Maurice, relating to the Popish plot ...
Reported to the House of Commons.   fo.
London, for Gabriel Kunholt, 1681
[Parliamentary votes and papers 1679, 1681]
[Narratives & Tryals III]   Wing S2572.
2137(32); 2251(34)

SERPENT (The) of deuision, 1590.
See LYDGATE (John).   **939(7)**

SERIOUS (A) and faithfull representation of the
judgements of ministers of the gospell within the
province of London.   4to.

*London, by M.B. for Samuel Gellibrand, and Ralph
Smith,* 1649   [Consutilia I]
Wing S2604.   **1427(8)**

SERMON (A) preach'd at the Chappel Royal in
the Tower, upon the death of ... Queen Mary.
4to.
*London, by J.D. for R.Mount, and sold by John
Whitlock,* 1695   Wing S2632.   **1528(17)**

SERRES (Jean de). A generall historie of France
... continued unto ... 1622.   fo.
[*London*] *by G.Eld, & M.Flesher,* 1624
Engr. title-page; engr. port. (Charrington p.103)
inserted.   STC 22246.   **2332**

SERVICE (The) ... of the common prayers, 1641.
See LITURGIES. *Church of Scotland.*   **1188(2)**

SETTLE (Elkanah). A narrative [of the Popish
plot].   fo.
*London, printed and are to be sold by Thomas
Graves for the author,* 1683   [Narratives &
Tryals III]   Wing S2700.   **2251(40)**

[————————] The notorious impostor, or ...
the life of W.Morrell, alias Bowyer.   4to.
London, for Abel Roper, 1692
[Consutilia I & VI]   Wing S2703.
1427(13); 1432(7)

[SEVEN Wise Masters of Rome.] Wisdoms
cabinet open'd; or, the famous history of the
Seven Wise Masters of Rome.   4to.
[*London, T.Haley*?, c.1680]   [Vulgaria III]
Woodcuts.   Title-page cropped.   **1192(6)**

[————————] The history of the Seven Wise
Masters of Rome.   8vo.
London, for M.Wotton, and G.Conyers, 1687
[Penny-Merriments III]   Woodcuts.
Wing H2185.   **364(5)**

SEVERAL. The severall humble petitions of
D.Bastwicke, M.Burton, M.Prynne. And of Nath.
Wickens ... to ... Parliament.   4to.
[*London*] 1641   [Consutilia III]
Wing S2765.   **1429(9)**

SEVILLE. Ordenanças de Sevilla.   fo.
([*Sevilla*] *por Andres Grande,* 1632)   Woodcut.
Gaselee 167.   **2098(2)**

———————— *Colegio ... en la Arte Maritima.*
Copia de las cedulas reales, 1681.
See CHARLES II, King of Spain.   **2140(2)**

SHADWELL (Thomas). The history of Timon of
Athens ... A play.   4to.
London, by J.M. for Henry Herringman, 1678
Wing S2846.   **1733(3)**

─────── The sullen lovers ... A comedy.
4to.
London, for Henry Herringman, 1670
Wing S2846. **1733(1)**

SHAFTESBURY (Anthony Ashley Cooper, 1st
Earl of). The case of Anthony Earl of Shaftesbury,
as it was argued before ... the King's Bench.   fo.
London, by K.P. for C.R., 1679
[Narratives & Tryals IV]   Wing C883. **2252(28)**

─────── The proceedings against the ...
Earl of Shaftesbury at the Old Baily, ... the
twenty fourth of November, 1681.
London, for H.Jones, 1681   [Narratives &
Tryals IV]   Wing P3553A. **2252(27)**

─────── The proceedings at the Sessions
House ... the 24th day of November, 1681 ...
against Anthony Earl of Shaftesbury.   fo.
London, for Samuel Mearne and John Baker, 1681
[Narratives & Tryals IV]   Wing P3564.
2252(26)

[───────] A seasonable speech [1659].
See TITUS (Silius). **1430(15)**

SHAKESPEARE (William). Comedies, histories,
and tragedies.   4th ed.   3 pts.   fo.
*London, for H.Herringman, and are to be sold by
Joseph Knight and Francis Saunders, 1685*
Engr. fp. (port., Charrington p.155).
Wing S2917; Diary 7 July 1664. **2635**

SHARP (John), Abp of York. A sermon preached
on the 28th of June.   3rd ed.   4to.
London, for Walter Kettilby, 1691
Wing S2994. **1573(1)**

[SHEERES (Sir Henry)] . A discourse touching
Tanger.   8vo.
London, for the author, 1680   Wing S3058;
Tangier Papers p.37 (3 Oct.1683). **558**

[───────] An essay on the certainty and
causes of the earth's motion on its axis.   4to.
London, for Jacob Tonson, 1698
MS corrections in unidentified hand.
Wing S3059; Tanner I, p.135. **1139**

SHELTON (Thomas). Tachy-graphia ... jam ...
Latinè edocta loqui.   8vo.
Londini, excusum pro Gulielmo Miller, 1671
[Short-hand Collection III]   Engr. pls.
Wing S3073; Carlton p.38. **402(1)**

─────── Tachygraphy.   8vo.
*London, printed by Thomas Milbourn, for Dorman
Newman, 1691*   [Short-hand Collection IV]
Engr. pls.   Wing S3084; Carlton p.29. **860(10)**

─────── A tutor to tachygraphy.   8vo.
London, for Samuel Cartwright, 1642
[Short-hand Collection III]   MS notes in
Pepys's hand.   Wing S3087; Carlton p.29.
402(11)

─────── Zeiglographia.   8vo.
*London, printed for Dor: Newman & Thomas
Sawbridge, 1685*   [Short-hand Collection IV]
Engr. title-page.   Wing S3096; Carlton p.39.
860(11)

SHEPHERDS. The shepheards kalender.   fo.
London, for Thomas Adams, 1618   Woodcuts.
STC 22422. **2127**

SHEPHERDS (The) garland of love.   12mo.
*London, for J.Wright, J.Clarke, W.Thackeray,
T.Passenger, 1682*   [Penny-Merriments II]
Woodcut. **363(40)**

SHEPPARD (William). Actions upon the case for
slander.   2nd ed.   8vo.
*London, printed for J.Starkey, T.Basset, T.Dring,
and J.Leigh, 1674*   Wing S3176. **908**

SHERINGHAM (Robert). De Anglorum gentis
origine disceptatio.   8vo.
*Cantabrigiæ, excudebat Joann.Hayes, impensis
Edvardi Story, 1670*   Wing S3236. **1069**

[SHERIDAN (Thomas)] . A learned discourse on
various subjects, viz. of the rise and power of
Parliaments.   8vo.
*London, printed, and are to be sold by H.Saw-
bridge, 1685*   Wing S3226. **416**

SHERLEY (Sir Anthony). [Sir Antony Sherley
his relation of his travels into Persia.   4to.
*London, [N.Okes] for Nathaniel Butter and
Joseph Bagfet, 1613]*   Wants title-page.
STC 22424. **1216(2)**

SHERLOCK (William). The case of the allegiance
due to soveraign powers stated.   4to.
London, for W.Rogers, 1691   [Consutilia I]
Wing S3269. **1427(2)**

─────── Concio ad sanctam synodum ...
XXX die Decembris [1701].   Ed.2.
Londini, impensis Gulielmi Rogers, 1702
[Convocation Pamphlets XII] **1698(4)**

[───────] The pretended expedient. In a
letter to the author.   4to.
[London] (for R.Sare, 1702)   [Convocation
Pamphlets X] **1696(2)**

[───────] A second letter to a friend,
concerning the French invasion.   4to.
*London, printed, and are to be sold by Randal
Taylor, 1692*   [Consutilia VI]
Wing S3339. **1432(23)**

─────── A sermon preach'd ... December
30.1694.   2nd ed.   4to.
London, for Will.Rogers, 1694
Wing S3358. **1528(5)**

─────────A vindication of the doctrine of the ... Trinity.   4to.
London, for W.Rogers, 1690
Wing S3376.   **1503**

SHIFTS (The) of Reynardine the son of Reynard the fox.   4to.
London, by T.J. for Edward Brewster, and Thomas Passenger, 1684   [Vulgaria IV]
Wing S3436.   **1193(9)**

SHIPWRIGHTS' COMPANY. [Charter, granted by James I in 1612.   2nd ed.]   4to.
(*London, by William Godbid*, 1677)   **1315**

[SHIRLEY (James)]. Love tricks: or, the school of complements.   4to.
London, for R.T., sold by Thomas Dring, junior, 1667   [Loose Plays I]   Wing S3477.
                                             1075(14)

[SHIRLEY (John), d.1679]. The life of the valiant and learned Sir Walter Raleigh, Knight. With his tryal at Winchester.   8vo.
London, printed by J.D. for Benj.Shirley, and Richard Tonson, 1677   Wing S3495.   **892**

[SHIRLEY (John), fl.1680-1702]. Brittains glory: or, the history of ... K.Arthur.   4to.
[London] by H.B. for J.Wright, J.Clark [etc.], 1684   [Vulgaria III]   Woodcut.
Wing M339.   **1192(8)**

─────────── The honour of chivalry. The second and third part, 1683.
See FERNÁNDEZ (Jerónimo).   **1190(2)**

[───────] The most delectable history of Reynard the fox: in heroic verse.   4to.
London, by A.M. and R.R. for Edward Brewster, 1681   [Vulgaria IV]   Woodcuts.
Wing S3512.   **1193(8)**

─────────── The renowned history ... of Guy, Earl of Warwick.   4to.
[London] for P.Brooksby, 1685   [Vulgaria III]
Woodcuts. Title-page cropped.
Wing S3516.   **1192(9)**

SHORT (A) account of Dr Bentley's humanity and justice to those authors who have written before him: with an honest vindication of Tho. Stanley.   8vo.
London, printed for Thomas Bennet, 1699
Wing S3534.   **1256(2)**

SHORT (A) compendium of the new ... sea-book, or, pilots sea-mirror [i.e. Die lichtende columne ofte zee-spiegel.]. Transl. ... by L.Childe.   4to.
London, by T.J. for George Hurlock, 1663
[Sea Tracts III]   **1079(7)**

SHORT (A) consideration of Mr.Erasmus Warren's defence of his exceptions against the theory of the earth, 1691.
See BURNET (Thomas).   **2271(2)**

SHORT defence of the last Parliament (*Author of*).
See DRAKE (James).

SHORT (A) introduction of grammar, 1662.
See LILY (William).   **886**

SHORT (A) state of some present questions in Convocation, 1703.
See GIBSON (Edmund), Bp of London.   **1696(19)**

SHORT (A) view of the late troubles in England, 1681.
See DUGDALE (Sir William).   **2605**

SHRENOCK (John). The youngmans guide in his way to heaven.   12mo.
[London] for J.Conyers [c.1680]   [Penny-Godlinesses]   Woodcut. Title-page cropped.
                                             365(4)

[SICILE, herald]. Le blazon des armes: auec les armes des princes ᴢ seigneurs de France.   8vo.
(*Paris, par Phelipe le Noir*) [c.1520]   Woodcuts.
Adams S1071.   **46(2)**

SIDNEY (Algernon). The arraignment, tryal & condemnation of Algernon Sidney, Esq; for high-treason ... November, 1683.   fo.
London, for Benj.Tooke, 1684   [Narratives & Tryals III]   Wing A3754.   **2253(7)**

─────────── The very copy of a paper delivered ... upon the scaffold on Tower-hill, ... Decemb.7.1683.   fo.
(*London, for R.H. J.B. and J.R., and are to be sold by Walter Davis*, 1683)   [Narratives & Tryals III]   Wing S3766.   **2253(8)**

SIDNEY (Sir Philip). The Countess of Pembroke's Arcadia.   13th ed.   fo.
London, for George Calvert, 1674   Engr. fp.
(port., Charrington p.156).   Wing S3770; Diary 2 Jan.1664/5.   **2214**

SIETE romances famosos, los dos de la muerte, que el Rey D.Enrique dió á su hermano el Rey Don Pedro.   4to.
(*Seuilla, por Juan Vejarano, à costa de Lucas Martin de Hermosa*) [c.1680]
Gaselee 76; Wilson p.315.   **1545(66)**

SIMON (Pedro). Primera parte de las noticias historiales de las conquistas de tierra firme en las Indias Occidentales.   fo.
Cuenca, en casa de Domingo de la Yglesia (1627)
Gaselee 168.   **2118(1)**

[SIMON (Richard)]. Disquisitiones criticæ [*sic*] de variis ... Bibliorum editionibus.   4to.
Londini, impensis Richardi Chiswel, 1684
Wing S3801.   **1560**

———————— Histoire critique des principaux commentateurs du Nouveau Testament. Tom.III. [*of* Histoire critique de l'Ancien et Nouveau Testament.] 2 pts. 4to.
Rotterdam, chez Reinier Leers, 1693　　**1820**

———————— Histoire critique des versions du Nouveau Testament. 4to.
Rotterdam, chez Reinier Leers, 1690　　**1819**

———————— Histoire critique du texte du Nouveau Testament. 4to.
Rotterdam, chez Reinier Leers, 1689　　**1818**

———————— Histoire critique du Vieux Testament. 4to.
Rotterdam, chez Reinier Leers, 1685　　**1864(1)**

———————— Opuscula critica adversus Isaacum Vossium. 2 pts. 4to.
Edinburgi, typis Joannis Calderwood, 1685
Wing S3803.　　**1864(2)**

———————— [*Sentiments de quelques théologiens* ...] Five letters concerning the ... Scriptures, 1690.
See LE CLERC (Jean).　　**481**

SIMPLE (The) cobler of Aggawam in America, 1647.
See WARD (Nathaniel).　　**1430(10)**

SIMPLICIUS. Commentarius in Enchiridion Epicteti [*with the text*], cum versione H.Wolfii et C.Salmasii animadversionibus et notis. (– Cebetis tabula ... Aurea carmina Pythagoræ.) [*Gk, Lat. & Arabic.*] 3 pts. 4to.
Lugduni Batavorum, typis Iohannis Maire, 1640
　　1548

SIMPSON (Sydrach). Reformation's preservation ... a sermon preached ... July 26.1643. 4to.
London, for Benjamin Allen, 1643
[Sermons Polemical VII] At end: MS imprimatur with signatures of Henry Elsinge, Clerk of the House of Commons, James Cranford, Joseph Caryll and Charles Herle; the first three being copies. Wing S3825.　　**1185(8)**

SINCLAIR (George). [The hydrostaticks. 4to.
Edinburgh, printed by George Swintoun, James Glen, and Thomas Brown, 1672]
Engr. title-page, diagrams. Wants printed title-page. Wing S3854.　　**1290**

SIR Francis Drake revived ... Being a summary ... of foure severall voyages ... Collected out of the notes of the said Sir Francis Drake [*etc.*]. 4to.
London, for Nicholas Bourne, 1653 (1652)
Engr. fp. (port., Charrington p.49).
Wing D2122.　　**1253**

SKAY (John). A friend to navigation. 4to.
London, by T.C[*otes*]., 1628 [Sea Tracts IV]
Woodcuts. STC 22592.　　**1080(5)**

SKELTON (John). Pithy pleasaunt and profitable workes of maister Skelton. 8vo.
London, imprinted by Thomas Marshe, [1568]
STC 22608.　　**228(1)**

SKENE (Sir John). De verborum significatione. The exposition of the terms ... in the foure buiks of Regiam majestatem, and uthers. 4to.
London, by E.G., 1641　　Wing C7681.　　**1007**

SKINNER (Stephen). Etymologicon linguæ Anglicanæ. fo.
Londini, typis T.Roycroft, apud H.Brome, R.Clavel [*etc.*], 1671　　MS notes in Daniel Waterland's hand. Wing S3947.　　**2259**

SKINNER (Thomas). Elenchi motuum nuperorum in Anglia, pars III. Siue, motus compositi. [A continuation of the work of G.Bate.] 8vo.
Londini, excudebat Guil.Godbid, prostant apud Mosem Pitt, 1676　　Wing S3948.　　**538**

[SLATIUS (Henricus)]. Fur prædestinatus: sive, dialogismus. 12mo.
Londini, impensis F.G., typis G.D., 1651
Wing S3982.　　**374(2)**

SLEIDAN (Joannes). De quatuor summis imperiis. Postrema ed. 16mo.
Amstelodami, apud Danielem Elzevirium, 1667　　**8**

———————— The general history of the reformation of the Church. fo.
London, printed by Edw.Jones, for Abel Swall, and Henry Bonwicke, 1689　　Engr. fp., ports (Charrington pp.34, 64, 98, 107, 116, 157).
Wing S3989.　　**2414**

SLEZER (John). Theatrum Scotiæ. Containing the prospects of their Majesties castles and palaces.
London, by John Leake for Abell Swalle, 1693
57 engr. pls.　　Wing S3993.　　**2838**

SLOANE (Sir Hans). Catalogus plantarum quæ in insula Jamaica sponte proveniunt. 8vo.
Londini, impensis D.Brown, 1696
Wing S3998.　　**835**

SLOETTEN (Henry Cornelius van). The isle of pines, 1668.
See NEVILLE (Henry).　　**1399(3)**

[SMALRIDGE (George), Bp of Bristol]. Some remarks upon the temper of the late writers about Convocations. 4to.
London, for A.Baldwin, 1701　　[Convocation Pamphlets XI]　　**1697(1)**

SMART (Peter). A catalogue of superstitious innovations ... Brought into Durham Cathedrall by Bishop Neal, and the Dean, and Prebendaries of the said Church. 4to.
London, for Joseph Hunscott, 1642
[Liturgick Controversies II]
Wing S4013.　　**1188(10)**

SMECTYMNUUS, *pseud.*
See MARSHALL (Stephen).

SMITH (Joannes), of Nimeguen. Antiquitates
Neomagenses.   4to.
*Noviomagi Batavorum, ex typographia Regneri
Smetii, 1678*   Engr. pls.   **1483**

SMITH (John), Captain. England's improvement
reviv'd: in a treatise of ... husbandry & trade by
land and sea.   4to.
*London, by Tho.Newcomb, for Benjamin South-
wood; and Israel Harrison, 1673*
Wing S4093.   **1732**

SMITH (John), clock-maker. Horological disquis-
itions.   8vo.
London, printed for Richard Cumberland, 1694
Table.   Wing S4106.   **833(2)**

SMITH (John), of Virginia. The seaman's grammar.
4to.
*London, and are to be sold by Andrew Kemb,
1653*   Wing S4123; Diary 13 March 1660/1.
1142(1)

———————— The sea-man's grammar and
dictionary ... enlarged.   4to.
*London, printed, and are to be sold by Randal
Taylor, 1691*   Engr. pl. inserted.
Wing S4124.   **1298**

SMITH (John), of Walworth. The narrative of
Mr.John Smith of Walworth ... containing a
further discovery of the late ... Popish plot.   fo.
*London, printed, and are to be sold by Robert
Boulter, 1679*   [Narratives & Tryals III]
Wing S4127.   **2251(41)**

SMITH (Richard), Bp of Chalcedon. Monita
quædam vtilia pro sacerdotibus, seminaristis,
missionariis Angliæ.   12mo.
Parisiis, 1647   **89**

SMITH (Thomas), Fellow of Magdalen College
Oxford. An account of the Greek church.   8vo.
*London, by Miles Flesher for Richard Davis, in
Oxford, 1680*   Wing S4232.   **1008**

———————— Catalogus librorum manuscript-
orum Bibliothecæ Cottonianæ.   fo.
Oxonii, e Theatro Sheldoniano, 1696
Engr. fp. (port., Charrington p.43).
Wing S4233.   **2730(1)**

———————— De Græcæ ecclesiæ hodierno
statu epistola. Ed. nova.   8vo.
*Trajecti ad Rhenum, apud Franciscum Halmam,
1698*   **1233(2)**

———————— Joannis Gravii, olim astronomiæ
in Academia Oxoniensi Professoris Saviliani, vita.
4to.
Londini, 1699   Wing S4234.   **1347**

———————— Remarks upon the manners,
religion and government of the Turks. Together
with a survey of the seven Churches of Asia ... and
a brief description of Constantinople.   8vo.
London, for Moses Pitt, 1678
Wing S4246.   **895**

———————— Two compendious discourses.
4to.
London, for S.Smith and B.Walford, 1699
Wing S4254.   **1349**

SMITH (Sir Thomas), Ambassador. Sir Thomas
Smithes voiage and entertainment in Rushia.   4to.
London, for Nathanyell Butter, 1605
[Consutilia V]   STC 22869.   **1431(8)**

SMITH (Sir Thomas), Secretary of State. The
Common-wealth of England.   12mo.
London, by R.Young for J.Smethwicke, 1640
STC 22867.   **222(2)**

SMITH (William). The vale-royall of England ...
performed by W.Smith ... publ. by D.King, 1656.
See KING (Daniel).   **2094**

SMITHSON (Samuel). The famous history of
Guy Earl of Warwick.   12mo.
*[London] for J.Clark, W.Thackeray, and T.Pass-
inger, 1686*   [Penny-Merriments I]
Woodcut.   Diary 6 March 1666/7.   **362(44)**

———————— The figure of nine.   8vo.
London, for J.Deacon, and C.Dennisson, [c.1690]
[Penny-Merriments I]   Wing S4355.   **362(20)**

SMITHURST (Benjamin). [Britain's glory, and
England's bravery ... To which is added, a continuation of the Historian's guide, from November,
1687 ... to June, 1689.   12mo.
London, for William Crook, 1689]   Wants all
except leaves I3-K5, containing the continuation
of S.Clarke's Historian's guide.   Wing S4356.
487(2)

SMYTHE (Sir John). Certain discourses ... concerning the formes and effects of diuers sorts of
weapons.   4to.
London, printed by Richard Johnes, 1590
STC 22883.   **924**

SNAKE (The) in the grass, 1698.
See LESLIE (Charles).   **1269**

SNAPE (Andrew). The anatomy of an horse.   fo.
*London, by M.Flesher for the authour, sold by
T.Flesher, 1683*   Engr. fp. (port., Charrington
p.157).   Wing S4382.   **2590**

SOAVE (Pietro), Polano, *pseud.*
See SARPI (Paolo).

SOBER (A) and temperate discourse, concerning
the interest of words in prayer, 1661.
See DAUBENY (Henry).   **1189(5)**

SOBER sadnes, 1643.
See WOMOCK (Laurence). **1430(7)**

SOLÍS (Antonio Alvarez).
See ALVAREZ SOLÍS (Antonio).

SOLÍS (Antonio de). Histoire de la conquête du Mexique ... Traduite de l'Espagnol.   4to.
Paris, chez Antoine Dezallier, (de l'imprimerie de Laurent Rondet,) 1691   Engr. pls.   **1870**

SOME cautions offered to the consideration of those who are to chuse members, 1695.
See HALIFAX (George Savile, 1st Marquis of).
1433(12)

SOME considerations about the raising of coin. In a second letter to Mr.Locke.   8vo.
London, printed for A. and J.Churchill, 1696
Wing S4481.   **796(3)**

SOME of the differences and alterations in the present common-prayer-book [1660].
See BURGESS (Cornelius).   **1188(6)**

SOME fruits of solitude, 1693.
See PENN (William).   **61**

SOME necessary considerations relating to all future elections of members to serve in Parliament, 1702.
See DRAKE (James).   **1437(8)**

SOME queries concerning the disbanding of the army.   4to.
[*London*] 1698   [Consutilia VII]
Wing S4560.   **1433(20)**

SOME reflections on that part of a book called Amyntor, 1699.
See CLARKE (Samuel), of St James's, Westminster.   **1082(4)**

SOME reflections on the eleventh section of Dr. D'Avenant's late book of essays, intituled, Peace at home.   4to.
London, 1704   **1382(2)**

SOME reflexions upon a treatise call'd Pietas Romana & Parisiensis, 1688.
See HARRINGTON (James), the younger.   **1873**

SOME remarks on the Bill for taking, examining and stating the Publick Accounts of the Kingdom. 4to.
London, printed in the year, 1702
[Consutilia XI]   **1437(3)**

SOME remarks upon the temper of the late writers, 1701.
See SMALRIDGE (George), Bp of Bristol.
1697(1)

SOME thoughts on a Convocation, 1699.
See HODY (Humfrey).   **1695(2)**

SOME useful reflections upon a pamphlet [by W. Paterson] called A brief account of the intended Bank of England. [By H.Chamberlen?]   4to.
[*London*, 1694]   [Consutilia VII]
Wants title-page.   Wing S4631 or 4632.   **1433(8)**

[SOMERS (John, 1st Baron)]. A brief history of the Succession ... Written for the satisfaction of the Earl of H.   fo.
[*London*, 1680]   Wing S4638.   **2565(2)**

[——————] Jura populi Anglicani: or the subjects right of petitioning.   4to.
London, 1701   [Consutilia XI]   **1437(10)**

[——————] The security of English-mens lives.   8vo.
London, printed for Benj.Alsop, 1682
Wing S4644.   **395**

SOMNER (William). Dictionarium Saxonico-Latino-Anglicum. ... Accesserunt Ælfrici Abbatis Grammatica.   fo.
Oxonii, excudebat Guliel.Hall, pro authore.
Prostant Londini, apud Danielem White, 1659
Wing S4663.   **2366**

—————— Julii Caesaris Portus Iccius illustratus: sive 1. Gul.Somneri ad Chiffletii librum de Portu Iccio, responsio ... 2. C.Du Fresne Dissertatio de Portu Iccio. Nova dissertatione auxit E.Gibson.   8vo.
Oxonii, e Theatro Sheldoniano, 1694   Engr. fp.
(port., Charrington p.159), map.   Wing S4666.
586

—————— A treatise of the Roman ports and forts in Kent ... Publish'd by J.Brome ... To which is prefixt the life of Mr.Somner (by W.Kennett). 2 pts.   8vo.
Oxford, at the Theater, 1693   Engr. fp. (port., Charrington p.159).   Wing S4669.   **844**

SOMNIUM navale, 1673.
See WOODROFFE (Benjamin).   **2057**

SOPHOCLES. Tragoediæ VII. Una cum ... scholiis. Ed. postrema. [*Gk & Lat.*]   2 pts.
Ἐν τῇ Κανταβριγίᾳ, ἐξετυπώθη παρ''Ιοαννου Φιελδου, αχξη [1668] (pt 1: 1665)   Wing S4691.
782

SOTO (Francisco de), S.J. Destierro de los malos cantares.   4to.
Sevilla, por Juan Cabeças, 1677
Gaselee 170; Wilson p.152.   **1545(11)**

SOUCHU DE RENNEFORT (Urbain). Relation du premier voyage de la Compagnie des Indes Orientales en l'isle de Madagascar.   12mo.
Paris, chez François Clouzier, 1668   **360**

SOULIGNÉ (De). The desolation of France demonstrated. 8vo.
London, printed for John Salusbury, 1697
Wing S4718. **1223**

SOUTH (Robert). Sermons preached upon several occasions. 8vo.
Oxford, by H.Hall, for Ric.Davis and Will.Nott, 1679 Wing S4743. **1215**

[SOUTHLAND (Thomas)]. Love a la mode. A comedy. 4to.
London, by J.C. for John Daniel, 1663
[Loose Plays I] Wing S4771; Diary 19 July 1663. **1075(11)**

SOUTHOUSE (Thomas). Monasticon Favershamiense. 8vo.
London, for T.Passenger, 1671 Engr. fp.
Wing S4772. **482**

[SOUVERAIN (Matthieu)]. Le Platonisme devoilé. 8vo.
Cologne, chez Pierre Marteau, 1700 **595**

SPAHER (Michael). A survey of the microcosme. Or the anatomie of the bodies of man and woman. fo.
London, by Joseph Moxon, and ... sold at his shop, 1675 Engr. pls. **2741**

SPAIN. *Treaties.* Tractatus pacis, inter Hispaniam et Unitum Belgium [30 Jan.1648]. 8vo.
Lugd. Batav., ex officinâ Elseviriorum, 1651 **449**

SPANHEIM (Friedrich), the elder. Dubiorum evangelicorum pars prima (− tertia). 3 vols in 2. 4to.
Genevæ, sumptibus Iacobi Chouët, 1639 **1739-40**

SPANHEIM (Friedrich), the younger. Histoire de la Papesse Jeanne ... tirée de la dissertation latine de M.de Spanheim [par J.Lenfant]. 12mo.
*Cologne, chez ******, 1694* Engr. title-page. **580**

———————— Historia Iobi. 4to.
Genevæ, sumptibus Petri Chouët, 1670 **1832**

SPANISH (The) history, 1678.
See RELATION des différends arrivés en Espagne. **1035**

[SPARKE (Michael)]. The narrative history of King James, 1651.
See NARRATIVE (The) history of King James ... **1259**

SPARROW (Anthony), Bp of Norwich. A rationale upon the Book of Common-Prayer. 12mo.
London, for T.Garthwait, 1668 Engr. title-page, engr. ports (Charrington pp.4, 82, 130).
Wing S4831. **428(1)**

SPARROW (Henry). Cupid's sports and pastimes. 12mo.
[*London*] *for W.Thackeray, 1684* [Penny-Merriments I] Woodcut. **362(43)**

SPECIMEN (A) of some errors ... in the History of the Reformation of the Church of England, 1693.
See WHARTON (Henry). **992**

SPEECH (A) in the Parliament of Scotland [1702?].
See KINCARDINE (Alexander Bruce, 4th Earl of). **1437(14)**

SPEECHES (The) and prayers of Major General Harison [and 9 others]. The times of their death. 4to.
[*London*] 1660 [Consutilia IV]
Wing S4874A. **1430(2)**

SPEED (John). The history of Great Britaine. 3rd ed. fo.
London, to be sold by George Humble, 1650
Engr. fp. (port., Charrington p.160), engr. title-page, pls. Wing S4880; Diary 19 & 21 Sept. 1666; 2 March 1666/7; 23 Oct. 1667. **2906**

———————— A prospect of the most famous parts of the world. fo.
London, by Iohn Dawson for George Humble, 1631 Engr. fp. (port., Charrington p.160), 22 engr. maps. STC 23040; Diary 26 Sept. 1660; 19 & 21 Sept. 1666. **2901(1)**

———————— The theatre of the empire of Great Britain. fo.
London, (Iohn Dawson) sold by George Humble, 1627 Engr. title-page, maps.
STC 23042. **2901(2)**

[SPEED (Robert)]. The counter scuffle. Whereunto is added The counter rat. 4to.
London, for T.Basset, R.Chiswell, M.Wotton [*etc.*], 1693 [Vulgaria III] Engr.
Wing S4898. **1193(19)**

SPEEDY (A) post, 1684.
See W.(J.). **1193(16)**

SPELMAN (Sir Henry). Concilia, decreta ... in re ecclesiarum orbis Britannici ... opera et scrutinio H.Spelman, 1639-64.
See ENGLAND. *Church of England.* **2818-9**

———————— De non temerandis ecclesiis, churches not to be violated. 5th ed. 8vo.
Oxford, by H.Hall, for Amos Curteyn, 1676
Wing S4923. **455**

———————— Glossarium archaiologicum. fo.
Londini, apud Aliciam Warren, 1664
Engr. fp. (map). Wing S4925; Diary 27 June, 7 July 1664. **2472**

—————————— The history and fate of sacrilege.
[*Pt.2 wanting.*] 8vo.
London, for John Hartley, 1698
Wing S4927. **1322**

—————————— Reliquiæ Spelmannianæ. fo.
Oxford, at the Theater for Awnsham and John Churchill, 1698 Engr. fp. (port., Charrington p.160). Wing S4930. **2705**

SPELMAN (Sir John). Ælfredi magni Anglorum Regis invictissimi vita. fo.
Oxonii, e Theatro Sheldoniano, 1678
7 engr. pls. Wing S4934. **2666**

SPENCER (John), Dean of Ely. De legibus Hebræorum ritualibus. fo.
Cantabrigiæ, ex officina Joan.Hayes, impensis Richardi Chiswel, Londini, 1685
Wing S4946. **2411**

—————————— A discourse concerning prodigies ... 2nd ed. (— A discourse concerning vulgar prophecies.) 2 pts. 8vo.
London, by J.Field for Will.Graves in Cambridge (for Timothy Garthwait), 1665
Wing S4948, 4949; Diary 1 June 1664. **920**

—————————— Dissertatio de Urim & Thummim.
8vo.
Cantabrigiæ, impensis Timoth.Garthwait, Londini, 1669 Wing S4950. **1032**

SPENSER (Edmund). The works.
London, by Henry Hills for Jonathan Edwin, 1679
Engr. fp. Wing S4965. **2307**

SPICER (John). Tables of interest, after the rate of five, six, seven and eight pounds per cent. per annum. 4to.
London, for J.Spicer, 1693
Wing S4973. **1484**

[SPINOZA (Benedict de)]. Opera posthuma. (Compendium grammatices linguæ Hebrææ.) 4to.
[*Amsterdam?*] 1677 **1376**

[—————————] Tractatus theologico-politicus, cui adiunctus est philosophia S.Scripturae interpres [by L.Meyer]. 2 pts. 8vo.
[*Amsterdam?*] 1674 **917**

[—————————] [*Tractatus theologico-politicus.*] Traitté des ceremonies superstitieuses des Juifs. [*Transl.*] 12mo.
Amsterdam, chez Jacob Smith, 1678 **73**

SPON (Jacob). Recherches curieuses d'antiquité. 4to.
Lyon, chez Thomas Amaulry, 1683 Engrs. **1953**

—————————— Voyage d'Italie, de Dalmatie, de Grece, et du Levant, fait aux années 1675 et 1676. 2 vols. 12mo.
Amsterdam, chez Henry & Theodore Boom, 1679
Engr. title-page, 34 engr. pls (port., Charrington p.160). **143-4**

SPORTS and pastimes [c.1680].
See M.(J.). **1193(6)**

SPOTTISWOOD (John), Abp of St Andrews. The history of the church and state of Scotland ... to the end of the reign of King James the VI ... In seven books. 4th ed. fo.
London, for R.Royston, 1677 Engr. fp., ports (Charrington pp.30, 160). Wing S5021. **2334**

[—————————] The history of the church and state of Scotland, pt II, 1677.
See BURNET (Gilbert), Bp of Salisbury. **2335**

SPRAT (Thomas), Bp of Rochester. The history of the Royal-Society. 4to.
London, by J.R. for J.Martyn, and J.Allestry, 1667 Engr. fp. (ports, Charrington pp.22, 32), engr. pls. Wing S5032; Diary 16 Aug.1667. **1529**

—————————— A letter from the Bishop of Rochester to the ... Earl of Dorset ... concerning ... the late ecclesiastical commission. 4to.
In the Savoy, by Edw.Jones, 1688
[Consutilia I] Wing S5033. **1427(6)**

—————————— The Bishop of Rochester's second letter to the ... Earl of Dorset. 4to.
In the Savoy, by Edward Jones, 1689
[Consutilia I] Wing S5049. **1427(7)**

—————————— Observations on Monsieur de Sorbier's voyage into England. 12mo.
In the Savoy, printed for John Martyn, and James Allestry, 1668 Wing S5036; Diary 13 Oct.1664; 19 May 1668. **492**

—————————— A relation of the late wicked contrivance of Stephen Blackhead and Robert Young. 2 pts. 4to.
In the Savoy, printed by Edward Jones, 1692 (1693) [Consutilia VI]
Wing S5046, 5051. **1432(9-10)**

[—————————] A true account and declaration of the horrid conspiracy against the late King. (— Copies of the informations and original papers.) 3rd ed. 2 pts. 8vo.
In the Savoy, printed by Thomas Newcomb, sold by Samuel Lowndes, 1686 (1685) Engr. plan.
Wing S5068A, S5030. **1137**

SPURSTOWE (William). Englands eminent judgments ... A sermon preached ... Novemb.5. 1644. 4to.
London, by E.G. for John Rothwell, 1644
[Sermons Polemical VII] Wing S5093. **1185(10)**

———————— Englands patterne and duty in it's monthly fasts. A sermon preached ... the 21 of July, An.Dom.1643. 4to.
London, for Peter Cole, 1643 [Sermons Polemical VII]   Wing S5094.   **1185(9)**

[STAFFORD (William)]. [A compendious or briefe examination of certayne ordinary complaints. *Wants all before **1.]* 4to.
(London, by Thomas Marshe, 1581)
[Consutilia V]   STC 23133a.   **1431(5)**

STAFFORD (William Howard, 1st Viscount). The speech ... immediately before his execution, Decemb.29.1680.   fo.
London, for W.Bailey, 1680 [Parliamentary votes and papers 1679, 1681]   Wing S5156.
2137(25)

———————— The tryal of William Viscount Stafford for high treason.   fo.
London, by the assigns of John Bill, Thomas Newcomb, and Henry Hills, 1680/1
[Parliamentary votes and papers 1679, 1681; Narratives & Tryals IV]   Wing T2238.
2137(24); 2252(15)

STAHL (Daniel). Regulæ philosophicæ ... Accessere ... Disputationes II ... Item, Doctrina Propositionum.   12mo.
Oxoniæ, impensis J.Webb, 1663   **409**

STALEY (William). The tryal of William Staley, Goldsmith; for speaking treasonable words.   fo.
London, for Robert Pawlet, 1678 [Narratives & Tryals I]   Wing T2237.   **2249(8)**

STALKER (John). A treatise of japaning.   fo.
Oxford, printed for, and sold by the author, 1688
24 engr. pls.   Wing S5187A; Tanner I, p.230[?].
2719

STANBRIDGE (John). Vocabula.   4to.
R.Pynson [*London*, 1496]
See Appendix.   **1305(4)**

STANHOPE (George), Dean of Canterbury. Of preparation for death and judgment. A sermon preached ... January 27.1694/5.   4to.
London, for R.Sare, 1695
Wing S5225.   **1528(7)**

STANLEY (Thomas). The history of philosophy. (— The history of the Chaldaick philosophy.) 2nd ed.   2 pts.   fo.
London (by Ralph Holt) for Thomas Bassett, Dorman Newman, and Thomas Cockerill, 1687
Engr. fp. (port., Charrington p.161), engr. pls.
Wing S5239.   **2587**

STAPLETON (Sir Miles). The tryal of Sr.M. Stapleton ... at York Assizes. 18 July 1681.   fo.
London, for Richard Baldwin, 1681
[Narratives & Tryals IV]   Wing T2217.
2252(21)

STAPLETON (Thomas). A fortresse of the faith.
Antwerpe, by Ihon Laet, 1565   Leaf Ss 4 defective.   STC 23232.   **1135(2)**

STAROWOLSKI (Szymon). Institutorum rei militaris, libri VIII.   12mo.
Florentiæ, sumptibus Ioannis Baptistæ, & Iosephi Corbi bibliopolarum Romæ, 1646   **84**

STATE (The) of the Protestants of Ireland under the late King James's government, 1691.
See KING (William), Abp of Dublin.   **1729**

STATE tracts: being a collection of several treatises relating to the Government. Privately printed in the reign of K.Charles II.   fo.
London, 1689   Wing S5329.   **2441(1)**

STATUS Ecclesiæ Gallicanæ, 1676.
See GEAVES (William).   **1782**

STATUTES.   *See* ENGLAND. *Statutes.*

STAUNTON (Edmund). Phinehas's zeal in execution of iudgment ... A sermon ... October 30. 1644.   4to.
London, by I.L. for Christopher Meredith, 1645
[Sermons Polemical VII]   Wing S5341.
1185(11)

STEEL (Laurence). Short writing, begun by nature; compleated by art.   12mo.
Sold in Bristoll by the author, & also by Charles Allen, and in London by Benjamin Clark and others, 1678   [Short-hand Collection IV]
20 engr. ll.   Wing S5380; Carlton, p.98.   **860(8)**

STEPHANUS.   *See* ESTIENNE.

[STEPHENS (William)]. An account of the growth of deism in England.   4to.
London, for the author, 1696   [Consutilia IX]
Wing S5459.   **1435(5)**

STERN (John). The last confession ... of Lieuten. John Stern.   fo.
London, for Richard Chiswell, 1682
[Narratives & Tryals IV]   Wing S5472.
2252(30)

STERRY (Peter). The spirits conviction of sinne ... In a sermon ... Novemb.26.1645.   4to.
London, by Matth.Simmons, for Henry Overton, and Benjamin Allen, 1645   [Sermons Polemical VII]   Wing S5485.   **1185(12)**

STEUCHUS (Augustinus), Eugubinus. Opera omnia.   Vols 1 & 2.   fo.
Venetiis, apud Dominicum Nicolinum, 1591 (1590)   Adams S1838.   **2460-61**

———————— Operum, tomus tertius.   fo.
Parisiis, apud Michaëlem Sonnium, 1577
Adams S1837.   **2462**

[STEVENSON (William)]. A right pithy,
pleasant, and merry comedy, entituled, Gammer
Gurtons needle.   4to.
*London, printed by Tho.Johnson, and are to be
sold by Nath.Brook, Francis Kirkman [etc.],*
1661   [Old Plays III]   Wing S5514.

1103(3)

STIER (Johann). Præcepta doctrinæ logicæ,
ethicæ, physicæ.   Ed. 5.   6 pts.   4to.
Londini, ex officina Rogeri Danielis, 1659
Engr. title-page.   Wing S5540.   **1456**

STILLINGFLEET (Edward), Bp of Worcester.
The Bishop of Worcester's answer to Mr.Locke's
letter.   8vo.
London, by J.H. for Henry Mortlock, 1697
Wing S5557.   **1261(1)**

——————— The Bishop of Worcester's answer
to Mr.Locke's second letter.   8vo.
London, by J.H. for Henry Mortlock, 1698
Wing S5558.   **1261(2)**

——————— A discourse concerning the
idolatry practised in the church of Rome.
2nd ed.   8vo.
London, by Robert White, for Henry Mortlock,
1671   Wing S5577.   **999**

——————— A discourse in vindication of the
doctrine of the Trinity.   2nd ed.   8vo.
London, by J.H. for Henry Mortlock, 1697
Wing S5586.   **1260**

[———————] The grand question, concerning
the Bishops right to vote in Parlament [*sic*] in
cases capital.   8vo.
London, for M.P. and sold by Richard Rumball,
1680   On title-page, in Pepys's hand, 'By Dr
Stillingfleet'.   Wing S5594.   **874**

——————— Irenicum. A weapon-salve for the
Churches wounds.   2nd ed.   4to.
London, printed by R.I. for Henry Mortlock, 1662
Wing S5597.   **1214**

——————— A letter to a deist.   8vo.
London, for Moses Pitt, 1682   Wing S5601.
1064

——————— Origines Britannicæ, or, the
antiquities of the British churches.   fo.
London, by M.Flesher for Henry Mortlock, 1685
Wing S5615.   **2362**

——————— Origines sacræ ... the grounds of
Christian faith.   4to.
London, by R.W. for Henry Mortlock, 1663
Wing S5617; Diary 12 Nov.1665.   **1274**

——————— A rational account of the grounds
of Protestant religion.   fo.
London, by Rob.White for Henry Mortlock, 1665
Wing S5624; Diary 21 Oct.1666.   **2325**

——————— A sermon preached ... November
13.1678.   5th ed.   4to.
London, by Margaret White, for Henry Mortlock,
1679   Wing S5653.   **1413(5)**

——————— The unreasonableness of
separation.   4to.
London, T.N. for Henry Mortlock, 1681
Wing S5675.   **1583**

STOBAEUS (Johannes). Κέρας ἀμαλθείας.
Ἐκλογαὶ ἀποφθεγμάτων καὶ ὑποθηκῶν. Sententiæ
ex thesauris Græcorum delectæ.   3 pts.   fo.
Aureliæ Allobrogum, pro Francisco Fabro, 1609
MS letter by Thomas Gale (Jan.1696/7) [? to
Pepys] and another MS sheet inserted.
Howarth p.266.   **2540**

——————— Dictà poetarum ... apud
J.Stobæum, 1623.
See DICTA poetarum ...   **1833**

STOKES (William). The vaulting-master: or, the
art of vaulting.   4to.
For Richard Davis, in Oxon., 1652
[Consutilia VIII]   Engr. fp. (port., Charrington
p.162), 15 engr. pls.   Wing S5728.   **1434(6)**

STOPFORD (Joshua). Pagano-papismus: or, an
exact parallel between Rome-pagan, and Rome-
Christian.   8vo.
London, by A.Maxwell, for R.Clavel, 1675
Wing S5744.   **735(1)**

——————— [The ways and methods of Rome's
advancement.]   8vo.
[*London, by A.M. for Robert Clavel,* 1675]
Wants title-page.   Wing S5746.   **735(2)**

STOW (John). Annales, or, a generall chronicle of
England. Continued ... by E.Howes.   fo.
Londini, (A.M.) impensis Richardi Meighen,
1631 (1632)   STC 23340.   **2318**

[———————] Certaine worthye manuscript
poems, 1597.
See S.(J.).   **29(4)**

——————— The survey of London ... Now
completely finished by A.M[unday]., H.D[yson].
and others.   fo.
*London, by Elizabeth Purslow, and are to be sold
by Nicholas Bourne,* 1633
Numerous MS and printed items inserted, mostly
concerning the 1690s. At pp.696-7 a note by
Pepys (14 Nov.1695) of information given him by
Gregory King, Lancaster Herald, about the
population of London in 1550 & in 1695. At end,
notes by Pepys (with extracts from poll-books
etc.) of the voting in the parliamentary elections
of 1690, 1695, 1698 & Nov.1701 in the city.
STC 23345; Naval Minutes p.321.   **2476**

STRADA (Famianus). [*De bello Belgico.*]
Histoire de la guerre de Flandre. [Transl.]
2 vols.   8vo.
Suivant la copie imprimée à Paris, 1665
24 engr. ports.   **1334-5**

—————————De bello Belgico. The history of the
Low-Countrey warres. [Transl.]   fo.
London, for Humphrey Moseley, 1650
Engr. ports (Charrington pp.3, 7, 10, 30, 34, 59,
89, 109, 131, 134, 136, 143, 161, 179.).
Wing S5777.   **2058**

STRAFFORD (Thomas Wentworth, 1st Earl of.).
The tryal of Thomas Earl of Strafford ... upon an
impeachment of high treason.   fo.
London, for John Wright, and Richard Chiswell,
1680   Engr. fp. (port., Charrington p.162).
Wing T2232.   **2389**

STRANGE (The) and wonderful history of Mother
Shipton.   12mo.
[*London*] *for W.H. and sold by J.Conyers* [1686]
[Penny-Merriments I]   Woodcut. Title-page
cropped.   Wing S5848.   **362(56)**

STRANGE (A) and wonderful relation of an old
woman that was drowned at Ratcliff High-way.
8vo.
London, for W.T. and sold by J.Blare [c.1680]
[Penny-Merriments II]   **363(27)**

STREAT (William). The dividing of the hooff: or,
seeming-contradictions throughout sacred
Scriptures.   4to.
*London, by T.H. for the author, and are to be
sold by W.Sheers*, 1654   Wing S5942.   **989**

STRICKLAND (John). A discovery of peace ... A
sermon ... 24th of April, 1644.   4to.
London, by M.Simmons for Henry Overton, 1644
[Sermons Polemical VII]   Wing S5969.
                                    1185(14)

—————————Gods work of mercy, in Sions
misery; a sermon preached ... Decemb.27.1643 ...
Whereunto is added, A catalogue of the names of
all the divines that preached before the Parliament
till this present.   4to.
London, by J.Raworth, for L.Fawne, 1644
[Sermons Polemical VII]   Wing S5970.
                                    1185(13)

STRINGER (Nathaniel). Rich redivivus, or Mr.
Jeremiah Richs shorthand improved.   3rd ed.
8vo.
*London, printed and are to be sould by Richard
Northcott*, 1686   [Short-hand Collection V]
Engr. fp. (port., Charrington p.143).
Wing S5977; Carlton pp.95-8.   **1111(2)**

[STRONG (Martin)]. An essay on the usefulness
of mathematical learning.   8vo.
Oxford, at the Theater for Anth.Peisley, 1701
                                         1090

STRONG (William). חבירן מלח
The commemoration and exaltation of mercy ...
A sermon ... Novemb.5.1646.   4to.
London, printed for Francis Tyton, 1646
[Sermons Polemical VII]   Pen-trials in un-
identified hands on front flyleaf.   Wing S6000.
                                    1185(15)

—————————The way to the highest honour ...
a sermon preached ... Feb.24.1646.   4to.
London, by T.H. for Iohn Saywell, 1647
[Sermons Polemical VII]   Wing S6013.
                                    1185(16)

STRUT (Thomas). The weaver's almanack. An
ephemeris for the year 1688.   8vo.
*London, printed by R.Holt, for the Company of
Stationers*, 1688   [Almanacks for the year 1688]
Wing A2407.   **425(28)**

STRUYS (Jan Janszoon). Les voyages en Moscovie,
en Tartarie, en Perse, aux Indes ... Relation d'un
naufrage par M.Glanius.   2 pts.   4to.
Amstredam, chés la veuve de Jacob van Meurs,
1681   Engr. fp., pls.   **1880**

STRYPE (John). Memorials of ... Thomas Cran-
mer.   2 pts.   fo.
London, for Richard Chiswell, 1694
Engr. fp. (port., Charrington p.44), engr. ports,
Charrington pp.23, 95, 116, 171.
Wing S6024.   **2434**

STUBBE (Edmund). Fraus honesta. Comoedia
Cantabrigiae olim acta.   12mo.
Londini, August.Math impensis Richardi Thrale,
1632   STC 23374.   **217(1)**

[STUBBE (Henry)]. A justification of the present
war against the United Netherlands.   4to.
London, for Henry Hills and John Starkey, 1672
Engr. fp, pls.   Wing S6050.   **1226(1)**

—————————A further justification of the
present war against the United Netherlands.   4to.
London, for Henry Hills, and John Starkey, 1673
Engr. pls.   Wing S6046.   **1226(2)**

STURMY (Samuel). The mariners magazine.
2nd ed.   2 pts.   fo.
*London, by Anne Godbid, for William Fisher,
Edward Thomas* [etc.], 1679   Engr. fp. (port.,
Charrington p.162), engr. title-page, diagrams.
                                         2196

SUCCESSION (The) to the Crown of England,
considered, 1701.
See DEFOE (Daniel).   **1436(4)**

SUCKLING (Sir John). Fragmenta aurea: a
collection of ... peices.   3rd ed.   2 pts.   8vo.
London, for Humphrey Moseley, 1658
Wing S6128; Diary 5 Sept.1664.   **905(1)**

———————— The last remains of Sir John Suckling. Being a full collection of all his poems and letters. 8vo.
London, for Humphrey Moseley, 1659
Wants portrait. Wing S6130. **905(2)**

SUETONIUS. The history of the twelve Caesars. 8vo.
London, printed for John Starkey, 1672
Engr. ports. Wing S6147. **975**

SUFFOLK (Charles Brandon, Duke of). The iustes of the moneth of Maye [c.1507].
See JOUSTS. **1254(1)**

SUITE de la civilité françoise, 1680.
See COURTIN (Antoine de). **135**

SULLY (Maximilien de Béthune, duc de). Memoires ou œconomies royales d'estat ... de Henry le grand. 4 vols in 3. fo.
Paris, chez Louis Billaine (vol.3: chez Augustin Courbé), 1664 (1662) Vol.1: engr. map, Carte du Bourdelois, du Perigord inserted. Wants sig.S. Vol.3: leaf Rrr4 bound at end of vol.4. **2593-5**

SULPITIUS (Joannes). Opus grammatices. 4to.
R.Pynson, London, 1498.
See Appendix. **1305(6)**

SUMMA conciliorum omnium ... Auctore F.Longo a Coriolano. fo.
Antuerpiæ, ex officina Plantiniana, apud Balthasarem Moretum, et uiduam Ioannis Moreti [etc.], 1623 (1622) **2680**

SUMMARY (A) defence of the Lower House of Convocation, 1703.
See HOOPER (George), Bp of Bath and Wells. **1697(15)**

SUMMARY (A) of the arguments for the Archbishop's right to continue the whole Convocation [1701].
See GIBSON (Edmund), Bp of London. **1695(8)**

SUMMARY (A) view of the articles exhibited against the late Bishop of St.David's, 1701.
See COOKE (Sir John). **1231**

SUNDERLAND (Robert Spencer, 2nd Earl of). The Earl of Sunderland's letter to a friend in London. Plainly discovering the designs of the Romish party. brs.
London, by J.Partridge, and M.Gilliflower, 1689
Wing S6177. **2441(2)**

SUPPLEMENT à l'histoire metallique de la republique de Hollande [of P.Bizot], 1690.
See BIZOT (Pierre). **1487**

SUPPLICATION. A supplicacion unto ... H.the. viij., 1534.
See BARNES (Robert). **958(2)**

SUPPLY (A) of prayer for the ships of this Kingdom that want ministers to pray with them.
London, for Iohn Field [1645]
[Liturgick Controversies II] Wing S6191. **1188(16)**

SURIREY DE SAINT REMY (Pierre). Memoires d'artillerie. 2 vols. 4to.
Paris, chez Jean Anisson, 1697 146 engr. pls. **1901-2**

SURIUS (Bernardinus). Le pieux pelerin, ou voyage de Jerusalem. 4to.
Brusselles, chez François Foppens, 1666
Engr. fp. (port., Charrington p.162), engr. title-page, map. **1810**

SURVEY (A) of France, 1618.
See DANETT (Thomas). **1429(7)**

SURVEY (A) of the buildings and encroachments on the river of Thames, on both sides, from London-Bridge ... to ... Lyme-house. [Signed by R.Haddock and 13 others.] Navy-Office, 30 30.Octob.84. fo.
[*London*, 1684] Bound in at end.
Wing S6198. **396**

SURVEY (A) of the pretended holy discipline, 1663.
See BANCROFT (Richard), Abp of Canterbury. **1651**

SWALLOW (John). Swallow. A new almanack for ... 1688. 8vo.
Cambridge, printed by John Hayes, 1688
[Almanacks for the year 1688]
Wing A2452. **425(24)**

SWAMMERDAM (Jan). Ephemeri vita: or the natural history and anatomy of the Ephemeron, a fly. [Transl.] 4to.
London, for Henry Faithorne, and John Kersey, 1681 [Consutilia IX] Engr. pls.
Wing S6233. **1435(1)**

———————— Histoire generale des insectes. [Transl.] 4to.
Utrecht, chez Guillaume de Walcheren, 1682
13 engr. pls. **1605**

SWENDSEN (Haagen). The tryals of H.Swendsen, S.Baynton, J.Hartwell and J.Spurr ... Nov.25.1702. fo.
London, for Isaac Cleave, 1703 [Narratives & Tryals VII] **2255(14)**

[SWETNAM (Joseph)]. The arraignmen[t] of lewd, idle, froward, and unconstant women. 4to.
London, by M.C. for T.Passenger, 1682
[Vulgaria III] Title-page cropped. **1192(23)**

SYDENHAM (Thomas). Tractatus de podagra et hydrope. 8vo.
Londini, typis R.N. impensis Gualt Kettilby, 1683
Wing S6320. **1119**

SYMBOLARUM in Matthæum tomus prior
(– alter), exhibens catenam Græcorum patrum.
[Ed. by] P.Possinus. [*Gk & Lat.*]   2 vols in 1.
fo.
Tolosæ, excudebat Ioannes Boude, 1646-7   **2568**

SYMMONS (Edward). A militarie sermon ...
Preached at Shrlwsbury [*sic*], May 19.1644.   4to.
Oxford, by Henry Hall, 1644   [Sermons
Polemical VII]   Wing S6347.   **1185(7)**

SYNAGOGUE (The): or the shadow of the
Temple, 1679.
See HARVEY (Christopher).   **480(2)**

SYNDICAT (Le) du pape Alexandre VII, 1669.
See LETI (Gregorio).   **41**

SYNODUS Anglicana, 1702.
See GIBSON (Edmund), Bp of London.   **1692**

T

T.(D.). Grammaire generale, 1664.
See LANCELOT (Claude).   **509**

T.(J.). Amyntor, 1699.
See TOLAND (John).   **1082(1)**

T.(S.). A case of conscience, 1643.
See TORSHELL (Samuel).   **1428(3)**

TABLE (A) to al the statutes [1570].
See ENGLAND. *Statutes.*   **1994(1)**

TABLEAU (Le) de la Croix representé dans les
ceremonies de la Ste. messe.   8vo.
Paris, chez F.Mazot, 1651 (1653)
54 engr. ll.   **872**

TABLES (Les) de la declinaison ... que fait le
soleil de la ligne equinoctiale, 1559.
See BISSELIN (Olivier).   **1077(10)**

[TABOUROT (Étienne)]. Les bigarrures, et
touches du Seigneur Des Accords.   Derniere ed.
5 pts.   12mo.
Rouen, chez David Geuffroy, 1626   **148**

TACHARD (Gui). Voyage de Siam des peres
Jesuites envoyés par le Roy.   12mo.
Amsterdam, chez Pierre Mortier, 1687
Engr. title-page, 30 engr. pls.   **683**

———————— Second voyage du père Tachard ...
au royaume de Siam.   12mo.
Amsterdam, chez Pierre Mortier, 1689   Engr.
title-page, 6 engr. pls.   **684**

TACITUS. The annales. The description of
Germanie. [*Etc.*] (3rd ed.) [Transl.]   2 pts.
fo.
(*London, by Arnold Hatfield for Iohn Norton*)
1604 (1605)   STC 23645.   **2096**

TAILOR (Robert). The hogge hath lost his pearle.
A comedy.   4to.
London, for Richard Redmer, 1614
[Old Plays II]   Autograph 'Nicholas Higginson'
on H4v, with title and author in different hand.
Title and author repeated in a third hand.
STC 23658.   **1102(2)**

TAISNIER (Joannes). A very necessarie and
profitable booke concerning nauigation ... Translated into Englishe, by R.Eden.   4to.
London, by Richarde Iugge [1579?]
[Sea Tracts III]   Engr. diagrams.   MS notes
in unidentified hand on title-page (obliterated),
and in margin, and at end draft or pen-trial:
'Thomas Bate after my most harty comendacions
unto you'.   STC 23659.   **1079(1)**

TALLENTS (Francis). A view of universal
history.   2 pts.
[*London*? c.1700]   8 charts.
Wing T131.   **2917**

TAMBURLAINE the greate, pts 1 & 2, 1605-6.
See MARLOWE (Christopher).   **1102(4, 4a)**

TA-MING Yung-li êrh-shih wu nien sui-tz'u
hsin-hai ta-t'ung li. [Official almanac for the 25th
year of the Yung-li period, 1671, issued by Cheng
Ching on behalf of the defunct Ming dynasty.]
[*Taiwan*, 1670?]   **1914(2)**

TANNER (John). Angelus Britannicus: an
ephemeris for ... 1688.   32nd impr.   8vo.
*London, printed by W.Horton, for the Company
of Stationers*, 1688   [Almanacks for the year
1688]   Wing A2525.   **425(25)**

———————— Angelus Britannicus: an
ephemeris for ... 1689.   33rd impr.   8vo.
*London, printed by W.H. for the Company of
Stationers*, 1689   [Almanacks for the year
1689]   Wing A2526.   **426(10)**

TANNER (Thomas), Bp of St Asaph. Notitia
monastica.   8vo.
Oxford, at the Theater, 1695   5 engr. pls.
Presented to Pepys by the author: Howarth,
pp.259-61.   Wing T144.   **1738**

TAPP (John). The sea-mans kalender.   4to.
London, by W.G. for George Hurlock, 1667
Volvelle.   **1142(3)**

TARIF ABENTARIQUE (Abulcacim), *pseud.*
See LUNA (Miguel).

TASBOROUGH (John). The tryal and conviction of J.Tasborough and A.Price, for subornation of perjury.   fo.
London, for Robert Pawlett, 1679/80
[Narratives & Tryals IV]   Wing T2161.   **2252(7)**

TAVERNIER (Jean Baptiste), Baron d'Aubonne.
A collection of several relations and treaties.
2 pts.   fo.
London, by A.Godbid and J.Playford, for Moses Pitt, 1680   Engr. pls, map.
Wing T250.   **2407**

———————— The six voyages through Turky, into Persia and the East-Indies. Made English by J.P. (— A new relation of the ... Seraglio.)   3 pts.
fo.
London, for R.L. and M.P., and are to be sold by John Starkey, and Moses Pitt, 1678 (1677)
23 engr. pls.   Wing T256.   **2406**

TAYLOR (Francis). Gods covenant the Churches plea: or a sermon preached ... Octob.29.1645.
4to.
London, by R.Cotes for Stephen Bowtell, 1645
[Sermons Polemical VII]   Wing T278.
1185(17)

TAYLOR (Jeremy), Bp of Down and Connor.
Antiquitates Christianæ ... In two parts. The first ... by J.Taylor ... the second ... by W.Cave.   fo.
London, by E.Flesher, and R.Norton, for R.Royston, 1678   Engr. fp., 18 engr. pls.
Wing T287A, C1588A.   **2599**

[————————] A discourse concerning prayer ex tempore.   4to.
[*London?*] 1646   [Liturgick Controversies II]
Wing T312.   **1188(13)**

———————— Σύμβολον θεολογικόν: or a collection of polemical discourses.   3rd ed.
2 pts.   fo.
London, by R.Norton for R.Royston, 1674
(1673)   Engr. fp. (port., Charrington p.163), engr. title-page, pl.   Wing T399.   **2640**

———————— The worthy communicant.   8vo.
London, by R.H. for Awnsham Churchil, 1683
Engr. title-page.   Wing T421.   **1124**

TAYLOR (John). Taylor on Thame Isis: or the description of the two famous riuers of Thame and Isis, who ... together, are called Thamisis, or Thames.   8vo.
London, by Iohn Haviland, 1632
STC 23803.   **2022(2)**

TEATRO (Il) d'onore, 1699.
See PARMA. Collegio de' Nobili.   **1451(1)**

TEISSIER (Antoine). Catalogus auctorum qui librorum catalogos, indices ... scriptis consign-arunt. Cum P.Labbæi Bibliotheca nummaria.
4to.
Genevæ, apud Samuelem de Tournes, 1686   **1861**

174

[TÉLLEZ (Gabriel)]. Los lagos de San Vicente.
4to.
[*Seville, Tomás López de Haro*, c.1683]
Gaselee 109.   **1553(3)**

[————————] El condenado por desconfiado.
Comedia famosa.   4to.
[*Seville, Tomé de Dios Miranda*, c.1678]
Gaselee 108.   **1553(15)**

TEMPIO (Il) nel tempio in occasione del battesimo del Serenissimo Infante primogenito ... di Rinaldo I. Duca di Modona.   4to.
Modona, per Bartolomeo Soliani, 1700
2 engr. pls.   Tanner II, p.19.   **1451(3)**

TEMPLE (Sir John). The Irish rebellion.   2 pts.
4to.
London, by R.White for Samuel Gellibrand, 1646
Wing T627.   **1536**

TEMPLE (Thomas). Christ's government in and over his people. Delivered in a sermon ...
Octob.26.1642.   4to.
London, for Samuel Gellibrand, 1642
[Sermons Polemical VII]   Wing T634.   **1185(18)**

TEMPLE (Sir William), Bart. An introduction to the history of England.   8vo.
London, for Richard and Ralph Simpson, 1695
Wing T638.   **1116**

———————— Letters ... In two volumes ...
Published by J.Swift. (— The third and last volume.)   3 vols.   8vo.
London, printed for J.Tonson, and A. and J. Churchil, and R.Simpson [etc.], 1700-1703
Engr. fp. (port., Charrington p.164).
Wing T641.   **1312-4**

[————————] Memoirs of what past in Christendom, from the war begun 1672 to the peace concluded 1679.   8vo.
London, printed by R.R. for Ric.Chiswell, 1692
Wing T642.   **1071**

[————————] Miscellanea.   8vo.
London, by A.M. and R.R. for Edw.Gellibrand, 1680   Wing T646.   **973**

———————— Miscellanea. The second part. In four essays.   8vo.
London, printed by T.M. for Ri. and Ra.Simpson, 1690   Wing T652.   **974**

———————— Observations upon the United Provinces of the Netherlands.   8vo.
London, printed by A.Maxwell for Sa.Gellibrand, 1673   Wing T656.   **1108**

TENISON (Thomas), Abp of Canterbury. Of idolatry: a discourse.   4to.
London, for Francis Tyton, 1678
Wing T704.   **1465**

———————— A sermon concerning holy resolution ... preached ... December 30th 1694.   4to.
London, for Ri.Chiswell, 1695
Wing T712.   **1528(4)**

———————— A sermon preached ... March 5. 1694/5.   4to.
London, for Ri.Chiswell, 1695
Wing T720.   **1528(9)**

———————— A true copy of the Archbishop of Canterbury's speech ... on ... February 19.1701/2. 4to.
(*London, for Ri.Chiswell*) [c.1702]
[Convocation Pamphlets X]   **1696(13)**

TENURE (The) of kings and magistrates, 1649.
See MILTON (John).   **1430(8)**

TERENCE. Comoediæ sex ... Accedunt Ælii Donati commentarius integer.   8vo.
Lugd.Batavorum, apud Franciscum Hackium,
1644   Engr. title-page.   **1134**

———————— Les comedies traduites en françois par Madame Dacier. [*Lat. & Fr.*]   3e ed.
3 vols.   12mo.
Amsterdam, chez George Gallet, 1699
Vol.1: Engr. title-page, 2 engr. pls.
Vol.2: Engr. fp.   Vol.3: 2 engr. pls.   **651-3**

TERMES (Les) de la ley, 1659.
See RASTELL (John).   **900**

TERRY (Edward). Ψευδελευθερια, or lawlesse liberty ... a sermon preached ... Aug.16.1646. 4to.
London, by Thomas Harper, and are to be sold by Thomas Slater, 1646
[Sermons Polemical VII]   **1185(19)**

———————— A voyage to East-India.   8vo.
London, by T.W. for J.Martin, and J.Allestrye,
1655   Engr. fp. (port., Charrington p.164), engr. pls, map.   Wing T782.   **497**

TERTULLIAN. Apologeticus et Ad Scapulam liber. Accessit M.Minucii Felicis Octavius.   2 pts. 12mo.
Cantabrigiæ, ex officina Joan.Hayes, impensis Henr.Dickinson & Rich.Green, 1686
Wing T784.   **66**

TESAURO (Emanuele). Patriarchæ sive Christi Servatoris genealogia ... Accessere Cæsarum elogia. 8vo.
Londini, ex officina Rogeri Danielis, 1657
Engr. title-page, 7 engr. pls.   Wing T791; Diary 23 Jan.1660/1.   **736**

TESDALE (Christopher). Hierusalem: or a vision of peace ... A sermon preached ... Aug.28.1644. 4to.
London, by R.Cotes, for Phil.Stephens, 1644
[Sermons Polemical VII]   Wing T792.
                                        1185(20)

THANKSGIVING. A thankes geuing to God vsed in Christes churche, 1551.
See LITURGIES. *Church of England.*   **228(2)**

THEAKER (Robert). A light to the longitude: or the use of an instrument called the seaman's director.   4to.
London, by William Godbid for William Fisher,
1665   [Sea Tracts IV]   Wing T844.   **1080(7)**

THEOCRITUS. Τὰ εὑρισκόμενα.   4to.
Oxoniæ, e Theatro Sheldoniano, impensis Sam. Smith, et Benj.Walford, 1699   Engr. fp.
Wing T852.   **1581**

THEODORUS VERAX, *pseud.*
See WALKER (Clement).

THEOLOGICAL (A) systeme, 1655.
See LA PEYRÈRE (Isaac de). Men before Adam.
                                        669

THERESA, St. La vie de la sainte Mere Terese de Iesus ... escrite par elle meme ... Nouvellement traduite ... en françois.   12mo.
Paris, chez Sebastien Huré, 1645   **451**

THESAURUS antiquitatum Romanarum, in quo continentur lectissimi quique scriptores ... congestus a J.G.Graevio.   12 vols.   fo.
Traject. ad Rhen. [&] *Lugd.Batav., apud Franciscum Halmam, Petrum vander Aa*, 1694-9
Engr. title-pages, engr. pls, maps, ports (Charrington pp.15 & 70). 4 MS drawings inserted at end.
                                        2780-91

THEVET (André). Histoire des plus illustres et scavans hommes de leurs siecles.   8 vols. 12mo.
Paris, chez François Mauger, 1671
Engr. fp. (port., Charrington p.20), title-page, ports.   **560-67**

THEVENOT (Jean de). Voyages.   5 vols. 12mo.
Paris, chez Charles Angot, 1689   Engr. fp., title-page, pls.   **772-6**

THIERS (Jean-Baptiste). Dissertations ecclésiastiques.   3 pts.   12mo.
Paris, chez Antoine Dezallier, 1688   **815**

———————— Histoire des perruques.   12mo.
Paris, aux dépens de l'Auteur, 1690   **914**

———————— Traité de la clôture des religieuses. 12mo.
Paris, chez Antoine Dezallier, 1681   **845**

THIRD (A) letter to a clergyman in the country (1702).
See ATTERBURY (Francis), Bp of Rochester.
                                        1697(8)

[THIS morning ...] [*Begins:*] Whitehall, August 29. 1695. This morning arrived here an express ... with the good news of the surrender ... of Namur. fo.
In the Savoy, by Edw.Jones, 1695   [Single leaf inserted between nos 3109 and 3110 of the London Gazette.]   Wing T937.   **2087**

THOMAS, à Kempis. De Christo imitando ... Interprete S.Castellione. Quibus adjungitur liber quartus Latine redditus.
Cantabrigiæ, ex officinâ Joh.Hayes, impensis G. Graves, 1685   Wing T949.   **213**

[————————] De imitatione Christi.   fo.
Parisiis, e Typographia Regia, 1640
Engr. title-page.   **2690**

————————— De l'imitation de Iesus-Christ, traduction nouuelle, par le sieur De Beüil.
3e ed.   16mo.
Paris, chez Charles Savreux, 1662
Engr. title-page, pls.   **339**

————————— Oraciones y meditaciones de la vida de Jesu Christo.   4to.
Brusselas, en casa de Francisco Foppens, 1661
Engr. title-page.   **1762**

THOMPSON (Nathaniel). The tryal of N.Thompson, W.Pain, and J.Farwell ... for ... publishing libels.   fo.
London, for Thomas Simmons, 1682
[Narratives & Tryals IV]   Wing T2207.
2252(31)

THORNDIKE (Herbert). Of religious assemblies, and the publick service of God.   8vo.
Cambridge, printed by Roger Daniel, and are to be sold ... in London, 1642   Wing T1054.   **828**

THORNTON (   ), Captain. Hereafter followeth the vttermost and [*sic*] course round about all Ireland.   4to.
[*London,* 1606]   [Sea Tracts II]
STC 24043.5.   **1078(6)**

[THORNTON (William)]. A vindication of the twenty third article of the Church of England.
4to.
London, for Thomas Bennet, 1702   **1772(2)**

THOROWGOOD (Thomas). Moderation iustified ... A sermon ... preached ... December 25.1644.
4to.
London, by I.L. for Christopher Meredith, and for Thomas Slater, 1645   [Sermons Polemical VII]   Wing T1069.   **1185(21)**

THOU (Jacques August de). Histoire de Monsieur De Thou des choses arrivées de son temps. Mise en françois.   3 vols.   [*No more published.*]   fo.
Paris, chez Augustin Courbé, 1659   **2650-52**

THREE (The) ladies of London, 1584.
See WILSON (Robert).   **1103(2)**

THREE letters concerning the present state of Italy, 1688.
See BURNET (Gilbert), Bp of Salisbury.   **679(2)**

THUCYDIDES. De bello Peloponnesiaco libri octo. [*Gk & Lat.*]   fo.
Oxoniæ, e Theatro Sheldoniano, impensis T.Bennet [*London*], 1696   2 engr. maps.
Wing T1133.   **2918**

————————— The history of the Grecian war ... translated ... by T.Hobbes.   2nd ed.   fo.
London, by Andrew Clark for Charles Harper, 1676   Engr. title-page, 4 engr. maps.
Wing T1134.   **2320**

THYSIUS (Antonius). Historia navalis.   4to.
Lugduni Batavorum, ex officina Joannis Maire, 1657   Naval Minutes, p.56.   **1824**

TILLOTSON (John), Abp of Canterbury. Apologie pour la religion protestante ... ou sermon sur le XXIV. de Josué v.XV ... Traduit de l'Anglois, par le Sieur P.Lorrain.   12mo.
La Haye, chez Abraham Arondeus, 1681   **67**

————————— A sermon preached November 5. 1678.   6th ed.   4to.
London, by J.D. for Brabazon Aylmer, and William Rogers, 1678   Wing T1231.   **1413(3)**

————————— A sermon preached ... the 27th of October [1692].   4to.
London, for Brabazon Aylmer, and William Rogers, 1692   [Consutilia VI]
Wing T1246.   **1432(14)**

TINDALL (Matthew). An essay concerning the laws of nations, and the rights of sovereigns.
4to.
London, for Richard Baldwin, 1694
[Consutilia VII]   Wing T1300.   **1433(11)**

TIRINUS (Jacobus). Commentarius in sacram Scripturam.   2 vols in 1.   fo.
Lugduni, sumptibus Ioannis Girin, & Bartholom. Riviere, 1672   **2596**

TIRSO DE MOLINA, *pseud.*
See TÉLLEZ (Gabriel).

TITI (Filippo), Abbot. Ammaestramento utile, e curioso di pittura scoltura et architettura nelle chiese di Roma.   12mo.
Roma, per Giuseppe Vannacci, 1686   **231**

[TITUS (Silius)]. A seasonable speech, made by a worthy member of Parliament in the House of Commons, concerning the other House. March 1659. [Also attributed to the Earl of Shaftesbury.]
4to.
[*London,* 1659]   [Consutilia IV]
Wing S2898.   **1430(15)**

[TOLAND (John)]. Amyntor: or, a defence of
Milton's life.   8vo.
London, printed, and are to be sold by the book-
sellers of London and Westminster, 1699
Wing T1760.   **1082(1)**

[————————] Christianity not mysterious.
8vo.
London, 1696   Wing T1762.   **1082(5)**

[————————] The danger of mercenary
Parliaments.   4to.
[*London,* c.1700]   [Consutilia XI]   **1437(5)**

TOM Double against Dr.D–v–n–t; or the learned
author of the Essays on peace at home and war
abroad.   8vo.
Sold by the booksellers of London and West-
minster, 1704   **1382(4)**

TOM Double return'd out of the country, 1702.
See DAVENANT (Charles).   **1380(2)**

TOM Tell Troath, or a free discourse touching
the manners of the tyme.   4to.
[*Holland*? c.1630]   [Consutilia II]
STC 23868.   **1428(13)**

TOM Thumb, his life and death.   12mo.
[*London*] *by J.M. for J.Clarke, W.Thackeray, and*
T.Passinger [c.1680]   [Penny-Merriments II]
Woodcuts.   **363(22)**

TOM Tram of the West [c.1680].
See CROUCH (Humphrey).   **362(41)**

TONGE (Simson). The narrative and case of
Simson Tonge.   fo.
London, printed for C.W., 1681
[Narratives & Tryals III]   Wing T1884A.
                    2251(42)

TOPSELL (Edward). The history of four-footed
beasts and serpents ... Collected out of the writings
of C.Gesner and other authors by E.Topsel. Whereunto is now added, The theater of insects ... By
T.Muffet. The whole revised.   fo.
London, by E.Cotes, for G.Sawbridge, T.Williams,
and T.Johnson, 1658   Woodcuts.
Wing G624.   **2521**

TORNIELLO (Francisco). Opera del modo de
fare le littere maiuscole antique.   4to.
[*Milan*] (*Gotardo da ponte,* 1517)
Woodcut diagrams.   Adams T809; Duff p.68.
                    1512(1)

TORRE (Carlo). Il ritratto di Milano.   4to.
Milano, per Federico Agnelli, 1674
7 engr. pls.   **1751**

TORRE FARFAN (Fernando de la). Fiestas de
la S.Iglesia metropolitana ... de Sevilla.   fo.
Seuilla, en casa de la viuda de Nicolàs Rodriguez,
1671   Engr. title-page, 20 engr. pls.
Gaselee 172.   **2144**

TORRE Y PERALTA (José de la). Aqui se contiene vn curioso romance, politico, y moral, que
haze vn soldado al ver vn retrato de Carlos
segundo.   4to.
(*Sevilla,* 1681)   Gaselee 173; Wilson p.235.
                    1545(21)

TORRE Y SEBIL (Francisco de la). La azuzena
de Etiopia. Comedia famosa, de F.de la Torre
[and J.Bolea].   4to.
[*Seville, Juan Cabezas,* c.1675]
Gaselee 171.   **1553(13)**

TORRIANO (Giovanni). Piazza universale di
proverbi italiani: or, a common place of Italian
proverbs. [*Ital. & Engl.*]   3 pts.
London, by F. and T.W. for the author, 1666
Wing T1928.   **2609**

———————— Vocabolario italiano & inglese ...
Formerly compiled by J.Florio.   fo.
London, by T.Warren for Jo.Martin, Ja.Allestry,
and Tho.Dicas, 1659   Wing T1920.   **2445**

[TORSHELL (Samuel)]. A case of conscience,
concerning flying in times of trouble.   4to.
London, for John Bellamie and Ralph Smith, 1643
[Consutilia II]   Wing T1934.   **1428(3)**

———————— The palace of justice ... A sermon
... before the Honorable House of Commons ...
12th of May, 1646.   4to.
London, by T.R. and E.M. for John Bellamy, 1646
[Sermons Polemical VII]   Wing T1940.
                    1185(22)

[TOUCHET (George)]. Historical collections ...
concerning the changes of religion ... in the reigns
of King Henry the eighth [to] Queen Elizabeth.
8vo.
[*London*] 1674   Wing T1954.   **848**

TOURNEFORT (Joseph Pitton de).
See PITTON DE TOURNEFORT (Joseph).

TOWNSHEND (Heywood). Historical collections:
or an exact account of ... the four last Parliaments
of Q.Elizabeth.   fo.
London, for T.Basset, W.Crooke, and W.Cademan,
1680   Wing T1991; Tangier Papers, p.105.
                    2311

TRACTATUS theologico-politicus, 1674.
See SPINOZA (Benedict de).   **917**

TRADES (The) increase, 1615.
See KAYLL (Robert).   **1079(5)**

TRADESCANT (John). Musæum Tradescant-
ianum: or, a collection of rarities.   8vo.
London, printed by John Grismond, sold by
Nathanael Brooke, 1656   Engr. ports, Charrington p.166.   Wing T2005.   **239**

TRAGEDY. The tragedie of Tancred and Gismund, 1592.
See WILMOT (Robert). **939(4)**

TRAITÉ. Traitté de l'aiman, 1687.
See ALENCÉ (Joachim d'). **489(1)**

TRAITÉ de la cour.
See DU REFUGE (Eustace). Arcana aulica ... **43**

TRAITÉ. Traitté des ceremonies superstitieuses, 1678.
See SPINOZA (Benedict de). Tractatus theologico-politicus. **73**

TRAITÉ des sources de la corruption ... aujourd'huy parmi les Chrestiens, 1700.
See OSTERWALD (Jean Frédéric). **667-8**

TREASON'S masterpiece, 1680.
See C.(C.). **750**

TREATISE (A) concernynge the diuision betwene the spiritualtie and temporaltie [1532?].
See SAINT GERMAN (Christopher). **368(1)**

TREATISE (A) of humane reason, 1674.
See CLIFFORD (Martin). **51**

TREATISE (The) of love. fo.
W.de Worde [*Westminster*, 1493]
See Appendix. **2051(2)**

TREATISE (A) of taxes, 1662.
See PETTY (Sir William). **1174(1)**

TREBY (Sir George). A collection of letters, 1681.
See COLLECTION (A) of letters ... **2251(43)**

[TRENCHARD (John)]. An argument, shewing, that a standing army is inconsistent with a free government. 4to.
London, 1697 [Consutilia VII]
Wing T2110. **1433(19)**

TRENT, Council of. Confessio fidei, 1642.
See VIA ad pacem ecclesiasticam ... **1012**

TRESCOT (Thomas). The zealous magistrate ... A sermon, preached in Exeter. 4to.
London, for Daniel Frere, 1642 [Sermons Polemical VII] Wing T2126. **1185(23)**

TRESOR (Le) des haranges, 1668.
See GILBAULT (L.). **547-8**

TRIAL. The tryal of T.Pilkington [*etc.*] for the riot at Guildhall, on Midsommer-Day, 1682. fo.
London, for Thomas Dring, 1683
[Narratives & Tryals IV] Wing T2231. **2252(32)**

TRIAL. A tryal of witches, 1682.
See HALE (Sir Matthew). A short treatise ... **904**

TRIALS. The tryals and condemnation of L.Anderson, alias Munson, W.Russel, alias Napper [and others] ... for high treason as Romish priests. fo.
London, for Thomas Collins and John Starkey, 1680 [Narratives & Tryals IV]
Wing T2243. **2252(6)**

TRIALS. The tryals and condemnation of T.White, alias Whitebread [and 4 others] all Jesuits and priests; for high treason. fo.
London, for H.Hills, T.Parkhurst, J.Starkey [*etc.*], 1679 [Narratives & Tryals I] Engr. port., Charrington p.50, inserted. Wing T2247.
2249(15)

TRIALS. The tryals of T.Walcot [and 4 others]. fo.
London, for Richard Royston, Benjamin Took, and Charles Mearn, 1683
[Narratives & Tryals V] Wing T2265. **2253(1)**

TRIANGULAR (A) canon logarithmical, 1695.
See NORWOOD (Richard). **1067(2)**

TRIGGE (Thomas). Calendarium astrologicum: or an almanack for ... 1688. 8vo.
London, printed by B.Griffin, for the Company of Stationers, 1688 [Almanacks for the year 1688] Wing A2570. **425(26)**

TRIGNY (de), *pseud.*
See LANCELOT (Claude).

[TRIMNELL (Charles), Bp of Winchester]. An answer to a Third letter to a clergyman in the country. 4to.
(*London, for R.Sare*, 1702) [Convocation Pamphlets X] 'Bp Trimnell' written above title in Daniel Waterland's hand. **1696(8)**

[——————] The late pretence of a constant practice to enter the Parliament ... consider'd and disprov'd. 4to.
(*London, for Richard Sare*) [c.1702]
[Convocation Pamphlets X] 'Bp Trimnell' written above title in Daniel Waterland's hand.
1696(5)

[——————] The late pretence of a constant practice to enter the Parliament ... in a second letter. 4to.
(*London, for Richard Sare*) [1702]
[Convocation Pamphlets X] 'Bp Trimnell' written above title in Daniel Waterland's hand.
1696(7)

[——————] A vindication of the proceedings of some members of the Lower House of the last Convocation. 4to.
[*London*] (*for Richard Sare*, 1702)
[Convocation Pamphlets IX] 'Bp Trimnell' written above title in Daniel Waterland's hand.
1695(8a)

TRINITY HOUSE, Deptford. The royal charter of confirmation granted by ... King James II to the Trinity-House of Deptford-Strond. 8vo. *London*, 1685   Engr. col. pls.   MS index inserted at end (25 leaves, in hand of one of Pepys's clerks).   Wing J381.   **1377**

TRISMOSIN (Salomon), *pseud.* La toyson d'or, ou la fleur de thresors ... Traduict de l'alemand. 8vo. *Paris, ches Charles Seuestre*, 1612 (1613) Engr. title-page, 22 woodcuts, coloured.   **862(1)**

TRITHEIM (Johann). Steganographia: hoc est: ars per occultam scripturam animi sui voluntatem absentibus aperiendi certa. (– Clavis.)   3 pts. 4to. *Darmbstadii, ex officina typographica Balthasaris Aulæandri, sumptibus Ioannis Berneri*, 1621   **1350**

TRIUMPHANT (The) weaver, 1682. *See* C.(R.).   **1193(14)**

TROGUS POMPEIUS. Justinus de historiis Philippicis, et totius mundi originibus (ex Trogo Pompeio). Interpretatione ... illustravit P.J. Cantel.   4to. *Parisiis, apud Fredericum Leonard*, 1677 Engr. title-page.   **1950**

TRUE (A) account and declaration of the horrid conspiracy, 1686. *See* SPRAT (Thomas), Bp of Rochester.   **1137**

TRUE (A) account of the behaviour, confession, and last dying speeches of the four criminals that were executed together with the paper writ by Captain Harrison's own hand ... on Friday the 15th of April, 1692.   brs. *London, printed for L.Curtiss*, 1692 [Consutilia VI]   **1432(3)**

TRUE (A) account of the late ... conspiracy against ... the Lord Protector.   4to. *London, by Thomas Newcomb*, 1654 [Consutilia III]   Wing T2381.   **1429(10)**

TRUE (The) and admirable history of patient Grissel.   4to. *London, for J.Wright, J.Clarke, W.Thackeray* [*etc.*], 1682   [Vulgaria IV]   Woodcut. Wing T2413.   **1193(2)**

TRUE (A) and compleat list ... of the ... Parliament of Ireland, 1692. *See* IRELAND. *Parliament.*   **1432(15)**

TRUE (A) and faithfull relation ... of what hath lately happened in Constantinople, 1622. *See* ROE (Sir Thomas).   **1431(12)**

TRUE (The) character of a church-man, 1702. *See* WEST (Richard).   **1696(12)**

TRUE. The true-lovers garland.   8vo. [*London*] *for J.Back*, 1687   [Penny-Merriments II]   Woodcut.   Wing T2742.   **363(46)**

TRUE (The) lover's new accademy.   12mo. [*London*] *for J.Conyers* [c.1680]   [Penny-Merriments II]   Woodcut.   **363(28)**

TRUE (A) narrative of the Popish-plot against King Charles I.   fo. *London, for Robert Harford*, 1680 [Narratives & Tryals III]   Wing T2805.   **2251(12)**

TRUE (The) picture of a modern Whig, 1701. *See* DAVENANT (Charles).   **1380(1)**

TRUE (The) portraiture of the kings of England, 1688. *See* PARKER (Henry).   **1430(17)**

TRUE (A) relation of the unjust, cruel, and barbarous proceedings against the English at Amboyna. [Publ. by the East India Company.] 4 pts.   12mo. *London, by Will.Bentley, for Will.Hope*, 1651 Engr. fp.   Wing T3065.   **79**

TRUE (The) Tom Double: or, an account of Dr. Davenant's late conduct and writings ... Part I. 4to. *London, by G.Croom, and sold by J.Nutt*, 1704   **1382(3)**

TRUE (The) tryal of understanding, 1687. *See* M.(S.).   **362(33)**

TRUTH brought to light, 1651. *See* NARRATIVE (The) history of King James ...   **1259**

TRUTH brought to light: or the gross forgeries of Dr.Hollingworth ... detected ... In a letter from Lieut.General Ludlow.   4to. *London*, 1693   Wing T3153.   **1286(9)**

TUBERO (Oratius), *pseud.* *See* LA MOTHE LE VAYER (François de).

TUCKNEY (Anthony). The balme of Gilead ... A sermon preached ... August 30.1643.   4to. *London, by Richard Bishop for Samuel Gellibrand*, 1643   [Sermons Polemical VII] Wing T3210.   **1185(24)**

TURBERVILL (Edward). The information of E.Turbervill ... at the Bar of the House of Commons.   fo. *London, by the assigns of John Bill, Thomas Newcomb, and Henry Hills*, 1680   [Narratives & Tryals III]   Wing T3252.   **2251(44)**

[TURNER (John)]. A vindication of the authority of Christian princes, over ecclesiastical synods. 8vo.
London, for A. and J.Churchil, 1701
[Convocation Pamphlets III]   **1689(4)**

TURNER (Thomas). The case of the bankers and their creditors more fully stated ... and a second time printed.   4to.
[*London*] 1675   [Consutilia I]
Wing T3337.   **1427(1)**

TURNER (William). An almanack for ... 1688. 8vo.
London, printed by J.Heptinstall, for the Company of Stationers, 1688   [Almanacks for the year 1688]   Wing A2598.   **425(27)**

TURNER (William), Dean of Wells. The huntyng of the Romyshe Vuolfe.   8vo.
[*Emden, E.van der Erve*, 1555?]
Autograph 'John Dawse' on title-page; MS notes on title-page and elsewhere in unidentified 16th-century hands.   STC 24356; Duff p.68.   **209(7)**

TURNOR (Thomas).   *See* TURNER (Thomas).

TWINUS (Johannes).   *See* TWYNE (John).

TWO divine hymns, 1700.
See PLAYFORD (Henry).   **2018(3)**

TWO (The) great questions consider'd, 1700.
See DEFOE (Daniel).   **1436(9)**

TWO groats-worth of wit for a penny ... Published by those famous astrologers Mr Rich.Saunders, and Dr.Coelson.   8vo.
[*London*] *printed for J.Coniers* [c.1680]
[Penny-Merriments I]   Woodcut.   **362(50)**

TWO hundred queries, 1684.
See HELMONT (Franciscus Mercurius van).   **415**

TWO papers of proposals concerning the discipline and ceremonies of the Church of England, 1661.
See BAXTER (Richard).   **1189(6)**

TWYNE (John). De rebus Albionicis, Britannicis atque Anglicis commentariorum libri duo.   8vo.
Londini, excudebat Edm.Bollifantus, pro Richardo Watkins, 1590   STC 24407.   **521**

TYNDALE (William). The obediēce of a Christen man.   8vo.
(*Marlborow in the lāde of Hesse, by Hans Luft* [or rather *Antwerp, J.Hoochstraten*], 1528)
Some leaves of sig.A defective; cropped at end.
STC 24446; Duff p.67.   **235**

—————————— The obedyence of a Christian man. 4to.
[*London, William Hill*, 1548]
STC 24448; Duff p.67.   **1028(1)**

—————————— The parable of the wycked mammon ... lately corrected.   4to.
(*London, by Wyllyam hill*) [1548]
STC 24458; Duff p.67.   **1028(2)**

TYSON (Edward). Orang-Outang, sive Homo sylvestris: or, the anatomy of a pygmie.   4to.
London, for Thomas Bennet, and Daniel Brown, and are to be had of Mr.Hunt, 1699
8 engr. pls.   Wing T3598.   **2036**

U

UBALDINI (Petruccio). A discourse concerninge the Spanishe fleete inuadinge Englande in ... 1588. Transl. [by R.Adams].   4to.
(*London, by A.Hatfield, and are to be sold at the shop of A.Rither*, 1590)   [Sea tracts I; Consutilia V]   Engr. title-page, pl.
1077(11) has autograph 'John Dagger' on title-page.   STC 24481.   **1077(11); 1431(23)**

—————————— Expeditionis Hispanorum in Angliam vera descriptio. [11 engr. maps by R.Adams to accompany P.Ubaldini's Discourse concerninge the Spanishe fleete.]   fo.
[*London*, 1590]   STC 24481a.   **2806**

[UDALL (Ephraim)]. The Bishop of Armaghes direction, concerning the lyturgy, and episcopall government. [Disavowed by J.Ussher, and attributed to E.Udall. Also published as 'Directions propounded ...'.]   4to.
London, 1660   [Liturgick Controversies II]
1188(7)

[——————————] Directions propounded ... to ... Parliament concerning the Booke of Common Prayer and episcopall government. [Also published as 'The Bishop of Armaghes direction...]
4to.
London, 1641   [Liturgick Controversies II]
Wing U7.   **1188(3)**

—————————— The good of peace ... A sermon preached ... the last day of July 1642.   4to.
London, by T.Badger, for Ph.Stephens and C. Meridith, 1642   [Sermons Polemical VIII]
Wing U9.   **1186(1)**

UNDERHILL (John). Newes from America, or, a new and experimentall discoverie of New England.
4to.
London, J.D[awson]*. for Peter Cole*, 1638
[Consutilia V]   Engr. pl.   STC 24518.
1431(18)

UNFORTUNATE Jack, 1681.
See SECOND (The) part of Unfortunate Jack.
362(28)

UNFORTUNATE (The) son; or, a kind wife is worth gold. 12mo.
[London] by J.M. for J.Deacon and C.Dennisson [168–?] [Penny-Merriments I] Woodcut.
Title-page cropped. 362(27)

UNLUCKY (The) citizen. 12mo.
London, by J.M. for J.Blare, 1686
[Penny-Merriments II] Woodcuts.
Wing U85. 363(17)

US (Les) et coûtumes de la mer, 1671.
See CLEIRAC (Estienne). 1849

USE (The) and manner of the ballot [1660].
See HARRINGTON (James), the elder. 1297(3)

USE (The) of daily publick prayers, 1641.
See CASAUBON (Méric). 1188(1)

USSHER (James), Abp of Armagh. An answer to a challenge made by a Jesuite ... To which is added, A discourse of the religion anciently professed by the Irish and British. (— A brief declaration of the universality of the church of Christ.) 3 pts.
4to.
London, for Benjamin Tooke, 1686-7
Wing U150, 170, 159. 1571

——————————— The Bishop of Armaghes direction, 1660.
See UDALL (Ephraim). 1188(7)

——————————— A briefe declaration of the universalitie of the Church of Christ ... A sermon ... the 20th of Iune 1624. 3rd impr. 4to.
London, by Iohn Dawson, for Ephraim Dawson, 1629 [Sermons Polemical VIII]
STC 24547. 1186(5)

——————————— De Romanæ ecclesiæ symbolo Apostolico vetere. 4to.
Oxonii, excudebat G.Hall, impensis J.S., et venales prostant apud Ric.Davis [etc.], 1660
Wing U168. 1021(2)

V

V.(J.), prisoner. The opinion of the Roman judges, 1643.
See VICARS (John). 1186(2)

V.(L.D.). Histoire des revolutions de Suede, 1695.
See VERTOT (René Aubert de). 670

V.(P.). La campagne du roy, 1678.
See PRIMI VISCONTI (Giovanni Battista), conte di San Maiole. 531

VALENTINE and Orson. 4to.
London, by J.R. for T.Passinger, 1685
[Vulgaria II] Woodcuts. Wing V30. 1191(2)

VALENTINE (Thomas). A charge against the Jews, and the Christian world, for not coming to Christ ... A sermon. 4to.
London, by M.S. for John Rothwell, 1647
[Sermons Polemical VII] Wing V24. 1185(25)

VALISE. La valize ouverte, 1680.
See PRÉCHAC (Jean de). 83(3)

VALLA (Laurentius). De linguæ Latinæ elegantia libri sex, unà cum libello de reciprocatione Sui & Suus. 8vo.
Cantabrigiæ, apud Eduardum Hall, 1688
Wing V46. 746

VALLE (Pietro della). The travels ... into East-India and Arabia Deserta. [Transl.] fo.
London, by J.Macock, for Henry Herringman, 1665 Wing V47. 2224

VALLEJO (Manuel de). Aqui se contienen quatro Loas famosas, que dos autores, Vallejo, y Acacio representaron en la Ciudad de Granada. 4to.
Seuilla, por Iuan de Ossuna, 1673
Gaselee 174; Wilson p.260. 1545(43)

VALLEMONT (Pierre le Lorrain de).
See LE LORRAIN DE VALLEMONT (Pierre).

VAREN (Bernhard). Descriptio regni Japoniæ et Siam. 8vo.
Cantabrigiæ, ex officina Joan.Hayes, impensis Samnelis [sic] Simpson, 1673
Wing V105. 1128

——————————— Geographia generalis ... Emendata ... ab I.Newton. Ed.2. 8vo.
Cantabrigiæ, ex officina Joann.Hayes, sumptibus Henrici Dickinson, 1681 Engr. pl. (diagrams).
Wing V107; Tanner II, p.21. 1157

[VARET (Alexandre Louis)]. The nunns complaint against the fryars. 8vo.
London, by E.H. for Robert Pawlett, 1676
Wing V110. 599

VARILLAS (Antoine). Ἀνέκδοτα ἑτερουιακα. Or, the secret history of the house of Medicis ... Made English by F.Spence. 8vo.
London, printed by R.E. for R.Bentley and S.Magnes, 1686 Wing V112. 957

——————————— Histoire de Charles IX.
Nouvelle ed. 2 vols. 12mo.
Cologne, chez Pierre Marteau, 1684 514-5

——————————— Histoire de François I. 2 vols.
12mo.
La Haye, chez Arnout Leers, 1684 544-5

———————— Histoire des revolutions arrivées dans l'Europe en matiere de religion. Vols 1 & 2. [Vols 3-6 wanting.]   12mo. *Paris, chez Claude Barbin*, 1686   **597-8**

———————— La pratique de l'education de Charles-quint.   2 vols.   8vo. *Paris, chez Claude Barbin*, 1685   **687-8**

VAUGHAN (Rice). A discourse of coin and coinage ... with a short account of our common law therein.   12mo. *London, by Th.Dawks, for Th.Basset*, 1675 Wing V131.   **448**

VAVASSEUR (François). De ludicra dictione. 4to. *Lutetiæ Parisiorum, apud Sebastianum Cramosium*, 1658   **1834**

VEGA (Garcilaso de la). The royal commentaries of Peru ... rendred into English by Sir P.Rycaut. 2 pts.   fo. *London, by Miles Flesher for Christopher Wilkinson*, 1688   Engr. fp. (port., Charrington p.148), engr. pls.   Wing G216.   **2431**

VEGA CARPIO (Lope Felix de). Alabanzas del glorioso Patriarca San Joseph, con tres romances. 4to. *(Sevilla, por Juan Cabeças*, 1681) Gaselee 177; Wilson p.143.   **1545(3)**

———————— El animal profeta. Comedia famosa.   4to. *[Seville, Tomás López de Haro*, 1679-83] Gaselee 175.   **1553(18)**

———————— La creacion del mundo, y primera culpa del hombre. Comedia famosa. (— Loa sacramental.)   4to. *[Seville, Juan Cabezas*, c.1676] Gaselee 176.   **1553(5)**

———————— El milagro por los zelos. Comedia famosa.   4to. *[Seville, Tomé de Dios Miranda*, c.1675] Gaselee 178.   **1553(20)**

———————— La obediencia laureada. Comedia famosa.   4to. *[Seville, Tomé de Dios Miranda*, c.1678] Gaselee 179.   **1553(23)**

VEITIA LINAGE (José de). Norte de la contratacion de las Indias occidentales.   2 pts.   fo. *Sevilla, por Iuan Francisco de Blas*, 1672 Engr. title-page.   Gaselee 180.   **2159**

VELASCO (Martin de). Arte de sermones.   4to. *Cadiz, por el Alferez Bartolomè Nuñez de Castro* [1677]   Q3, 4 misbound.   Engr. pl. Gaselee 181.   **1270(1)**

VELLEIUS PATERCULUS (Marcus). Historiæ Romanæ ... libri duo. Interpretatione et notis illustravit R.Riguez ... in usum Delphini.   4to. *Parisiis, apud Fredericum Leonard*, 1675 Engr. title-page.   **1917**

VENN (Thomas). Military & maritime [*sic*] discipline in three books.   3 pts.   fo. *London, by E.Tyler, and R.Holt, for Rob.Pawlet* [*etc.*], 1672   Engr. fp, title-page, pls. Wing V192.   **2195**

VENNER (Tobias). Via recta ad vitam longam. (— The baths of Bathe. — A brief ... treatise concerning ... tobacco.)   3 pts.   4th impr.   4to. *London, for Abel Roper*, 1660   Engr. fp. (port., Charrington p.170).   Wing V196.   **1425**

VENNING (Ralph). The Christian's temptations and tryals ... Preached by Mr.Ralph Vennings [*sic*].   12mo. *London, for Charles Passinger* [c.1674] [Penny-Godlinesses]   **365(40)**

VERAX (Theodorus), *pseud.* *See* WALKER (Clement).

VERE (Sir Francis). The commentaries ... Published by W.Dillingham.   fo. *Cambridge, by John Field*, 1657   Engr. pls (ports, Charrington pp.128, 170).   Wing V240.   **2015**

VERGILIUS (Polydorus). De inventoribus rerum libri VIII. Et De prodigiis libri III.   12mo. *Amstelodami, apud Danielem Elzevirium*, 1671 Engr. title-page.   **107**

———————— Historiæ Anglicæ libri XXVII ... ex nova ed. A.Thysii.   8vo. *Lugduni Batavorum (typis Philippi de Cro-y) sumptibus Joannis Maire*, 1651 (1649)   **1229**

VERGILIUS MARO (Publius).   *See* VIRGIL.

VERINI (Giovanni Battista). Incipit liber primus (— quartus) elementorum litterarum.   4to. *[Toscolano, A.Paganini*, c.1530] Adams V570; Duff p.69.   **1512(2)**

VERO (Il) modo di visitare le quattro chiese di Roma, per pigliare il Santissimo Giubileo dell' Anno Santo.   12mo. *Roma, per il Buagni*, 1700   Woodcuts.   **145(4)**

VERSTEGAN (Richard). Restitution of decayed intelligence in antiquities.   8vo. *London, for Samuel Mearne, John Martyn, and Henry Herringman*, 1673   Pls.   Wing V271; Naval Minutes, p.22.   **834**

VERTOT (René Aubert de). Histoire de la conjuration de Portugal en 1640.   12mo. *Sur l'imprimé de Paris, à Amsterdam, chez Henry Desbordes*, 1689   **242**

[——————] Histoire des revolutions de Suede.   2 vols in 1.   12mo.
Paris, chez Michel Brunet, 1695   670

VETERES de re militari scriptores. (– G.Stewechii ... Commentarius.)   2 vols.   8vo.
Vfsaliæ [sic] Clivorum, ex officina Andreæ ab Hoogenhuysen, 1670   Engr. title-pages, pl., diagrams.   1328-9

VETUS Codex.
See ENGLAND. *Parliament. Placita Parlamentaria.*
                              2121

VIA ad pacem ecclesiasticam in qua continentur confessio fidei, secundum Conc. Trid., confessio fidei Augustana [*etc.*]. [Ed. by H.Grotius.]   8vo.
[*Paris, Gilles Morel*] 1642   1012

[VICARS (John)]. The opinion of the Roman judges touching imprisonment, and the liberty of the subject ... A sermon preached ... Jan.25.
4to.
[*London*] 1643   [Sermons Polemical VIII]
On title-page, in hand of one of Pepys's clerks:
'J.Vicars, School-maʳ at Christ's Hospitall'.
Wing V320.   1186(2)

——————— Unholsome henbane between two fragrant roses.   4to.
(*London, for John Rothwell*, 1645)
[Liturgick Controversies II]   Wing V332.
                              1188(12)

VICTORINUS (Georgius). Siren coelestis centum harmoniarum, duarum, trium, & quatuor vocum.
Editio altera. Suprema.   4to.
Londini, ex typographeo Iohannis Norton, 1638
STC 24715.   *See also below*, vol.IV.   1730(2)

VIE (La) de Corneille Tromp, lieutenant-general de Hollande & de West-Frise.   12mo.
La Haye, chez Etienne Foulque, 1694
Engr. fp. (port., Charrington p.167).   591

VIE (La) de Gaspard de Coligny, 1686.
See COURTILZ DE SANDRAS (Gatien).   530

VIE (La) et les actions memorables du Sr. Michel de Ruyter, 1677.
See PIÉLAT (Barthélemy).   74

VIEW (A) of the new directory, 1645.
See HAMMOND (Henry).   1188(15)

VIGENÈRE (Blaise de). Traicté des chiffres, ou secrètes manières d'escrire.   4to.
Paris, chez Abel L'Angelier, 1586
Adams V743.   1911

VILLASEÑOR (Juan de). Historia general de las grandezas, y excelencias de España.   fo.
Madrid, por Roque Rico de Miranda, 1681
Gaselee 183.   2139(1)

VILLAULT (Nicolas), Sieur de Bellefond.
A relation of the coasts of Africk called Guinee ... faithfully Englished.   12mo.
London, for John Starkey, 1670
Wing V387.   384

VINCENT, of Beauvais. The myrrour ... of the worlde [1490] & [1529?].
See IMAGE du Monde.   1941(1), (2)

VINCENT (Nathaniel). The day of grace ...
A sermon.   12mo.
[*London*] *by A.M. for J.Conyers*, 1687
[Penny-Godlinesses]   365(12)

VINCENT (Thomas). One of Mr Vincent's last sermons.   12mo.
London, for T.Passinger, 1685
[Penny-Godlinesses]   365(35)

VINDICATION (A) of King Charles the Martyr, 1693.
See WAGSTAFFE (Thomas).   1286(11)

VINDICATION (A) of some among our selves against the false principles of Dr.Sherlock, 1692.
See HICKES (George).   1436(3)

VINDICATION (A) of the author of the Right of the Archbishop to continue, 1702.
See GIBSON (Edmund), Bp of London.   1696(9)

VINDICATION (A) of the authority of Christian princes, over ecclesiastical synods, 1701.
See TURNER (John).   1689(4)

VINDICATION (A) of the deprived Bishops, 1692.
See DODWELL (Henry).   1436(2)

VINDICATION (A) of the late sermon, 1680.
See B.(A.).   1183(23)

VINDICATION (A) of the proceedings ... of the last Convocation, 1702.
See TRIMNELL (Charles), Bp of Winchester.
                              1695(8a)

VINDICATION (A) of the twenty third article of the Church of England, 1702.
See THORNTON (William).   1772(2)

VINEGAR and mustard: or, wormwood lectures, 1686.
See WADE (John).   362(48)

VINES (Richard). The authours, nature, and danger of haeresie ... A sermon preached ... the tenth of March 1646.   4to.
London, by W.Wilson for Abel Roper, 1647
[Sermons Polemical VIII]
Wing V545.   1186(4)

──────────── The impostures of seducing
teachers discovered; in a sermon ... April 23, 1644.
4to.
London, by G.M. for Abel Roper, 1644
[Sermons Polemical VIII]   Wing V557.
1186(3)

VIRGIL. Opera ... notis illustravit C.Ruæus.
2.ed.   4to.
Parisiis (ex typographia Dionysii Thierry) apud
Simonem Benard, 1682   **1946**

──────────── The works ... Transl. into English
verse; by Mr.Dryden. Adorn'd with a hundred
sculptures.   fo.
London, for Jacob Tonson, 1697   Engr. fp., pls
(some inserted), engr. ports inserted, Charrington
p.50.   Wing V616.   **2947**

──────────── An essay upon two of Virgil's
Eclogues, and two books of his Æneis ... towards
the translation of the whole. By J.Harrington.
8vo.
London, by T.C. for Thomas Brewster, 1658
Wing V627.   **533(2)**

──────────── The .xiii. bukes of Eneados ...
Translatet ... into Scottish metir, bi ... G.Douglas.
4to.
Londō [W.Copland], 1553
STC 24797; Duff p.70.   **1652**

──────────── Æneis: the third, fourth, fifth and
sixth books. Transl. by J.Harrington.   8vo.
London, by J.Cottrel, for Henry Fletcher, 1659
Wing V618.   **533(3)**

VIRGINIA, colony. A declaration of the state of
the colony and affaires in Virginia ... By his
Majesties Counseil for Virginia.   4to.
London, by Thomas Snodham, 1620
[Consutilia III]   STC 24841.6.   **1429(5)**

VISCONTI (Primi).
See PRIMI VISCONTI (Giovanni Battista), conte
di San Maiole.

VISION (The) of Pierce Plowman, 1550.
See LANGLAND (William).   **1302**

VISSCHER (Nicolaus), the elder. Speculum
Zelandiæ ... gelegen inde eylanden en de
graeflijckheyt van Zeelandt.   fo.
[c.1660]   36 engr. pls.   **2809(1)**

──────────── Theatrum præcipuarum urbium
ducatus Brabantiæ ... Flandriæ et Zelandiæ.   fo.
[*Amsterdam*?] 1660   36 engr. pls.   **2809(2)**

VITRUVIUS. Les dix livres d'architecture,
corrigez et traduits ... en françois.   fo.
Paris, chez Jean Baptiste Coignard, 1673
Engr. title-page, 64 engr. pls.   **2915**

──────────── Abregé des dix livres d'architect-
ture de Vitruve.   12mo.
Paris, chez Jean Baptiste Coignard, 1674
11 engr. pls.   **676**

VITUS (Ricardus).   *See* WHITE (Richard).

VOICE. The voyce of the Lord in the Temple.
4to.
London, by T.Paine for Francis Eglesfield, 1640
[Consutilia II]   STC 24870.   **1428(6)**

[VORAGINE (Jacobus de), Abp of Genoa].
[Legenda aurea ... the Golden legende. Transl. by
W.Caxton.]   fo.
(*London [Wynkyn de Worde]* 1527)
Leaves A1-3, 7, 8 missing; yy6-8 defective.
Woodcuts.   STC 24880; Duff p.71; Diary
10 Apr. 1668.   **2040**

VOS (Marten de). Vita, passio, et resurrectio
Iesu Christi, varijs iconibus à ... M.de Vos expressa,
ab A.Collart ... excisis.   fo.
[*Antwerp, c.1620*]   Engr. title-page, 51 engr.
pls.   **2233**

VOSSIUS (Gerardus Johannes). De quatuor artibus
popularibus, de philologia, et scientiis mathemat-
icis.   3 pts.   4to.
Amstelædami, ex typographeio Ioannis Blaeu,
1660   **1586**

──────────── Dissertationes tres de tribus
symbolis.   Ed. 2.   4to.
Amstelædami, ex typographeio Ioannis Blaeu,
1662   **1021(1)**

──────────── G.J.Vossii et clarorum virorum
ad eum epistolæ. Collectore P.Colomesio.
2 pts.   fo.
Londini, typis R.R. & M.C., impensis Adielis
Mill, 1690   Wing V691A.   **2313**

──────────── Harmoniæ evangelicæ, 1656.
See BIBLE. *Latin. Gospel Harmonies.*   **1533**

──────────── Theses theologicæ et historicæ.
4to.
Bellositi Dobunorum [i.e. Oxford], excudebat
W.T., impensis W.W., 1628   STC 24882.7.
1272

VOSSIUS (Isaac). [De motu marium.] Le guidon
de la navigation ... Traduit du Latin.   4to.
Paris, chez Francois Clousier, 1665   **1531(1)**

──────────── [De motu marium.] A treatise
concerning the motion of the seas and winds ...
Translated.   8vo.
London, by H.C. for Henry Brome, 1677
2 engr. pls (diagrams).   Wing V706.   **584**

[────────────] De poematum cantu. Et viribus
rythmi.
Oxonii, e theatro Sheldoniano, prostant Londini
apud Rob.Scot, 1673   Wing V699.   **1565**

——————— De septuaginta interpretibus.
(Appendix.)   2 pts.   4to.
Hagæ-Comitum, ex typographia Adriani Vlacq,
1661-3   **1868**

——————— De Sibyllinis.   2 pts.
Oxoniæ, e theatro Sheldoniano, venales prostant
apud Mosem Pitt Londini, 1680
Wing V701.   **1567**

——————— Observationum ad Pomp.Melam
appendix.   4to.
Londini, prostant apud Robertum Scott, 1686
Wing V704.   **1851(2)**

——————— Variarum observationum liber.
4to.
Londini, prostant apud Robertum Scott, 1685
Wing V707.   **1851(1)**

VOYAGE (Le) de Beth-el, 1678.
See FOCQUEMBERGUES (Jean de).   **6**

VOYAGE d'Espagne, 1665.
See BRUNEL (Antoine de).   **1827**

VOYAGE. Voiage du monde de Descartes, 1691.
See DANIEL (Gabriel).   **577**

VOYAGES (The) and travels of ... Sir Francis
Drake.   4to.
London, by M.H. and I.M. for P.Brooksby, 1683
[Vulgaria III]   **1192(11)**

W

W.(Sir A.). The court ... of King James, 1650.
See WELDON (Sir Anthony).   **62(1)**

W.(E.). No præexistence, 1667.
See WARREN (Edward).   **1428(18)**

W.(J.). Mercury, 1641.
See WILKINS (John), Bp of Chester.   **784**

W.(J.). A speedy post.   12th ed.   4to.
London, by M.H. and J.M. for William Thackeray,
1684   [Vulgaria IV]   Woodcut.
Wing W70.   **1193(16)**

W.(J.). Vinegar and mustard, 1686.
See WADE (John).   **362(48)**

W.(L.). A merry dialogue between Andrew and
his sweet heart Joan.   8vo.
[*London*] *by A.M. for J.Deacon, and C.Dennisson*
[c.1680]   [Penny-Merriments I]   Woodcut.
                                       362(5)

W.(O.). The Greek and Roman history illustrated,
1692.
See WALKER (Obadiah).   **811**

W.(R.). A right excellent comoedy called The
three ladies of London, 1584.
See WILSON (Robert).   **1103(2)**

W.(W.). Antidotum Britannicum.   8vo.
London, for Richard Sare, 1681
Wing W140.   **467(1)**

[WADE (John)]. Vinegar and mustard: or, worm-
wood lectures ... Taken verbatim in short writing
by J.W.   12mo.
[*London*] *by J.B. for J.Clark, W.Thackeray, and*
T.Passinger, 1686   [Penny-Merriments I]
                                       362(48)

WADSWORTH (Thomas). Christ in the clouds.
6th ed.   12mo.
[*London*] *for Charles Passinger, 1682*
[Penny-Godlinesses]   **365(36)**

[WAGSTAFFE (Thomas)]. A defence of the
vindication of K.Charles the martyr.   4to.
London, printed by W.Bowyer, 1699
Wing W206.   **1082(2)**

[——————] The rights and liberties of
Englishmen asserted.   4to.
London, printed for A.Baldwin, 1701
[Consutilia XI]   **1437(9)**

[——————] A vindication of King Charles
the martyr.   8vo.
London, for Joseph Hindmarsh, 1693
On title-page, 'Madam Eliz:Martin' and, in Pepys's
hand, 'By Mr.Wagstaffe'.   Wing W218.
                                       1286(11)

WAKE (William), Abp of Canterbury. An appeal
to all the true members of the Church of England.
8vo.
London, for Richard Sare, 1698   [Convocation
Pamphlets III]   Wing W229.   **1689(2)**

——————— The authority of Christian
princes over their ecclesiastical synods.   8vo.
London, for R.Sare, 1697   [Convocation
Pamphlets III]   Wing W230.   **1689(1)**

[——————] An exposition of the doctrine
of the Church of England.   4to.
London, for Richard Chiswell, 1686
Wing W243.   **1544(2)**

[——————] A letter from a country
clergyman ... touching some reproaches cast upon
the Bishops.   4to.
(*London, printed and sold by John Nutt, 1702*)
[Convocation Pamphlets X]   **1696(4)**

———————Of our obligation to put our trust in God ... In a sermon.   5th ed.   4to.
London, for R.Sare, 1695   Wing W251.
1528(15)

———————The state of the Church and clergy of England.   fo.
London, for R.Sare, 1703   **2330**

WAKEMAN (Sir George). The tryals of Sir G.Wakeman, W.Marshall, W.Rumley, and J.Corker for high treason.   fo.
London, for H.Hills, T.Parkhurst, J.Starkey [etc.], 1679   [Narratives & Tryals I]
Wing T2259.   **2249(16)**

WALCOT (Thomas). A true copy of a paper written by Capt.Tho.Walcott ... after his condemnation.   fo.
(London, for Timothy Goodwin, 1683)
[Narratives & Tryals V]   Wing W285.   **2253(6)**

———————The tryals of T.Walcot [and 4 others], 1683.
See TRIALS. The tryals ...   **2253(1)**

WALKER (Anthony). A true account of the author of a book entituled Εἰκὼν Βασιλικὴ.   4to.
London, printed for Nathanael Ranew, 1692
Wing W310.   **1286(5)**

[WALKER (Clement)]. Anarchia Anglicana ... The second part ... By Theodorus Verax [i.e. Clement Walker].   4to.
1649   Engr. pl.   Wing W317.   **1148(2)**

[———————] The High Court of Justice. Or Cromwells new slaughter-house in England. Being the III. part of the Historie of Independencie.   4to.
1651   Wing W325.   **1148(3)**

[———————] The history of Independency. The fourth and last part ... By T.M.Esquire [i.e. C.Walker.]   4to.
London, printed for H.Brome, and H.Marsh, 1660
Wing W331A.   **1148(4)**

[———————] Relations and observations ... upon the Parliament begun Anno Dom.1640.
2 pts.
1648   Wing W334.   **1148(1)**

———————The triall of Lieut.Collonell John Lilburne [1649].
See LILBURNE (John).   **1430(6)**

WALKER (Ellis). Epicteti Enchiridion ... a poetical paraphrase, 1692.
See EPICTETUS.   **829**

WALKER (George). A sermon preached ... Januarie 29th.1644.   4to.
London, by T.B. for Nathaniel Webb, 1645
[Sermons Polemical VIII]   Wing W364.
1186(6)

WALKER (Henry). A sermon, preached in the King's Chappell at Whitehall on ... July 15.1649.
4to.
[*London*] 1649   [Sermons Polemical VIII]
Wing W385.   **1186(7)**

[WALKER (Obadiah)]. The Greek and Roman history illustrated by coins & medals.
London, printed by G.Croom, for William Miller, and Christopher Wilkinson, 1692
Wing W397.   **811**

[———————] Of education. Especially of young gentlemen.   5th impr.   12mo.
Oxford, at the Theater for Amos Curteyne, 1687
Wing W403.   **678**

WALKER (William). Βαπτισμῶν διδαχή. The doctrine of baptisms.   8vo.
London, for Robert Pawlet, 1678
Wing W417.   **1232**

WALLACE (James). An account of the islands of Orkney.   8vo.
London, for Jacob Tonson, 1700   Engr. fp.
(map), engr. pl.   Wing W491.   **1294**

WALLER (Edmund). Poems, &c.   4th ed.   8vo.
London, printed for Henry Herringman, 1682
Engr. fp., pl. (ports, Charrington p.173).
Wing W516.   **1155**

WALLIS (John). Opera mathematica.   3 vols.
fo.
Oxoniæ, e Theatro Sheldoniano, 1699 (1693-5)
Engr. fps (ports, Charrington p.173).
MS note inserted in vol.1 (extract of letter from Wallis to Dr John Fell, 8 Apr.1685). *See below*, vol.V.   Wing W597; Howarth, pp.258, 273-4.
2646-8

———————A treatise of algebra ... With some additional treatises.   3 pts.   fo.
London, by John Playford, for Richard Davis, Oxford, 1685 (1684)   Engr. fp. (port., Charrington p.173), engr. pls (diagrams).   Wing W613.
2396(1)

WALSH (Sir Robert), Bart. A true narrative and manifest ... relating unto plots.   fo.
[*London*] *for the author*, 1679   [Narratives & Tryals I]   Wing W644.   **2249(7)**

WALSINGHAM. The foundation of the chapel of Walsingham.   4to.
R.Pynson [*London*, 1496]
See Appendix.   **1254(6)**

WALSINGHAM'S manual, 1655.
See DU REFUGE (Eustace).   **43**

WALTON (Isaak). The life of Dr.Sanderson, late Bishop of Lincoln ... To which is added, some short tracts.   2 pts.   8vo.
London, for Richard Marriott, 1678   Engr. fp.
(port., Charrington p.150).   Wing W667.   **1016**

WANLEY (Nathaniel). The wonders of the little
world.   fo.
*London, for T.Basset, R.Cheswel [sic], J.Wright,
and T.Sawbridge*, 1678
Wing W709; Howarth, p.328.   **2671(1)**

WANTON Tom: or, the merry history of Tom
Stitch the taylor.   12mo.
*[London] for R.Butler, and sold by Richard
Kell*, 1685   [Penny-Merriments I]
Wing W716.   **362(13)**

WARD (John). God iudging among the gods ...
A sermon ... March 26.1645.   4to.
London, by I.L. for Christopher Meredith, 1645
[Sermons Polemical VIII]   Wing W773.
                                     1186(8)

WARD (Nathaniel). A sermon preached ...
June 30.1647 ...   4to.
*London, by R.I. for Stephen Bowtell and
William Bishop*, 1649   [Sermons Polemical VIII]
Wing W785.   **1186(9)**

[————————] The simple cobler of Aggawam
in America. Willing to help mend his native
country ... By Theodore de la Guard [i.e. N.Ward].
4to.
*London, by John Dever & Robert Ibbitson, for
Stephen Bowtell*, 1647   [Consutilia IV]
Wing W786.   **1430(10)**

WARD (Seth), Bp of Salisbury. A philosophicall
essay towards an eviction of the being and
attributes of God.   5th ed.   8vo.
*Oxford, by Leonard Lichfield, and are to be sold
by Thomas Bartlet*, 1677   Wing W826.   **523**

WARE (Sir James). De Hibernia & antiquitatibus
ejus disquisitiones.   8vo.
*Londini, typis J.Grismond, impensis Jo.Crook &
Thomæ Heath*, 1654   2 engr. maps.
Wing W843.   **1033**

————————————— The historie of Ireland, 1633.
See HANMER (Meredith).   **2000**

WARNING (A) to wicked livers; or ... the life and
death of John Duncalf.   8vo.
London, for J.Conyers [c.1680]
[Penny-Godlinesses]   **365(6)**

WARRE (James). The touch-stone of truth.
3rd impr.   8vo.
*London, by Aug.Mathewes, and are to be sold by
Thomas Iones*, 1630   STC 25091.   **557**

[WARREN (Edward)]. No præexistence.   4to.
London, by T.R. for Samuel Thomson, 1667
[Consutilia II]   'E.W[arren]' spelt out on title-
page in unidentified hand.   Wing W957.
                                     1428(18)

WARREN (Erasmus). A defence of the discourse
concerning the earth before the flood.   4to.

London, for John Southby, 1691
Wing W963.   **1527**

————————————— Geologia: or, a discourse concerning the earth before the deluge.   4to.
London, for R.Chiswell, 1690   **1526**

WARREN (John). The potent potter; or, a sermon
preached ... 19. of April 1649.   4to.
*London, by T.R. & E.M. for Nathaniel Webb and
William Grantham*, 1649   [Sermons Polemical
VIII]   Wing W976.   **1186(10)**

WARRINGTON (Henry Booth, 1st Earl of). The
late Lord Russel's case.   fo.
London, for Awnsham Churchill, 1689
[Narratives & Tryals V]   Wing D878.   **2253(3)**

————————————— The tryal of Henry Baron Dela-
mere for high treason.   fo.
London, for Dorman Newman, 1686
[Narratives & Tryals V]   Wing T2189.
                                     2253(20)

WARWICK (Edward Rich, Earl of). The several
tryals of Edward Earl of Warwick ... and Charles
Lord Mohun ... for the murder of Mr.R.Coote.
2 pts.   fo.
[London] by Edward Jones, for Jacob Tonson,
1699   [Narratives & Tryals VII]
Wing S2813.   **2255(3)**

WARWICK (Sir Philip). A discourse of government.
8vo.
London, for Samuel Lowndes, 1694
Wing W991.   **1421**

————————————— Memoires of the reigne of King
Charles I. with a continuation to the happy
restauration of King Charles II.   8vo.
London, for Ri.Chiswell, 1701   Engr. fp. (port.,
Charrington p.174).   **1300**

WASE (Christopher). Considerations concerning
free-schools, as settled in England.   8vo.
*Printed at the Theater in Oxford, and are to be
had there. And in London at Mr Simon Millers*,
1678   Wing W1015.   **1222**

[WATT (Joachim von)]. A worke entytled of ye
olde god ʊ the newe. [Transl. by W.Turner.]
8vo.
(*London, by me Iohan Byddell*, 1534)
STC 25127; Duff p.51.   **60**

WAYS. The wayes and meanes whereby an equal
& lasting commonwealth may be suddenly introduced, 1660.
See HARRINGTON (James), the elder.   **1297(2A)**

WEALTH discovered, 1661.
See CRADOCK (Francis).   **1174(2)**

WEBB (John). An historical essay endeavoring a probability that the language of the Empire of China is the primitive language.　8vo.
London, for Nath.Brook, 1669　Engr. map.
Wing W1202.　　　　　　　　　　831(2)

WEBSTER (John), dramatist. The Dutchesse of Malfy, a tragedy.　4to.
London, for Robert Crofts [1657-64]
[Loose Plays I]　Wing W1222; Diary 2, 6 Nov. 1666.　　　　　　　　　　1075(6)

WEBSTER (John), physicist. Metallographia: or, an history of metals.　4to.
London, by A.C. for Walter Kettilby, 1671
Wing W1231.　　　　　　　　　　1480

WEDNESDAY'S fast.　4to.
W.de Worde [*Westminster*, 1500]
See Appendix.　　　　　　　　　　1254(3)

WEEVER (John). Ancient funerall monuments within ... Great Britaine.　fo.
London, by Thomas Harper, sold by Laurence Sadler, 1631　Woodcuts.
STC 25223.　　　　　　　　　　2103

─────────── The mirror of martyrs, or the life ... of ... Sir John Old-castle.　8vo.
[*London*] *by V.S. for William Wood*, 1601
STC 25226.　　　　　　　　　　29(5)

[WELDON (Sir Anthony)]. The court and character of King James. Written and taken by Sir A:W:　8vo.
London, by R.I. and are to be sold by John Wright, 1650　Engr. port. (Charrington p.85) inserted.　Wing W1273; Diary 10 Feb. 1664/5.
　　　　　　　　　　62(1)

WELLS (Edward). Elementa arithmeticæ.　8vo.
Oxoniæ, e Theatro Sheldoniano. Excudebat Johan.Croke, 1698　Wing W1286.　1741

─────────── A treatise of antient and present geography together with a sett of maps.　· 8vo.
Oxford, at the Theater, 1701　Engr. fp.　1394

─────────── A new sett of maps.　fo.
Ib., 1701　38 engr. maps.　　　2989

[WELLWOOD (James)]. An answer to the late K.James's last declaration.　4to.
London, for Richard Baldwin, 1693
[Consutilia VII]　Wing W1302.　1433(3)

─────────── Memoirs of the most material transactions in England for the last hundred years. 3rd ed.　8vo.
London, for Tim.Goodwin, 1700
Wing W1308.　　　　　　　　　　1414

WELLWOOD (William). An abridgement of all sea-lawes.　8vo.

London, by the assignes of Ioane Man and Benjamin Fisher, 1636　STC 25238; Naval Minutes, pp.137-8.　　　　　　309

─────────── De dominio maris.　4to.
Hagæ-comitum, ex typographia Adriani Vlac, 1653　Naval Minutes, p.118.　1024(2)

[WEST (Richard)]. The principles of Mr.Atterbury's book ... consider'd.　4to.
London, printed, and sold by J.Nutt, 1701
[Convocation Pamphlets IX]　'R.West D.D.' written on title-page in Daniel Waterland's hand.
　　　　　　　　　　1695(5)

[───────────] The true character of a churchman.　4to.
London, for A.Baldwin, 1702　[Convocation Pamphlets X]　'Dr R:West' written on title-page in Daniel Waterland's hand.　1696(12)

WESTFEILD (Thomas). A sermon preached ... on the fourteenth day of November.1641.　4to.
London, by J.Raworth, for J.Partridge, 1641
[Sermons Polemical VIII]　Wing W1419.
　　　　　　　　　　1186(11)

WESTMINSTER ASSEMBLY. The confession of faith: together with the larger and lesser catechisms.　3rd ed.　12mo.
London, for the Company of Stationers, sold by Tho.Parkhurst and Dorman Newman, 1688
Wing C5798.　　　　　　　　　　636

─────────── A directory for the publique worship of God. [Drawn up by the Westminster Assembly.]　4to.
London, for Evan Tyler, Alexander Fifield, Ralph Smith [*etc.*], 1644　[Liturgick Controversies II] M3 cropped.　Wing D1544.　1188(14)

WESTMINSTER SCHOOL. Principi juventutis Gulielmo ... Duci Glocestriæ ... scholæ Westmonasteriensis alumni ... hæc carmina mœrentes consecrant.　fo.
Londini, excudebat Edv.Jones, 1700
Wing W1471.　　　　　　　　　　2287

WETENHALL (Edward), Bp of Cork. Scripture authentick, and faith certain.　8vo.
London, for H.F. and J.K., and sold by Edw.Evets, 1686　Wing W1515.　　　968

[WHARTON (Henry)]. A defence of pluralities. 8vo.
London, for Robert Clavel, 1692
Wing W1561.　　　　　　　　　　962(1)

─────────── Fourteen sermons.　8vo.
London, for Ri.Chiswell, 1697　Engr. fp. (port., Charrington p.175).　Wing W1563.　1291

─────────── Historia de episcopis & decanis Londinensibus: necnon ... Assavensibus ... ad annum 1540.　8vo.

Londini, impensis Ri.Chiswell, 1695
Wing W1565.   **1311**

——————————— One and twenty sermons.   8vo.
London, for Ri.Chiswell, 1698   Engr. fp. (port.,
Charrington p.175).   Wing W1566.   **1292**

[———————] A specimen of some errors in
the History of the Reformation ... by G.Burnet ...
By A.Harmer [i.e. H.Wharton].   4to.
London, printed for Randall Taylor, 1693
MS letter of H.Wanley to Pepys (3 Feb.1702/3)
inserted, with collation of the bidding prayer
printed at pp.166-8 with MS in Lambeth Library.
See also below, vol.V.   Wing W1569.   **992**

WHEARE (Degory). The method and order of
reading ... histories ... Added, an appendix ... by
N.Horseman.   8vo.
London, printed by M.Flesher, for Charles Brome,
1685   Wing W1592.   **929**

WHELER (Sir George). A journey into Greece.
fo.
*London, for William Cademan, Robert Kettlewell,
and Awnsham Churchill*, 1682   Engr. pls (maps).
Wing W1607.   **2132**

WHINCOP (John). Gods call to weeping and
mourning ... a sermon ... January 29.1644.   4to.
*London, by John Field for Nathaniel Web and
William Grantham*, 1646   [Sermons Polemical
VIII]   Wing W1663.   **1186(12)**

——————————— Israels tears for distressed Zion ...
a sermon ... Sept.24.1645.   4to.
London, by R.C. for Andrew Crooke, 1645
[Sermons Polemical VIII]   Wing W1664.
                                        1186(13)

WHISTON (James). England's calamities dis-
cover'd, with a proper remedy.   4to.
*London, for the author, sold by Joseph Fox,
R.Clavel, and T.Minton*, 1696   [Consutilia VII]
Wing W1686.   **1433(16)**

WHISTON (William). A new theory of the earth.
8vo.
London, R.Roberts, for Benj.Tooke, 1696
7 engr. pls.   Wing W1696.   **1384**

——————————— A short view of the chronology of
the Old Testament.   4to.
*Cambridge, the University Press, for B.Tooke,
London*, 1702   **1637**

WHITAKER (Jeremiah). The danger of greatnesse
... A sermon preached ... the 14th day January
1645.   4to.
London, by G.M. for John Bellamie, 1646
[Sermons Polemical VIII]   Wing W1711.
                                        1186(15)

——————————— Eirenopoios, Christ the settlement
of unsettled times. In a sermon preached ...
the 25. of January. [1642].   4to.
London, for John Bellamy and Ralph Smith, 1642
[Sermons Polemical VIII]   Wing W1712A.
                                        1186(14)

WHITBOURNE (Richard). A discourse and
discouery of New-found-land.   4to.
London, by Felix Kyngston, for William Barret,
1620   [Consutilia III]   STC 25372.   **1429(4)**

——————————— A discourse containing a louing
inuitation ... to aduenturers ... in the New-found-
land.   2 pts.   4to.
London, by Felix Kyngston, 1622
[Consutilia III]   STC 25375a.   **1429(3)**

WHITE (John). The troubles of Jerusalems
restauration ... In a sermon preached ...
Novemb.26.1645.   4to.
*London, by M.Simmons for John Rothwel, and
Luke Fawne*, 1646   [Sermons Polemical VIII]
MS corrections.   Wing W1784.   **1186(16)**

WHITE (Richard). Historiarum Britanniæ insulæ
... libri nouem priores.   5 pts.   8vo.
(*Duaci, ex officina Gulielmi Riuerij*) *apud
Carolum Boscardum*, (1597-)1602
Adams W91.   **550**

WHITE (Thomas), Jesuit. The last speeches [of
T.White and 4 others, 1679].
See LAST (The) speeches of the five notorious
traitors ...   **2251**

——————————— The tryals ... of T.White [and 4
others], 1679.
See TRIALS. The tryals and condemnation of
T.White ...   **2249(15)**

WHITE (Thomas), almanac-maker. White 1688.
A new almanack for ... 1688 ... Calculated for the
meridian of Todington in Bedfordshire.   8vo.
*London, printed by Bernard White for the
Company of Stationers*, 1688   [Almanacks for
the year 1688]   Wing A2727.   **425(29)**

WHITEBREAD (Thomas), *pseud.*
See WHITE (Thomas), Jesuit.

[WHITELOCK (Sir Bulstrode)]. Memorials of the
English affairs.   fo.
London, for Nathaniel Ponder, 1682
Wing W1986.   **2679**

WHITFELD (Henry). The light appearing more
and more, 1651.
See MAYHEW (Thomas).   **1428(1)**

WHITFORDE (Richard). [The boke called the
Pype or Tonne, of the lyfe of perfection.]   4to.
(*london, by me Robert Redman*, 1532)
Wants sig.K; title-page defective.
STC 25421; Duff p.72.   **1036(2)**

WHITTLE (John). An exact diary of the late
expedition of ... the Prince of Orange ... to his
arrival at White-Hall.   4to.
London, for Richard Baldwin, 1689
[Consutilia VI]   Wing W2044.   **1432(19)**

[WHITTINGHAM (William)]. A briefe discourse
of the troubles begun at Frankeford in Germany,
An.Dom.1554. About the Booke of Common
Prayer.   4to.
London, by G.Bishop, and R.White, for Tho.
Underhill, 1642   [Liturgick Controversies II]
Wing W2045.   **1188(11)**

WHOLE (The) art of palmestry [c.1685].
See R.(W.).   **363(9)**

WHOLE (The) duty of man, 1702.
See ALLESTREE (Richard).   **1083**

WHOLE (The) prophecies of Scotland, England,
France, Ireland, and Denmark.   12mo.
Edinburgh, printed by the heir of Andrew Ander-
son, 1680   Wing W2060.   **358(3)**

WICKED (The) life and penitent death of Tho:
Savage.   8vo.
London, for J.Back [c.1685]   [Penny-
Godlinesses]   Woodcut.   Wing W2078.
365(37)

WICLIF (John). Two short treatises, against the
Orders of the Begging Friars.   4to.
Oxford, by Ioseph Barnes, 1608
STC 25589.   **958(3)**

——————Wickliffes wicket, or a learned
and godly treatise of the Sacrament.   4to.
At Oxford, printed by Joseph Barnes, and are to
be sold by John Barnes [*London*] , 1612
STC 25592.   **1336(2)**

WICQUEFORT (Abraham van). L'ambassadeur
et ses fonctions.   2 vols.   4to.
La Haye, chez Jean & Daniel Steucker, 1681
(1680)   **1508-9**

——————Memoires touchant les ambassadeurs et les ministres publics.   8vo.
La Haye, chez Jean & Daniel Steucker, 1677   **705**

WILDE (George). A sermon preached upon ...
the third of March in St.Maries church Oxford.
4to.
Oxford, by Leonard Lichfield, 1643
[Sermons Polemical VIII]   Wing W2160.
1186(17)

[WILDMAN (John)]. Putney proiects ...
Composed by ... John Lawmind [i.e. J.Wildman].
4to.
London, 1647   [Consutilia IV]
Wing W2171.   **1430(11)**

WILKINS (John), Bp of Chester. A discourse
concerning the gift of prayer ... — Ecclesiastes.
2 pts.   8vo.
London, by A.M. and R.R. for Edw.Gellibrand,
1678   Wing W2183.   **944**

——————A discovery of a new world.
4th ed.   2 pts.   8vo.
London, printed by T.M. & J.A. for John Gilli-
brand, 1684   Wing W2186.   **1121**

——————An essay towards a real character,
and a philosophical language.   2 pts.   fo.
London, for Sa:Gellibrand, and for John Martyn,
1668   Engr. pls (diagrams).
Wing W2196; Diary 4 June 1666; 30 Nov.1667;
15, 17, 27 May, 5 July & 2 Dec.1668; Naval
Minutes p.177.   **2356**

——————Mathematical magick.   8vo.
London, for Edw.Gellibrand, 1680   Engr. fp.
(port., Charrington p.176), pls.
Wing W2200.   **802**

[——————] Mercury, or the secret and
swift messenger.   8vo.
London, printed by I.Norton, for Iohn Maynard,
and Timothy Wilkins, 1641   Autograph on
title-page: 'Guil⁹ Adderley. 1648. Pinnar. Middlesex'.   Wing W2202.   **784**

——————Of the principles and duties of
natural religion ... To which is added a sermon
preached at [the author's] funerals by W.Lloyd.
2 pts.   8vo.
London, by A.Maxwell, for T.Basset, H.Brome,
R.Chiswell, 1675   Engr. fp. (port., Charrington
p.176).   Wing W2204.   **1159**

——————Sermons preach'd upon several
occasions before the King.   8vo.
London, by H.Cruttenden for Robert Sollers,
1677   Wing W2213.   **925**

WILKINSON (Henry), Captain. The information of
Capt.Hen.Wilkinson.   fo.
London, printed for Henry Wilkinson, 1681
[Narratives & Tryals III]   Wing W2218.
2251(45)

WILKINSON (Henry), of Christ Church, Oxford.
The gainefull cost ... A sermon preached ... the
27 of November.   4to.
London, for Chr.Meredith and Sa.Gellibrand, 1644
[Sermons Polemical VIII]   Wing W2222.
1186(18)

——————Miranda, stupenda ... a sermon
preached ... July 21.1646.   4to.
London, by T.B. for Christopher Meredith and
Samuel Gellibrand, 1646   [Sermons Polemical
VIII]   Wing W2224.   **1186(19)**

WILLIAM, Abp of Tyre. Belli sacri historia.   fo.
Basileæ (per Nicolaum Brylingerum et Ioannem Oporinum, 1549)   Autograph on title-page 'Thomas Lord Wentworth'; marginal notes in same hand.   *For continuation see* HEROLDT (Johann), Basilius.   Adams W176.   **2270(1)**

WILLIAM III, King of England. By the King and Queen, A proclamation for dissolving this present Parliament, and declaring the speedy calling another. 6 Feb.1689 [1690].   brs.
London, by Charles Bill and Thomas Newcomb, 1689   Wing W2530.   **1967(6)**

——————— By the King and Queen, a proclamation. Whereas ... divers passes ... have been forged. 9 Mar.1692/3.   brs.
London, by Charles Bill and the executrix of Thomas Newcomb, 1692/3   [*Inserted between nos 2851 & 2852 of the London Gazette.*]
Wing W2551.   **2087**

——————— By the King, a proclamation, commanding all Papists and reputed Papists to depart from the cities of London and Westminster. 11 Jan.1701.   brs.
London, by Charles Bill and the executrix of Thomas Newcomb, 1701   [*Inserted between nos 3774 & 3775 of the London Gazette.*]   **2090**

——————— His Majesties most gracious speech to both Houses of Parliament, on ... the third day of December, 1697.   fo.
London, by Charles Bill, and the executrix of Thomas Newcomb, 1697   Wing W2411.
2156(5)

——————— Whereas the necessity of affairs does require speedy advice. (23) Dec.1688.   brs.
[*London*] *for Awnsham Churchill,* 1688
Endorsed in Pepys's hand: 'The Prince of Orange's Invitation to ye Members of any of ye Parliament's of Charles ye 2d etc. to ye Ld Mayr, Aldermn and Comon Councill of London to meet him at St James's ye 26th of this inst Decr.'
Wing W2495.   **1967(2)**

WILLIAM, of Occam. A dialogue betwene a knyght and a clerke concernynge the power spiritual and temporall.   8vo.
(*London, in the house of Thomas Berthelet*) [1532?]   STC 12511.   **368(2)**

[WILLIAMS (John), Bp of Chichester]. A declaration of the sense of the Archbishops and Bishops ... concerning the ... proceedings of certain clergy-men at the execution of Sir John Freind. [By J.Williams?]   4to.
[*London*] *for John Everingham,* 1696
[Consutilia IX]   Wing W2699.   **1435(6)**

[———————] A defence of the Arch-bishop's sermon on the death of her late Majesty.   4to.
London, for J.Harris and A.Bell, 1695
Wing W2700.   **1528(10)**

WILLIAMS (John), Minister. The school of godliness.   12mo.
[*London*] *for P.Brooksby* [c.1680]   [Penny-Godlinesses]   Woodcut.   **365(16)**

WILLIAMS (Sir William). The speech ... to the Honourable House of Commons, upon the electing of him speaker in the Parliament at Oxford, Monday the 21st day of March, 1680.   fo.
London, for Gabriel Kunholt, sold ... by Langley Curtis, 1680 [1681]   [Parliamentary votes and papers 1679, 1681]   Wing W2780.
2137(29)

WILLIS (Edmond). An abbreviation of writing by character.   2nd ed.   8vo.
London, printed by George Purslowe, and are to bee sold by Nicholas Bourne, and by Philemon Stephens, 1627   [Short-hand Collection IV]
STC 25742; Carlton, p.22.   **860(12)**

WILLIS (John). The art of stenographie: or, short writing.   6th ed.   16mo.
London, for Robert Willis, sould by W.Iones, 1618
[Short-hand Collection III]   STC 25744a.6;
Carlton p.12.   **402(3)**

——————— The art of stenographie.
12th ed.
London, for Henry Seile, 1639   [Short-hand Collection III]   With the engraved title-page of the 10th ed.   STC 25746.7; Carlton p.15.
402(10)

——————— Mnemonica; or, the art of memory.   8vo.
London, printed and are to be sold by Leonard Sowersby, 1661   Wing W2812.   **310**

——————— The school-master to the art of stenography.   2nd ed.   8vo.
London, for Henry Seyle, 1628   [Short-hand Collection III]   STC 25751; Carlton p.17.
402(6)

——————— The school-master to the art of stenography.   3rd ed.   8vo.
London, by R.L. for Henry Seile, 1647
[Short-hand Collection III]   Engr. pl.
Wing W2813; Carlton p.18.   **402(13)**

WILLIS (Richard), Bp of Winchester. Concio ad sanctam synodum ... xx die Octobris [1702].
4to.
Londini, impensis Matthei Wotton, 1702
[Convocation Pamphlets XII]   **1698(6)**

WILLIS (Thomas). Two discourses concerning the soul of brutes ... Englished by S.Pordage.   fo.
London, for Thomas Dring, Ch.Harper, and John Leigh, 1683   7 engr. pls.   Wing W2856.   **2321**

WILLUGHBY (Francis). De historia piscium libri IV. (– Icthyographia.) 2 pts. fo.
Oxonii, e Theatro Sheldoniano (sumptibus Societatis Regalis), 1686 (1685)   Engr. title-page, 186 engr. pls.   Wing W2877.   **2713**

———————— The ornithology ... Transl. into English ... To which are added three ... discourses ... By J.Ray. fo.
London, by A.C. for John Martyn, 1678 80 engr. pls.   Wing W2880.   **2607**

WILMOT (Robert). The tragedie of Tancred and Gismund ... By R.W[ilmot and others].   4to.
London, by Thomas Scarlet, and are to be solde by R.Robinson, 1592   [Old Plays I] STC 25764a.   **939(4)**

WILSON (Arthur). The history of Great Britain, being the life and reign of King James the first. fo.
London, for Richard Lownds, 1653   Engr. fp. (port., Charrington p.85).   Wing W2888.   **2168**

WILSON (George). A compleat course of chymistry. 8vo.
London, printed, and sold at the author's house; and by Walter Kettilby, 1699   6 engr. pls (diagrams).   Wing W2892.   **1029**

WILSON (John). Andronicus Comnenius: a tragedy. 4to.
London, for John Starkey, 1664   [Loose Plays II]   Wing W2912.   **1604(1)**

[————————] The cheats. A comedy.   4to.
London, for G.Bedell, and T.Collins; and Cha. Adams, 1664   [Loose Plays II] Wing W2916.   **1604(4)**

———————— The projectors. A comedy.   4to.
London, for John Playfere; and William Crook, 1665   [Loose Plays II]   Wing W2923.
   1604(6)

WILSON (Robert). The coblers prophesie.   4to.
London, by Iohn Danter for Cuthbert Burbie, 1594   [Old Plays III]   STC 25781.   **1103(5)**

[————————] [The pedlers prophecie.   4to.
London, by Thomas Creede, sold by William Barley, 1595]   [Old Plays I]   Wants title-page.   STC 25782.   **939(3)**

———————— A right excellent comoedy called The three ladies of London.   4to.
London, by Roger Warde, 1584   [Old Plays III] STC 25784.   **1103(2)**

WILSON (Thomas). Davids zeale for Zion. A sermon preached ... April 4.[1641].   4to.
London, for Iohn Bartlet, 1641   [Sermons Polemical VIII]   Wing W2947.   **1186(20)**

———————— Jerichoes down-fall ... a sermon preached ... Septemb.28.1642.   4to.
London, for John Bartlet, 1643   [Sermons Polemical VIII]   Wing W2948.   **1186(21)**

WINCHILSEA (Heneage Finch, 2nd Earl of). A true and exact relation of the late prodigious earthquake & eruption of Mount Ætna.   4to.
In the Savoy, by T.Newcomb, 1669 [Consutilia VIII]   Engr. fp.
Wing W2967.   **1434(8)**

WING (John). Ὀλύμπια δώματα or an almanack for ... 1688 ... Calculated ... to the ... town of Stamford. 8vo.
Cambridge, printed by John Hayes, 1688 [Almanacks for the year 1688]   Wing A2779.
   425(30)

———————— Ὀλύμπια δώματα or an almanack for ... 1689 ... Calculated ... to the ... town of Stamford. 8vo.
Cambridge, printed by John Hayes, 1689 [Almanacks for the year 1689]   Wing A2780.
   426(8)

[WINSTANLEY (William)]. The delectable history of poor Robin.   12mo.
London, for J.Conyers [c.1680]   [Penny-Merriments I]   Woodcut. Title-page cropped.
Wing D898A.   **362(19)**

———————— The honour of merchant-taylors, wherein is set forth the noble acts, valliant deeds, & heroick performances of merchant-taylors in former ages.   4to.
London, by P.L. for William Whitwood, 1668 [Vulgaria IV]   Engr. fp. (port., Charrington p.17), woodcuts.   Wing W3064; Diary 10 Aug. 1668.   **1193(13)**

———————— The lives of the most famous English poets.   8vo.
London, by H.Clark, for Samuel Manship, 1687 Engr. fp. (port., Charrington p.179). Inserted at end: MS index (in hand of one of Pepys's clerks).   Wing W3065.   **902**

———————— Poor Robin. An almanack, 1688-9.
See POOR Robin ...

WISDOM. The wisdome of Doctor Dodypoll. [*A comedy.*]   4to.
London, by Thomas Creede, for Richard Oliue, 1600   [Old Plays I]   STC 6991.   **939(9)**

WISDOMS cabinet open'd [c.1680].
See SEVEN Wise Masters of Rome.   **1192(6)**

WISEMAN (Sir Robert). The law of laws: or, the excellency of the civil law.   2 pts.   8vo.
London, for R.Royston, and are to be sold by Richard Green, Cambridge, 1686 (1685) Wing W3114.   **1034**

WIT and mirth: or, Pills to purge melancholy, 1699.
See PLAYFORD (Henry).   654

WITSEN (Nicolaas). Aeloude en hedendaegsche scheeps-bouw en bestier.   fo.
Amsterdam, by Casparas Commelijn Broer en Jan Appelaer, 1671   Engr. title-page, 109 engr. pls.
2220

WOLSEY (Thomas), Cardinal. [Rules.]
See COLET (John). Æditio.   424(4)

WOMANS (The) brawl: or, Billingsgate against Turn-Mill-Street.   12mo.
[*London*, c.1680]   [Penny-Merriments II]
Woodcut.   Wants title-page.   363(1)

[WOMOCK (Laurence)]. Sober sadnes.   4to.
[*Oxford*]*for W.Webb*, 1643   [Consutilia IV]
Wing W3352.   1430(7)

WONDERFUL (The) adventures ... of young Shon ap Morgan.   12mo.
[*London*] *for J.Deacon* [c.1680]   [Penny-Merriments II]   363(14)

[WOOD (Anthony à)]. Athenæ Oxonienses. An exact history of all the writers and bishops who have had their education in ... Oxford.
2 vols in 1.   fo.
London, for Tho.Bennet, 1691-2
Wing W3382, 3383A.   2822

—————————— Historia et antiquitates Universitatis Oxoniensis. [Transl.]   2 vols in 1.
Oxonii, e Theatro Sheldoniano, 1674   Engr. title-page (ports, Charrington p.32), engr. map.
Wing W3385.   2895

[WOODHEAD (Abraham)]. An historical narration of the life and death of ... Jesus Christ.   4to.
Oxford, printed at the Theater, 1685
Wing W3448.   1854

—————————— Pietas Romana, 1687.
See MEYDEN (Theodor van).   665

WOODHOUSE (John). Woodhouse, 1688. A new almanack for ... 1688. (A prognostication for ... 1688.)   8vo.
London, printed by R.E. (– by J.M.) for the Company of Stationers, 1688   [Almanacks for the year 1688]   Wing A2867.   425(31)

[WOODROFFE (Benjamin)]. Somnium navale sive poema in expeditionem navalem.   fo.
Oxonii, e theatro Sheldoniano, 1673
Wing W3471.   2057

WOODWARD (Daniel). Vox Uraniæ: an almanack ... for ... 1688.   8vo.
London, printed by J.D. for the Company of Stationers, 1688   [Almanacks for the year 1688]
Wing A2895.   425(32)

[WOODWARD (John)]. Brief instructions for making observations in all parts of the world.   4to.
London, for Richard Wilkin, 1696
[Consutilia IX]   Wing W3509.   1435(4)

—————————— An essay toward a natural history of the earth.   8vo.
London, printed for Ric.Wilkin, 1695
Wing W3510.   1241

WORD (The) of God the best guide, 1689.
See BIBLE. *English. Selections.*   823(1)

WORLD (A) of wonders, 1607.
See ESTIENNE (Henri).   2034

WORK. A worke entytled of ye olde god ʓ the newe, 1534.
See WATT (Joachim von).   60

WOTTON (Sir Henry). Reliquiæ Wottonianæ.
3rd ed.   8vo.
London, printed by T.Roycroft, for R.Marriott, F.Tyton, T.Collins, and J.Ford, 1672
Engr. fp. (port., Charrington p.181).
Wing W3650.   915

WOTTON (William). Reflections upon ancient and modern learning. 2nd ed. With a dissertation upon the epistles of Phalaris ... by Dr.Bentley.
2 pts.   8vo.
London, by J.Leake, for Peter Buck, 1697
Wing W3659.   1152

WRIGHT (Abraham). Five sermons, in five several styles.   8vo.
[*London*] *for Edward Archer*, 1656
Wing W3685; Diary 6 Sept.1668.   151

WRIGHT (Edward). Errors in nauigation ... Whereto is adioyned ... the Earle of Cumberland his voyage to the Azores.   2 pts.   4to.
London, printed for Ed.Agas, 1599   Engr. map, diagrams.   STC 26019a.   949(1)

—————————— Certaine errors in navigation ... With many additions that were not in the former edition.   2 pts.   4to.
London, by Felix Kingstō, 1610   Engr. title-page, diagrams.   STC 26020.   949(2)

WRIGHT (James). A compendious view of the late tumults.   8vo.
London, printed by Edw.Jones, for S.Lownds, 1685   Wing W3692.   950

[—————————] Historia histrionica: an historical account of the English-stage.   8vo.
London, by G.Croom, for William Haws, 1699
Wing W3695.   1293

WRIGHT (John Michael). An account of His Excellence Roger Earl of Castlemaine's Embassy ... now made English.   fo.

London, by Tho.Snowden for the author, 1688
Engr. fp., 16 engr. pls.   Wing W3702.   **2603**

WRIGHT (Simeon). The several informations of
S.Wright, T.Launders and R.Perkin, concerning
the horrid Popish plot.   3 pts.   fo.
London, for Thomas Simmons (Richard Baldwin)
1681   [Narratives & Tryals III]
Wing S2767A.   **2251(29-31)**

[WRIGHT (William)]. A letter to a Member of
Parliament; occasioned by a Letter to a Con-
vocation-man.   4to.
London, for W.Rogers, 1697   [Convocation
Pamphlets IX]   'W.Wright Esqr a Lawyer'
written on title-page in hand of Daniel Waterland.
Wing W3715.   **1695(1)**

WYCHERLEY (William). The plain-dealer.
A comedy.   2nd ed.   4to.
London, for James Magnes and Richard Bentley,
1678   Wing W3750.   **1733(2)**

WYCLIFFE (John).   *See* WICLIF (John).

WYE (Thomas). A briefe discourse ... in maner of
a dialogue, betwene Baldwyne & a sayler.   8vo.
London, by Robert Waldegraue, 1580
STC 26057.7.   **96(2)**

WYNNE (Henry). The description and uses of
the general horological-ring: or universal ring-dyal.
12mo.
*London, printed by A.Godbid and J.Playford, for
the author*, 1682   Engr. diagram.   **232(2)**

X

XENOPHON. History of the affairs of Greece ...
Transl. by J.Newman.
London, printed by R.H. for William Freeman,
1685   Wing X19.   **963**

——————— Κύρου παιδείας βιβλία ή. De Cyri
institutione libri octo.   4to.
Etonæ, in Collegio Regali, 1613   On front
flyleaf Pepys has written the price ('2s.'), and (in
Greek) his name and the date: Ἐκ τῶν τοῦ
Σαμουὴλ Πήπυς. αχμθ [1649].
STC 26065.   **1304**

——————— Κύρου παιδεία: or, the institution
and life of Cyrus the Great ... Made English.
8vo.
*London, printed for Matthew Gilliflower, and
James Norris*, 1685   Engr. fp.
Wing X10.   **971**

XIMÉNEZ SEDEÑO (Francisco).
See JIMÉNEZ SEDEÑO (Francisco).

Y

YARRANTON (Andrew). England's improvement
by sea and land. (– The second part.)   2 vols.
4to.
*London, printed by R.Everingham for the author,
and are to be sold by T.Parkhurst, and N.Simmons
(and Thomas Simmons)* 1677-81   15 engr. pls.
Wing Y13, 13A.   **1341-2**

YOUNG (The) clerks guide, 1690.
See HUTTON (Sir Richard).   **966**

YOUNG. The young-man's last legacy.   8vo.
[London] for J.Deacon, 1687
[Penny-Godlinesses]   **365(15)**

YOUNG (Robert). A true copy of the paper
delivered ... to the ... Ordinary, at Tyburn, on the
19th of April, 1700.   brs.
(London, for E.Mallet, 1700)   [Consutilia VI]
Wing Y75.   **1432(11)**

YOUNG (Thomas). Hopes incouragement ...
A sermon preached ... February 28.1643.   4to.
London, for Ralph Smith, 1644   [Sermons
Polemical VIII]   Wing Y92.   **1186(22)**

Z

ZAYAS Y SOTOMAYOR (Maria de). Primera,
y segunda parte de las novelas amorosas. Correg-
idas ... en esta ultima impression.   8vo.
Madrid, por Ioseph Fernandez de Buendia, 1664
Gaselee 185.   **1552(2)**

ZEALE (John). A narrative of the phanatical
plot.   fo.
[London] for the author, 1683   [Narratives &
Tryals III]   Wing Z10.   **2251(46)**

ZOUCH (Richard). Cases and questions resolved
in the civil law.   8vo.
Oxford, by Leon.Lichfield, for Tho.Robinson,
1652   Wing Z17.   **299**

——————— The jurisdiction of the Admiralty
of England asserted, against Sr.E.Coke's Articuli
admiralitatis.   8vo.
London, for Francis Tyton, and Thomas Dring,
1663   Wing Z22; Tangier Papers p.10 (*bis*:
31 Aug., 3 Sept.1683).   **785**

Appendix

CATALOGUE OF INCUNABULA   *by J. C. T. Oates*

BARTHOLOMAEUS, Anglicus. De proprietatibus rerum.   fo.

[*W. de Worde, Westminster*, 1495]   **2126**

Wants leaves 1-4 (title-page, prologue of the translator John Trevisa, and most of Lib.i) and 6 (blank). The last leaf (end-title and device) has been bound at the beginning. The missing text has been supplied in MS by one of Pepys's clerks 'from One of a later Edition by a complete Century, greatly different from this both in Form and Phrase'. A note by Daniel Waterland adds ambiguously: 'This Edition appears to be Berthelet's of 1535: And the Supplemental part is taken from Bateman's Edition of 1582. forty-seven years later in the same Century'. In fact, all the transcript was made from a copy of Berthelet's edition.

GW 3414; Duff, Fifteenth Century, 40; Duff p.5; STC 1536.

BEDFORD (Jasper Tudor, Duke of). The epitaph of Jasper, Duke of Bedford.   4to.

R. Pynson [*London*, 1496]   **1254(5)**

$a^6 b^4$ (not $A^6 B^4$, as stated by Duff).

Jasper, Duke of Bedford, died 21 December 1495. Thomas Tanner's attribution of this poem to John Skelton (*Bibliotheca*, etc., p.676) is not accepted by Dyce (*Poetical Works of Skelton*, ii. 388). The author writes in the character of (and perhaps actually was) one Smert or Smart, the Duke's falconer.

Duff, Fifteenth Century, 233; Duff p.57; STC 14477 = 22605.

BOOK (The) of hawking, hunting, and heraldry.   fo.

St Albans, 1486   **1985**

Wants the first leaf (blank), e f^8 (*Book of hunting*), and d 8, f 10 (last) of the *Book of heraldry*. At the beginning a note by Daniel Waterland on the printed editions of the book and its authorship; in the same hand on first d4v: 'The copy here is imperfect, wanting 16 Leaves of the same edition; as appears from the Copy in Bp More's Library, now the Royal Library belonging to the University.'

GW 4932 (but reading blasyng at second c 1 r, compylyt at f9r, 1.17); Duff, Fifteenth Century, 56; Duff p.5; STC 3308.

BOOK (The) of hawking, hunting, and heraldry. — The treatise of fishing.   fo.

W. de Worde, Westminster, 1496   **1984**

Wants the last leaf. At the beginning a note by Daniel Waterland similar to the one at the beginning of No.1985.

GW 4933 (but reading abowte at first b 1 r, men. at i4v, 1.12, and [red] (I^5) at second a 1 r); Duff, Fifteenth Century, 57; Duff p.6; STC 3309.

CESSOLIS (Jacobus de). The game of chess.   fo.

W. Caxton [*Westminster*, c.1478]   **1945**

Wants the first leaf (blank) and most of the last. Rubricated in red (initials and paragraph-marks).

Caxton's second edition. The text missing at the end has been supplied in MS by one of Pepys's clerks, who transcribed it (see his note at the beginning) in 1699 from the copy of Caxton's first edition which belonged to John Moore, then Bishop of Norwich. He also added transcripts of the dedication and explicit (beginning: *And therefore my ryght redoubted lord*) which were printed in that edition (but not in this): that explicit being replaced in this second edition by a sentence for which the scribe had no printed model, he completed the last two full lines as best he could thus: Thenne late eue [*ry man of whatever*] / condycion he be that redyth or herith this [*lityll & simple book*] / ... Moore's copy is now in the University Library, Cambridge.

GW 6533; Duff, Fifteenth Century, 82; Duff p.14; STC 4921; De Ricci 18(5), wrongly stating that the woodcuts are coloured.

CHASTISING (The) of God's children.   fo.

[*W.de Worde, Westminster*, c.1494]   **2051(1)**

Contemporary marginal notes (mostly cropped). E3v: 'Memorandum that I George Bassendyne'; G 1v: a drawing of a jester and another person, with legends: 'The prolege of these to wyse persones', 'I haue brought unto your mastershype an napple'; at end: 'here endeth the one and thyrtey salmeys H D', in a hand which has inserted chapter-numbers beginning on G 1r.

GW 6583 (but reading chapytres at 2v, col.2, l.36); Duff, Fifteenth Century, 85; Duff p.15; STC 5065; De Ricci 104(12).

CHAUCER (Geoffrey). The Canterbury tales.   fo.

W. Caxton [*Westminster*, c.1484]   **2053**

Wants the first leaf (blank), a 2 (Caxton's *Prohemye*), and c4, 5 (end of Chaucer's Prologue); sig. b misbound.

Rubricated in red (initials). Scribbles and pen-trials, including some names, on several leaves; p 6v, 7r: two crude drawings of persons ('mr̄o catlin' and 'mr̄o ionson').

GW 6586 (but reading texte not trete at sig. B of Pt 3; GW's transcript of sig. b in Pt 2 properly belongs to the description of Pt 1); Duff, Fifteenth Century, 88; Duff p.15; STC 5083; De Ricci 23(5).

CHRISTINE de Pisan. The book of the feat of arms and chivalry.   fo.

W. Caxton [*Westminster*], 14 July 1489   **1938(1)**

Wants the last leaf (blank).

GW 6648 (but reading Eplicit not Explicit at 2v, l.31, and dyuerſe not diuerſe, kyng not king at 143v, ll.3, 12); Duff, Fifteenth Century 96; Duff p.15; STC 7269; De Ricci 28(14).

CHRONICLES of England.   fo.

[*W.de Machlinia, London*, 1486]   **1997**

Wants all before D 2 (35 leaves), aa 1 & 8, and cc 8.

The text missing at the beginning has been supplied by a transcript in the hand of one of Pepys's clerks of leaves ij-b 6 of Caxton's first edition (1480) followed by six printed leaves (b 7, 8, c 1-4) from his second edition (1482). A note at the beginning says that this work was done in 1692 and that the transcript was made from the copy (now in the University Library, Cambridge) which belonged to John Moore, then Bishop of Norwich. F 8r: 'Thomas mason one'.

GW 6673; Duff, Fifteenth Century, 99; Duff p.16; STC 9993.

CHRONICLES of England.   fo.

W. Caxton, Westminster, 8 October 1482

Six leaves only (b 7, 8, c 1-4) inserted in No.1997.

GW 6671; Duff, Fifteenth Century, 98; Duff p.16; STC 9992; De Ricci 30(15).

DONATUS (Aelius). Ars minor (Donatus pro pueris).   4to.

R.Pynson [*London*, 1500]   **1305(1)**

a 1r: 'Su̅ libr̄ Jo: Jhonson pret xxᵈ'.

GW 8944; Duff, Fifteenth Century, 132; Duff p.19; STC 7017.

——————— **Accidence.**   4to.

W.de Worde, Westminster [1499]   **1305(2)**

Duff, Fifteenth Century, 134; Duff p.20; STC 7010.

HIGDEN (Ranulph). Polycronicon. fo.
W.Caxton [Westminster, after 2 July 1482]   **2063**

Wants leaves 30³ and 30⁶ (supplied by leaves B 1-4 from De Worde's edition of 1495), also the blank leaves 1, 21, 25, 256, & 450 (last). Rubricated in red (initials, paragraph-marks, marginal headings). Several long marginal notes by Daniel Waterland concerning the printed editions and the date of Trevisa's translation, as variously stated in the manuscripts; Waterland has noted at Lib.vii, cap.44: 'Explicit MS. Lat. Higden: Coll: Johñ. Cant.' Leaves 2r & 22r: 'Constat liber iste Thome Andro recte Medice.'

Duff, Fifteenth Century, 172; Duff p.32; STC 13438; De Ricci 49(2).

──────────── **Polycronicon.** fo.
W.de Worde, Westminster, 13 April 1495

Four leaves only (B1-4) inserted in No.2063.

Duff, Fifteenth Century, 173; STC 13439.

HORMAN (William). Introductorium linguae latinae. 4to.
W.de Worde [Westminster, 1495]   **1305(5)**

Duff, Fifteenth Century, 231; Duff p.34; STC 13809.

IMAGE du Monde. The mirror of the world. fo.
W.Caxton [Westminster, 1490]   **1941(1)**

Duff, Fifteenth Century, 402 (but reading the not the/ at 4v, l.1, and AMEN/ not AMEN at 87v, l.12); Duff p.69; STC 24763; De Ricci 95(2).

INFORMATIO puerorum. 4to.
R.Pynson [London, c.1500]   **1305(3)**

Duff, Fifteenth Century, 223; Duff p.33; STC 14078.

MAYNERIIS (Maynus de). Dialogus creaturarum moralisatus. fo.
G.Leeu, Gouda, 6 June 1481   **2002(2)**

Wants the first leaf (blank); l⁸, itself misbound, misbound before k⁸. Rubricated in red; some woodcuts partly coloured. c5r: 'Rocherde marcetun'.

Duff p.18; Campbell, Annales de la typographie néerlandaise, 561; Polain, Catalogue des livres imprimés au quinzième siècle des bibliothèques de Belgique, 1264 (but reading Per not Pre and mensis innij not iunij in the colophon).

MIRK (John). Liber festivalis. – Quattuor sermones. (2 pts.) fo.
R.Pynson [London, 1493]   **1944**

Pt 1 wants the first leaf (probably blank), g6, h6, & k7. At the end are two leaves of manuscript in the hand of one of Pepys's clerks containing 'The Form of Bydding of Bedys Exhibited in ye Specimen publish'd 1693 against Dr. Burnet's History of ye Reformation.'

Duff, Fifteenth Century, 303-4; Duff pp.49, 54; STC 17960.

PEROTTUS (Nicolaus). Grammatica. – GUARINUS, Veronensis. De arte diphthongandi. Regulae de crescentiis genitivorum. 4to.
N.de la Barre, Paris, 1 June 1498   **1305(7)**

Duff p.52 (inaccurate: 1v, GRĀMATICA, (l.7) Iem; 132r, M.cccc.xcviii; 132v, woodcut of the Nativity (73 x 52mm.) within border-pieces, including Ph. Renouard, Marques, Nos 528 (scroll with name only) and 532; foliated, not paginated).

REYNARD the fox.   fo.

[*W. Caxton, Westminster*, 1489]   **1796**

Wants the last two leaves (i 5, 6).

The only recorded copy of Caxton's second edition. A conclusion to the text has been supplied by one of Pepys's clerks. The source of his transcript has not been identified; it is not the text of Caxton's first edition, and its beginning does not fit the text as it ends on i6v. On the first recto: 'John Awdeley', 'John Audley'.

Duff, Fifteenth Century, 359 (but reading suche not such at 2v, l.13); Duff p.54; STC 20920; De Ricci 88.

ROTE (The) or mirror of consolation.   4to.

W. de Worde, Westminster, [1499]   **1254(4)**

A 5, 6 misbound between A 2 and A 3. The outer and lower margins of the title-page cut away; on its upper margin: 'Nico: Atkinson.'

Duff, Fifteenth Century, 365; Duff p.55; STC 21335.

STANBRIDGE (John). Vocabula.   4to.

R. Pynson [*London*, 1496]   **1305(4)**

Duff, Fifteenth Century, 373; Duff p.58; STC 23177.

SULPITIUS (Joannes). Opus grammatices.   4to.

R. Pynson, London, 1498   **1305(6)**

Duff, Fifteenth Century, 389; Duff p.66; STC 23426.

TREATISE (The) of love.   fo.

W. de Worde [*Westminster*, 1493]   **2051(2)**

Wants B2, 5. Contemporary marginal notes (as 2051(1)). A5r: 'Harry Dane'.

Duff, Fifteenth Century, 399; Duff p.68; STC 24234; De Ricci 105(7).

WALSINGHAM. The foundation of the chapel of Walsingham.   4to.

R. Pynson [*London*, 1496]   **1254(6)**

Wants the first leaf (short title & woodcut?).

For some discussion of the question whether this the unique copy was once Richard Smith's, see *The Library*, Fifth ser., xiii.269-70: cf. 1254(3).

Duff, Fifteenth Century, 412; Duff p.24; STC 25001.

WEDNESDAY'S fast.   4to.

W. de Worde [*Westminster*, 1500]   **1254(3)**

For some discussion of the question whether this the unique copy was once Richard Smith's, see *The Library*, Fifth ser., xiii.269-70: cf. 1254(6).

Duff, Fifteenth Century, 413; Duff p.71; STC 24224.

LIST OF 'COLLECTIONS'

The library contains 17 'collections' in which Pepys gathered into one or more volumes pamphlets and other small items relating to a single theme. In all of them except his 'Convocation Pamphlets' he inserted lists of contents.

In this list the publication dates are given as approximate in those cases where the collections contain items which, for whatever reason, lack dates.[1] The titles are in some cases slightly abbreviated.

Shorthand Collection 29 items; 1588-1692	13, 401, 402, 860, 1111
Penny-Merriments 114 chapbooks and one broadside ballad; c.1652-c.1687	362-4
Penny-Godlinesses 46 chapbooks; c.1679-c.1687	365
Almanacks for the year 1688 32 items	425
Almanacks for the year 1689 13 items	426
Old Plays English; 27 items, 1565-1617	939, 1102-3
Loose Plays English; 28 items; c.1638-1689	1075, 1604
Sea Tracts 35 items; 1559-1682	1077-80
Sermons Polemical 172 items; 1625-80	1179-86
Liturgick Controversies 36 items; 1607-87	1187-9
Vulgaria Popular literature; 51 pamphlets; c.1637-c.1693	1190-3
Naval Pamphlets 16 items; 1636-95	1399
Consutilia 182 miscellaneous pamphlets; c.1528-c.1703	1427-38
Convocation Pamphlets 68 items; 1697-1703	1689-98
News-Pamphlets Newsbooks; 430 items; 1660-66	1744-7

1. I.e. because they were published without dates, or because the title-page is lacking, or because the dates have been completely or partially removed by cropping.

Parliamentary Votes and Papers **2137**

    33 items (2 in MS) relating to the Second Exclusion Parliament Oct. 1679-
Jan. 1681 and the Oxford Parliament, March 1681

Narratives & Tryals **2249-55**

    238 items (4 in MS) concerning the Popish Plot and Exclusion crisis; 1678-82

The following missing books were not included in the MS. slip catalogue completed in 1898. All (except no.351) were noted as missing in 1906-7 when the contents of the library were checked by F.Sidgwick[1]. No.300 has been missing since at least 1744[2].

The descriptions given here derive from the titles in Pepys's own catalogue. The identifications are mostly those proposed by Sidgwick, and are necessarily tentative.

Bale's Martyrdom of Sir John Oldcastle.   130(1)
    Apparently STC 1276, 1277 or 1278.

Segar's Disswasive from a Court-Life — about 1549.   130(2)
    Possibly a work by Francis Seager, author of 'The School of Virtue'; R.B.Mc-
    Kerrow suggested that it might be A.de Guevara's A Dispraise of the Life of a
    Courtier, 1548 (STC 12431)

Sr.Ken.Digby's Discourse of the Sympathetick Powder, in an Assembly at
Montpelier.   234
    Wing lists four English editions (D1435-8); there were also French, German
    and Latin versions.

The Affair of ye Queen of Scots, in Scotch — 1566.   300
    This was apparently the work by Buchanan — STC 3981 or 3982.

Chess ... the Game ... Barbier.   351
    This must have been an edition of J.Barbier's revision of A.Saul's The Famous
    Game of Chesse-Play; STC and Wing each record two editions.

Skelton (Poet Laureat) his Satyr against Wolsey; printed in the Cardinal's Life-
time.   458
    An edition of *Why come ye not to court?* or *Colin Clout*?

English Liturgy in French.   549
    Presumably a French translation of the Book of Common Prayer.

---

1. *Bibliotheca Pepysiana*, pt II (1914), pp.xviii-xix. The omission of no.351 from his list must have been accidental. There is also a MS volume missing: see below, vol.V.
2. Ib., p.xix.